READINGS IN ECONOMICS

READINGS IN ECONOMICS

Seventh Edition

Paul A. Samuelson

Institute Professor
Massachusetts Institute of Technology

McGraw-Hill Book Company

New York St. Louis San Francisco Düsseldorf Johannesburg Kuala Lumpur London
Mexico Montreal New Delhi Panama Rio de Janeiro Singapore Sydney Toronto

1 2 3 4 5 6 7 8 9 0   BABA   7 9 8 7 6 5 4 3

Library of Congress Cataloging in Publication Data

Samuelson, Paul Anthony, 1915-   ed.
    Readings in economics.

    1. Economics—Addresses, essays, lectures.
I. Title.
HB34.S3 1973   330′.08   73-8677
ISBN 0-07-054542-1
ISBN 0-07-054543-X (pbk.)

This book was set in Times by Rocappi, Inc.
The editors were Jack R. Crutchfield, Michael Elia, and Annette Hall;
the designer was J. E. O'Connor; and the production supervisor was Ted Agrillo.
The printer and binder was George Banta Company, Inc.

PREFACE

This seventh edition of *Readings in Economics* is an anthology designed to supplement any of the well-known elementary textbooks used in beginning economics courses. Out of the embarrassment of riches now available, I have tried to select the most interesting, relevant, and representative writers. In this edition, I have increased the emphasis on criticism—from both the Right and the Left—of mainstream economics.

Great names appear. You are not educated if you have never read a page of Malthus, Ricardo, Karl Marx, Henry George, Maynard Keynes—or, for that matter, J. K. Galbraith, Milton Friedman, Ralph Nader, James Tobin, and Robert Solow.

Should blood be sold or given? Should advertising be subjected to penalty taxes? Should there be price-wage guidelines or "benign neglect"? New times bring new questions to the fore, and the old chestnuts in the standard anthologies aren't good enough for today's reader.

Experience in some hundreds of classrooms shows that the debate format best suits the nonprofessional economist. In these *Readings,* you can find Simon Kuznets versus Walt Rostow on developmental take-offs; Solow versus the Club of Rome; Galbraith and Friedman versus the world; Ernest Mandel on Marx's theory of alienation, and Irving Kristol on the other side; Assar Lindbeck's economics of the New Left against Baran and Sweezy and Hymer and Roosevelt. This is the stuff out of which knowledge can grow.

As editor I have cut the original texts. Though no new words are put into any author's mouth, some of his throat clearings have been selectively omitted. Since no one should rely on these edited versions for a definitive text of the originals, there has been no need to annoy the reader with those vexing signs of deletions. And the headings and subheadings, useful to punctuate incomplete texts, are generally my handiwork as editor and should not be held against the authors.

Finally, I have written introductions to the essays, provided biographical data about the authors, and supplied questions to guide the readings. Although the order of arrangement has been integrated with the 1973 ninth edition of Samuelson's *Economics,* these *Readings* have been found useful in the past with a variety of alternative texts. (A few intrepid instructors have even built an entire course around them alone.)

My acknowledgments are many. Particular thanks go to the coeditors of previous editions. Felicity Skidmore (Institute of Research on Poverty, University of Wisconsin), Dean Robert L. Bishop of M.I.T., President John C. Coleman of Haverford, my earlier collaborators, have left their indelible marks on the work. Annette Hall and Peggy Dutka of McGraw-Hill, and Norma Wasser, my editorial coworker—all know my indebtedness to them. But only I know how much I again owe to instructors and countless readers for suggestions and criticisms.

Paul A. Samuelson

CONTENTS

CONTENTS BY AUTHOR

Author	Title	Reading Number

1

BASIC ECONOMIC CONCEPTS AND NATIONAL INCOME

The Nature of Economics

Readings 1 and 2

Economics is a social science, and therefore cannot attain the exactitude and precision of the hard physical sciences. In Reading 1, one of the most eminent economists of all time sets down his definition of economics.

In Reading 2, a modern historian meets head on the ethical problems with respect to indoctrination and objectivity that any professors of the social sciences face.

Alfred Marshall, gigantic Victorian, long was professor of economics at Cambridge University, England; he trained a whole generation of economists all over the world, including Lord Keynes. Gordon Wright is head of the history department at Stanford University.

Questions to guide the reading

Do you think a professor should avoid "taking sides"? Is it possible for him to do so? Can beginning students be trusted to choose among competing arguments?

Can money measure the important elements of life? Are people spiritually better off when the material basis of life is mismanaged and deficient?

Can economists make controlled experiments? Can astronomers? Can meteorologists? Which do you think is more exact as a science, astronomy or biology?

Reading 1

Definition of Economics

Alfred Marshall

Economics is a study of men as they live and move and think in the ordinary business of life. But it concerns itself chiefly with those motives which affect, most powerfully and most steadily, man's conduct *in the business part of his life*.

Everyone who is worth anything carries his higher nature with him into business; and, there as elsewhere, he is influenced by his personal affections, by his conceptions of duty and his reverence for high ideals. And it is true that the best energies of the ablest inventors and organizers of improved methods and appliances are stimulated by a noble emulation more than by any love of wealth for its own sake. But, for all that, the steadiest motive to ordinary business work is the desire for the pay which is the material reward of work.

The pay may be on its way to be spent selfishly or unselfishly, for noble or base ends; and here the variety of human nature comes into play. But the motive is supplied by a definite amount of money: and it is this definite and exact money measurement of the steadiest motives in business life, which has enabled economics far to outrun every other branch of the study of man.

Just as the chemist's fine balance has made chemistry more exact than most other physical sciences; so this economist's balance, rough and imperfect as it is, has made economics more exact

From Alfred Marshall, *Principles of Economics,* 8th ed. (Macmillan and Co. Ltd., London, 1920). Reprinted by permission of The Macmillan Company, New York, and Macmillan & Co., Ltd., London.

than any other branch of social science. But of course economics cannot be compared with the exact physical sciences: for it deals with the ever changing and subtle forces of human nature.

It is essential to note that the economist does not claim to measure any affection of the mind in itself, or directly; but only indirectly *through its effect*. No one can compare and measure accurately against one another even his own mental states at different times: and no one can measure the mental states of another at all except indirectly and conjecturally by their effects. Of course various affections belong to man's higher nature and others to his lower, and are thus different in kind. But, even if we confine our attention to mere physical pleasures and pains of the same kind, we find that they can only be compared indirectly by their effects. In fact, even this comparison is necessarily to some extent conjectural, unless they occur to the same person at the same time.

Economists watch carefully the conduct of a whole class of people, sometimes the whole of a nation, sometimes only those living in a certain district, more often those engaged in some particular trade at some time and place: and by the aid of statistics, or in other ways, they ascertain how much money on the average the members of the particular group they are watching are just willing to pay as the price of a certain thing which they desire, or how much must be offered to them to induce them to undergo a certain effort or abstinence that they dislike.

The measurement of motive thus obtained is not indeed perfectly accurate; for if it were, economics would rank with the most advanced of the physical sciences; and not, as it actually does, with the least advanced.

Reading 2

One Side, All Sides—Or No Sides

Gordon Wright

Some years ago, at the end of my course, I solicited written criticisms from those students who had survived the experience and were still conscious. One of the most intriguing responses ran thus: "During the course I swayed back and forth in my emotions. At first I thought the lectures were provacitive [*sic*]; now I think they are indoctrinary. I am not against freedom of speech; I am glad you have ideas and are consistent, but your lectures are very subtly indoctrinating the class without the class realizing it. . . ." Having delivered this thunderbolt, my anonymous critic offered a constructive suggestion: "Continue as you are, but at the beginning of the course warn the students and state when you express your thesis that it is yours." A somewhat rueful footnote was appended: "I know you did this, but do it oftener."

Perhaps I ought to have shrugged off this complaint, or consoled myself with the thought that Socrates too had once been accused of surreptitiously corrupting the young. Better still, I might have sought reassurance by challenging my critic's grasp of the nature of history as a discipline. True, he had not fallen into the common error of demanding total objectivity in the classroom; like most of us today, he had abandoned the positivist fallacy that humanists can be as neutral as chemists, and that we can all agree if we simply stick to "verifiable facts." But he did demand something almost as difficult: a clear separation of judgment and fact, with each judgment (like each pack of cigarettes) carefully labeled "DANGEROUS."

I could not quite shake off the feeling that my critic had found a chink in my academic armor, and had drawn a bit of blood. After all, I had always believed that teaching and preaching are

From Gordon Wright, "One Side, All Sides—Or No Sides." Reprinted from *Stanford Today,* Winter, 1965, ser. 1, no. 11, © 1966 by the Board of Trustees of Leland Stanford Junior University. Reprinted abridged with kind permission of the author and publisher.

two quite different things, and that any attempt to impose one's own value judgments in the classroom is (as the French say) an abuse of confidence. Had I been unwittingly misleading students by a false appearance of objectivity? If some bias is inescapable when man studies man, is it not safer for the teacher to flaunt his prejudices, to preach and proselyte without restraint, so that even the most naïve student will be on guard against "subtle indoctrination"?

This is a plausible thesis; and I know some teachers (at Stanford and elsewhere) who subscribe to it. Indeed, one administrator at a fine California university has frankly set out to staff his sector of the campus with dedicated right-wing doctrinaires on the dubious ground that the rest of the campus is loaded with left-wingers. Presumably these two legions of crusaders, clashing in the free market place of ideas, will fight it out until Truth finally prevails. I am not so sure myself that this is the best way to arrive at Truth, to advance learning, or even to educate students. Certainly the presence of some strong-minded partisans of a

given system or idea will add savour to a campus, and ought to frighten nobody. But a faculty heavily loaded with true believers, either of one simonpure variety or of several rival sects, would be likely to spend most of its energy either in indoctrination campaigns or in civil war.

There is, nevertheless, a real dilemma here; it confronts any teacher whose concern is human behavior, either past or present. If aloof objectivity is impossible and if flagrant partisanship may be destructive, is there any sort of middle ground that might be any better? I myself believe that the answer is affirmative—but only if certain difficult conditions are met.

In the first place, the teacher seeking that middle ground must possess a high degree of that rare trait called intellectual integrity: a willingness to face all the facts, even those that may jolt his own deeply-held beliefs. In the second place, he must really subscribe to the dictum of the late Judge Learned Hand: "The spirit of liberty is the spirit which is not too sure that it is right."

Population and Economics

Readings 3 and 4

Economics is about people. Population relative to natural and man-made resources and to technical knowledge is a prime determinant of economic well-being. Here we meet the man and ideas that led Thomas Carlyle to put the persistent stigma of "the dismal science" on economics. The Reverend Thomas Robert Malthus (1766–1834) was a distinguished member of the classical school in economics. Despite his other contributions to the growing science of economics he is primarily remembered today for his gloomy analysis of population trends. He argues in this famous passage that, in the absence of moral restraint, population must forever tend to outstrip the available means of subsistence.

This analysis, which for a time seemed irrelevant to the American scene, is now coming back into the world spotlight. Jay Forrester's *World Dynamics* and the 1971 MIT study *Limits to Growth*, sponsored by the Club of Rome, are really old Malthus speaking through a computer.

Population presents a new outlook and problem today. Pollution and environmental blight have alerted the advanced nations to the danger of rapidly expanding population. Ansley J. Coale, director of the Office of Population Research at Princeton University, is a leading authority on demography. In Reading 4 he puts the whole subject into an informed perspective.

Questions to guide the reading

Do you agree with Darwin and Malthus that left to herself, Nature would cause species numbers to explode, leading inevitably, through the laws of diminishing returns, to a jeopardization of decent living standards? Just how is the law of diminishing returns involved?

If each couple wants to have three or more children per family, and modern medicine keeps virtually all children alive, what is the prospective long-term population trend? What does this imply for privacy, air and water pollution, and a serene environment in an advanced economy? What would it imply for an impoverished economy? Alternatively, what are the ultimate consequences of a desire to have less than two children per couple? To have exactly 2.11, the replacement requirement at which there is no ultimate growth?

Why does Dr. Coale make no mention of Malthus? If writing about Asia, would he worry about future famine and not merely about the ecological amenities of life?

Why not ZPG (zero population growth) *now*? Do you agree with Coale's next-to-the-last paragraph?

Reading 3

Population Growth and Poverty

Thomas R. Malthus

In an inquiry concerning the improvement of society, the mode of conducting the subject which naturally presents itself, is,

1. To investigate the causes that have hitherto impeded the progress of mankind towards happiness; and,

2. To examine the probability of the total or partial removal of these causes in future.

The principal object of the present essay is to examine the effects of one great cause intimately united with the very nature of man; which, though it has been constantly and powerfully operating since the commencement of society, has been little noticed by the writers who have treated this subject. The facts which establish the existence of this cause have, indeed, been repeatedly stated and acknowledged; but its natural and necessary effects have been almost totally overlooked; though prob-

ably among these effects may be reckoned a very considerable portion of that vice and misery, and of that unequal distribution of the bounties of nature, which it has been the unceasing object of the enlightened philanthropist in all ages to correct.

The cause to which I allude, is the constant tendency in all animated life to increase beyond the nourishment prepared for it.

It is observed by Dr. Franklin, that there is no bound to the prolific nature of plants or animals, but what is made by their crowding and interfering with each other's means of subsistence. Were the face of the earth, he says, vacant of other plants, it might be gradually sowed and overspread with one kind only, as for instance with fennel: and were it empty of other inhabitants, it might in a few ages be replenished from one nation only, as for instance with Englishmen.

From T. R. Malthus, *An Essay on the Principle of Population* (Reeves and Turner, London, 1878, 8th ed.).

This is incontrovertibly true. Through the animal and vegetable kingdoms Nature has scattered the seeds of life abroad with the most profuse and liberal hand; but has been comparatively sparing in the room and the nourishment necessary to rear them. The germs of existence contained in this earth, if they could freely develop themselves, would fill millions of worlds in the course of a few thousand years. Necessity, that imperious, all-pervading law of nature, restrains them within the prescribed bounds. The race of plants and the race of animals shrink under this great restrictive law; and man cannot by any efforts of reason escape from it.

Population has this constant tendency to increase *beyond* the means of subsistence, and it is kept to its necessary level by these causes. The subject will, perhaps, be seen in a clearer light, if we endeavour to ascertain what would be the natural increase of population, if left to exert itself with perfect freedom; and what might be expected to be the rate of increase in the productions of the earth, under the most favourable circumstances of human industry.

The potential rate of increase of population. It will be allowed that no country has hitherto been known, where the manners were so pure and simple, and the means of subsistence so abundant, that no check whatever has existed to early marriages from the difficulty of providing for a family, and that no waste of the human species has been occasioned by vicious customs, by towns, by unhealthy occupations, or too severe labour. Consequently in no state that we have yet known, has the power of population been left to exert itself with perfect freedom.

In the northern states of America, where the means of subsistence have been more ample, the manners of the people more pure, and the checks to early marriages fewer, than in any of the modern states of Europe, the population has been found to double itself, for above a century and a half successively, in less than twenty-five years. In the back settlements, where the sole employment is agriculture, and vicious customs and unwholesome occupations are little known, the population has been found to double itself in fifteen years. Even this extraordinary rate of increase is probably short of the utmost power of population. Sir William Petty supposes a doubling possible in so short a time as ten years.

But, to be perfectly sure that we are far within the truth, we will take the slowest of these rates of increase, a rate in which all concurring testimonies agree, and which has been repeatedly ascertained to be from procreation only.

It may safely be pronounced, therefore, that *population, when unchecked,* goes on doubling itself every twenty-five years, or *increases in a geometrical ratio.*

The potential rate of increase of food production. The rate according to which the productions of the earth may be supposed to increase, it will not be so easy to determine. Of this, however, we may be perfectly certain, that the ratio of their increase in a limited territory must be of a totally different nature from the ratio of the increase of population. A thousand millions are just as easily doubled every twenty-five years by the power of population as a thousand. But the food to support the increase from the greater number will by no means be obtained with the same facility. Man is necessarily confined in room. When acre has been added to acre till all the fertile land is occupied, the yearly increase of food must depend upon the melioration of the land already in possession. This is a fund, which, from the nature of all soils, instead of increasing, must be gradually diminishing. But population, could it be supplied with food, would go on with unexhausted vigour; and the increase of one period would furnish the power of a greater increase the next, and this without any limit.

From the accounts we have of China and Japan, it may be fairly doubted, whether the best-directed efforts of human industry could double the produce of these countries even once in any number of years. There are many parts of the globe, indeed, hitherto uncultivated, and almost unoccupied; but even in new colonies, a geometrical ratio increases with such extraordinary rapidity, that the advantage could not last long. If the United States of America continue increasing, which they certainly will do, though not with the same rapidity as formerly, the Indians will be driven further and further back into the country, till the whole race is ultimately exterminated, and the territory is incapable of further extension.

The science of agriculture has been much studied in England and Scotland; and there is still a great portion of uncultivated land in these countries. Let us consider at what rate the produce of this island might be supposed to increase under circumstances the most favourable to improvement.

If it be allowed that by the best possible policy, and great encouragements to agriculture, the average produce of the island could be doubled in the first twenty-five years, it will be allowing, probably, a greater increase than could with reason be expected.

In the next twenty-five years, it is impossible to suppose that the produce could be quadrupled. It would be contrary to all our knowledge of the properties of land. It must be evident to those who have the slightest acquaintance with agricultural subjects, that in proportion as cultivation extended, the additions that could yearly be made to the former average produce must be gradually and regularly diminishing.

Let us suppose that the yearly additions which might be made to the former average produce, instead of decreasing, which they certainly would do, were to remain the same; and that the produce of this island might be increased every twenty-five years, by a quantity equal to what it at present produces. The most enthusiastic speculator cannot suppose a greater increase than this. In a few centuries it would make every acre of land in the island like a garden.

It may be fairly pronounced, therefore, that, considering the present average state of the earth, *the means of subsistence,* under circumstances the most favourable to human industry, *could not possibly be made to increase faster than in an arithmetical ratio.*

The potential rates of increase of population and food compared. The necessary effects of these two different rates of increase, when brought together, will be very striking. Let us call the population of this island eleven millions; and suppose the present produce equal to the easy support of such a number. In the first twenty-five years the population would be twenty-two millions, and the food being also doubled, the means of subsistence would be equal to this increase. In the next twenty-five years, the population would be forty-four millions, and the means of subsistence only equal

to the support of thirty-three millions. In the next period the population would be eighty-eight millions, and the means of subsistence just equal to the support of half that number. And, at the conclusion of the first century, the population would be a hundred and seventy-six millions, and the means of subsistence only equal to the support of fifty-five millions, leaving a population of a hundred and twenty-one million totally unprovided for.

Taking the whole earth, instead of this island, emigration would of course be excluded; and, supposing the present population equal to a thousand millions, the human species would increase as the numbers 1, 2, 4, 8, 16, 32, 64, 128, 256, and subsistence as 1, 2, 3, 4, 5, 6, 7, 8, 9. In two centuries the population would be to the means of subsistence as 256 to 9; in three centuries as 4096 to 13 and in two thousand years the difference would be almost incalculable.

In this supposition no limits whatever are placed to the produce of the earth. It may increase for ever and be greater than any assignable quantity; yet still the power of population being in every period so much superior the increase of the human species can only be kept down to the level of the means of subsistence by the constant operation of the strong law of necessity, acting as a check upon the greater power.

Of the general checks to population, and the mode of their operation

The ultimate check to population appears then to be a want of food, arising necessarily from the different ratios according to which population and food increase. But this ultimate check is never the immediate check, except in cases of actual famine.

The immediate check may be stated to consist in all those customs, and all those diseases, which seem to be generated by a scarcity of the means of subsistence; and all those causes, independent of this scarcity, whether of a moral or physical nature, which tend prematurely to weaken and destroy the human frame.

These checks to population, which are constantly operating with more or less force in every society, and keep down the number to the level of the means of subsistence, may be classed under two general heads—(i) the preventive, and (ii) the positive checks.

The preventive and positive checks described.

(i) The *preventive* check, as far as it is voluntary, is peculiar to man, and arises from that distinctive superiority in his reasoning faculties, which enables him to calculate distant consequences. The checks to the indefinite increase of plants and irrational animals are all either positive, or, if preventive, involuntary. But man cannot look around him, and see the distress which frequently presses upon those who have large families; he cannot contemplate his present possessions or earnings, which he now nearly consumes himself, and calculate the amount of each share, when with very little addition they must be divided, perhaps, among seven or eight, without feeling a doubt whether, if he follow the bent of his inclinations, he may be able to support the offspring which he will probably bring into the world. In a state of equality, if such can exist, this would be the simple question. In the present state of society other considerations occur. Will he not lower his rank in life, and be obliged to give up in great measure his former habits? Does any mode of employment present itself by which he may reasonably hope to maintain a family? Will he not at any rate subject himself to greater difficulties, and more severe labour, than in his single state? Will he not be unable to transmit to his children the same advantages of education and improvement that he had himself possessed? Does he even feel secure that, should he have a large family, his utmost exertions can save them from rags and squalid poverty, and their consequent degradation in the community?

These considerations are calculated to prevent, and certainly do prevent, a great number of persons in all civilised nations from pursuing the dictate of nature in an early attachment to one woman.

If this restraint do not produce vice, it is undoubtedly the least evil that can arise from the principle of population. Considered as a restraint on a strong natural inclination, it must be allowed to produce a certain degree of temporary unhappiness; but evidently slight, compared with the evils which result from any of the other checks to population; and merely of the same nature as many other sacrifices of temporary to permanent gratifi-

cation, which it is the business of a moral agent continually to make.

When this restraint produces vice, the evils which follow are but too conspicuous. A promiscuous intercourse to such a degree as to prevent the birth of children, seems to lower, in the most marked manner, the dignity of human nature. It cannot be without its effect on men, and nothing can be more obvious than its tendency to degrade the female character, and to destroy all its most amiable and distinguishing characteristics. Add to which, that among those unfortunate females, with which all great towns abound, more real distress and aggravated misery are, perhaps, to be found, than in any other department of human life.

When a general corruption of morals, with regard to the sex, pervades all the classes of society, its effects must necessarily be, to poison the springs of domestic happiness, to weaken conjugal and parental affection, and to lessen the united exertions and ardour of parents in the care and education of their children:—effects which cannot take place without a decided diminution of the general happiness and virtue of the society; particularly as the necessity of art in the accomplishment and conduct of intrigues, and in the concealment of their consequences necessarily leads to many other vices.

(ii) The *positive* checks to population are extremely various, and include every cause, whether arising from vice or misery, which in any degree contributes to shorten the natural duration of human life. Under this head, therefore, may be enumerated all unwholesome occupations, severe labour and exposure to the seasons, extreme poverty, bad nursing of children, great towns, excesses of all kinds, the whole train of common diseases and epidemics, wars, plague, and famine.

On examining these obstacles to the increase of population which I have classed under the heads of preventive and positive checks, it will appear that they are all resolvable into *moral restraint, vice,* and *misery.*

Of the preventive checks, the *restraint from marriage* which is not followed by irregular gratifications may properly be termed moral restraint.

Promiscuous intercourse, unnatural passions, violations of the marriage bed, and improper arts to conceal the consequences of irregular connexions, are preventive checks that clearly come under the head of *vice*.

Of the positive checks, those which appear to arise unavoidably from the laws of nature, may be called exclusively misery; and those which we obviously bring upon ourselves, such as wars, excesses, and many others which it would be in our power to avoid, are of a mixed nature. They are brought upon us by vice, and their consequences are misery.

The mode of operation of preventive and positive checks.   The sum of all these preventive and positive checks, taken together, forms the immediate check to population. In every country some of these checks are, with more or less force, in constant operation; yet, notwithstanding their general prevalence, there are few states in which there is not a constant effort in the population to increase beyond the means of subsistence. This constant effort as constantly tends to subject the lower classes of society to distress, and to prevent any great permanent melioration of their condition.

These effects seem to be produced in the following manner. The constant effort towards population, which is found to act even in the most vicious societies, increases the number of people before the means of subsistence are increased. The food, therefore, which before supported eleven millions, must now be divided among eleven millions and a half. The poor consequently must live much worse, and many of them be reduced to severe distress. The number of labourers also being above the proportion of work in the market, the price of labour must tend to fall, while the price of provisions would at the same time tend to rise. The labourer therefore must do more work, to earn the same as he did before.

During this season of distress the discouragements to marriage and the difficulty of rearing a family are so great, that the progress of population is retarded. In the mean time, the cheapness of labour, the plenty of labourers, and the necessity of an increased industry among them, encourage cultivators to employ more labour upon their land, to turn up fresh soil, and to manure and improve more completely what is already in tillage, till ultimately the means of subsistence may become in the same proportion to the population, as at the period from which we set out. The situation of the labourer being then again tolerably comfortable, the restraints to population are in some degree loosened; and, after a short period, the same retrograde and progressive movements, with respect to happiness, are repeated.

One principal reason why this oscillation has been less remarked, and less decidedly confirmed by experience than might naturally be expected, is, that the histories of mankind which we possess are, in general, histories only of the higher classes. We have not many accounts that can be depended upon, of the manners and customs of that part of mankind, where these retrograde and progressive movements chiefly take place.

Reading 4

Controlling the Population Explosion

Ansley J. Coale

Population growth in the United States

I shall begin a discussion of population with a brief description of recent, current, and future population trends in the United States. Our population today is a little over 200 million, having increased by slightly more than 50 percent since 1940. I think it is likely to increase by nearly 50 percent again in the 30 years before the end of the century.

This rate of increase cannot continue long. If it

From Ansley J. Coale, "Man and His Environment," *Science*, vol. 170, pp. 132–136, Oct. 9, 1970. Copyright 1970 by the American Association for the Advancement of Science. Reprinted by permission of the author and the publisher.

endured throughout the next century, the population would reach a billion shortly before the year 2100. Within six or seven more centuries we would reach one person per square foot of land area in the United States, and after about 1500 years our descendants would outweigh the earth if they continued to increase by 50 percent every 30 years.

Every demographer knows that we cannot continue a positive rate of increase indefinitely. The inexorable arithmetic of compound interest leads us to absurd conditions within a calculable period of time. Logically we must, and in fact we will, have a rate of growth very close to zero in the long run.

The only questions about attaining a zero rate of increase for any population is when and how such a rate is attained. A zero rate of increase implies a balance between the average birth and death rates, so the choice of how to attain a zero rate of increase is a choice between low birth and death rates that are approximately equal. The average growth rate very near to zero during mankind's past history has been attained with high birth and death rates—with an average duration of life that until recently was no more than 30 or 35 years. I have no difficulty in deciding that I would prefer a zero rate of growth with low rather than high birth and death rates, or with an average duration of life in excess of 70 years, as has been achieved in all of the more advanced countries of the world, rather than the life that is "nasty, brutish, and short."

When? The remaining question then is *when* should our population growth level off.

A popular answer today is "immediately." In fact a zero rate of increase in the United States starting immediately is not feasible and I believe not desirable. The reason is the age composition of the population that our past history of birth and death rates has left to us. We have an especially young population now because of the postwar baby boom. One consequence is that our death rate is much lower than it would be in a population that had long had low fertility. Therefore, if we were to attain a zero growth rate immediately, it would be necessary to cut the birth rate about in half. For the next 15 or 20 years, women would have to bear children at a rate that would produce only a little over one child per completed family.

At the end of that time we would have a very peculiar age distribution with a great shortage of young people. The attendant social and economic disruptions represent too large a cost to pay for the advantages that we might derive from reducing growth to zero right away.

In fact, a more reasonable goal would be to reduce fertility as soon as possible to a level where couples produced just enough children to insure that each generation exactly replaced itself. If this goal (early attainment of fertility at a replacement level) were reached immediately, our population would increase 35 to 40 percent before it stabilized. The reason that fertility at the mere replacement level would produce such a large increase in population is again the age distribution we have today. There are many more people today under 20 than 20 to 40, and when the relatively numerous children have moved into the childbearing ages, they will greatly outnumber the persons now at those ages.

Population and pollution

The connection between the current growth in our population and the deterioration of our environment of which we have all become aware is largely an indirect one. There seems little doubt that the rapid increase in the production of goods has been responsible for the rapid increase in the production of bads, since we have made no effective effort to prevent the latter from accompanying the former. But per capita increase in production has been more important than population growth. It has been calculated that if we were to duplicate the total production of electricity in the United States in 1940 in a population enjoying the 1969 per capita usage of energy, the population could be only 25 million rather than 132 million people there were in 1940. Population has increased by 50 percent, but per capita use of electricity has been multiplied several times. A similar statement can even be made about the crowding of our national parks. The population has increased by about 50 percent in the last 30 years—attendance in national parks has increased by more than 400 percent.

A wealthy industrial urban population of 100 million persons would have most of the pollution problems we do. In fact, Sydney, Australia, has problems of air and water pollution and of traffic jams, even though the total population of Australia is about 12 million in an area 80 percent as big as the United States. There is no doubt that slower population growth would make it easier to improve our environment, but not much easier.

Policies that would affect the growth of population

We must, at some time, achieve a zero rate of population, and the balance should surely be achieved at low birth and death rates rather than at high rates. What kinds of policies might be designed to assure such a level of fertility or, more generally, to produce the fertility level that is at the moment socially desirable?

Birth control. These are policies that would, through education and the provision of clinical services, try to make it possible for every conception to be the result of a deliberate choice, and for every choice to be an informed one, based on an adequate knowledge of the consequences of bearing different numbers of children at different times. A component of such a set of policies would be the development of more effective means of contraception to reduce the number of accidental pregnancies occurring to couples who are trying to avoid conception.

Legal abortion. These are policies that call for a substantial government role and I think that an effective government program in these areas is already overdue. I personally believe that education in the consequences of childbearing and in the techniques of avoiding pregnancy, combined with the provision of contraceptive services, should be supplemented by the provision of safe and skillful abortion upon request. I am persuaded by experience in Japan and eastern Europe that the advantages of abortion provided under good medical auspices to cause the early termination of unwanted pregnancies are very important to the women affected, as is evident in the fact that when medically safe abortion has been made available at low cost, the number of abortions has initially been as great or greater than the number of live births. Later there is a typical tendency for women to resort to contraception rather than repeated abortions.

The reason I favor abortion is that such a high proportion of births that occur today [less true, perhaps, after 1973 than in 1970] are unwanted, and because a large number of desperate pregnant women (probably more than a half a million annually) resort to clandestine abortions today, with high rates of serious complications. In contrast, early abortion, under skilled medical auspices, is less dangerous than tonsillectomy, and substantially less dangerous than carrying a child to full term.

Deliberate policy; not chance

If it is true that the elimination of unwanted pregnancies would reduce fertility very nearly to replacement, it must be conceded that this outcome is fortuitous. It is highly unlikely that over a substantial period of time the free choice by each couple of the number of children they want would lead exactly to the socially desirable level of fertility. The erratic behavior of fertility in America and in other advanced industrialized countries in the last 30 or 40 years is ample evidence that when fertility is voluntarily controlled, the level of fertility is subject to major fluctuations, and I see no logical reason to expect that on average people would voluntarily choose a number of children that would keep the long-run average a little above two per couple. In other words, we must acknowledge the probable necessity of instituting policies that would influence the number of children people want. However, there is no need for haste in formulating such policy, since, as I have indicated, improved contraceptive services combined with a liberal provision of abortion would probably move our fertility at present quite close to replacement, and a gradual increase in population during the next generation would not be a major addition to the problems we already face.

Policies intended to affect people's preferences for children should be designed within the framework of our democratic traditions. They should be designed, for example, to encourage diversity and permit freedom of choice. The ideal policy would affect the decision at the margin and not try to impose a uniform pattern on all. I do not think that people who prefer to have more than the average number of children should be subject to ridicule or abuse.

To design policies consistent with our most cherished social and political values will not be easy, and it is fortunate that there is no valid reason for hasty action.

Pricing under Capitalism

Reading 5

All economies have one problem in common: relatively limited resources to be allocated among the unlimited wants of their people. Indeed an economic system may be viewed as a way in which a society organizes itself to answer certain fundamental questions: What goods and services shall be produced? How shall they be produced? For whom shall they be produced? At the core of the American economic system, there is a much-lauded but little understood mechanism for answering these questions: the free marketplace.

The late Sumner H. Slichter, long a professor of economics at Harvard University and a prolific writer on the American economy, here describes how this system relies on the motivations of individual freedom, self-interest, and profit to give it its forward thrust, and how it relies too on the forces of competition to check the accumulation of power in the marketplaces. The picture was a qualified one even at the time of Slichter's writing; it is still more qualified today as we increasingly modify the market mechanisms with one restraint or another. But none of those modifications lets us escape from the necessity of beginning with an understanding of the market system in its purer forms. Society may or may not want to operate in a totally free private enterprise world; but it must at least know that bench mark if intelligent choices are to be made.

Questions to guide the reading

The market mechanism described here was eloquently discussed by an early and towering figure in economics, Adam Smith, in this manner:

Every individual necessarily labors to render the annual revenue of the society as great as he can. He generally indeed, neither intends to promote the public interest, nor knows how much he is promoting it. . . . he intends only his own security; and by directing that industry in such a manner as its produce may be of the greatest value, he intends only his own gain, and he is in this, as in many other cases, led by an invisible hand to promote an end which was no part of his intention. Nor is it always the worse for the society that it was no part of it. By pursuing his own interest he frequently promotes that of the society more effectually than when he really intends to promote it. I have never known much good done by those who affected to trade for the public good. (*The Wealth of Nations,* Book IV, Chap. II, 1776.)

How does this "Invisible-Hand" mechanism work in, say, getting resources to move where they are most desired by consumers, or arriving at prices that serve to clear the marketplaces?

What is the nature of the system of values on which such a free-market society might be built? To what extent are these values that might be shared by men in the Soviet Union, or in one of the newly developing countries of Africa?

What is the rationale on which we have chosen in our economy to interfere at some points with the workings of the market system? Have we succeeded in finding what Adam Smith could not find, an effective way of pursuing the public good by strategic direct intervention rather than by the exclusive use of the free markets?

Free Private Enterprise

Sumner H. Slichter

Possible forms of economic organizations

Every economic system must provide some way of doing three fundamental things: (1) getting goods produced; (2) determining what share each person shall have in the total product; and (3) regulating the consumption of goods, that is, determining who shall consume this good and who that. The manner in which these three basic economic processes are performed stamps the economic system with its most essential characteristics. How does the existing economic order organize and regulate the production, distribution, and consumption of goods?

There are several ways in which these activities *might* be organized and regulated:

1. On the basis of family autonomy. Each family might produce everything which it uses, relying upon others for nothing. In such a society there would be no trade.

2. On a communistic basis. What is produced and what each person does might be determined by the group as a whole and the product might be the property of the group, to be divided in accordance with socially determined rules.

3. On a despotic basis. The things produced and the tasks of each person might be decided by a despot or a despotic class, the product in all or in part being the property of the despot to be shared with the others as he saw fit.

4. On the basis of custom and heredity. Instead of choosing his own work or having it selected for him by the group or a despot, each person might be born into his occupation. He might be expected to do the thing which his father did, and other occupations might be closed to him. Likewise the share of each person in the product and the things

which he is permitted or forbidden to consume might also be determined by custom.

All of these methods of organizing and controlling economic activities have been more or less prevalent in the past and, indeed, instances of them still exist. They are not, however, the methods which prevail today in the United States. It may seem a strange way of doing, but we organize industry by, in effect, saying to each individual, "Choose your own occupation. Produce what you like. What you do, to whom you sell, what or from whom you buy, the prices you get or give, are all your own concern. You are free, subject to a few restrictions, to produce whatever you wish regardless of whether or not it is needed, regardless of whether or not too much of it already exists. You are likewise free to refrain from engaging in any occupation no matter how acute may be the shortage of goods or how pressing the need for your help. You are free to buy from whoever is willing to sell and to sell to whoever is willing to buy. You are equally free to refuse to buy or sell whenever you please and for any reason or no reason."

This is what we mean by *free private enterprise.* Under it the government confines itself in the main to the suppression of fraud and violence and to the enforcement of contracts. It does not itself engage in or attempt to guide the course of industry. It pursues a "let alone" or "hands off" policy. Let us now see how, under free enterprise, the three fundamental economic processes of production, distribution, and consumption take place.

How free enterprise organizes production

Why does not a system of freedom, in which each person is at liberty to pursue whatever occupation

From Sumner H. Slichter, *Modern Economic Society* (Henry Holt and Company, Inc., New York, 1928). Reprinted with kind permission of the publisher.

he pleases and to produce whatever he wishes, result in hopeless chaos? Why do not many essential articles fail to get made and why does not the output of many things far exceed the demand for them? How can we get along without a central directing body to discover how much different things are in demand and to tell each of us what to produce?

To put the problem specifically, how does New York City each day obtain about the quantity of milk that it demands? Of the thousands of people engaged in supplying New York with milk, almost none knows either how much the city consumes or how much is being produced. And yet, despite this ignorance, New York each day receives about the amount of milk that it demands. There is neither a great surplus nor a shortage. Milk does not spoil because there is no one to consume it, and babies do not go without it because too small a supply reaches the city on some days. At the same time, other cities in the neighborhood are also receiving their daily supply from the same territory. Each uses a different quantity, yet each receives about the amount it demands.

The guide upon which we rely is the profit in making different goods, which, of course, depends upon the prices which they command and the cost of producing them. Suppose, for example, that New York failed to receive enough milk to satisfy the demand. Rather than go without milk or drink less, many people would be willing to pay more. Consequently the price would promptly rise. This would tend to end the shortage. More milk would be shipped to New York and less to other places. This would continue until there was no greater profit in selling milk in New York than elsewhere.

Just as price regulates the distribution of milk between cities, so it also determines the total amount produced in the country as a whole. Failure of the supply to keep pace with the demand would cause the price to rise. The greater profit to be had from the sale of milk would cause farmers to produce more of it. Some farmers, who had been separating their milk and selling the cream to be made into butter, might turn to the sale of whole milk. Others might abandon raising grain, stock, or fruit and enter dairy farming. As the output of milk increased, the price, of course, would drop. This would continue until producing milk was no more attractive than alternative branches of farming. If, furthermore, the demand for milk were to fall off or the supply to increase faster than the demand, farmers, in order to dispose of their supply, would be compelled to lower the price. Milk production would become a less profitable occupation, men would be deterred from entering it, and some of those already engaged in it might be led to abandon it or at least to reduce their output. And this would continue until the price rose and milk production became no less attractive than alternative occupations.

Price also determines in large measure where and how goods are made. Because living in New York City is expensive, it might seem a poor place in which to locate a factory. But the great stream of immigrants who for many years entered the country at New York and who were reluctant to undertake a long journey through a strange country provided the city with a bountiful supply of cheap labor. To take advantage of this, many industries, such as the needle trades, grew up in or near the East Side. At one time the Genesee valley in western New York was an important wheat region and Rochester, at the falls of the Genesee, was a great milling center. As the urban population in the East has grown, the greater profits in dairying and in fruit and truck raising have driven wheat raising to the West. The same is true of sheep raising. At one time, New York State contained nearly 5,000,000 sheep; now it has less than one-tenth that number. The growth of urban population has made dairying so profitable that most farmers cannot afford to raise sheep in New York.

Whether goods shall be made by hand or by machinery is often a question of money costs. Shall houses be built of wood or brick? As long as our immense forests were far from exhaustion, wooden houses were the almost universal rule. In Europe, where timber is less plentiful, frame dwellings are the exception. We still use timber to a greater extent than do most countries, but the cost of certain woods, such as white pine, has caused us to use cheaper varieties—Norway pine, hemlock, spruce, Douglas fir. Shall land be farmed intensively or extensively? The English obtain about twice as many bushels of wheat per acre as do the Americans, but we obtain about twice as many bushels per man. The reason is that in England, where land is relatively expensive, it is economized by the use of more labor and less land. Here where labor is expensive in comparison with land, labor is economized by the use of more land and less labor.

How shares in the output of industry are determined

In our highly specialized society, each of us, at the best, contributes to industry's output very few things. One man may produce wheat, another wood, another milk, another cattle, another corn. In fact, most men do not contribute even one complete product. Hundreds of workers combine their efforts to make a suit of clothes, a pair of shoes, an automobile, or a telephone.

Although each individual makes a very specialized contribution to the product of society, each wishes to obtain from that output hundreds of articles. The man who produces only wheat desires flour, butter, sugar, clothing, shoes, hats, magazines, furniture, services of doctors, dentists, lawyers, and much else. If he contributes 2,000 bushels of wheat to society's stock of goods, how much is he entitled to withdraw?

Just as prices determine what things are produced, in what proportions, and by what methods, so, under free enterprise, they also determine the share of each person in the output of industry. If our imaginary wheat grower, who has produced a crop of 2,000 bushels, obtains $1.25 for each bushel, he is thereby enabled to purchase articles valued at $2,500. Just how much this is, will depend upon the price of shoes, hats, sugar, and the various other things which he desires. The next year he may work harder and produce 2,400 bushels. In the meantime, however, the price of wheat may drop to 75 cents a bushel. Hence, despite the fact that he has worked harder and raised more wheat, he has only $1,800 to spend for goods. And if, perchance, prices in general have risen, each of his dollars will buy him less than the year before. In a word, what share a man receives in the product of industry is determined by the prices of what he has to sell quite as much as by how industriously and efficiently he labors.

How consumption is regulated under free enterprise

There are many ways in which we might determine what goods each person shall consume. We might undertake to ascertain the peculiar needs of each and see that he was afforded some special opportunity to obtain the things which would satisfy them. Or we might study the ability of different persons to use goods to the advantage of the rest of us and arrange for men of outstanding ability to receive the things which they require in order to be of greatest service to the community.

To a limited extent, we do regulate consumption upon the basis of either needs or ability to use goods advantageously. Schooling is considered so important that many governments supply a certain amount of it free or below cost. Police and fire protection, parks, playgrounds, and, to some extent, transportation, communication, and insurance are also considered so essential that they are provided by the government. Fellowships and scholarships, awarded to students of special promise, are among the few attempts which we make to place goods within reach of those who can use them to special advantage.

Under a system of free enterprise, however, which permits men to buy whatever they can get on the best terms that they can obtain, neither need nor ability to use goods for the benefit of others necessarily has much to do with determining how goods are consumed. Of far greater importance are the prices of different commodities and the ability of different persons to pay these prices.

In some respects, the control of consumption by price and ability to pay works out very satisfactorily. Suppose, for example, that unfavorable weather or blight made it likely that the potato crop would be exceptionally small. It is obvious that we should need to consume potatoes sparingly, making more than customary use of substitutes. If, on the other hand, the outlook were for a large crop, it would be to our interest to use more potatoes than usual. In each case, price produces the desired effect. If the prospects are for a small crop, the higher price induces sparing consumption; if a large crop seems probable, the low price encourages larger consumption. Because skilled labor is scarce, it is desirable that we economize it by using its products sparingly. The high wages of skilled craftsmen make their products expensive and encourage consumers to avoid wasting them. Commodities which can be made only at great risk of accidental or industrial disease should also be used sparingly. In so far as these hazards cause workmen to demand higher wages, they increase the price of the products and limit their consumption.

Although the regulation of consumption by prices usually encourages the economizing of scarce goods, it does so in a manner not altogether satisfactory. If consumption must be reduced this should perhaps be accomplished by those using less who can do so with the smallest inconvenience and sacrifice. As a matter of fact, the well-to-do, who are best supplied, are least induced by higher prices to curtail their purchases. It is the poor, who can least afford to reduce their consumption, who get along with less when the supply falls short. In periods of severe food shortage, such as often occur during war time, the regulation of consumption by ability to pay works such hardship that it is sometimes superseded by a system of rationing.

Some claims on behalf of free enterprise

Since free enterprise is the principal method by which our economic activities are organized and controlled, our study of modern industrial society must very largely consist of an inquiry into how freedom works under present-day conditions— such as machine industry, huge corporations, and science applied to business. But before we proceed further with our analysis, it will be helpful to become familiar in a general way with some of the claims which have been made in behalf of free enterprise. The "obvious and simple system of natural liberty," as Adam Smith called freedom of enterprise, has been regarded as the one and only way in which men might attain the maximum satisfaction of their desires with a minimum outlay of sacrifice. It is true that this extreme view has been accepted by few economists of repute and that since the middle of the last century, it has been increasingly under attack. Nevertheless it has had and still does have a wide acceptance by the general public and by certain schools of politicians, and it is appealed to frequently in political controversies. And even though we no longer spend much time discussing whether or not we can *always* trust free enterprise to regulate economic activity better than any other method, we are frequently compelled to decide whether or not it is the best way of controlling a specific economic activity under specific circumstances. Consequently the claims which have been made on its behalf are still very live issues.

The reasoning in support of the belief that freedom of enterprise is the maximum of satisfaction at the minimum of cost is very simple. Each individual, it is said, is better able than any one else to judge his own interests. If men are at liberty to spend their money as they choose, they will naturally purchase those things that will yield them the most satisfaction. Consequently the very commodities which give consumers the greatest pleasure are the most profitable for business enterprises to produce. Likewise, if men are free to use such methods of production as they wish, they will select those which involve the least cost per unit of output. With the goods which give the greatest gratification being made by the methods which are least costly, it follows, according to the theory, that there will be the maximum surplus of satisfaction over sacrifice.

Some assumptions of the theory of free enterprise

But if this result is to follow, two things would appear to be necessary: (1) goods must go to the consumers who will derive the greatest pleasure from them, and (2) the tasks of making goods must be assigned to the workers who can perform them with the least sacrifice for each unit of product. Does freedom of enterprise cause either goods or jobs to be distributed in this manner?

We have already seen that under a system of free enterprise goods tend to get into the hands of those who offer the best prices for them. But how then can they be consumed so as to yield the maximum of satisfaction? Are the people who are willing and able to pay most for goods also those who will derive the most satisfaction from using them? If they are not, it would appear possible to increase the surplus of satisfaction over sacrifice by causing goods to be distributed more in accordance with needs and less in accordance with ability to pay. We have no way of comparing the amount of pleasure which two persons derive from consuming an article. And yet it seems ridiculous to assert that ability to derive satisfaction from goods is proportionate to ability to pay for them. Assume that A and B each wish a pair of shoes. A, who is well-to-do, is willing to pay $12; B, who is poor, will offer only $7. Obviously A will get the shoes. But because he is rich and well supplied with shoes, an additional pair is only a slight convenience to him. B, poor and scantily supplied, has urgent need for another pair. It seems clear that the sum total of satisfaction would be greater if B obtained the shoes, and yet it seems equally clear that under freedom of enterprise they will go to A.

We are no better able to compare the pains suffered by different persons than we are the pleasures which they enjoy. Nevertheless it does not appear probable that freedom of enterprise necessarily causes jobs to be distributed so as to result in a minimum sacrifice for each unit of output—so that, for example, persons who can do heavy work with least fatigue will be given heavy work. Rather jobs tend to go to those who are willing to do the most work for the least money. Now the fact that X is willing to do a job for a dollar a day less than Y does not necessarily mean that X finds the task less onerous or unpleasant than Y. It may simply mean that he needs the money more and is willing to work at a lower rate in order to get it.

In face of the fact that ability to derive pleasure from goods does not appear to correspond to capacity to pay for them and that jobs are not necessarily given to the men who can do them with the least sacrifice for each unit of product, how can it be asserted that industrial liberty results in a maximum of satisfaction over sacrifice? But the exponents of free enterprise are not without a reply. To interfere with liberty in order to bring about a distribution of goods upon the basis of needs rather than ability to pay, or in order to cause jobs to be assigned to those who perform them with least sacrifice, might have the *immediate* effect of increasing the surplus of satisfaction over sacrifice. But this result, it is said, would be short lived. Men have the greatest incentive to improve their efficiency when they are free to compete for any jobs which they desire and to spend their income as they see fit. Were this incentive diminished by distributing jobs to those who could perform them with the least sacrifice and goods to those who would derive the most pleasure from them, output would inevitably decline. What would be gained by a different distribution of goods and jobs would be lost through smaller production.

The significance of competition

But how is it possible for us to trust business enterprises with so much freedom? In other branches of human relations, laws to regulate conduct seem to be quite essential. Why should industry be an ex-

ception to this general rule? If we leave business concerns free to make anything they like by any methods which they see fit, what is to prevent them from supplying the public with poorly made or adulterated goods or from using methods that are cheap in terms of dollars but expensive in terms of human sacrifice? Might not the sum total of pleasure be greater and of pain be less if the state enforced certain standards of quality or prohibited the use of certain methods of production?

The theory of free enterprise does not, it is important to emphasize, assert that restraints upon human selfishness are not needed. It simply assumes that they are provided by *competition.* This, according to the theory, is the great regulative force which establishes effective control over economic activities and gives each of us an incentive to observe the interests of others. Thus business establishments are deterred from furnishing adulterated or poorly made goods by the fear that customers may shift their patronage to rivals. Likewise the enterprises which fail to protect their men against accidents or industrial disease or which work them unusually hard, are penalized by the refusal of laborers to work for them except at a higher wage than other employers pay.

The mere existence of competition, however, is not enough. For it to perform satisfactorily the protective function attributed to it, certain very definite conditions must be present.

To begin with, an appreciable proportion of buyers and sellers must be willing to discriminate against those sellers or buyers who ignore, and in favor of those who take account of, the welfare of others. Otherwise, of course, no one has an economic incentive to pay attention to the well-being of his fellows. Assume, for example, that an enterprise pollutes a stream by dumping refuse and chemicals into it. From the standpoint of the firm, this may be an economical method of production. But from the standpoint of the community it is an expensive one because it kills the fish, spoils the stream for bathing, and makes it foul and ill-smelling. But competition will not stop the pollution unless an appreciable number of consumers, wage earners, or investors refuse to deal with the firm which is responsible—that is, unless a substantial number of consumers refuse to buy from it, or wage earners to work for it, or investors to put money into it. But if the enterprise charges no more than its rivals for goods of equal grade, offers equally attractive conditions of employment, and pays as high dividends, who has an interest in discriminating against it? Perhaps the very fact that the enterprise pollutes the stream enables it to offer better terms than its rivals. Or take the case of child labor—another method of production cheap in dollars and cents but expensive in terms of human cost. If the firms which employ children are able, *because of that very fact,* to sell for less or to pay higher wages to adults or higher profits to investors, who is going to discriminate against them? Under these circumstances, does not competition positively encourage the employment of children?

But willingness to discriminate between those who consider the interests of others and those who do not is insufficient. Competition protects consumers against inferior ware only when they know good quality from bad; it protects laborers from unguarded machines only when they know which employers have and which have not guarded their machines. In other words, competition is an efficient protective agency only when buyers or sellers have the information necessary to make intelligent choices. It fails, for example, to protect consumers against milk from tubercular cattle because the ordinary buyer of milk has no way of distinguishing the milk of healthy cows from that of diseased.

The information needed for intelligent choices may be available, and yet many buyers or sellers may be too ignorant, too careless, too neglectful of their own interests to use it. If, for example, workmen show no disposition to shun plants which are notoriously dangerous or unsanitary, what incentive have employers to improve conditions?

Some issues raised by free enterprise

The whole theory that industrial liberty results in a maximum net satisfaction rests, it will be recalled, upon the assumption that each individual knows his own interests better than any one else and consequently can make his own decisions better than any one can make them for him. Is this true? May not free enterprise fail to yield the greatest possible satisfaction precisely *because* it results in choices which are molded too much by impulse, habit, prejudice, ignorance, or clever sales talk and too little by reflection, investigation of facts, or comparison of alternative opportunities? Under the system of economic freedom, choices are largely a matter of individual decision.

This means that they are usually made in a hurry and by amateurs who have little opportunity to obtain expert advice. This situation may not be inevitable, but it exists. And yet millions of individuals, each attempting to decide for himself about the purchase of scores of articles concerning which he knows little, are an easy prey for ingenious selling and advertising experts. It may be true, as the theory of free enterprise asserts, that each individual knows his own desires better than any one else, but of what good is this if he has time to investigate neither what he is buying nor what he might buy, or if he is prevented by a skillful salesman from reflecting very much as to what he really does wish after all? Hence, when we find the United States spending more for tobacco than for education, the explanation may be, not that we desire tobacco more than education, but simply that the facilities for getting people to buy tobacco are more efficient than those for persuading them to pay for education. A representative body which could employ experts to investigate people's needs and desires and to test products might be able to spend a considerable portion of consumers' money with greater satisfaction to them than they could obtain by spending it themselves.

Role of government

Perhaps the most striking aspect of the theory of free enterprise is its assertion that intervention of the government in economic activities is unnecessary. The theory, as we have said, does not deny that restraints on human selfishness are needed. It simply asserts that we can trust competition to provide them. But closer inquiry reveals that the defenders of free enterprise do not trust competition to do all things. However much they trust it to guard the lives and limbs of workmen against dangerous machinery or to protect consumers against injurious foods, they do not rely upon it to enforce contracts or to prevent fraud. But the same reasoning which is used to prove that the government need not intervene on behalf of wage earners and consumers can be employed to show that laws are not required to guard business men against fraud or breach of contractual obligations. Would not a customer who refused to pay his bills soon experience difficulty in getting dealers to sell to him, and would not an enterprise which violated its contracts find other concerns unwilling to deal with it?

Is not the aid of the courts in these matters as superfluous as laws to protect workmen against dangerous machines or consumers against adulterated wares?

This inconsistency in the theory of free enterprise is to be explained by its origin. The theory was invented several hundred years ago to justify the demand of business men for release from oppressive legal restrictions. That the makers of the theory should have had greater faith in the capacity of competition to protect workmen against loss of life or limb than in its capacity to protect business men against bad debts is not surprising. When the rights of business were involved, it seemed quite proper for the government to lend the aid of its courts; only when the interests of consumers or wage earners were at stake did competition become a perfect protective instrument and intervention by the government "paternalistic" and "an unwarranted invasion of private rights."

Because the theory of free enterprise assumes that competition is needed to prevent freedom from being abused, it must also assume that competition is a more economical method of production than monopoly. Otherwise the claim that freedom results in the greatest satisfaction and the least sacrifice could not be correct. In many instances, however, it seems reasonably certain that monopoly is more economical than competition. The clearest cases are the so-called "octopus" industries, such as gas, electric light and power, water, railway, and street railway, which must run wire, pipe, or rails close to each consumer in order to deliver the service. It is the cost of duplicating this part of the plant which makes competition in these industries so uneconomical. In the oil industry, the desire of each landowner to obtain as much of the oil as possible causes him to put down an excessive number of wells along the edge of his property, thus diminishing the pressure under which the oil is held, substantially reducing the quantity which can be recovered, and greatly increasing the cost of getting it. Or consider the wastefulness of competition in distributing milk. With only a few customers in each block, a driver must travel many miles to reach several hundred customers. A study of competitive milk distribution in Rochester, New York, indicated that 2,509 miles of travel were necessary to distribute milk which a monopoly could deliver with 300 miles of travel. Competition required 356 men, 380 horses, and 305 wagons; a monopoly, it was estimated, would need 90 men, 80 horses, and 25 horsedrawn trucks. In most other industries, the case against competition is less clear, but undoubtedly there are many in which monopoly would be more economical.

The exponents of economic freedom answer that, even though monopoly is more economical at any given time, it may be less so in the long run. The search for new and cheaper methods of production needs, it is said, the spur of competition. In other words, competition more than makes up for its wastes by stimulating the development of better techniques.

Although the theory that government intervention in industry is unnecessary presupposes the existence of competition, the very absence of state interference often results in monopoly. This is not surprising. Indeed, it would be strange if business men left at liberty to do as they like, should not frequently combine to exploit the public rather than compete to serve the public. Consequently the government may find itself compelled to intervene either to enforce competition or to regulate monopoly. Either policy, of course, is a departure from the principle of free enterprise.

Reading 6

The market system is all around us. We buy and sell, and use money as the medium of exchange, with such ease that we often miss seeing just what functions the market and the exchange medium fulfill for us. Sometimes we need to get an unusual, even artificial perspective on this system in order to understand it. Then perhaps we can come at long last to feel about markets as Monsieur Jourdain came to feel about prose in Molière's *Le Bourgeois Gentilhomme:* "By my faith! for over forty years I've been speaking prose without knowing anything about it."

R. A. Radford found an unusual vantage point from which to view markets in his experiences as a British prisoner of war in Germany during World War II. Here he saw, in microcosm, the emergence of complex markets out of a simple barter system; he saw a medium of exchange—cigarettes—emerge to perform the same functions that less "useful" money performs for us. The very simplicity of the story he tells has made this article a minor classic in economics. To understand its full flavor is to know the world around us better than we knew it before.

Questions to guide the reading

Why did a system of exchange develop among the prisoners, and what is the parallel case for exchange in the world outside the prison camp?

What determined how elaborate or simple this prison market system became? What determines the extent to which we develop and use markets in everyday life?

The Economic Organisation of a P.O.W. Camp

R. A. Radford

Introduction

After allowance has been made for abnormal circumstances, the social institutions, ideas and habits of groups in the outside world are to be found reflected in a Prisoner of War Camp. It is an unusual but a vital society.

One aspect of social organisation is to be found in economic activity, and this, along with other manifestations of a group existence, is to be found in any P.O.W. camp. True, a prisoner is not dependent on his exertions for the provision of the necessaries, or even the luxuries of life, but through his economic activity, the exchange of goods and services, his standard of material comfort is considerably enhanced. And this is a serious matter to the prisoner: he is not "playing at shops" even though the small scale of the transactions and the simple expression of comfort and wants in terms of cigarettes and jam, razor blades and writing paper, make the urgency of those needs difficult to appreciate, even by an ex-prisoner of some three months' standing.

Nevertheless, it cannot be too strongly emphasised that economic activities do not bulk so large

in prison society as they do in the larger world. There can be little production; as has been said the prisoner is independent of his exertions for the provision of the necessities and luxuries of life; the emphasis lies in exchange and the media of exchange.

Everyone receives a roughly equal share of essentials; it is by trade that individual preferences are given expression and comfort increased. All at some time, and most people regularly, make exchanges of one sort or another.

Although a P.O.W. camp provides a living example of a simple economy which might be used as an alternative to the Robinson Crusoe economy beloved by the textbooks, and its simplicity renders the demonstration of certain economic hypotheses both amusing and instructive, it is suggested that the principal significance is sociological. True, there is interest in observing the growth of economic institutions and customs in a brand new society, small and simple enough to prevent detail from obscuring the basic pattern and disequilibrium from obscuring the working of the system. But the essential interest lies in the

From R. A. Radford, "The Economic Organisation of a P.O.W. Camp," *Economica*, vol. 12, 1945. Reprinted with kind permission of the editor.

universality and the spontaneity of this economic life; it came into existence not by conscious imitation but as a response to the immediate needs and circumstances. Any similarity between prison organisation and outside organisation arises from similar stimuli evoking similar responses.

The following is as brief an account of the essential data as may render the narrative intelligible. The camps of which the writer had experience were Oflags and consequently the economy was not complicated by payments for work by the detaining power. They consisted normally of between 1,200 and 2,500 people, housed in a number of separate but intercommunicating bungalows, one company of 200 or so to a building. Each company formed a group within the main organisation and inside the company the room and the messing syndicate, a voluntary and spontaneous group who fed together, formed the constituent units.

Between individuals there was active trading in all consumer goods and in some services. Most trading was for food against cigarettes or other foodstuffs, but cigarettes rose from the status of a normal commodity to that of currency. RMk.s existed but had no circulation save for gambling debts, as few articles could be purchased with them from the canteen.

Our supplies consisted of rations provided by the detaining power and (principally) the contents of Red Cross food parcels—tinned milk, jam, butter, biscuits, bully, chocolate, sugar, etc., and cigarettes. So far the supplies to each person were equal and regular. Private parcels of clothing, toilet requisites and cigarettes were also received, and here equality ceased owing to the different numbers despatched and the vagaries of the post. All these articles were the subject of trade and exchange.

The development and organisation of the market

Very soon after capture people realised that it was both undesirable and unnecessary, in view of the limited size and the equality of supplies, to give away or to accept gifts of cigarettes or food. "Goodwill" developed into trading as a more equitable means of maximising individual satisfaction.

We reached a transit camp in Italy about a fortnight after capture and received ¼ of a Red Cross food parcel each a week later. At once exchanges, already established, multiplied in volume. Starting with simple direct barter, such as a non-smoker giving a smoker friend his cigarette issue in exchange for a chocolate ration, more complex exchanges soon became an accepted custom. Stories circulated of a padre who started off round the camp with a tin of cheese and five cigarettes and returned to his bed with a complete parcel in addition to his original cheese and cigarettes; the market was not yet perfect. Within a week or two, as the volume of trade grew, rough scales of exchange values came into existence. Sikhs, who had at first exchanged tinned beef for practically any other foodstuff, began to insist on jam and margarine. It was realised that a tin of jam was worth ½ lb. of margarine plus something else; that a cigarette issue was worth several chocolates issues, and a tin of diced carrots was worth practically nothing.

In this camp we did not visit other bungalows very much and prices varied from place to place; hence the germ of truth in the story of the itinerant priest. By the end of a month, when we reached our permanent camp, there was a lively trade in all commodities and their relative values were well known, and expressed not in terms of one another—one didn't quote bully in terms of sugar—but in terms of cigarettes. The cigarette became the standard of value. In the permanent camp people started by wandering through the bungalows calling their offers—"cheese for seven" (cigarettes)—and the hours after parcel issue were Bedlam. The inconveniences of this system soon led to its replacement by an Exchange and Mart notice board in every bungalow, where under the headings "name," "room number," "wanted" and "offered" sales and wants were advertised. When a deal went through, it was crossed off the board. The public and semipermanent records of transactions led to cigarette prices being well known and thus tending to equality throughout the camp, although there were always opportunities for an astute trader to make a profit from arbitrage. With this development everyone, including non-smokers, was willing to sell for cigarettes, using them to buy at another time and place. Cigarettes became the normal currency, though, of course, barter was never extinguished.

The unity of the market and the prevalence of a single price varied directly with the general level of organisation and comfort in the camp. A transit camp was always chaotic and uncomfortable: people were overcrowded, no one knew where anyone else was living, and few took the trouble to find out. Organisation was too slender to include an Exchange and Mart board, and private advertisements were the most that appeared. Consequently a transit camp was not one market but many. The price of a tin of salmon is known to have varied by two cigarettes in 20 between one end of a hut and the other. Despite a high level of organisation in Italy, the market was morcellated in this manner at the first transit camp we reached after our removal to Germany in the autumn of 1943. In this camp—Stalag VIIA at Moosburg in Bavaria—there were up to 50,000 prisoners of all nationalities. French, Russians, Italians, and Jugo-Slavs were free to move about within the camp; British and Americans were confined to their compounds, although a few cigarettes given to a sentry would always procure permission for one or two men to visit other compounds. The people who first visited the highly organised French trading centre with its stalls and known prices found coffee extract—relatively cheap among the tea-drinking English—commanding a fancy price in biscuits or cigarettes, and some enterprising people made small fortunes that way. (Incidentally we found out later that much of the coffee went "over the wire" and sold for phenomenal prices at black market cafes in Munich: some of the French prisoners were said to have made substantial sums in RMk.s. This was one of the few occasions on which our normally closed economy came into contact with other economic worlds.)

Eventually public opinion grew hostile to these monopoly profits—not everyone could make contact with the French—and trading with them was put on a regulated basis. Each group of beds was given a quota of articles to offer and the transaction was carried out by accredited representatives from the British compound, with monopoly rights. The same method was used for trading with sentries elsewhere, as in this trade secrecy and reasonable prices had a peculiar importance, but as is ever the case with regulated companies, the interloper proved too strong.

The permanent camps in Germany saw the highest level of commercial organisation. In addition to the Exchange and Mart notice boards, a shop was organised as a public utility, controlled by representatives of the Senior British Officer, on a no profit basis. People left their surplus clothing, toilet requisites and food there until they were sold at a fixed price in cigarettes. Only sales in cigarettes were accepted—there was no barter—and there was no higgling. For food at least there were standard prices: clothing is less homogeneous and the price was decided around a norm by the seller and the shop manager in agreement; shirts would average say 80, ranging from 60 to 120 according to quality and age. Of food, the shop carried small stocks for convenience; the capital was provided by a loan from the bulk store of Red Cross cigarettes and repaid by a small commission taken on the first transactions. Thus the cigarette attained its fullest currency status, and the market was almost completely unified.

It is thus to be seen that a market came into existence without labour or production. The B.R.C.S. may be considered as "Nature" of the textbook, and the articles of trade—food, clothing and cigarettes—as free gifts—land of manna. Despite this, and despite a roughly equal distribution of resources, a market came into spontaneous operation, and prices were fixed by the operation of supply and demand. It is difficult to reconcile this fact with the labour theory of value.

Actually there was an embryo labour market. Even when cigarettes were not scarce, there was usually some unlucky person willing to perform services for them. Laundrymen advertised at two cigarettes a garment. Battle-dress was scrubbed and pressed and a pair of trousers lent for the interim period for twelve. A good pastel portrait cost thirty or a tin of "Kam." Odd tailoring and other jobs similarly had their prices.

There were also entrepreneurial services. There was a coffee stall owner who sold tea, coffee or cocoa at two cigarettes a cup, buying his raw materials at market prices and hiring labour to gather fuel and to stoke; he actually enjoyed the services of a chartered accountant at one stage. After a period of great prosperity he overreached himself and failed disastrously for several hundred cigarettes. Such large-scale private enterprise was rare but several middlemen or professional traders existed. The padre in Italy, or the men at Moosburg who opened trading relations with the French, are examples: the more subdivided the market, the less perfect the advertisement of prices, and the less stable the prices, the greater was the scope for these operators. One man capitalized his knowledge of Urdu by buying meat from the Sikhs and selling butter and jam in return: as his operations became better known more and more people entered this trade, prices in the Indian Wing approximated more nearly to those elsewhere, though to the end a "contact" among the Indians was valuable, as linguistic difficulties prevented the trade from being quite free. Some were specialists in the Indian trade, the food, clothing or even the watch trade. Middlemen traded on their own account or on commission. Price rings and agreements were suspected and the traders certainly cooperated. Nor did they welcome newcomers. Unfortunately, the writer knows little of the workings of these people: public opinion was hostile and the professionals were usually of a retiring disposition.

One trader in food and cigarettes, operating in a period of dearth, enjoyed a high reputation. His capital, carefully saved, was originally about 50 cigarettes, with which he bought rations on issue days and held them until the price rose just before the next issue. He also picked up a little by arbitrage; several times a day he visited every Exchange or Mart notice board and took advantage of every discrepancy between prices of goods offered and wanted. His knowledge of prices, markets and names of those who had received cigarette parcels was phenomenal. By these means he kept himself smoking steadily—his profits—while his capital remained intact.

Sugar was issued on Saturday. About Tuesday two of us used to visit Sam and make a deal; as old customers he would advance as much of the price as he could spare us, and entered the transaction in a book. On Saturday morning he left cocoa tins on our beds for the ration, and picked them up on Saturday afternoon. We were hoping for a calendar at Christmas, but Sam failed too. He was left holding a big black treacle issue when the price fell, and in this weakened state was unable to withstand an unexpected arrival of parcels and the consequent price fluctuations. He paid in full, but from his capital. The next Tuesday, when I paid my usual visit, he was out of business.

Credit entered into many, perhaps into most, transactions, in one form or another. Sam paid in advance as a rule for his purchases of future deliveries of sugar, but many buyers asked for credit, whether the commodity was sold spot or future. Naturally prices varied according to the terms of sale. A treacle ration might be advertised for four cigarettes now or five next week. And in the future market "bread now" was a vastly different thing from "bread Thursday." Bread was issued on Thursday and Monday, four and three days' rations respectively, and by Wednesday and Sunday night it had risen at least one cigarette per ration, from seven to eight, by supper time. One man always saved a ration to sell then at the peak price: his offer of "bread now" stood out on the board among a number of "bread Monday's" fetching one or two less, or not selling at all—and he always smoked on Sunday night.

The cigarette currency

Although cigarettes as currency exhibited certain peculiarities, they performed all the functions of a metallic currency as a unit of account, as a measure of value and as a store of value, and shared most of its characteristics. They were homogeneous, reasonably durable, and of convenient size for the smallest or, in packets, for the largest transactions. Incidentally, they could be clipped or sweated by rolling them between the fingers so that tobacco fell out.

Cigarettes were also subject to the working of Gresham's Law. Certain brands were more popular than others as smokes, but for currency purposes a cigarette was a cigarette. Consequently buyers used the poorer qualities and the Shop rarely saw the more popular brands: cigarettes such as Churchman's No. 1 were rarely used for trading. At one time cigarettes hand-rolled from pipe tobacco began to circulate. Pipe tobacco was issued in lieu of cigarettes by the Red Cross at a rate of 25 cigarettes to the ounce and this rate was standard in exchanges, but an ounce would produce 30 home-made cigarettes. Naturally, people with machine-made cigarettes broke them down and re-rolled the tobacco, and the real cigarette virtually disappeared from the market. Hand-rolled cigarettes were not homogeneous and prices could no longer be quoted in them with safety:

each cigarette was examined before it was accepted and thin ones were rejected, or extra demanded as a make-weight. For a time we suffered all the inconveniences of a debased currency.

Machine-made cigarettes were always universally acceptable, both for what they would buy and for themselves. It was this intrinsic value which gave rise to their principal disadvantage as currency, a disadvantage which exists, but to a far smaller extent in the case of metallic currency;— that is, a strong demand for non-monetary purposes. Consequently our economy was repeatedly subject to deflation and to periods of monetary stringency. While the Red Cross issue of 50 or 25 cigarettes per man per week came in regularly, and while there were fair stocks held, the cigarette currency suited its purpose admirably. But when the issue was interrupted, stocks soon ran out, prices fell, trading declined in volume and became increasingly a matter of barter. This deflationary tendency was periodically offset by the sudden injection of new currency. Private cigarette parcels arrived in a trickle throughout the year, but the big numbers came in quarterly when the Red Cross received its allocation of transport. Several hundred thousand cigarettes might arrive in the space of a fortnight. Prices soared, and then began to fall, slowly at first but with increasing rapidity as stocks ran out, until the next big delivery. Most of our economic troubles could be attributed to this fundamental instability.

Price movements

Many factors affected prices, the strongest and most noticeable being the periodical currency inflation and deflation described in the last paragraphs. The periodicity of this price cycle depended on cigarette and, to a far lesser extent, on food deliveries. At one time in the early days, before any private parcels had arrived and when there were no individual stocks, the weekly issue of cigarettes and food parcels occurred on a Monday. The non-monetary demand for cigarettes was great, and less elastic than the demand for food: consequently prices fluctuated weekly, falling towards Sunday night and rising sharply on Monday morning. Later, when many people held reserves, the weekly issue had no such effect, being too small a portion of the total available. Credit allowed people with no reserves to meet their non-monetary demand over the weekend.

The general price level was affected by other factors. An influx of new prisoners, proverbially hungry, raised it. Heavy air raids in the vicinity of the camp probably increased the non-monetary demand for cigarettes and accentuated deflation. Good and bad war news certainly had its effect, and the general waves of optimism and pessimism which swept the camp were reflected in prices. Before breakfast one morning in March of this year, a rumour of the arrival of parcels and cigarettes was circulated. Within ten minutes I sold a treacle ration, for four cigarettes (hitherto offered in vain for three), and many similar deals went through. By 10 o'clock the rumour was denied, and treacle that day found no more buyers even at two cigarettes.

More interesting than changes in the general price level were changes in the price structure. Changes in the supply of a commodity, in the German ration scale or in the make-up of Red Cross parcels, would raise the price of one commodity relative to others. Tins of oatmeal, once a rare and much sought after luxury in the parcels, became a commonplace in 1943, and the price fell. In hot weather the demand for cocoa fell, and that for soap rose. A new recipe would be reflected in the price level: the discovery that raisins and sugar could be turned into an alcoholic liquor of remarkable potency reacted permanently on the dried fruit market. The invention of electric immersion heaters run off the power points made tea, a drag on the market in Italy, a certain seller in Germany.

In August, 1944, the supplies of parcels and cigarettes were both halved. Since both sides of the equation were changed in the same degree, changes in prices were not anticipated. But this was not the case: the non-monetary demand for cigarettes was less elastic than the demand for food, and food prices fell a little. More important however were the changes in the price structure. German margarine and jam, hitherto valueless owing to adequate supplies of Canadian butter and marmalade, acquired a new value. Chocolate, popular and a certain seller, and sugar, fell. Bread rose; several standing contracts of bread for cigarettes were broken, especially when the bread ration was reduced a few weeks later.

In February, 1945, the German soldier who drove the ration wagon was found to be willing to exchange loaves of bread at the rate of one loaf for a bar of chocolate. Those in the know began selling bread and buying chocolate, by then almost unsaleable in a period of serious deflation. Bread, at about 40, fell slightly; chocolate rose from 15; the supply of bread was not enough for the two commodities to reach parity, but the tendency was unmistakable.

The substitution of German margarine for Canadian butter when parcels were halved naturally affected their relative values, margarine appreciating at the expense of butter. Similarly, two brands of dried milk, hitherto differing in quality and therefore in price by five cigarettes a tin, came together in price as the wider substitution of the cheaper raised its relative value.

Enough has been cited to show that any change in conditions affected both the general price level and the price structure. It was this latter phenomenon which wrecked our planned economy.

Paper currency—Bully Marks

Around D-Day, food and cigarettes were plentiful, business was brisk and the camp in an optimistic mood. Consequently the Entertainments Committee felt the moment opportune to launch a restaurant, where food and hot drinks were sold while a band and variety turns performed. Earlier experiments, both public and private, had pointed the way, and the scheme was a great success. Food was bought at market prices to provide the meals and the small profits were devoted to a reserve fund and used to bribe Germans to provide grease paints and other necessities for the camp theatre. Originally meals were sold for cigarettes but this meant that the whole scheme was vulnerable to the periodic deflationary waves, and furthermore heavy smokers were unlikely to attend much. The whole success of the scheme depended on an adequate amount of food being offered for sale in the normal manner.

To increase and facilitate trade, and to stimulate supplies and customers therefore, and secondarily to avoid the worst effects of deflation when it should come, a paper currency was organised by the Restaurant and the Shop. The Shop bought food on behalf of the Restaurant with paper notes and the paper was accepted equally with the cigarettes in the Restaurant or Shop, and passed back to the Shop to purchase more food. The Shop acted as a bank of issue. The paper money was backed 100 per cent. by food; hence its name, the Bully Mark. The BMk. was backed 100 per cent. by food: there could be no over-issues, as is permissible with a normal bank of issue, since the eventual dispersal of the camp and consequent redemption of all BMk.s were anticipated in the near future.

Originally one BMk. was worth one cigarette and for a short time both circulated freely inside and outside the Restaurant. Prices were quoted in BMk.s and cigarettes with equal freedom—and for a short time the BMk. showed signs of replacing the cigarette as currency. The BMk. was tied to food, but not to cigarettes: as it was issued against food, say 45 for a tin of milk and so on, any reduction in the BMk. prices of food would have meant that there were unbacked BMk.s in circulation. But the price of both food and BMk.s could and did fluctuate with the supply of cigarettes.

While the Restaurant flourished, the scheme was a success: the Restaurant bought heavily, all foods were saleable and prices were stable.

In August parcels and cigarettes were halved and the Camp was bombed. The Restaurant closed for a short while and sales of food became difficult. Even when the Restaurant reopened, the food and cigarette shortage became increasingly acute and people were unwilling to convert such valuable goods into paper and to hold them for luxuries like snacks and tea. Less of the right kinds of food for the Restaurant were sold, and the Shop became glutted with dried fruit, chocolate, sugar, etc., which the Restaurant could not buy. The price level and the price structure changed. The BMk. fell to four-fifths of a cigarette and eventually farther still, and it became unacceptable save in the Restaurant. There was a flight from the BMk., no longer convertible into cigarettes or popular foods. The cigarette reestablished itself.

But the BMk. was sound! The Restaurant closed in the New Year with a progressive food shortage and the long evenings without lights due to intensified Allied air raids, and the BMk.s could only be spent in the Coffee Bar—relict of the Restaurant—or on the few unpopular foods in the

Shop, the owners of which were prepared to accept them. In the end all holders of BMk.s were paid in full, in cups of coffee or in prunes. People who had bought BMk.s for cigarettes or valuable jam or biscuits in their heyday were aggrieved that they should have stood the loss involved in their restricted choice, but they suffered no actual loss of market value.

Price fixing

Along with this scheme came a determined attempt at a planned economy, at price fixing. The Medical Officer had long been anxious to control food sales, for fear of some people selling too much, to the detriment of their health. The deflationary waves and their effects on prices were inconvenient to all and would be dangerous to the Restaurant which had to carry stocks. Furthermore, unless the BMk. was convertible into cigarettes at about par it had little chance of gaining confidence and of succeeding as a currency. As has been explained, the BMk. was tied to food but could not be tied to cigarettes, which fluctuated in value. Hence, while BMk. prices of food were fixed for all time, cigarette prices of food and BMk.s varied.

The Shop, backed by the Senior British Officer, was now in a position to enforce price control both inside and outside its walls. Hitherto a standard price had been fixed for food left for sale in the shop, and prices outside were roughly in conformity with this scale, which was recommended as a "guide" to sellers, but fluctuated a good deal around it. Sales in the Shop at recommended prices were apt to be slow though a good price might be obtained: sales outside could be made more quickly at lower prices. (If sales outside were to be at higher prices, goods were withdrawn from the Shop until the recommended price rose: but the recommended price was sluggish and could not follow the market closely by reason of its very purpose, which was stability.) The Exchange and Mart notice boards came under the control of the Shop: advertisements which exceeded a 5 per cent. departure from the recommended scale were liable to be crossed out by authority: unauthorised sales were discouraged by authority and also by public opinion, strongly in favour of a just and stable price. (Recommended prices were fixed partly

from market data, partly on the advice of the M.O.)

At first the recommended scale was a success: the Restaurant, a big buyer, kept prices stable around this level: opinion and the 5 per cent. tolerance helped. But when the price level fell with the August cuts and the price structure changed, the recommended scale was too rigid. Unchanged at first, as no deflation was expected, the scale was tardily lowered, but the prices of goods on the new scale remained in the same relation to one another, owing to the BMk., while on the market the price structure had changed. And the modifying influence of the Restaurant had gone. The scale was moved up and down several times, slowly following the inflationary and deflationary waves, but it was rarely adjusted to changes in the price structure. More and more advertisements were crossed off the board, and black market sales at unauthorised prices increased: eventually public opinion turned against the recommended scale and authority gave up the struggle. In the last few weeks, with unparalleled deflation, prices fell with alarming rapidity, no scales existed, and supply and demand, alone and unmellowed, determined prices.

Public opinion

Public opinion on the subject of trading was vocal if confused and changeable, and generalisations as to its direction are difficult and dangerous. A tiny minority held that all trading was undesirable as it engendered an unsavoury atmosphere; occasional frauds and sharp practices were cited as proof. Certain forms of trading were more generally condemned; trade with the Germans was criticised by many. Red Cross toilet articles, which were in short supply and only issued in cases of actual need, were excluded from trade by law and opinion working in unshakable harmony. At one time, when there had been several cases of malnutrition reported among the more devoted smokers, no trade in German rations was permitted, as the victims became an additional burden on the depleted food reserves of the Hospital. But while certain activities were condemned as anti-social, trade itself was practised, and its utility appreciated, by almost everyone in the camp.

More interesting was opinion on middlemen

and prices. Taken as a whole, opinion was hostile to the middleman. His function, and his hard work in bringing buyer and seller together, were ignored; profits were not regarded as a reward for labour, but as the result of sharp practices. Despite the fact that his very existence was proof to the contrary, the middleman was held to be redundant in view of the existence of an official Shop and the Exchange and Mart. Appreciation only came his way when he was willing to advance the price of a sugar ration, or to buy goods spot and carry them against a future sale. In these cases the element of risk was obvious to all, and the convenience of the service was felt to merit some reward. Particularly unpopular was the middleman with an element of monopoly, the man who contacted the ration waggon driver, or the man who utilised his knowledge of Urdu. And middlemen as a group were blamed for reducing prices. Opinion notwithstanding, most people dealt with a middleman, whether consciously or unconsciously, at some time or another.

There was a strong feeling that everything had its "just price" in cigarettes. While the assessment of the just price, which incidentally varied between camps, was impossible of explanation, this price was nevertheless pretty closely known. It can best be defined as the price usually fetched by an article in good times when cigarettes were plentiful. The "just price" changed slowly; it was unaffected by short-term variations in supply, and while opinion might be resigned to departures from the "just price," a strong feeling of resentment persisted. A more satisfactory definition of the "just price" is impossible. Everyone knew what it was, though no one could explain why it should be so.

As soon as prices began to fall with a cigarette shortage, a clamour arose, particularly against those who held reserves and who bought at reduced prices. Sellers at cut prices were criticised and their activities referred to as the black market. In every period of dearth the explosive question of "should non-smokers receive a cigarette ration?" was discussed to profitless length. Unfortunately, it was the non-smoker, or the light smoker with his reserves, along with the hated middleman, who weathered the storm most easily.

The popularity of the price-fixing scheme, and such success as it enjoyed, were undoubtedly the result of this body of opinion. On several occasions the fall of prices was delayed by the general support given to the recommended scale. The onset of deflation was marked by a period of sluggish trade; prices stayed up but no one bought. Then prices fell on the black market, and the volume of trade revived in that quarter. Even when the recommended scale was revised, the volume of trade in the Shop would remain low. Opinion was always overruled by the hard facts of the market.

Curious arguments were advanced to justify price fixing. The recommended prices were in some way related to the calorific values of the foods offered: hence some were overvalued and never sold at these prices. One argument ran as follows:—not everyone has private cigarette parcels: thus, when prices were high and trade good in the summer of 1944, only the lucky rich could buy. This was unfair to the man with few cigarettes. When prices fell in the following winter, prices should be pegged high so that the rich, who had enjoyed life in the summer, should put many cigarettes into circulation. The fact that those who sold to the rich in the summer had also enjoyed life then, and the fact that in the winter there was always someone willing to sell at low prices were ignored. Such arguments were hotly debated each night after the approach of Allied aircraft extinguished all lights at 8 P.M. But prices moved with the supply of cigarettes, and refused to stay fixed in accordance with a theory of ethics.

Conclusion

The economic organisation described was both elaborate and smooth-working in the summer of 1944. Then came the August cuts and deflation. Prices fell, rallied with deliveries of cigarette parcels in September and December, and fell again. In January, 1945, supplies of Red Cross cigarettes ran out: and prices slumped still further: in February the supplies of food parcels were exhausted and the depression became a blizzard. Food, itself scarce, was almost given away in order to meet the non-monetary demand for cigarettes. Laundries ceased to operate, or worked for £s or RMk.s: food and cigarettes sold for fancy prices in £s, hitherto unheard of. The Restaurant was a memory and the BMk. a joke. The Shop was empty and the Exchange and Mart notices were full of unaccepted offers for cigarettes. Barter increased in volume, becoming a larger proportion of a smaller volume of trade. Thus, the first serious and prolonged food shortage in the writer's experience, caused the price structure to change again, partly because German rations were not easily divisible. A margarine ration gradually sank in value until it exchanged directly for a treacle ration. Sugar slumped sadly. Only bread retained its value. Several thousand cigarettes, the capital of the Shop, were distributed without any noticeable effect. A few fractional parcel and cigarette issues, such as one-sixth of a parcel and twelve cigarettes each,

led to monetary price recoveries and feverish trade, especially when they coincided with good news from the Western Front, but the general position remained unaltered.

By April, 1945, chaos had replaced order in the economic sphere: sales were difficult, prices lacked stability. Economics has been defined as the science of distributing limited means among unlimited and competing ends. On 12th April, with the arrival of elements of the 30th U.S. Infantry Division, the ushering in of an age of plenty demonstrated the hypothesis that with infinite means economic organisation and activity would be redundant, as every want could be satisfied without effort.

Reading 7

Widespread agreement could quickly be found for the proposition that we need much capital to sustain and improve our high standard of living in the United States. But what is implied in this approval?

To the economist, "capital" is a word with too many popular meanings. It requires a quite specific meaning if it is to convey a concept with analytical significance in understanding how our economy operates. This definition is found in using the word to refer to either (1) man-made factors of production or (2) goods that have been produced by the economic system not to satisfy present consumption but to aid in further production. In this sense, a nation's stock of *real capital* consists of the improved land, buildings, equipment, and inventories that are used to produce other goods and services. So defined, capital can come into existence only by diverting some of today's scarce resources from the production of "final" goods for present consumption to the production of "intermediate" goods for use in further production. Why would a society choose to follow such an "indirect" or "roundabout" way of satisfying its wants? And why do some societies rely more on capital-intensive productive processes than other societies?

The Austrian economist Eugen von Böhm-Bawerk (1851–1914) is best known for his writings on capital and interest. Here he describes how and why capital intensive or "roundabout" methods of production work to man's advantage.

Questions to guide the reading

How do other popular uses of the word "capital" relate to the definition employed here?

If capital-intensive or roundabout methods of production yield greater results than direct methods, why do we not immediately adopt the most roundabout or the most indirect methods of production available?

Capital and Roundabout Production

Eugen von Böhm-Bawerk

The end and aim of all production is the making of things with which to satisfy our wants; that is to say, the making of goods for immediate consumption, or Consumption Goods. We combine our own natural powers and natural powers of the external world in such a way that, under natural law, the desired material good must come into existence. But this is a very general description indeed of the matter, and looking at it closer there comes in sight an important distinction which we have not as yet considered. It has reference to the *distance* which lies between the *expenditure of human labour* in the combined production and *the appearance* of the desired good. We either put forth our labour just before the goal is reached, or we, intentionally, take a *roundabout* way. That is to say, we may put forth our labour in such a way that it at once completes the circle of conditions necessary for the emergence of the desired good, and thus the existence of the good *immediately* follows the expenditure of the labour; or we may associate our labour first with the more remote causes of good, with the object of obtaining, not the desired good itself, but a proximate cause of the good; which cause, again, must be associated with other suitable materials and powers, till, finally,—perhaps through a considerable number of intermediate members,—the finished good, the instrument of human satisfaction, is obtained.

Enhanced productiveness of roundabout method

The nature and importance of this distinction will be best seen from a few examples. A peasant requires drinking water. The spring is some distance from his house. There are various ways in which he may supply his daily wants. First, he may go to the spring each time he is thirsty, and drink out of his hollowed hand. This is the most direct way; satisfaction follows immediately on exertion. But it is an inconvenient way, for our peasant has to take his way to the well as often as he is thirsty.

And it is an insufficient way, for he can never collect and store any great quantity such as he requires for various other purposes.

Second, he may take a log of wood, hollow it out into a kind of pail, and carry his day's supply from the spring to his cottage. The advantage is obvious, but it necessitates a roundabout way of considerable length. The man must spend, perhaps, a day in cutting out the pail; before doing so he must have felled a tree in the forest; to do this, again, he must have made an axe, and so on. But there is still a third way; instead of felling one tree he fells a number of trees, splits and hollows them, lays them end for end, and so constructs a runnel or rhone which brings a full head of water to his cottage. *Here, obviously, between the expenditure of the labour and the obtaining of the water we have a very roundabout way, but, then, the result is ever so much greater.* Our peasant need no longer take his weary way from house to well with the heavy pail on his shoulder, and yet he has a constant and full supply of the freshest water at his very door.

Another example. I require stone for building a house. There is a rich vein of excellent sandstone in a neighbouring hill. How is it to be got out? First, I may work the loose stones back and forward with my bare fingers, and break off what can be broken off. This is the most direct, but also the least productive way. Second, I may take a piece of iron, make a hammer and chisel out of it, and use them on the hard stone—a roundabout way, which, of course, leads to a very much better result than the former. Third method—Having a hammer and chisel I use them to drill a hole in the rock; next I turn my attention to procuring charcoal, sulphur, and nitre, and mixing them in a powder, then I pour the powder into the hole, and the explosion that follows splits the stone into convenient pieces—still more of a roundabout way, but one which, as experience shows, is as much superior to the second way in result as the second was to the first.

From Eugen von Böhm-Bawerk, *Positive Theory of Capital* (1891).

The lesson to be drawn from these examples is obvious. It is—that *a greater result is obtained by producing goods in roundabout ways than by producing them directly.* Where a good can be produced in either way, we have the fact that, by the indirect way, a greater product can be got with equal labour, or the same product with less labour. But, beyond this, the superiority of the indirect way manifests itself in being the only way in which certain goods can be obtained.

A fundamental law

That roundabout methods lead to greater results than direct methods is one of the most important and fundamental propositions in the whole theory of production. It must be emphatically stated that the only basis of this proposition is the experience of practical life. Economic theory does not and cannot show *a priori* that it must be so; but the unanimous experience of all the technique of production says that it is so. And this is sufficient; all the more that the facts of experience which tell us this are commonplace and familiar to everybody. But *why* is it so?

In the last resort all our productive efforts amount to shiftings and combinations of matter. We must know how to bring together the right forms of matter at the right moment, in order that from those associated forces the desired result, the product wanted, may follow. But, as we saw, the natural forms of matter are often so infinitely large, often so infinitely fine, that human hands are too weak or too coarse to control them. We are as powerless to overcome the cohesion of the wall of rock when we want building stone as we are, from carbon, nitrogen, hydrogen, oxygen, phosphor, potash, etc., to put together a single grain of wheat. But there are other powers which can easily do what is denied to us, and these are the powers of nature. There are natural powers which far exceed the possibilities of human power in greatness, and there are other natural powers in the microscopic world which can make combinations that put our clumsy fingers to shame. If we can succeed in making those forces our allies in the work of production, the limits of human possibility will be infinitely extended. And this we have done.

Nature of capitalist production

The condition of our success is, that we are able to control the materials on which the power that helps us depends, more easily than the materials which are to be transformed into the desired good. Happily this condition can be very often complied with. Our weak yielding hand cannot overcome the cohesion of the rock, but the hard wedge of iron can; the wedge and the hammer to drive it we can happily master with little trouble. We cannot gather the atoms of phosphorus and potash out of the ground, and the atoms of carbon and oxygen out of the atmospheric air, and put them together in the shape of the corn or wheat; but the organic chemical powers of the seed can put this magical process in motion, while we on our part can very easily bury the seed in the place of its secret working, the bosom of the earth. Often, of course, we are not able directly to master the form of matter on which the friendly power depends, but in the same way as we would like it to help us, do we help ourselves against it; we try to secure the alliance of a second natural power which brings the form of matter that bears the first power under our control. We wish to bring the well water into the house. Wooden rhones would force it to obey our will, and take the path we prescribe, but our hands have not the power to make the forest trees into rhones. We have not far to look, however, for an expedient. We ask the help of a second ally in the axe and the gouge; their assistance gives us the rhones; then the rhones bring us the water. And what in this illustration is done through the mediation of two or three members may be done, with equal or greater result, through five, ten, or twenty members. Just as we control and guide the immediate matter of which the good is composed by one friendly power, and that power by a second, so can we control and guide the second by a third, the third by a fourth, this, again, by a fifth, and so on,—always going back to more remote causes of the final result—till in the series we come at last to one cause which we can control conveniently by our own natural powers. This is the true importance which attaches to our entering on roundabout ways of production: every roundabout way means the enlisting in our service of a power which is stronger or more cunning than the human hand; every extension of the roundabout way means an addition to the powers which enter into the service of man, and the shifting of some portion of the burden of production from the scarce and costly labour of human beings to the prodigal powers of nature.

The kind of production which works in these wise circuitous methods is nothing else than what economists call Capitalist Production, as opposed to that production which goes directly at its object. And Capital is nothing but the complex of intermediate products which appear on the several stages of the roundabout journey.

Supply and Demand Pricing

Reading 8

Economics textbooks carry pictures of downward-sloping demand curves. Usually these are hypothetical examples. How does an industry go about getting statistical estimates of these important schedules? Since early in this century economists have devoted much energy and ingenuity to such measurements.

Here Professors Nisbet and Vakil present their findings on the demand curve for marijuana among a student population. The higher the price per ounce, the fewer ounces will be bought per month. The results seem fairly realistic when checked two ways: by reported guesses as to what one would do, and by actual purchases. But of course it is not possible, in a social science like economics, to make the exact controlled experiments that yield the high precision of the natural sciences.

Professors Nisbet and Vakil are in the economics department at Evergreen State College, Olympia, Washington.

Questions to guide the reading

How would you go about determining the demand schedule of a group of college students for movie going? For foreign travel?

Would the fact that possession of marijuana is illegal subtract from the precision with which such a demand curve can be estimated? Does a cut in Q of slightly more than 1 per cent when P rises by 1 per cent seem reasonable or unreasonable to you? How do you arrive at your opinion?

Estimates of Demand Curve for Marijuana among UCLA Students

Charles T. Nisbet and Firouz Vakil

It is the purpose of this note to add some economic considerations to the growing literature on drug use by offering some estimates of the price demand for marijuana.

The sample and the data

The data were gathered through the use of an anonymous mail questionnaire. Out of the 926 re-

From Charles T. Nisbet and Firouz Vakil, "Some Estimates of Price and Expenditure Elasticities of Demand for Marijuana among U.C.L.A. Students," *The Review of Economics and Statistics,* vol. LIV, no. 4, November 1972. Reprinted in abridgment with the kind permission of the authors and the publisher.

spondents, 52.8 per cent claimed to have never tried marijuana and were classified as "non-smokers," while 47.2 per cent said they have tried marijuana and were classified as "smokers." Out of the 437 "smokers," 184 were "purchasers" and 253 were "non-purchasers," obtaining marijuana only from friends.

The intent of the questionnaires was to obtain data with respect to how much marijuana[1] in "lids" (ounces) a consumer, at a given income, is purchasing [per month] and would be willing to purchase when facing a number of alternative prices.[2]

Each individual purchaser was thus asked to trace out his particular demand function. The objections to the derivation of this type of hypothetical demand function are well known: people have not thought out in advance what they will do when confronted with such a hypothetical situation, snap judgments cannot inspire great confidence, expectation of a particular action may diverge from actual action when confronted with the concrete situation. Additional data on actual prices and the corresponding quantities demanded were also collected.[3]

The results

[Figure 1 gives, in lieu of a technical table of statistical results, a picture of the demand curve estimated from the results of the survey. The size of the four points indicates how many of the 184 respondents corresponded to each average price level: thus, 132 students bought near $10 an ounce, 32 bought near $6.75, 32 bought near $15.95, and 1 student claimed to have bought at $25.

The straight line marked *DD* was fitted by the authors to the market data. They point out, however, that if each of the 184 points were plotted on

[1] Note that the unit of consumption is a "lid" (or ounce of dried marijuana).
[2] Students were asked to indicate how much their *use* of marijuana changes with variations in prices per unit of time so the increased quantity demanded at lower prices would not represent stocking up or hoarding.
[3] Stigler suggests that when quizzed, individuals tend to see fewer substitution possibilities than when confronted with a higher price. Consequently demand curves based on market surveys tend to be less elastic than empirically estimated demand curves using marking data.

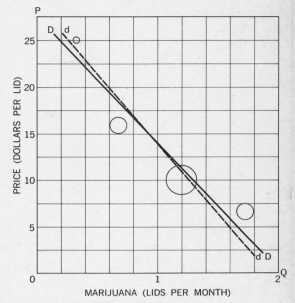

Figure 1   Demand curve for pot.

the diagram, there would be very considerable scattering around the line of best fit. Since the demand was estimated two ways—by what people actually bought in the market (as shown in *DD*) and by what they *guessed* they would do if confronted with different prices—the broken curve marked *dd* shows a slightly different demand curve from personal guessing. As expected, this is slightly less responsive to price than is *DD:* people apparently underestimate how much they'll actually feel forced to cut down by price.

Did those with higher incomes demand more? Strangely not in this UCLA sample. Perhaps those with more income were more afraid to "get busted" for illegal acts.]

Conclusions

(1) The individual college student's demand curve for marijuana exhibits the standard characteristics prescribed by conventional economic theory.

(2) Estimates of price elasticities around the going market price ranged from −0.40 to −1.51 depending on the type of data used and on the functional form. It is likely that a price elasticity slightly greater than one would give a reasonable

estimate [i.e., each 1 per cent cut in P might well cause a bit more than 1 per cent rise in Q].

(3) The price elasticity data suggest that policies designed to restrict supply, such as "operation intercept," may be effective in reducing the quantity consumed of marijuana. However, rising prices of marijuana may also encourage substitutes to other more harmful drugs.

Readings 9, 10, and 11

"You can't interfere with the laws of supply and demand" is obviously a nonsensical statement, since governments do it all the time. They put maximum ceilings on rents, on interest rates, and, in time of war, on food prices generally. But strong believers in the virtue of a market-pricing system, like Professor Milton Friedman of the University of Chicago, argue in effect: "If you do interfere with the laws of supply and demand, despite your good intentions, you are likely to create social *inefficiency.*"

What libertarians like Dr. Friedman do not always stress is that there may be a clash between "efficiency" and "humanitarian equity." New York City rent controls may end up destroying some housing; but the practice also, for a long time, transfers income to the poor from presumably more affluent landlords. Critics of laissez faire say: "An efficient system that is inhumane may well be worse than an inefficient system that will be humane." To which libertarians reply: "You may well end up getting inefficiency *and* inhumanity."

Obviously, no a priori argument can settle these questions of value judgment and likely fact. These three *Newsweek* columns of Professor Friedman set forth a provocative view.

Questions to guide the reading

What good are low rents if you can't find an apartment at such rates? Similarly, it is illegal loan sharks who often lobby for *low* legal interest ceilings, knowing that legitimate money will dry up at such rates, driving desperate people into the clutches of the illegal loan sharks. (Small loans involve so much administrative, investigative, and forfeiture costs as to necessitate rates more like 20 per cent per year than 6 per cent. But loan sharks often extort hundreds of per cent a year—if not per month!)

Those lucky enough to get an apartment at controlled rents or a loan at ceiling rates benefit. Often these are poor and deserving people. Hence, can these interferences with supply and demand be all bad? Does Professor Friedman go into the question of how you would weigh the good effects on the distribution of income against the bad effects of distorting inefficiencies? If so, where? If not, why not?

Is it the case that only a "monster" would be against legal standards for housing of migrant farm workers? Does Professor Friedman argue that the housing conditions of migrants are other than wretched on the average? Or does he argue that trying to improve the situation will actually throw the migrants out of jobs and hurt *them* in the end? What about those who manage to keep jobs and who do get better housing? How can one weigh their gain against other people's loss?

Reading 9

Roofs or Ceilings

Milton Friedman

In 1946, George Stigler and I published a pamphlet attacking the legal ceilings that had been imposed on rents during World War II and were then still in effect. We argued that the ceilings, by keeping rents artificially low to those persons who were fortunate enough to live in controlled dwellings, encouraged the waste of housing space and, at the same time, discouraged the construction of additional dwellings. Hence our title, "Roofs or Ceilings."

Nationwide ceilings were subsequently abolished. However, localities were given the option to continue them. New York City—with that unerring instinct for self-destruction that has brought it to its present condition—is the only major city still controlling rents under this option.

A recent [1971] article by Richard Stone in the *Wall Street Journal,* "Shortage of Housing in New York Gets Worse Every Day," brought this ancient pamphlet vividly back to mind. At a time when there is so much talk about imposing new price controls, this cautionary tale is worth pondering.

The New York story

Reports Stone: "The dimensions of the New York shortage are vast. The rental vacancy rate is below 1 per cent . . . Private building is at near-paralysis . . . Increasing numbers of landlords simply give up, abandoning buildings they can neither afford to maintain nor sell at any price. Tenants, left with no heat, water or electricity vacate such buildings in a matter of days. When that happens, blight swallows up whole neighborhoods, almost overnight."

"Every day there are fewer housing units available in New York City than the day before."

"New York's archaic rent-control law keeps the marginally poor whose fortune is improving from moving out of slum neighborhoods."

Others go to great lengths to find a rent-controlled apartment, including keeping "track of obituaries to divine what deaths are creating rent-control vacancies."

"Partly because of rent control, rents on private housing built since 1947—housing that doesn't come under the law—skyrocketed over the past decade . . . After fierce public outcry, the city last summer passed a law holding annual increases to 5 per cent. To no one's surprise, several major builders responded by withdrawing from the city."

Or, as we wrote in our 1946 pamphlet: "Rent ceilings cause haphazard and arbitrary allocation of space, inefficient use of space, retardation of new construction. The legal ceilings on rents are the reason there are so few places for rent. Because of the excess of demand over supply, rental property is now rationed [in New York] by various forms of chance and favoritism. As long as the shortage created by rent ceilings remains, there will be a clamor for continued rent controls. This is perhaps the strongest indictment of ceilings on rent. They, and the accompanying shortage of dwellings to rent, perpetuate themselves, and the progeny are even less attractive than the parents."

Housing and grapefruit

Do not suppose that this sad tale reflects anything special about housing. During World War II, when price control was nearly universal, black markets, and rationing by chance, favoritism, and bribery developed in steel, meat, bananas—you name it. Since World War II, there have been major crises in gold and foreign exchange—because governments have tried to fix the prices of both. When the price of the dollar was fixed too low in terms of other currencies, there was a "dollar shortage"; more recently, when it has been fixed too high, there has been concern about balance-of-payments deficits. The price system is a remarkably efficient system for bringing buyers and sellers together; for assuring that the quantities some people want to buy will match the quantities other people want to sell. Immobilize the price system and something else—if only chaos and queues—must take its place.

Would you like to see a shortage of grapefruit in New York that will get worse with every day? Let New York impose and effectively enforce a ceiling price on grapefruit below the market price. Let Washington do so, and the shortage will be nationwide. And you can substitute any product you wish for "grapefruit," provided you add the qualification that the ceiling price be "effectively enforced." That is the direction in which the well-meaning people who are talking about legal price-and-wage control are pushing us. They should be condemned to hunting for an apartment in New York.

Reading 10

Defense of Usury

Milton Friedman

In 1787, Jeremy Bentham published a lengthy pamphlet entitled, "Defense of Usury; Shewing the Impolicy of the Present Legal Restraints on the Terms of Pecuniary Bargains." The pecuniary bargains he was concerned with were loans between individuals or business enterprises. The legal restraints were limits on interest rates paid or received. Usury was and is the popular term for charging interest rates in excess of legal limits.

Bentham makes an overwhelmingly persuasive case for the proposition he sets forth at the beginning of the pamphlet, "viz. that *no man of ripe years and of sound mind, acting freely, and with his eyes open, ought to be hindered, with a view to his advantage, from making such bargain, in the way of obtaining money, as he thinks fit: nor* (what is a necessary consequence) *any body hindered from supplying him, upon any terms he thinks proper to accede to.*"

Conviction versus practice

During the nearly two centuries since Bentham's pamphlet was published, his arguments have been widely accepted by economists and as widely neglected by politicians. I know of no economist of any standing from that time to this who has favored a legal limit on the rate of interest that borrowers could pay or lenders receive—though there must have been some. I know of no country that does not limit by law the rates of interest—and I doubt that there are any. As Bentham wrote, "in great political questions, wide indeed is the distance between conviction and practice."

Bentham's explanation of the "grounds of the prejudices against usury" is as valid today as when he wrote: "The business of a moneylender . . . has no where, nor at any time, been a popular one. Those who have the resolution to sacrifice the present to future, are natural objects of envy to those who have sacrificed the future to the present. The children who have eat their cake are the natural enemies of the children who have theirs. While the money is hoped for, and for a short time after it has been received, he who lends it is a friend and benefactor: by the time the money is spent, and the evil hour of reckoning is come, the benefactor is found to have changed his nature, and to have put on the tyrant and the oppressor. It is an oppression for a man to reclaim his own money: it is none to keep it from him."

Bentham's explanation of the "mischief of the anti-usurious laws" is also as valid today as when he wrote that these laws preclude "many people, altogether, from the getting the money they stand in need of, to answer their respective exigencies."

For still others, they render "the terms so much the worse . . . While, out of loving-kindness, or whatsoever other motive, the law precludes a man from *borrowing*, upon terms which it deems too disadvantageous, it does not preclude him from *selling*, upon any terms, howsoever disadvantageous." His conclusion: "The sole tendency of the law is to heap distress upon distress."

Who is hurt?

Developments since Bentham's day have increased the mischief done by usury legislation. Economic progress has provided the ordinary man with the means to save. The spread of banks, savings-and-loan associations, and the like has given the ordinary man the facilities for saving. For the first time in history, the working class may well be net lenders rather than net borrowers. They are also the ones who have fewest alternatives, who find it hardest to avoid legal regulations, and who are therefore hardest hit by them.

Under the spur of [Congressman] Wright Patman and his ilk, the Federal Reserve now [1970] limits the interest rate that commercial banks may pay to a maximum of 4½ per cent for small savers but to 7½ per cent for deposits of $100,000 or more. And the deposits of small savers have been relatively stable or growing, while those of large depositors have been declining sharply because they have still better alternatives.

That is the way the self-labeled defenders of the "people" look after their interests—by keeping them from receiving the interest they are entitled to. Along with Bentham, "I would . . . wish to learn . . . why the legislator should be more anxious to limit the rate of interest one way, than the other? Why should he set his face against the owners of that species of property more than of any other? Why he should make it his business to prevent their getting *more* than a certain price for the use of it, rather than to prevent their getting *less?* . . . Let any one that can, find an answer to these questions; it is more than I can do."

Reading 11

Migrant Workers

Milton Friedman

The old saw is that the Quakers went to the New World to do good and ended up doing well. Today, well-meaning reformers go to Washington to do good and end up doing harm.

A recent *Wall Street Journal* story gives a striking example—the effects in Michigan of stricter Federal and state standards for housing migrant farm workers. The intent: to improve the conditions of a group of low-paid workers. The result: to hurt the workers, the farmers and consumers.

"Higher labor costs," says the story, "have prompted many growers . . . to switch to mechanized harvesting in recent years, lessening demand for migrant workers. That trend has intensified in the last two years, as government agencies have implemented stricter housing regulations for grow-

ers participating in their migrant-worker placement programs . . .

"State and Federal officials estimate that mechanization could eliminate from 6,000 to 10,000 jobs in Michigan this summer that were previously done by migrants . . . License applications [for migrant camps] are down 11 per cent so far this summer . . .

"Nonetheless, approximately 50,000 migrant workers, mostly Mexican-Americans from Southwest Texas, are expected to come into Michigan looking for work this summer. That's about the same number that came through last year."

Mechanization is a good thing if it is a response to a decline in the number of persons seeking jobs as migrant workers at low wages. That would mean that the former migrant workers have found better employment opportunities. Mechanization is a bad thing if it is a response to higher labor costs imposed arbitrarily from the outside. That simply wastes capital to replace people who are forced into unemployment on even less desirable jobs.

Who is helped, who hurt?

Migrant workers are clearly hurt. It is small comfort to an unemployed migrant worker to know that, if he could get a job, he would have better housing. True, the housing formerly available may have been most unsatisfactory by our standards. However, the migrant workers clearly regarded it, plus the accompanying jobs, as the best alternative available to them, else why did they flock to Michigan? It is certainly desirable that they have better alternatives available to them, but until they do, how are they helped by eliminating alternatives, however unsatisfactory, that are now available? That is simply biting off their noses to save our faces.

Farmers are clearly hurt. The cost of migrant labor has been raised. That is why they are mechanizing. The machines limit the rise in cost but do not eliminate it. Costs would be lower if farmers could hire migrant labor on *terms that would be mutually satisfactory to them and the laborers.* But they are not permitted to do so.

Consumers are clearly hurt. At the higher costs, less food will be harvested, so making food prices higher than they otherwise would be.

Producers of mechanized farm equipment are helped by having a larger market. But in the main, they simply produce harvesting equipment instead of other equipment.

The only other people who are helped are the do-gooders responsible for this type of legislation and for these effects. They have the highminded satisfaction of promoting a noble cause. The good intention is emblazoned forth for all to see. The harm is far less visible, much more indirect, much harder to connect with the good-hearted action. Besides, the harm is mostly to someone else.

Is this case unique?

This case is not in any way unique, except that it happens to be more obvious than most. I know hardly any do-gooder legislation of this kind—whether it be minimum-wage laws or rent control or urban renewal or public housing or fair-employment legislation—which, on examination of its full consequences, does not do more harm than good—and more harm as judged by the intentions of the well-meaning people who sponsor such legislation.

Will the liberals ever learn this lesson of experience? So far, the clear failure of government program after government program to achieve its objective has simply led to a clamor for still larger, still more expensive, still more far-reaching programs—to do still more harm. It is about time that the liberals asked themselves whether the fault may not be in the system they favor—doing good at other people's expense—rather than in the way the system is operated. It is about time that they appealed to their heads as well as their hearts.

Readings 12 and 13   A Dialogue on Blood and Money

Shoes and bread we buy for money. Supply and demand rules. But blood we get mostly free. People *sell* their mousetraps, but they voluntarily *donate* their blood through the Red Cross or some other community agency.

Richard Titmuss, a sociologist at the London School of Economics and Political Science until his death in 1973, received much attention for his book that compares Britain's completely voluntary system of blood giving with the American voluntary-plus-commercial-donor system. This serves as a critique of American capitalism.

The first piece, an enthusiastic *Newsweek* column, gives my own initial reaction to the argument—which parallels that of many reviewers of good will.

The second piece, by Kenneth J. Arrow of Harvard University, subjects the Titmuss argument to more careful scientific and philosophic scrutiny. Professor Arrow received a Nobel Prize in Economics in 1972, being the youngest ever to win that award. He is an expert on both risk and social values. Because he is widely known for his broad social sympathies, Arrow's evaluation is all the more valuable. It is a good example of deep economic analysis applied to human welfare.

Questions to guide the reading

Sometimes there are temporary blood shortages. Would these be possible, or probable, in a straight supply-and-demand system?

What if other countries just don't have the solidarity and altruism of the British islanders? How would Titmuss's idealism cope with that real possibility? And how would a good test to screen out hepatitis affect one's view of the best system?

Reading 12

Free Blood in England, Bought Blood in the United States

Paul A. Samuelson

Vilfredo Pareto, the great turn-of-the-century sociologist and mathematical economist, once attended a scientific congress. He listened with impatience to some spokesmen of the then popular "German historical school," which we today might think of as involving a blend between the economic iconoclasm of the young left and the humorless caution of middle age.

What left Pareto especially indignant was the claim, "There is no such thing as economic law." According to what may be apocryphal legend, Pareto later had his revenge.

Encountering his antagonist Gustav Schmoller on the street, Pareto raised his coat collar and shuffled forward to whine, "Where can I get a good dinner for 10 pfennigs?"

"For 10 pfennigs? No one can possibly get a good dinner anywhere for that."

"Aha," Pareto replied, "so there does exist economic law after all!"

What is the moral of this little tale? Does it demonstrate, for example, what I was brainwashed to believe in my innocent student days, that "there is no such thing as a free lunch"? Indeed, it was not until I had studied advanced economics that it even occurred to me to wonder what the no-free-lunch dogma was itself supposed to mean and be telling us about economic reality and feasible policy.

Angels, not angles

I mention this because I have just been reading a remarkable, too-little-known book, "The Gift Relationship: From Human Blood to Social Policy," by Richard M. Titmuss of the London School of Economics.

The author compares our American system of providing blood with that of the British. Here the issue is something more vital than mere lunch. Blood to the dying or postoperative patient is the nutrient of life itself.

No Englishman pays even a shilling for all the blood his doctors prescribe for him. And blood is more plentiful there than in this most affluent country of the world.

Where's the catch? you will ask. We all know that medicine is "socialized" in Great Britain; so, although the patient does not pay directly for the blood that he receives, surely the long-suffering middle classes are bled white by the tax system so that paupers can live parasitically on the red cells and energies of their betters?

From "Paul A. Samuelson on Blood," *Newsweek,* September 13, 1971. Reprinted with the kind permission of the publisher.

Wrong again. No one pays for the blood—not the state, not the patient, not the Red Cross.

Something for nothing? Yes, something for nothing and that something which poets have rightly symbolized as the most precious of all things.

No one pays for blood in England because no donor receives anything for his gift. That is, nothing except the "mere" satisfaction from giving. When I give blood in England that does not give me a surer claim on blood at a future date when I may need it. It does not give my child a preferred place in the queue for blood. All I get is the anonymous pleasure of knowing that I have helped my fellow man.

The next time you hear the expression "perfidious Albion," think of this remarkable example of social solidarity. When you read that British GNP is lagging, remind yourself of English courtesy in the bus queue and at the customs.

Blood and money

Meanwhile, what's the situation back here at home? The first thing to notice is that although we rely on monetary supply and demand to give us our daily bread, most of our blood and plasma is quite divorced from the market mechanism. More than two-thirds does come from donors who receive no cash in return.

To be sure, not all of this is completely voluntary. When a favorite teacher has a child dying of leukemia, all of his students and colleagues are urged to give blood. Often a consumer of blood, or his associates, are under specific compulsion to repay in kind for blood used. Not infrequently emotional blackmail is resorted to in this good cause.

But when all is said and done, the supply of voluntary blood in America falls increasingly behind the need for it. Recourse must be had to commercial donors.

We have in our everyday language the not very nice words "blood money." Today we should add the pejorative phrase "money blood." In terms of quality (red cells, hepatitis risk), the blood you get for a buck is simply not as good as that you get for love.

This should not surprise anyone. Wise people have always known that the love you get for love is better than the love you get for money.

Reading 13

Does Money Really Destroy Giving?

Kenneth J. Arrow

Richard Titmuss is justly distinguished for his devotion to the welfare of society at large and particularly to those who have received the least of society's benefits. His latest and much-noticed study, *The Gift Relationship: From Human Blood to Social Policy* focuses specifically on the workings of a particular system, that by which blood is made available for transfusions in the United States and in the United Kingdom. This study is intended to illuminate a much broader landscape: the limits of economic analysis, the rival uses of exchange and gift as modes of allocation, the collective or communitarian possibilities in society as against the tendencies toward individualism.

Thesis: Commerce corrupts

Perhaps the flavor of the lessons he wants us to learn can best be suggested by a somewhat lengthy quotation of his final two paragraphs:

From our study of the private market in blood in the United States, we have concluded that the commercialization of blood and donor relationships represses the expression of altruism, erodes the sense of community, lowers scientific standards, limits both personal and professional freedoms, sanctions the making of profits in hospitals and clinical laboratories, legalizes hostility between doctor and patient, subjects critical areas of medicine to laws of the marketplace, places immense social costs on those least

From Kenneth J. Arrow, "Gifts and Exchanges," *Philosophy and Public Affairs,* Princeton University Press, vol. 1, no. 4, Summer 1972. Reprinted, in abridgment, with the kind permission of the author and the publisher.

able to bear them—the poor, the sick, and the inept—increases the danger of unethical behavior in various sectors of medical science and practice, and results in situations in which proportionately more and more blood is supplied by the poor, the unskilled, the unemployed, Negroes and other low-income groups, and categories of exploited human populations of high blood yielders. Redistribution in terms of blood and blood products from the poor to the rich appears to be one of the dominant effects of the American blood-making systems.

Moreover, on four testable non-ethical criteria the commercialized blood market is bad. In terms of economic efficiency it is highly wasteful of blood; shortages, chronic and acute, characterize the demand-and-supply position and make illusory the concept of equilibrium. It is administratively inefficient and results in more bureaucratization and much greater administrative, accounting, and computer overheads. In terms of price per unit of blood to the patient (or consumer), it is a system which is five to fifteen times more costly than voluntary systems in Britain. And, finally, in terms of quality, commercial markets are much more likely to distribute the contaminated blood; the risks for the patient of disease and death are substantially greater. Freedom from disability is inseparable from altruism.

The present essay is a series of reflections on the issues raised by Titmuss' evidence and assertions.

Giving in economics

It is obvious that the allocation of goods and services is not accomplished entirely by exchange, as standard economic models would hold. Clearly this is true for such impalpable goods as respect, love, or status. But even when we confine ourselves to goods whose allocation the economist believes himself capable of analyzing with his tools, the donation of blood for transfusions is only one example of a large class of unilateral transactions in which there is no element of payment in any direct or ordinary sense of the term. Formal philanthropy has always been a prominent element of all economic systems. The whole structure of government expenditures is a departure from the system of mutual exchange.

There is another and very important sense in which a more subtle form of giving affects the allocation of economic resources. It can be argued that the presence of what are in a slightly old-fashioned terminology called *virtues* in fact plays a significant role in the operation of the economic system. Titmuss calls attention to the great value of truthfulness on the part of blood donors; the most serious risk in blood transfusion is the possible transmission of serum hepatitis from donor to recipient. Since no adequate test has yet been devised for the presence of hepatitis in the blood, its detection depends essentially on the willingness of the donor to state correctly whether or not he is suffering from that disease. This is a prototype of many other similar situations in economic life. The process of exchange requires or at least is greatly facilitated by the presence of several of these virtues (not only truth, but also trust, loyalty, and justice in future dealings).

Finally, there is a broader set of issues raised by Titmuss. The picture of a society run exclusively on the basis of exchange has long haunted sensitive observers, especially from the early days of the capitalist domination. The ideas of community and social cohesion are counterposed to a drastically reduced society in which individuals meet only as buyers and sellers of commodities.

Commercial U.S. versus altruistic U.K.

The starting point of Titmuss' analysis and reflections is the basic fact that in the United Kingdom the supplying of blood for transfusions is completely voluntary and unpaid, while in the United States there is a mixed system with both commercial and noncommercial blood banks and with payments of various kinds. According to Titmuss' estimates, based on admittedly unsatisfactory surveys, about one-third of the United States supply (including derivatives such as plasma, plasma fractions, and red blood cell concentrates) comes from paid blood donors. Nor are the rest considered to be truly voluntary; by Titmuss' standards a donor is considered to be voluntary only if the recipient is unknown to him and there are no social sanctions enforcing the donation. Thus only 9 percent of the United States donors are regarded as voluntary. About one-half give blood free of charge, but in most cases they are in effect replacing blood given to relatives.

In the United Kingdom there are no paid donors. However, it does turn out that in the case of 28 percent of the British donors either they or their families have received blood transfusions.

A rough impression suggests that unpaid donations are distributed among socio-economic classes more or less in proportion to the relative size of each class. Paid donors, on the contrary, are drawn almost exclusively from the lower-income categories, including the unemployed.

Even in the United Kingdom the percentage of the eligible population that gives blood is actually very small, only 6 percent according to Titmuss' estimates. Titmuss does not comment on this fact. The picture of a broadly altruistic society seems somwhat blurred when we realize what a small fraction of the population is in fact functioning altruistically.

Is it a case of either . . . or?

Economists typically take for granted that since the creation of a market increases the individual's area of choice it therefore leads to higher benefits. Thus, if to a voluntary blood donor system we add the possibility of selling blood, we have only expanded the individual's range of alternatives. But this is emphatically not the view held by Titmuss. On the contrary, he states, "as this study has shown comparatively, private market systems in the United States and other countries . . . deprive men of their freedom to choose to give or not to give" (p. 239). Shortly thereafter he continues: "In a positive sense we believe that policy and processes should enable men to be free to choose to give to unnamed strangers. They should not be coerced or constrained by the market. In the interests of the freedom of all men, they should not, however, be free to sell their blood or decide on a specific destination of the gift. The choice between these claims—between different kinds of freedom—has to be a social policy decision; in other words, it is a moral and political decision for the society as a whole" (p. 242). I can find no support in the evidence for the existence of such a dilemma. Indeed, it is not easy to see what kind of evidence would be relevant. It may be that the spread of commercial services in the United States was itself due to the failure of the voluntary services to supply enough blood, to give one simple hypothesis. The comparison might indeed indicate that the United States is a less altruistic society than the United Kingdom, but it would not show

that commercial blood-giving was a cause rather than an effect.

Why should it be that the creation of a market for blood would decrease the altruism embodied in giving blood? I do not find any clear answer in Titmuss. Evidently Titmuss must feel that attaching a price tag to this activity anywhere in the system depreciates its value as a symbolic expression of faith in others. But note that this is really an empirical question, not a matter of first principles. Do people in fact perceive the signals as Titmuss suggests? Would they, were the moral questions expounded with greater clarity?

Is giving really more efficient? And necessarily?

The aspect of Titmuss' work that will probably have the most striking effect is his argument and evidence that a world of giving may actually increase efficiency in the operation of the economic system. This is on the face of it a dramatic challenge to the tenets of the mainstream of economic thought.

Risk to blood receivers.   Titmuss presents a powerful indictment of the efficiency of blood-giving in the United States. With regard to the imposition of unnecessary risks on recipients, dramatic evidence has been advanced by Titmuss. The essential problem is that the use of infected blood in transfusions can lead to serum hepatitis in the recipient. A number of American investigators have shown that there is a remarkably high rate of post-transfusion serum hepatitis, an incidence which may reach 3 to 4 percent. Hepatitis is a serious illness and occasionally fatal. There seems to be very clear evidence that it is the commercial blood that is the primary source of hepatitis. Titmuss cites statistics showing that the risk of infection from blood given by prison and skid row populations is over ten times as great as from the population in general. On the other hand, the incidence of post-transfusion serum hepatitis in the United Kingdom is apparently less than 1 percent.

Further evidence comes from such comparisons as are possible with other countries. In West Germany, where evidently most of the blood is supplied commercially, post-transfusion hepatitis is estimated at 14 percent; in Japan, where virtually all the blood is commercial, the incidence is between 18 and 25 percent. According to data Titmuss could locate, commercial blood was very common in most countries and overwhelmingly so in the U.S.S.R., where about 50 percent of the blood is paid for at a very high rate. In Sweden, usually regarded as a society oriented toward collectivism, all of the blood is paid for. It is gathered by the state, not by commercial blood banks. The percentage of commercial blood in East Germany exceeds that in West Germany.

The basic problem here is one that has many parallels. The commodity or service offered has uncertain characteristics. The buyer is not really in a position to know what it is that he is buying. There is at the present time no test that can accurately detect whether a given blood donor is capable of transmitting hepatitis. Usually the donor will know that he has had hepatitis, and therefore his truthfulness in recording his past history is of the utmost importance.

The situation is one alluded to earlier, that the virtue of truthfulness in fact contributes in a very significant way to the efficiency of the economic system. A voluntary donor system is from this point of view self-enforcing. Anyone whose motive for giving is to help others, but who suffers from hepatitis and is aware of the implications of this, will of course refrain from giving. On the other hand, a commercial blood donor, especially one driven by poverty, has every incentive to conceal the truth.

To repeat, the two key features of the situation are uncertainty about the quality of the service and a difference between the degrees of knowledge possessed by buyer and seller. One can think of many parallels. A good example is the question of automobile safety. The seller is supplying a complex machine. The details of both design and construction are inevitably better known to the seller than to the buyer. In these circumstances it seems clear to me that the price system is no insurance of efficiency in all respects. Some alternative system of determining quality and providing assurance for buyers is needed. One such candidate is a sense of social responsibility on the part of the seller. In this context, ethical behavior can be regarded as a socially desirable institution which facilitates the achievement of economic efficiency in the broad sense.

Risk to blood sellers. It also appears that commercial blood-giving leads to risks to the donors, though less serious than those to the recipients. Commercial blood donors have some incentive to give blood more frequently than is desirable from the point of view of their health.

For many purposes, particularly the treatment of anemia, only the red blood cells are needed. There has been developed a new process called plasmapheresis. Here the red blood cells are separated from the plasma in which they float and the plasma is then reinjected into the body of the donor. Under these conditions donations can be, and are, made much more frequently. Several donations a week can be made, or so it is held. The collection of red blood cells for plasmapheresis is almost exclusively commercial, being carried out by or on behalf of the pharmaceutical companies. The fact that a very substantial income can be had through frequent donations means at least the potentiality of serious risk to the donors. There is, however, very little evidence of any damage actually having taken place.

Waste of blood. A third apparent inefficiency in the United States system, according to Titmuss, is a very substantial amount of wastage of the blood collected; persistent shortages are also observed. Blood deteriorates after being drawn from a donor, and for most purposes it must be used within twenty-one days of collection. It appears that about 30 percent of the blood is wasted [in the U.S., as compared to perhaps 10 percent wastage in the U.K.]. He notes that elective surgery is occasionally postponed because of the shortage of blood. It is asserted that no such shortages exist in the United Kingdom; a study by two economists that arrives at the opposite conclusion is abruptly dismissed by Titmuss as having been badly designed.

Although Titmuss links wastage of blood to the commercial system, he really gives no theoretical explanation of this link. I cannot conceive what it is. One would be much more tempted to explain a greater wastage of blood in the United States, if such exists, by the generally decentralized nature of the American blood collection system. It should be noted that the voluntary system is quite chaotic as far as its organization is concerned. It is possible that, in the absence of a clear system of meeting shortages of a perishable commodity in one place with surpluses from another, such a system would perform much less efficiently than the British National Health Service. I find no clear evidence that commercialism per se is the key factor here.

Giving and the social order

Titmuss here and throughout his work is interested in still broader issues. For him the marketplace is basically subversive of the ideal social order. Some of his chapter titles are suggestive: "Blood and the Marketplace," "Economic Man: Social Man." He greatly fears that "the myth of maximizing economic growth can supplant the growth of economic social relation" (p. 199).

A case serves Titmuss as an empirical springboard for his general attack on the commercialization of society. The blood supply in Kansas City was regarded as subject to the antitrust laws because blood was treated as a commodity. It is the latter point that disturbs Titmuss and arouses his ire. He generalizes from this to the whole treatment of medical care as a commodity.

Malpractice suits in U.S.   He notes, with appropriate statistics, that malpractice suits have become increasingly prevalent in the United States. The cost of malpractice insurance is rising, the settlements are growing in size as well as in number. All this is contrasted with the British situation, in which malpractice suits are apparently quite negligible in number and seriousness.

What do these observations in fact tell us? Titmuss, without giving a detailed theoretical explanation, suggests in a general sort of way that the commercialization of medical practice is accompanied by a legitimization of doctor-patient hostility.

One can, it seems to me, look at this matter somewhat differently. The ideal of Titmuss could be interpreted as that of a world where doctors and hospitals are protected from the consequences of their errors, at least as far as legal proceedings are concerned. After all, there is one very important relevant question: Are the malpractice suits justified? We have to reckon with the idea that there is a lot of malpractice in the United States. To discourage suits, then, would simply be a way of denying compensation to legitimate victims for the costs imposed upon them, and of minimizing a method of exerting pressure on doctors who perform badly.

What is disturbing, in this case as in many others, is that an appeal against the marketplace and its coldness has a way of slipping into a defense of privilege. Maine [in his 1861 classic, *Ancient Law*] spoke of the difference between status and contract. It is very easy indeed for "community" to slip over into "status."

Elitism?

Indeed, there is something of a paradox in Titmuss' philosophy. He is especially interested in the expression of impersonal altruism. It is not the richness of family relationships or the close ties of a small community that he wishes to promote. It is rather a diffuse expression of confidence by individuals in the workings of a society as a whole. But such an expression of impersonal altruism is as far removed from the feelings of personal interaction as any marketplace. Indeed, the small number of blood donors in the United Kingdom suggests, if I were to generalize as freely as Titmuss does, the idea of an aristocracy of saints. This is a way of social life that seems to have worked remarkably well in the British context, while proving capable of catastrophic consequences in the Soviet Union.

*   *   *

Despite—and in part because of—its flaws, Titmuss' book is a resonant evocation of central problems of social value. It has greatly enriched the quality of social-philosophical debate.

Business Organization and the Corporate Conscience

Readings 14 and 15   Debate on Galbraith

The discussion a book evokes is sometimes as valuable as the work itself. And the second round of a debate may be more valuable than the first. Robert Solow, brilliant professor of economics at M.I.T. and one-time member of the Kennedy New Frontier economic team, wrote a brilliant critique of the *New Industrial State*. Professor John Kenneth Galbraith of Harvard wrote a brilliant reply. Brilliant salvos were going off all over the place. Then Robin Marris, Fellow of King's College, Cambridge, England, who has actually done serious research work on the motives and behavior of the modern corporation, joined in the debate. Reading 14 is his affirmation that Galbraith is on to something new and good; Reading 15 is Solow's evaluation of what Galbraith's contribution adds up to.

Questions to guide the reading

You and your parents buy Fords and Chevrolets, Ivory soap and Tide detergent, RCA and Zenith television sets. Looking back on last year's expenditures, are there any purchases you really regret? Which were merely the result of persuasive advertising and unconscious conditioning? Why did you not buy Edsels when you did buy Mustangs?

If Marris is right and managers become obsessed with the cancer of growth even at the expense of profits, how can we account for the fact that General Mills sold off its animal-food lines in order to conserve capital for more lucrative undertakings? If managers are absolute monarchs, why not dispense with dividends and grow even faster?

If Solow is right, could we get out of a depression by more advertising? Since successful long-run profit maximization will lead to growth in directions of greatest advantage, how can we differentiate such behavior from actions to maximize growth for its own sake?

Reading 14

Galbraith: *Oui*

Robin Marris

I have volunteered to intervene in the Solow-Galbraith controversy, which began in the Fall issue of this journal, because I have some doubts whether, at the end of the day, the lay reader was left clear about the basic issues.

It is true that Galbraith relies largely on assertion (or, shall we say, on persuasive writing) in contrast to large-scale evidence to make his case—especially his case about advertising. It is also true that, by a great deal of hard work and by pains-

From Robin Marris, "Galbraith, Solow, and the Truth about Corporations," *The Public Interest,* No. 11, Spring, 1968. Copyright © 1968 National Affairs, Inc. Reprinted with kind permission of the author and publisher.

taking development of mathematical and statistical methods, economists over the last twenty years have learned to work more scientifically. But, for reasons which seem to be as much cultural as technical, the leading exponents of the new methods have chosen largely to confine themselves within the framework of the traditional assumptions. The form of their experiments has tended to preclude answering many of the questions here in debate. The influence of advertising, for example, has not been tested, but when the question arises it is customary to say that the traditional framework, now endowed with statistical flesh, provides a reasonable explanation of observed behavior, so that it is probably unnecessary to worry about Madison Avenue. If asked for a further opinion, exponents of this school usually themselves resort to assertions; specifically, they assert that the effects of large-scale advertising largely cancel themselves out, leaving the broad pattern of consumer expenditure undisturbed. Solow's review of Galbraith followed this line of argument almost precisely.

If the great majority of applied economists in this country are really so sure that they already know the answer, i.e., they are sure that most advertising results in a stand-off, the profession has clearly been guilty of a grave dereliction of duty to the public. They should have been shouting loudly and with one voice, "Here is an activity that has no significant net economic effect, good or bad; it is a total waste; it should be prohibited like arson." The discussion would then be thrown back into the sociological arena. I personally regard the cultural effects of advertising as debasing to language, to truth, and to logic, and as especially despicable because advertising is known to be most effective where the consumer has the least capacity to obtain the information necessary to evaluate products. There are sociologists who argue that the modern style of advertising (especially television) has a function in integrating the working class into the mass society and that the less well-educated obtain satisfaction from being wooed by advertisers. It is true that it is mostly the educated who scoff at advertising. We know from British experience that the working class positively prefers commercial programs and that BBC's audience is largely confined to the better educated. On the other hand, one has to count the cost of the recent effects in the United States of parading television

commercials before people living in squalid conditions who can see no hope of buying many of the goods displayed. These are sorts of questions which economists have not equipped themselves to judge, and here I would align myself with Galbraith (in his rejoinder) in a plea for the broadening of both economics and sociology.

The myth of "consumers' sovereignty"

This said, I must confess that the picture which, in my book, I drew in support of my own theory was more complex than Galbraith's and put considerably less emphasis on the effects of advertising as such. The picture was not strictly confirmed by "hard" evidence, although it is considerably supported by evidence drawn from the work of sociologists and market researchers. I saw the process by which consumer tastes develop as a complicated interaction of personal influence (meaning the influence of consumers on other consumers), greatly helped at critical points by advertising and marketing efforts generally. Sociologists have shown, in rather carefully designed experiments, that consumption decisions are effectively influenced, on the one hand, by a variety of advertising media and, on the other, by the recommendations of other persons known to the individual consumer. Each factor—advertising and personal recommendation—is responsible, very broadly, for about an equal share of the total result. The experiments cannot contribute directly to the present controversy, because they relate to decisions between alternative brands of the same product at given prices; but they remain suggestive.

The implications for the "affluent society" thesis, and for economic theory, are also clear. A complex, dynamic, socio-economic system of this kind must be considered to be something like a biological phenomenon. Chance constellations of small individual factors at a particular time can have a considerable influence on the future direction of a plant's development. The needs, interests, and performance of producers are a particularly potent example of such influence, and one way of reading Galbraith is to take "advertising" as a portmanteau word for all these kinds of effects. In any event, once we accept this kind of picture, the notion of "consumers' sovereignty" becomes vague, to say the least, and we are provided with a virtually complete justification for a wide range of political action to impose social value judgments in the direction of consumption patterns. Here, quite likely, Solow would want to raise his hand and say, "I do not disagree." But the fact remains that the notion of consumers' sovereignty, essentially an *economic* theory, retains very considerable political force in defense of the status quo. Anyone who doubts the close political relationship should take a look at an advertisement in the January 1968 issue of *Fortune* magazine, paid for by the Magazine Publishers' Association. This advertisement pointed to the alleged relative economic failure of East Germany, as compared with West Germany, in a defense of the activity of United States mass media in fostering demand for a wide range of, and variety among, individual consumers' goods (using the example of stuffed olives). A dramatic juxtaposition of a representation of the Berlin Wall was clearly intended to create a mental association between political repression and government intervention in the pattern of consumption.

The large corporation

The other basic issue between Galbraith and Solow concerned the role of the large corporations. Of course it is true that important sectors of the American economy are still traditionally organized. Supermarkets were an important social innovation, and still more important was the discovery that they can be operated successfully by quite small businesses. But does Solow or anyone else *really* believe that these small-business sectors have a significant influence on the speed and pattern of economic development? The drive of our system comes manifestly from the large-scale sector, now increasingly including the government as well as the large "profit-making" corporations.

And there is a major exception that marvelously tests the rule. The temporary visitor to this country cannot help being impressed by the apparently general dissatisfaction with the economic and social performance in the field of urban development, dissatisfaction which ranges from the fact of the existence of slums (and the associated difficulty in providing low-cost housing) to the more general question of the adequacy of city planning, the development of the suburbs, and so on. From

overseas, the United States appears so prosperous that the "urban" problem is widely assumed to be no more than a euphemism for the race problem. But is it a coincidence that the production sector most closely concerned (namely the construction industries and the real estate business) happens to represent the most prominent exception to the rule of "managerial" capitalism? In this sector, medium-scale organization is typical, and large-scale organizations are usually owned by traditional capitalists. In particular, the free market in urban land (which is at the bed of this whole sea of troubles) displays one of the purest forms of traditional capitalism still surviving. And the cream of the joke is that most qualified observers of the scene other than economists are asking that the great managerial corporations come to the rescue.

Galbraith, on the other hand, thinks that the "Technostructure" cannot or will not undertake the task, because its performance would lack technical virtuosity. I am not convinced. Although put across with characteristic force, the argument is not in fact very strong. There is not firm evidence that, if money were provided for massive urban projects on a scale comparable with current military and space programs, opportunities for exercising technical virtuosity would not be found or would be rejected, especially if the new programs made liberal use of such labels as "Componentization Research" and "Systems Analysis." Galbraith's later argument (in his chapter on the Cold War), that one reason why this kind of money is not in practice available is the indirect political (and indirectly bellicose) influence of the existing Technostructure, is much more convincing, but was not referred to by Solow.

The real world of the firm

When we reach the core of the debate—i.e., the economic theory of corporate behavior—the truth is that Solow was disingenuous, but that Galbraith had left out vital elements and laid himself open to legitimate attack. What Solow omitted to tell was that my theory implies that *in spite* of the existence of "an important discipline in the capital market," the real-world system almost certainly behaves very differently from the way implied in the conventional theory: the conventional theory would imply that corporations would choose to grow considerably more slowly and reward stockholders significantly better. Galbraith, however, in failing to meet the argument that profits are needed for growth, failed to explain how this divergence can occur. In offering to put the record straight, I am motivated not only by vanity, but also by the conviction that an accurate theory about corporate growth is essential for a correct understanding of a wide range of contemporary problems of economic and social policy. The theory cannot be made simple, but can be summarized as follows.

A growing corporation faces two problems: the problem of creating a growing demand for its products, and the problem of financing the necessary growth of capacity. The corporation may strive to be as efficient as possible, in the sense of squeezing the maximum profit from its existing markets; but the search for (or creation of) *new* markets inevitably costs money (in research, marketing, and losses from failures), and so, as the growth process is accelerated, the average return realized on the *total* assets of the corporation must be *adversely* affected (even if the development expenditure is deployed as efficiently as possible).

Profits and/or growth

A decision by the management to grow at a certain rate, and to choose the consistent retention ratio, must also evidently imply a unique level and expected rate of growth of the dividend; and so, in a rational stock market, the decision must imply a unique current price and prospective capital gain in the corporation's stock. Up to a point, actual or potential stockholders may be content to see increased growth creating prospects of future gain at the expense of current dividends; beyond this point, any further increase in the growth rate chosen by the management must have a depressing effect on the stock price. There is no reason to suppose that a growth-oriented management will always refrain from accelerating beyond this point; and if they go too far they will undoubtedly lay themselves open to a variety of dangers (e.g., a take-over raid). I suggested in my theory that we might describe a typical "managerial" objective as maximum growth subject to a *minimum* on the stock price.

Solow said that my theory, in recognizing the minimum stock-price constraint, "came closer to

the conventional view." On the contrary, in the conventional view management exists only to serve stockholders, and the essential technical problem is to find decision rules that would establish the policy which will, in fact, *maximize* the price of the stock. The two theories become "similar" only in the special conditions where the minimum and maximum position lie close together. These conditions are most improbable; in other words, the traditional theory is literally a "special case."

Because large-scale, professional management, not personally owning large supplies of finance, has such predominant technical advantages in the modern economy; because, although it may *use* stockmarket investors and bankers, it no longer *depends* on them; because the (not insubstantial) true capitalists who remain in our system avoid speculating in large manufacturing businesses unless these are going very cheap (they prefer real estate); because the other potential take-over raiders are typically themselves management-controlled—because of all this and much more, it is inevitable that the safe minimum level of the price of a corporation's stock will be significantly lower, and the safe maximum growth rate correspondingly higher, than the values which would be chosen by a management that really did care only for the welfare of the stockholders. Numerical calculations based on statistical observation suggest that a rather growth-conscious management could typically grow almost twice as fast, setting the stock market value at all times about one-third lower, as compared to the values which would be obtained in an otherwise comparable corporation dominated by stockholders who knew all the facts. Furthermore, the growth-oriented management could safely continue the policy indefinitely, even if there were quite a number of others who chose to behave otherwise. Since the growth-oriented managements will by definition be located in the faster growing corporations, this type of behavior must in time drive out other types—a process which, I suggest, has been going on for some time. The further the process goes, the weaker is the power of the stock market to resist. Since the growth-oriented firms are technically efficient, they display not unattractive levels and growth rates of dividends, the incentive to resistance is dampened, and the latent preference for slower growth and higher current dividends remains un-recognized.

Furthermore, because managements, in foster-ing growth, also create technical progress, new wants, new goods, and a generally different dy-namic environment, the implications of the two types of theory cannot easily be compared. We cannot possibly assert that it would necessarily be in the public interest to compel managements to conform to the traditional norm; we might very likely make many people worse off and few better off. Galbraith, however, imposed the value judg-ment (the "affluent-society" thesis) that the higher rate of consumer innovation resulting from "man-agerial" behavior by the corporations is undesir-able, because it is biased against the expression of leisure preferences and against the development of "public" goods. He does not, however (as maybe does Solow in saying "it might perhaps be better if companies were forced more often into the capital market") suggest that the remedies lie in the direc-tion of the traditional model.

The conclusion I draw (and it is an implication which I suspect to be one of the causes of the con-siderable ideological drive of "neoclassical" eco-nomics in the United States) would probably be disliked by both parties: namely, that once the classical idealization of capitalism is thus de-stroyed, there is no *economic* case for its superior-ity over socialism. Consequently, the attempt to impose capitalism all around the world, in some cases virtually by force, can only be justified on political grounds. The latter, however, seem to get thinner every day. In the miserable developing countries of the "free" world, where we cheerfully give aid to almost any form of dictatorship pro-vided no industries are nationalized (the case of Tito being a historical freak, much disliked by the Congress, I understand), there is no dearth of greedy *profit* maximizers, many living in consider-able luxury. What the non-affluent majority of the world's population so badly needs is a much greater number of *growth* maximizers.

The need for "restructuring"

More domestic and less inflammatory implications of the truth about the corporations are varied and pervasive. I will conclude with an example which may be of some topical interest. Suppose it is de-

sired to get the corporations interested in replacing slums with wholesome low-rental dwellings, and suppose that the political conditions for the neces-sary diversion of national resources have already been created. Suppose federal contracts provide a massive injection of technical stimulus into the construction sector. We would still face the diffi-culty that low-income housing is an unprofitable line of business. This keeps out the traditionally motivated corporation and also discourages the growth-motivated corporation, because it means growing in directions that offer a particularly unfavorable relationship between growth and pro-fitability, and consequently, means low "equilib-rium" rates of growth in accordance with the the-ory. Under present conditions, therefore, a growth-oriented management undertaking these desirable activities *will be penalized in terms of its own motives*—a point which, once seen, appears rather obvious, but is not in fact generally well understood, and seems to have been missed by Galbraith.

Solow and many of his colleagues would then say, of course, that here is a perfect example of the traditional assumptions being good enough for policy purposes. On the contrary, it provides an excellent example of the serious practical errors which can result from that attitude. Suppose a cer-tain senator, who may be nameless, proposes a scheme of tax credits to firms which will undertake socially oriented urban renewal projects. On the traditional assumptions, the function of the sub-sidy is simply to compensate stockholders for a reduced pre-tax rate of return. In my kind of model, the function is to compensate the manage-ment for lost growth-opportunity by offsetting the reduction in cash flow. If we follow this through, we will find that the size of the tax credit needed to obtain a given amount of housing would be sub-stantially smaller, and the general political appeal of the project consequently more attractive.

Finally, I would suggest, if we were to "restruc-ture" our economic system so that the units of pro-duction were endowed with the social norm of growth maximization (subject to financial con-straints), and were freed from the embarrassments of stockholders and other trappings of private property, manipulation of the financial rules to offset various kinds of built-in bias, and generally to foster a good society, would be much easier. We would be freed from the inhibitions and costs resulting from our archaic but powerful custom of assigning a private owner or part owner to most of our means of production. We should be able to concentrate on the task of finding the most effi- cient ways of organizing all the things we want to do, and to stop wasting our time discussing whether the old corporations did, or were supposed to, "maximize profits." But that is a longer story.

Reading 15

Galbraith: *Non*

Robert M. Solow

Marris comments at length on the influence of advertising in the management of consumer demand, and on the theory of corporate behavior. On the first, he does not endorse Galbraith's view of the utter helplessness of the consumer, but he does agree that the success of salesmanship undermines conventional presumptions about the beneficence of market processes. On the second, he presents a theory which corresponds roughly with Galbraith's more impressionistic sketch, but which, because of its greater precision, offers less freedom to draw picturesque implications. I shall say a word about each subject.

On advertising

Here one must be clear what the question is. No one who believes, as I do, that profit is an important business motive could argue that advertising has no influence on the willingness of consumers to buy a given product at a given price. After all, how could I then account for the fact that profit-seeking corporations regularly spend billions of dollars on advertising? Nor did I exactly "resort to assertion." What I said was: "I have no great confidence in my own casual observations either. But I should think a case could be made that much advertising serves only to cancel other advertising, and is therefore merely wasteful." I should think it obvious that this almost *has* to be true—i.e., that much advertising merely cancels other advertising—for otherwise there would be nothing to stop both the cigarette industry and the detergent industry from expanding their sales to their hearts' desire and to the limits of consumers' capacity to carry debt. And what would stop each individual manufacturer of cigarettes and detergents from doing the same?

No, that is hardly the issue. I have no wish to deny that an individual seller can shift the relation between his sales and the price he charges by incurring advertising or other selling costs. There is even a lot of conventional theory about that. It is important that the evidence Marris cites relates, as he admits, to consumers' "decisions between alternative brands of the same product at given prices." I suppose, on common sense grounds, that it must be relatively easy to affect such decisions by advertising. That is why essentially all tobacco companies advertise—because each is forced to offset the advertising of any one of their number, or lose sales. It must be harder to influence the consumer's choice between purchases of cigarettes and purchases of beer, and much harder still to influence his distribution of expenditures among such broad categories as food, clothing, automobiles, housing. It is open to legitimate doubt that advertising has any detectable effect at all on the sum total of consumer spending or, in other words, on the choice between spending and saving.

My remarks were directed primarily to this last proposition. I wanted to show how shaky the foundations are for the naïve belief that not only the fortunes of individual companies, but also the viability of capitalism, rests on the success of the Madison Avenue shock troops, because without them the flow of consumer spending would dry up.

I suspect Marris would agree with me on this

point. He goes on to ask why, if much advertising is merely wasteful, economists are not in favor of prohibiting it. Well, as a principle, that does seem to border on the tyrannical. But it has sometimes occurred to me that there might be some point in taxing advertising expenditure, and I gather from conversation with other economists that they have had the same thought. If we do not push it very hard, that is perhaps because up to now there have been more important causes to promote, with a considerably greater chance of success.

That leaves the difficult question of the status of the notion of consumers' sovereignty. Once sellers of commodities can influence, even if not control, consumers' preferences among commodities, it becomes a much less persuasive defense of laissez-faire to say that the system caters to consumers' preferences. Since I am not much of a believer in laissez-faire anyway, that doesn't disturb me. But I am not, for a number of reasons, prepared to accept Marris' leap to apparently wholesale political steering of the direction of consumption. In the first place, to the extent that competition induces sellers to offset one another's advertising campaigns, the seriousness of the problem is tempered and we are back again to waste (and the possibility of taxation as a remedy). Second, there is already piecemeal political intervention in the direction of consumption, beginning with pure-food-and-drug legislation, the mild policing of deception in labeling and advertising, and the various other consumer-protection laws recently proposed or enacted. There would seem to be plenty of room for strengthening and extending such devices. Moreover, just because the formation of consumer preferences is inescapably a social process, it is not clear by what standard Marris' proposal is superior to what we have now. Indeed, "collective political action . . . to steer the direction of consumption" might simply centralize taste-making powers in the hands of a government certainly more powerful and probably more nearly monolithic than even the world of large corporations. I am not sure I want exclusive access to the formation of my tastes to rest with the government of an Eisenhower or a Johnson (or a Douglas-Home or a Wilson). Probably neither does Marris, and in practice we might accept the same sort of policies.

On corporate behavior

Marris has summarized, with quite wonderful economy, his own theory of corporate behavior. It is a self-contained determinate theory, with implications that are testable at least in principle. Like any theory, this one raises two questions. Does it tell a true story? And, if it does, what are its larger implications about economic life?

As I mentioned in my review of Galbraith, it is not easy to invent a clear-cut statistical test of the Marris theory of corporate growth against the more standard model of long-run profit maximization anchored by a target rate of return. I suggested that this is because the two theories do not have drastically different implications. Marris objects; like any student of advertising, he would like to stress the differences between his own product and Brand X. I should have been more precise. The two theories need not have very different implications, but they may. Whether they do depends on the height of the minimum acceptable-rate-of-return (or stock price) in Marris' model. The higher it is, or the closer to the target rate of return, the more similar a Marris economy will be to mine. I am uncertain about the source of Marris' conviction that the differences are in fact large, since so far as I know his theory has not yet been given a large-scale run against the facts. One would like to know, for example, how well it does as a predictor of plant and equipment spending.

In the meanwhile, we are reduced to casual empiricism about the assumptions and implications of the Marris theory. This is hardly the place to discuss the matter in detail. I will simply say that the theory, interesting and attractive as it is, seems to me to rest on two fairly weak assumptions. The first is that for a given corporation in a given environment there must be a well-defined relation between its rate of growth (of output) and its rate of return on capital, independent of the absolute size of the corporation. It is not enough for the theory that, with everything else momentarily given, a corporation's profitability should depend on how rapidly it is trying to expand its sales and its capacity. What is required is that this relation hold for long intervals of time during which the corporation is actually growing. Both at the beginning of the period, when the company is small, and at the end, when it is large, it has to be true that to a particular, more or less steady rate of growth of x per cent a year corresponds the same more or less steady rate of profit of y per cent a year. This is not outlandish, but I think the assumption rests on too simple a view of the business of sales promotion, and on insufficient attention to the production-cost side of the problem.

The second dubious assumption is the one that names growth of sales as the prime object of the corporation. Marris does not simply assert this; he argues it with care and sociological circumstance in his book. He gives two versions: a management may "choose to go for a certain growth rate," or else it may seek "maximum growth subject to a minimum on the stock price." In a more technical statement of the theory he can allow profits and growth to be two separate objectives which have to be weighed against each other. The more weight a corporation attaches to profits and the less to growth, the more nearly it will behave according to the conventional theory.

There is certainly a lot of talk in the business press about growth and expansion. But this, by itself, is hardly support for the Marris-Galbraith doctrine. In the first place, the alternative theory—that corporations maximize long-run profits more or less, and expand whenever they earn more than a target rate of return—also entails that successful companies will be growing most of the time, and will no doubt be talking about it. In the second place, one must keep in mind that the federal government taxes long-term capital gains only half as heavily as dividends, and under some circumstances considerably less than that. Retention and reinvestment of earnings—i.e., internally financed growth—is the obvious way for a corporation to convert dividends into capital gains for its shareholders, including its officers. So devotion to growth is quite consistent with profit-maximization if profit is interpreted as the after-tax return to the stockholder.

Theories that emphasize the separation of ownership and control tend to ignore the fact that, if the common stockholder cannot control the policy of the corporation he owns, he can arrange to own a different corporation by merely telephoning his broker. He can even buy shares in a mutual fund that will tailor a portfolio to his expressed preferences between current dividends and capital gains. Indeed, such theories generally tend to ignore the large-scale institutional investors, whose presence on the other side of the market makes the balance of power between management and owner look a little different.

This would seem to be important, even within the framework of Marris' theory. He admits that some corporations can be more growth-oriented and less profit-oriented than others. If any substantial number of stockholders strongly favors immediate profits over growth, their demands can be mobilized by institutional investors. Corporate managements are sure to be found or created who will be prepared to get their kicks by catering to these demands.

I realize that these casual remarks about the plausibility of assumptions can never be decisive. For that we will have to wait for serious empirical testing. And if I am right that the two theories could turn out to have similar implications, we may have to wait even longer—but of course it will matter less. By the way, Marris' discussion of the problem of getting private firms interested in the construction of low-rent housing seems to me to favor my view of the matter at least as much as it does his. It turns out that low-income housing is now an unattractive business to be in, on the assumptions of either theory. When you get right down to the nitty-gritty, the difference is merely the size of the subsidy needed to obtain a given amount of housing, and there is probably room for more than one opinion about that, too.

On Ideology

Marris considers his theory to be subversive of the existing order. Since the consumer is presumably manipulated and the stockholder presumably ignored, no intellectual case remains for capitalism as an efficient economic system. Even leaving aside the question whether this argument applies to the regulated mixed economy of today, it is the damnedest argument for socialism I ever heard. Who would storm the Winter Palace so that units of production could be "endowed with the social norm of growth maximization (subject to financial constraints)" even if "manipulation of the financial rules to offset various kinds of built-in bias . . . would be much easier"?

Marris also suspects that only an ideological drive can explain the persistence with which economists in the United States cling to some (incomplete) confidence in market mechanisms. I would not deny that some academic disputes have a genuine ideological content. But I would also assert that there is far less ideology wrapped up in academic economics in the United States than a man from Cambridge, England, can possibly realize. (One of Cambridge's most distinguished economists, with whom I had been carrying on a rather abstract controversy, once said to me at a party: "You're not a reactionary; so why don't you agree with me?" I thought it was a good question.) In fact, I don't think that my argument with Galbraith and Marris is really ideological in character. My own view is that any economic system can be made to work, if you go at it cleverly. But to do that, you have to get the analysis right. If Marris' theory of the firm turns out to work better, which is conceivable, I will buy it cheerfully.

Readings 16 and 17

Critics have damned historic capitalism as being heartless and indifferent to human welfare and suffering. Careful study of the actual operations of competitive markets revealed to economic experts that human welfare in a market system is not necessarily dependent upon the altruistic motivations of businessmen and laborers. Today, however, we live in a mixed economy, not in historic capitalism. And it is persuasively argued by many thinkers that the modern large corporation has developed a soul and a social conscience.

Instead of eavesdropping on scholars, let us turn (in Reading 16) to the businessman beast himself to hear what he says he is actually doing. Eli Goldston is a highly successful corporate executive, being President of Eastern Gas and Fuel Associates. Mr. Goldston also finds time to serve on many public-policy commissions and governmental advisory bodies. Thus he was on the Democratic Advisory Council set up by Senator Edward Kennedy in Massachusetts. When Goldston asserts that he and men like him in other large corporations are obsessed with maximizing their company per share earnings and the future market value of the companies stock price, he is speaking from *inside* observation of the technostructure.

In Reading 17 a brilliant economic analyst and polemicist of the "Chicago" free-market school pooh-poohs the notion that the system relies on, or should rely on, social motivations of even the largest corporations.

Jack Hirshleifer is professor of economics at the University of California at Los Angeles.

Questions to guide the reading

Adam Smith said that if people pursued their self-interest in competitive markets, they would be led—as if by an "Invisible Hand"—to secure the maximum of social well-being. Do you think this holds true, with respect to free enterprise in heroin? Advertising expenditures on or off Madison Avenue? Farm production? Sweatshop labor? How important is the assumption of "perfection of competition"?

We know that people often rationalize. Often too, they unconsciously distort reality in this process. On its own merits does the Goldston argument strike you as having the ring of truth or is it self-deception and propaganda?

Could Hirshleifer be correct about the limited freedom of a small-scale competitor and yet be wrong about the 100 largest corporations? What would happen if a Christ-like altruist became head of a large corporation? Could he change the system?

Reading 16

The Real Truth about Profit Maximizing

Eli Goldston

Net profit per share is more important to professional managers than many current theorists assume. Observations about business by one immersed in it may lack the breadth and depth of a scholarly inquiry and, above all, its historical perspective. But without endorsing the discredited barnyard aphorism that only a hen can judge a good egg, perhaps an active businessman can add some new knowledge of business to what is usually reported by academic observers.

My comments will apply principally to *big business*—business with substantial *public stock ownership*. Small, proprietary businesses are an important element in the American economy, but they are not likely to be significant in changing the way business generally participates in major social problems. I believe my observations should, however, be pertinent over quite a range of business sizes. Just as styles and manners tend to drift out from Cafe Society or the Jet Set through society columns, so the structure, staffing, procedures, and objectives of *Fortune's* 500 Largest Industrials spread through the business press to the rest of business. A wise government will make use of this "trickle-down" theory and try first to get the business "influentials" or "opinion leaders" to accept new programs.

Big business firms today often differ from the customary descriptions of American corporate enterprise in a number of ways: ownership, structure, exposure, motivation and measurement, character of decision-makers, objectives, and product. I will emphasize the factors that make for greater participation by private firms in solving social problems.

Characteristics of contemporary American business

Ownership. The degree of *separation between owners and managers* of modern big business has been overstated. So has the alleged ability of incompetent or unaggressive management to survive and even to perpetuate itself by selecting its successors. The number of shareholders in United States corporations has risen from about 6.5 million to over 24 million during the past fifteen years. Those economists who feel that a corporate manager can turn his back on stock prices and no longer feel any real pressure for earnings performance should try coming home to find that the cleaning woman who owns ten shares of his company's stock wants to know if she should buy more. They should try going to a cocktail party that develops into an impromptu shareholders' meeting or attending a dinner party where the hostess has the cleaning woman's question—except that, in addition, she plans to report on the stock to her investment club.

The firms where unaggressive management can relax are typically ones where a founding family is still powerful enough to keep control and affluent enough not to press for profit maximization. Except in such firms, ownership is proving to be an increasingly strong influence on management. Repeated successes in unseating poor managements by "takeovers," "overhead tenders," and "forced mergers" have demonstrated that the owners of a contemporary American business more often than not insist on and can demand growing profits. "Performance-minded" investment trusts have speeded the process, for they no longer automatically vote with incumbent management or sell off their stock. Instead they look for, follow, and even back "raiders" in undervalued situations, convinced that nothing can be bought so cheap as a company under poor management about to be replaced.

Banks are still occasionally reluctant to finance "overhead tenders," but they have raised their sights from the days when it was assumed that

From Eli Goldston, "New Prospects for American Business," *Daedalus,* Journal of the American Academy of Arts and Sciences, Winter 1969. Reprinted with kind permission of the author and publisher.

about $500,000 for expenses and $50,000,000 in capital was the absolute maximum a "raider" could raise. Managements are no longer safe behind these financial limitations, as witness the takeover of United Gas by Pennzoil in 1966 largely by the use of bank loans. United Gas management, owning 3.3 per cent of a market equity of $442 million, was not safe.

Both the number and value of tender offers have increased spectacularly. In 1960, there were 25 tender offers with a total value of $186 million. By 1965, there were 75 with a total value of $951 million, and 1967 went well over the $1 billion mark. In the first six months of 1968, the 1967 total was exceeded. Not only shareholders, but institutional lenders and public creditors are intent on profitable performance, and they may bring quiet but considerable pressure, the existence or true nature of which is seldom publicly revealed. Those economists who believe that size and inertia provide a safe moat for an incompetent but incumbent management should follow Hodson's "Beauties Between the Balance Sheets" or *Finance Magazine*'s "Wolves of Wall Street," which list companies selling below break-up value. Watching the names of the listed firms disappear suggests that the moat is loaded with amphibian sharks who are not above crawling out to devour those they are intended to defend.

Structure. The degree to which large enterprises can once again be personally directed is not yet fully appreciated. With modern technology, a business enterprise can truly be the shadow of one man. Communication is instant, so rapidly improved that it is difficult to realize that as recently as 1929 even the President of the United States did not have a telephone in his office. Personal transportation makes it possible for any executive group to be assembled anywhere in the world within forty-eight hours. Data-handling technology applied to budgeting, forecasting, accounting by profit centers, and control by variances brings small and early deviations quickly to the attention of top management. The applications of business simulation with third-generation *computers permit the choice of policies to be isolated in a small top-management group working on long-range planning and leaving operations to carefully watched line managers.* The clearer separation between policy and operations permits the elimination of vast clerical staffs and the accompanying middle management, making the corporate apparatus more responsive and personalized. This separation also heightens concern with profit in both policy and operating decision-making; objectives and reasons for decisions cannot remain fuzzy under modern procedures.

Exposure. Greater disclosure requirements by the S.E.C., the growth of security analysis as a profession, and broader public stock ownership have combined since World War II to create what many corporate managements regard as well-nigh indecent exposure. Also of importance have been continuous expansion of commonly accepted accounting principles, increasing detail of reports to regulatory authorities, and the stock exchange dictum: "If in doubt, announce it." Together these forces have released an unprecedented flow of business data, all making up the *public performance scoreboard.*

Security analysts of brokerage firms, institutions, and mutual funds hammer on the doors of management requesting interviews and pressing invitations to speak at their weekly meetings in forty-one cities. Since 1948, the number of security analysts has increased from 1,600 to 11,000, so that there are almost five full-time students for each of the 2,296 companies listed on all United States exchanges. Their findings appear in *The Wall Street Transcript,* a trade publication whose circulation has gone from 500 in 1963 to 7,500 in 1967, and their judgments are summarized in the *Wall Street Journal,* whose circulation has increased from 56,500 in 1945 to over 1 million today. The number of "owners" has also soared, which greatly increases the attention given to all these materials. No manager can publish a report bare of progress and can assume that he is sunning on an isolated beach where his nakedness will be unnoticed.

Motivation and measurement. As management feels ownership influence more and more and as its exposure increases, it will be even more concerned with the public scoreboard that records the market value of stock and the price-earnings ratio.

This will be reinforced by the trend to greater stock ownership among managers themselves. Managers have become owners in varying degrees—to some extent by ordinary purchases, but more often through stock options granted as a performance incentive. At present, 860 companies listed on the New York Stock Exchange (two thirds of the total) have stock option plans. A recent study indicates that within this group the median number of shares authorized under the plans equals nearly 3 per cent of the outstanding stock. Although this is a modest percentage of the total market equity of a company, it usually represents a substantial percentage of the total net worth of management.

For the new manager, the lure of personal financial gain is thus linked to that of publicized good performance; he seeks good results for reasons both of personal gain and of team pride. He realizes a significant part of his compensation through market appreciation and therefore tends to appraise his own performance, even if his functions are non-financial, by the stock exchange scoreboard that operates from 10:00 A.M. to 3:30 P.M. each market day and displays the market opinion of the management team to which he belongs. One should think of big business in the United States as something like a highly competitive professional sport in which the players have intertwined desires for greater personal wealth and for team victory. The teams are organized and guided by coaches who, like athletic coaches, must be smart enough to understand the management of people and the changing rules of a complex game, but also simple-minded enough to regard winning as being terribly important. Government planners might usefully study American professional baseball players.

Character of the decision-makers.   Today's typical top-management decision-maker has had advanced professional business education after an A.B. in economics, engineering, or accounting. He is pragmatic and goal-oriented to earnings per share, but he also shares the middle-class American notions of team competition, fair play, observance of the rules of the game, rewards calibrated to results (with some modest recognition of length of service), and the ability of the individual to make himself into pretty much what he wishes. He has a stern regard for honesty and for the importance of paying one's own way. He looks on taxes as an expense and would no sooner think of cheating on them than of cheating a supplier or customer. But he considers taxes an important and controllable expense and is interested in *exploiting all proper allowances, deductions, and exemptions.* This well-trained, law-abiding, profit-motivated entrepreneurial administrator, fully in command of his own operations, can easily be guided by a government that understands him and the game he is playing.

The memory of the electric equipment price fixing case and of General Motors' clash with Ralph Nader is too recent for me to suggest that all professional managers fit this description. But such incidents, which put the machinery of business decision into an opaque box for idealistic bright college graduates, are less likely to happen when some of these young men, with a fresh concept of the role of business in society, mature into top business leadership. I am not suggesting that violations of law or morality will cease or that private enterprise can be moved by social concern to do the uneconomic. Nor will business decisions be based upon uncertain and unquantifiable concerns about the impact of a general urban crisis on a particular firm. But an atmosphere of understanding and commitment can be developed so that reasonable incentives will work.

Summary

With the clear focus of business on a public scoreboard where growth in earnings per share is the major criterion, it is easy to understand that earnings growth has become the consuming objective of American business.

Reading 17

Capitalist Ethics—Tough or Soft?

Jack Hirshleifer

> I have never known much good done by those who affected to trade for the public good. It is an affectation, indeed, not very common among merchants, and very few words need be employed in dissuading them from it.
>
> Sometimes it is said that man cannot be trusted with the government of himself. Can he, then, be trusted with the government of others?

Few world outlooks have been responsible for greater social mischief than the ideology or social philosophy which might be called "sentimental socialism"—the cluster of ideas centering upon a contrast between the evil capitalist ethic and its supposedly superior socialist counterpart. Sentimental socialists maintain, for one thing, that, since the system of private enterprise for profit rewards pursuit of self-interest, it cannot serve the general interest. Consequently, a system banning selfish private enterprise for profit is bound to encourage economic activity in the public interest in the place of the proscribed private interest.

What is sentimental here is the belief that a change in social organization is all that is required to abolish human selfishness. As Mr. Dooley said, "A man that'd expect to train lobsters to fly in a year is called a lunatic; but a man that thinks men can be turned into angels by an election is called a reformer and remains at large." Among sentimental socialists are such disparate modern thinkers as Albert Einstein, Jawaharlal Nehru, and R. H. Tawney. Sentimental or "soft" socialism has an extraordinary appeal to gentle physicists, nonmaterialistic statesmen, Unitarian ministers, and social workers—to mention just a few vulnerable categories. By way of contrast, it is worth mentioning that Karl Marx was primarily a realistic or "tough" socialist. He despised the Utopians with their proposed ethical reconstitutions of society. Basically, Marx understood both capitalism and socialism as systems of power relations developing out of an ineluctable historical process.

Proponents of capitalism have often, on varying grounds, attacked the beautiful image of beneficent socialism as a false picture. Alternatively, there have been attempts to construct an ideology of capitalism which will be less vulnerable to socialist criticism.

When business preaches

Such an attempt appears in a recent article by James C. Worthy, a vice-president of a leading American corporation, entitled "Religion and Its Role in the World of Business."[1] "Soft socialism" regards the business system as convicted of encouraging selfishness and, consequently, of failing to serve humanity. Speaking before a religious conference, an audience which he may (perhaps wrongly) have suspected of being especially likely to hold a soft view of human nature, Worthy propounded an ideology which might be called "sentimental capitalism" as the answer to sentimental socialism. Admitting that selfishness is socially harmful, Worthy declares that businessmen, despite appearances, are really unselfish. In Worthy's view, the reason for the businessman's odd behavior is the outmoded theory of laissez faire economics, which justifies and condones "rational" conduct based exclusively on self-interest. Businessmen, influenced by this ideology, feel constrained to explain their behavior in these terms.

There are several interesting things about this defense of capitalism—that capitalists are really not selfish after all. The first is that, as a defense, it

[1] 31 J. Business 293 (1958).

From Jack Hirshleifer, "Capitalist Ethics—Tough or Soft?," *The Journal of Law and Economics,* October, 1959, The University of Chicago Law School. Reprinted with kind permission of the author and publisher.

is a hopeless failure. There are many reasons why this argument must fail, but perhaps the most conspicuous reason is that it is untrue. Instances of "generous" practice whether or not masked by "selfish" talk may exist, but they are not the characteristic examples that come immediately to mind as representative of business behavior. One doubts, for example, that the cigarette companies are giving serious consideration these days to stopping sales of their product merely because there is a strong suspicion that cigarette smoking causes lung cancer. Industries often ask to be relieved of tax burdens and only rarely that their taxes be increased.

Of course, selfishness is not limited to capitalists, in our society, or in any other. A gentle physicist may rise to wrath when someone steals his ideas or perhaps only disagrees with them; a nonmaterialistic statesman may call on the troops when the populace of a province prefers another government. Even socialist writers are rarely unconcerned with their royalties—unless, indeed, as is likely in a socialist society, this concern becomes trivial because of the more pressing need to keep head and neck firmly attached.

What does all this prove? Simply that all the world is largely governed by self-interest, and all the world knows it. Consequently, the assertion that capitalists are exempt from this failing is unlikely to win many converts to capitalism.

No need for shame

The second interesting—even amazing—thing about Mr. Worthy's argument is that he, as defender of the capitalist system, completely misunderstands the fundamental nature of that system as viewed by the laissez faire ideology he attacks. Worthy's basic ideas are expressed in the following sentences:

The ideas of fair play and self-restraint are essentially religious. They help keep dog-eat-dog practices in check and enable the economy to operate without strict governmental supervision and control: self-restraint rather than legal restraint is the rule. . . .

The great weakness of laissez faire economics (both the earlier and the later variety) is not so much the reliance on individual freedom and the distrust of government controls but rather the absence—indeed, the explicit denial in official business theory—of any

responsibility of the businessman to anyone but himself. . . .

The principle that self-interest is a sufficient guide for personal and public policy (that private vices make for public good) makes the demand for greater public control inevitable. . . .

In other words, the alternatives Worthy recognizes are self-restraint or legal restraint. But the essence of the laissez faire idea is that there is a third form of "restraint" against antisocial practices—not so frail a reed as the hope of self-restraint, nor such a threat to individual freedom as legal restraint. I refer, of course, to the *market* restraint of competition. Under laissez faire, if a business charges high prices, either because of inefficiency or because it is attempting to exploit its position, competitors rush in to serve the public in the place of the firm which is failing to do so. It is competition, not self-interest or the lack of it, which forces businessmen (if they wish to succeed) to give the public what it wants at the lowest attainable price.

The third interesting point in Mr. Worthy's presentation is his implicit acceptance of the ideas of the "new managerialism"—that the corporate manager (the typical "capitalist" of today) should serve the interest of all affected groups (owners, employees, customers, suppliers, and the community) rather than seek profits (i.e., serve stockholders) alone. No one can represent conflicting interests; he can at best mediate among them. Where there are conflicting masters, the servant is responsible to none. In this interpretation "unselfishness" of managers who deal with corporate funds (other people's money) may not be much of a virtue.

Selfishness better than sentiment

On all these grounds, a sentimental defense of capitalism cannot be accepted. Is it possible to give a tough-minded defense of capitalism—that is, to show that, taking people as they really are, capitalism can convert their energies to useful social results more effectively than other systems? The answer to this question, I believe, is "Yes."

Under the system of private enterprise for profit, men enjoy the opportunity to receive high returns if they provide people with goods and services that people are willing to pay for. The disciplining rod is competition; if some producers do not fill an existing public need or do not fill it well, others can begin to do so. In this system everyone can be selfish—consumers buy what they like, businessmen produce what they can sell, laborers work for whoever pays most—but the market forces them to serve one another's interests, the laborer by working, the employer by paying labor and organizing production, and the consumer by paying for the final product. (Of course, it is not true that everyone *must* be selfish under this system—all who choose to serve others without reward may do so, but the choice is their own.) To be sure, the system has more or less serious failings: among those usually cited are the arbitrariness of the distribution of inherited wealth, and possible divergences between what the public wants and what it ought to have. These and other real objections to the capitalist system can be raised, but it remains to be shown how alternative systems will perform better. Capitalism has the decisive merit, at least, of being based on human motives as they actually are.

If we ask how an actual socialist system would have to cope with the same motives, we see that the consumers, managers, workers, and government officials of a socialist system can on no reasonable ground be assumed to be less selfish than their equivalents in a capitalist society. The distinctive characteristic of the socialist system is that it encourages and gratifies a rather different aspect of human self-interest. The main rewards in capitalism go to those who serve others through providing services and products for which others are willing to pay. In a socialist system, the monopolization of the economic (together with the political) sphere by government eliminates the check of competition. The great rewards will then go not to those who serve the public but to those who control government and thereby *rule* the public.

Checks and balances

Corresponding to the alternative "soft" and "tough" defenses which have been given for the private enterprise system in the economic sphere, it is of interest to note that there are both sentimental and realistic defenses for democracy in the political realm. The sentimental argument runs that the people are "good" (unselfish) and so deserve to rule. The unsentimental argument, in contrast, says that all are humanly selfish—rulers and ruled alike. Democracy is a good system because it sets up a regularized procedure whereby those in the seats of power are held in check by the necessity for election by the people they govern. As in the economic sphere, the test of a desirable social system is not whether the group to whom it grants power constitutes an unselfish class but whether the holders of power are effectively checked in their exercise of it.

Reading 18

Ralph Nader has been called the *fifth estate.* He has spearheaded the consumerism movement. He is a grimly dedicated man who cannot be bought off or discouraged. Nader's Raiders strike terror in the heart of the Galbraithian giant corporations.

The quintessence of Naderism is contained in the present selection, which goes far beyond the narrow question of whether autos are safe and legislators corrupt.

Questions to guide the reading

If it's a free country, why is it involuntary for me to buy patent medicines or cosmetics that experts find lacking in quality? Why doesn't competition persuade sellers not to give short weight or adulterated quality? Are Nader's names for his "sub-economies" very well chosen: involuntary, transfer, controlled market, corporate socialism, compulsory consumption, expendable? What might be better names? Give examples of big business exercising big influence on government.

A Citizen's Guide to the American Economy

Ralph Nader

This year the gross national product of the United States will exceed one trillion dollars, while the economy will fail to meet a great many urgent human needs. This contrast between the statistics of growth and the fact of economic deprivation in America has become more and more evident to the public during the past decade—especially in such dramatic cases as that of the medical care industry, which has received vastly higher payments from both the government and patients, while the quality of medical care itself remains unchanged or has become worse.

Indeed, the quality of life is deteriorating in so many ways that the traditional statistical measurements of the "standard of living" according to personal income, housing, ownership of cars and appliances, etc., have come to sound increasingly phony.

Nevertheless the methods used to understand the economic system have remained rigid ones. The current analyses of and arguments about "national income levels," "inflation," and "government spending" do little to trace the precise ways in which the operations of the economy affect the life of the consumer. Nor do such analyses make political judgments or assign responsibilities so as to effectively change the consumer's situation. We have all heard arguments about the need to change national priorities in allocating public funds for defense, health, education, welfare, pollution control, etc. But such proposals have so far failed to take account of the ways in which portions of reallocated public funds may be siphoned off or misused before any are used for the purposes originally intended.

Wastes of the corporate economy

Meanwhile, the impact on our lives of the largest economic force of all, the corporate economy, has been badly neglected. Most formal inquiries into a more just and efficient use of national wealth have failed to measure how the citizen's dollars are being wasted and depreciated in the market place and his taxes converted into corporate property and income. Instead these studies focus mainly on "aggregate consumer spending" without asking specifically what consumers receive in return.

What are needed now are analyses of the corporate economy that will do what economists for the most part have failed to do: show how corporations, by their control of both the market and government, have been able to divert scarce resources to uses that have little human benefit or are positively harmful. Such studies will have to take account of facts that economists now tend to ignore because they find them untidy or because they cannot fit them into prevailing economic theory. But as they are carried out, they will show the folly of pouring more dollars into the sieve of an irresponsible corporate system.

The sub-economies.   To encourage more inquiry into the institutionalized abuses of unchecked corporate power, I would like to outline some of the major categories in which the abuses fall and to give a few of the many possible examples of how they work. I call these categories "sub-economies."

In each case, the consumer's dollars are inexcusably wasted or his taxes misused.

1. The involuntary sub-economy

By this I mean the billions that consumers would not have paid if they knew or could control what they were getting, or if corporations observed elementary standards of honesty, safety, and utility in producing and selling the things that are bought.

Consumers are now spending billions of dollars for products sold under false pretenses: meat and poultry that are adulterated with fat and water; patent medicines, mouthwashes, and "aids" to beauty and diet that do far less than they are said to do or nothing at all. Both the Food and Drug Administration and the National Academy of Sciences have compiled lists of drugs, patent medicines, and mouthwashes that are valueless for the purposes they advertise and often harmful as well, as in the case of certain antibiotics.

Worthless drugs alone cost consumers one billion dollars a year. The Federal Trade Commission estimates that another billion is wasted on fraudulently sold home improvements or repairs. Equally flagrant is the short-weighting, short-counting, and short-measuring of consumer purchases. A report in the *Wall Street Journal* [August, 1971] "The pennies add up fast enough," the *Journal* said, "that estimates by state officials of the total US loss from short-weighting start at $1.5 billion a year and rise to as high as $10 billion a year."

All these expenses—and I could list many more—were clearly involuntary: the consumers did not get what they thought they were paying for.

Defective, costly goods.   Quite as serious are what might be called "secondary consumer expenditures": the consumer may get something he wants, such as a car, but its defects are such as to force him to incur more costs. The fragile recessed bumpers of most automobiles are a case in point. Collisions at under ten miles per hour have been costing $2 billion a year for damages that could easily have been avoided if these cars had had effective bumpers.

The "accident-injury industry," composed of companies and professionals providing insurance and medical, legal, and repair services, is now being paid about $12 billion a year. Many of them would not have to be paid for at all if cars were sensibly and safely designed, as could be done without increasing the over-all cost of making cars.

These involuntary expenditures imposed by the auto industry have become fairly familiar. Less well understood is the way in which many different products, including packaged food, soft drinks, and gasoline, are sold through incredibly expensive advertising of their brand names for which the consumer must bear the cost, but for which he receives nothing of additional value.

The staff of Senator Hart's anti-trust committee estimates, moreover, that deceptive packaging and promotion in the food industry alone are causing consumers to lose $14 billion a year, for example, by pushing the large "economy" sized boxes of food that in fact cost more per unit than medium sized boxes.

Next step for consumer movement.   The consumer movement has had some limited success in improving regulatory action against deceptive sales practices and the safety standards of some products, notably cars, and in encouraging private litigation. Its main achievement has been to create an awareness among consumers that they are being gypped and endangered.

But it has yet to devise the economic and political machinery that will counter-balance or deplete the power of corporations to impose involuntary expenditures.

2. The transfer sub-economy

It is in the *transfer sub-economy* that the prices for goods and services may rise unconscionably as they move from the supplier of raw materials to the manufacturer, and then to the wholesaler, the retailer, and the consumer. It is not simply that a rise in the price of steel will cause a rise in the price of steel products. The economists know that such increases will escalate sharply as they pass from one shared monopoly or oligopoly of steel buyers and sellers to another, until they reach the consumer.

To the extent that such price rises are unchecked by effective competition, consumer bargaining, public exposure, or government anti-trust standards at each stage of the economic process, it becomes easier to transfer costs all along the line.

The moral.   The lesson of this story is that we can no longer depend, as classical market theory held, on consumer response alone to encourage efficiency and competition that will result in higher quality. In a complex multi-layered economy it is necessary that countervailing economic power be brought to bear at each level of the buying and selling process, however remote from the consumer. This is the only way to prevent excessive transfers of costs and to encourage efficiency and innovation.

We are very far from such a situation now. When railroad and trucking groups obtain rate increases from the all too compliant ICC, the large supermarkets and other retail chains rarely say a word; they calmly transfer the new costs on to the consumer. Since most of the railroads and truckers raise their rates uniformly, the supermarkets have no choice among competing transport services; and so the consumer is forced to pay the bill.

3. The controlled market sub-economy

By this I mean the thousands of arrangements that make it possible for corporations to avoid competition over the price, quantity, and quality of things made and sold, so that the value of what buyers receive is often outrageously distorted, by comparison with what the value would be if the market was not controlled.

Many of the practices in this sub-economy are violations of the anti-trust laws that have become both familiar and tolerated: price fixing, product fixing—for example the auto industry's entrenchment of the internal combustion engine—shared monopolies, etc. They also include other barriers to entry into the market such as excessive restrictions on occupational licenses, oil import quotas, the tying up of patents, and other devices that blatantly serve special economic interests while causing consumers and workers to suffer losses.

How much do they lose? The Federal Trade Commission has estimated that if highly concentrated industries were broken up by the anti-trust laws into more competitive companies so that the four largest firms in any industry would not control more than 40 percent of that industry's sales, prices would fall *by 25 percent or more.* This estimate applies to such major industries as autos, steel, copper, aluminum, containers, chemicals, detergents, canned soups, cereals. Nevertheless the figure represents only a small proportion of the unjustifiable costs to the consumer that result from the controlled market.

Stodgy oligopolists. It is not just a question of price fixing. Concentrated industries can for years resist the innovations that would make them more efficient. The basic oxygen furnace was not used by the big steel firms until 1963, thirteen years after it was developed by a small Austrian steel company. The controlled market, moreover, blocks the individual or small business inventors who are still the source of so many of the really new techniques in our society.

Such inventors find that their chances of entering the market or selling their work to established companies are dim when their ideas would not only serve the consumer but also disturb existing capital commitments or ways of doing business.

The major corporations will go to fantastic lengths to avoid competition over value. The merchandising in the supermarkets attempts to substitute elaborate games of chance, trading stamps, coupons, and other gimmicks—for all of which the consumer finally pays—for decisions based on the price and quality of the goods themselves.

Mini-monopolies. The price and quality of goods and services are also distorted by what might be called "mini-monopolies." Millions of consumers throughout the country have little choice except to use the only bank or finance company or pharmacy in their town. In company towns they must use the company store. Many specialty markets, such as hospital equipment or drugs, are monopolized by one or a few firms, making competition all the more impossible. Even the legally sanctioned monopolies, such as public utilities, usually manage to regulate the public agencies that are supposed to regulate them. The effect on the consumer is the same as if these businesses were private monopolies illegally controlling the market.

4. The corporate socialism sub-economy

[This] brings us to the *corporate socialism sub-economy* which includes both a) corporate pressure on government to unjustifiably transfer public funds and privileges to corporate control and b) withholding of proper payments and other obligations from the government by the corporations that owe them.

Tax loopholes. The tax system has become, to a disgraceful degree, an indirect subsidy to corporations and other privileged groups. Many of the glaring tax loopholes that slip through Congress each year are in effect huge payments by the government of money it would otherwise have received: for example the depletion allowances for oil and minerals, the tax dodges allowed to the real estate, timber, and cattle industries, the uses of the capital gains tax that favor the very rich.

Thanks to the oil depletion allowance, among other loopholes, the Atlantic Richfield Oil Company, to take an extreme example, had a net income of $797 million, while paying no federal tax whatever, from 1962 until 1968, when it paid at the rate of 1.2 percent.

These "tax expenditures" by the federal government have their local counterparts in the gross underpayment of property taxes by mineral companies, real estate developers, and commercial and industrial property owners. A preliminary estimate shows that local taxpayers are paying a subsidy of at least $7 billion a year to such interests when they allow them to evade property taxes.

Before national priorities can even be determined, it is crucial that Congress and the public know how much money is being spent by the government through the tax system. Tax expenditures now amount to roughly $45 billion a year but there is no systematic way of knowing precisely how much is being spent for what purposes.

What is needed, first of all, is an annual federal tax expenditure budget which will show exactly how much money the government loses for each tax privilege that is granted and just where that money goes instead.

But a tax expenditure budget will be only a beginning of a reform of the tax system, for the pressures from private interests and from the executive itself to increase tax subsidies are bound to continue.

Recently, for example, the Treasury Department issued its new proposals—the "ADR system"—for allowing depreciations for tax purposes. This system would allow fast write-offs of business equipment without any relation to the useful life of such equipment—the traditionally accepted measure of depreciation for tax purposes.

ADR would mean a tax subsidy to business of over $3 billion a year—more than Nixon's welfare reform proposals (which would cost $2.1 billion). More than a dozen tax authorities, including the former Commissioner of Internal Revenue and experts from the Harvard, Yale, and Pennsylvania law schools, have stated that this multi-billion-dol-

lar tax break is an illegal use of Presidential power.

Government subsidies to industries. The direct subsidies paid for agriculture, shipping, business promotion, and "research" are quite as important—and as much neglected by Congress—as the indirect subsidies paid by the tax system. The Department of Agriculture, for example, is now spending over $4 billion each year for its subsidy programs.

Who evaluates these payments and the reasons for making them? As it happens, big corporate farms receive the lion's share and Congress does not question the inequities that result.

Agriculture is only one sector of this sub-economy where hard questions must be asked if the public usefulness of *existing* tax dollars is to be improved. The inflated contract and procurement practices of the government are another. Waste and mismanagement in defense contracting, and the consequent multi-billion-dollar "cost-over-runs" have become commonplace—e.g., the $2 billion overrun paid Lockheed for the C5A. But who is looking into the waste in other government contracting—from the leasing of buildings at inordinate cost to the billions of dollars paid for research in "think tanks" and advice from private consulting firms? Many of these studies are worthless, expensive, used mainly to delay policy decisions and to get the agencies who commission them off the hook. Others are wholly ignored.

If only the grossest forms of waste and corruption in federal, state, and local procurement practices were investigated and eliminated many billions of dollars would be saved and political life itself would get a badly needed shake-up.

Better government buying. The General Services Administration, the purchasing and housekeeping agency of the federal government, suggested that state and local governments cooperate in setting up systems of centralized purchasing direct from manufacturers, thus bypassing the 20 to 30 percent mark-up of the wholesalers. If they did this, they would save between $6 and $7 billion a year.

This recommendation was not followed, nor did the GSA pursue it. The wholesalers' trade association immediately launched a campaign against it in Congress. The wholesalers' association has plenty of political muscle and uses it on all levels of government.

The great illusion of the public is that it is protected by the conscience of public officials, when in fact aggressive monitoring of these officials and those they deal with is constantly needed.

5. The compulsory consumption sub-economy

Unlike the other aspects of the economy that have been discussed here, the *compulsory consumption sub-economy* is not part of any recognized system of economic exchange—but it has grave economic effects. I am referring to the compulsory consumption of environmental pollution and compulsory exposure to occupational health and safety hazards. These reduce the *quality* of the gross national product and thus diminish the value of the citizen's dollar, even when they do not directly compel people to pay for medical treatment, for example.

We are just beginning to calculate the billions of dollars that pollution costs in damages to health, in cleaning costs, and in damage to property, resources, and agricultural crops. Air and water pollution are each costing at least $14 billion a year. (The yearly damage to California crops alone from air pollution runs to $45 million a year.) The costs to the unborn, or to the environment in the future, have not even been estimated.

Safety and health hazards on jobs in factories, foundries, mines, and other work places are also a form of compulsory consumption. They now cause three times as many injuries as street crime: 15,000 sudden deaths last year, uncounted thousands of deaths resulting from occupational disease, 2.5 million disabling injuries, several million cases of less serious injuries and illness.

Clearly the forced consumption of pollution—gases, chemicals, coal and cotton dust—is a silent and sometimes invisible form of violence which compels people to pay insurance, medical, and other costs, including the loss of wages. The polluting corporations inflict these burdens on workers when, for only a fraction of the money they force others to pay, they could have prevented much of the pollution in the first place.

Enforcing corporate responsibility.   The power of corporations to pollute, in short, is far too great

for them to exercise responsibly. General Motors, by virtue of the engines it designs and the plants it operates, has been responsible for over 30 percent of the estimated tonnage of US air pollution. Is there any city street where the citizen can escape the pollution of GM engineering when he breathes?

Between 1967 and 1969 GM spent $250 million to change its slogan on billboards, dealers' signs, and other promotional material to read "GM Mark of Excellence." With the same funds it could have easily developed a workable non-polluting engine.

Restoring Schumpeterian dynamism.   We may expect two developments to occur if certain industries are successfully challenged in the market and by public protest.

First, many industries would be displaced or diminished as superior technologies are invented and sold on their merits. Cleaner and cheaper sources of energy for cars and power plants, for example, will increasingly pose the threat of displacement to large industries. So will safer and more effective non-chemical methods of pest control eventually diminish the chemical pesticides industry.

Second, new services are already emerging to show businesses how to reduce telephone, utility, and insurance bills, for example.

These, it should be said, are just the kinds of changes that are called for by the theory of capitalism; they are what Joseph Schumpeter, perhaps the leading theoretician of the capitalist economy, had in mind when he wrote of the "creative destruction" of inferior or obsolete industries under capitalism. But in fact, such developments are being discouraged and suppressed by politically entrenched corporate institutions.

6. The expendable sub-economy

[This] is composed mostly of poor people who are being excluded from the services of the economy at large. It is not simply that the poor pay more: they are not being allowed to buy.

In every large city, insurance and banking firms commonly "red line"—or refuse to do business with—people in the poor districts. What has happened is that *Fortune*'s Five Hundred largest corporations have decided that they have less and less need for the business of the poor.

Urban blight.   But by cutting off the funds needed for housing, for financing small business, and for municipal bonds in the low income areas of the cities, the banks and other lenders are causing the deterioration of the urban economy and injuring the well-being of millions of people.

The government, moreover, has become a willing partner in such discrimination. It provides fast tax write-offs for airplanes, computers, bulldozers, and trucks, causing loan money to flow in these directions and not toward loans to the poor and those who have more urgent needs. It provides tax inducements for slum landlords who are allowed to depreciate slum property at an accelerated rate and to pay capital gains taxes on profits from sales—a process which is quickly repeated by the next slum landlord.

Equalizing loan opportunity.   The federal government should ensure that all segments of the borrowing public be given equitable treatment so far as restrictions on borrowing are concerned. Several methods are available to accomplish this.

One is to provide for different Federal Reserve Board requirements for different kinds of loans. For example, the FRB could require a reserve requirement of 5 percent against residential loans and one of 20 percent against non-productive corporate loans, such as loans to conglomerates to acquire yet another company.

Another method would be to link certain kinds of deposits to certain kinds of loans. In return for the benefits they receive from the federal ceilings on interest rates, as well as from other government programs, the banks could be required to make time deposits available when there is a shortage of funds for home mortgages and home construction.

Like so many of the other economic forces I have dealt with here, the banking system needs systematic surveillance and is not getting it.

Specious apologetics for business as usual

Apologists for the present corporate system will argue that the sub-economies I have described so generally here are justified because they support industries, create jobs, generate income. But it should be clear that their operations and the kinds of needs they satisfy are, to a great extent, neither desirable nor socially responsible; in many cases they are not legal.

Restoring effective competition.   For most of this century there has been declared a national consensus in favor of competition, as well as numerous laws designed to encourage it, but both have been for the most part betrayed. When they have not, the benefits for the citizen have been dramatic [e.g., $40 million saving in one year to D.C. consumers, when a new supermarket chain competed down prices of the three dominant chains]. Indeed each of the sub-economies I have described subverts values that are deeply rooted in American life.

On from GNP to Net Economic Welfare.   What has been tragic is the general failure to understand how this has occurred. Fundamentally new ways must be found to make both government and corporations accountable. We should pursue the suggestion already made by some social critics for a "social accounts system" which would enable government and citizens to evaluate whether programs of education, medicine, and transportation, for example, were improving or deteriorating in quality. (The current inclusion of such activities in the gross national product has nothing whatever to say about their quality.)

We are wasting 25 per cent!   Senator Philip Hart has estimated that of the $780 billion spent by consumers in 1969, about $200 billion purchased *nothing* of value. By nothing of value he meant just that: over $45 billion was drained away by monopolistic pricing, for example, and over $6 billion by oil import quotas which drive up the prices of fuel oil and gasoline. His estimate, and it is only a preliminary one, shows how crucial is the need to evaluate how corporate and government wealth is being used—or misused—for individual and social purposes.

Program for action

Such evaluations simply have not been made in our corporate political economy—not by our blinkered economists, certainly, and not by the government or the corporations themselves. Indeed the corporations have effectively blocked both the government and independent researchers from collecting and analyzing such information. Even the data on pollution must be fought for if it is to be extracted from corporations by government agencies and individuals bringing law suits. The task of the consumer movement now is to gather and analyze and disseminate this type of information by demanding it from the three branches of government and by mounting private actions by consumer groups to publicize it. Such information is the currency of economic democracy, the first tool for changing the perception of citizens and society itself.

Organized Labor

Reading 19

Human labor is perhaps the most important factor of production. In the modern mixed economy a large fraction of the labor force belongs to the trade union movement which, in contrast to the union movements of the totalitarian countries, really is free to engage in independent collective bargaining. The public at large both approves of, and is uneasy about, organized labor. Here a leading expert on the economics of labor describes the dynamics of the American labor movement.

George W. Taylor, professor of economics at the University of Pennsylvania, was long a leading labor arbitrator, member of the War Labor Board, and adviser on labor matters to presidents of both political parties.

Questions to guide the reading

When workers band together to improve their working conditions and wages, why are they any different from collusive monopolists out to improve their own well-being at the expense of the rest of the community? Is labor merely a commodity like anything else? Is bargaining power "equal" in the absence of unions? Why is the right to strike a crucial issue in the realm of collective bargaining?

The Role of Labor Unions

George W. Taylor

It has been said: "Man stands always at the beginning and at the end of an era." The one we presently survey looms as the most heroic of all the epics. In the newest era, the impact of science and technology upon traditional social and economic theory has consequences in many ways as revolutionary as the more widely-recognized effect upon older theories of war and international cooperation. In perspective, however, one sees essentially an intensification of the "normal" propensity of social systems to dissolve and to reform in response to changed environments.

From George W. Taylor, "The Role of Labor Unions," The Benjamin Franklin Lecture Series, 1961–1962, Mar. 29, 1962, University of Pennsylvania Wharton School of Finance and Commerce. Reprinted with kind permission of the author.

In the Eighteenth Century, Adam Smith created little controversy when he first expounded economic individualism as the key to promotion of national welfare.

Perhaps it was fortunate that even while the "Wealth of Nations" was still a best-seller, economic individualism was giving way to the organization as the dominant institution. A synthetic but powerful "person"—the corporation—was created without benefit of Adam's rib. More and more, the individual had to adjust to the status of a worker for the corporation and, later on, as a member of the union organization. The government might still leave the individual alone, but the organization did not and doubtless could not if its economic function was to be performed. Where was it said: "One trouble about laissez-faire was that nobody ever made clear who was to leave what alone"? At any event, the organizational revolution produced the business corporation and, later as a countervailing power, the labor union.

The notable extent to which the organizational laissez-faire doctrine has become a part of "traditional wisdom" was recently revealed when certain management representatives, who have long opposed the labor union idea, rushed to the ramparts in staunch defense of free collective bargaining. The government had suggested, in a tentative feeling-out move, that under present emergency conditions the public interest would have to be specifically taken into account in private wage and price determinations. Of course, organized labor was also there telling the government to keep its grasping hands off. Here was a stark expression of the creed: "Whatever is good for the corporation and the unions automatically and adequately conserves the national interest."

As the response of a democratic country to the challenges to ideals and safety, leaders in both the public and private sectors have a responsibility to work at inventing new ways and means to create new institutions, or adjust the old ones, in order to assure the mutual compatibility of governmental and private decisions. The definition of the private system which will best enhance the odds for national safety and survival in the current world environment is being formulated. As Barbara Ward put it: "The fundamental question is whether we in the West are able to confront the challenge of our times. And here we face the agonizing diffi-culty that some of the creative responses we need to make run deeply against the grain of our traditional thinking."

Unions and collective bargaining

This paper will be focused mainly upon the kind of creative responses necessary to make union functions and the process of collective bargaining workable in the new environment. May I propose that in industrial relations, more than in any area, federal policy and private decision-making "come uneasily face to face." These subjects, moreover, are deeply involved in the value determinations that will shape Western civilization.

There is so much prating about the "dignity of man" in the more flashy oratory of the day that the good term unfortunately has become quite shop-worn. One hesitates considerably in even using the phrase. There is still a considerable "bite," however, to the concomitant notion that, in a democracy such as ours, the conditions under which one man becomes subject to the direction of his fellow, for the latter's profit, is an important determinant of the emphasis that is placed upon the conservation of human values.

As a nation we have become increasingly concerned, especially since 1929, about effecting a fair and equitable balance between the conflicting goals of efficiency in production and the preservation of human values. The invisible hand of the market place did not provide compensation for men injured on the job, wages as a matter of right for men out of work, pensions for retired workers, or freedom from unjustified discharges. Much of the strength of this country, I believe, has derived from a strong drive for efficiency in competition moderated, however, by an inherent compassion in the utilization of one factor of production—labor. Here is the really revolutionary idea of the past century.

In the United States, employees in the key sectors of the economy seek to attain their personal objectives through union organization. The institution is designed primarily to exert a strong bargaining position in the making of labor contracts with the employers. This unique orientation of the labor movement in the United States has elements of the mysterious to labor leaders in other democracies where a far greater reliance is placed upon political action. The importance of the decisions made in the private sector of our economy is matched in no other country in the world. This is in large part the case because of the so-called job-consciousness of the American worker. We are indebted to the late Selig Perlman for observing that in our so-called job-conscious unionism: ". . . the Hegelian dialectic nowhere occurs, nor is cognizance taken of 'labor's historical mission.' What monopolizes attention is labor combating competitive menaces . . . labor bargaining for the control of the job."

It is significant that labor unions did not initiate the current movement in the United States for governmental guides to be used in wage and price determination. And, no more than employers, do unions see any merit in the kind of national bargaining for a general wage policy that is practiced in some other democratic countries. Decentralized private decision-making in the wage and price areas has been our way of life. It is the economists and those in the governmental agencies who are in the van of the national planning movement. In their own ways, they seek to express the national interests vis-a-vis those who make private decisions and to reflect an insistent public demand for protection against inflation. How can national planning needs be provided for under a decentralized decision-making system in which great power resides in the private institutions?

It seems to me that, in their model building, most economists underrate not only the private power centers but the importance of the functions assigned to a labor union in the United States. Its primary responsibility is to the employees directly represented and not to the model builders. The terms of a labor contract with an employer must meet the fundamental expectations of employees—at least the terms must be appraised by them as preferable to a strike. Most labor agreements must be validated by a majority vote of a union meeting.

The script is generally adhered to by most unions. There have been notable deviations, however, such as those recently revealed in the investigations of the Senate Committee headed by Mr. McClellan. The evidence showed how easy it is for the dialogue of collective bargaining to be short-circuited by a dictatorial union leader who, glorifying either "effectiveness" or personal power,

views the accommodation process as an unnecessary nuisance. But, the public demands that the script be followed. Accordingly, legislators pass laws to limit the power of all union leaders and to make them more responsive to the demands of the employees they represent. There is some incongruity between that thrust of legislation and the now insistent call upon the unions to exercise retraint in establishing employment terms.

Most unions do seek to carry out the functions so crucial in a democracy of channeling employee dissent to the bargaining table and of dissipating it through negotiated terms accepted by the employees as well as by the employer. Outstanding union leaders are well aware of the mediation element in their jobs. To begin with, they have to moderate the extreme demands of the membership which can't possibly be secured. The question of "democracy in unions," it has always seemed to me, concerns the procedures employed for this purpose and especially for mediating intra-union differences. For example, is priority to be given to the demands of older men for improved pensions rather than the claims of younger men for unemployment benefits? The assignment of priorities becomes more arduous as prospective wage increases are limited. Management also has a stake in "satisfying the men," and the public interest is involved. The efficiency of performance on the job, we believe, is related to the acceptability of employment terms. We differ from the totalitarians on this point but continue to be glad for the difference.

Thus, those calls upon the unions to exercise restraint in the national interest are, in essence, the assignment to union leaders of the responsibility for inducing the employees they represent to moderate their expectations. The reasons have to be clear, convincing and intelligible to "the man on the street," and they have yet to be formulated. In my opinion, the 25-hour week gained in New York by Local 3 of the International Brotherhood of Electrical Workers represents unwarranted, preferred treatment for a select group. It is reported, however, that the membership voted 5,000 to 3 to strike if necessary to gain this objective. Maybe they didn't read the national economic analyses. Even so, a national problem about gold balances is vital to the economists, understandable to most union leaders, but more remote than the moon to most employees. They have all they can do to hold a job, meet installment charges, and keep the crab grass out of the front lawn. They want those high-prized work rules which, so lightly dismissed by the rest of us as featherbedding, make their lives more secure and comfortable. Nor is there anything unusual about all this. People in every walk of life cherish the special vested interest they have staked out for themselves even if only through squatters rights. The state of mind that underlies featherbedding is neither an invention nor a monopoly of organized labor. Professor Aaron has cynically observed: "The popular feeling that there is something immoral about featherbedding may be appropriately described as a selective revulsion to unearned increment not elsewhere observable in the economy." The willingness of employees to give up their featherbedding in the national interest might conceivably be enhanced if the rest of us would lead the way.

The difficult mediation process which begins within the union continues in collective bargaining. Here the expectations of the employees have to be reconciled with the management need to minimize competitive costs and to maintain profits margins sufficient for capital expansion. Just as the employer has an interest in proper performance of the union function, the employees are dependent for their job security upon a proper performance of the management collective bargaining function.

In my opinion, the several steps designed to reconcile diverse objectives in collective bargaining have never been more difficult or exacting. This is because of the acceleration of technological change, the pressures of national and world competition, the claim upon resources for national programs, and the need to stabilize prices—all coming to a head at the same time. Employee demands are not limited to increased standards of living for those likely to keep their jobs, but include increasingly costly provisions for those who will be displaced. A double wage claim has to be dealt with. Competition, and national planning, introduces road blocks to price increases at a time when increased corporate earnings are sought to support the capital formation so vital to sound economic growth. There just isn't enough increased productivity in sight to meet all the demand upon it.

In addition, the strike as a traditional means of inducing agreement in collective bargaining has become less and less tolerable. Not only can strikes interfere with constructive economic growth but the answers fashioned out of trial by economic combat often do not, in this day and age, adequately resolve the issues that caused the work stoppage in the first place.

Clearly, the need is for an agreement based upon analytic processes rather than economic power arbitrament. A much higher standard of performance is thus required of collective bargaining between the labor and management institutions in the 1960's if the country is to survive with freedom and thus to advance the historic mission of Western civilization.

In the process, the standard objectives of collective bargaining have to be modified to the fact of national emergency as a way of life. For, as far ahead as one can project, vast resources will be diverted year after year to maintain a huge military establishment, to assist people in underdeveloped nations to raise their living standards, and to meet relentless Communist pressures throughout the world. A greater share of the Gross National Product doubtless will be absorbed in providing better education "at every level and in every discipline," and improved medical care for more people.

All this means that the overhead costs of keeping the country in business have grown to mammoth proportions. And, these overhead costs have to be met before increases in the production of goods and services can be allocated to the enhancement of our own personal standards of living. Little short of nonsensical is the current tendency to pin responsibility solely upon the hourly-rated workers, especially those in the mass production industries, for becoming more productive and for curbing their expectation. They are truly a part of the picture but no more than the rest of us.

Cooperation between the public and the private sectors

A number of stubborn propositions can be identified: (1) in terms of the virtually unlimited claims upon even mighty resources, ours is not an affluent society at all but one of limited means, (2) the resources we do possess should be fully utilized—

idle or ineffectively used plant and service facilities and high rates of employment are incompatible with the needs of the times, (3) accelerated economic growth and higher productivity in all endeavors are a must in order to meet as many pressing needs as is possible, (4) even if economic performance is vastly improved, priorities will still have to be specified, (5) changes are necessary in those existing institutions, including collective bargaining, which now serve essentially to balance conflicting private interests without particular regard for the general welfare.

Particularly in evolving priorities, of which voluntary restraints are a part, close cooperating between decision-makers in the private and public sectors is called for. In other words, the democratic principles of participation, accommodation and consent should be recognized as providing an element of strength not available to the totalitarian nations.

The evolving collective bargaining

The people of this country have had a genius for creating institutional forms to effectuate their value judgments. This has been evident, during the past generation, in the historic transformation of industrial relations in the United States. We have moved in important industries from unilateral decision-making by management toward co-determination by management and organized workers. Substitution of the two-party system for the one-party system for determining conditions of employment was one of the responses made to the devastating depression of the 1930's. Then came World War II and, as a result of agreement between labor and employer representatives, public members served with these parties on the War Labor Board to insure that the national interests were taken into account along with those of employees and management. A temporary three-party system was evolved. The principles of participation and consent were applied during World War II in an unprecedented manner to formulate and administer a national wage policy. When concern about inflation became the dominant national mood, changes in industrial relations were made by enactment of the Taft-Hartley Act in 1947. On the record, it can be concluded that collective bargaining is an institution adaptable to changing circumstances. The main adaptations now being urged arise from the growing intolerance of strikes and the public interest in the substantive terms of private wage agreements.

The right to the strike

Just why is it that we have adhered so staunchly, even ritualistically, to the notion that in a democratic society the right to strike must be preserved. Considerable costs to everyone can be entailed in the exercise of that right. How can it be argued that the fair and equitable solution to the problems at the workplace can best be found in trial by economic combat?

One can wonder about the efficacy of the strike as a means of bringing about agreement. Yet, even the late Senator Robert Taft, in devising a procedure in 1947 to protect the public interest in public emergency disputes, insisted that while a strike might be temporarily enjoined for 80 days, the employee right to engage in a concerted stoppage should thereafter be reinstated in the absence of a settlement agreement. He accepted the traditional principles that: (1) only by agreement between those directly affected can the terms of employment be established in a democracy and (2) the strike is the only available device for inducing the essential compromise and agreement and (3) it provides an assurance against the terms of employment being imposed by the government.

There is, however, no certainty that the economic and social costs will always be viewed as a fair price to pay in allowing adherence to these principles. During the protracted steel strike of 1959, for instance, the public demand for compulsory arbitration mounted insistently when it seemed as though the complete stoppage of this basic industry could bring the public to its knees before bringing the parties to terms. In the even more exacting recent world moreover, intolerance of the strike has become more general. The need is apparent for a better and less costly means for motivating agreement. A social invention is called for.

To be sure, the total number of strikes has been declining and the average length of a shut-down has been decreasing. Since 1947, strike losses have averaged less than one-third of one percent of total working time. This is probably less than the working hours lost because of layoffs. As is so often the case, the overall statistics don't tell the whole story. A series of short stoppages by a few men on the missile sites do not make big statistics but can impair critical defense programs. By withdrawing their services, a small group of tug-boat operators can bring New York City to its knees in a few days. Little strikes can make big trouble. And, there are the occasional big, industry-wide strikes that may be averaged out in the national statistics but nevertheless have some adverse effect on nearly everybody in the year of occurrence. Some day perhaps, the function now assigned to the strike because of lack of a better technique, will appear no more sensible than bloodletting as an earlier surgical practice.

Whether or not an acceptable substitute for the strike can be designed depends mainly upon those in the private sector although governmental assistance can be accorded to those who are receptive. A considerable recognition of public responsibility is a prerequisite for the formulation of a creative response in this area. A number of initial efforts are encouraging.

An illustration of purposeful experimentation is the procedure for dealing with labor disputes at the missile and space sites. At each location, a Missile Site Labor Relations Committee has been established. It consists of representatives from manufacturing and construction concerns, various labor organizations, contracting agencies along with mediators assigned by the Federal Mediation and Conciliation Service. These committees are to "forecast impending problems, arrange for their settlement before they become acute, using fully all existing voluntary procedures and devising new adequate procedures where none exist." The unions have agreed not to call any strikes. Unauthorized or so-called wild-cat strikes still occur and this has led impatient men to call for compulsory arbitration to fix employment terms. Even the neophytes in industrial relations know, however, that a legislative ban on strikes doesn't eliminate work stoppages. It only makes them illegal. Procedures worked out by the affected parties which are relied upon to resolve disputes ordinarily settled by strikes is the indicated course of action in a democracy.

Significant experimentation is also under way in having informed outsiders participate in collective bargaining at the invitation of the union and management. The third parties have sometimes been authorized to recommend settlement terms before resort is made to a work stoppage. In its present form, this is a new development. Through private mediation by third-party participants who have the authority to recommend terms, I have no doubt that work stoppages can be minimized. Nor will the substantive terms be any less attentive to the public interest than is presently the case. Indeed, to a limited degree, the public interest will be given a more emphatic expression. Perhaps, it is this very possibility which accounts, in some measure, for the opposition of many companies and unions to third-party participation. Yet, the third-party participants do operate within the limits of the private institution. Any recommendations, if they are to be effective, must be geared to terms which can form the basis for agreement between the union and the management.

In my opinion, there is a strong likelihood that the public interest in avoiding strikes, in an increasingly interdependent society and at a time when the effective utilization of resources is a national necessity, will result increasingly in the designation of third parties to participate in collective bargaining and in their authorization to make recommendations for settlement terms if that becomes necessary. This would be an institutional change short of arbitration and the specification of employment terms by the outsiders. The indicated "voluntary" response of unions and management would be a natural result of an increasing public intolerance of work stoppages with its "or else" implications.

Public interest in the terms of settlement

Collective bargaining conducted without any work stoppages at all might still be inadequate. Negotiated terms fully acceptable to the private parties of direct interest could, nevertheless, be obstructive to the attainment of major national goals. Under present circumstances, it is not safe to look upon all wage and price determinations as exclusively involving private interests. But, in a democracy, neither can they be construed as strictly a governmental affair.

Existing institutional arrangements are not adequate to fix conditions of employment in this context. Over the past 20 years, one President after another has called upon unions and management in general terms to exercise voluntary restraint. One trouble with this approach is in the generality. How much restraint is necessary under varying circumstances? What relative degrees of restraint are to be exercised in wage determination as compared to price determination? Would a likely result be the inclusion of prices and profit margins among the subjects dealt with by collective bargaining in order to determine whether or not a certain wage would require a price increase? And, how can a responsibility for national planning be undertaken by private decision-makers whose job it is to serve the particular interests of constituencies which can dis-elect them? More questions are raised than are answered by the call for restraint in general.

If the public involvement in these private decisions is real, and I believe this is the case, an effective enunciation of the required restraint has to be expressed in micro-economic terms, i.e., for ready insertion into the equation which has to be resolved in the private sector. In World War II, for example, the guide lines were in terms of the relation between wage-rates and the Consumer Price Index, comparative wage-rates and the like. Experience shows, moreover, that to be effective a public wage policy should be created through the cooperative endeavors of public, union and management representatives. It cannot be created by public representatives alone.

Among the obstacles to tackling the problem is the fact that the dimensions of today's challenge are not fully perceived or certainly not publicly admitted, by many important leaders in the private sector. How else can one interpret these recently reported remarks of a steel executive: "From a broad philosophical standpoint, most businessmen feel that in a competitive system, you serve the national interest in pursuing your private interest." Or, the outright rejection by Mr. George Meany, President of the A.F.L.-C.I.O., of Secretary Goldberg's suggestion that "the role of government is to assert the national interest." To Mr. Meany, that is an infringement upon "the rights of free people and free society." The institutional laissez-faire policy has become rather thoroughly embedded.

The democratic approach

A recognition of the urgency of today's problems is a prerequisite for purposeful cooperation between governmental and private decision-makers to devise institutional forms for meeting the question: how are the vital goals of national planning to be achieved while the strengths of the private enterprise system are maintained? Devising an adequate answer to the question is a big part of the task of making democracy work in the new world environment.

The old faith in democracy was "simple and confident." It has been described as a belief in "the civilization of the dialogue, where everybody talked with everybody else above everything, where nobody tried to get his way by force or fraud, where everybody was content to abide by the decision of the majority as long as the dialogue could continue." This might have constituted, once upon a time, a fairly reasonable facsimile of the accommodation process. But, that was certainly before the emergence of that complex web of interdependence in which we are enmeshed. Yet, the democratic concept of self-government based upon an accommodation of conflicting interests through reason and persuasion remain "perhaps the most potent idea of modern history." Improved institutional forms provide the best hope for maintaining and furthering the democratic idea in a world in which people are developing a willingness to be told what to do. In the words of Robert M. Hutchins: ". . . if our hopes of democracy are to be realized, the next generation is in for a job of institutional remodeling the like of which has not been seen since the Founding Fathers." One need not go that far while still visualizing institutional adjustments as the most promising way of adapting our negotiating processes, including collective bargaining, to the demands of life in the second half of the Twentieth Century.

Government and Taxation

Readings 20 and 21   A Dialogue on the Proper Economic Role of the State

No question was more hotly debated in the 1960s than the proper economic role of government. Here is a debate on the subject before a Swarthmore College audience between a conservative and a liberal.

George J. Stigler is Walgreen Professor at the Graduate School of Business of the University of Chicago and a world authority on microeconomics. Though a trifle shorter than J. K. Galbraith, Stigler is considered by some connoisseurs to be even wittier. At times each of the debaters has served as adviser to Republican and Democratic administrations, respectively.

Paul A. Samuelson is Institute Professor at M.I.T. He served as economic adviser to senator, candidate, and president-elect John F. Kennedy.

Questions to guide the reading

Since we cannot expect perfection in this world, do you think that Dr. Stigler is being overly critical in pointing out governmental errors? Was the wartime development of the atomic bomb an exception to Stigler's first rule? How does its success affect your judgment on rule 2? Is uniform mistreatment always worse than discrimination? Is it contemptuous of the poor to insist that money which they are given not be badly spent?

From Abraham Lincoln's statement, can you judge what he would think about today's SEC, control of thalidomide, of marijuana, of heroin? Can such problems be settled by aphorisms? How can you measure "freedom" when in the absence of coercive rules you may even have less of it? When one man's freedom is another man's coercion in a tight, little world? Is impersonality always a bad thing? Under centralism there would be one big employer: Is that a good thing? In what ways is a market system coercive?

Reading 20

The Government of the Economy

George J. Stigler

No doubt this is the best of all possible worlds, for the time being. But even in the best of possible worlds, a good many things happen that displease us. Without exception we are shocked when a tranquilizer is sold, and its use by pregnant women leads to tragic deformities in babies. We are all distressed when there is extensive unemployment and personal suffering. Most of us are displeased when a strike closes down a railroad or a port or the airlines. Some of us are deeply annoyed when the price of soybeans falls. A few of us are outraged when an increase is announced in the price of steel, but this particular few is not unimportant.

There was an age when social dissatisfaction

From George J. Stigler, "The Government of the Economy," *A Dialogue on the Proper Economic Role of the State,* Selected Paper No. 7, Graduate School of Business, University of Chicago. Reprinted by permission of George J. Stigler.

was kept in the house. All evils were ancient evils, and therefore necessary evils which served at least to keep men humble and patient. This resignation to imperfection has almost vanished in modern times—the hereafter in which all problems are solved has been moved up to two months after the next election. And government has become the leading figure in almost every economic reform. I propose to discuss what governments can do in economic life, and what they should do.

The question of what governments can do, what they are capable of doing, will strike many Americans, and for that matter most non-Americans, as an easy one. For it is a belief, now widely held and strongly held, that the government can, if it really puts its mind and heart to a task, do anything that is not palpably impossible. The government, we shall all admit, cannot really turn the number π into a simple fraction by legislative mandate, nor can a joint resolution of the houses of Congress confer immortality. But with a will, the government can see to it that fully 85 per cent of the male population, and a few women, are taught several infinite series for calculating π, and with a will, the government can prolong human life appreciably by suitable medical and social insurance programs.

An article of faith

This acceptance of the omnipotence of the state does not represent a generalization of experience; it is not a product of demonstrated effectiveness in bending events to the wise or foolish designs of policy. *On the contrary, the belief is an article of faith, indeed an article of almost desperate faith.* It is not an intrinsically absurd belief; there is no rigorous logical demonstration that the state cannot turn sows' ears into silken purses. There is also no logical demonstration that all men cannot become saints, but the number of saintly men has not yet risen to the level where the census makes it a separate statistical category.

Our faith in the power of the state is a matter of desire rather than demonstration. When the state undertakes to achieve a goal, and fails, we cannot bring ourselves to abandon the goal, nor do we seek alternative means of achieving it, for who is more powerful than a sovereign state? We demand, then, increased efforts of the state, tacitly

assuming that where there is a will, there is a governmental way.

Yet we know very well that the sovereign state is not omnipotent. The inability of the state to perform certain economic tasks could be documented from some notorious failures. Our cotton program, for example, was intended to enrich poor cotton farmers, increase the efficiency of production, foster foreign markets, and stabilize domestic consumption. It is an open question whether 28 years of our farm program have done as much for poor cotton farmers as the trucking industry. Again, the Federal Trade Commission is the official guardian of business morals, including advertising morals. I am reasonably confident that more would have been achieved if one of the F.T.C.'s 48 years of appropriations had been devoted to a prize for the best exposé of sharp practices.

That there should be failures of governmental policy is not surprising, nor will the failures lead us to a blanket condemnation of governmental activity in economic life. Invariable success, after all, is found in only a few places. What is surprising is *how little we know about the degree of success or failure of almost all governmental intervention in economic life.* And when I say how little we know, I expressly include the people whose business it should be to measure the achievements, the professional economists.

When we have made studies of governmental controls that are sufficiently varied in scope and penetrating in detail, we may be able to construct a set of fairly useful generalizations about what the state can do. But society will not wait upon negligent scholars before meeting what seem to be pressing issues. The remainder of my talk cannot wait either, so I am driven to present what I consider plausible rules concerning feasible economic controls.

Stigler's laws

What economic tasks can a state perform? I propose a set of rules which bear on the answer to the question, but I shall not attempt a full argument in support of them—it must suffice to give an illustrative case, a plausible argument. It must suffice partly because full proofs have not been accumulated, but partly also because I wish to have time to discuss what the state should do, which is considerably less than what it can do.

RULE 1: The state cannot do anything quickly.

It would be unseemly to document at length the glacial pace of a bureaucracy in double step. A decent respect for due process lies behind some of the procedural delays, and poses a basic issue of the conflicting demands of justice and efficiency in economic regulation. But deliberation is intrinsic to large organizations: not only does absolute power corrupt absolutely; it delays fantastically. I would also note that initiative is the least prized of a civil servant's virtues, because the political process allots much greater penalties for failure than rewards for success.

Size vs. control

RULE 2: When the national state performs detailed economic tasks, the responsible political authorities cannot possibly control the manner in which they are performed, whether directly by governmental agencies or indirectly by regulation of private enterprise.

The lack of control is due to the impossibility of the central authority either to know or to alter the details of a large enterprise. An organization of any size—and I measure size in terms of personnel—cannot prescribe conduct in sufficient detail to control effectively its routine operations: it is instructive that when the New York City subway workers wish to paralyze their transportation system, they can do so as effectively by following all the operating instructions in literal detail as by striking.

Large organizations seek to overcome the frustrating problems of communication and command by seeking and training able executives, who could be described more accurately as able subordinates. But to get a good man and to give him the control over and responsibility for a set of activities is of course another way of saying that it is impossible for the central authorities to control the activities themselves. As the organization grows, the able subordinate must get able subordinates, who in turn must get able subordinates, who in turn must get able subordinates, who in turn—well, by the time the organization is the size of the federal government, the demands for ability begin to outstrip the supply of even mediocre genes.

I estimate, in fact, that the federal government is at least 120 times as large as any organization can be and still keep some control over its general operations. It is simply absurd to believe that Congress could control the economic operations of the federal government; at most it can sample and scream. Since size is at the bottom of this rule, two corollaries are:

1. Political control over governmental activity is diminishing.

2. The control exercised by a small city is much greater than the control exercised over General Motors by its Board of Directors.

Uniformity of treatment

RULE 3: The democratic state strives to treat all citizens in the same manner; individual differences are ignored if remotely possible.

The striving for uniformity is partly due to a desire for equality of treatment, but much more to a desire for administrative simplicity. Thus men with a salary of $100,000 must belong to the Social Security system; professors in New York must take a literacy test to vote; the new automobile and the 1933 Essex must be inspected; the most poorly co-ordinated driver and the most skillful driver must obey the same speed limits; the same minimum wage must be paid to workers of highly different productivities; the man who gives a vaccination for small pox must have the same medical credentials as a brain surgeon; the three-week-old child must have the same whiskey import allowance as a grown Irishman; the same pension must be given to the pilot who flew 100 dangerous missions as to the pilot who tested a Pentagon swivel chair; the same procedure must be passed through to open a little bank in Podunk and the world's largest bank in New York; the same subsidy per bale of cotton must be given to the hillbilly with two acres and the river valley baron with 5,000 acres. We ought to call him Uncle Same.

RULE 4: The ideal public policy, from the viewpoint of the state, is one with identifiable beneficiaries, each of whom is helped appreciably, at the cost of many unidentifiable persons, none of whom is hurt much.

The preference for a well-defined set of beneficiaries has a solid basis in the desire for votes, but it extends well beyond this prosaic value. The political system is not trustful of abstract analysis, nor, for that matter, are most people. A benefit of $50 to each of one million persons will always seem more desirable than a $1 benefit to each of 150 million people, because one can see a $50 check, and hence be surer of its existence.

The suspicion of abstract theory is of course well-founded: most abstract theories recorded in history have been false. Unfortunately it is also an abstract theory, and a silly one, that says one should believe only what he can see, and if the human race had adhered to it we would still be pushing carts with square wheels.

You do not need to be told that someone is always hurt by an economic policy, which is only a special case of the basic economic theorem that there is no such thing as a free lunch. On the other hand, I do not say that all political lunches are priced exorbitantly.

RULE 5: The state never knows when to quit.

One great invention of a private enterprise system is bankruptcy, an institution for putting an eventual stop to costly failure. No such institution has yet been conceived of in the political process, and an unsuccessful policy has no inherent termination. Indeed, political rewards are more closely proportioned to failure than to success, for failure demonstrates the need for larger appropriations and more power. This observation does not contradict my previous statement that a civil servant must avoid conspicuous failure at all costs, for his failure is an unwise act, not an ineffectual policy.

The two sources of this tenacity in failure are the belief that the government must be able to solve a social problem, and the absence of *objective* measures of failure and success.

Let me emphasize as strongly as I can that each of these characteristics of the political process is a source of strength in some activities, as well as a limitation in other activities. If the state could move rapidly, contrary to Rule 1, and readily accepted abstract notions, contrary to Rule 4, our society would become the victim of every fad in morals and every popular fallacy in philosophy. If the state could effectively govern the details of our lives, no tyranny would ever have been overthrown. If the state were to adapt all its rules to individual circumstances, contrary to Rule 3, we would live in a society of utter caprice and obnox-

ious favoritism. If the state knew when to quit, it would never have engaged in such unpromising ventures as the American Revolution, not that I personally consider this our best war. But what are virtues in the preservation of our society and its basic liberties are not necessarily virtues in fixing the wages of labor or the number of channels a television set can receive.

These rules, and others that could be added, do not say that the state cannot socialize the growing of wheat or regulate the washing of shirts. What the rules say is that political action is social action, that political action displays reasonably stable behavioral characteristics, and that *prescriptions of political behavior which disregard these characteristics are simply irresponsible*. To say, after describing a social economic problem, that the state must do something about it, is equivalent in rationality to calling for a dance to placate an angry spirit. In fact the advantage is with the Indians, who were sure to get some useful exercise. The state can do many things, and must do certain absolutely fundamental things, but it is not an Alladin's lamp.

State's proper economic role

I propose merely to sketch what I believe is the proper treatment of certain classes of important economic problems.

Class 1: monopoly.   The fear of monopoly exploitation underlies a vast network of public regulation—the control over the so-called public utilities, including the transportation and communication industries and banking institutions, as well as traditional antitrust policies. The proper methods of dealing with monopoly, in their order of acceptability, are three:

1. The maintenance or restoration of competition by the suitable merger prevention policies, which we now fail to use in areas such as rail and air transport, and by the dissolution of monopolies. This method of once-for-all intervention provides the only really effective way of dealing with monopoly.

It will be said that for technological reasons even a modest amount of competition is unattainable in many areas. I believe these areas are very few in number. Even when a community can have only one electric company, that company is severely limited by the long-run alternatives provided by other communities.

2. Where substantial competition cannot be achieved—and I do not ask for perfect competition—the entry into the field is often controlled by the state—for example the TV channels are allocated by the FCC. Here auctioning off the channels seems the only feasible method of capturing the inherent monopoly gains. The history of regulation gives no promise that such gains can be eliminated.

3. In the few remaining cases in which monopoly cannot be eliminated or sold to the monopolist, monopolies should be left alone, simply because there is no known method of effective control.

Class 2: poverty. A community does not wish to have members living in poverty, whatever the causes of the poverty may be. The maximum level of socially tolerable poverty will vary with the society's wealth, so poor societies will stop short at preventing plain starvation, but Texans will demand, through the oil embargoes that Presidents Eisenhower and Kennedy found expedient to accept, also Cadillacs and psychiatrists in their minimum poverty budget. I consider treatment of poverty a highly proper function of the state, but would propose that it be dealt with according to two principles:

1. Direct aid should take the form of direct grants of money, and only this form. If the poor would rather spend their relief checks on food than on housing, I see no reason for denying them the right. If they would rather spend the money on whiskey than on their children, I take it that we have enforceable laws to protect children.

2. The basic problem of poverty from the social viewpoint, however, is not the alleviation of current need but equipping the people to become self-supporting.

In fact, so-called liberal policies in this area often seem to me to be almost studied in their callousness and contempt for the poor. Many ameliorative policies assume that the poor are much poorer in intelligence than in worldly goods, and must be cared for like children. Few people ask of a policy: What will be the effects on the poor who are not beneficiaries? If we tear down a slum, and rehouse half the people better at public cost, the only response to a query about the other half will be—we must do this for them too. Much of our welfare program has the macabre humor of a game of musical chairs.

Class 3: economic distress. I define economic distress as experiencing a large fall in income, or failing to share in a general rise, but without reaching some generally accepted criterion of poverty. Here my prescriptions would be:

1. Compensation for losses in the cases in which the distress is clearly and directly caused by governmental policy.

2. Exactly the same kind of treatment of distress as of poverty in other respects: Direct grants in the short-run; policies to foster the mobility of resources in the long-run.

Class 4: consumer and worker protection. Since unpunished fraud is profitable, it must be punished. I doubt whether many people realize how strong are the remedies provided by traditional law, and in particular how effective the actions of people who have been defrauded. I am confident that research in this area would suggest methods of vastly increasing the role of *self-policing* in the economy.

It is otherwise with the alleviation of consumer incompetence. In order to preserve the dignity and freedom of the individual in my society, I shall if I must pay the price of having some fail wholly to meet the challenge of freedom.

We should not, however, accept dramatic episodes as a measure of need; we should not simply assume that there is a useful law for every problem; and we should not lazily accept remedies which take freedom from 97 men in order to give protection to three.

And now I close. I consider myself courageous, or at least obtuse, in arguing for a reduction in governmental controls over economic life. You are surely desirous of improving this world, and it assuredly needs an immense amount of improvement. No method of displaying one's public-spiritedness is more popular than to notice a problem and pass a law. It combines ease, the warmth of benevolence, and a suitable disrespect for a less enlightened era. What I propose is, for most people, much less attractive: Close study of the comparative performance of public and private economy, and the dispassionate appraisal of special remedies that is involved in compassion for the community at large. I would urge you to examine my views in the most critical spirit, if I thought it

necessary; I do urge you to attempt the more difficult task of exercising your critical intelligence in an appraisal of the comfortable wishfulness of contemporary policy.

Reading 21

The Economic Role of Private Activity

Paul A. Samuelson

Introduction: matter and antimatter

Thoreau, disapproving of the Mexican War, would not pay his taxes and was put in jail for civil disobedience. His Concord neighbor, Emerson, went to visit him down at the hoosegow and called out: "Henry, what are you doing in there?" Thoreau replied, "Waldo, what are you doing out there?" You will have perceived my point. One way of approaching the question, "What is the proper role of Government?" is to ask, "What is the proper role of non-Government?"

Abraham Lincoln is supposed to have said somewhere:

I believe the government should do only that which private citizens cannot do for themselves, or which they cannot do so well for themselves.

One would think this is supposed to be saying something. Let us try it in its converse form.

I believe the private economy should be left alone to do those activities which, on balance after netting out all advantages and disadvantages, it can best do.

Obviously what I have stated is an empty tautology. It is no more helpful than the usual answer from Dorothy Dix to a perplexed suitor that merely says, "Look into your own heart to see whether you truly love the girl. And then after you have made up your mind, I am sure it will be the right decision."

But are these mere tautologies? Do the two Lincolnesque statements say exactly the same thing? There is a certain literal sense in which they can be

interpreted to be saying the same thing. But we all bring to the words we hear certain preconceptions and attitudes.

I think Lincoln meant to imply in his formulation that *there is needed a certain burden of proof that has to be established by anyone who proposes that the government do something.* The balance of advantage in favor of the government must be something substantial or you should stand with the *status quo* of private enterprise.

Why? Lincoln does not say. But he takes it for granted that his listeners will understand that "personal liberty" is a value for its own sake and that some sacrifice of "efficiency" is worth making at the optimal point where activity is divided so as to maximize the total net advantage of "efficiency *cum* liberty" and vice versa.

Overture to the program

So much for introduction. My Act I has prepared the way for what is to follow. In Act II, I want to examine the conditions under which efficiency is realizable by free enterprise or *laissez faire.* This is familiar ground, but too familiar and needs re-examination.

Then in Act III, I want to raise some questions about the notion that absence of government means increase in "freedom." Is "freedom" a simply quantifiable magnitude as much libertarian discussion seems to presume? In case the clock catches me somewhere in Act II, let me give you a hint of the kind of thing I have in mind: Traffic

From Paul A. Samuelson, "The Economic Role of Private Activity," *A Dialogue on the Proper Economic Role of the State,* Selected Paper No. 7, Graduate School of Business, University of Chicago. Reprinted by permission of Paul A. Samuelson.

lights coerce me and limit my freedom, don't they? Yet in the midst of a traffic jam on the unopen road, was I really "free" before there were lights? And has the algebraic total of freedom, for me or the representative motorist or the group as a whole, been increased or decreased by the introduction of well-engineered Stop Lights? Stop Lights, you know, are also Go Lights.

Then I shall conclude on what may seem a *nihilistic* note, but which I hope is actually a *liberating* one.

Technical requirements for competitive optimality

My friend George Stigler points out certain defects of government action. By itself, that is like pointing out certain defects of marriages. What we need to know is, "What are the alternatives? Celibacy? Cold baths? Violent exercise?" Jesting aside, Professor Stigler obviously hopes that the market can undertake most tasks "efficiently" and "equitably." I, too, so hope. But what are the strict conditions for optimal performance by private markets? Here are a bit of heroic assumptions:

1. Each person's tastes (and values) depend only upon his separable consumptions of goods. I.e., there must be no "consumption externalities."

2. Strict constant-returns-to-scale prevails.

3. Perfect competition, in senses too numerous to list here, prevails.

4. The interpersonal distribution of property (inclusive of personal attributes) is ethically correct initially or is to be made so by ideal lump-sum transfers of a perfectly nondistorting type.

Then, and only then, has it been rigorously proved that perfect competitive equilibrium is indeed optimal. So strict are these conditions that one would have thought that the elementary consideration that a line is infinitely thinner than a plane would make it *a miracle for these conditions to be met.* Real life optimality, or an approach to it, would seem to cry out—not merely for departure from *laissez faire*—but for never having been remotely near to *laissez faire*.

And note this. We each belong to many circles: The U.S.A., the Elks, the Samuelson family, the office pool, etc. In almost none of these relationships is the organizing principle that of decentralized competitive pricing. Let the descendants of Abraham Lincoln ponder over that one.

Division of responsibilities

It is a lucky accident that so much of economic life can be performed reasonably well by markets. But a long list of important cases arises where economics suggests that government should intervene:

1. Monopoly needs to be fought tooth and nail.

2. "Externalities"—the pollution of our environment, the rubbing of our elbows together—cry out for laws, zoning ordinances, concise rules of the road, taxes and subsidies.

3. The distribution of income and of opportunity—as between white and black, rich and poor, genetically lucky and unlucky—cries out for governmental measures to reduce inequality. Professor Stigler says the poor should be taught to get prosperous by their own efforts. He overlooks the fact that extensive statistical study shows that much of poverty—perhaps more than half today—is hopeless poverty. The old can never become young; the lame can never become whole; the disadvantaged 21-year-old—and perhaps 3-year-old—will never in his lifetime overcome his handicaps. An affluent society can afford to treat its underdogs humanely—just as tycoons and kings have been able to provide well for their incompetent and mediocre offspring.

All this is commonplace and obvious today. And Abraham Lincoln—reborn in 1975 or 1984—would be the first to proclaim it.

The nature of freedom

But enough of these technicalities. Let me repeat some reflections on freedom that I presented recently at a conference on Individualism in the Twentieth Century.

Adam Smith, our patron saint, was critical of state interference of the pre-Nineteenth Century type. And make no mistake about it: Smith was right. Most of the interventions into economic life by the State were *then* harmful both to prosperity and freedom. What Smith said needed to be said. In fact, much of what Smith said still needs to be said: *Good intentions by government are not enough;* acts do have consequences that had better be taken into account if good is to follow. (Thus, the idea of a decent real wage is an attractive one. So is the idea of a low interest rate at which the needy can borrow. Nonetheless, the attempt *by law* to set a minimum real wage at a level much above the going market rates, or to set a maximum interest rate for small loans at what seem like reasonable levels, inevitably does much harm to precisely the people whom the legislation is intended to help. Domestic and foreign experience—today, yesterday and tomorrow—bears out the Smithian truth. Note that this is not an argument against *moderate* wage and interest fiats, which may improve the perfection of competition and make businessmen and workers more efficient.)

Smith himself was what we today would call a pragmatist. He realized that monopoly elements ran through *laissez faire*. When he said that Masters never gather together even for social merriment without plotting to raise prices against the public interest, he anticipated the famous Judge Gary dinners at which the big steel companies used to be taught what every oligopolist should know. Knowing the caliber of George III's civil service, Smith believed the government would simply do more harm than good if it tried to cope with the evil of monopoly. Pragmatically, Smith would, if he were alive today, favor the Sherman Act and stronger anti-trust legislation, or even public utility regulation generally.

The Invisible Hand again

One hundred per cent individualists skip these pragmatic lapses into good sense and concentrate on the purple passage in Adam Smith where he discerns an Invisible Hand that leads each selfish individual to contribute to the best public good. Smith had a point; but he could not have earned a passing mark in a Ph.D. oral examination in explaining just what that point was. Until this century, his followers—such as Bastiat—thought that the doctrine of the Invisible Hand meant one of two things: (a) that it produced maximum feasible total satisfaction, somehow defined; or (b) that it showed that anything which results from the voluntary agreements of uncoerced individuals must make them better (or best) off in some important sense.

Both of these interpretations, which are still held by many modern libertarians, are wrong. They neglect Assumption 4 of my earlier axioms for non-government. This is not the place for a technical discussion of economic principles, so I shall be very brief and cryptic in showing this.

First, suppose some ethical observer—such as Jesus, Buddha, or for that matter, John Dewey or Aldous Huxley—were to examine whether the total of social utility (as that ethical observer scores the deservingness of the poor and rich, saintly and sinning individuals) was actually maximized by 1860 or 1962 *laissez faire*. He might decide that a tax placed upon yachts whose proceeds go to cheapen the price of insulin to the needy might increase the total of utility. Could Adam Smith prove him wrong? Could Bastiat? I think not.

Of course, they might say that there is no point in trying to compare different individuals' utilities because they are incommensurable and can no more be added together than can apples and oranges. But if recourse is made to this argument, then the doctrine that the Invisible Hand maximizes total utility of the universe has already been thrown out the window. If they admit that the Invisible Hand will truly maximize total social utility *provided the state intervenes so as to make the initial distribution of dollar votes ethically proper,* then they have abandoned the libertarian's position that individuals are not to be coerced, even by taxation.

In connection with the second interpretation that anything which results from voluntary agreements is in some sense, *ipso facto,* optimal, we can reply by pointing out that when I make a purchase from a monopolistic octopus, that is a voluntary act: I can always go without Alka-Seltzer or aluminum or nylon or whatever product you think is produced by a monopolist. Mere voluntarism, therefore, is not the root merit of the doctrine of the Invisible Hand; what is important about it is the system of checks and balances that comes under perfect competition, and its measure of validity is at the technocratic level of efficiency, not at the ethical level of freedom and individualism. That this is so can be seen from the fact that such socialists as Oscar Lange and A. P. Lerner have advocated channeling the Invisible Hand to the task of organizing a socialistic society efficiently.

The impersonality of market relations

Just as there is a sociology of family life and of politics, there is a sociology of individualistic competition. It need not be a rich one. Ask not your neighbor's name; enquire only for his numerical schedules of supply and demand. Under perfect competition, no buyer need face a seller. Haggling in a Levantine bazaar is a sign of less-than-perfect competition. The telephone is the perfect go-between to link buyers and sellers through the medium of an auction market, such as the New York Stock Exchange or the Chicago Board of Trade for grain transactions. Two men may talk hourly all their working lives and never meet.

These economic contacts between atomistic individuals may seem a little chilly or, to use the language of winetasting, "dry." This impersonality has its good side. Negroes in the South learned long ago that their money was welcome in local department stores. Money can be liberating. It corrodes the cake of custom. Money does talk. Sociologists know that replacing the rule of status by the rule of contract loses something in warmth; it also gets rid of some of the bad fire of olden times.

Impersonality of market relations has another advantage, as was brought home to many "liberals" in the Joseph McCarthy witch-hunting era of American political life. Suppose it were efficient for the government to be the one big employer. Then if, for good or bad, a person becomes in bad odor with government, he is dropped from employment, and is put on a black list. He really then has no place to go. The thought of such a dire fate must in the course of time discourage that freedom of expression of opinion which individualists most favor.

Many of the people who were unjustly dropped by the federal government in that era were able to land jobs in small-scale private industry. I say small-scale industry because large corporations are likely to be chary of hiring names that appear on anybody's black list.

Wheat growers anonymous

Many conservative people, who think that such men should not remain in sensitive government work or in public employ at all, will still feel that they should not be hounded into starvation. Few want for this country the equivalent of Czarist Russia's Siberia, or Stalin Russia's Siberia either. It is hard to tell on the Chicago Board of Trade the difference between the wheat produced by Re-

publican or Democratic farmers, by teetotalers or drunkards, Theosophists or Logical Positivists. I must confess that this is a feature of a competitive system that I find attractive.

We have seen how a perfect model of competitive equilibrium might behave if conditions for it were perfect. The modern world is not identical with that model. As mentioned before, there never was a time, even in good Queen Victoria's long reign, when such conditions prevailed.

Whatever may have been true on Turner's frontier,[1] the modern city is crowded. Individualism and anarchy will lead to friction. We now have to coordinate and cooperate. Where cooperation is not fully forthcoming, we must introduce upon ourselves coercion. When we introduce the traffic light, we have by cooperation and coercion, although the arch individualist may not like the new order, created for ourselves greater freedom.

The principle of unbridled freedom has been abandoned. It is now just a question of haggling about the terms! On the one hand, few will deny that it is a bad thing for one man, or a few men, to impose their wills on the vast majority of mankind, particularly when that will involves terrible cruelty and terrible inefficiency. Yet where does one draw the line? At a 51 per cent majority vote? Or, should there be no actions taken that cannot command unanimous agreement—a position which such modern exponents of libertarian liberalism as Professor Milton Friedman are slowly evolving toward. Unanimous agreement? Well, virtually unanimous agreement, whatever that will come to mean.

The principle of unanimity is, of course, completely impractical. My old friend Milton Friedman is extremely persuasive, but not even he can keep his own students in unanimous agreement all the

[1] Density of population produces what economists recognize as external economies and diseconomies. These "neighborhood effects" are often dramatized by smoke and other nuisances that involve a discrepancy between private pecuniary costs and social costs. They call for intervention: zoning, fiats, planning, regulation, taxing, and so forth.

But too much diluteness of the gas also calls for social interfering with *laissez faire* individualism. Thus, the frontier has always involved sparse populations in need of "social overhead capital." In terms of technical economics jargon this has the following meaning: when scale is so small as to lead to unexhausted increasing returns, free pricing cannot be optimal and there is a *prima facie* case for cooperative intervention.

time. Aside from its practical inapplicability, the principle of unanimity is theoretically faulty. It leads to contradictory and intransitive decisions. By itself, it argues that just as society should not move from *laissez faire* to planning because there will always be at least one objector—Friedman if necessary—so society should never move from planning to freedom because there will always be at least one objector. Like standing friction, it sticks you where you are. It favors the *status quo*. And the *status quo* is certainly not to the liking of arch individualists. When you have painted yourself into a corner, what can you do? You can redefine the situation, and I predicted some years ago that there would come to be defined a privileged *status quo,* a set of natural rights involving individual freedoms, which alone requires unanimity before it can be departed from.

At this point the logical game is up. The case for "complete freedom" *has been begged, not deduced.* So long as full disclosure is made, it is no crime to assume your ethical case. But will your product sell? Can you persuade others to accept your axiom when it is in conflict with certain other desirable axioms?

Not by reasoning alone

The notion is repellent that a man should be able to tyrannize over others. Shall he be permitted to indoctrinate his children into any way of life whatsoever? Shall he be able to tyrannize over himself? Here, or elsewhere, the prudent-man doctrine of the good trustee must be invoked, and in the last analysis his peers must judge—*i.e.,* a committee of prudent peers. And may they be peers tolerant as well as wise!

Complete freedom is not definable once two wills exist in the same interdependent universe. We can sometimes find two situations in which choice A is more free than choice B in apparently every respect and at least as good as B in every other relevant sense. In such singular cases I will certainly throw in my lot with the exponents of individualism. But few situations are really of this simple type; and these few are hardly worth talking about, because they will already have been disposed of so easily.

In most actual situations we come to a point at which choices between goals must be made: do you want this kind of freedom and this kind of hunger, or that kind of freedom and that kind of hunger? I use these terms in a quasi-algebraic sense, but actually what is called "freedom" is really a vector of almost infinite components rather than a one-dimensional thing that can be given a simple ordering.

Where more than one person is concerned the problem is thornier still. My privacy is your loneliness, my freedom to have privacy is your lack of freedom to have company. Your freedom to "discriminate" is the denial of my freedom to "participate." There is no possibility of unanimity to resolve such conflicts.

The notion, so nicely expounded in a book I earnestly recommend to you, Milton Friedman, *Capitalism and Freedom* (Chicago, 1962), that it is better for one who deplores racial discrimination to try to persuade people against it than to do nothing at all—but, failing to persuade, it is better to use no democratic coercion in these matters— such a notion as a *general* precept is arbitrary and gratuitous. Its arbitrariness is perhaps concealed when it is put abstractly in the following form: If free men follow Practice X that you and some others regard as bad, it is wrong in principle to coerce them out of that Practice X; in principle, all you ought to do is to try to persuade them out of their ways by "free discussion." One counter-example suffices to invalidate a general principle. An exception does not prove the rule, it disproves it. As a counter-example I suggest we substitute for "Practice X" the "killing by gas of 5 million suitably-specified humans." Who will agree with the precept in this case?

Only two types would possibly agree to it: (1) those so naive as to think that persuasion can keep Hitlers from cremating millions; or (2) those who think the *status quo,* achievable by what can be persuaded, is a pretty comfortable one after all, even if not perfect. When we are very young we fall into the first category; when old and prosperous, into the second; perhaps there is a golden age in between. *The notion that any form of coercion whatever is in itself so evil a thing as to outweigh all other evils is to set up freedom as a monstrous shibboleth.* In the first place, absolute or even maximum freedom cannot even be defined unambiguously except in certain special models. Hence one is being burned at the stake for a cause that is only a slogan or name. In the second place, as I have shown, coercion can be defined only in terms of an infinite variety of arbitrary alternative *status quo.*

The precept "persuade-if-you-can-but-in-no-case-coerce" can be sold only to those who do not understand what it is they are buying. This doctrine sounds a little like the "Resist-Not-Evil" precepts of Jesus or Gandhi. But there is absolutely no true similarity between the two doctrines, and one should not gain in palatability by being confused with the other.

Marketplace coercion, or the Hegelian freedom of necessity

Libertarians fail to realize that *the price system is, and ought to be, a method of coercion.* Nature is not so bountiful as to give each of us all the goods he desires. We have to be coerced out of such a situation, by the nature of things. That is why we have policemen and courts. That is why we charge prices, which are high enough relative to limited money to limit consumption. The very term "rationing by the purse" illustrates the point. Economists defend such forms of rationing, but they have to do so primarily in terms of its efficiency and its fairness. Where it is not efficient—as in the case of monopoly, externality, and avoidable uncertainty—it comes under attack. Where it is deemed unfair by ethical observers, its evil is weighed pragmatically against its advantages and modifications of its structure are introduced.

Classical economists, like Malthus, always understood this coercion. They recognized that fate dealt a hand of cards to the worker's child that was a cruel one, and a favorable one to the "well-born." John Stuart Mill in a later decade realized that mankind, not Fate with a capital F, was involved. Private property is a concept created by and enforced by public law. Its attributes change in time and are man-made, not Mother-Nature-made.

Nor is the coercion a minor one. Future generations are condemned to starvation if certain supply-and-demand patterns rule in today's market. Under the freedom that is called *laissez faire,* some

worthy men are exalted; and so are some unworthy ones.[2] Some unworthy men are cast down; and so are some worthy ones. The Good Man gives the system its due, but reckons in his balance its liabilities that are overdue.

Anatole France said epigrammatically all that needs to be said about the coercion implicit in the libertarian economics of *laissez faire.* "How majestic is the equality of the Law, which permits both rich and poor alike, to sleep under the bridges at night." I believe no satisfactory answer has yet been given to this. It is certainly not enough to say, "We made our own beds and let us each lie in them."[3] For once Democracy rears its pretty head, the voter will think: "There, but for the Grace of God and the Dow-Jones averages, go I." And he will act.

The whole matter of proper government policy involves issues of ethics, coercion, administration, incidence, and incentives that cannot begin to be resolved by semantic analysis of such terms as "freedom," "coercion," or "individualism."

A final law

At the end I must lay down one basic proposition. If you remember only one thing of what I say, let it be this. If you don't remember anything of what I say, let this be the last thing you forget.

There are no rules concerning the proper role of government that can be established by *a priori* reasoning.

This may seem odd to you: for to state the rule that there are no rules may sound like a self-contradiction, reminiscent of the breakfast cereal box that contains an exact picture of itself . . . of itself . . . of itself. . . . However, no Bertrand Russell theory of types is involved here. For, my proposi-

---

[2] "I am kept from attending college because my family is———————." To discern the coercion implicit in a competitive pricing system, note that any of the following can be substituted into the blank space: Negro, bourgeois, Jewish—*or poor.*

[3] If one disagrees with Malthus and France and thinks that we all had equal opportunities and *have* made the beds we are to lie in, our judgment of *laissez faire* improves—as it should. But note it is because of its fine welfare results, and *not because the kind of freedom embodied in it is the end-all of ethics.*

tion—call it Samuelson's Law if you like—does not claim to be established by Reason, but merely to be a uniformity of experience. Whose experience? My experience, and that of every (I mean, almost every) man of experience.

If I am wrong it will be easy to prove me wrong: namely, by stating one valid nontrivial proposition about the proper role of government derived by cogent *a priori* reasoning alone. After I have digested it, I shall have no trouble in eating my own words.

Let me illustrate by a few rules that have been proposed and that will pass neither the test of experience nor of logic.

JEFFERSON'S LEMMA: That government is best which governs least.

I waive the formal objection that there exists no least positive real number. Just as the only good Injun is alleged to be a dead one, this says that the best government would be one which committed suicide. By a social compact and constitution, anarchy would be proclaimed.

Taken *literally,* no one—certainly not Jefferson—will buy this dictum of zero government. Such sweeping rules are like soap bubbles: Literally take them and you find nothing in your hands to take. In this they differ from the Pythogorean or other theorem about Euclidean space derived by logic: Imagine saying "I believe the three angles of a plane triangle add up to 180°—but of course, not to the degree of taking the belief literally."

Here is another proposed law.

ACTON'S CONJECTURE: "All power corrupts, and absolute power corrupts absolutely."

Of course Lord Acton didn't say quite this in his letter to Bishop Creighton; nor did he profess to deduce it *a priori.* Yet, since Lord Acton was unfamiliar with the anthropology of the Samoan islands, neither he nor anyone else, with the possible exception of Margaret Mead, can testify to its universal correctness. Even within the experience of the history known to 19th Century Cambridge Dons, this cannot be established unless the words "corrupt" and "power" be defined tautologically. The Spearman rank correlation coefficient between the power of rulers and their abusive rulings is certainly not $+1$; to say the correlation is positive in a wide sampling of history is to say something interesting, but this is the kind of non-sweeping *empirical* uniformity which I am pleading for in this lecture as against dogmatic arguments from the nature of things.

Here is another branch whose graft never took on the tree of wisdom.

COLIN CLARK'S LAW: The role of government must be held below a ceiling of 25 per cent of the national income.

This is not a two-halves truth or even, I fear, a 25 per cent truth. A number of nations whom we all point to as having accomplished miracles in the last decade never had the erudition to know of Clark's Law or the instinctive good sense to desist from violating it. That Western Germany, the showplace of free enterprise, should collect 34 per cent of her national income for taxes is as shocking and thoughtless a violation of Clark's natural law as that a column of mercury should, after 30 vertical inches, neglect to remember that Nature abhors a vacuum.

I could go on. But why do so? My point is made: No *a priori* reasoning has yet been found to demarcate the role of non-government and of government. However, I must not be dogmatic. Having found cause to reject laws of Jefferson, Acton, and Clark, I must out of courtesy and caution reserve judgment on any laws that Professor Stigler may unveil. For, as I learned when our friendship began long ago, George Stigler can do almost anything—anything but be boring.

Reading 22

Government expenditure does much to help those with low incomes. Graduated income taxation further helps to equalize economic opportunity and mitigate the extremes of economic inequality.

Along with these conventional programs against poverty, a new program has captured the imagination of economists—the "negative income tax," which actually has the government pay out money to the poor, rather than collect it from them.

Yale's James Tobin, Sterling Professor of Economics, explores this new idea.

Questions to guide the reading

If people with low incomes receive payments from the government as a matter of right, will that hurt their pride? Blunt their economic incentives? Can we afford the negative income tax without raising tax rates on the middle- and high-income groups?

The Negative Income Tax

James Tobin

Assuring living standards in the absence of earning capacity

People who lack the capacity to earn a decent living need to be helped, but they will not be helped by minimum wage laws, trade union wage pressures, or other devices which seek to compel employers to pay them more than their work is worth. The more likely outcome of such regulations is that the intended beneficiaries are not employed at all.

A far better approach is to supplement earnings from the public fisc. But assistance can and should be given in a way that does not force the recipients out of the labor force or give them incentive to withdraw. Our present system of welfare payments does just that, causing needless waste and demoralization. This application of the means test is bad economics as well as bad sociology. It is almost as if our present programs of public assistance had been consciously contrived to perpetuate the conditions they are supposed to alleviate.

The welfare mess

These programs apply a strict means test. The amount of assistance is an estimate of minimal needs, less the resources of the family from earnings. The purpose of the means test seems innocuous enough. It is to avoid wasting taxpayers' money on people who do not really need help. But another way to describe the means test is to note that it taxes earnings at a rate of 100 per cent. A person on public assistance cannot add to his family's standard of living by working. Of course, the means test provides a certain incentive to work in order to get off public assistance altogether. But in many cases, especially where there is only one adult to provide for and take care of several children, the adult simply does not have enough time and earning opportunities to get by without financial help. He, or more likely she, is essentially forced to be both idle and on a dole. The means test also involves limitations on property holdings which deprive anyone who is or expects to be on public assistance of incentive to save.

In a society which prizes incentives for work and thrift, these are surprising regulations. They deny the country useful productive services, but that economic loss is minor in the present context. They deprive individuals and families both of work experience which could teach them skills, habits, and self-discipline of future value and of

From James Tobin, "On Improving the Economic Status of the Negro," *Daedalus*, Journal of the American Academy of Arts and Sciences, Fall, 1965. Reprinted with kind permission of the author and publisher.

the self-respect and satisfaction which comes from improving their own lot by their own efforts.

Public assistance also encourages the disintegration of the family. The main assistance program, Aid for Dependent Children, is not available if there is an able-bodied employed male in the house. In most states it is not available if there is an able-bodied man in the house, even if he is not working. All too often it is necessary for the father to leave his children so that they can eat. It is bad enough to provide incentives for idleness but even worse to legislate incentives for desertion.

The bureaucratic surveillance and guidance to which recipients of public assistance are subject undermine both their self-respect and their capacity to manage their own affairs. In the administration of assistance there is much concern to detect "cheating" against the means test and to ensure approved prudent use of the public's money. Case loads are frequently too great and administrative regulations too confining to permit the talents of social workers to treat the roots rather than the symptoms of the social maladies of their clients. The time of the clients is considered a free good, and much of it must be spent in seeking or awaiting the attention of the officials on whom their livelihood depends.

A better plan

The defects of present categorical assistance programs could be, in my opinion, greatly reduced by adopting a system of basic income allowances, integrated with and administered in conjunction with the federal income tax. In a sense the proposal is to make the income tax symmetrical. At present the federal government takes a share of family income in excess of a certain amount (for example, a married couple with three children pays no tax unless their income exceeds $3700). The proposal is that the Treasury pay any family who falls below a certain income a fraction of the short-fall. The idea has sometimes been called a negative income tax.

The payment would be a matter of right, like an income tax refund. Individuals expecting to be entitled to payments from the government during the year could receive them in periodic installments by making a declaration of expected income and expected tax withholdings. But there would be a fi-nal settlement between the individual and the government based on a "tax" return after the year was over, just as there is now for taxpayers on April 15.

A family with no other income at all would receive a basic allowance scaled to the number of persons in the family. For a concrete example, take the basic allowance to be $400 per year per person. It might be desirable and equitable, however, to reduce the additional basic allowance for children after, say, the fourth. Once sufficient effort is being made to disseminate birth control knowledge and technique, the scale of allowances by family size certainly should provide some disincentive to the creation of large families.

A family's allowance would be reduced by a certain fraction of every dollar of other income it received. For a concrete example, take this fraction to be one third. This means that the family has considerable incentive to earn income, because its total income including allowances will be increased by two-thirds of whatever it earns. In contrast, the means test connected with present public assistance is a 100 per cent "tax" on earnings. With a one-third "tax" a family will be on the receiving end of the allowance and income tax system until its regular income equals three times its basic allowance.

Families above this "break-even" point would be taxpayers. But the less well-off among them would pay less taxes than they do now. The first dollars of income in excess of this break-even point would be taxed at the same rate as below, one-third in the example. At some income level, the tax liability so computed would be the same as the tax under the present income tax law. From that point up, the present law would take over; taxpayers with incomes above this point would not be affected by the plan.

Pictures of a plan

The best way to summarize the proposal is to give a concrete graphical illustration. On the horizontal axis of Figure 1 is measured family income from wages and salaries, interest, dividends, rents, and so forth—"adjusted gross income" for the Internal Revenue Service. On the vertical axis is measured the corresponding "disposable income," that is, income after federal taxes and allowances. If the

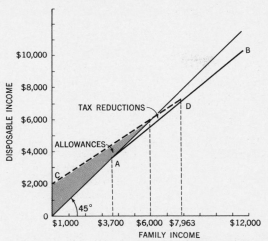

Figure 1 Illustration of proposed family allowance plan (married couple with three children).

family neither paid taxes nor received allowance, disposable income would be equal to family income; in the diagram this equality would be shown by the 45° line from the origin. Disposable income above this 45° line means the family receives allowances; disposable income below this line means the family pays taxes. The line OAB describes the present income tax law for a married couple with three children, allowing the standard deductions. The broken line CD is the revision which the proposed allowance system would make for incomes below $7963. For incomes above $7963 the old tax schedule applies.

Beneficiaries under Federal Old Age Survivors and Disability Insurance would not be eligible for the new allowances. Congress should make sure that minimum benefits under OASDI are at least as high as the allowances. Some government payments, especially those for categorical public assistance, would eventually be replaced by basic allowances. Others, like unemployment insurance and veterans' pensions, are intended to be rights earned by past services regardless of current need. It would therefore be wrong to withhold allowances from the beneficiaries of these payments, but it would be reasonable to count them as income in determining the size of allowances, even though they are not subject to tax.

Prudent cost

Although the numbers used above are illustrative, they are indicative of what is needed for an effective program. It would be expensive for the federal budget, involving an expenditure of perhaps fifteen billion dollars a year. Partially offsetting this budgetary cost are the savings in public assistance, on which governments now spend five and six-tenths billion dollars a year, of which three and two-tenth billion are federal funds. In addition, savings are possible in a host of other income maintenance programs, notably in agriculture. The program is expensive, but it need not be introduced all at once. The size of allowances can be gradually increased as room in the budget becomes available. This is likely to happen fairly rapidly.

I sometimes refer to programs which make up for lack of earning capacity as stopgaps, but that is not entirely fair. Poverty itself saps earning capacity. The welfare way of life, on the edge of subsistence, does not provide motivation or useful work experience either to parents or to children. A better system, one which enables people to retain their self-respect and initiative, would in itself help to break the vicious circle.

2

DETERMINATION OF NATIONAL INCOME AND ITS FLUCTUATIONS

Modern Theories of Income Determination and Forecasting

Readings 23 and 24

"We are all post-Keynesians now" is a slogan that reflects the gradual acceptance of the modern theory of income determination. It was not always so. The late President Hoover used to refer, in his retirement, to the doctrines of "Keynes and Marx" as if they were more or less synonymous.

In Reading 23, Galbraith describes the slow penetration of Keynesian techniques of thought. In Reading 24, Henry Hazlitt rejects the scientific validity of Keynesian analysis.

Henry Hazlitt long wrote an economic column for *Newsweek*.

Questions to guide the reading

Is it unhealthy for radically new doctrines to be first regarded with suspicion and hostility, with the burden of proof being put against them? How can you reconcile Lord Keynes' liking for individualism and the middle classes with his insistence that laissez faire would have to be modified by the macroeconomic programs of fiscal and monetary policy if full employment and reasonable price stability were to be attained?

Could a conservative, primarily interested in business profits and hostile to the working classes, find modern theories of income determination helpful to his cause?

Reading 23

How Keynes Came to America

John Kenneth Galbraith

> I believe myself to be writing a book on economic theory which will largely revolutionize—
> not, I suppose, at once but in the course of the next ten years—the way the world thinks
> about economic problems.
>
> *Letter from J. M. Keynes to George Bernard Shaw, New Year's Day, 1935.*

The most influential book on economic and social policy so far in this century, *The General Theory of Employment, Interest and Money,* by John Maynard Keynes, was published twenty-nine years ago last February in Britain and a few weeks later in the United States. A paper-back edition is now available in the United States for the first time, and quite a few people who take advantage of this bargain will be puzzled at the reason for the book's influence. Though comfortably aware of their own intelligence, they will be unable to read it. They will wonder, accordingly, how it persuaded so many other people—not all of whom, certainly were more penetrating or diligent. This was only one of the remarkable things about this book and the revolution it precipitated.

By common, if not yet quite universal agreement, the Keynesian revolution was one of the

John Kenneth Galbraith, "How Keynes Came to America," *New York Times Book Review*, May, 1965. © 1965 by The New York Times Company. Reprinted with kind permission of the author and publisher.

great modern accomplishments in social design. It brought Marxism in the advanced countries to a total halt. It led to a level of economic performance that now inspires bitter-end conservatives to panegyrics of unexampled banality. Yet those responsible have had no honors and some opprobrium. For a long while, to be known as an active Keynesian was to invite the wrath of those who equate social advance with subversion. Those concerned developed a habit of reticence. As a further consequence, the history of the revolution is, perhaps, the worst told story of our era.

It is time that we knew better this part of our history and those who made it, and this is a little of the story. Much of it turns on the almost unique unreadability of "The General Theory" and hence the need for people to translate and propagate its ideas to government officials, students and the public at large. As Messiahs go, Keynes was deeply dependent on his prophets.

A modern classic

"The General Theory" appeared in the sixth year of the Great Depression and the fifty-third of Keynes's life. It is a measure of how far the Keynesian revolution has proceeded that its central thesis now sounds rather commonplace. Until it appeared, economists, in the classical (or non-socialist) tradition, had assumed that the economy, if left to itself, would find its equilibrium at full employment. Increases or decreases in wages and in interest rates would occur as necessary to bring about this pleasant result. If men were unemployed, their wages would fall in relation to prices. With lower wages and wider margins, it would be profitable to employ those from whose toil an adequate return could not previously have been made. It followed that steps to keep wages at artificially high levels, such as might result from the ill-considered efforts by unions, would cause unemployment. Such efforts were deemed to be the principal cause of unemployment.

Movements in interest rates played a complementary role by insuring that all income would ultimately be spent. Thus, were people to decide for some reason to increase their savings, the interest rates on the now more abundant supply of loanable funds would fall. This, in turn, would lead to increased investment. The added outlays

for investment goods would offset the diminished outlays by the more frugal consumers. In this fashion, changes in consumer spending or in investment decisions were kept from causing any change in total spending that would lead to unemployment.

Keynes argued that neither wage movements nor changes in the rate of interest had, necessarily, any such agreeable effect. He focused attention on the total of purchasing power in the economy—what freshmen are now taught to call aggregate demand. Wage reductions might not increase employment; in conjunction with other changes, they might merely reduce this aggregate demand. And he held that interest was not the price that was paid to people to save but the price they got for exchanging holdings of cash, or its equivalent, their normal preference in assets, for less liquid forms of investment. And it was difficult to reduce interest beyond a certain level. Accordingly, if people sought to save more, this wouldn't necessarily mean lower interest rates and a resulting increase in investment. Instead, the total demand for goods might fall, along with employment and also investment, until savings were brought back into the line with investment by the pressure of hardship which had reduced saving in favor of consumption. The economy would find its equilibrium not at full employment but with an unspecified amount of unemployment.

What to do

Out of this diagnosis came the remedy. It was to bring aggregate demand back up to the level where all willing workers were employed, and this could be accomplished by supplementing private expenditure with public expenditure. This should be the policy wherever intentions to save exceeded intentions to invest. Since public spending would not perform this offsetting role if there were compensating taxation (which is a form of saving), the public spending should be financed by borrowing—by incurring a deficit. So far as Keynes can be condensed into a few paragraphs, this is it.

Before the publication of "The General Theory," Keynes had urged his ideas directly on President Roosevelt, most notably in a famous letter to *The New York Times* on December 31, 1933: "I lay overwhelming emphasis on the increase of national purchasing power resulting from government expenditure which is financed by loans." And he visited F.D.R. in the summer of 1934 to press his case, although the session was no great success; each, during the meeting, seems to have developed some doubts about the general good sense of the other.

In the meantime, two key Washington officials, Marriner Eccles, the exceptionally able Utah banker who was to become head of the Federal Reserve Board, and Lauchlin Currie, a former Harvard instructor who was director of research and later an economic aide to Roosevelt (and later still a prominent victim of McCarthyite persecution), had on their own account reached conclusions similar to those of Keynes as to the proper course of fiscal policy. When "The General Theory" arrived, they took it as confirmation of the course they had previously been urging.

Paralleling the work of Keynes in the thirties and rivaling it in importance, though not in fame, was that of Simon Kuznets and a group of young economists and statisticians at the University of Pennsylvania, the National Bureau of Economic Research and the United States Department of Commerce. They developed the now familiar concepts of National Income and Gross National Product and their components and made estimates of their amount. Included among the components of National Income and Gross National Product was the saving, investment, aggregate of disposable income and the other magnitudes of which Keynes was talking. As a result, those who were translating his ideas into action knew not only what needed to be done but how much. And many who would never have been persuaded by the Keynesian abstractions were compelled to belief by the concrete figures from Kuznets and his inventive colleagues.

The "other Cambridge"

However, the trumpet—if the metaphor is permissible for this particular book—that was sounded in Cambridge, England, was heard most clearly in Cambridge, Massachusetts. Harvard was the principal avenue by which Keynes's ideas passed to the United States.

In the late thirties, Harvard had a large community of young economists, most of them held there by the shortage of jobs that Keynes sought to cure.

They had the normal confidence of their years in their ability to remake the world and, unlike less fortunate generations, the opportunity. They also had occupational indication of the need. Massive unemployment persisted year after year. It was degrading to have to continue telling the young that this was merely a temporary departure from the full employment norm, and that one need only obtain the needed wage reductions.

Paul Samuelson of M.I.T., who, almost from the outset, was the acknowledged leader of the younger Keynesian community, has compared the excitement of the young economists, on the arrival of Keynes's book, to that of Keats on first looking into Chapman's Homer. Here was a remedy for the despair that could be seen just beyond the Yard. It did not overthrow the system but saved it. To the non-revolutionary, it seemed too good to be true. To the occasional revolutionary, it was. The old economics was still taught by day. But in the evening, and almost every evening from 1936 on, almost everyone discussed Keynes.

This might, conceivably, have remained a rather academic discussion. As with the Bible and Marx, obscurity stimulated abstract debate. But in 1938, the practical instincts that economists sometimes suppress with success were catalyzed by the arrival at Harvard from Minnesota of Alvin H. Hansen. He was then about fifty, an effective teacher and a popular colleague. But most of all he was a man for whom economic ideas had no standing apart from their use.

The economists of established reputation had not taken to Keynes. Faced with the choice between changing one's mind and proving that there is no need to do so, almost everyone opts for the latter. So it was then. Hansen had an established reputation, and he did change his mind. Though he had been an effective critic of some central propositions in Keynes's "Treatise on Money," an immediately preceding work, and was initially rather cool to "The General Theory," he soon became strongly persuaded of its importance.

He proceeded to expound the ideas in books, articles and lectures and to apply them to the American scene. He persuaded his students and younger colleagues that they should not only understand the ideas but win understanding in others and then go on to get action. Without ever seeking to do so or being quite aware of the fact, he became the leader of a crusade. In the late thirties Hansen's seminar in the new Graduate School of Public Administration was regularly visited by the Washington policy-makers. Often the students overflowed into the hall.

The officials took Hansen's ideas, and perhaps even more his sense of conviction, back to Washington. In time there was also a strong migration of his younger colleagues and students to the capital. Among numerous others were Richard Gilbert, now a principal architect of Pakistan's economic development, who was a confidant of Harry Hopkins; Richard Musgrave, now of Princeton, who applied Keynes's and Hansen's ideas to the tax system; Alan Sweezy, now of California Institute of Technology, who went to the Federal Reserve and the W.P.A.; George Jaszi, who went to the Department of Commerce; Griffiths Johnson, who served at the Treasury, National Resources Planning Board and the White House; and Walter Salant, now of the Brookings Institution, who served in several Federal agencies. Keynes himself once wrote admiringly of this group of young Washington disciples.

Washington learns

The discussions that had begun in Cambridge continued through the war years in Washington. One of the leaders, a close friend of Hansen's but not otherwise connected with the Harvard group, was Gerhard Colm of the Bureau of the Budget. Colm, a German refugee who made the transition from a position of influence in Germany to one of influence in the United States in a matter of some five years, played a major role in reducing the Keynesian proposals to workable estimates of costs and quantities. Keynesian policies became central to what was called post-war planning and designs for preventing the re-emergence of massive unemployment.

Meanwhile, others were concerning themselves with a wider audience. Seymour Harris, another of Hansen's colleagues and an early convert to Keynes, became the most prolific exponent of the ideas in the course of becoming one of the most prolific scholars of modern times. He published half a dozen books on Keynes and outlined the ideas in hundreds of letters, speeches, memoranda, Congressional appearances and articles. Professor Samuelson, mentioned above, put the Keynesian

ideas into what became (and remains) the most influential textbook on economics since the last great exposition of the classical system by Alfred Marshall. Lloyd Metzler, now of the University of Chicago, applied the Keynesian system to international trade. Lloyd G. Reynolds, at a later stage, gathered a talented group of younger economists at Yale and made that university a major center of discussion of the new trends.

Business chimes in

Meanwhile, with the help of the academic Keynesians, a few businessmen were becoming interested. Two New England industrialists, Henry S. Dennison of the Dennison Manufacturing Company in Framingham and Ralph Flanders of the Jones and Lamson Company of Springfield, Vermont (and later United States Senator from Vermont) hired members of the Harvard group to tutor them in the ideas. Before the war they had endorsed them in a book, in which Lincoln Filene of Boston and Morris E. Leeds of Philadelphia had joined, called "Toward Full Employment." In the later war years, the Committee for Economic Development, led in these matters by Flanders and the late Beardsley Ruml, and again with the help of the academic Keynesians, began explaining the ideas to businessmen.

In Washington during the war years the National Planning Association had been a center for academic discussion of the Keynesian ideas. At the end of the war Hans Christian Sonne, the imaginative and liberal New York banker, began underwriting both N.P.A., and the Keynesian ideas. With the C.E.D., in which Sonne was also influential, N.P.A. became another important instrument for explaining the policy to the larger public. (In the autumn of 1949, in an exercise of unparalleled diplomacy, Sonne gathered a dozen economists of strongly varying views at Princeton and persuaded them to sign a specific endorsement of Keynesian fiscal policies. The agreement was later reported to the Congress in well-publicized hearings by Arthur Smithies of Harvard and Simeon Leland of Northwestern University.)

The Full Employment Act

In 1946, ten years after the publication of "The General Theory," the Employment Act of that year gave the Keynesian system the qualified but still quite explicit support of law. It recognized, as Keynes had urged, that unemployment and insufficient output would respond to positive policies. Not much was said about the specific policies but the responsibility of the Federal Government to act in some fashion was clearly affirmed. The Council of Economic Advisers became, in turn, a platform for expounding the Keynesian view of the economy and it was brought promptly into use.

Those who nurture thoughts of conspiracy and clandestine plots will be saddened to know that this was a revolution without organization. All who participated felt a deep sense of personal responsibility for the ideas; there was a varying but deep urge to persuade.

Something more was, however, suspected. And there was some effort at counter-revolution. Nobody could say that he preferred massive unemployment to Keynes. And even men of conservative mood, when they understood what was involved, opted for the policy—some asking only that it be called by some other name. The Committee for Economic Development, coached by Ruml on semantics, never advocated deficits. Rather it spoke well of a budget that was balanced only under conditions of high employment. Those who objected to Keynes were also invariably handicapped by the fact that they hadn't (and couldn't) read the book. It was like attacking the original Kama Sutra for obscenity without being able to read Sanskrit.

Reaction on the Charles River

Harvard, not Washington, was the principal object of attention. In the fifties, a group of graduates of mature years banded together in an organization called the Veritas Foundation and produced a volume called "Keynes at Harvard." It found that "Harvard was the launching pad for the Keynesian rocket in America." But then it damaged this not implausible proposition by identifying Keynesianism with socialism, Fabian socialism, Marxism, Communism, Fascism and also literary incest, meaning that one Keynesian always reviewed the works of another Keynesian. More encouragingly, the authors also reported that "Galbraith is being groomed as the new crown prince of Keynesism (sic)." The university

was unperturbed, the larger public sadly indifferent. The book evidently continues to have some circulation on the more thoughtful fringes of the John Birch Society.

Another and more influential group of graduates pressed for an investigation of the Department of Economics, employing as their instrument the visiting committee that annually reviews the work of the department on behalf of the Governing Boards.

It was conducted by Clarence Randall, then the exceptionally articulate head of the Inland Steel Company, with the support of Sinclair Weeks, a manufacturer, former Senator and tetrarch of the right wing of the Republican Party in Massachusetts. In due course, the committee found that Keynes was, indeed, exerting a baneful influence on the Harvard economic mind and that the department was unbalanced in his favor. The department, including the members most skeptical of Keynes's analysis—no one accepted all of it and some very little—unanimously rejected the committee's finding. So did President James Bryant Conant. There was much bad blood.

In ensuing years there was further discussion of the role of Keynes at Harvard and of related issues. But it became increasingly amicable, for the original investigators had been caught up in one of those fascinating and paradoxical developments with which the history of the Keynesian (and doubtless all other) revolutions is replete. Shortly after the committee reached its disturbing conclusion, the Eisenhower Administration came to power.

Mr. Randall became a Presidential assistant and adviser. Mr. Weeks became Secretary of Commerce and almost immediately was preoccupied with the firing of the head of the Bureau of Standards over the question of the efficacy of Glauber's salts as a battery additive. Having staked his public reputation against the nation's scientists and engineers on the issue (as the late Bernard De Voto put it) that a battery could be improved by giving it a laxative, Mr. Weeks could hardly be expected to keep open another front against the economists. But much worse, both he and Mr. Randall were acquiring a heavy contingent liability for the policies of the Eisenhower Administration. And these, it soon developed, had almost as strong a Keynesian coloration as the department at Harvard.

Eisenhower retreat

President Eisenhower's first Chairman of the Council of Economic Advisers was Arthur F. Burns of Columbia University and the National Bureau of Economic Research. Mr. Burns had credentials as a critic of Keynes. In his introduction to the 1946 annual report of the National Bureau, called "Economic Research and the Keynesian Thinking of Our Times," he had criticized a version of the Keynesian underemployment equilibrium and concluded a little heavily that "the imposing schemes for governmental action that are being bottomed on Keynes's equilibrium theory must be viewed with skepticism." Alvin Hansen had replied rather sharply.

But Burns was (and is) an able economist. If he regarded Keynes with skepticism, he viewed recessions with positive antipathy. In his 1955 Economic Report, he said, "Budget policies can help promote the objective of maximum production by wisely allocating resources *first between private and public uses;* second, among various government programs." (Italics added.) Keynes, reading these words carefully, would have strongly applauded. And, indeed, a spokesman for the N.A.M. told the Joint Economic Committee that they pointed "directly toward the planned and eventually the socialized economy."

After the departure of Burns, the Eisenhower Administration incurred a deficit of no less than $9.4 billions in the national income accounts in the course of overcoming the recession of 1958. This was by far the largest deficit ever incurred by an American Government in peacetime; it exceeded the *total* peacetime expenditure by F.D.R. in any year up to 1940. No administration before or since has given the economy such a massive dose of Keynesian medicine. With a Republican Administration, guided by men like Mr. Randall and Mr. Weeks, following such policies, the academic Keynesians were no longer vulnerable.

The new conventional wisdom

Presidents Kennedy and Johnson have continued what is now commonplace policy. Advised by Walter Heller, a remarkably skillful exponent of Keynes's ideas, they added the new device of the deliberate tax reduction to sustain aggregate demand. And they abandoned, at long last, the doubletalk by which advocates of Keynesian policies combined advocacy of measures to promote full employment and economic growth with promises of a promptly balanced budget. "We have recognized as self-defeating the effort to balance our budget too quickly in an economy operating well below its potential," President Johnson said in his 1965 report. Now, as noted, Keynesian policies are the new orthodoxy. Economists are everywhere to be seen enjoying their new and pleasantly uncontroversial role.

We have yet to pay proper respect to those who pioneered the Keynesian revolution. Everyone now takes pride in the resulting performance of the economy. We should take a little pride in the men who brought it about. It is hardly fitting that they should have been celebrated only by the reactionaries. The debt to the courage and intelligence of Alvin Hansen is especially great. Next only to Keynes, his is the credit for saving what even conservatives still call capitalism.

Reading 24

Keynesian and Other Present-day Heresies

Henry Hazlitt

Shortly after the appearance of John Maynard Keynes's *General Theory of Employment, Interest, and Money* in 1936, the doctrines enunciated in it conquered the academic world and have dominated it ever since. But in the decade beginning in 1955 a frontal counterattack was launched. In

From Henry Hazlitt, "The Development of Economic Thought," *National Review*, New York, November 1965. Reprinted with kind permission of the author and publisher.

1959 the present writer published *The Failure of the "New Economics,"* with the subtitle, *An Analysis of the Keynesian Fallacies;* a year later I brought together in an anthology, *The Critics of Keynesian Economics,* articles written by some twenty distinguished economists over the preceding twenty-four years which directly or indirectly refuted the Keynesian contentions. Then, in 1963, Professor W. H. Hutt, Dean of the Faculty of Commerce at the University of Cape Town, published his brilliant and thoroughgoing *Keynesianism—Retrospect and Prospect.*

Retreat

There are now, at long last, definite signs of a crack-up of the Keynesian ideology. I wish I could report that this is the result of recent criticisms of its internal confusions and contradictions, but the plain truth seems to be that it is cracking up because the remedies based on it are so obviously not working as advertised. What is happening is precisely the result predicted by Jacob Viner in the same year the *General Theory* appeared: "In a world organized in accordance with Keynes's specifications there would be a constant race between the printing press and the business agents of the trade unions."

It would be wrong to give the impression that retreat from the pure Keynesian ideology on the part of the leading Keynesians has been open and avowed. But it can be detected by the shrewd analyst. In an article in *The South African Journal of Economics* of last June, W. H. Hutt pointed out that Samuelson and half a dozen other Keynesians have quietly abandoned Keynes's crucial concept of an "unemployment equilibrium." It was precisely this, however, that they had originally hailed as "the shattering new insight" that had "wrought a revolution in thought." Instead, they are now explaining unemployment as chiefly the result of "money wage rates that are sticky and resistant to downward price movements." In brief, they have returned to the old "classical" explanation of unemployment.

Fellow travelers

I would be misleading the reader if I implied that the bulk of economic discussion in the last decade has circled around the books I have mentioned. Vance Packard and others have enjoyed the greatest sales and attention—for books which give the reader the impression that American industry is chiefly engaged in turning out, wastefully and irrationally, all sorts of silly products that the American public does not need but can be hornswoggled into believing that it wants. And the most discussed and most influential economics book in the last decade has been J. K. Galbraith's *The Affluent Society* (1958). Where the older socialists told us that the trouble with capitalism was that it couldn't produce the goods, Galbraith told us that its trouble was that it was producing altogether too many, but they were all the wrong goods. Therefore, we should tax the "private sector" even more onerously to force it to support an even bigger "public sector"—i.e. still more public spending, more welfare-statism and more socialism.

At the same time, those who were endorsing the Galbraith theme saw no inconsistency in also supporting the theme that the American economy was not "growing" fast enough. In any case, their remedy was the same—various forms of government inflation and other interventions to achieve this faster growth. W. W. Rostow's *The Stages of Economic Growth* was a typical product of this forced-growth mania.

Requiem

The economic theory and practice of a decade cannot be judged merely from its books. Almost every non-Communist government in the world was, and is, practicing Keynesian policies to the accompaniment of Keynesian rationalizations. These policies consist of continuous currency and credit expansion, artificially low interest rates, increased government spending, and budget deficits. When such policies result in inflation, in balance of payments deficits, and in rising prices and wages, the remedy adopted is not to abandon the policies, but to try to offset them by such devices as further import restrictions, penalties and prohibitions on foreign investment, price controls, "wage policies," and "income policies"—in brief, to further government controls that move in the totalitarian direction. And this is the current direction of government economic policy the world over.

Inflation

Readings 25 and 26

Inflation, which means a general rise in the price level, may be mild or severe. The United States has not experienced what most observers would call a severe inflation for many years. Yet the widespread concern over Vietnam and post-Vietnam price rises of better than 5 per cent per annum suggests that the fears of runaway inflation may have a powerful grip on American thought.

Certainly the stories of what much more rapid inflations have done to creditors and debtors, to different groups of income receivers, and to political and social institutions in other times and places deserve our careful attention. How do men accommodate themselves to periods of unrestrained price rises? And what is left in the wake of such periods?

Here are two case reports on severe inflations. Frank D. Graham, former professor of economics at Princeton University, describes the burdens placed upon the German society by one of the most spectacular inflations in history—the post-World War I German inflation of 1919–1923.

Internal monetary reform and a revised plan for German reparations (the Dawes Plan, adopted in 1924) finally halted the German inflation, but the case of Chile offers the unusual experience of a nation struggling decade after decade with substantial price increases almost constantly eroding the purchasing power of the currency. Yet this prolonged inflation has not developed into the type of galloping hyperinflation that has wrought havoc in other countries. This puzzling experience is described by Joseph Grunwald, expert on Latin America.

Questions to guide the reading

What common characteristics are there in the two inflations described?

What lessons are there in these case studies for the United States today?

Reading 25

Hyperinflation: Germany 1919–1923

Frank D. Graham

Germany, in common with other warring countries, departed from the gold standard at the outbreak of hostilities in 1914. On November 20, 1923, the German paper mark, after having fallen to an infinitesimal fraction of its former value, was made redeemable in the newly introduced renten-mark at a trillion to one. The rentenmark, after a short but honorable existence during which its gold value remained substantially stable at that of the original gold mark, was supplemented by the present [1930] standard reichsmark.

The regime of inconvertible and depreciating

From Frank D. Graham, *Exchange, Prices and Production in Hyper-Inflation Germany, 1920–1923* (Princeton University Press, Princeton, N.J., 1930). Reprinted with kind permission of the publisher.

paper money thus ran for a little less than a decade. The progress of depreciation was, however, very unevenly distributed over these ten years. During most of the war period the exchange value of the mark did not fall greatly from par with the dollar and if, when the issue of the conflict was no longer in doubt, it sank heavily, it was still quoted in December 1918 at more than twelve American cents. During the peace negotiations, however, German exchange continued to fall fast. This downward movement persisted till February 1920 when the descent was checked at just a shade below one cent per mark, that is, at about ¹⁄₂₄ of its pre-war value. A quick recovery then set in which carried the rate to nearly 3¢ in May. Though there was some reaction from this figure relative stability at a level of from 1½ to 2¢ was attained in June. By early 1920 the period of immediate adjustment to post-war conditions may therefore be considered to have been completed. Not until September 1921 did the value of the mark again fall below one American cent and as late as June 1922 it still sold for about ¹⁄₃ of a cent. From then onward the decline was vertiginous till the final collapse in November 1923. At the latter date forty-two billion (42,000,000,000) marks were worth but a single American cent. Without a complete ouster of the currency concerned, no corresponding depreciation appears in the long and varied annals of monetary history. Never before had a paper money fallen at so rapid a rate over such an extended period.

Reparations or scapegoat

While the payments of cash reparations in 1921 undoubtedly played an important part in promoting the decline in the currency, and while the sanctions imposed on Germany in 1923 led to the ultimate collapse, this is, of course, by no means the whole story. Reparations gravely affected public finances but the fiscal difficulties were far from being solely due to this cause. It is true that, if a more soundly conceived and executed reparations policy had been adopted by the creditor Powers, inflation of the currency might perhaps have been stayed by the vigorous measures of reform of the public finances initiated in Germany in 1920. But inflation had none the less proceeded far before any cash reparations whatever had been paid and it was accelerated after they had been entirely suspended. Its roots went back into the early war period and it was, in many German quarters, nurtured rather than repressed. The war administration had looked with a much too friendly eye on inflationary policies. The initial impetus thus given was never checked and long after the war was over the Reichsbank was entirely too pliable in its attitude toward both governmental and private borrowing.

The attitude of the Reichsbank was but one aspect of a fairly general complacency toward currency depreciation. The burden of the great internal government debt, piled up during and immediately after the war, meant exceedingly high taxes unless it should be lightened by a decline in the value of the counters in which it was expressed. Though currency depreciation meant confiscation of the property of holders of the government debt it was the line of least resistance for the Treasury and was thus not unwelcome in official circles. The policy of inflation had, in addition, powerful support from influential private quarters.

Inflation was therefore combated but half-heartedly at best. Though several of the administrations of the years 1920 to 1923 made valiant attempts to arrest its progress they could not summon the sustained powers necessary to success. It may well be doubted whether a stable standard could in any case have been set up while immense reparations debts were plaguing the situation. But this must remain an open question. So long as wealth and income were being merely transferred by the decline in the value of the monetary unit and not, as a sum, diminished, so long as scapegoats could be found to assume the burdens and yield of their substance to those who knew how to profit from the situation, projects of reform were treated cavalierly. It was only when enterprisers, instead of surely profiting from inflation as they long did, were suddenly plunged into a sea of uncertainties, only when business activity passed from the stage of exhilaration to panic, only when resistance to a further assumption of losses on the part of the public at large became general, that influential opinion veered to a conviction of the necessity of restoring a stable standard. The pass to which matters had then come is shown in Table 1.

Table 1 Treasury Bills Discounted by the Reich, Issues of Paper Currency, Index of Wholesale Prices, and Index of Dollar Exchange Rates against Paper Marks: 1919–1923 (value figures in millions of marks)

End of month	Total amount of Treasury bills discounted by the Reich*	Total issues of paper currency (except emergency currency)	Index of wholesale prices† 1913 = 1	Index of dollar exchange rates in Berlin‡ 1913 = 1
1919 Dec.	86,400	50,065	8.03	11.14
1920 June	113,200	68,154	13.82	9.17
Dec.	152,800	81,387	14.40	17.48
1921 June	185,100	84,556	13.66	17.90
Dec.	247,100	122,497	34.87	43.83
1922 June	295,200	180,169	70.30	89.21
July	308,000	202,626	100.59	159.60
Aug.	331,600	252,212	192.00	410.91
Sept.	451,100	331,876	287.00	393.04
Oct.	603,800	484,685	566.00	1,071.94
Nov.	839,100	769,500	1,154.00	1,822.30
Dec.	1,495,200	1,295,228	1,475.00	1,750.83
1923 Jan.	2,081,800	1,999,600	3,286.00	11,672.00
Feb.	3,588,000	3,536,300	5,257.00	5,407.00
Mar.	6,601,300	5,542,900	4,827.00	4,996.00
April	8,442,300	6,581,200	5,738.00	7,099.00
May	10,275,000	8,609,700	9,034.00	16,556.00
June	22,019,800	17,340,500	24,618.00	36,803.00
July	57,848,900	43,813,500	183,510.00	262,030.00
Aug.	1,196,294,700	668,702,600	1,695,109.00	2,454,000.00
Sept.	46,716,616,400	28,244,405,800	36,223,771.00	38,113,000.00
Oct.	6,907,511,102,800	2,504,955,700,000	18,700,000,000.00	17,270,129,000.00
Nov.	191,580,465,422,100	400,338,326,400,000	1,422,900,000,000.00	1,000,000,000,000.00
Dec.	1,232,679,853,100	496,585,345,900,000	1,200,400,000,000.00	1,000,000,000,000.00

* Practically all government borrowing after 1919 was in the form of discounted Treasury bills. The figure for November 1923 is as of the 15th of that month.
† In the index number of wholesale prices from December 1919 to December 1922 inclusive the figures represent monthly averages. From January to June, 1923, statistics are available for specific days three times a month, and from July to December, 1923, weekly. The figures in the table are for the latest available date in each month.
‡ The December 1919 figure for the index number of exchange rates is a monthly average. All other figures for this index are end-of-month quotations.

Sources of data: (1) *Zahlen zur Geldentwertung in Deutschland 1914 bis 1923;* Statistisches Reichsamt, Verlag von Reimar Hobbing, Berlin, 1925, pp. 6–10, 16–18, 46–7. (2) *Germany's Economy, Currency and Finance.* Zentral-Verlag G.m.b.H., Berlin, 1924, p. 63.

The masses of the urban population were living from hand to mouth, nay, had nothing in their hands but worthless bits of paper which the farmers would no longer accept in exchange for grain. Food riots were general. Political dissolution was in imminent prospect and armed revolt had already raised its head. Affairs were indeed so black that it is clear, in retrospect, that they actually facilitated the reform by imbuing the people with the resolution of despair.

Inflation and social upheaval

Inflation had shaken the social structure to its roots. The changes of status which it caused were profound. No such shifting of property rights, in time of peace, had ever before taken place. Great numbers of families of long established wealth and position were reduced to beggary at the very time that new or additional fortunes of staggering magnitude were being accumulated. The old middle class well-nigh disappeared and a new group came into prominence. There was less change in the condition of the masses—they had not so much to lose—but the wiping out of savings, insurance, and pensions pressed heavily upon the worker even if his losses did not parallel those of some of the better-to-do social classes.

The drama, and particularly the tragedy, of the time have left an indelible impression of the evils of inflation on the minds of the generation which lived through it. The most striking effects were in the realm of the distribution of wealth rather than in production but there were periods, principally in the final stages of depreciation, when the great majority of the population was in extreme want and perhaps even more distressing uncertainty. When prices were rising hourly by leaps and bounds, when the purchasing power of present and prospective receipts of money was vanishing before it could be spent, or would even be acquired, the population of a so highly specialized exchange society as Germany, was subjected to a well-nigh intolerable strain.

Reading 26

Chronic Inflation: Twentieth-century Chile

Joseph Grunwald

There is some evidence that Chile's price inflation started as far back as the late 1870s. Since the beginning of the official consumer price index in 1928, there have been only about four years, but not consecutive ones, during which it may be said that relative price stability existed.

Chile's very severe depression of the 1930s and the influence of the war years of the forties brought a very erratic pattern of price movements during those two decades. On the average, the yearly price increase was roughly 10 per cent during the thirties and 20 per cent during the forties. The inflation rate increased somewhat during the first years of the fifties, but in the middle of 1953 a price explosion took place which brought the yearly inflation rate to over 80 per cent by 1955.

With the 1956 anti-inflation program the inflation rate dropped to 38 per cent in 1956 and 17 per cent in 1957. Price increases were higher in 1958 and 1959, reaching about 35 per cent annually, but since the end of 1959 a relative stability has been attained.

Inflation became a way of life and was institutionalized into the legal and socio-economic structure of the country, each sector of the economy constructing its own defense apparatus.

The wage and salary sectors achieved the right to legal wage readjustments in some relation to the cost-of-living index. These income adjustments applied not only to wages and salaries but also to pensions, retirement and other social security incomes. The other mechanism for the salaried

From Joseph Grunwald, "The 'Structuralist' School of Price Stabilization and Economic Development: The Chilean Case," in Albert O. Hirschman (ed.), *Latin American Issues* (The Twentieth Century Fund, New York, 1961). Reprinted with kind permission of the publisher.

classes was price control and subsidized imports of certain basic consumer items.

The self-employed and profit-earning groups defended themselves first through anticipating the inflation by increasing their prices even before the annual wage adjustments came around, and following this up by further price increases after the wage adjustments were given. Second, the credit mechanism also served as an inflation defense for the more substantial businesses. Increases in costs due to wage adjustments and price increases of raw materials were readily absorbed through relatively easy access to credit for the privileged groups, while for others credit was sharply rationed or unavailable.

The government sector defended itself against inflation through the printing press. It is clear that deficit spending became unavoidable as government revenues were based upon the previous period's assessments compared to current pricing for government expenditures.

Nearly all of the sectors of the community hedged through the building up of inventories. This applied also to consumer groups, who bought consumer goods for storage rather than for use.

It is not surprising that this inflation spirit developed a finesse and cleverness in handling the pressures of price increases in all sectors. Although most of the defense mechanisms employed were in themselves quite inflationary, there is little doubt that they brought a certain self-confidence to the community which helped to stave off panic.

The curious aspect of Chile's inflation history of close to a century is that the country never experienced runaway inflation. One would think that, once a country reaches such high rates of price increases as Chile did, hyperinflation would follow almost automatically. There is no satisfactory answer to this. The fact is that not enough money was printed for hyperinflation to develop. But if the forces that made the authorities "print money" were so strong as to maintain a 20 or more per cent yearly inflation for many years, what stopped those forces from compelling a snowballing monetary expansion? Probably the social pressures were not strong enough, and perhaps public confidence was greater than is generally thought. But if among the factors of hyperinflation is public panic, then the defense mechanisms which the Chilean community has built up over the years have helped to avoid it—no matter how inflationary these mechanisms may be in themselves.

Readings 27 and 28   Debate on Creeping Inflation

The American record in the 1950s was one of moderate or "creeping" inflation. The impact of this was widely and emotionally discussed throughout the decade, but the concern reached a peak when prices continued to rise even in the midst of a mild recession in 1958. Was this a portent of inevitable inflation even when jobs were scarce? Did it mean that more severe inflation must follow as soon as employment picked up once again? And what difference did inflation make?

Creeping inflation's critics were numerous. Its defenders were rarer. One of the most articulate defenders was the late Sumner H. Slichter, professor of economics at Harvard University. His view that a modest amount of inflation was both inevitable and healthy in any economy committed to high levels of employment and growth attracted considerable attention, and drew forth the rebuttal in Reading 28 by Jules Backman, professor of economics at New York University. The main issue with which they are concerned was somewhat eclipsed in the early 1960s by the stability of prices which appeared to stem from too high a rate of unemployment. But an economy that sought a way back to a point near full employment had to ask itself once again after 1965: Can we have stable prices too? See Readings 66, 67, and 68 by Burns, Eckstein, and Galbraith for a debate on wage-price guideposts and controls.

Questions to guide the reading

Were there significant changes in the American economy in the 1960s to lend greater weight to one side or the other in this debate on inflation?

How might Americans be able to protect themselves against a steady inflation that hovered around 2 per cent per annum? How adequate are the assurances that inflation will not be likely to go much beyond that point in the near future?

Reading 27

The Case for Creeping Inflation

Sumner H. Slichter

The principal economic issue dividing the American people today is the issue of growth of the economy vs. stability of the price level. Mr. Eisenhower has declared that a stable price level "is an indispensable condition for achieving vigorous and continuing economic growth" and has placed strong emphasis on the prevention of inflation in his State of the Union message, his budget message, and his economic report.

His critics accuse him of discouraging growth in order to stabilize the price level. The A.F.L.-C.I.O. Economic Policy Committee has charged that Mr. Eisenhower's program is "a sure-fire prescription for stagnation." The Joint Congressional Economic Committee, under the chairmanship of Senator Paul H. Douglas of Illinois, is about to start hearings on the problem of reconciling full employment, an "adequate" rate of growth and price stability.

Is it true, as Mr. Eisenhower says, that there is no conflict between vigorous economic growth and a stable price level? Or must permanent inflation be accepted as a necessary condition to maximum growth? And if maximum growth entails creeping inflation, what will be the consequences for the economy? Will the United States price itself out of world markets? Will confidence in the dollar be undermined and will there be a disastrous flight from the dollar with creeping inflation developing into a gallop? Will creeping inflation produce great suffering among recipients of fixed incomes? Or are the consequences of creeping inflation greatly exaggerated?

The inflation of the 1950's in the United States has been caused by a mixture of strong demand for goods and a strong upward push of costs, but the principal reason the price level has increased and slow inflation must be expected to continue more or less indefinitely is the strong tendency for labor costs to rise faster than output per man-hour. During the past ten years, for example, hourly compensation of employes in private industry outside agriculture has risen more than twice as fast as output per man-hour.

The unions explain this by asserting that wages were simply chasing prices up, but the facts refute the claims of the union spokesmen. In *every one* of the past ten years the percentage rise in the hourly compensation of workers exceeded the percentage rise in the consumer price index. Furthermore, in nine out of the past ten years, the rise in hourly compensation of workers exceeded the rise in the wholesale prices of finished goods. Wages were not chasing prices up; on the contrary, prices were chasing wages, and were falling behind each year.

The tendency for wages to outrun output per man-hour is bound to occur in an economy of private enterprise and powerful trade unions whenever the demand for goods is strong—that is, whenever the conditions are favorable for rapid growth. Wages could be prevented from outrunning output per man-hour if the bargaining power

From Sumner H. Slichter, "Argument for 'Creeping' Inflation," *New York Times Magazine,* Mar. 8, 1959. Reprinted with kind permission of the publisher.

of unions were weakened and the bargaining power of employers strengthened by the maintenance of a fairly high rate of unemployment.

Some members of the Board of Governors of the Federal Reserve System, some members of the Council of Economic Advisers and some private economists have proposed that tight credit policies be used to create the amount of unemployment necessary to keep wages from rising faster than productivity and to keep the price level steady. The amount of unemployment needed would vary with the phase of the business cycle, the vigor of foreign competition and the year-to-year fluctuation in the size of crops, but recent experience indicates that an unemployment rate of 5 to 8 per cent would be required.

Stagnation vs. growth

Fostering unemployment in order to keep wages from outrunning productivity, however, would mean retarding the growth of the economy. Hence the conflict between maximum growth and stable prices is real—the community must decide which it prefers. There is little doubt which way the decision will go because the loss to the community from a retarded rate of growth would increase at a compound rate and would soon become intolerably burdensome. Suppose that the economy, which is capable of increasing its productive capacity at the rate of 4 per cent a year, were held to a growth of only 2 per cent a year in order to keep the price level steady. At the end of ten years the economy would have a productive capacity more than 26 percentage points less than it would have had at the greater rate of growth.

What about the long run effects of creeping inflation? Would not creeping inflation bring frequent recessions, so that in the long run more real growth would be achieved under a stable price level? There is no doubt that rapid growth entails the risk of recession, but the occasional recessions that accompany a high rate of growth need not be severe. Much progress has been made in building up resistance of the economy to contraction. The recession of 1958 illustrates this progress. The drop in business investment and the liquidation of inventories were moderately severe, but personal income and retail sales remained remarkably steady. As a result, the recession was both mild

and short. In view of the growing capacity of the economy to resist contraction, one must reject the view that a stable price level is a necessary condition to the maximum rate of growth.

Best of two worlds?

Are not changes possible in our institutions, policies, or business practices that would enable us to avoid creeping inflation and at the same time realize our maximum growth potential? There are many changes that would diminish the tendency for prices to rise, but none of them would assure that unions would not push up wages faster than industry could raise output per man-hour in the strong sellers' markets that would characterize a rapidly growing economy.

The *possibility of price and wage controls may be dismissed,* partly because the people would not tolerate controls in time of peace and partly because controls are easily evaded by changing the quality of goods and by introducing substitute goods. Strong public hostility to excessive union wage claims will have some effect on wages, but not much. Union members expect their officers to get all that they can for the members and would displace officers whom they suspected of failing to represent them faithfully. Union members, however, are not immune to public opinion, and strong public hostility to excessive demands will tend to weaken by a small amount the upward pressure of unions on wages.

What about the possibility of *curbing* the *power of the trade unions by organization on the part of employers, by depriving unions of some of their present privileges and immunities, or by imposing new restrictions on unions?* More organization among employers would help, but too much should not be expected from it. The employers are organized for dealing with unions in the steel industry, the coal industry, the railroad industry, and at the local level in many of the building trades, but in none of these industries have employers been able to prevent wages from outrunning output per man-hour.

Depriving unions of some of their present extraordinary privileges, such as the use of coercive picketing to force people to join or the conscription of neutrals in labor disputes, would remove some glaring injustices, but would have little effect upon the bargaining power of most unions. Breaking up some of the large unions, as has been suggested by George Romney and others, would have consequences that are hard to predict. Unions would lose some of their present ability to support strikes by some members while other members work and pay special assessments into a strike fund. Nevertheless, the new unions might drive hard bargains. There would be rivalries among them and each would have a strong desire to make a good showing.

Thus, if there were three or four unions in the automobile industry, each might feel a strong urge to make a better settlement than any of the others. Hence, breaking up the unions might increase their militancy and make reasonable settlements with them more difficult.

Promoting productivity

But whatever the possible results of the breaking up of unions, that step is not going to be taken. The American workers want their unions, and any effort to destroy or seriously weaken organized labor would cause the workers to rally to the support of the unions and make them stronger and more aggressive than ever.

The most promising methods of checking the tendency of rising labor costs to push up prices are new methods of management that enlist the ingenuity and imagination of the men at the machines and benches in reducing the ratio of labor costs to income from sales. Experience in more than a score of plants shows that amazing things begin to happen when workers share in a plant-wide bonus, based upon their success in narrowing the ratio of labor costs to income from sales, and are given good opportunities to discuss their ideas regularly with management. The common interest that everyone in the plant has in reducing labor costs produces an almost startling degree of teamwork and cooperation.

The new methods of management were introduced a few years ago by the late Joseph Scanlon, and his work is being carried out by his followers. But a generation or more will probably be required to spread the new methods throughout industry and adapt them to enterprises of various sizes and kinds. Eventually American industry will drastically modify its methods of handling labor and draw on the great capacity of rank and file

workers to contribute to improvements in technology. The new methods of management may or may not be adequate to prevent wages from outrunning productivity, but they hold more promise for checking rising labor costs than any device that has yet been developed.

If a generation or so will be required for new methods of management to check the rise in labor costs, what will happen in the meantime? Fears that the United States will be priced out of world markets are far-fetched. Prices in most other important industrial countries have been rising in recent years even faster than in the United States. Between 1950 and 1957, for example, the increase in the index of wholesale prices in Britain was more than twice as large as in the United States. In Sweden and Norway it was more than three times as large, in France almost three times as large, in West Germany almost twice as large, in Austria four times as large.

No one knows, of course, whether prices in other industrial countries will continue to rise faster than in the United States. Since the principal industrial countries are in competition with one another and since they all are more or less subject to the same influences (such as powerful trade unions and an insistent popular demand for social services that precludes important reductions in taxes), all of the industrial countries are likely to experience about the same movement of the price level.

The competitive position of the United States is very strong, especially in manufacturing. This is indicated by the fact that our exports of finished manufactures are nearly three times as large as our imports. But if important industrial countries were to succeed in underselling us on a broad scale, that would not be a calamity for us. On the contrary, it would help us check inflation by stiffening the resistance of American employers to union demands and by encouraging employers to cut prices.

Also ill-founded are fears that creeping inflation will precipitate a flight from the dollar and that creeping inflation will sooner or later become a gallop. Every country in Europe has had creeping inflation during the past ten years. The idea has become pretty well accepted that a continued drop in the purchasing power of money is to be expected. And yet in virtually all countries the rise in prices between 1953 and 1957 was considerably less than in the period 1948 to 1953.

As for a general flight from the dollar, the practical question arises: "Where is the money to go?" Other currencies have limited attractiveness because almost any country one might name has economic and political problems as formidable as those confronting the United States. Flight into commodities is not satisfactory because the future price of each commodity depends upon specific market conditions (supply, demand, competition of substitutes) far more than on what happens to the general price level. Some shifting of investment is bound to occur and already has occurred, but the process tends to limit itself.

For example, if the price level is expected to rise 2 per cent a year, a good bond yielding nominally 5 per cent has a true yield of 3 per cent. Such a bond may be as attractive as a stock that has been bid up so that it yields only 2.5 per cent.

Adjusting to the Inevitable

Our conclusion is that there is no immediate prospect that conflict can be avoided in advanced industrial countries between the desire for the maximum possible economic growth on the one hand and a stable price level on the other hand. This conflict is created by the rise of the relatively new institution of collective bargaining which is too well established and produces too many important benefits to be disturbed simply because it produces creeping inflation.

But the prospect that we shall be living under creeping inflation does call for various common sense adaptations and adjustments. Efforts should be made to speed the adoption of the new methods of management that automatically reward workers for helping reduce the ratio of labor costs to sales income. Pension plans, including the Federal old-age and survivors' insurance plan, should be adapted to creeping inflation. This means that they should either be fitted with escalator clauses or revised every now and then to compensate for the rise in the price level.

People should review their investment policies and should not hold long-term bonds or other long-term fixed-income investments unless the yield is sufficient to compensate them for the probable annual loss in purchasing power. Long-term wage contracts should contain escalator clauses. But in general, people should realize that living under creeping inflation in the future will not be essentially different from living under creeping inflation in the past—in fact, prices will probably rise considerably less in the next ten years than in the past ten.

Most important of all, people should realize that the alternative to creeping inflation is a fairly substantial amount of chronic unemployment. The problems of creeping inflation are a small price to pay for avoiding the much greater problems of unemployment and a rate of growth that falls far short of our potential.

Reading 28

The Case against Creeping Inflation

Jules Backman

There is a general agreement that economic growth is indispensable for a strong America. However, there has been considerable public debate about the ideal rate of growth and how to achieve it.

One school of thought asserts that "an inescapable cost" of a desirable rate of growth is creeping inflation. It holds that the alternatives are "creeping inflation and economic growth" or "price stability and unemployment." In this way, creeping inflation is given "respectability by association," while price stability is subject to "guilt by association."

The second school of thought holds not only

From Jules Backman, "The Case against Creeping Inflation," *New York Times Magazine*, May 3, 1959. Reprinted with kind permission of the author and publisher.

that we can have both a desirable rate of growth and stable prices, but that we can maintain our growth only by keeping prices stable.

Creeping inflation refers to a price rise of 2 per cent or 3 per cent a year. Professor Sumner Slichter, one of the exponents of the first school, states that this type of "slow inflation must be expected to continue more or less indefinitely." Such an annual rate of increase does not seem to be very large, but an annual rise of 2 per cent will wipe out half of the purchasing power of the dollar in thirty-five years, and a 3 per cent rate will result in a similar reduction in less than twenty-five. This is the simple arithmetic of creeping inflation.

Nevertheless, apologists for creeping inflation argue that it is unavoidable if we are to achieve the rate of economic growth which is necessary to enable us to attain our aspirations at home and to meet the threat from Russia. They explain that it is inevitable because labor costs rise more rapidly than output per man-hour. According to this argument, trade unions are so powerful that these excessive increases in wages and other labor costs could be stopped only by stringent governmental monetary and fiscal controls. The result of such curbs would be large-scale unemployment, which would limit economic growth. We are told that we must, therefore, accept creeping inflation as a lesser evil.

There is no disagreement concerning objectives between the creeping inflationists and those who are opposed. We are agreed that our goal is a maximum achievable rate of economic growth. We are agreed that unemployment is undesirable and exacts a high social cost. We are agreed that inflation—creeping or any other kind—is not desirable as a way of life. We disagree as to the means by which we may achieve our goals. The creeping inflationists say that we cannot achieve all three goals, that we must choose among them. The anti-creeping inflationists say we can achieve growth, a minimum level of unemployment *and* price stability.

The arguments against creeping inflation may be summarized as follows: (1) it slows long-term economic growth; (2) it makes recessions worse; (3) it hurts fixed-income groups and savers; (4) not everyone can be protected against it by "escalator clauses"; (5) it leads to galloping inflation; (6) it is not inevitable in an expanding economy.

(1) Creeping inflation slows long-term economic growth

There is general agreement that to meet the threat of the expanding Russian economy our own economy must continue to grow as rapidly as possible. Some say we must step up our rate of growth to about 5 per cent a year as compared with our long-term record of about 3 per cent. While the difference between 3 per cent and 5 per cent appears to be small, it becomes enormous with the passage of time. With a growth rate of 3 per cent, total output of goods and services in our economy increases fourfold in about fifty years. With a 5 per cent rate of increase, on the other hand, total output in a half century would be more than ten times as large as it is at present.

Everyone is in favor of the highest possible rate of economic growth. But there are practical limits to expansion which must be faced. When we exceed these limits the pressures for inflation become intensified. President Eisenhower properly has pointed out that a stable price level is "an indispensable condition" for achieving the maximum growth rate in the long run.

History does not support the assumption that economic growth must be accompanied by rising prices. Economic growth has occurred in many periods of stable or declining prices. Two such major periods in the nineteenth century—the Eighteen Twenties and Eighteen Thirties and the last third of the century—were periods of declining prices. During the Nineteen Twenties, when prices remained relatively stable, national output rose about 4 per cent a year. On the other hand, from 1955 to 1957, when prices crept upward almost 3 per cent a year, national output rose less than 2 per cent annually.

Two major factors have contributed to economic growth in this country: higher productivity and an expanding population. Two-thirds of our 3 per cent annual rate of growth has been accounted for by rising output per man-hour, about one-third by increasing population. Increases in productivity, therefore, provide the key to future economic growth. Output per man-hour is affected by many factors but the most important has been the investment in new machines and equipment. The magnitude of such investments depends upon the level of savings. Savings will be discouraged by creeping inflation, and thus long-term economic growth will be stultified.

Confronted by creeping inflation, savers are more interested in speculating—to protect themselves against losses in purchasing power—than in providing capital for industry. There is ample evidence of this tendency in the rampant speculation now taking place in stocks. If inflation should continue to be a threat, more and more persons would try to protect themselves in this manner. The result would be a speculative binge which would ultimately collapse. Such a development could only act to retard economic growth.

To stimulate economic growth it is necessary to create an environment in which savings will be encouraged and business will be willing to convert those savings into new plant and equipment. Price stability encourages savings, while tax incentives could be used to induce new investments. This is the road to greater economic growth.

Creeping inflation also interferes with business planning. When protection against price rises becomes a dominant factor, business men are not likely to plan boldly for expansion. One result is an adverse impact on job creation.

(2) Creeping inflation makes recessions worse

It is true that fear of higher prices may give a temporary stimulus to the economy. But this development induces speculation in inventories. Eventually, the inventories become burdensome, then the economy experiences a setback. The 1948-49 downturn properly has been described as an inventory recession. Inventory liquidation also was significant in the 1953-54 and 1957-58 recessions.

When protection against tomorrow's higher costs becomes a major factor in industry decisions to expand capacity today, the net result tends to be overexpansion—followed by a sharp decline in new investment in plant and equipment. The current lag in the capital goods industries reflects the aftermath of the overexpansion of 1955-57. Thus, creeping inflation means more cyclical unemployment. It is not an alternative to unemployment; it is a significant cause of unemployment. And it is little solace to those who become unemployed that they may have received overtime pay during the boom.

We normally anticipate that there will be 2.5 to 3 million workers unemployed even when the economy is operating at full speed. This frictional unemployment usually is short-term, representing individuals changing jobs or seasonally unemployed (as in the construction, apparel or retail trades). Therefore, when we have a total of 4.3 million unemployed, our real problem is how to create about 1.5 million jobs. The economic cost of unemployment must be measured in terms of this smaller figure.

The hardships attending unemployment should not be minimized. The price in terms of broken homes, loss of self-respect, loss of national output, and related developments is a heavy one indeed. This is why every effort must be directed to adopting the proper policies to reduce unemployment.

Creeping inflation exacts a double toll: first, a loss in the buying power of our money; second, added unemployment. It carries a high price tag.

(3) Creeping inflation hurts fixed-income groups and savers

Persons with fixed or relatively fixed incomes—those who live on proceeds of life-insurance policies, pensioners, those who work for non-profit organizations, government employes and bondholders—are hardest hit by any cut in the purchasing power of money. Ask the pensioner who planned his retirement twenty years ago how he gets along today with the dollars that buy less than half of what they bought then.

With an increasing number of senior citizens in our population, and with the growth of private pension plans, this is a matter of serious national concern. The hardships experienced by these persons can be just as tragic as those suffered by the unemployed.

In addition, families with savings accounts, United States Savings Bonds and other types of savings find their purchasing power steadily eroding. These various forms of savings aggregate about $400 billions. Every increase of 1 per cent in the price level, therefore, wipes out $4 billions in purchasing power.

This problem cannot be evaluated in terms of one-year or two-year results. As we noted earlier, creeping inflation could cut the total value of savings in half within twenty-five to thirty-five years. This is a heavy cost and cannot be ignored.

Nor can workers escape the adverse effects of

creeping inflation. Higher prices cut the purchasing power of wages and benefits received under security programs. The part of a wage increase which is excessive is taken away—in whole or in part—by price inflation. Reduced profits mean reduced incentives to invest in new plant and equipment; one result is fewer job opportunities. And unemployment, which thus may attend excessive labor-cost increases, means that those who hold their jobs obtain part of their higher real earnings at the expense of those who lose their job or who fail to obtain jobs.

(4) Not everybody can be protected against creeping inflation by "escalator clauses"

It is significant that not even the apologists for creeping inflation regard it as something to be encouraged. Rather, we are told it is an evil which must be tolerated and to which adjustment must be made. One suggestion is that "escalator clauses," such as those now contained in many union contracts, might be extended to pensioners, insurance beneficiaries, bondholders and the like. This proposal acknowledges the ill effects of inflation, but suggests that the burden could be neutralized.

But not everybody can ride the escalator. It is the height of folly to imagine that we can inflate without some groups paying the price.

Professor Slichter has suggested that under the conditions of creeping inflation people "should not hold long-term bonds or other long-term fixed-income investment unless the yield is sufficient to compensate them for the probable annual loss in purchasing power." What would happen to our financial system if bondholders should attempt to liquidate their investments en masse? The basic weakness of the apology for creeping inflation is reflected in the recognition of the problem in this area.

(5) Creeping inflation leads to galloping inflation

Psychology plays an important role in economic decisions. As the purchasing power of money steadily erodes, more and more persons will seek to protect themselves against future price rises. The resulting flight from money into goods would accelerate the rate of increase in prices. Creeping

inflation could then become galloping inflation, and finally runaway inflation.

It is true that such a development would require support from monetary and fiscal inflation. But that this support would be forthcoming seems probable as long as we persist in tolerating wage inflation and insist upon full employment.

(6) Creeping inflation is not inevitable in an expanding economy

Many factors are at work today to raise or hold up prices. They include the agricultural support program, the high level of Federal, state and local government spending, the increases in various sales and excise taxes, featherbedding and make-work rules, controls affecting imports and the steady expansion in private debt.

The primary cause of creeping inflation, however, as Professor Slichter has pointed out, is wage inflation—labor costs rising faster than output per man-hour. When wage inflation abates, price inflation also is moderated. It is noteworthy that, despite business recovery in the past year, consumer prices have remained stable and wholesale prices have risen only fractionally. This temporary stability reflects the likelihood that output per man-hour has risen more rapidly than the long-term rate (a typical recovery performance), and that, as a result, wage inflation has been at a minimum—perhaps even nonexistent—for the economy as a whole during this period.

The basic problem, then, is to counteract wage inflation. Two factors make this difficult. One is the national objective to maintain full employment, the other is the growth of powerful labor unions.

The full-employment policy makes it difficult to impose those stringent monetary and fiscal checks to rising prices which would create deflation and unemployment. The national concern over unemployment has assured union leaders that their wage policies will be underwritten by new inflationary measures when necessary. In other words, full-employment policies have increased the bargaining strength of the unions.

The problem of wage inflation could be ameliorated if union leaders and the workers they represent accepted the fact that our average standard of living cannot rise faster than national productivity. Only as we produce more can we obtain more goods and services, or more leisure, or some combination of both.

However, since it is the job of union leaders to get as much for their members as fast as they can, there is little point in criticizing them for taking full advantage of the present situation.

We can make more progress by taking action on two fronts:

First, the power of the unions must be curbed. There is little agreement on how this may be accomplished. Some students of the problem have suggested applying the antitrust laws to limit unions' monopoly power. Others have proposed more drastic remedies, such as limiting the power to strike, or curbing the size of unions.

Each of these proposals involves serious difficulties which must be carefully evaluated. Possibly some other solution will be forthcoming. However, unless some means is found to curb excessive union power and its abuse, this source of pressure for creeping inflation will continue.

Second, the Employment Act of 1946 should be amended to include the goal of stabilizing the purchasing power of the dollar as well as the goal of maintaining high-level employment. This would provide a guide against which to measure proposed policies. It would not mean wage or price controls. Individual prices would continue to fluctuate as at present but public policy would have as one objective the prevention of marked changes in the general price level.

Uncertainty would be substituted for the present certainty that inflationary wage increases will be supported by governmental actions. The new element of uncertainty might impose some restraint upon unions. It might also make industry less willing to grant excessive wage increases because it would make their recovery through higher prices less certain.

One important caution must be noted. There is no magic in a stable price level. Stability of prices during the Nineteen Twenties did not prevent the most catastrophic depression in modern history. Stability of prices from 1952 to early 1956 did not prevent the 1954 recession—or the 1955–1957 boom. General price stability may conceal important disparities in price relationships or in cost-price relationships which in turn upset the effective functioning of the economy. In other words, general price stability is not a cure-all for the problem of the business cycle.

Nevertheless, if these limitations are kept in mind, the inclusion of the goal of price stability in the Employment Act will focus national attention on inflation and its causes. The public will be made aware of the dangers that are inherent in monetary and fiscal inflation with their impact upon total demand, wage inflation with its impact on costs, and other policies which act to raise or hold up prices. And, certainly, full awareness of the sources—and evils—of creeping inflation is an indispensable step in mobilizing public opinion against inflationary policies.

Monetary and Federal Reserve Policy

Reading 29

The total money supply is manufactured out of the monetary base, i.e., from "currency held by the public plus the reserves held by the commercial banks and upon which their deposit-component-of-the-money-supply is based (as modified by changes in legal reserve requirements)." If the Federal Reserve is to control the money supply, it must contrive the right total of this high-power money base.

The Federal Reserve Bank of St. Louis is sometimes regarded as the single captured province of the Chicago school of monetarism. In any case, analysts rely on it for up-to-date statistics bearing upon modern macroeconomics. This particular reading was originally written by staff members Leonall C. Andersen and Jerry L. Jordan of the St. Louis Reserve Branch.

Questions to guide the reading

You can lead a horse to water but you can't make him drink. That old saying is sometimes used to argue that controlling the monetary base is not enough. Excess reserves may pile up and thwart you. Do you think that this explains what happened in the Great Depression of 1929 to 1933 when the monetary base was made to grow but when the total money supply actually declined much in consequence of the fact that people were pulling their money out of the banks? But is such a recurrence likely in a modern mixed economy?

The Monetary Base—Explanation and Analytical Use

Federal Reserve Bank of St. Louis

The monetary base recently has achieved prominence as a measure of monetary influence on the economy. Other aggregates often used are the money stock defined as currency plus demand deposits held by the nonbank public, money plus time deposits at commercial banks, member bank reserves, bank credit, liquid assets, and total credit. Other frequently used measures of monetary actions include market interest rates and so-called marginal reserve measures such as member bank excess reserves, borrowings from Reserve banks, and free reserves.

Those who find the monetary base to be a measure of monetary influence give two reasons for doing so. First, there is a significant body of monetary theory which incorporates the monetary base as an important link between Federal Reserve monetary actions and their ultimate impact on income, output, and prices. Second, among all the variables cited above as measures of monetary actions, the monetary authorities have the most complete control over the monetary base, and the base reflects the actions of these authorities more directly than the other measures do.

The article explains the monetary base concept, and then discusses its role in monetary analysis, briefly developing some of the arguments for using the base as a measure of monetary actions.

Monetary base concepts

Three concepts are used in this article to compute the monetary base. These are the "source base," "reserve adjustments," and the sum of these two, called the "monetary base."

The source base. The "source base" is derived from a consolidated monetary balance sheet of the Federal Reserve System and the United States Treasury.[1] Table 1 presents this consolidated balance sheet. According to column one of this table, the source base is the sum of Federal Reserve credit (Federal Reserve holdings of U.S. Government securities, member bank borrowing from Reserve banks, and Federal Reserve float), the nation's gold stock, and U.S. Treasury currency outstanding *less* Treasury deposits at Reserve banks, Treasury cash balances, and other deposits and accounts at Reserve banks.

For ease of computation, the source base is [also] frequently measured by summing the monetary liabilities of the Federal Reserve and the

---

[1] The term "source base" used in this article is the same magnitude which Friedman-Schwartz-Cagan call "high-powered money," and which Brunner-Meltzer call the "monetary base."

From "The Monetary Base—Explanation and Analytical Use," Federal Reserve Bank of St. Louis, August 1968. Reprinted with kind permission of the publisher.

Table 1   Calculation of the Source Base—June 1968—Monthly Averages of Daily Figures* (millions of dollars)

Sources of base		Uses of base	
Federal Reserve credit:		Member bank deposits	
Holdings of securities	+51,396†	at Federal Reserve	+21,350
Discounts and advances	+ 705	Currency held by banks	+ 5,566
Float	+ 1,712	Currency held by the public	+41,900
Gold stock	+10,369		
Treasury currency outstanding	+ 6,744		
Treasury deposits at Federal Reserve	− 960		
Treasury cash holdings	− 973		
Other deposits and other			
Federal Reserve accounts	− 177		
Source Base	68,816		68,816

* Data are not adjusted for seasonal variation.
† Includes acceptances of $90 million not shown separately.
Source: Board of Governors of the Federal Reserve System, Federal Reserve *Bulletin.* The sources and uses of the base are a rearrangement of data contained in the first table appearing in the Financial and Business Statistics section of the *Bulletin*—"Member Bank Reserves, Federal Reserve Bank Credit, and Related Items."

Treasury. These liabilities, consisting of member bank deposits (reserves) at Reserve banks and currency held by banks and the nonbank public, are referred to as *uses of the base* and are listed in column two of Table 1. These uses of the base are equal to the source.

Reserve adjustments.   Because of changes in laws and regulations and in the distribution of deposits among banks subject to different regulations, adjustments must be made in the source base in order to maintain comparability over time. "Reserve adjustments" allow for the effects of changes in reserve requirements on member bank deposits, and for changes in the proportion of deposits subject to different reserve requirements (reserve city member banks versus country member banks versus nonmember banks, demand deposits versus time deposits, and recently the over and under $5 million reserve requirement differentials on both demand and time deposits). These reserve adjustments are expressed as dollar amounts which are positive when average reserve requirements fall and negative when they rise.

The monetary base.   The monetary base is defined in this article as the source base plus reserve

adjustments. In deriving a seasonally-adjusted time series for the monetary base, the source base was first seasonally adjusted and then the month's reserve adjustment amount was added to this magnitude. There are no discernible seasonal movements in the latter. The chart (p. 113) presents the time series for the monetary base since January 1947.

Analytical use of the monetary base

This section discusses factors influencing the supply of the monetary base and the demand for the base. It concludes with a brief discussion of the adjustment process by which the amount of the base demanded is brought into equilibrium with the amount supplied by monetary authorities. This adjustment process establishes the monetary base as a strategic economic variable for monetary management and for interpreting actions of such management.

Supply of the monetary base.   The supply of the monetary base is substantially under the complete control of the Federal Reserve System. Recent studies [by Brunner and others] have found that movements in Federal Reserve credit dominate movements in other sources of the source base,

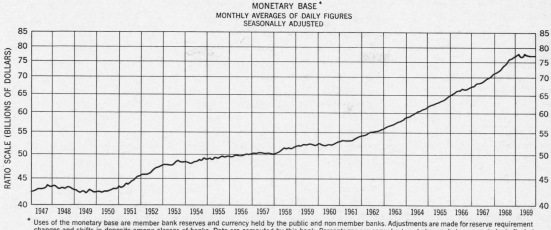

MONETARY BASE *
MONTHLY AVERAGES OF DAILY FIGURES
SEASONALLY ADJUSTED

* Uses of the monetary base are member bank reserves and currency held by the public and non member banks. Adjustments are made for reserve requirement changes and shifts in deposits among classes of banks. Data are computed by this bank. Percentages are annual rates of change between periods indicated. They are presented to aid in comparing most recent developments with past "trends."
Latest data plotted: June preliminary.

and therefore determine most of the movements of the monetary base.[2] Evidence has also been presented that Federal Reserve open market operations are able to offset, to a high degree, seasonal and irregular movements in other components of the source base. Consequently, the Federal Reserve, if it so chooses, is able to achieve desired levels of the monetary base for purposes of economic stabilization.

Demand for the monetary base.

Demand for the monetary base consists of the demand of *commercial banks* for excess reserves and required reserves and the demand of the non-bank public for currency (Table 1, Column 2). Banks' demand for required reserves is a derived demand reflecting the demands for private demand deposits, Government demand deposits, net interbank deposits, and time deposits. Demand for the monetary base consequently reflects economic decisions made by commercial banks, the nonbank *public,* and the *Government.* Therefore, all of the factors influencing the decisions of each of these sectors influence the demand for the monetary base. Some of the

[2] Although member bank borrowing from Reserve banks and changes in the gold stock and float are not under the direct control of monetary authorities, it is generally believed that open market operations may be used to offset short-term changes in these and other accounts in order to achieve a desired level of the monetary base.

factors influencing each of these sectors are discussed below:

Total demand. Total demand for the monetary base is the summation of sector demands; it is therefore influenced by the factors determining individual sector demands. Consequently total demand for the base (given wealth, interest rates paid on time deposits and other forms of savings accounts, and the Federal Reserve discount rate) is positively related to economic activity and prices of real assets, and negatively related to a wide variety of short-term market interest rates.

The adjustment process.

Most recent developments in monetary theory, which pertain to the determination of economic activity, stress the role of assets, both financial and real, and the market adjustment of asset holdings through the relative price mechanism. The monetary base, according to some economists, is an asset which monetary authorities supply to the economy. Since the supply of this asset can be controlled by the Federal Reserve System, banks and the nonbank public must adjust their holdings of real and other financial assets so as to bring the amount demanded of the monetary base equal to the amount supplied. In the process of adjustment, economic activity, prices of real assets, and interest rates are changed.

There is a "weak" and a "strong" view regarding the role of the monetary base. The weak view embodies the process just outlined and goes no further. The strong view also adopts this adjustment process, but then extends the analysis with additional hypotheses and empirical tests. It holds that the monetary base is the main determinant of the money stock, which, in turn, is *a good indicator of the thrust of monetary forces.* Furthermore, according to the strong view the monetary base is the proper measure of Federal Reserve monetary actions. Whichever view one adopts, changes in the monetary base are held as ultimately leading to changes in the growth of total demand for goods and services.

There are differences between the two views regarding *the strength and predictability of the influence of monetary forces on economic activity.* The weak view holds that other factors, such as *fiscal actions, or shifts in the demand for goods and services,* also influence to a considerable degree changes in economic activity. As a result, the influence of monetary forces is not very predictable. The strong view recognizes these other influences on economic activity, but maintains that monetary forces are the dominant influence and that their influence is highly predictable.

According to the strong view, if the monetary base were to expand at a trend rate of 6 per cent, total demand would adjust to vary around a trend rate consistent with, but not necessarily the same as, the rate of expansion in the base. If the rate of growth in the monetary base were reduced by monetary authorities, total demand would slow and vary around a lower trend rate. Sources of variations around an established trend in economic activity result from changes in fiscal actions and other independent forces.

Summary

The monetary base can be controlled by the Federal Reserve System and is directly influenced by its actions, even though other economic variables are used as guides by monetary managers. Moreover, reliable data for the source base, the main component of the monetary base, are readily available from the balance sheets of the Federal Reserve System and the Treasury. Monetary managers, therefore, have up-to-date information on the major factors affecting movements in the monetary base. Such knowledge makes it possible for them to offset, by open market operations, movements in these other factors in order to achieve a change in the monetary base appropriate for economic stabilization.

Interpretations of movements in the monetary base are not obscured by short-run movements in Government demand deposits or movements between demand and time deposits. Such movements frequently lead to disagreements among monetary analysts regarding the proper interpretation of changes in the money stock, money plus time deposits, and bank credit. Movements in market interest rates and marginal reserve measures are also subject to these same problems of interpretation.

Whether one takes the weak or the strong view, the Federal Reserve System, by varying the supply of the monetary base, causes commercial banks and the nonbank public to adjust their spending on real and financial assets so as to bring the amount demanded of the base into equilibrium with the amount supplied. In the course of these adjustments, the pace of economic activity is affected.

Three points should be noted: the monetary base is under the *direct control of the Federal Reserve System,* it may be *changed by monetary managers* in a predictable manner, and such changes have *an important influence on output, employment, and prices.* These considerations lead to the conclusion that the monetary base is an important magnitude for those interested in monetary management.

Readings 30 and 31   *First Debate on Monetarism*

For centuries philosophers and economists have noted as no coincidence that vast increases in the supply of money have been accompanied by tremendous increases in the price level. This doctrine became known as the "Quantity Theory of Money." Like many basic ideas, the Quantity Theory became so familiar and began to seem so simple that a later generation of economists became inclined to disparage its significance. In this lecture, Professor Milton Friedman of the University of

Chicago reasserts in an emphatic manner the merits of the Quantity Theory. Professor Friedman, who is a leading spokesman for the University of Chicago School of Libertarian economists, is well known for the brilliance of his analytical and empirical researches; Candidate Barry Goldwater called upon him for economic counsel in the presidential campaign of 1964, and so did Richard Nixon in 1968 and 1972.

The present discussion shows why monetarism now deserves ample investigation. Indeed, later Readings 69 and 70 by Friedman and Heller, along with 71 by Samuelson, carry forward the discussion introduced in the present two readings.

Since the issues dealt with here are quite technical, not every reader can be expected to master every last nuance of the discussions. Intermediate and advanced courses are the places for more exhaustive inquiry into these disputed matters.

Questions to guide the reading

What is the testimony of some of the great galloping inflations of history concerning the role of money? Why does the author doubt that inflation is necessary to promote economic development and growth?

Since total spending depends upon the velocity with which money circulates, what is the evidence that velocity tends to be constant as people allegedly hold the same number of weeks' stock of money?

Check the reasons for the eclipse and comeback of money. Summarize in your words the crucial dispute between monetarists and eclectic post-Keynesians. Could crude Keynesianism be right in 1938 but quite wrong in 1970? Could the crude monetarist position be right at one time and wrong at another?

What are the causal links between Fed action and GNP? Does it matter if V is a constant, or if it is speeded up by higher interest rates? What effects on V would withdrawal of government bonds as result of open-market Fed purchases make? Give an example of a hill of evidence to show M has an effect. Does that mean other actions have no effect? In plain words, what does the St. Louis study claim to show?

Can controlled experiments decide between competing theories? Why not? [Added in proof: Ray Fair of Princeton, reviewing the forecasting errors of a dozen models, reported in 1973 that the St. Louis Fed's monetarist model ended last.] If the 1969 tax surcharge was slow and weak in having effects, is that cogent reason to adopt the rule of a constant rate of growth of the M supply? Do the later Friedman and Heller readings change your opinions about the debate here?

Reading 30

The Quantity Theory of Money Vindicated

Milton Friedman

Like an old-fashioned preacher delivering a Sunday sermon, I can provide the audience with texts for my talks. The text for this talk is "Cherchez la monnaie." By inflation, I shall mean a steady and sustained rise in prices. I shall deal primarily with open inflation, which is to say, an inflationary pro-

From Milton Friedman, *Inflation: Causes and Consequences* (Asia Publishing House, New York, 1963). Copyright by the Council for Economic Education, Bombay, India. Reprinted with kind permission of the author and publisher.

cess in which prices are permitted to rise without being suppressed by Government price controls or similar techniques.

It is widely asserted that inflation is inevitable in a country that is trying to force the pace of development. The argument generally runs something like this. A country that is trying to force the pace of development places heavy pressure upon the available resources. The pressure upon the resources means an increase in demand which can be met only by a rise in prices. In consequence, it is said, the process of development will surely force a rise in prices. This argument, however, confuses *physical* magnitudes with *money* magnitudes. The pressure on resources during the course of development affects relative prices. It tends to make the prices of those things for which the demand is particularly great in the course of development, high compared with the prices of other things. It need not, however, affect the absolute price level.

Everything depends on how the real resources, which are employed in the course of development, are acquired. If the real resources are acquired by Government, for example, through taxes or through borrowing from the public, or if the real resources are acquired by private enterprises and individuals by using their own savings for the purpose of investment, there will be no pressure of monetary demand. There will be a shift of demand away from certain things towards other things, and this will produce the shift in physical resources required. On the other hand, if the printing press, or any of its more sophisticated modern variants, is used to try to acquire resources, then, of course, there will tend to be inflation and price rise. The view that development makes inflation inevitable is misleading and arises from confusing physical magnitudes in the economy with monetary magnitudes.

The phenomenon of prices changing by more than the difference between the change in output and the change in money stock is often observed and the reason is not far to seek. When prices are going down, money becomes a more desirable way in which to hold assets; its value is increasing day by day; hence people have a strong tendency, if they expect the price decline to continue, to hold a larger fraction of their wealth in the form of money. On the other side of the picture, when prices are going up, money becomes a less desirable form in which to hold assets. In consequence, people tend to economise on their money balances; velocity tends to increase. How much velocity will change depends on whether the fall in prices or the rise in prices is anticipated. Generally, when inflation has started after a period of roughly stable prices, people initially do not expect prices to continue rising. They regard the price rise as temporary and expect prices to fall later on. In consequence, they have tended to increase their monetary holdings and the price rise has been less than the rise in the stock of money. Then as people gradually become wise to what is going on, they tend to re-adjust their holdings. Prices then rise more than in proportion to the stock of money. Eventually people come to expect roughly what is happening and prices rise in proportion to the stock of money.

Progress with prices falling

Numerous examples can be cited to demonstrate that inflation is not inevitable in the course of economic development, that it has little or nothing to do with the pressure on real resources, but rather with monetary institutions and the monetary policies which are followed. One of the most dramatic goes back nearly a century to the fifteen years following the Civil War.

During the Civil War itself (1861–65), Government resorted to printing money in order to finance the war—the famous "greenbacks"—with the result that by the end of the war, the price level had more than doubled. The United States wanted to return to the gold standard at the pre-war parity. In order to do this, prices had to be cut in half to bring them into line with prices in the rest of the world. And they were in fact cut in half. The decline owed little to deliberate policies followed by the Government. It was the result rather of an extraordinarily high rate of economic growth in that 15-year period. By all the statistical evidence available, that 15-year period saw a more rapid rate of economic growth than almost any other period in the whole history of the United States. According to the estimates which Simon Kuznets has constructed of income in the United States since 1869, the decade of the 1870s shows a higher rate of growth than any decade from 1869 to 1959.

Kuznets himself thinks, and I agree with him, that his estimates over-state the rise in the early decades. But whatever index you look at, whether the expansion of railroads, increase in traffic on railroads and canals and so on, shows that period to have been a period of very rapid growth. Output considerably more than doubled; and since the stock of money rose only a trifle, prices were cut in half.

I do not cite this example to suggest that declines in prices promote economic growth. I cite it rather because it is such an extreme example to contradict the widely believed notion that a price rise is somehow inevitable, or, if not inevitable, at any rate highly desirable, in order to promote economic growth. In the American case, I do not believe that the decline in prices produced economic growth. On the contrary, it was the economic growth, which had its origin in very different sources, which produced the decline in prices. Neither do I mean to suggest that this experience is a model for anybody to follow. The fall in prices created real difficulties. It stimulated political discontent and controversy; there was a long recession from 1873 to 1879 and so on. Very likely, the economic growth would have been the same if a monetary policy had been followed which would have meant stable prices, and other difficulties would have been less. Yet the fact remains that economic growth was entirely consistent with falling prices.

Other less dramatic examples are ready at hand. In the United States from 1879, when the U.S. went back on gold, to 1896, prices fell at the rate of something like 2 to 3 per cent a year. From 1896 to 1913, prices rose at the rate of something like 2 to 3 per cent a year. Yet these two periods show almost precisely the same rate of economic growth as judged by the growth in national product. Again, in the same period from 1870 to 1890 or 1895, prices were falling in the United Kingdom; from 1890 or 1895 to 1913 prices were rising. Yet the estimates of real national output constructed some years ago show that the rate of increase in output was faster during the period of falling prices than during the period of rising prices. In more recent times, since the end of the second World War, countries like Italy and West Germany have had very rapidly rising outputs with roughly constant or mildly rising prices. Since

something like 1953 or 1954, Greece has had a very rapid rate of economic growth with highly stable prices. In the early years after the War, Japan had a substantial price rise and also a substantial rise in output. Since then, the rise in output has continued but prices have been roughly stable.

I hasten to add that examples can also be cited when rises in prices went along with expansion of output. What I am arguing is not that falling prices are inevitable in the course of economic expansion but only that rising prices are not inevitable, though they may occur. For example, in addition to the cases in the United States and the United Kingdom that I have given, there is the great period of the price revolution in Europe in the 15th and 16th centuries, to which I shall return in another connection. That was a period when the pace of economic development quickened throughout Europe along with a steady and long continued rise in prices. Or again, to take the recent post-war experience, over the past 10 years or so, Israel has been experiencing a rate of price rise of roughly 10 per cent a year—not a negligible rate of price rise by anybody's calculation. Yet it has also experienced a rate of rise in real income of the order of something like 10 per cent a year. So clearly, while inflation is not an inevitable accompaniment of development, neither does it necessarily prevent development. The basic forces making for economic growth are much more fundamental than the question of whether prices are rising or falling.

False causes of inflation

I should like to spend a bit more time examining analytically the causes of inflation because the emphasis I have just been placing on the stock of money as the culprit is widely regarded as old-fashioned and out of date. Most modern writers today attribute inflation to very different kinds of causes. They say it is the result of attempted investment exceeding desired savings; or of a wage push on the part of employees; or of a profit push on the part of employers and entrepreneurs; or of the inability to increase the output of food as rapidly as the increase in output of other things; and so on in infinite variety and diversity. Now these explanations may, in one sense, be correct. If any of these factors produces a rise in the stock of money, it will produce inflation. But if it does not produce a rise in the stock of money, it will not produce inflation.

The reasons why these explanations are so popular are not far to seek. There are, I think, two main reasons. The first is the natural tendency to confuse what is true for the individual with what is true for the society as a whole. The most interesting and important thing about economics as a science is precisely that almost everything that is true for the individual is wrong for the society and almost everything that is true for the society as a whole is wrong for the individual. One individual can affect the price of hardly anything he buys. Yet, all individuals together make the price what it is. In the particular case of inflation, to each individual separately, the price rise is not in any way connected with the fact that somehow or other a printing press has been turning out those loose pieces of paper we like to carry around in our pockets. The individual entrepreneur raises his prices because, on the one hand, his costs have gone up and, on the other, he finds he can still sell his product at higher prices. We never see the fact that that higher price in turn is ultimately the result of the creation of more money. That is one reason. A second and equally important reason is that, so far as the printing of money is concerned, in modern days, the Government has a near-monopoly.

Nobody likes to blame himself for bad things that occur. Though many people like inflation because it helps them personally, nonetheless almost everyone thinks it is a bad thing on the whole and nobody likes to admit that he is responsible for inflation. It is far easier for Government to attribute inflation to the profiteers, or the bad trade unions that insist on pushing up the wages, or the intractability of agricultural producers who are unable to expand food than it is for Government or government officials to say, *mea culpa*.

Keynesian fallacies

Though these are the two main reasons why inflation tends to be attributed to everything except money, there is a third supplementary reason which has been especially important in the last 20 years or so. That is something that happened purely in the intellectual sphere, namely, the Keynesian revolution in economic thought in the 1930s, which led many economists to reduce the role assigned to money. The reason why I think that it is not really a basic explanation is because the emphasis on non-monetary explanations is not a new thing. One can go back one or two thousand years and more and find that every time there is inflation, two explanations are offered. One explanation is that the amount of money has increased. The other explanation is that something special has happened: wage-earners have pushed up their wages; profiteers have been active; there has been a blockade of the country and as a result supplies could not come in; and so on and on.

As I have already noted, these two separate explanations are not necessarily contradictory. The non-monetary factors may, on some occasions, be the cause of the monetary expansion.

One thing is clear from the historical record. The actual sources of monetary expansion have been very different at different times and in different places. Hence, if a theory of inflation is going to deal not with the expansion of the stock of money but with what brought it about, it will be a very pluralistic theory which will have many possible sources of inflation. For example, in the early days, when actual coin was the medium of circulation, inflations tended to be produced by such devices as sweating and clipping.

A modern technological invention has largely put an end to that particular source of inflation, the invention being the milling of coins. In addition, the use of pieces of paper, bank notes, instead of actual coins, has also reduced opportunities for that kind of inflation. Another source of expansion in the nominal stock of money has been what the history books always refer to as "crying up" or "crying down" the nominal value of money. Again, a major source of inflation in the past has been discovery of new sources of gold or of silver, or technological changes which have increased the possibility of extracting silver or gold from ores. Printing money to pay for war has always been one of the major sources of inflation. Full employment policy is, however, a modern invention for producing inflation.

Cherchez la monnaie

Whenever these or other factors have led to a substantially greater expansion in the stock of money than the current rate of increase in output, they have led to inflation. If you are going to regard them as causes, you will, as I said, be fated to have many explanations. I know of no exception to the proposition that there has been a one to one relation between substantial rises in prices and substantial rises in the stock of money.

Why should money be so critical a factor in price level behaviour? Why should it occupy such a central role in the process? The key to an answer is the difference between the *nominal* quantity of money, the quantity of money expressed in terms of rupees, dollars, or marks or what have you, and the *real* quantity of money, the quantity of money expressed in terms of the goods and services it will buy or the number of weeks of income it is equal to.

People seem to be extraordinarily stubborn about the real amount of money that they want to hold and are unwilling to hold a different amount, unless there is a real incentive to do so. This is true not only over time but over space. Let me give a few striking figures. I shall refer only to currency in circulation, excluding deposits, since currency is more comparable among the countries I want to deal with.

In India, the amount of currency that is held by people amounts to roughly seven weeks' income. That is to say, if you calculate the aggregate income received by all Indians during a seven weeks' period, the resulting sum is roughly equal to the amount of currency that is held by all the people and all the business enterprises in India.

Let us now turn to Yugoslavia, a country that is vastly different in many respects from India. Yugoslavia has a Communist Government and extensive centralised control over economic activity. It has a different kind of agriculture, different social customs and traditions. Yet the people of Yugoslavia hold in the form of currency something like 6¼ weeks' income, remarkably close to the figure for India.

Greece is a royalist country with a king and queen and a very different economic structure from either Yugoslavia or India. Yet its people hold in the form of currency almost the same amount as in Yugoslavia, a little over 6 weeks' income. In Turkey, they hold a little over 5 weeks' income. In the United States, they hold about 4¼ weeks' income in the form of currency. In Israel they hold about 4¼ weeks' income also, although the level of income in Israel is one-third or one-

quarter of that in the United States. Here we have countries with every variety of economic system, with real incomes varying over a range of 15 or 20 to one and yet currency holdings, expressed in terms of weeks' income, vary over a range of decidedly less than 2 to 1.

How money affects prices

Given that people are so stubborn about the amount they hold in the form of money, let us suppose that, for whatever reasons, the amount of money in a community is higher than people want to hold at the level of prices then prevailing. They find that although on the average they would like to hold, let us say, the 7 weeks' income that they hold in India, they are actually holding, say, 8 weeks' income. What will happen? Here again it is essential to distinguish between what happens to the individual and what happens to the community. Each individual separately thinks he can get rid of his money and he is right. He can go out and spend it and thereby reduce his cash balances. But for the community as a whole the belief that cash balances can be reduced is an optical illusion. The only reason I can reduce my cash balances in nominal terms is because somebody else is willing to increase his. One man's expenditures are another man's receipts. People as a whole cannot spend more than they as a whole receive. In consequence, if everybody in the community tries to cut the nominal amount of his cash balances, they will on the average be frustrated. The amount of nominal balances is fixed by the nominal quantity of money in existence and no game of musical chairs can change it. But people can and will try to reduce their cash balances and the process of trying will have important effects. In the process of trying to spend more than they are receiving, people will bid up the prices of all sorts of goods and services. Nominal incomes will rise and real cash balances will indeed be reduced, even though nominal balances are not affected. The rise in prices and incomes will bring cash balances from 8 weeks' income to 7 weeks' income. People will succeed in achieving their objective, but by raising prices and incomes rather than by reducing nominal balances. In the process, prices will have risen by about an eighth. This in a nutshell is the process whereby changes in the stock of money exert their influence on the price level.

Reading 31

Monetarism Objectively Evaluated

Paul A. Samuelson

There are fashions within science. Nowhere is the oscillating pendulum of opinion more marked in the field of economics than in the area of money. By the end of the 1930s, after the so-called Keynesian revolution, courses and textbooks continued to be devoted to money. But in fact money had almost completely dropped out of them and the emphasis had shifted to analysis of income determination in terms of such Keynesian concepts as the multiplier and the propensity to consume.

Comeback of money

If the market quotation for monetary theory sagged in the decade after 1936, by the early 1950s there were unmistakable signs of a comeback. It was Professor Howard S. Ellis of the University of California who coined in those years the expression, "the rediscovery of money." And the famous Accord of 1951, which gave back to the Federal Reserve its freedom to pursue an autonomous monetary policy independently of the needs and desires of President Truman's Treasury, was the objective counterpart of the reappearance of money in the theoretical models of academic scholars.

Of course, we cannot expect recovery to take place at the same time in all markets. Within Britain, the historic home of central banking, the news of the revival of money was late in coming; and even later in being believed. As recently as 1959 the prestigious Radcliffe Report, technically known as the Committee on the Working of the Monetary System, devoted upwards of 3½ million words to the subject. Yet the unanimous conclusion of this distinguished group of British academics and men of finance was, in the end, that money as such did not matter.

Often, if a stock goes down too far in *price,* in reaction it may subsequently go up too far. There

is danger of this in the case of monetary theory. A crude monetarism is now stalking the land. In the present article I wish to provide a scientifically objective evaluation of the issues and a balanced history of the oscillations in monetary doctrines.

Friedman and the Chicago School

Undoubtedly the popularity of monetarism can be traced in large part to one man, namely Professor Milton Friedman of the University of Chicago. His monumental *Monetary History of the United States, 1867–1960,* written with Mrs. Anna Schwartz, is the bible of the movement; and let me say as an infidel that it is a classic source of data and analysis to which all scholars will turn for years to come. In addition to this scholarly work, Professor Friedman has published numerous statistical studies in learned economic journals. He has testified before Congress and lectured before lay groups. His influential columns in *Newsweek* and writings for the financial press have hammered away at one simple message:

It is the rate of growth of the money supply that is the prime determinant of the state of aggregate dollar demand. If the Federal Reserve will keep the money supply growing at a steady rate—say 4 to 5 percent by one or another definition of the money supply, but the fact of steadiness being more important than the rate agreed upon—then it will be doing all a central bank can usefully do to cope with the problems of inflation, unemployment, and business instability.

Fiscal policy as such has no independent, systematic effect upon aggregate dollar demand. Increasing tax rates, but with the understanding that money growth remains unchanged, *will have no effect* in lessening the degree of inflation; it will have no *independent* effect in increasing the level of unemployment in a period of deflation; changes in public expenditure out of the budget (it being understood that the rate of growth of the money supply is held unchanged) will also have *no lasting effects on inflationary or deflationary gaps.*

In the past, budgetary deficits and budgetary surpluses have often been accompanied by central bank creation of new money or deceleration of growth of new money. Therefore, many people have wrongly inferred that fiscal deficits and surpluses have *predictable* expansionary and contracting effects upon the total of aggregate spending. But this is a complete confusion. *It is the changes in the rate of growth of the money supply which alone have substantive effects.* After we have controlled or allowed for monetary changes, fiscal policy has negligible independent potency.[1]

This is my summary of the Friedman-type monetarism. No doubt he would word things somewhat differently. And I should like to emphasize that there are many qualifications in his scientific writing which do not logically entail the *simpliste* version of monetarism outlined above. Indeed it is one of the purposes of this article to demonstrate and emphasize the point that the weight of the evidence on money, theoretical and empirical, does not imply the correctness of crude monetarism.

Among the central bankers of the world, financial journalists, statesmen and politicians, business and academic economists, and men of affairs generally, monetarism seems almost paradoxically simple and perverse. Can President Nixon really suppose that it makes no difference for the control of the 1969–70 American inflation, whether or not he proposes to extend into 1970 the tax surcharge? Professor Friedman is but one of his advisers, and it is evident that Paul McCracken, Chairman of the Council of Economic Advisers, and Arthur F. Burns, the new chairman of the Federal Reserve

Board named by Nixon, do *not* see eye to eye with Friedman in this matter.

Yet Professor Friedman does not stand alone. His mountains of data, cogency of reasoning, and formidable powers of patient persuasion have raised unto him a host of followers. Graduates of the Chicago workshops in monetary theory carry to new universities the message. A number of other scholars, such as Professors Allan Meltzer at Carnegie-Mellon University in Pittsburgh and Karl Brunner of Ohio State University, have also produced research in support of monetarism. Professor Harry Johnson leads the campaign to export monetarism to the British Isles. One of our twelve regional Federal Reserve Banks, that of St. Louis, has carried the torch for monetarism, providing up-to-date numerical information on the vagaries of the money supply, and promoting quantitative research on the lagged potency of money. Distinguished graduates of the University of Chicago, such as Dr. Beryl Sprinkel of the Harris Trust Company Bank in Chicago, and Dr. James Meigs, of the First National City Bank of New York, profess to be monetarists who improve the accuracy of their business forecasts by concentrating primarily on money. At one time or another the editorial pages of the influential *Washington Post* and *New York Times* have become permeated by monetarism. Finally, the Joint Economic Committee of Congress, when it was under the chairmanship of Senator William Proxmire, reacted strongly against the use of fiscal policy as a stabilization device, and recommended to the Federal Reserve Board that it never permit the money supply to grow at rates widely different from some agreed-upon constant.

Keynes and Keynesians

Thus monetarism is a movement to reckon with. I believe monetarism could be deemed fruitful, to the degree that it has pushed economists away from a *simpliste* Keynesian model, popular in the United States during the Great Depression and still lingering on in Britain, and made economists more willing to recognize that monetary policy is an important stabilization weapon, fully coordinate with fiscal policy as a macro-economic control instrument. However, my reading of the development of modern economic doctrine does

---

[1] Professor Friedman is careful to specify that fiscal policy does have important effects upon the *composition* of any given total of gross national product. Thus increases in government expenditures will pull resources out of the private sector into the public. John Kenneth Galbraith might like this but Milton Friedman does not. Also, increasing taxation relative to public expenditure, although having no independent effect on aggregate demand, will tend to lower consumption and reduce interest rates. This contrived increase in thriftiness will move the mix of full-employment output in the direction of more rapid capital formation; it will speed up the rate of growth of productivity and real output, and will increase the rate of growth of real wages. If the trend of the money supply remains unchanged, this will tend toward a lower price level in the future or a less rapidly rising one. (See the introduction to Reading 69 for Friedman's exact wording.)

not suggest to me that the post-Keynesian position that I myself hold, and of which Professor James Tobin of Yale and Franco Modigliani of M.I.T. are leading exponents, has been materially influenced by monetarism. Indeed, speaking for myself, the excessive claims for money as an exclusive determinant of aggregate demand would, if anything, have slowed down and delayed my appreciation of money's true quantitative and qualitative role.[2]

Keynes vs. Keynesians

Although the neglect of money is often said to be a characteristic of Keynesian economists and a heritage of the analysis in Keynes' 1936 classic *General Theory of Employment, Interest and Money,* it is doubtful that Keynes himself can be properly described as ever having believed that "money does not matter." If one writes down in the form of equations or graphs the boney structure of the *General Theory,* he sees that money enters into the liquidity-preference function in such a way that an increase in the money supply lowers interest rates, thereby inducing an increase in investment, and through multiplier mechanism causes a rise in employment and production, or, if employment is already full and output at capacity levels, causes upward pressure on the price level.

For a quarter of a century before 1936, Keynes was the principal exponent of monetary theory and the inheritor of the Cambridge tradition of Marshall and Pigou. Although the *General Theory* did represent the repudiation of some of the doctrines Keynes espoused in his 1930 *Treatise on Money,* it represented a continuation and culmination of many of those monetary doctrines. At frequent intervals in the last decade before Keynes' death in 1946, he affirmed and reaffirmed in print

and private correspondence his faith that, if the long-term interest rate could be brought down low enough, monetary policy could play an effective role in curing depression and stagnation.[3]

Post-Keynesianism

How is it that some Keynesians should ever have become identified with the doctrine that money does not matter? Most converts to Keynesianism became converts during the slump years of the late 1930s. Then the deep-depression polar case did seem to be the realistic case. It is a sad fact about many scholars that they learn and unlearn nothing after the age of 29, so that there exist in chairs of economics around the world many economists who still live mentally in the year 1938. For 1938, when the interest rate on Treasury Bills was often a fraction of a fraction of a fraction of a percent, even a monetarist might despair of the potency of central bank monetary policy.

As one who lived through those times, I can testify by recall how money got lost so that it could later be rediscovered. First, multiple correlation studies by people like Jan Tinbergen, of the Netherlands, who pioneered for the League of Nations macrodynamic models of the business cycle, invariably found that such variables as interest rates turned up with *zero or perversely-signed weights in their estimating equations.* Second, case studies at the Harvard Business School and elsewhere invariably registered the result that *the cost and availability of credit was not a significant determinant of business behavior and investment.* Third,

---

[2] To clarify my point, let me state my belief that Professor Friedman has been a force of the first magnitude in getting economists generally to realize the desirability of flexible exchange rates. He, and Professors Frank Knight and Henry Simons at Chicago before him, deserve an honored place in the history of economic thought in influencing economists to appreciate the merits of market pricing as against direct government interventions. But I do not believe that the positions today of the Tobins and Modiglianis of the modern scene would be very different if a Chicago School had never existed.

[3] When an author writes as much as did Keynes, it is inevitable that certain of his passages might seem to contradict others. There are *some* of his paragraphs written in the 1930s that do seem to play down the quantitative potency of monetary policy in times of deep depression. And those many writers, such as Sir John Hicks, Sir Roy Harrod, Professor James Meade, and the late Oskar Lange, who have codified the *General Theory* in the form of simple equations and graphs, are able to formulate a "deep-depression" polar case in which money does not matter (either because the liquidity-preference schedule displays infinite elasticity at a "liquidity trap," or the marginal efficiency schedule of investment displays complete inelasticity to interest rate changes). But note that this is not the general case of the *General Theory,* but only a special polar case, just as the classical quantity theory of money is the special case at the opposite pole.

large-scale questionnaire surveys, like those emanating from Oxford and associated with the names of Sir Robert Hall, Sir Hubert Henderson, Sir Roy Harrod, Charles Hitch, and Phillip Andrews, uniformly recorded answers denying the importance of interest rates and monetary conditions. Fourth, as Professor Alvin Hansen and other contemporary writers noted, the inflow to the States of billions of dollars of gold resulting from distrust of Hitler's Europe, produced almost a controlled experiment in which the reserves of the banking system were vastly expanded and yet no commensurate expansion in business activity or even in the total money supply was achieved. Finally, it was fashionable in those days for theorists to argue that interest was a negligible cost where short-term investment projects were involved, and where long-term projects were involved the irreducible uncertainties of expectations served to dwarf the importance of the interest rate as a controlling variable.

However realistic it may have been in the 1930s to denigrate the importance of money, and with hindsight I do believe that even this may have been overdone, still in the high-employment epoch that is characteristic of the post-World War II years there was little excuse to remain frozen in an archaic denial of money. This is not the place to sketch in detail the evolution of post-Keynesian analysis. Already in the war years, Professor Modigliani in a justly famous article had shown the logical need for placing greater emphasis upon stocks as against flows than had been done by the *General Theory* and its first commentators.

Professor Pigou, in a handsome recantation of his first rejection of the *General Theory,* supplied in the 1940s an important influence of the real money stock as it acts directly on the propensity to consume even in the absence of the interest rate effects that had been recognized in the *General Theory.* Recognition of this "Pigou effect" served to reconcile the deep cleavage between neoclassical theory and the Keynesian revolution: theoretically a sufficiently large decline in the wage rate and the price level could, with a fixed quantum of money, restore full employment; practically no one—and certainly not Pigou—advocated such hyper-deflation as a practicable program to combat unemployment.

How it works

By the 1950s and 1960s a body of analysis and data had been accumulated which led to a positive, strong belief that open-market and discount operations by the central bank could have *pronounced macroeconomic effects upon investment and consumption spending in the succeeding several months and quarters.* One of the principal preoccupations of the post-Keynesian economists, which is to say of the ruling orthodoxy of American establishment economics, has been to trace out the *causal* mechanisms whereby monetary and fiscal variables produce their effects upon the total of spending and its composition.

Thus, an open-market purchase of Treasury bills by the Fed first bids up bond prices and lowers their yield; this spreads to *a reduction* in *yields* on competing securities, such as longer-term government bonds or corporate bonds or home mortgages. The lowering of interest costs will typically be accompanied by *a relaxation in the degree of credit rationing,* and this can be expected *to stimulate investment spending* that would otherwise not have taken place. The lowering of interest rates generally also brings about an *upward capitalization of the value of existing assets,* and this increase in the money value of wealth can be expected to have a certain *expansionary influence on consumer spending,* and in a degree on business spending for investment. As a limit upon the stimulus stemming from money creation by orthodox open-market operations, must be reckoned the fact that as the central bank pumps new money into the system, it is in return taking from the system *an almost equal quantum of money substitutes* in the form of government securities. In a sense the Federal Reserve or the Bank of England is merely a dealer in second-hand assets, contriving transfer exchanges of one type of asset for another, and in the process affecting the interest rate structure that constitutes the terms of trade among them.

What needs to be stressed is the fact that one cannot expect money created by this process of central-bank open-market operations *alone,* with say the fiscal budget held always in balance, to have at all the same functional relationship to the level of the GNP and of the price index that could be the case for money created by gold mining or money created by the printing press of national governments or the Fed and used to finance public expenditures in excess of tax receipts. Not only would the creation of these last kinds of money involve a flow of production and spendable income in their very *act of being born,* but in addition the community would be *left permanently richer* in its ownership of monetary wealth. In money terms the community *feels* richer, in money terms the community *is* richer. And this can be expected to reflect itself in a higher price level or a lower rate of unemployment or both.

By contrast, money created through conventional central-bank operations quite divorced from the financing of fiscal deficits or the production of mining output does not entail an equivalent permanent increase in net wealth as viewed by people in the community. Post-Keynesians emphasize that extinguishing the outstanding interest-bearing public debt, whether by a capital levy or by open-market purchase of it, does rationally make the community *feel poorer* than would be the case if the same amount of money existed and the public debt had been unreduced. All men are mortal. Most men do not concern themselves with the wellbeing of their remote posterity. Hence, government bonds as an asset are not completely offset in their minds by the recognition of the liability of paying in perpetuity taxes to carry the interest on those bonds. Only if people live forever, foreseeing correctly the tax payments they (or the posterity as dear to them in the most remote future as is their own lifetime wellbeing) must make on account of the perpetual future interest payments on government bonds—only then would it be true to say that retirement of public debt would have no substantive effects upon the reckoning of wealth, the levels of spending, and the level of prices generally. Rejecting such a perpetual-life model as extreme and unrealistic, we must debit against an increase in money through open-market operations a partial offset in the form of retirement of some of the outstanding public debt.

Finally, to clarify the significant difference between the post-Keynesian analysis which most modern economists believe to be plausible as against the tenets of monetarism, I must point out that even when the money supply is held constant:

1. Any significant changes in thriftiness and the propensity to consume can be expected to have systematic independent effects on the money value of current output, affecting average prices or aggregate production or both.

2. Likewise an exogenous burst of investment opportunities or animal spirits on the part of business can be expected to have systematic effects on total GNP.

3. Increases in public expenditure, or reductions in tax rates—and even increases in public expenditure balanced by increases in taxation—can be expected to have systematic effects upon aggregate GNP.

All these tenets of the modern eclectic position are quite incompatible with monetarism. (Indeed that is the differentiating definition by which we distinguish the Chicago School monetarism from the post-Keynesian positions with which it has so much overlap.) The eclectic position is incompatible with monetarism, but it is not incompatible with a *sophisticated* version of the Quantity Theory of Money. For as soon as one follows the logic of neoclassical analysis (expecting that less of any kind of inventory will be held if, other things equal, the cost of holding it has gone up) and postulates that the *velocity of circulation of money is a rising function of the interest rate,* the post-Keynesian (and even the simple Keynesian) model becomes compatible with the Quantity Theory. One way of looking at Keynesian liquidity preference is as *a theory of the velocity of circulation.*

Faulty logic

When post-Keynesians study recent economic history, they find that interest rates and money do enter into their estimating equations and with the theoretically expected algebraic signs. Case studies bear out the importance of investment decisions of the cost and availability of credit. Properly phrased questionnaires to business elicit answers that point in the same direction. And plausible theories to explain how businessmen make their investment decisions and how they ought to also bear out the fact that monetary policy does matter. So there is simply no excuse for living in a 1938 dream world in which money does not matter.

The bearing of all this on monetarism is well illustrated by an incident a few years ago at an American Bankers Association symposium where leading academic economists were commenting upon Professor Friedman's writings. Professor James Tobin went to the blackboard and wrote down three sentences:

1. MONEY DOES NOT MATTER.
2. MONEY MATTERS.
3. MONEY ALONE MATTERS.

He went on to say: Professor Friedman produces evidence to prove that the first proposition, Money doesn't matter, is false: he purports to have demonstrated from this that the third proposition, Money alone matters, is true; whereas the correct logical conclusion is that the second proposition, Money does matter, is all that follows. And on that there is no quarrel among leading modern macroeconomic economists.

Power and cogency of relevant evidence. I think there is much wisdom in this. When Professor Friedman defends monetarism, as for example in a late-1968 debate at New York University with new economist Walter Heller [see Reading 70], he refers to a mountain of evidence that supports monetarism. But how many members of the thousands in the overflow crowd attending that debate were able to appraise that evidence to see whether it supports the proposition 2, that money matters, rather than the central tenet of monetarism, that (when it comes to predictable systematic effects on aggregate demand and on inflationary or deflationary gaps) money alone matters? Sir Ronald Fisher, the greatest statistician of our age, pointed out that replication a thousandfold of an inconclusive experiment does nothing to add to its value. In terms of the language of statistics, most of the evidence compiled about money has little or no power to differentiate between propositions 2 and 3. Let me illustrate.

Anecdotes about incidents. A typical bit of historical evidence put forth to support monetarism goes like the following. "In 1919, after World War I, the U.S. Treasury wished to stabilize the interest rate. Keeping the Discount Rate constant resulted in a great increase in the money supply and in strong inflation. Then, early in 1920 on an identifiable date, the Treasury changed its policy; there followed a sharp reduction in the growth of the money supply; there followed a collapse of prices and the Recession of 1920-21. Ergo mone-

tarism is true." But surely, for our purpose, this is a complete *non sequitur*. If we accept the chronology as given, it should indeed give pause to some witness before the Radcliffe Committee who argues that money never matters. But a whole range of mountains of evidence of this type does not tell us whether other factors—such as fiscal policy— may not also have an independent influence on the pace of inflation. Replicating a refutation does not add commensurately to its weight, so I shall forebear from giving other examples of similar reasoning.

Cyclical leads and lags. But let me mention a different kind of evidence sometimes adduced for monetarism. The rate of change of the money supply precedes by 16 months or so, on the average but with great variance, the turndowns in the business cycle. Now it is easy to show that this set of facts fits in as well with an ultra-Keynesian model as with an ultra-Friedman model. Indeed in an unpublished paper, Professor Tobin has shown that the kind of Keynesian model that only a Radcliffe Committee member could still believe in does *better* than the monetarist model in fitting those facts. And let me add that those facts on timing are not very impressive facts. Those who play seriously the game of looking for leading indicators to predict business activity find the money-change series only one of many straws to indicate the way the wind is blowing. And not one of the more useful straws. Moreover, according to the most thorough studies, those by Dr. Geoffrey Moore of the National Bureau of Economic Research and Dr. Julius Shiskin of the U.S. Census Bureau, the money-change indicator has been scoring less well in recent decades than in earlier times.

Actually, in the 50 years since Warren Persons of Harvard initiated these leads and lags studies, the stock of money always tended to be one of the laggards rather than leaders in business cycle findings. Instead of turning up in the *A* group of leaders, money and interest rates tended to appear in the *C* group of laggards. Subsequent work by Arthur F. Burns and Moore at the National Bureau tended to confirm this finding. Indeed it is only in recent years that research is beginning to show signs that Money itself turns down and up as early as, or before, general GNP does—and, ironically, I believe this is probably to be explained by the fact that the Federal Reserve has been disregarding the advice of the monetarists and has tried to do some advance forecasting so that it can lean against the winds of recession before they begin to blow very hard.

What does a monetarist do when confronted with the fact that his causal factor, money, does not empirically lead his response factor, general business? One desperate artifice is to change his focus from the *stock* of money to its *time derivative, its rate of growth.* It is a mathematical fact that any periodic fluctuation that behaves a bit like a sine curve will have its derivative turndown a quarter cycle before itself; so if money itself does not lag business by as much as one quarter, one cannot help but get some lead at turning points by using the rate of change of money. But by that kind of frivolous action, one could use the derivative of production, its rate of change, to predict the turning points of the stock of money: or, with recognition of noise in the data, use production's own rate of change to predict its turning points.

Dimensional traps.   Obviously, we have to find the reason for using dM/dt, the rate of change of money, rather than M, the stock of money, as our causal variable. One ridiculous argument for using the former is dimensional: both the level of GNP and the rate of growth of the money supply are measured in terms of dollars *per year.* Therefore, relate GNP and dM/dt, not GNP and M. This argument is ridiculous because the whole basis of the quantity theory of money is that V, the velocity of circulation of money or its reciprocal, is the dimensional constant that exists to relate the stock of money and the flow of national product. Professor Friedman, more than any other modern economist, has sloshed through the mountains of Yugoslavia to demonstrate that every peasant holds seventeen-weeks' purchasing power in his pockets. The whole demand-for-money concept is for the purpose of making hypotheses about how that number 17 will change when interest rates, branch banking, or price expectations change. Moreover, there is involved a profound misunderstanding of how dimensional analysis is to be used in any science. The behavioral equation of a simple pendulum has for its very purpose the relating of two dimensionally different magnitudes—the

position of the pendulum as measured in centimeters or dimensionless angular degrees and its acceleration as measured in centimeters per time squared. Nor is this a special example: Newton's universal law of gravitation, the greatest system of the world produced by man's thoughts, relates dimensionally different magnitudes in precisely the way that Dr. Friedman criticizes.

Trial by simple correlation.   Let me mention one last kind of evidence that allegedly bears out the position of monetarism. Dr. Friedman, with the collaboration of Dr. David Meiselman, prepared for our Commission on Money and Credit a comparison of which does better for prediction: a simple correlation of money with GNP, or a simple correlation of some kind of Keynesian multiplicand with GNP or a related measure. They end up with a somewhat larger Pearsonian correlation coefficient for money. Ergo, monetarism is correct; Keynesianism has been defeated in a trial of honor. In my view this is simply silly. I waive the fact that the choice of variables and periods selected for the study has been subject to much criticism and debate. The post-Keynesian position which I adhere to does not believe in either of the simple theories set up as straw men, and is not particularly interested in which has the higher simple correlation coefficient. Even the St. Louis Federal Reserve Bank, a bastion of monetarism, when it came to compare either simple theory with an eclectic combination of both—which was still, in my eyes, an overly simple model and not one optimally formulated at that—they found that there was a statistically significant reduction in unexplained variance from a combination of the two simple theories.

The St. Louis Fed studies

I do not wish to conclude with the impression that there is no possible evidence that would convert me to monetarism. Its tenets are clear cut and are operationally refutable in principle. Thus, a November 1968 study by the St. Louis Federal Reserve Bank, using what is technically called a reduced-form 4-quarter lagged regression model, found that money had a significant positive effect on GNP in the 1952-68 sample period. Tax-rate changes had no significant effect. Public-expenditure changes had weak positive effects for two quarters, followed by weak negative effects two quarters later that wiped out any net steady-state effect. Now I do not believe that such a reduced form analysis correctly specifies the macroeconomic model that needs to be estimated. But if it were not for this fundamental and fatal objection, I would say that evidence like this does have a bearing on whether proposition 3 of the monetarists or proposition 2 of the post-Keynesians is more correct. Although space does not permit a proper evaluation of the St. Louis study here, I shall devote a few words to it because it is the only part of the mountains of evidence that are advanced in favor of monetarism that would, if it were correct, have power and relevance in favor of the monetarist position that the money supply alone matters. As already seen, all the other evidence is germane only to the nondisputed issue as to whether it is true that money does not at all matter.

First, it is at first blush impressive that by money alone one can at least retroactively "explain" in the usual multiple-correlation sense about half the total variance in the change in GNP. But when one examines the whole sample, inclusive of the fifties and the sixties, one sees that all the good fit is in the sixties. The multiple-correlation coefficient (R^2 to be technical) is not at all large in the fifties. We thus are confronted essentially with only one epoch, one experiment upon which to base our new monistic faith in monetarism. And those of us who know the 1960s, who were part of the decisions made and who have a much more intimate feel for the causations than can be given in one crude statistical time series, cannot in accordance with the best modern theories of Bayesian inference believe that the 1960s are best understood in terms of a "money only matters" model. (Specifically, our cross-sectional judgmental data suggest that if Kennedy had frozen the budget at a low balanced level and then made the M supply grow as it did, the vector of economic development would have been very different—in contrast to a crude use of the St. Louis reduced-form equations.)

Second, the so-called reduced-form technique of the St. Louis multiple correlation cannot hope to identify correctly the true causal role of fiscal and monetary policy. I have used that technique on

fabricated examples in which money did not alone matter, and it has given the false answer that money does alone matter. Gramlich, Gramley, Davis, and a number of other writers have criticized it on this account and have suggested alternatives. Not all the criticisms prove to be telling, but I believe that when all the record is in the eclectic position will be the only tenable one.

Third, it is a logical corollary of the monetarist interpretation of events itself that the St. Louis study should exaggerate the potency of money. Friedman, Meiselman, Meltzer and Brunner, numerous St. Louis Fed writers have all insisted that the Federal Reserve tends to commit the crime of trying to stabilize interest rates rather than the rate of growth of the money supply. Ad nauseam they charge the Fed with an excessive preoccupation with the false criterion of net free reserves. Well, let us take them at their word. As Tobin says, they cannot have it both ways. What would be the consequence of applying the St. Louis reduced-form technique to a model in which the Fed committed the crime of increasing M whenever an exogenous upthrust in GNP tended to destabilize interest rates? Suppose we contrive a model in which money doesn't matter at all but in which the Fed has a criminal fascination for net free reserves and all the other magnitudes that the monetarists abhor and warn against? The answer is this: "Where M does not matter, the St. Louis technique will infer that it really does matter! Where M matters a little, the St. Louis methods will be biased toward the verdict that M matters much, or exclusively." I myself do not conclude from this that the St. Louis studies are of no interest. Indeed they are the only fresh evidence I have seen in 15 years; the rest is persuasive rehash of what has not been in doubt in sophisticated circles. But all the evidence leads me to the prediction that mechanisms like those in the FRB-MIT model of Professor Modigliani will prove to be most useful for description and policy.

Crucial tests in 1966–1967 and 1968–1969

Personally, as a scientist, I would cheerfully accept *any hypothesis that would deliver the goods and explain the facts.* As a fallible human being, I do not relish having to change my mind but if economists had to hang from the ceiling in order to do their job, then there would be nothing for it than to do so. But monetarism does not deliver the goods. I could make a fortune giving good predictions to large corporations and banks based on monetarism if it would work. But I have tried every version of it. And none do.

To this there are two standard answers. The first is that nothing works well. Fine tuning is an illusion. There is much "noise" in the data. No one can claim that monetarism would enable the Federal Reserve to iron out all the variation in the economy. All we can say for it is that stabilizing the growth rate of money is the best policy that the ingenuity of man can ever arrive at. All this involves what I call the chipmunk syndrome. The nimble monetarist sticks his neck out in an occasional prediction: that prediction is not always free of ambiguity, but it does seem to point qualitatively in one direction, often a direction counter to the conventional wisdom of the moment: then if subsequent events do seem to go in the indicated direction, the prediction is trumpeted to be a feather in the cap of monetarism. If, as is happening all the time, events do not particularly go in that direction—or if as happens often, events go somewhat in a direction that neither competing theory has been subjected to a test of any resolving power—the chipmunk pulls in his head, saying that there is no way of fine tuning the economy or making completely accurate predictions.

The other argument against the view that monetarism simply does not work is the assertion, "Monetarism does work. So and so at the Blank bank uses it and he beats the crowd in batting average." I believe this to be a serious and important subject for investigation. Let me therefore, because of space limitations, confine myself to a few observations based upon preliminary investigations of the matter.

1. Those analysts who use their monetarism *neat* really do *not* perform well.

2. A number of bank economists, who give great weight to the money factor but who *also* pay attention to what is happening to defense spending and inventories and a host of other factors, seem to me to have compiled an excellent record at forecasting. Not a perfect record. Who has a perfect record? And not, as far as quantitative studies known to me suggest, a better record than the best macroeconomic forecasters who do not con-

sciously put special stress on the money factor (but who do not neglect it either!). In short, it is impossible to separate "flair" in forecasting from success attributable primarily to use of money-supply variables.

3. The years 1966–67 are often referred to as years of a crucial test in which monetarism defeated Keynesianism. I have gone over all the main forecasts used by both schools during that period and I must report that this is a misapprehension. There was *wide range* of forecasts by practitioners of both schools: there was a *wide overlap* between these two ranges. On the whole, the monetarists averaged better and *earlier* in their perception of the slowdown beginning to be seen in late 1966 in consequence of the money crunch of 1966. And one would expect this to be the case from an eclectic viewpoint since the independent variable of money received the biggest alteration in *that* period. But many of the monetarists went overboard in predicting a recession in 1967 of the National Bureau type: indeed some of the more astute monetarists warned their brethren against following the logic of the method, lest it discredit the method! And some of the largest squared errors of estimate for 1967 that I have in my files came from dogmatic monetarists who did not heed the warning from inside their own camp.

4. Again, the year 1969 is thought by some to provide a test of some power between the two theories. Yet I, who am an eclectic, have my own GNP forecast for the year nicely bracketed by the two banks that have been most successful in the past in using monetarism in their projections. And though I must admit that the last part of 1968 was stronger than those who believe in the potency of fiscal policy and the mid-1969 tax surcharge to be, I do not interpret that extra strength as being a negation of any such potency or as due solely or primarily to the behavior of money during the last 12 months. Without the tax surcharge, I believe the GNP would have surprised us by soaring even faster above predictions. Since history cannot be rerun to perform controlled experiments, I cannot prove this. But the weight of all the evidence known to me does point in this direction. In a soft science like economics, that is all even the best practitioner can say.

Conclusion

The bulk of my remarks have been critical of an overly simple doctrine of monetarism. But they must not be interpreted as supporting the view that money does not matter. There are parts of the world, particularly in Britain and the Commonwealth, where it might be better to believe in overly simple monetarism than in overly simple denial of the role of money.

In the *Sunday Telegraph* (London, December 15, 1968) I was able to invert the Tobin syllogisms to isolate the fatal flaw in the reasoning of the Radcliffe Report. The Radcliffe Committee heard much convincing testimony to show that there ex-isted no invariable velocity of circulation of money to enable one to predict GNP accurately from the money supply alone. In effect then, Radcliffe established the falsity of Tobin's third proposition, Money alone matters. And, in a *non sequitur,* they concluded the truth of his first proposition, that Money does not matter. For all their talking around the subject of liquidity as a substitute concept for money alone, they and the fossil-Keynesians who hailed their report should have recognized the fact that both theory and experience give to money (along with fiscal and other variables) an important role in the macroeconomic scenario of modern times.

Deficits and the Public Debt

Readings 32, 33, and 34

There is no subject in political economy more interesting to people than the public debt. And there is no subject on which the mythology of the man in the street is more misinformed than that of the public debt and deficit financing. Fortunately, in the 1960s progress was made in public understanding and acceptance of the scientific aspects of the matter. But these readings remind us that endemic in the minds of uninformed laymen remain tragic illusions.

Reading 32 is by the late Harry F. Byrd, long a Democratic Senator from Virginia, an unreconstructed believer in orthodox finance and limited government. Reading 33 is by Maurice Stans, a certified public accountant, Eisenhower's Director of the Bureau of the Budget, and Secretary of Commerce in Nixon's first administration. Reading 34 is by one of the world's most eminent economic scientists, Professor James Tobin, Sterling Professor of Economics at Yale and member of President Kennedy's first Council of Economic Advisers.

Questions to guide the reading

Why are analogies between private and public finance misleading? In particular, if the ability of the government to bear the interest costs of the public debt depends primarily upon the taxable incomes of the nation, why should not the burden of the public debt be a manageable one even if it were to grow by more per year than the largest peacetime deficit we have ever had—$12 billion in 1959, during Eisenhower's term, which is less than a growth rate of 4 per cent per annum in an economy that has a money GNP growth rate of 6 or more per cent per annum?

If the real assets of a nation are to grow, how much can debt grow without impairing the ratios of a healthy society? Why is failure to have GNP grow the greatest danger that a society with debt can ever face?

Reading 32

The Evils of Deficit Spending

Senator Harry F. Byrd

As I see it, balancing the budget without resorting to legerdemain or unsound bookkeeping methods is certainly in the category of our No. 1 problems.

Beginning with 1792, the first fiscal year of our Federal Government, and through 1916, Federal deficits were casual and usually paid off in succeeding years. In this 124-year period there were 43 deficit years and 81 surplus years. As late as July 1, 1914, the interest-bearing debt was less than $1 billion.

In Andrew Jackson's administration the public debt was paid off in toto, an achievement in which President Jackson expressed great pride.

It can be said for this first 124 years in the life of our Republic we were on a pay-as-you-go basis. In that period I think it can be accurately said that we laid the foundation for our strength today as the greatest nation in all the world.

It is disturbing these days to hear some economists argue the budget should not be balanced and that we should not begin to pay off the debt because, they allege, it will adversely affect business conditions. Have we yielded so far to the blandishments of Federal subsidies and Government support that we have forgotten our Nation is great because of individual effort as contrasted to state paternalism?

Evils of deficit spending

Here are some of the evils of deficit spending:

The debt today is the debt incurred by this generation, but tomorrow it will be debt on our children and grandchildren, and it will be for them to pay, both the interest and the principal.

It is possible and in fact probable that before this astronomical debt is paid off, if it ever is, the interest charge will exceed the principal.

Protracted deficit spending means cheapening the dollar. Cheapened money is inflation. Inflation is a dangerous game. It robs creditors, it steals pensions, wages, and fixed income. Once started, it is exceedingly difficult to control. This inflation has been partially checked but the value of the dollar dropped slightly again in the past year. It would not take much to start up this dangerous inflation again.

Public debt is not like private debt. If private debt is not paid off, it can be ended by liquidation, but if public debt is not paid off with taxes, liquidation takes the form of disastrous inflation or national repudiation. Either is destructive of our form of government.

Today the interest on the Federal debt takes more than 10 percent of our total Federal tax revenue. Without the tremendous cost of this debt our annual tax bill could be reduced 10 percent across the board.

Budget reform?

Proposals have been advocated changing our budgetary system. There are two which recur with persistency, and I want to warn you of them.

First, there is the proposal for a cash budget. Those who advocate the cash budget are suggesting that the Government pay its routine bills with savings of the citizens who have entrusted protection of their old age and unemployment to the guardianship of the Federal Government. These trust funds were established from premiums paid by participants in social security, unemployment insurance, bank deposit insurance programs, etc. Not a cent of these funds belongs to the Government.

Second, some are advocating a capital budget which means that so-called capital expenditures should not be considered as current expenditures in the budget.

Those who advocate the so-called capital budget must start out with the fallacious assumption that the Government is in business to make a

From a speech by Senator Harry F. Byrd reprinted in *Congressional Record*, vol. 101, pt. 4, 84 Congress, 1 Session, May 4, 1955.

profit on its citizens. To my knowledge the Federal Government has never made a bona fide profit on any Government operation.

They must assume that debt contracted by a Federal agency is not a debt of the Federal Government and a burden on all of the taxpayers.

I am an old-fashioned person who believes that a debt is a debt just as much in the atomic age as it was in the horse and buggy days.

A capital budget must assume that Government manufacturing plants, such as atomic energy installations, are in commercial production for a profit, and that Government stockpiles are long-time investments for profit instead of precautions against emergencies when they would be completely expendable with no financial return.

Likewise, it must assume that the agriculture surplus program is primarily a long range investment deal instead of a prop for annual farm income to be used when needed on a year-by-year basis.

While the vastness and complexity of the Federal Government of the United States necessarily makes budgeting difficult, the so-called conventional budget currently in use offers the best approach to orderly financing with fullest disclosure.

What is needed for a better fiscal system is fuller disclosure of Federal expenditures and responsibility for them—not less, as inevitably would be the case with so-called cash and capital budgets.

With full disclosure of the Federal expenditure situation, the American people then would have an opportunity to decide whether they wanted to recapture control and bring the rate of spending into balance with the rate of taxing and thus reduce the tremendous Federal debt burden we are now bearing.

At home we can get along without Federal usurpation of individual, local, and State responsibilities, and we can get along without Federal competition in business whether it be hotels, furs, rum, clothing, fertilizer, or other things.

The Bible says if thine eye offend thee pluck it out. I say if the Federal Government should not engage in such activities, we should first stop new invasions and then gradually, if not abruptly, eliminate the old intrusions. When we do these things we shall balance the budget, for lower taxes and reduced debt. There will be no further need for trick budgets and debt-ceiling evasions and hiding taxes. The Government will be honest in itself, and honest with the people.

Reading 33

The Need for Balanced Federal Budgets

Former Secretary of Commerce Maurice H. Stans

The federal government should have a balanced budget; its expenditures, especially in times like these, should not exceed its income. Of this I am deeply convinced.

As a matter of fact, I find it difficult to understand why there are still some people who do not seem to agree. Even though I have now been an official of the government almost four years and know by hard experience that there are at least two sides to all public questions, on this one the facts speak eloquently for themselves. And the arguments that are marshalled in opposition to show that a balanced budget is unimportant—or that it

can be safely forsaken for lengthy periods of time—certainly seem unsound. It is true that we as a nation have been extremely fortunate in maintaining our fundamental strengths thus far despite the heavy deficit spending of the past thirty years. But we cannot count on being lucky forever; and more and more the consequences of past profligacy are now catching up with us.

Let us look at some of the facts:

1. It is a fact that in 24 of the last 30 years (i.e., up to 1959) the federal government has spent more than it has received.

2. It is a fact that last fiscal year (1958) the fed-

From Maurice H. Stans, "The Need for Balanced Federal Budgets," *Annals of the American Academy of Political and Social Science,* 1959. Reprinted with kind permission of the author and publisher.

eral government had a deficit (12.5 billion dollars) larger than ever before in time of peace.

3. It is a fact that the federal government debt is now 290 billion dollars (in 1959) and that the annual cost of carrying that debt is more than 10 per cent of the budgeted income of the government—and has been going up.

4. It is a fact that our economy is operating at a higher rate of activity than it ever has before and that the standard of living it is producing for all America is far beyond that of any other country in the world.

5. It is a fact that in times of high economic activity there is competition among business, consumers, and government for the productive resources of the country; if government, by indulging in high levels of spending in such times, intensifies that competition, it openly invites inflation.

6. It is a fact that with an unbalanced budget, federal borrowings to raise the money to spend more than income tend to add to the money supply of the country and therefore are inflationary.

7. It is a fact that the purchasing power of the dollar has declined more than 50 per cent in the last twenty years. Today we spend more than $2.00 to get what $1.00 would buy in 1939.

8. And finally, it is a fact that all too often in history inflation has been the undoing of nations, great and small.

True, there are many people who still feel that a bit of inflation is a tolerable, if not a good, thing. I think they fail to see that a bit of inflation is an installment on a lot of inflation—a condition in which nobody can hope to gain.

Those of our citizens who believe that inflation is not undesirable simply overlook the history of nations. Inflation is an insidious threat to the strength of the United States. Unless we succeed in exercising a tighter rein over it than we have been able to up to this point, I am afraid that we will all lose—as individuals, as a nation, and as a people.

In my view, the facts that I have recited clearly demonstrate the need for:

1. Containing federal expenditures within federal income—which means balancing the budget—in fiscal years 1960 and 1961.

2. Establishing the principle of a balanced budget—including some surplus for reduction of the national debt—as a fiscal objective for the prosperous years ahead.

These are the standards on which fiscal integrity for the nation should rest. These are the standards by which the force of inflation induced by reckless fiscal policy can be averted. Yet in 24 of the last 30 years we have not been able to attain them.

Let us look at some of the circumstances which have caused heavy federal spending in the past and have, perhaps, made us insensitive to the dangers of deficits.

Looking back

Over the last three decades the federal government has spent 264 billion dollars more than it has received. The six years in which there was an excess of income over expense produced negligible surpluses in relation to the deficits of the other years.

We need hardly be reminded of the cause of most of those deficits. In the earlier years it was depression; in the middle years it was war; in recent years it has been war again and then recession.

In the depression years it was not possible to balance the budget; while government services and costs were growing by popular demand, federal revenues declined as a result of economic inactivity. The efforts made to balance the budget by increasing tax rates in 1930 and 1932 and in 1936 and 1938 were apparently self-defeating.

As for the expenditure side of the budget, the decade of the 1930's produced a great deal of talk about "pump-priming" and "compensatory spending"—federal spending which would compensate in poor times for the decline in business and consumer demand and thus lend balance and stability to the economy. The theory was, of course, for the federal government to spend proportionately larger amounts during depression times and proportionately smaller amounts during good times—to suffer deficits in poor years and enjoy surpluses in prosperous years, with the objective of coming out even over the long pull.

Then, in the early 1940's came World War II. During the war years, the federal government's expenditures vastly exceeded its income, and huge further deficits were piled up. In retrospect, most students of wartime economic developments now agree that we did not tax ourselves nearly enough.

We did not pay enough of the costs of war out of current income. We created a large debt while suppressing some of its inflationary consequences with direct economic controls, but the suppression was only temporary.

Depression and war, although major factors, were not the only reasons for increased federal expenditures and deficits during the past thirty years. It was more complex than that. In the 1930's the national philosophy of the responsibilities of the federal government underwent a major change. The country's needs for economic growth and social advancement were gradually given increased recognition at the federal level.

The aim of economic growth, of social advancement, and of "compensatory" economic stability became intertwined. Many federal activities of far-reaching implications were established in ways which affected federal expenditures for very long periods of time—if not permanently. Social security, greatly increased support for agriculture, rural electrification, aids to home owners and mortgage institutions, public housing, public power developments like the Tennessee Valley Authority and other multipurpose water resource projects, and public assistance grants are just a few examples. All of them, however, remained as federal programs after World War II. And we were actually fighting in that war before federal spending for work relief could be stopped.

The immediate postwar period was marked by dramatic demobilization. Nevertheless, many of the major costs of war lingered on. The maintenance in the postwar period of even the reduced and relatively modest structure of our Armed Forces was far more costly than anything that existed in the way of the machinery of war prior to 1940. The war also left us with greatly increased expenditure commitments for interest on public debt, for veterans, and for atomic energy. The Marshall Plan and the mutual security program followed in succession. It became obvious next, that the cold war was going to be expensive. Then, with the Korean aggression, it became necessary to rearm and, even after the shooting stopped, the peacetime striking force and defensive machinery we had to maintain continued expenditures at levels that far exceeded in cost anything we had earlier imagined.

Thus, the postwar growth of the budget has been partly in the area of national security, partly deferred costs of World War II, and partly the inheritance of activities and ways of thinking that characterized the depression of the 1930's. We have now learned that many of the programs the federal government initiated in the 1930's were neither temporary nor "compensatory" in character. Moreover, we have not only retained many of them, but we have also greatly expanded them in the postwar period. Since World War II we have seen large increases in federal expenditures for urban renewal, public health, federal aid for airports and highways, new categories and a higher federal share of public assistance grants, aid to schools in federally impacted areas, great liberalization in aid to agriculture, as well as new programs for science, education, and outer space.

The present

What can we conclude from all of this?

It seems to me that in the first place we must recognize that the compensatory theory of federal spending has failed thus far and offers little hope for the future unless we exert a more forceful and courageous determination to control the growth of federal spending. The major spending programs which originated in the depression years have in most cases persisted in the following decades. A work relief project could be turned off when we started to fight a war, but most of the programs established in the 1930's developed characteristics of a far more permanent sort.

An example can be found in the program of the Rural Electrification Administration (REA). This program was started in 1936 when only a minority of farm families enjoyed the benefits of electricity. Today, 95 per cent of our farms receive central station electric service. We have invested 4 billion dollars in this program, at 2 per cent interest. Nonetheless, indications are that future demands for federal funds will be even greater as the REA cooperatives continue to grow.

The startling fact is that three out of four new users currently being added are nonfarm users. About one-half of REA electric power goes to industries, communities, or nonfarm families. The reasonable approach is that rural electric cooperatives should now be able to get some of their financing from other than government sources, especially for nonfarm purposes that compete with taxed private industry.

Inability to turn off expenditures is not all that is wrong with the compensatory theory of the pre-war period. Initially, it deals largely with the spending side of the fiscal equation whereas the income side now appears to be playing a more important part. Today—with corporate income tax rates at 52 per cent—any substantial reduction of corporate earnings produces an immediate pro-portionate and large loss to the federal treasury. Personal income taxes also respond, though less sharply, to a fall in national production and em-ployment. Thus, when times take a turn for the worse, federal revenues decline promptly and sub-stantially.

Couple this with enlarged social obligations in times of recession or depression—unemployment compensation, public assistance, and so on—and you have substantial leverage of a more or less automatic character for the production of federal deficits in times of depressed economic activity. To do more than this—to deliberately step up expen-ditures still more, for public works and other con-struction—runs grave risks. There is, first, the risk that an anti-recession expenditure program cannot be turned off after the recession, but instead repre-sents a permanent increase in the public sphere at the expense of the private. Second, it is difficult to start programs quickly, so the major impact may come long after the need for the economic stimula-tion has passed. Both of these risks mean that anti-recession actions can well represent an inflationary danger for the post-recession period. The danger is there even if, as some believe, positive governmen-tal intervention is required to counter recessions. It is more grave, however, if—and I believe this was proved true in 1958-59—the economy is vig-orous and resilient enough to come out of a tem-porary recession and to go on through a revival period to new prosperous peaks without any direct financial federal interference.

I think we may conclude that it is inevitable that our nation will be faced with large budgets in the years ahead. This is particularly true for the defense obligations which our country has as-sumed, for its international undertakings to pro-vide economic and military assistance to other free nations, and as a result of many programs which have been started over the years—major programs

for water resource development, agriculture, veter-ans' benefits, low-cost housing, airways modern-ization, and space exploration—all these and many others have taken on a permanent quality which makes it clear that federal budgets will be large budgets in our lifetimes.

There is still another conclusion which springs from this short recitation of the history of the last thirty years. It is that the federal government has assumed more and more responsibility for activi-ties which formerly were regarded as being under the jurisdiction of state and local governments. More and more the federal government as as-sumed responsibility for public assistance, hous-ing, urban renewal, educational aid to areas with federal installations, and many other programs that are now supported by federal grants-in-aid to the states. All this, of course, contributes to the conclusion that these federal programs are not only large at the present time, but have a built-in durability—a staying power with which we must reckon as a fact of life.

I think these thoughts are well summarized in the words of Mr. Allen Sproul, former President of the New York Federal Reserve Bank, who re-cently said:

Government, in our day, touches upon the economic life of the community in an almost bewildering vari-ety of ways, but its overall influence comes into focus in the consolidated cash budget and, in a subsidiary way, in the management of the public debt. When we abandoned the idea of taxation for revenue only and admitted, as we must, a more important role of Gov-ernment in economic affairs, we thought up a tidy little scheme called the compensatory budget. This envisaged a cash budget balanced in times of real prosperity, in deficit in times of economic recession and in surplus in times of inflationary boom. What we have got is a budget that may throw up a shaky surplus in times of boom, but that will surely show substantial deficits in times of recession. The bias, over time, is toward deficits, with only wobbly con-tracyclical tendencies.

Looking ahead

It seems to me that as we move into another de-cade it will be essential to recognize that unless we have a more positive program for operating our federal government within its income, the forces that have gained such tremendous momentum in the past will perpetuate the tradition of deficits—to the great disadvantage of the country as a whole.

Assuming a continuous, but not uninterrupted, economic growth for the country, accompanied by ever-increasing, but not uninterrupted, growth of federal revenues, we should nevertheless expect that the growth of programs started in the past will have a strong tendency to absorb the expected additional revenues—unless aggressive controls are exercised by an alert administration and a statesmanlike Congress during those years.

On those occasions when the economy recedes from its way of growth, we must expect great leverage to be exerted toward the building up of additional deficits. We must learn to live with recession-induced deficits as a matter of necessity, but we should not take un-needed actions which mortgage our nation's future with both more debt and an inflationary potential.

Conclusions

It seems to me to follow from these facts and analyses that it should be the policy of the federal government to strive determinedly for a balanced budget at all times, for, clearly, if it does not, the forces at work to upset financial stability will surely prevail as a matter of momentum.

As we move into the next decade we have the lessons of the three past decades to guide us:

1. Federal programs persist and in most cases grow. As demand expands, the programs expand. It is extremely difficult to curtail them. Their growing costs—and a growing economy—must be reckoned with realistically. This means that actions should be taken to reduce or to end them as they accomplish the purposes for which they were initiated (eighteen such proposals were made in President Eisenhower's budget message for the fiscal year 1960).

2. In times of recession, it is important to avoid doing things as temporary expedients which will become longer range programs and create major problems later on. We have plenty of these as carry-overs from earlier days; we should avoid creating new ones for the years ahead.

3. We must, of course, learn to live with deficits when major national emergencies threaten or exist in our country. But we should resolve to create equivalent surpluses later on to offset such deficits.

The lesson is clear. We should pay as we go, and if we are to look for debt reduction or tax reduction on a sound footing—as we should—we must do more than this. We must plan for substantial budgetary surpluses in good years—or we will surely contribute to further dangerous inflation in the years ahead.

Reading 34

Deficit, Deficit, Who's Got the Deficit?

James Tobin

For every buyer there must be a seller, and for every lender a borrower. One man's expenditure is another's receipt. My debts are your assets, my deficit your surplus.

If each of us was consistently "neither borrower nor lender," as Polonius advised, no one would ever need to violate the revered wisdom of Mr. Micawber. But if the prudent among us insist on running and lending surpluses, some of the rest of us are willy-nilly going to borrow to finance budget deficits.

In the United States today one budget that is usually left holding a deficit is that of the federal government. When no one else borrows the surpluses of the thrifty, the Treasury ends up doing so. Since the role of debtor and borrower is thought to be particularly unbecoming to the federal government, the nation feels frustrated and guilty.

Unhappily, crucial decisions of economic policy too often reflect blind reactions to these feelings. The truisms that *borrowing is the counterpart of*

From James Tobin, *National Economic Policy* (Yale University Press, New Haven and London, 1966). Reprinted with kind permission of the author and publisher.

lending and *deficits the counterpart of surpluses* are overlooked in popular and Congressional discussions of government budgets and taxes. *Both guilt feelings and policy are based on serious misunderstanding of the origins of federal budget deficits and surpluses.*

Private surpluses

American *households* and *financial institutions* consistently run financial surpluses. They have money to lend, beyond their own needs to borrow. Figure 1 shows the growth in their combined surpluses since the war; it also shows some tendency for these surpluses to rise in periods of recession and slack business activity. Of course, many private households have financial deficits. They pay out more than their incomes for food, clothing, cars, appliances, houses, taxes, and so on. They draw on savings accounts, redeem savings bonds, sell securities, mortgage houses, or incur installment debt. But deficit households are far outweighed by surplus households. As a group American *households* and *non-profit institutions* have in recent years shown a net financial surplus averaging about $15

billion a year—that is, households are ready to lend, or to put into equity investments, about $15 billion a year more than they are prepared to borrow. In addition, *financial institutions* regularly generate a lendable surplus, now of the order of $5 billion a year. For the most part these institutions—banks, savings and loan associations, insurance companies, pension funds, and the like—are simply intermediaries which borrow and relend the public's money. Their surpluses result from the fact that they earn more from their lending operations than they distribute or credit to their depositors, shareowners, and policyholders.

Who is to use the $20 billion of surplus funds available from households and financial institutions? *State and local governments* as a group have been averaging $3-4 billion a year of net borrowing. Pressures of the expanding populations of children, adults, houses, and automobiles, plus the difficulties of increasing tax revenues, force these governments to borrow in spite of strictures against government debt. *Unincorporated businesses,* including farms, absorb another $3-4 billion. To the rest of the world we can lend perhaps $2 billion a year. We cannot lend abroad—net—more than the surplus of our exports over our imports of goods and services, and some of that surplus we give away in foreign aid. We have to earn the lendable surplus in tough international competition. Recent experience shows clearly that when we try to lend and invest too much money abroad, we either have to borrow it back or else pay in gold.

These borrowers account for $8-10 billion. The remainder—some $10-12 billion—must be used either by *nonfinancial corporate business* or by the *federal government.* Only if corporations as a group take $10-12 billion of external funds, by borrowing or issuing new equities, can the federal government expect to break even. This is, moreover, an understatement of what is required to keep the federal debt from rising, for the federal government itself provides annually $3 to $4 billion of new lending; the Treasury would have to borrow to finance these federal lending programs even if the government absorbed no *net* funds from the economy. It is *gross* federal borrowing that offends the conservative fiscal conscience, whether or not the proceeds are used to acquire other financial assets.

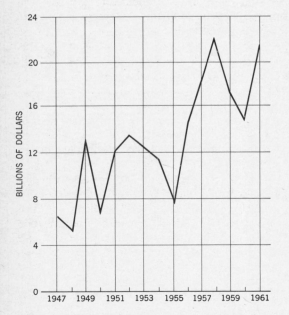

Figure 1 Financial surpluses of consumers, nonprofit institutions, and financial institutions, 1947–61.
Source: Board of Governors of the Federal Reserve System

Which is it to be?

The moral is inescapable, if startling. If you would like the federal deficit to be smaller, the deficits of business must be bigger. Would you like the federal government to run a surplus and reduce its debt? Then business deficits must be big enough to absorb that surplus as well as the funds available from households and financial institutions.

That does not mean that business must run at a loss—quite the contrary. Sometimes, it is true, unprofitable businesses are forced to borrow or to spend financial reserves just to stay afloat; this was a major reason for business deficits in the depths of the Great Depression. But normally it is businesses with good profits and good prospects that borrow or sell new shares of stock, in order to finance expansion and modernization. As the President of American Telephone and Telegraph can testify, heavy reliance on outside funds, far from being a distress symptom, is an index and instrument of growth in the profitability and worth of the corporation. The incurring of financial deficits by business firms—or by households and governments for that matter—does not usually mean that such institutions are living beyond their means and consuming their capital. Financial deficits are typically the means of accumulating nonfinancial assets—real property in the form of inventories, buildings, and equipment.

When does business run big deficits? When do corporations draw heavily on the capital markets? The record is clear: when business is very good, when sales are pressing hard on capacity, when businessmen see further expansion ahead. Though corporations' internal funds—depreciation allowances and plowed-back profits—are large during boom times, their investment programs are even larger.

The facts of experience

Figure 2 shows the financial deficits or surpluses of corporate business and of the federal government since the war. Three facts stand out. First, the *federal government has big deficits when corporations run surpluses or small deficits and vice versa.* Second, *government surpluses and business deficits reach their peaks in periods of economic expansion,*

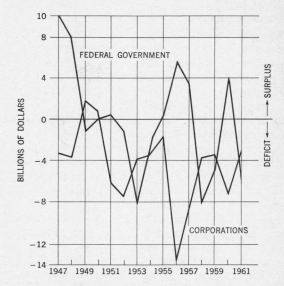

Figure 2 Net financial surpluses and deficits of the federal government and of nonfinancial corporations, 1947–61.
Source: Board of Governors of the Federal Reserve System

when industrial capacity is heavily utilized, as in 1947–48, 1951–52, and 1956–57. Third, the combined deficit of corporate business and the federal government is greater now than in the early postwar years; this is the counterpart of the upward trend in available surpluses shown in Figure 1.

Recession, idle capacity, unemployment, economic slack—these are the enemies of the balanced government budget. When the economy is faltering, households have more surpluses available to lend, and business firms are less inclined to borrow them.

The federal government will not succeed in cutting its deficit by steps that depress the economy, perpetuate excess capacity, and deter business firms from using outside funds. Raising taxes and cutting expenses seem like obvious ways to balance the budget. But because of their effects on private spending, lending, and borrowing, they may have exactly the contrary result. Likewise, lowering taxes and raising government expenditures may so stimulate private business activity and private borrowing that the federal deficit is in the end actually reduced.

Misleading parables

This may seem paradoxical, and perhaps it is. Why is it that the homely analogy between family finance and government finance, on which our decisive national attitudes toward federal fiscal policy are so largely based, misleads us? If John Jones on Maple Street is spending $8,700 a year but taking in only $8,000, the remedy is clear. All Mr. Jones need do to balance the family budget is to live resolutely within his income, either spending some $700 less or working harder to increase his earnings. Jones can safely ignore the impact of either action on the incomes and expenditures of others and the possible ultimate feedback on his own job and income. The situation of the President on Pennsylvania Avenue, spending $87 billion a year against tax revenues of $80 billion, is quite different. Suppose that he spends $7 billion less, or tries through higher tax rates to boost federal revenues by $7 billion. He cannot ignore the inevitable boomerang effect on federal finances. These measures will lower taxpayers' receipts, expenditures, and taxable incomes. The federal deficit will be reduced by much less than $7 billion; perhaps it will even be increased.

Incidentally, many of the very critics who are most vocal in chiding the government for fiscal sin advocate policies that would make fiscal virtue even more elusive. They want to keep private borrowing in check by the use of tight credit policies and high interest rates. They want to increase corporations' *internal* flow of funds by bigger depreciation allowances and higher profit margins, making business still less dependent on external funds to finance investment, even in boom times. When these apostles of sound finance also tell the government to shun external finance, have they done their arithmetic? If everyone is self-financing, who will borrow the surpluses?

The price we pay

The nation is paying a high price for the misapplied homely wisdom that guides federal fiscal policy. The real toll is measured by unemployment, idle capacity, lost production, and sluggish economic growth. But fiscal conservatism is also self-defeating. It does not even achieve its own aim, the avoidance of government deficits. Federal fiscal and monetary policies consciously and unashamedly designed to stimulate the economy would have sufficient justification in economic expansion itself. But they might well "improve" the federal budget too—by inducing business to use the private surpluses that now have no destination other than a rising federal debt.

3

THE COMPOSITION AND PRICING OF NATIONAL OUTPUT

Microeconomic Pricing

Reading 35

Gold played an historical role in the monetary system. This puts it into the general category of macroeconomics. Since 1968, though, the official monetary tier of gold has been sealed off from the free-tier market. Supply and demand rules in the Zurich and London free markets for gold.

Jewelers, dentists, gangsters, and hoarders provide the growing demand for free gold. The supply of gold comes from the dwindling mines of South Africa and Russia and, on a smaller scale, from Canada and the U.S. West.

However, as David Williams, of the International Monetary Fund, trained earlier at the London School of Economics, makes clear here, the dominant influences on the supply and demand for gold have come from speculators. Whenever speculators think financial crises will force devaluation of the dollar and collapse of the post-1968 two-tier system, the free price of gold soars as high as $70 an ounce. When quiet reigns on the monetary front, gold's price meanders.

Questions to guide the reading

If speculation and hoarding become unimportant, what would growing industrial use for gold and declining productivity of mines imply for the long-run trend of the price of gold? What would wholesale abandonment of official gold and dumping of it on the free market do to the short-run price of gold? Could that fall below $38 per ounce?

Free Gold: A Supply-Demand Market

David Williams

Gold is a commodity which is used in increasing amounts in the technologically advanced industries and for medical and associated purposes; with the rise in real incomes, gold is also increasingly demanded for making into jewelry and personal adornments; in addition, gold has been an important form of private saving. Unlike almost all other metals—with the exception of silver—gold has also had a long and somewhat glamorous history as a commodity used for monetary purposes.

Establishment of the two-tier system

[However, the tier of free-market gold has now been effectively divorced from the official monetary tier.]

The Governors of the seven central banks—those of the United States, the United Kingdom, Belgium, Germany, Italy, the Netherlands, and Switzerland—met in Washington on the weekend of March 17, 1968. They decided that they would no longer intervene in the private gold markets to

From David Williams, "The Gold Markets, 1968–72," *Finance and Development* (a publication of the International Monetary Fund and the World Bank Group), vol. 9, no. 4, December 1972. Reprinted with kind permission of the IMF and the World Bank.

maintain the price of gold in those markets within 1 per cent of the official price of $35 an ounce [$38 an ounce after 1971]—i.e., they would no longer sell gold to the private markets. Furthermore, in view of the prospective establishment of the special drawing right facility they believed the then existing stock of monetary gold was sufficient and they no longer felt it necessary to buy gold from the market. They also agreed that they would not sell gold to monetary authorities to replace gold sold in private markets.

The agreement of 1968 led to a separation of the official gold market—in which transactions would take place at the official price of [$38] per fine ounce—and the private gold market—in which the price for gold would be freely determined in accordance with supply and demand conditions. The two-tier gold market was thereby established.

Effects of the two-tier Gold System

The agreement of 1968 radically transformed both the private international gold markets and official gold policies. First, the price of gold would fluctuate in the international private markets and could diverge from its official price as the leading central banks would no longer stabilize prices. Second, it could be expected that all newly mined gold would be sold in the private markets. Third, the international monetary functions of gold were to be maintained on the basis of the then existing official holdings of gold; the gold reserves of central banks would change mainly as a result of official transactions between themselves and not as a result of transactions between central banks and the private markets. Private speculation in gold would no longer affect the total of world liquidity and newly mined gold and private gold holdings would in principle be treated in private markets as are other commodities.

The London bullion market was the most important international gold market. The leading bullion brokers in London decided to have a gold fixing twice daily—at the traditional time of 10:30 A.M. and again at 3 P.M. At those times, the price for gold is set—or fixed—at a level which satisfies demand. However, transactions take place at prices other than the fixed price during the day, though these trading prices are normally closely related to the fixing price.

Furthermore, partly in view of the fluctuating free market price of gold, the London market lost its pre-eminence as an international gold market. The Zürich bullion market, for instance, gained in relative importance, especially because of the role of the leading Swiss commerical banks in dealing in gold.

Long-run developments affecting gold markets

One of the factors influencing the gold market has already been noted—the increasing demand for gold. In most fields of technology, no substitute for gold appears to be in sight so that rising prices do not appear to affect the demand very greatly. In addition, both artistic and long-term hoarding demands for gold seem relatively more responsive to changes in the level of real incomes and in social habits than to changes in the price of gold. Thus, the increase in demand seems likely to continue.

In contrast to the continued rise in demand for gold, the outlook for increases in the supply of newly mined gold is less certain. Old mines are being worked out, and few new gold discoveries are being made. The volume of gold production since 1965 has been relatively stable or, in some years, has fallen. In addition, there is no assurance that a higher gold price would greatly stimulate over the short run an increase in production; it would seem more likely to have the effect of maintaining output over the longer run. In short, then, the outlook seems to be of a long-run quantitative rise in the demand for gold and, possibly, a stable, if not falling, gold output. Under such conditions, some long-term upward pressure on prices would seem probable.

In principle, the official price for gold should not exert any marked influence on the private gold markets (and vice versa) since the private and official gold markets have been separated since March 1968. In practice, uncertainty regarding the official price has had a continuing influence on the private gold markets.

For example, on the one hand, a deliberate demonetization of gold, or prolonged running down of these stocks by sales of gold in the free market, would fundamentally alter the balance of supply in the gold markets and lead to a fall in prices. On the other hand, heavy reliance on gold in official international settlements would raise the issue of whether there are sufficient stocks of gold for this purpose—and this too has implications for the long-run future official price of gold.

Gold price cycles

Over the past four years [1968 to early 1973] the free market price of gold rose from $35 per fine ounce [in] March 1968 to a peak of $70 in early August 1972. However, the price of gold has fluctuated considerably since the two-tier system was instituted. As can be seen in the chart, the free market price for gold shows three distinct changes between March 1968 and August 1972.

For the first 16 months following the establishment of the two-tier gold system, gold prices generally rose in the private markets—from about $38 per fine ounce on April 1, 1968 to almost $44 per fine ounce during the first five months of 1969. Susbstantial falls in prices also occurred. During most of 1968, day-by-day price changes were comparatively large.

Uncertainty about the maintenance of the official price of gold at $35 influenced the working of the free gold markets not only directly, but also indirectly through developments in the foreign exchange markets.

In fact, during most of 1968 and early 1969, the demand for gold was relatively strong in view of comparatively unstable conditions in the foreign exchange markets. The chief significance for the private gold market of developments in the foreign exchange markets was the likely effects that possible exchange rate changes might have had on the official price of gold. This led to somewhat distorted conditions in the markets and induced considerable market speculation which led to unsustainably high prices for gold.

Conditions in the private gold markets began to change significantly during the second half of 1969 and a dramatic fall in prices occurred. Between the end of May and December 1969, the price for gold in London fell from $43.225 per fine ounce to its then official price of $35 per fine ounce. In early January 1970, the price fell to $34.75 and then

Gold prices in London, April 1968–August 1972.

moved fairly closely around its official price until about September 1970.

This rapid and prolonged fall in prices was due to a number of factors which influenced both the demand for, and supply of, gold on the market. The prospective activation of the SDR facility in 1969 [i.e., the decision of the IMF to create "paper gold" as a supplement or replacement to official monetary gold]; the growing balance of payments deficit of South Africa and the increasing amounts of gold being offered for sale on the private market which, in the absence of heavy short-term speculative demand, were more than sufficient to meet normal industrial and long-term hoarding demand; and developments in the international money markets—Euro-dollar [interest] rates increased sharply thereby increasing the effective cost of holding gold—and the greater [1969] stability in the foreign exchange markets.

These developments affected the outlook for a possible change in the official price of gold—which had been the dominant factor influencing the international gold markets since prior to the devaluation of sterling in November 1967. In particular, the activation of the SDR facility not only dispelled uncertainty regarding a possible global shortage of international reserves, but also ensured that a part of the growth of international reserves would be in the form of a gold type asset. Furthermore, the Executive Directors of the Fund on December 30, 1969 decided that South Africa could sell gold to the Fund in certain circumstances—in particular, with regard to the price for gold in the London market, when it fell to its official price of $35 per fine ounce, and to the balance of payments position of South Africa. As a consequence of this decision, some gold would possibly flow into official reserves; furthermore, an effective floor price was established in the London market at $35 per fine ounce.

The third significant change in prices began in the autumn of 1970 when prices began to rise. Between that time and the summer of 1972, the trend of prices was generally sharply upward, with only comparatively short periods of relative stability and small technical declines in prices. Taking the period as a whole, prices rose from about $36 per fine ounce at the beginning of September 1970 to $70 per fine ounce by the first week of August 1972. During the first five months of 1972—and especially during May and June 1972—the rise in prices accelerated sharply.

For most of this period the international monetary system was under increasing strain. After August 15, 1971—when the United States suspended the convertibility of the U.S. dollar into gold and other reserve assets—the system experienced its greatest crisis since the abandonment of the gold standard in the early 1930s. A few points can be noted with respect to the reaction of the private gold market and the free market price for gold during this period of strain and eventual crisis in the system.

First, and most important, was the pervasive influence of speculation—induced by growing instability in the exchange markets—regarding the official price of gold.

Second, over the last two years the leading international gold markets have become "thinner" in the sense that the volume of readily tradable gold at a given price has diminished. The supply of gold on the market is now determined largely by the amount of gold offered by the gold producing countries, sales by the U.S.S.R. and East European countries, and by short-term speculative gold holders who trade in response to expected price changes. The large overhang of gold which characterized the market for about two years after the inception of the two-tier system has been partly absorbed by industrial and other users, while a large part of the remainder has disappeared into hoards and is unlikely to be reoffered to the market.

The fundamental change in the supply position of gold in the private markets has resulted in sharp movements in prices when even relatively small changes in demand have occurred. In this sense the private gold markets have become relatively more unstable over time.

Third, to a far greater extent than hitherto, a rise in prices has tended to accelerate as speculative activity has fed upon itself. However, subsequent declines in prices have not largely been in reaction to fundamental changes in expectations and demand, but have resulted from technical adjustments to temporarily overbought positions and other factors essentially of a short-term financial nature (e.g., changes in Euro-dollar deposit rates). In conditions of relative calm, prices have not fallen, as might have been expected, but have remained steady.

To some extent, of course, part of the rise in prices can be attributed to a reduction in the supply of gold offered on the market, particularly by South Africa, at a time when demand for the metal—especially for industrial purposes—was buoyant. However, the relatively high price of gold in the private markets in the middle months of 1972 reflected a large premium in the light of the uncertainty regarding future developments in the international monetary system.

Conclusion

As a result of the establishment of the two-tier system in March 1968, the level of official gold reserves no longer changes as a result of fluctuations in the private demand for gold nor, except to the extent that the Fund purchases gold from South Africa, as a result of fluctuations in world gold output. The official supply of gold is relatively fixed. Indeed, the future role of gold in the international monetary system is uncertain.

In the private markets, fluctuations in the price of gold have reflected reactions to developments in the international monetary system and, in particular, to the future official role of gold in the system. Such fluctuations are, perhaps, explainable not only because of the relatively large official stocks of gold in existence—equivalent to about 30 years' output—but also because of the possibility (which took place on May 8, 1972) of changes in the official price of gold.

Furthermore, since the inception of the two-tier system, the supply of gold placed on the market is falling in relation to demand because central banks no longer generally sell gold in the market. Under conditions of crisis or acute uncertainty, reaction in the private gold market tends to be exaggerated and the price of gold shows a rapid rise. In this sense the private gold markets are relatively unstable markets.

The private gold markets are unlikely to function in broadly the same manner as other commodity markets until, at least, the psychological link between the private and official gold markets is broken. To a considerable extent this will depend on the relative importance of the future role of gold as a monetary asset.

Reading 36

Economists, properly, put stress on marginal-cost pricing. In this reading an eminent economist, who has spent a good deal of time with the electricity authorities in Britain, discusses some of the practical difficulties in applying marginal-cost pricing.

Ralph Turvey achieved fame as a scholar at the London School of Economics while still very young. He left his post as Reader there to go into government service, serving as Joint Deputy Chairman of the National Board for Prices and Incomes before becoming an economic consultant.

Questions to guide the reading

What if marginal-cost curves are very irregular and wavy? Or suppose a firm produces many heterogeneous products. Is it easy to make controlled experiments to determine what the incremental effects on total cost are of changes in particular outputs? Is a crude approximation to marginal cost still not better than old-fashioned reliance on average costs? What are the problems of losses that you may encounter if you do adhere to marginal-cost pricing, and what thorny problems for subsidization does this entail?

Practical Problems of Marginal-cost Pricing

Ralph Turvey

Let us assume that the management of a public utility is firmly convinced of two things: that marginal-cost pricing leads to efficient resource allocation and that efficient resource allocation is something which they ought to strive to achieve. We shall not ask whether they are right in holding these twin beliefs. We simply enquire what there is to stop them from introducing full-blooded marginal-cost pricing in the course of the next couple of years.

I shall talk about four important difficulties and obstacles, one after the other. I shall not argue that they are insuperable but merely that they exist.

1. Ignorance

The first obstacle is *the difficulty of estimating the marginal cost* of any specified item of output. The accountants may well be ready to use their cost allocations to produce an answer. If, as frequently happens, they have allocated joint costs between products and have not treated bygones as bygones, it is necessary to disregard the answer they give. This requires tact. It is then necessary to do one or both of two things:

1. Go back to the *raw* accounting data, add to them if necessary, and *analyze them.*

2. Get engineers to *plan and cost* the finite increment in capacity necessary to produce a finite increment in output and divide the cost by the size of the increment.

These are the approaches of *statistical cost analysis* and *engineering cost analysis* respectively.

There are no major difficulties in statistical cost analysis—assuming that the necessary skilled staff is available—but there are hundreds of minor ones! Thus, take the simple problem of estimating the marginal cost of meter-reading by a cross-section regression of meter-readers' wages against the number of meters read. The facts are there, of course, but getting them out can be a big job.

As another example, consider the problem of estimating the cost of periodical vehicle maintenance. Job-time records may provide information about labor cost, but what about spare parts? If detailed information is available about the stocks of hundreds of different parts, an enormous amount of labor is necessary to work out average spare-part cost per overhaul.

Now it may be urged, quite rightly, that these are small cost items. Quite so, but the sum of a large number of small cost items may constitute an appreciable fraction of the relevant total.

A good description of a very large-scale costing exercise undertaken by the 2 Canadian railways has been provided in a recent paper. Just to measure the yard-switching minutes required in handling any particular category of traffic, one of many variables, required that each of the 2 railways employed "a team of from *eight to ten men* with yard experience working *for a six-month period* to analyze only the yards in Western Canada."

In view of the difficulties of this analysis, it is natural to turn to engineering cost analysis so far as capacity costs are concerned. What we would like to know is the capital cost of reinforcing the distribution system to meet anticipated load growth. The key word here is "reinforce." It is fairly easy to construct an abstract model of a new distribution system of given topology to meet a load uniformly distributed over a virgin plain. Such models are constructed in order to examine the optimum choice of voltage levels, transformer ratings, and cable sizes as a function of equipment costs and of load density. But such models tell us very little either about the costs of providing for a specified new load at a particular point, given the existing distribution system, or about average incremental costs over a whole administrative area.

An analytical approach to incremental distribution capital costs is thus not possible. Reinforce-

From Ralph Turvey, "Practical Problems of Marginal-cost Pricing in Public Enterprise: England," in Almarin Phillips and Oliver E. Williamson (eds.), *Prices: Issues in Theory, Practice, and Public Policy* (University of Pennsylvania Press, Philadelphia, 1968). Reprinted with the kind permission of the author and publisher.

ment is an *ad hoc* business. On the whole, it is rarely called for purely as a result of cost-minimization. A transformer, for instance, is hardly ever replaced because the saving in expected future running costs will outweigh the capital cost of the changeover. The effective impulse to capital expenditure is usually either thermal overloading or a need to avoid voltage drop. In either case, what matters is the fact that load growth has caused (or will soon cause) certain physical limits to be passed. Cost calculations only come in when it is not obvious which is the cheapest of several alternative methods of reinforcement.

2. Complexity

Electricity may be supplied to consumers at several voltage levels and, since it cannot be stored, is a different commodity in each hour of the year. An [ideal, administrative costs aside] tariff would reflect differences of both kinds. It would also have to vary geographically, since costs do so, and its general level would depend on the degree of system reliability of supply offered, this being an aspect of quality which cannot be differentiated between consumers.

Even this statement is an oversimplification. It nevertheless serves to show that "pure" marginal-cost pricing is nonoperational. Prices have to reflect a *weighted average* of marginal costs over periods of time, over geographical areas, and so on. The gain from more accurate cost-reflection in a tariff must be weighed against the costs of greater accuracy in choosing the optimal point.

Being a platitude, this last statement is not helpful. There is thus a real problem to be faced in applying marginal-cost pricing, namely, the problem referred to above of specifying the items of output. A simple example of the problem is to be found in urban transport; in London underground train rides are *priced according to distance,* while New York subway rides are priced *at a flat rate,* but Professor Vickrey (of Columbia) proposed pricing them *by time of day.* Thus here we have two alternative multiple-output specifications and one simple one from which to choose.

Clearly the choice cannot be made unless we know how the consumer reacts to the change in tariff structure. Thus a knowledge of night and day demand elasticities with respect to both night and day prices is required even when, as assumed here, marginal costs are constant. Yet it is difficult to see how this knowledge can be obtained; in the probable absence of ready-made cross-section data for econometric analysis, the only way of acquiring the necessary information seems to be by experiment. The difficulties of this need no emphasis.

Although these examples leave out many of the factors involved in tariff-making, they suffice to display the difficulties of marginal-cost pricing in practice. It is laborious and expensive to obtain detailed statistical information about the load curves of a sample of consumers. Any tariff can only be approximately correct and the choice of it necessitates a great deal of judgment. This is so even when the only relevant considerations are the matters dealt with so far. We shall now go on to examine some other considerations which make matters even more difficult.

3. Financial objectives

Privately owned public utilities presumably want to make profits—subject to any ceiling imposed by public authorities—while publicly owned public utilities are frequently required to aim at some minimum level of profits. In either case this creates an obstacle to marginal-cost pricing if the revenue it would provide is less than total accounting costs, including the ceiling or target level of profits.

It is tempting (to economists) to say that this obstacle arises only if there are *economies of scale so that long-run marginal cost is below long-run average cost.* Now Vinerian long-run average-cost curves show whether or not the total cost of a new firm built from scratch is greater or less than x per cent of what the total cost of that firm would have been if it had been built x per cent as large. Since public utilities are not built from scratch at one set of relative prices and with a given technology, but grow through time with changing relative prices and improving technology, the concept is wholly inappropriate. To attempt to cram the analysis into the Procrustean boot of a single cost curve is to confuse matters right at the start.

The point is that total accounting costs are a complicated time-integral of a *historical dynamic* process and that expansion costs may depend not only upon present prices and technology but also upon the stock of capital inherited from the past. Thus in an integrated system, the operating mode of new plant, and hence incremental system costs, will depend on how it fits in with existing plant.

Whatever the reasons for it, an excess of total accounting costs over the revenue from marginal-cost pricing obviously constitutes an obstacle to marginal-cost pricing. So what can be done? There are three possibilities: (1) reduce accounting costs; (2) raise the average cost to consumers of output without raising the marginal cost to them; (3) give up marginal-cost pricing.

The first way involves either a subsidy or a capital reconstruction. An example of the latter, though not one inspired by a desire for marginal-cost pricing, is *the writing off* by the British government of £400 million of the National Coal Board's debt to the Exchequer of £960 million. This kind of thing would obviously be rather unpopular among the stockholders of investor utilities, however. Like subsidies, it takes the discussion beyond the framework of decision-making by the public utility itself, so I shall not pursue the matter here.

The second way, in its pure form, involves eating into consumer surplus without affecting resource allocation. *Thus the fixed charge paid by telephone subscribers can be raised while the charge per call is left equal to marginal cost per call.* The trouble is that the scope for this kind of behavior is limited, both by distributional considerations (to which I refer in the next section) and by the circumstance that such a fixed charge is, in effect, the sale to consumer of a license to buy. Now the price attached to this license must be uniform for each class of consumers, and somewhere within each class there will be consumers who are at the margin. An annual subscription for the right to travel on a rapid transit system would shift the odd out-of-town customer to cabs. A higher fixed charge for a telephone would put off a few potential consumers. Thus, in many cases, setting a stiff price on the license to buy will involve a departure from marginal-cost pricing.

This, then, brings us to the third way. Instead of pricing so as to maximize the sum of consumers' and producer's surpluses, i.e., setting prices at marginal cost all along the line, we now price so as to maximize this sum subject to the constraint that

the producer's surplus shall be sufficient for his total receipts to cover his total accounting costs.

But this brings us from practice to theory, so, rather than confirming whether this is the right maximand from the point of view of optimal resource allocation, and rather than deducing its implications for the price to marginal-cost ratios for different outputs, I merely note that financial considerations can generate a real obstacle to marginal-cost pricing and pass on to the next item in my list.

4. Political considerations

Deviations from marginal-cost pricing may be freely chosen by the management of a public utility, or forced upon them, in order to achieve or avoid particular results. It is convenient to call these "political" factors, meaning by this merely that they raise issues outside the professional expert competence of the management, involving issues of public policy.

Not all political considerations interfere with marginal-cost pricing. A prohibition on the import of cheap fuel or the requirement that a proportion of new transmission be undergrounded for amenity reasons would both raise marginal costs without impeding marginal-cost pricing. But in other cases, where pricing itself raises political issues, the ability to reflect marginal costs in prices may be reduced.

This can often happen where it is felt that *the consumers who would be adversely affected by the introduction of marginal-cost pricing are particularly deserving.* Old-age pensioners, farmers, the inhabitants of remote areas and newspaper readers provide examples. Of course, economists are in the habit of recommending that such deserving groups should receive an explicit subsidy from the taxpayer in preference to an implicit cross-subsidy from other consumers of the same products. But though this position may sometimes win some support, it usually does not. A classic example of this is the requirement that railways continue to run their urban commuter services at a loss, being permitted neither to raise the fares nor to cut down on the service. Similarly, bus undertakings have often been required to provide unremunerative rural routes as a condition of getting the profitable routes through densely populated areas. The

United States Post Office charges extremely low rates for second-class mail, largely on the grounds that newspapers provide a very valuable public service, and charges nothing for reading matter for the blind. Similarly, Greek members of parliament do not pay for their telephone calls and telegrams (with the result that their constituents visiting Athens frequently ask to use their telephone), the parents of large families in France pay extra low rail fares and Swedish university students pay concessionary prices at the state opera. In none of these cases, so far as I know, is the motive that of a monopolist seeking to exploit different elasticities of demand.

The costs of electricity distribution are a decreasing function of load density. This suggests that marginal-cost pricing would involve higher electricity tariffs in less-developed parts of a country. In fixing their tariff for bulk supplies, the *tarif vert,* Electricité de France concluded, however, that such tariffs would jeopardize development in the underdeveloped "departments". It was therefore decided, "as a matter of policy, to assign to all the departments which are not yet industrialized— practically two-thirds of the national territory—a fictitious consumption density, which "anticipates the later development" of consumption. Distribution costs have thus been lowered, over two-thirds of the country, to the level observed in the departments which have already become industrialized.

None of the 12 area boards in England and Wales charges a higher tariff to rural consumers in any given consumer class than to urban consumers in the same class. It may be that a desire to aid rural consumers played some part in this, but I fancy that practical administrative considerations are much more important. The problem of drawing and constantly revising a defensible dividing line between urban and rural areas in a small country is enough to deter anyone who is not totally insensitive to public relations.

Finally, there is a major difficulty in introducing marginal-cost pricing which, though in a sense the most trivial political obstacle, can nevertheless not be neglected. This is that unless a public utility is in the happy situation where all costs are falling rapidly, any change in its tariff structure is bound to make some consumers worse off. These consumers will complain, while those who are made better off will keep quiet. Even if those adversely affected do not constitute a group "politically" deemed worthy of special treatment, the mere fact that they will complain is significant.

A management sufficiently devoted to the ideal of marginal-cost pricing might be ready to weather the storm. But complainants can lobby their representatives in the legislature, raise their grievance with consultative councils, petition regulatory commissions, call for public enquiry, refuse to pay their bills, go on strike, and kick up a shindig in a myriad of ways. Now this upsets other people even if, as we are assuming for the sake of argument, it fails to upset the management. But the other people who get upset may succeed in transmitting the shock to the management. In the end, then, even the purest of mortals has to keep an ear to the ground and, like us of coarser clay, include a quiet life as one of the variables in his objective function.

Reading 37

In a perfectly competitive market, no one producer can have any sizable impact upon the quantities produced or the prices charged. The market is impersonal; Producer A has no occasion to think about what any specific Producer B may do, simply because there are hundreds or even thousands of B's in the market. But in cases of oligopoly (few sellers), every producer if he is wise will think long and hard about the actions of the remaining few producers. Producer A knows—and sometimes fears—Producer B. The structure of prices in such a market is often a fascinating study in mutual trust and, sometimes, distrust.

One of the landmark cases under the Sherman Antitrust Act resulted in the Supreme Court's order to break up the giant American Tobacco Company in 1911. What emerged thereafter was an industry of few sellers. There has been no evidence of collusion or overt contact among the successor firms to the original American Tobacco Company. But the handful of producers have been keenly aware of one another's presence.

William H. Nicholls, professor of economics at Vanderbilt University, discusses some of the more interesting features of pricing in this industry. The price leadership picture which he draws with such fine detail is an invaluable supplement to textbook discussions of oligopoly.

Questions to guide the reading

From the point of view of the consumer, what is gained by having oligopoly and price leadership in the cigarette industry in contrast with the near-monopoly of the pre-1911 era?

What are likely to be the most critical considerations entering into any one cigarette manufacturer's decision to go along with or to hold out against a price change elsewhere in the industry? What then are the preconditions for effective price leadership?

Price Leadership: The Case of the Cigarette Industry

William H. Nicholls

> Evolution is not a force but a process. . . .
> *John Viscount Morley*

This is a summary and appraisal of cigarette price policies since the Tobacco Trust was dissolved by Court action in 1911. After a brief summary of the principal trends in the cigarette market during 1911–50, we try to analyze the process by which present cigarette policy evolved. We shall be primarily concerned with the means by which the uncertainties inherent in the circular interdependence of a noncollusive, oligopolistic market structure were resolved.

A. Principal trends in the cigarette market, 1911–50

The most important single characteristic of the American cigarette market has been the highly dynamic nature of the demand for cigarettes. During 1911–50, cigarette production in the United States increased from 10 to 393 billions and per capita consumption increased nearly twentyfold. Furthermore, these trends were almost wholly uninterrupted, production falling below previous levels only during 1920–21, 1931–33, and 1949. With the

demand curve for cigarettes shifting so steadily upward, each of the four major successor firms to the Tobacco Trust (American Tobacco, Reynolds Tobacco, Liggett and Myers, and Lorillard) could, in considerable part, direct large advertising outlays to extending the aggregate market to its own advantage rather than to taking old customers away from its principal rivals. Their combined advertising expenditures not only contributed to the expansion of total cigarette consumption, but, during most of the period, greatly strengthened their position relative to the rest of the industry. Thus, having inherited 80 per cent of the nation's cigarette business from the Trust, the four successor companies had achieved a market position of perhaps 97 per cent by 1925 and controlled 98 per cent as late as 1931 (Table 1). During the 1930's, the development of the first significant independent competition since the dissolution reduced the position of the successor companies to 74 per cent, more than half of their loss being attributable to the rise of lower-priced "economy" brands, which

From William H. Nicholls, *Price Policies in the Cigarette Industry* (Vanderbilt University Press, Nashville, Tenn., 1951). Reprinted with kind permission of the author and publisher.

Table 1   Summary of Market Positions of Principal Cigarette Companies, Selected Years, 1911–50

Year	Total sales as per cent of U.S. cigarette production										Total U.S. production (billions)
	Amer.	L.& M.	Rey.	Lor.	4 Co's.	BW	PM	All other	3 major brands	Economy brands	
1911	37.1	27.8	0	15.3	80.2	...	...	19.8	...	...	10
1925	21.2	32.0	41.6	1.9	96.7	...	...	3.3	82	...	82
1931	39.4	22.7	28.4	7.0	97.6	0.2	0.3	1.9	86	0.3	117
1939	22.7	21.6	23.7	5.7	73.7	10.6	7.0	8.7	66	14.8	181
1950	30.9	18.7	26.9	5.5	82.0	6.1	11.0	1.8	68	0.9	393

had taken over 15 per cent of the domestic market by 1939. However, by 1950—thanks largely to the virtual disappearance of the economy brands—the successor companies' position had recovered to 82 per cent. The three major brands alone (Lucky Strike, Camel, Chesterfield)—which have always received the bulk of the industry's advertising outlays—increased their relative importance from 82 to 86 per cent during 1925-31, fell back sharply to 66 per cent in 1939, and accounted for 68 per cent by 1950.

Among the four successor firms, the relative distribution of cigarette sales has fluctuated widely since the dissolution (Table 1). The years 1911-25 were characterized by the rise of Reynolds (which had received no cigarette business from the Trust) to a position of dominance (45 per cent in 1923) and the precipitous decline of Lorillard. During 1925-31, American rapidly pushed far into the lead (39 per cent in 1931)—largely at the expense of Reynolds—while Lorillard for the first time showed some vitality. Between 1931 and 1939, all four companies suffered important setbacks, with American showing the greatest loss of relative position, Liggett & Myers the least. While continuing to show a decline in relative position, Reynolds held a slight lead (with 24 per cent) in the latter year. Since 1939, American has again definitely taken over first place (31 per cent in 1950) although Reynolds has also experienced a relative gain.

Since 1927 (with the exception of 1934 and 1944), Liggett & Myers has never ranked higher than third place in the American cigarette market. Even prior to that time, Liggett & Myers followed a conservative, non-aggressive price and advertising policy, with Reynolds largely setting the pace. After 1927, either Reynolds or American took the lead in most basic policy decisions and their relative positions have fluctuated widely over the years, in contrast with Liggett & Myers' more stable market percentage. Throughout most of the period since the dissolution, Lorillard has been of relatively minor importance in the cigarette market, not having produced more than 8 per cent of the nation's cigarettes since well before 1925. Of the five principal independents which grew to significant size—during the 1930's, two (Brown & Williamson and Philip Morris) outranked Lorillard by 1939. Since the latter date, Philip Morris has continued to expand its market position considerably but the other principal independents (including Brown & Williamson) have rapidly lost ground.

Since the dissolution, the list prices of the major cigarette brands have been relatively inflexible. During the 38 years 1913-50 inclusive, the price of Camel cigarettes was changed 20 times, exclusive of 5 increases (two of them by amounts greater than the tax) resulting from changes in federal cigarette taxes and one upward adjustment in OPA's cigarette price ceiling not related to a tax increase. The list price of Camels ranged from $4.00 to $8.00 per thousand over this period. Had the tax been constant at its present rate throughout 1913-50, however (and had earlier list prices been increased by exactly the amount of the difference in tax rates), the range would have been narrowed to $6.00-$8.50, the lowest price falling in 1933 and the highest in 1919-21. During

1913-23—before virtually identical list and net prices of the three major brands became the rule—the list price of Camels (adjusted to present tax rates) ranged from $6.25 to $8.50, with 9 price changes not associated with tax increases. During the much longer period of virtual list-price identity 1923-50, however, the range (at present tax rates) was $6.00-$8.00, with only 11 price changes (plus one OPA increase) unrelated to tax increases. Thus, during the 27 years of virtual list-price identity the number of price changes only slightly exceeded that during the earlier 11-year period and the range of prices was somewhat less.

Because of the large and fixed federal cigarette tax, however, even these relatively inflexible list prices have resulted in more flexible net prices to manufacturers after dealer discounts and tax. Thus, the range in the net price of Camels during 1913-50 was $1.85 (1933) to $4.05 (1919-21). During 1913-23, the range was $2.28-$4.05 and, during 1923-50, $1.85 to $3.56 (1950), or 3.4 cents a package. If one eliminates two special periods of price-cutting—that of 1928-29 within the Big Four and that of 1933-36 directed against independent competition—and the wartime period of price controls, the range in net prices is narrowed to $2.51-$3.56, or 2.1 cents a package, during a total period of 17 years since 1923. These data underline the barriers which the large federal tax has imposed against price competition, the extreme severity of the 1933 price cuts, and the more moderate price policy which the major firms have followed since 1937.

The price history of the three major brands during 1912-23 reflected many of the characteristics which one associates with the concept of competitive price behavior. Diverse price differentials did exist among the three brands as they were introduced, and the timing and extent of changes in prices and discounts varied considerably from one brand to another. While Reynolds' influence on the price policies of its two major competitors was already discernible, the latter companies did sometimes take independent action in price changes. Despite the frequent diversity of list prices among the three brands, discounts were usually adjusted openly or secretly to bring net prices fairly closely in line—a result still consistent with a process of price competition.

When the three major firms moved to virtual list and net price identity in August 1923, however, any resemblance to competitive price behavior disappeared.

Combined net profits of the three major companies grew from 50 to 106 million dollars during 1923-31, a period in which they accounted for 90 per cent or more of total cigarette production. During the same period, their rates of earnings on net worth increased from 15-20 per cent to 17-22 per cent. Their loss of business to independents, and the resulting severe price reductions of 1933, cut their net profits in half and their earnings to 8-13 per cent in that year. By 1940, their net profits had recovered to 73 million dollars and their earnings to 13-17 per cent, despite a continued loss of relative market position. The coming of price controls brought a tremendous increase in their absolute and relative sales but by 1943 had resulted in a reduction in their combined net profits to 57 million dollars (just above their 1933 low) and earnings of 10-13 per cent. With the price increases of 1946-50, their combined profits at last passed the previous peak of 1933, amounting to 108-111 million dollars in 1948-50, when they earned 12-16 per cent on net worth. This rate of earnings approached their 1932-39 average of 13-17 per cent but still fell short of their average earnings of 18-21 per cent during 1924-31. Nonetheless, it is clear that the three major companies have consistently enjoyed earnings well above normal competitive levels and that the effects of potential and actual competition over many years have not been sufficient to eliminate significant amounts of monopoly profits.

B. The process of revising incorrect anticipations under oligopoly

Since 1911, the American cigarette market has been characterized by oligopoly. Because the great bulk (68-91 per cent) of the nation's cigarettes has been produced and sold by three successor firms, no one of them could ignore the influence of its own price decisions upon the sales (hence price policies) of the other firms or, in turn, the influence of their resultant price policies upon its own sales. Even the smallest of the three major firms, Liggett & Myers, recognized this circular interdependence clearly in stating that its cigarette prices depend "to a considerable extent upon what its chief competitors are doing and what they are likely to do in respect of price changes." Such recognition did not spring full-blown from the dissolution decree. But during 1917-23—after the three major brands had been introduced—each of the three firms certainly came to realize that circular interdependence did exist. It then became incumbent upon each firm to try to judge correctly the nature of this interdependence. For, until it knew what assumptions to make as to the extent and timing of any interactions which it might set in motion by a change in its own policies, it could not correctly assess the probable *ultimate* effects of this change upon its own profits. The simplest way to have eliminated these oligopolistic uncertainties would have been outright merger or formal collusion. But, operating under the shadow of the recent dissolution decree, the successor firms could hardly avail themselves of these alternatives. Hence, a policy of experimentalism—by which the three companies tried out different price differentials and different timings of price changes (and responses to price changes)—was forced upon them.

There is ample evidence in the price history of 1917-23 that the major firms' original anticipations of rival reactions were incorrect. This was especially true during the earlier part of the period when price *increases* were the order of the day. An outstanding example of incorrect anticipations was American's unsuccessful attempt to lead in a price increase in September 1918. It is obvious that American expected its major rivals to follow upward and seriously underestimated the costliness (in loss of sales) of its policy in the event that they failed to do so. Out of this experience, American apparently revised its anticipations of rival reactions, becoming understandably reluctant to initiate price changes thereafter. While Reynolds was less unfortunate in leading price increases during 1918-19 even its success was mixed, with American once following upward all the way, once only in part. In the latter case, Reynolds then cut below American, which (through secret discounts) moved to the same level as Reynolds. Reynolds used similar techniques in following Liggett & Myers' one initial price *increase* only part way, and in following American's single initial price *decrease* by an even larger price cut, in each case thereby establishing the price level to which the original price leader then moved. Obviously,

each of these price changes again reflected uncertainty as to what rival reactions would be. But, by its own choice of policies, Reynolds made it clear that a failure to follow its lead completely would result in its returning to lower prices but created a serious doubt as to whether it would itself follow its rivals' leads. While the latter doubts might have led to new conflicts and uncertainties, these were resolved by an increasing willingness of the other firms to concede a position of price leadership to Reynolds.

Uncertainties regarding probable rival reactions to initial price *cuts* were more easily diminished. During the period of price decreases 1921-22, American and Reynolds both discovered that the other would promptly meet price cuts in full, thereby making it possible for each to anticipate correctly the other's reaction to a price decrease. Although reluctant to conform with this policy, Liggett & Myers' resistance to price cuts during 1921-22 probably revealed the costliness of such a policy and brought it around to the same point of view. Experience with secret rather than open price differentials was apparently found to be an unsatisfactory technique (probably because they did not remain secret) of increasing sales, being little used after 1919.

The market situation of 1917-23 had all the elements which, according to general theory, would result in a highly unstable or even chaotic outcome. Unquestionably, each of the three major firms was originally extremely uncertain as to the extent and timing of its rivals' reactions to a price change. Furthermore, the fact that each firm at times tried to initiate price changes (Table 2) implies that each aspired to a position of price leadership in order that it might set that price which would correspond most closely to its own maximum-profit position. Yet, while there were indeed elements of instability during this period, the impressive fact is the pattern of order which rather quickly emerged. Such an outcome—particularly in view of the fact that there was apparently no formal collusion of any kind—is in itself remarkable and stands in sharp contrast with theoretical predictions of extreme instability. This outcome would suggest that anticipations as to rival reactions, while initially incorrect, can be gradually revised with experience until they become both correct and compatible. While it is impossible to

Table 2 Summary of Price Leadership among the Three Major Cigarette Companies, 1917–50

Time period	Company initiating price change	Number of successful leads			Number of unsuccessful leads		
		Upward	Downward	Total	Upward	Downward	Total
1917–23	Reynolds	2	2	4	0	0	0
	American	0	1	1	1	0	1
	Liggett & Myers	1	0	1	0	0	0
	Uncertain	2	0	2	0	0	0
1924–39	Reynolds	4	1	5	0	0	0
	American	0	2	2	0	0	0
	Liggett & Myers	0	0	0	0	0	0
1940–50 (ex. OPA)	Reynolds	2	0	2	0	0	0
	American	2	0	2	1	0	1
	Liggett & Myers	0	0	0	2	0	2
1917–50 (ex. OPA)	Reynolds	8	3	11	0	0	0
	American	2	3	5	2	0	2
	Liggett & Myers	1	0	1	2	0	2
	Uncertain	2	0	2	0	0	0

predict, on purely theoretical grounds, that such revisions will converge or the paths by which convergence may be reached, the concrete fact in the cigarette industry is that they did so.

Although American and Liggett & Myers subordinated their aspirations for price leadership to Reynolds' claims only reluctantly, Reynolds meanwhile enforced its own claims with considerable restraint. As a result of this element of "give and take," price competition (such as there was) was keep within reasonable bounds. And, reluctance and restraint notwithstanding, Reynolds' position of price leadership—particularly in the more uncertain area of price *increases*—was gradually recognized, reinforced by its steadily growing strength in the cigarette market. Once this became true, remaining uncertainties could be (and were in August 1923) easily resolved by standardizing dealer discounts—so that identical list prices automatically produced the identical net prices to manufacturers which had tended to result anyway—and by making responses to changes in the leader's price, whether upward or downward, complete and immediate.

We may conclude that the crucial step in eliminating oligopolistic uncertainty in the cigarette industry was the mutual recognition that one of the three firms was to act as price leader, particularly on price increases. For this step eliminated the problem of a "kinked" demand curve which would otherwise have faced each of the three firms. Such a discontinuous demand curve would result if each oligopolist believed that "rivals will quickly match price reductions but only hesitatingly and incompletely (if at all) follow price increases." Under this pattern of expected behavior, the demand curve for the product of each oligopolist would have a kink at the existing price. The part above the kink would be more elastic, indicating the given firm's loss of business if it should raise its price, other prices remaining unchanged at the old level. The lower part would be more inelastic, showing the given firm's gains of business if its price cuts were at all times matched by its rivals.

American's unsuccessful efforts to bring about a general price increase in 1918 and its experience with matched price cuts during 1921–22 were undoubtedly such as to convince it of the reality of the "kink." Had the other two firms (especially Reynolds) had precisely the same experience, any one of them would have been extremely reluctant to lead in a price increase because of the belief (verified by experience) that the others would not follow upward. Under such circumstances, cigarette prices would have been highly insensitive to changes in cost or demand, hence extremely rigid. Furthermore, unless the existing price was initially at the level which would maximize their joint profits, the final price would also have to be below that level. Thus, the advantages of mutual recognition of one *(any one)* of the oligopolists as price leader become obvious. For, once the price leader (Reynolds) could correctly anticipate that its price increases would be followed, the "kink" in its demand curve disappeared and it could raise prices with impunity. What the other firms lost in initiative was far more than offset by the gains in certainty as to the "rules of the game" on price increases, which made greater joint profits possible.

C. Factors favoring a policy of cigarette-price identity

A striking characteristic of cigarette policies after 1923 was that a policy of price identity (rather than differential prices) among the major brands evolved.

Between August 1923 and May 1951, there was a total of only 15 days on which the list (and net) prices of the three major brands differed because of a rival's delay in responding to an initial price change on one of the brands. At all other times (except 1923-28 and 1946-49, when minute price differences of 3-5 cents a thousand existed among them), the three major brands had (apart from what was apparently a small amount of price-shading) absolutely identical list prices, dealer discounts and net prices. The fourth major successor-company brand (Old Gold), while probably never important enough to have upset the common price policy had Lorillard shown more independence, also conformed fully with the policy of price-identity except for a small 10-cent-per-thousand differential during 1928-29. Thus, the prices of the three (or four) brands moved together, either upward or downward, with an almost perfect harmony of amplitude and timing. The same was true for the major standard brands of Philip Morris and Brown & Williamson after 1940, by which time these two independents had successfully established themselves in the standard-brand field.

To be sure, substitution (though imperfect) in consumption established certain narrow limits upon the extent to which price differentials might be profitable. But at least, within these limits, they became possible. Hence, a policy of price identity or price differentials among the several brands became a matter of deliberate choice, based upon expectations of the relative profitability of alternative courses of action. Why, then, was it a policy of price *identity,* and not one of price differentials, which emerged?

First, at the time the three major brands were introduced, there was already certain "customary" retail-price classes (10, 15, and 20 cents a package) which the three companies apparently felt it necessary to respect. These "customary" price classes introduced a very strong element of discreteness into price policies and favored pricing for identical retail prices as compared with so great a minimum price differential as 5 cents. (During the years since 1930, the rapid increase in odd-cents state taxes has effectively destroyed such discreteness in cigarette prices. But, in the early history of the industry, "customary" or "convenient-coin" prices undoubtedly exercised an important influence on cigarette price policies.)

Second, the concentration of advertising on the three brands served to set them apart (in the minds of consumers) as a particular class of product differing from non-advertised minor brands. The effect of such advertising was probably such as to diminish the elasticity of demand for the three brands as a class, while tending to break down the imperfections of substitution within the product class. As a consequence, the elasticity of demand for any one of the three brands was probably increased—a result further enhanced by the steadily growing increment of new, unattached smokers. Because of the small number of firms, sensitivity to the prices of rival products was greatly increased, thereby reducing the likelihood that any given firm could successfully maintain a significant price differential below other brands. Again, therefore, a strong tendency toward identical prices would have been expected.

Third, the tendency of consumers to judge quality by price created a further barrier to departures from price identity among the three brands. We have argued that the existence of discrete price classes, with advertising concentrated upon a single price class, encouraged price identity within that class. But it is equally probable that, as they became accustomed to price identity among the major advertised brands, consumers increasingly judged the extent to which the three brands were close substitutes (in terms of quality) by their common price. Because of this perverse psychology created by product differentiation, an unmatched price cut on one major brand might cause consumers to associate lower price with lower quality—particularly if the lower price forced a significant reduction in the firm's advertising outlays—so that they would remain with (or soon shift back to) the higher-priced brands. While this factor favoring price identity among the major advertised brands can easily be exaggerated, it is noteworthy that the two principal independent brands (Philip Morris, Raleigh) which finally succeeded in attaining volume sales in the standard-brand price class, did so by initially selling in a *higher* price class, lowering their prices only after they had become established. On the other hand, with minor exceptions, none of the economy brands has yet entered the standard-brand price class after becoming established at lower prices, which made significant advertising outlays prohibitive.

Fourth, the growth of cigarette taxes has increasingly diminished the prospect of gains from unmatched price cuts below other brands and favored even unmatched price increases. Since the dissolution, federal, state and local governments have pyramided taxes upon cigarettes. These taxes have almost invariably been specific rather than graduated or *ad valorem,* and have now reached so high a proportion (50 per cent or more) of the retail price as to make even an unmatched price cut (a price differential below competing brands) of questionable value. Thus—in a state levying a three-cent-per-package cigarette tax in addition to the seven-cent federal tax—suppose that the manufacturer of any one of the major brands of cigarettes had been successful in establishing an unmatched price cut of one cent a package at retail at 1949 prices. To achieve this 5-per cent reduction in the retail price, he would have had to reduce his own final net price by 12 per cent. The effect of present taxes upon the economy-brand manufacturer is even more severe—a 15-per cent reduction in net price would have been required to reduce the retail price by 5 per cent, and an 18-per cent reduction to reduce the retail price by a full cent. Thus, combined cigarette taxes—being so large and unrelated to retail price—have been an increasingly important factor favoring continued price identity.

The effect of these various factors was undoubtedly to strengthen the tendency of oligopolistic competition to result in a policy of price identity. Given this tendency, absolute price identity was obviously superior to small departures from price identity as a means of eliminating the uncertainties of oligopoly. Even small and variable differences in list prices, discounts and net prices might arouse suspicions that rivals were not living up to the mutually-recognized "rules of the game." Prices and discounts, being the most precisely measurable and most fully publicized variables of market policy, could also be reduced to foolproof "rules" more easily than quality of product (blend, packaging, etc.) and quantity of advertising.

But none of these reasons is enough to explain fully the acceptance of price leadership among the major producers. Why, in particular, were the other firms always willing to follow Reynolds' price *increases?* Because, on balance, they recognized the advantages to themselves in doing so. In most instances, they were "glad to follow" because they "saw the opportunity to make some money," "to reinstate . . . our earnings," or "to increase income." Again, counsel for Liggett & Myers stated it most clearly. "The opportunity to increase sales by not following [was] illusory," since such an action was certain to force "the others . . . to return to the lower figure." Hence, if it is believed that "the higher price will not adversely affect public buying of this type of product, or invite new competition into the field, obviously each has the most natural and legitimate of reasons for following the increase." Even so, why was recognition of a *single* price leader among the dominant firms necessary? The answer lies in the elimination of the kink in the demand curves of the oligopolists. Obviously, no one of the three firms was sufficiently dominant to establish prices to which its rivals would react purely competitively because, individually, they had no influence over price. Rather, their circular interdependence was so great that—unless the kink was eliminated by mutual acceptance of a common leader for price increases—prices might be frozen despite significant increases in costs or demand. If so, it would become impossible to readjust to changing market conditions in such a way as to hope to achieve and maintain a position of maximum joint profits for the dominant group.

Hence, while Reynolds may at times have turned its position as price leader somewhat to its own advantage, its declining market position after 1923 increasingly put upon it the burden of establishing for the group a price policy which rather promptly reflected changing market conditions, if its position of leadership was to be maintained. American's price cuts of 1933 indicate its belief that, at that time, Reynolds had failed to do so since 1931. On the other hand, Reynolds' price increases of 1929, 1934 and 1937 undoubtedly did represent appropriate adjustments to increased demand and costs, enhancing the willingness of the others to follow. Significantly, there is no evidence that, during 1924–39, American even considered leading in a price increase, higher costs or otherwise. And, while frequently justifying its willingness to follow upward on the basis of costs, Liggett & Myers admitted that trends in costs merely determined "whether we followed gladly or whether we followed reluctantly." Even rising costs did not cause Liggett & Myers to give any thought to leading in a price increase because, as "third seller," it did not wish "to take a chance" on doing so. In any case, the high relative importance of selling costs to total costs probably forced the price leader to give his principal attention to changing demand factors rather than to changing production costs.

Since the direction (if not identical amplitude and timing) of all other price increases of 1924–39 might have been expected in terms of changing market conditions, it was the 1931 price increase which provided the acid test for the common price policy. If ever there was a time when a refusal to follow a price increase might have appeared likely to pay off in increased relative sales, it was then. Yet is 1931, as well as at other times, American and Liggett & Myers apparently believed that their retention of the lower price would result only in temporary gains since Reynolds would then restore its price to its previous lower level, whereas their gains would be permanent if they matched Reynolds' increase. American confirmed this by saying that—in conjunction with a lower price policy on its cigarette substitutes (roll-your-own and pipe tobacco)—it "naturally saw the opportunity to make some money" and "reserve[d] the

right to make price changes downward" if its expectations were not fulfilled.

On the other hand, Liggett & Myers officials thought the increase "was a mistake" and "ill-advised." Why, then, did Liggett & Myers follow—especially if it really believed that its current sales position was so weak that it was, for once, "doubtful of its ability to force the [other two] manufacturers . . . to cancel their increases"? Why shouldn't such a doubt have encouraged rather than discouraged an independent price policy? Both American and Liggett & Myers replied that their failure to follow would have given Reynolds a sufficient increment of advertising funds to prevent them from substantially increasing their sales at the lower price. Such an argument is wholly unconvincing and completely inconsistent with their belief in the absolute necessity of fully matching price decreases.

In view of past experience—reinforced by the depressed economic conditions of 1931—it seems absurd to suppose that the failure of either American or Liggett & Myers to follow Reynolds' price increase would not have forced a cancellation of that increase. Hence, the former companies must have believed that the possibility of increased joint profits at the higher common price was sufficiently great to warrant the experiment, while the possible gains from resisting the change were temporary, hence "illusory." By following upward, as Liggett & Myers clearly recognized, each firm ran "the risk of retaliation by consumers, but that retaliation [would], based on price, be visited on all rivals equally. . . . For a manufacturer to suffer with other manufacturers a loss of sales may be unpleasant but it is not fatal; one of the leading sellers will presumably readjust its price as soon as the effects of the excessive price are obvious." Of course, the real risk was that aggregate elasticity of demand for cigarettes had been underestimated by the price leader—that is, that the "retaliation of consumers" would be *so great* that profits would be diminished rather than increased. It was recognized, however, that—if experience led to a diminution of profits—a joint price reduction could correct the situation.

According to Liggett & Myers, had it refused to follow the 1931 price increase, it would have run the greater risk "of losing [its relative] position in the market . . . which [as of the fate of Lorillard shows, it might] never be able to regain." While fully applicable to a failure to follow a price decrease, such a statement is obviously invalid with regard to a price increase (Liggett & Myers' arguments to the contrary notwithstanding). Nonetheless, Liggett & Myers are undoubtedly correct in its belief that "the inertia of custom, plus extensive advertising, tend to assure a well established manufacturer his existing share of the market provided he does not permit his competitors to do anything drastically different from himself." To be sure, in an oligopolistic market situation, "imitation minimizes risk"—the risk of oligopolistic price uncertainties. By the elimination of this risk, the maximization of the dominant firm's joint profits was largely assured.

Reading 38

How does the auto industry stand up to Galbraith's charge that much money and ingenuity are spent today in making the consumer want not genuine transportation efficiency and comforts, but mere emulative conspicuous and invidious consumption? This reading is a careful calculation of the costs that could have been avoided if the 1949 American car had been stabilized.

Franklin Fisher is a professor of econometrics at M.I.T.; Zvi Griliches is a professor of economics at Harvard University; and Carl Kaysen, long a professor at Harvard, is now Director of the Institute of Advanced Study at Princeton.

Questions to guide the reading

If people want variety and novelty, should they get it, provided they can afford it? What would one propose be done with the money—and, more important, the resources—saved by having less frequent changes in automobile models?

The Costs of Automobile Model Changes since 1949

Franklin M. Fisher, Zvi Griliches, and Carl Kaysen

This paper reports estimates of the costs to the economy of the changes in private automobile specifications that took place during the fifties. In such costs are included not only the costs to the automobile manufacturers themselves of special retooling for new models but also the direct costs of producing larger, heavier, and more powerful cars, as well as the costs of automatic transmissions, power brakes, and the like. Finally, we include the secondary costs not paid out by the automobile companies but paid nevertheless by the consuming public in the form of increased expenditures for gasoline necessitated by the "horsepower race."

Throughout, we concentrate on the cost of the resources that would have been saved had cars with the 1949 model lengths, weights, horsepowers, transmissions, etc., been produced in every year. As there was technological change in the industry, we are thus assessing not the resource expenditure that would have been saved had the 1949 models themselves been continued but rather the resource expenditure that would have been saved had cars with 1949 specifications been continued but been built with the developing technology as estimated from actual car construction cost and performance data.

In thus assessing the costs of automobile model change, we do not mean to deny that such changes also brought benefits. Indeed, it is quite clear that

From Franklin M. Fisher, Zvi Griliches, and Carl Kaysen, "Abstract and the Costs of Automobile Model Changes since 1949," *American Economic Review*, May, 1962. Reprinted with kind permission of the authors and publisher.

most or all of the changes involved were in fact desired by the consuming public (perhaps after advertising) and that the automobile companies were satisfying such desires. Nevertheless, the costs estimated seem so staggeringly high that it seems worth while presenting the bill and asking whether it was "worth" it, in retrospect.

The consumer pays

The largest component of the cost of model changes since 1949 turns out to be the higher costs of automobile construction (as measured by automobile prices) attendant on higher horsepowers, greater lengths, greater weights, and so forth. As the cost of a given specification varies with technological change (in particular, that of horsepower clearly declines over time), such costs were estimated by a series of cross-section regressions of the list prices of a given year's models on the specifications thereof. From these regressions, estimates of the cost of construction of the average 1949 car in each successive year (given the retooling expenditures which actually took place) were constructed and compared with the average list price of actual models. Optional equipment was separately costed, as were advertising expenditures. The results showed an average cost per car (in current prices) over 1956–60 of $454 for size and horsepower plus about $116 for optional equipment and $14 for advertising. The total estimated costs of such items thus averaged about 3.3 billion dollars per year for the same period.

These estimates, however, make no allowance for the retooling expenditures which would have been saved had 1949 specifications actually been continued; they merely estimate the saving from producing cars with such specifications given the actual retooling expenditures. Accordingly, we next estimated the saving in retooling expenditure that would have occurred in the absence of model change, basing our estimates on the expenditures for special tools reported by the automobile companies to the Securities and Exchange Commission and charged by them to profit and loss. We concluded that, again in current prices, such savings would have averaged about $99 per car over the 1956–60 period, total savings coming to about 560 million dollars per year.

The total costs of model change as estimated so far came to about $700 per car (more than 25 per cent of purchase price) or about 3.9 billion dollars per year over the 1956–60 period. However, unlike the costs so far considered, there are other costs of model changes which are not exhausted with the construction of the car but are expended over its life. Chief among these (and the only one estimated by us) is the additional gasoline consumption due to changes in transmissions and especially to increases in horsepower.

This part of the study was broken into halves. First, we estimated the relation between over-all gasoline mileage as reported by *Consumer Reports* and the "fuel economy factor" reported by the same source. This analysis was divided by type of transmission and number of forward speeds. We then proceeded (much as in our analysis of direct costs) to analyze the technologically changing relationship between advertised horsepower and displacement (the principal component of the fuel economy factor) by means of a series of cross-section regressions using the engines produced in successive model years. We interpreted the results in terms of engine redesign to secure higher horsepower at given displacement and used them to compute the displacement that could have been secured for the 1949 model horsepowers. We then used the relation between displacement and gasoline consumption via the fuel economy factor to estimate the gasoline consumption that would have been obtained with 1949 horsepowers. The result showed that whereas actual gasoline mileage fell from 16.4 miles per gallon in 1949 to 14.3 miles per gallon ten years later, then rising to about 15.3 in 1960 and 1961, the gasoline mileage of the average 1949 car would have *risen* to 18.0 miles per gallon in 1959 and 18.5 in 1961. This meant that the owner of the average 1956–60 car was paying about $40 more per 10,000 miles of driving (about 20 per cent of his total gasoline costs) than would have been the case had 1949 models been continued.

We then utilized these results to compute the cost of such additional gasoline consumption by the car stock, estimating this to average about 968 million dollars per year over the 1956–60 period in current prices. Moreover, since such additional expenditure continues over the life of the car, we estimated that even if 1962 and all later model years were to see a return to 1949 specifications, the 1961 present value (in 1960 prices) of additional gasoline consumption by cars already built through 1961 discounted at 10 per cent would be about 7.1 billion dollars.

Bill and bill of indictment

We thus estimated costs of model changes since 1949 to run about 5 billion dollars per year over the 1956–60 period with a present value of future gasoline costs of 7.1 billion. If anything, these figures are underestimates because of items not included. As stated at the outset, most of these costs were stated in the price of the car and it is difficult not to conclude that car owners thought the costs worth incurring at the time of purchase. Whether, in retrospect, this means that they were in fact worth incurring is a question we do not attempt to answer.

Readings 39 and 40   Debate on Advertising

The wastes of a market system have often been criticized. Billions are spent each year on advertising to persuade us consumers to buy one thing rather than another. Some of our most creative talent goes into catchy jingles, flamboyant illustrations, Pavlovian conditioning of buyers, and far-fetched claims for products. Some consumers benefit from new information, whether they are conscious of it or not. Some do not. Some gain misinformation. In any case, TV, newspapers, and magazines are viable in their present form because of the present system of advertising revenue.

Sven Lindqvist, a journalist and author, was one member appointed to Sweden's Royal Commission on Advertising. Here he gives reasons why he favors taxing advertising (and, to preserve competitive newspapers, using the proceeds to subsidize weaker newspapers). Kenneth Boulding, famous American economist (and social scientist, poet, and pacifist), decades ago proposed such a tax on advertising. Nicholas Kaldor in Britain has arrived at similar conclusions.

Lester Telser, professor of economics at the University of Chicago, subjects advertising to economic analysis. He concludes that the patterns make sense: that consumers do benefit, and that competitive information is made better by advertising.

The reader must score the debate.

Questions to guide the reading

Investigation shows that soap and cigarettes get advertised much in all countries. Does that mean society has a rational social interest in permitting or encouraging this? For health reasons we banned TV advertising of cigarettes. Did that hurt or help the big companies? It helped them, sent their stocks up in the years that immediately followed. What, if anything, can one conclude from this?

Can you stop the "bad" in advertising without killing off the "good," too? Do only the highbrows really dislike advertising? Someone must pay if we are to see super-bowl games. Why not those consumers who buy advertisers' products? Why not, in a free country, let any economic activity go on between consenting adults that will pay for itself? Formulate your views on these controversial matters.

Reading 39

The Case for Taxed Advertising

Sven Lindqvist

> In the case of monopolistic competition, the state's main duty is to prevent too many resources from flowing into the industry and being wastefully used. A careful taxation system could do much in this direction, especially in the elimination of selling costs. The taxation of advertising would seem to be a method of raising revenue that has few objections; it is surprising that it has not been tried except in a very small way.
>
> *Kenneth E. Boulding, Economic Analysis, 1941.*

On May 27, 1972, Sweden's parliament, the Riksdag, decided to introduce a tax on advertising. The new tax is collected from publishers and printers. It amounts to 6 per cent on advertisements in daily newspapers and 10 per cent on other advertisements. The revenue is to be used in an effort to check the monopolization of the press. By giving economically weak dailies production grants, it is hoped that the future existence of a free, and politically differentiated press will be secured.

The original motives for the proposal were not connected with press policies, but with consumer policies. The proposal for an advertising tax was born within the Royal Commission on Advertising. This commission was appointed in 1966 to investigate whether advertising should be permitted in the TV programs of the publicly owned and controlled Radio Sweden.[1] The Commission was given the instructions to make a comprehensive survey of Swedish advertising. These are some of its findings:

1. A poll among companies showed that advertising expenses in 1965-1967 amounted to 2.4 per cent of private consumption, and grew by some 10 per cent a year, considerably faster than private consumption.

2. Most of the advertising expenditure was concentrated to only a small number of companies. 1,700 companies accounted for 85 per cent of the advertising expenditure. 255 companies in manu-

[1] There are no commercial TV or radio stations in Sweden.

facturing and commerce, with one-third of the total turnover, accounted for 60 per cent of the advertising expenditure.

3. Advertising expenses were also highly concentrated to certain commodity groups. One-half of the advertising of manufacturers and importers concerned ten commodity groups—among them tobacco and spirits, automobiles, cosmetics, detergents, coffee, chocolate and gasoline. It did not seem likely that the consumers' need of information would be correspondingly concentrated on precisely these commodity groups.

4. The intensity factor of advertising—that is the relation between a company's advertising expenses and its turnover—showed variations between different commodity groups that could hardly be explained as rational.

Why should the intensity factor be six times higher for detergents than for washing machines? Why do wrist watches have twice as high an intensity factor as cameras—and cameras an intensity factor five times as high as toys? Why does toothpaste have an intensity factor of advertising 133 times as high as eggs?

5. The statistical analysis of these variations showed that the consumers' need for information rarely was the reason. In other words, it is not the needs of the buyer, but the needs of the seller that determine the advertising intensity of a product.

A high advertising intensity is more than anything else connected with the competition for shares of markets with few producers.

6. A poll among 150 decision-makers in some 40

From Sven Lindqvist, "The Case for Taxed Advertising," *Viewpoint,* released by the Swedish Information Service, New York, June 21, 1972. Reprinted in abridgment with the kind permission of the author and the publisher.

companies showed that the companies seldom make any real analysis of their advertising needs. Old patterns, the actions of competitors and various pressure groups within and outside the company play a considerably greater role than rational deliberations.

7. A poll with 122 consumers in two Swedish cities, who were asked in which way they take advantage of advertising, showed that the consumers do not give advertising much credit as a source of information—the same result as shown by previous similar polls. The only ads that are more systematically used for the gathering of information are the ads with food prices from the big supermarket chains before the weekends.

On the whole, the results of these investigations painted the picture of rising costs for a highly irrational activity that is of little value to the consumers.

Advertising in sellers', not buyers', interest

The explanation can be sought in the terms of the rules of the market economy itself. Its fundamental principle is that consumer demand should guide production.

But the consumer's demand for *advertising* does not guide the production of advertising. It can be strongly questioned whether there is such a demand at all. Instead, what guides the businessman is the power of advertising to increase the *demand for his products*. The advertising costs are then included in the price of the products that are advertised (or in the price of other products). Thus, in the end they are paid by whoever buys these products.

But the consumers have no possibility of deciding the volume or the aims of advertising. Normally they cannot choose between buying the same product with, or without the advertising costs the seller has sunk into the product. Advertising thus avoids being governed by the normal mechanisms of the market economy.

Where the consumers are unable to exert their influence, the society can take over the governing function. Here are a few examples of such measures:

One of the investigations of the Commission on Advertising, made in 1967-68, showed that one-fifth of all advertisements were misleading or conflicting in some other way with the basic rules for advertising of the International Chamber of Commerce. In 1970, a Consumer Ombudsman was appointed to supervise advertising and to stop misleading ads.

On the suggestion of another royal commission a Consumers' Office was created to, among other things, try to influence the producers' information to the buyers.

Several other governing measures are under consideration within the Commission on Advertising. From the very beginning one of them, the advertising tax, aroused special interest.

Government revenue from advertisers?

The Commission had been appointed to investigate the possible introduction of TV commercials. The big companies were lobbying for access to this advertising medium. To the government, commercials on TV could mean a new source of revenue of some importance. The government might, in other words, be able to make some money on an extension of the advertising business.

But the investigation of the Commission showed that such an extension would not be in the interest of the consumers. Was there, then, no way of giving the government extra revenue from a measure that would be correct in view of the policies on advertising—namely the curbing of excessive advertising?

Yes, there was such a measure. It had been suggested by Kenneth E. Boulding 30 years ago. The measure was to put a tax on advertising.

Taxing evil. The Commission worked for two years on a proposal to impose a 50 per cent ad tax on the 2,000 companies whose advertising costs are above $20,000 a year. As for fiscal revenues, and in several other respects, such a tax would have similar effects as introducing TV commercials—but for the consumers the effect would be the opposite. It would lead to a limitation, instead of an increase of competitive advertising.

Coupled with this model was the possibility of granting tax exemption to companies that were prepared to make an agreement with the Consumers' Office to include adequate consumer information in their advertising.

Opposition from the interests. The original proposal met with heavy opposition, however, partly from the business organizations that were represented in the Commission, partly from the press, which in it saw a threat to its advertising revenue.

In order to make it politically acceptable, the proposal was trimmed—first within the Commission, then by the Ministry of Finance, and finally in the Riksdag.

The tax, in its final form, is not justified mainly by the need to curb advertising, but by the need to support the press.

Much still to be accomplished

I am one of the members of the Commission who most ardently advocated an advertising tax. What should I say about the result?

Trend toward press monopoly. In my opinion it is highly questionable whether this advertising tax will be able to check the monopolization of the press. The combination of an ad tax and press subsidies certainly leads to a redistribution of revenue from the big monopoly papers to smaller dailies. But the market mechanisms are working in the opposite direction so strongly that this might, at its best, only delay the monopolization.

If we wish to secure the future publication of several dailies within the same distribution area, strong measures are needed. One such could be compulsory spreading of advertising, which would mean that an ad placed with one paper also has to go into the other dailies in that area. Perhaps all the ads should be printed in a special advertising section that would be distributed with all the daily newspapers in the area.

Too little. In my opinion it is also highly questionable whether the advertising tax will be able to curb excessive advertising. A 6–10 per cent tax is not enough to check the increase of advertising costs. At its best, this increase will be delayed for a year or two. A general advertising tax, as the one that has now been approved by the Riksdag, will not only curb the big advertisers, as was the original intent, it will also curb classified ads for lost kittens and used cars. Finally, with the present design of the tax it will be difficult, or next to impossible, to exempt companies that are willing to provide adequate information to the consumers.

From my point of view, the main advantage of the advertising tax is that it has, at least for the time being, prevented TV commercials from being introduced in Sweden.

Reading 40

Some Aspects of the Economics of Advertising

L. G. Telser

Introduction

High on the list of controversial economic topics stands advertising. The critics of advertising claim it abuses consumer confidence, shapes and sometimes vulgarizes taste, and creates abnormal, unjustified profits. To these critics advertising is the leading symbol of materialistic Western civilization and of capitalism in particular. There is once more talk of a tax on advertising and of limitations on the advertising of some products, particularly medicines and cigarettes.

Nowadays there are few defenders of advertisers, and even these speak humbly and possibly without conviction. In intellectual circles it is risky to one's reputation of intelligence and/or honesty to defend advertising.

What seems most lacking in the debate is an attempt to understand the functions of advertising, its uses, and its prevalence. Indeed, some aspects

From L. G. Telser, "Some Aspects of the Economics of Advertising," *The Journal of Business*, The University of Chicago Press, vol. 41, no. 2, April 1968. Copyright © 1968 by the University of Chicago. Reprinted in abridgment with the kind permission of the author and the publisher.

of advertising pose problems of considerable intellectual challenge, whose study will aid protagonists on all sides of the debate on advertising.

Some do, some don't

Advertising comes in many forms. Not all goods are advertised to the same extent, if at all, and different goods are advertised in different media. A conspicuous form of advertising is on television, and even larger sums in total are spent on advertising in the other media—newspapers, magazines, radio, billboards, and direct mail.

Some commodities are more advertised in one medium than in another. For example, retailers generally concentrate their advertising in newspapers. Large mail-order houses use media with a national audience and spend large sums preparing and mailing catalogues. Some nationally distributed goods such as automobiles and cigarettes are advertised in many media, while others such as breakfast cereals are advertised mostly on television. Some commodities are not advertised at all, such as locomotives, contraceptives, and glass eye balls. Consumer goods are much more advertised than industrial products.

What explains these differences in the usage of advertising by commodity and by media?

Advertising outlays on a given commodity change over time. For example, in the 1920's cigarettes were more advertised than in the 1930's, and, more recently, cigarettes [were, until the TV ban] again heavily advertised. Two breakfast cereals, General Mills' Wheaties and Kelloggs' Corn Flakes, were much more advertised than they are now. Kodak Instamatic cameras and Polaroid Land cameras are now more advertised than they will be in the future. What explains these changes over time?

Inevitable as death and taxes

Total advertising outlays as a percentage of national income show remarkable stability over time. In the United States this ratio has remained between 2 and 3 per cent of national income annually, except for some changes over the business cycle. The percentage rises somewhat when business is slack and falls somewhat when business is more active. What explains the secular stability of this ratio and its behavior over the business cycle?

Advertising is only one means of promoting the sale of goods and services. Personal selling is the older method, and more is spent on salesmen than on advertising. Moreover, one cannot understand the determinants of advertising expenditures without considering the problem of explaining total selling outlays.

There are wide differences in personal selling. In supermarkets there are salesmen who are little more than clerks; at auto dealers there are salesmen who are anything but clerks. Industrial-goods salesmen often provide their customers with technical advice, and detail men give physicians considerable information about drugs. Some goods are sold mainly through the efforts of salesmen, while others rely mainly on advertising and still others, notably drugs, depend on both personal selling and advertising.

There is a logic to these methods of promotion. This is shown by a comparison between two independent sets of data on advertising in the 1930's, one collected in England by Kaldor and Silverman and the other in the United States by the Federal Trade Commission. Advertising as a percentage of sales for the same products in the two countries is remarkably close. This can be no coincidence. Basic factors inherent in the market, the product, and the tastes of consumers explain these similarities.

Advertising and big profits

Study of the problems just cited advances our understanding of the determinants of advertising outlays and throws light on the contention that advertising is a means to abnormally high profits. In its most naive form this belief rests on some easily available statistics.

The Fortune list of the five hundred largest companies gives the ten companies with the highest rate of return on invested capital. Frequent members of this list are such large advertisers as Gillette, Avon, American Home Products, and Alberto Culver. Other companies among the golden ten are those that spend large sums on research and development.

The moral seems clear. The road to riches requires a firm to spend on research and development and advertising. Indeed, were matters really so simple, it would be hard to explain why all companies do not travel the same road to riches.

Omitted crucial assets. Alas the figures are fallacious, because they cling to old-fashioned accounting conventions that define capital as consisting only of investments in tangible items such as plant, equipment, and inventories. However, the true capital of a company includes expenditures that yield a return long after the initial outlays. Advertising expenditures together with research and development have this property. Yet the typical balance sheet omits them.

The relevant rate of return on the firm's true capital is much lower than the Fortune figures suggest.

A short history of advertising

To understand the present state of advertising, a brief glance at its history is helpful. Advertising is among the oldest of man's activities, probably first appearing in conjunction with the oldest profession.

Advertising in its modern form began in England in the middle of the nineteenth century, together with the popular press. This is no accident. The large circulation of penny newspapers provided a ready audience for advertising messages not long overlooked by businessmen. Proprietary medicines were among the first major advertisers in these newspapers, and more respectable products, such as tea, cocoa, and sewing machines, did not lag far behind.

It is the United States that deserves the credit for the rapid improvement and development of advertising. A pioneer user was Kellogg, who originally promoted health foods as a proprietary remedy for alimentary problems but soon recognized the larger possibilities in selling his wares as breakfast cereals. The modern national advertising campaign can be said to have begun with the introduction of the first domestic blend of cigarettes, Camels, in 1913. Cigarette makers continued to innovate in advertising, particularly by their use of radio in the twenties and thirties.

Monopoly or competition?

Important changes in methods of distribution were helped by the emergence of advertising. The local shop and retailer played a smaller role, and self-service stores offering customers packaged, branded, and nationally advertised goods at lower prices grew rapidly. Competition among retailers became keener, because with the new sales methods it was easier for consumers to shop in several stores in search of the lowest price for a standard, branded item. At the same time, manufacturers became more involved in distribution.

Kaldor and others claim that the heavier expenses of the new methods of promotion gave monopoly power to the manufacturer. This last point is important, and I shall have more to say about it.

Why do it?

To say that business firms advertise because they find this to be profitable, although true, does not advance our understanding of the subject. We must look more closely at the mechanism of advertising.

To this end let us consider how advertisers choose media for a given product, say, baby food. Potential customers are mothers of babies. Hence the advertiser wants media whose audience includes a sizeable number of females in this category. Television programs such as baseball games might be less suitable than weekly comedy programs after 8:00 P.M.

In general the advertiser will attempt to allocate the funds in his advertising budget among the various media so as to obtain the maximum number of potential customers for his product. This may seem obvious, yet it goes far in explaining why some products are more advertised than others.

Some products have so few potential customers that it does not pay to advertise them in any media, for example, glass eye balls. Such products are more efficiently promoted in other ways—by the use of salesmen or simply by relying on the buyers ability to find the sellers for themselves, say, with the help of directories. This also explains why industrial products are less advertised than consumer products. There are fewer customers of industrial products, and it would be wasteful to convey advertising messages to them via the standard media. If there are enough industrial customers to support a trade journal, this journal will also contain pertinent advertising. The same is true of hobbyists. It is probably better to advertise chess sets in a chess magazine than in *Life* [or *Time*]. Indeed, without advertising many specialized magazines could not survive.

The same considerations explain the greater advertising of new than of established products. To illustrate, it is instructive to examine changes in advertising outlays on cigarettes during the past fifty years. At first cigarettes were a new product competing with cigars. During the twenties, advertising outlays were large and directed at women. By the thirties, penetration of both male and female markets had reached high and stable levels so that advertising outlays dropped to a point sufficient to maintain awareness among existing customers and to contact new potential customers as they came of age. After World War II there were new varieties—long cigarettes, filtered and mentholated ones, etc. To sell these new brands there were sharply increased advertising outlays. The ultimate reason for the appearance of the new brands was the connection between smoking and lung cancer and not the advertising in itself.

Brand loyalty: Benefiting from created fads

It is widely believed that advertising can reduce competition by the creation of brand loyalty for the advertised brands. This proposition is testable by comparing the brand-share stability of two classes of products, one which is more advertised and the other which is little advertised. The brand shares in the heavily advertised product class should be more stable over time than brand shares in the little-advertised product group.

I tested this proposition by comparing the share stability of a group of toiletries and cosmetics, a heavily advertised product class, with a group of food items, a much less advertised product class. Contrary to the hypothesis, brand-share stability is *lower* for the more advertised than for the less advertised group. The life-span of a brand in the cosmetic-toiletry category is shorter than for a product in the foods category.

Creative obsolescence.   The explanation is clear. The high level of advertising results from the high frequency of introduction of new products in the cosmetic class. Far from creating brand *loyalty,* the high advertising outlays are the result of brand

disloyalty. Consumers become dissatisfied with the existing brands of cosmetics, toiletries, and toothpaste and are constantly ready to test the promise of new varieties—promises hardly capable of fulfilment.

Similar reasoning explains the large sums spent in promoting drugs. There is frequent introduction of new drugs. To gain acceptance for these new products, the drug companies spend large sums on detail men and advertising. If the drug companies spent smaller sums in accelerating the acceptance of new products, they would obtain a lower rate of return and would also spend less on research and development.

The conclusion is that some of the large advertising outlays are explained by the rapid rate of introduction of new products. It also appears that advertising by itself seems incapable of maintaining consumer acceptance of a product that is found to be unsatisfactory.

Advertising and concentration

Closer study of the relation between advertising and competition is possible. One measure of competition in an industry, widely accepted by economists, is the concentration of sales among the four leading firms in the industry. The larger the share of the total going to the four leading firms, the less the competition. If advertising reduces competition, then there ought to be high levels of advertising in those industries in which the leading firms have a large share of total sales and low levels of advertising in industries where the leading firms have small shares.

This seems to be true in some industries, for instance, soaps, cigarettes, and breakfast cereals, but it is false in other industries, drugs, and cosmetics. The best way to test the proposition is to examine the data for all consumer-product industries.

Such an examination shows a negligible positive association between advertising intensity and concentration. In other words, the exceptions to the hypothesis nearly outweigh the conforming cases. Changes in concentration and advertising intensity ought to move in the same direction according to the hypothesis that advertising lessens competition. The data for the period 1947–57 show, if anything, the opposite relation—an inverse association between changes in advertising intensity and changes in concentration.

The weakness of the hypothesis claiming a positive association between advertising and monopoly is shown by another fact. Industries that make industrial goods hardly advertise and yet may be highly concentrated. Thus if all manufacturing industries were examined to determine the relation between advertising intensity and the concentration of sales among the leading firms, no systematic pattern would emerge. Advertising levels are better explained by the factors I have discussed above than by the state of competition in the industry. Characteristics of the customers of the product, their number, and the cost of contacting them by various media are much more important in explaining the level of advertising.

Temporary profits

Although a continuously high rate of profit year after year is a symptom of monopoly, occasional high profits are not, even if these may result from a successful advertising campaign. Some highly advertised consumer products strike the public fancy and yield a handsome return, and this can also happen to unadvertised goods for much the same reasons. Examples of the latter abound—best sellers, hula hoops, *Gone with the Wind,* and miniskirts. Neither Xerox nor IBM owes its profits to advertising. Conspicuous examples of success due to advertising are offset by the more numerous and unpublicized failures (the Edsel?). The result is an average rate of return.

Despite these facts there are some who believe that advertising is an unusually powerful money-maker. The case for a tax on advertising had better rest on firmer ground than the contention that advertising lessens competition, as evidenced by the high profits that advertising can generate—a position defended by [former] Assistant Attorney General Donald Turner.

In a static economy there would be less advertising. Information about goods and services, terms of sale, and the identity of buyers and sellers would not become obsolete. Catalogues and directories would never be changed. People would continue to use the same things in the same way. To the extent that advertising conveys pertinent infor-

mation about such changes, it facilitates economic growth.

Honesty the best long-run policy?

My analysis so far has dealt mostly with the more technical aspects of advertising. I have not said whether advertising is sufficiently informative, whether trivial product differences are over-emphasized, whether advertising is truthful or deliberately misleading, whether there is too much advertising, whether support of television out of advertising receipts debases the quality of television entertainment, and whether advertising stimulates too much useless change.

Central to many of these questions is the undeniable fact that as the economy grows richer it yields a larger array of complicated consumer goods. To purchase wisely requires a high degree of competence that only a specialist can acquire. This expertise cannot be obtained from a careful study of the content of advertising messages. The potential for abuse is present. Is it only the fear of government controls that checks the cupidity of the advertiser?

Surely not. To obtain the continued patronage of a satisfied clientele is often the goal of business enterprise, and not out of altruism. For experience has shown this to be the profitable course.

Moreover, consumers can judge the quality of goods and services indirectly in many ways. They test the reliability of sellers through long experience. Department stores and mail-order retailers act in effect as expert buyers on behalf of their customers. These retailers have the knowledge to buy goods and get good value for their money. Competition forces them to sell these goods jointly with their expertise at reasonable prices. Nor is experience the sole mentor of consumers. Guaranties and warranties guard their interest.

Finally, in cases of serious damage consumers can resort to the courts. Manufacturers of defective articles are liable for the damage they cause, and the risk of costly law suits increases their incentive to control the quality of their products. A wide reputation engendered by advertising in itself forces sellers to exercise closer watch on quality of products. This can be understood by comparison with a state in which consumers of defective articles do not know the maker and, therefore, do not know who ought never be patronized again. It is interesting to note that one of the arguments in the Soviet Union for the recent introduction of advertising and brand names is the desire to give factories stronger incentive to improve the quality of consumer goods.

Why so little disinterested information?

The market also meets the demand for information about consumer goods in direct ways. A few magazines specialize in reporting to their readers about the attributes of numerous articles by brand. Nevertheless, some kinds of potentially useful information are strangely absent. Thus advertisers rarely compare their own products directly with competing wares. Most advertising is mere puffing, and very little is critical. Magazines and newspapers are also deficient because they do not provide their readers with news about consumer products. Perhaps because of pressures from advertisers there are few columns containing news about consumer items, although this might be expected to have considerable interest to many readers. The only consumer products criticized in newspapers and magazines are plays, books, movies, and television programs.

Public regulating

Though experience acquaints consumers with the good and bad qualities of products, it is sometimes a slow and costly teacher. Partly for this reason there has never been sole reliance on market forces. Weights and measures were among the earliest subjects of government control. The government inspects, controls, and licenses many goods and services ranging from meats to elevators, drugs, and physicians.

The Federal Trade Commission scrutinizes advertising and prosecutes for false or misleading statements. At the same time, advertising of a product is considered to confer an implicit warranty that makes the manufacturer liable for faulty performance.

Sweeping rules for additional regulation cannot be laid down, and I believe that each case has to be judged on its merits.

Advertising and pay TV

In closing I can hardly forbear comment on how the introduction of pay television can lead to improvement in the quality of television entertainment. The sponsorship of television by advertisers pressures networks to produce programs that will appeal to a mass audience at the expense of gratifying minority tastes.

Under a system of pay television it would be possible to have programs appealing to smaller audiences who are willing to pay for them directly. Giving more scope to market forces in television would increase variety and quality, just as similar market forces in publishing permit high-quality magazines to survive with a relatively small circulation. Pay television can develop in many ways, and community antennas, CA-TV, give promise of leading to viable pay television, provided they are allowed to do so without hindrance from the Federal Communications Commission.

Reading 41

Conventional views of competition in our economy tend to look at the practices of different firms in the same industry or product market. But one of the most challenging views on markets has been that which looked beyond an industry or a product to the end use and found competition in the whole process of innovations to meet that end need through new products or processes. That view makes it abundantly clear that, just as competition is dynamic, so too is our understanding of its workings.

The late Joseph Schumpeter was professor of economics at Harvard University and is the major name associated with this view. Here he argues that certain of the most criticized aspects of capitalism are in fact essential features in its record of progress. The literature of economics has few pieces to stand alongside the work of Schumpeter.

Questions to guide the reading

Is the Schumpeter view of competition at odds with or complementary to the view of, say, Slichter?

Are there important prerequisites in order for the process of "creative destruction" to be operative? Are those conditions met within all or most of the American economy?

What are the implications of the Schumpeter view for current antitrust policy in the United States?

Capitalism and Economic Progress

Joseph A. Schumpeter

We have a considerable body of statistical data descriptive of a rate of "progress" [under capitalism] that has been admired even by very critical minds. On the other hand, we have a body of facts about the structure of the economic system and about the way it functioned. We wish to know whether that type of economy was favorable, irrelevant, or unfavorable to the performance we observe.

Profits vs. welfare?

Unlike the class of feudal lords, the commercial and industrial bourgeoisie rose by business success. Bourgeois society has been cast in a purely economic mold. Prizes and penalties are measured in pecuniary terms. Going up and going down means making and losing money. This, of course, nobody can deny. But I wish to add that, within its own frame, that social arrangement is, or at all events was, singularly effective. The promises of wealth and the threats of destitution that it holds out, it redeems with ruthless promptitude. Wherever the bourgeois way of life asserts itself sufficiently to dim the beacons of other social worlds, these promises are strong enough to attract the large majority of supernormal brains and to identify success with business success. They are not proffered at random; yet there is a sufficiently enticing admixture of chance: the game is not like roulette, it is more like poker. Spectacular prizes much greater than would have been necessary to call forth the particular effort are thrown to a small minority of winners, thus propelling much more efficaciously than a more equal and more "just" distribution would, the activity of that large majority of businessmen who receive in return very modest compensation or nothing or less than nothing, and yet do their utmost because they have the big prizes before their eyes and overrate their chances of doing equally well. Similarly, the threats are addressed to incompetence. But though the incompetent men and the obsolete methods are in fact eliminated, sometimes very promptly, sometimes with a lag, failure also threatens or actually overtakes many an able man, thus whipping up *everyone,* again much more efficaciously than a more equal and more "just" system of penalties would. Finally, both business success and business failure are ideally precise. Neither can be talked away.

He who innovates

In most cases the man who rises first *into* the business class and then *within* it is also an able businessman and he is likely to rise exactly as far as his ability goes. This fact, so often obscured by the auto-therapeutic effort of the unsuccessful to deny it, is much more important than anything that can be gleaned from the pure theory of the capitalist machine.

But is not all that we might be tempted to infer from "maximum performance of an optimally se-

From Joseph A. Schumpeter, *Capitalism, Socialism, and Democracy* (Harper & Brothers, New York, 1942). Reprinted with kind permission of Mrs. Joseph A. Schumpeter and the publisher.

lected group" invalidated by the further fact that it aims at maximizing profits instead of welfare? Outside of the bourgeois stratum, this has of course always been the popular opinion. Economists have sometimes fought and sometimes espoused it.

The so-called classical economists disliked many things about the social institutions of their epoch and about the way those institutions worked. They fought the landed interest and approved of social reforms—factory legislation in particular—that were not all on the lines of *laissez faire*. But they were quite convinced that within the institutional framework of capitalism, the manufacturer's and the trader's self-interest made for maximum performance in the interest of all. Confronted with the problem we are discussing, they would have had little hesitation in attributing the observed rate of increase in total output to relatively unfettered enterprise and the profit motive.

It is exceedingly difficult, at this hour of the day, to do justice to these views. They were of course the typical views of the English bourgeois class, and bourgeois blinkers are in evidence on almost every page the classical authors wrote. No less in evidence are blinkers of another kind: the classics reasoned in terms of a particular historical situation which they uncritically idealized and from which they uncritically generalized. Most of them, moreover, seem to have argued exclusively in terms of the English interests and problems of their time. This is the reason why, in other lands and at other times, people disliked their economics, frequently to the point of not even caring to understand it. But it will not do to dismiss their teaching on these grounds. A prejudiced man may yet be speaking the truth. Propositions developed from special cases may yet be generally valid. And the enemies and successors of the classics had and have only different but not fewer blinkers and preconceptions; they envisaged and envisage different but not less special cases.

From the standpoint of the economic analyst, the chief merit of the classics consists in their dispelling, along with many other gross errors, the naïve idea that economic activity in capitalist society, because it turns on the profit motive, must by virtue of that fact alone necessarily run counter to the interests of consumers.

This later analysis we will take in two strides—as much of it, that is, as we need in order to clarify our problem. Historically, the first will carry us into the first decade of this century, the second will cover some of the postwar developments of scientific economics. Frankly I do not know how much good this will do the non-professional reader; like every other branch of our knowledge, economics, as its analytic engine improves, moves fatally away from that happy stage in which all problems, methods, and results could be made accessible to every educated person without special training. I will, however, do my best.

The profit motive under perfect competition

The first stride may be associated with two great names revered to this day by numberless disciples—so far at least as the latter do not think it bad form to express reverence for anything or anybody, which many of them obviously do—Alfred Marshall and Knut Wicksell. Their theoretical structure has little in common with that of the classics, but it conserves the classic proposition that in the case of perfect competition the profit interest of the producer tends to maximize production. It even supplies almost satisfactory proof. It can be shown that firms which cannot by their own individual action exert any influence upon the price of their products or of the factors of production they employ will expand their output until they reach the point at which the additional cost that mus be incurred in order to produce another small increment of product (marginal cost) just equals the price they can get for that increment. And this can be shown to be as much as it is in general "socially desirable" to produce. Where this is so, there exists a state of equilibrium in which all outputs are at their maximum and all factors fully employed. This case is usually referred to as perfect competition.

The profit motive under monopolistic competition

Let us take the second stride. The classics recognized cases of "monopoly," and Adam Smith himself carefully noticed the prevalence of devices to restrict competition and all the differences in flexibility of prices resulting therefrom. But they looked upon those cases as exceptions and, moreover, as exceptions that could and would be done away with in time. If we look more closely at the conditions that must be fulfilled in order to produce perfect competition, we realize immediately that outside of agricultural mass production there cannot be many instances of it. A farmer supplies his cotton or wheat in fact under those conditions: from his standpoint the ruling prices of cotton or wheat are data, though very variable ones, and not being able to influence them by his individual action he simply adapts his output; since all farmers do the same, prices and quantities will in the end be adjusted as the theory of perfect competition requires. But this is not so even with many agricultural products—with ducks, sausages, vegetables and many dairy products for instance. And as regards practically all the finished products and services of industry and trade, it is clear that every grocer, every filling station, every manufacturer of gloves or shaving cream or handsaws has a small and precarious market of his own which he tries to build up and to keep by price strategy, quality strategy, "product differentiation," and advertising. Thus we get a completely different pattern which there seems to be no reason to expect to yield the results of perfect competition. In these cases we speak of Monopolistic Competition. Their theory has been one of the major contributions to [recent] economics.

The work of oligopoly

There remains a wide field of substantially homogeneous products such as steel ingots, cement, cotton gray goods and the like—in which the conditions for the emergence of monopolistic competition do not seem to prevail. This is so. But in general, similar results follow for that field inasmuch as the greater part of it is covered by largest-scale firms which, either individually or in concert, are able to manipulate prices even without differentiating products—the case of Oligopoly.

As soon as the prevalence of monopolistic competition or of oligopoly or of combinations of the two is recognized, many of the propositions which economists used to teach with the utmost confidence become either inapplicable or much more difficult to prove. The "beneficial" competition of the classic type seems likely to be replaced by "predatory" or "cut-throat" competition or simply

by struggles for control in the financial sphere. These things are so many sources of social waste, and there are many others such as the costs of advertising campaigns, the suppression of new methods of production (buying up of patents in order not to use them) and so on. And most important of all: under the conditions envisaged, equilibrium no longer guarantees either full employment or maximum output in the sense of the theory of perfect competition. It *may* exist without full employment; it is *bound* to exist, so it seems, at a level of output below that maximum mark, because profit-conserving strategy, impossible in conditions of perfect competition, now not only becomes possible but imposes itself.

Well, does not this bear out what the man in the street (unless a businessman himself) always thought on the subject of private business? Has not modern analysis completely refuted the classical doctrine and justified the popular view? Is it not quite true after all, that there is little parallelism between producing for profit and producing for the consumer and that private enterprise is little more than a device to curtail production in order to extort profits which then are correctly described as tolls and ransoms?

These conclusions are in fact almost completely false. Yet they follow from observations that are almost completely true. But economists and popular writers have once more run away with some fragments of reality they happened to grasp. These fragments themselves were mostly seen correctly. But no conclusions about capitalist reality as a whole follow from such fragmentary analyses.

Most important of all, the modern standard of life of the masses evolved during the period of relatively unfettered "big business." If we list the items that enter the modern workman's budget and from 1899 on observe the course of their prices not in terms of money but in terms of the hours of labor that will buy them—i.e., each year's money prices divided by each year's hourly wage rates—we cannot fail to be struck by the rate of the advance which, considering the spectacular improvement in qualities, seems to have been greater and not smaller than it ever was before. If we economists were given less to wishful thinking and more to the observation of facts, doubts would immediately arise as to the realistic virtues of a theory that would have led us to expect a very different result. Nor is this all. As soon as we go into details and inquire into the individual items in which progress was most conspicuous, the trail leads not to the doors of those firms that work under conditions of comparatively free competition but precisely to the doors of the large concerns—which, as in the case of agricultural machinery, also account for much of the progress in the competitive sector—and a shocking suspicion dawns upon us that big business may have had more to do with creating that standard of life than with keeping it down.

The process of creative destruction

The essential point to grasp is that in dealing with capitalism we are dealing with an evolutionary process. It may seem strange that anyone can fail to see so obvious a fact which moreover was long ago emphasized by Karl Marx.

Capitalism is by nature a form or method of economic change and not only never is but never can be stationary. And this evolutionary character of the capitalist process is not merely due to the fact that economic life goes on in a social and natural environment which changes. Nor is this evolutionary character due to a quasi-automatic increase in population and capital or to the vagaries of monetary system. The fundamental impulse that sets and keeps the capitalist engine in motion comes from the new consumers' goods, and new methods of production or transportation, the new markets, the new forms of industrial organization that capitalist enterprise creates.

The contents of the laborer's budget, say from 1760 to 1940, did not simply grow on unchanging lines but they underwent a process of qualitative change. Similarly, the history of the productive apparatus of a typical farm, from the beginnings of the rationalization of crop rotation, plowing and fattening to the mechanized thing of today—linking up with elevators and railroads—is a history of revolutions. So is the history of the productive apparatus of the iron and steel industry from the charcoal furnace to our own type of furnace, or the history of the apparatus of power production from the overshot water wheel to the modern power plant, or the history of transportation from the mail-coach to the airplane. The opening up of new markets, foreign or domestic, and the organizational development from the craft shop and the factory to such concerns as U.S. Steel illustrate the same process of industrial mutation—if I may use that biological term—that incessantly revolutionizes the economic structure *from within*, incessantly destroying the old one, incessantly creating a new one. This process of Creative Destruction is the essential fact about capitalism. It is what capitalism consists in and what every capitalist concern has got to live in.

Long-run progress vs. short-run efficiency

Since we are dealing with a process whose every element takes considerable time in revealing its true features and ultimate effects, there is no point in appraising the performance of the process [as] of a given point of time; we must judge its performance over time, as it unfolds through decades or centuries. A system that at *every point* of time fully utilizes its possibilities to the best advantage may yet in the long run be inferior to a system that does so at *no* given point of time, because the latter's failure to do so may be a condition for the level or speed of long-run performance.

Second, since we are dealing with an organic process, every piece of business strategy acquires its true significance only against the background of that process and within the situation created by it. It must be seen in its role in the perennial gale of creative destruction; it cannot be understood irrespective of it or, in fact, on the hypothesis that there is a perennial lull.

But economists look at the behavior of an oligopolist industry—an industry which consists of a few big firms—and observe the well-known moves and countermoves within it that seem to aim at nothing but high prices and restrictions of output. They accept the data of the momentary situation as if there were no past or future to it and think that they have understood what there is to understand if they interpret the behavior of those firms by means of the principle of maximizing profits with reference to those data. In other words, the problem that is usually being visualized is how capitalism administers existing structures, whereas the relevant problem is how it creates and destroys them.

In capitalist reality as distinguished from its textbook picture, competition which counts [is] the competition from the new commodity, the new technology, the new source of supply, the new type of organization (the large-scale unit of control for instance)—competition which commands a decisive cost or quality advantage and which strikes not at the margins of the profits and the outputs of the existing firms but at their foundations and their very lives. This kind of competition is so much more important that it becomes a matter of comparative indifference whether competition in the ordinary sense functions more or less promptly; the powerful lever that in the long run expands output and brings down prices is in any case made of other stuff.

It is hardly necessary to point out that competition of the kind we now have in mind acts not only when in being but also when it is merely an ever-present threat. It disciplines before it attacks. The businessman feels himself to be in a competitive situation even if he is alone in his field. In many cases, though not in all, this will in the long run enforce behavior very similar to the perfectly competitive pattern.

Many theorists take the opposite view which is best conveyed by an example. Let us assume that there is a certain number of retailers in a neighborhood who try to improve their relative position by service and "atmosphere" but avoid price competition and stick as to methods to the local tradition—a picture of stagnating routine. As others drift into the trade that quasi-equilibrium is indeed upset, but in a manner that does not benefit their customers. The economic space around each of the shops having been narrowed, their owners will no longer be able to make a living and they will try to mend the case by raising prices in tacit agreement. This will further reduce their sales and so, by successive pyramiding, a situation will evolve in which increasing potential supply will be attended by increasing instead of decreasing prices and by decreasing instead of increasing sales.

Such cases do occur, and it is right and proper to work them out. But as the practical instances usually given show, they are fringe-end cases to be found mainly in the sectors furthest removed from all that is most characteristic of capitalist activity. Moreover, they are transient by nature. In the case of retail trade the competition that matters arises not from additional shops of the same type, but from the department store, the chain store, the mail-order house and the supermarket which are bound to destroy those pyramids sooner or later. Now a theoretical construction which neglects this

essential element of the case neglects all that is most typically capitalist about it; even if correct in logic as well as in fact, it is like *Hamlet* without the Danish prince.

Monopolistic practices

Both as a fact and as a threat, the impact of new things considerably reduces the long-run scope and importance of practices that aim, through restricting output, at conserving established positions and at maximizing the profits accruing from them. We must now recognize the further fact that restrictive practices of this kind, as far as they are effective, acquire a new significance in the perennial gale of creative destruction, a significance which they would not have in a stationary state or in a state of slow and balanced growth. In either of these cases restrictive strategy would produce no result other than an increase in profits at the expense of buyers. But in the process of creative destruction, restrictive practices may do much to steady the ship and to alleviate temporary difficulties. This is in fact a very familiar argument which always turns up in times of depression and, as everyone knows, has become very popular with governments and their economic advisers—witness the NRA. While it has been so much misused and so faultily acted upon that most economists heartily despise it, those same advisers who are responsible for this invariably fail to see its much more general rationale.

Robin Hood to protect the innovators

Practically any investment entails, as a necessary complement of entrepreneurial action, certain safeguarding activities such as insuring or hedging. Long-range investing under rapidly changing conditions, especially under conditions that change or may change at any moment under the impact of new commodities and technologies, is like shooting at a target that is not only indistinct but moving—and moving jerkily at that. Hence it becomes necessary to resort to such protecting devices as patents or temporary secrecy of process. But these protecting devices which most economists accept as normal elements of rational management are only special cases of a larger class comprising many others which most economists condemn although they do not differ fundamentally from the recognized ones.

If for instance a war risk is insurable, nobody objects to a firm's collecting the cost of this insurance from the buyers of its products. But that risk is no less an element in long-run costs if there are no facilities for insuring against it, in which case a price strategy aiming at the same end will seem to involve unnecessary restriction and to be productive of excess profits. Similarly, if a patent cannot be secured or would not, if secured, effectively protect, other means may have to be used in order to justify the investment. Among them are a price policy that will make it possible to write off more quickly than would otherwise be rational. Again, means may have to be devised in order to tie prospective customers to the investing firm.

In analyzing such business strategy [as] of a given point of time, the investigating economist or government agent sees price policies that seem to him predatory and restrictions of output that seem to him synonymous with loss of opportunities to produce. He does not see that restrictions of this type are, in the conditions of the perennial gale, incidents, often unavoidable incidents, of a long-run process of expansion which they protect rather than impede. There is no more of paradox in this than there is in saying that motorcars are traveling faster than they otherwise would *because* they are provided with brakes.

Creators not crooks

This stands out most clearly in the case of those sectors of the economy which at any time happen to embody the impact of new things and methods on the existing industrial structure. The best way of getting a vivid and realistic idea of industrial strategy is indeed to visualize the behavior of new concerns or industries that introduce new commodities or processes (such as the aluminum industry) or else reorganize a part or the whole of an industry (such as, for instance, the old Standard Oil Company).

As we have seen, such concerns are aggressors by nature and wield the really effective weapon of competition. Their intrusion can only in the rarest of cases fail to improve total output in quantity or quality, both through the new method itself—even if at no time used to full advantage—and through the pressure it exerts on the preexisting firms. On the one hand, largest-scale plans could in many cases not materialize at all if it were not known from the outset that competition will be discouraged by heavy capital requirements or lack of experience. Even the securing of advantages that run counter to the public's sense of fair play—railroad rebates—move, as far as long-run effects on total output alone are envisaged, into a different light; they *may* be methods for removing obstacles that the institution of private property puts in the path of progress. In a socialist society that would be no less necessary. They would have to be secured by order of the central authority.

On the other hand, enterprise would in most cases be impossible if it were not known from the outset that exceptionally favorable situations are likely to arise which if exploited by price, quality and quantity manipulation will produce profits adequate to tide over exceptionally unfavorable situations. Again this requires strategy that in the short run is often restrictive. In the majority of cases, however, it is so successful as to yield profits far above what is necessary in order to induce the corresponding investment. These cases then provide the baits that lure capital on to untried trails. Their presence explains in part how it is possible for so large a section of the capitalist world to work for nothing: in the midst of the prosperous twenties just about half of the business corporations in the United States were run at a loss, at zero profits, or at profits which, if they had been foreseen, would have been inadequate to call for the effort and expenditure involved.

Ideology refuted

All this is of course nothing but the tritest common sense. But it is being overlooked with a persistence so stubborn as sometimes to raise the question of sincerity. And it follows that, within the process of creative destruction, there is another side to industrial self-organization than that which these theorists are contemplating. "Restraints of trade" of the cartel type as well as those which merely consist in tacit understandings about price competition may be effective remedies under conditions of depression. As far as they are, they may in the end produce not only steadier but also greater expansion of total output than could be secured by an entirely uncontrolled onward rush that cannot fail to be studded with catastrophes.

Even as now extended, however, our argument does not cover all cases of restrictive or regulating strategy, many of which no doubt have that injurious effect on the long-run development of output which is uncritically attributed to all of them. And even in the cases our argument does cover, the net effect is a question of the way in which industry regulates itself in each individual case. It is certainly as conceivable that an all-pervading cartel system might sabotage all progress as it is that it might realize, with smaller social and private costs, all that perfect competition is supposed to realize. This is why our argument does not amount to a case against state regulation. It does show that there is no general case for indiscriminate "trust-busting" or for the prosecution of everything that qualifies as a restraint of trade. Rational as distinguished from vindictive regulation by public authority turns out to be an extremely delicate problem which not every government agency, particularly when in full cry against big business, can be trusted to solve. But our argument, framed to refute a prevalent *theory* and the inferences drawn therefrom about the relation between modern capitalism and the development of total output, yields another outlook on facts and another principle by which to interpret them. For our purpose that is enough.

Reading 42

An earlier selection (page 150) told of price leadership in an industry of few sellers. Stability was maintained in the cigarette industry without overt collusion. But, the law notwithstanding, producers in some industries have participated in direct but secret conspiracies to bring price stability into their businesses. Few recent instances have been as dramatic as the one involving some of the nation's largest manufacturers of electrical equipment. Here were big names and big stakes caught up in an economic drama that produced both angry finger pointing and quieter soul searching in and out of the business world.

John Brooks, novelist and free-lance writer on business subjects, goes well beyond the traditional economist's approach to this famous law case. The economic issues are here, but so too are the moral issues and above all the communications issues raised by this critical and puzzling chapter in our business history.

Questions to guide the reading

What light does the case throw on the difficulties in maintaining stability in oligopolistic markets in the absence of direct collusion? From the public point of view, are the results here substantially different from those to be expected under conditions of legal and effective price leadership?

What are our most effective defenses against a recurrence of this type of conspiracy?

Communication and Collusion: The Case of the Electrical Industry

John Brooks

Among the greatest problems facing American industry today, one may learn by talking with any of a large number of industrialists who are not known to be especially given to pontificating, is "the problem of communication." This preoccupation with the difficulty of getting a thought out of one head and into another is something the industrialists share with a substantial number of intellectuals and creative writers, more and more of whom seem inclined to regard communication, or the lack of it, as one of the greatest problems not just of industry but of humanity. (A few avantgarde writers and artists have given the importance of communication a backhanded boost by flatly and unequivocally proclaiming themselves to be against it.) As far as the industrialists are concerned, I admit that in the course of hearing them invoke the word "communication"—often in an almost mystical way—over the past few years I have had a lot of trouble figuring out exactly what they meant. The general thesis is clear enough; namely, that everything would be all right, first, if they could get through to each other within their own organizations, and, second, if they, or their organizations, could get through to everybody else. What has puzzled me is how and why, in this day when the foundations sponsor one study of communication after another, individuals and organizations fail so consistently to express themselves understandably, or how and why their listeners fail to grasp what they hear.

Recently, I acquired a two-volume publication of the United States Government Printing Office entitled *Hearings Before the Subcommittee on Antitrust and Monopoly of the Committee on the Judiciary, United States Senate, Eighty-seventh Congress, First Session, Pursuant to S. Res. 52,* and after a fairly diligent perusal of its 1,459 pages I think I begin to see what the industrialists are talking about. The hearings, conducted in April, May, and June, 1961, under the chairmanship of Senator Estes Kefauver, of Tennessee, had to do with the now famous price-fixing and bid-rigging conspiracies in the electrical-manufacturing industry, which had already resulted, the previous February, in the imposition by a federal judge in Philadelphia of fines totaling $1,924,500 on twenty-nine firms and forty-five of their employees, and also of thirty-day prison sentences on seven of the employees. Since there had been no public presentation of evidence, all the defendants having pleaded either guilty or no defense, and since the records of the grand juries that indicted them were secret, the public had had little opportunity to hear about the details of the violations, and Senator Kefauver felt that the whole matter needed a good airing. The

transcript shows that it got one, and what the airing revealed—at least within the biggest company involved—was a breakdown in intramural communication so drastic as to make the building of the Tower of Babel seem a triumph of organizational rapport.

Verdict rendered

In a series of indictments brought by the government in the United States District Court in Philadelphia between February and October, 1960, the twenty-nine companies and their executives were charged with having repeatedly violated Section 1 of the Sherman Act of 1890, which declares illegal "every contract, combination in the form of trust or otherwise, or conspiracy, in restraint of trade or commerce among the several States, or with foreign nations." (The Sherman Act was the instrument used in the celebrated trust-busting activities of Theodore Roosevelt, and along with the Clayton Act of 1914 it has served as the government's weapon against cartels and monopolies ever since.) The violations, the government alleged, were committed in connection with the sale of large and expensive pieces of apparatus of a variety that is required chiefly by public and private electric-utility companies (power transformers, switchgear assemblies, and turbine-generator units, among many others), and were the outcome of a series of meetings attended by executives of the supposedly competing companies—beginning at least as early as 1956 and continuing into 1959—at which noncompetitive price levels were agreed upon, nominally sealed bids on individual contracts were rigged in advance, and each company was allocated a certain percentage of the available business. The government further alleged that, in an effort to preserve the secrecy of these meetings, the executives had resorted to such devices as referring to their companies by code numbers in their correspondence, making telephone calls from public booths or from their homes rather than from their offices, and doctoring the expense accounts covering their get-togethers to conceal the fact that they had all been in a certain city on a certain day. But their stratagems did not prevail. The federals, forcefully led by Robert A. Bicks, then head of the Antitrust Division of the Department of Justice, succeeded in exposing them, with considerable help from some of the conspirators themselves, who, after an employee of a small conspirator company saw fit to spill the beans in the early fall of 1959, flocked to turn state's evidence.

The economic and social significance of the whole affair may be demonstrated clearly enough by citing just a few figures. In an average year, a total of more than one and three-quarter billion dollars is spent to purchase machines of the sort in question, nearly a fourth of it by federal, state, and local governments (which, of course, means the taxpayers), and most of the rest by private utility companies (which are inclined to pass along any rise in the cost of their equipment to the public in the form of rate increases). To take a specific example of the kind of money involved in an individual transaction, the list price of a 500,000-kilowatt turbine-generator—a monstrous device for producing electric power from steam power—may be something like sixteen million dollars. Actually, manufacturers have sometimes cut their prices by as much as 25 percent in order to make a sale, and therefore, if everything is aboveboard, it may be possible to buy the machine at a saving of four million dollars; if representatives of the companies making such generators hold a single meeting and agree to fix prices, they may, in effect, increase the cost to the customer by the four million. And in the end, the customer is almost sure to be the public.

Caught red-handed

In presenting the indictments in Philadelphia, Bicks stated that, considered collectively, they revealed "a pattern of violations which can fairly be said to range among the most serious, the most flagrant, the most pervasive that have ever marked any basic American industry." Just before imposing the sentences, Judge J. Cullen Ganey went even further; in his view, the violations constituted "a shocking indictment of a vast section of our economy, for what is really at stake here is the survival of . . . the free-enterprise system." The prison sentences showed that he meant it; although there had been many successful prosecutions for violation of the Sherman Act during the seven decades since its passage, it was rare indeed for executives to be jailed. Not surprisingly, there-

fore, the case kicked up quite a ruckus in the press. The *New Republic,* to be sure, complained that the newspapers and magazines were intentionally playing down "the biggest business scandal in decades," but the charge did not seem to have much foundation. Considering such things as the public's apathy toward switchgear, the woeful bloodlessness of criminal cases involving antitrust laws, and the relatively few details of the conspiracies that had emerged, the press in general gave the story a good deal of space, and even the *Wall Street Journal* and *Fortune* ran uncompromising and highly informative accounts of the debacle; here and there, in fact, one could detect signs of a revival of the spirit of old-time anti-business journalism as it existed back in the thirties. After all, what could be more exhilarating than to see several dignified, impeccably tailored, and highly paid executives of a few of the nation's most respected corporations being trooped off to jail like common pickpockets? It was certainly the biggest moment for business-baiters since 1938, when Richard Whitney, the president of the New York Stock Exchange at the time, was put behind bars for speculating with his customers' money. Some called it the biggest since Teapot Dome.

To top it all off, there was a prevalent suspicion of hypocrisy in the very highest places. Neither the chairman of the board nor the president of General Electric, the largest of the corporate defendants, had been caught in the government's dragnet, and the same was true of Westinghouse Electric, the second-largest; these four ultimate bosses let it be known that they had been entirely ignorant of what had been going on within their commands right up to the time the first testimony on the subject was given to the Justice Department. Many people, however, were not satisfied by these disclaimers, and instead, took the position that the defendant executives were men in the middle, who had broken the law only in response either to actual orders or to a corporate climate favoring price-fixing, and who were now being allowed to suffer for the sins of their superiors. Among the unsatisfied was Judge Ganey himself, who said at the time of the sentencing, "One would be most naïve indeed to believe that these violations of the law, so long persisted in, affecting so large a segment of the industry, and finally, involving so many millions upon millions of dollars, were facts unknown to those responsible for the conduct of the corporation. . . . I am convinced that in the great number of these defendants' cases, they were torn between conscience and approved corporate policy, with the rewarding objectives of promotion, comfortable security, and large salaries."

Scapegoats needed

The public naturally wanted a ringleader, an arch-conspirator, and it appeared to find what it wanted in General Electric, which—to the acute consternation of the men endeavoring to guide its destinies from company headquarters, at 570 Lexington Avenue, New York City—got the lion's share of attention both in the press and in the Subcommittee hearings. With some 300,000 employees, and sales averaging some four billion dollars a year over the past ten years, it was not only far and away the biggest of the twenty-nine accused companies but, judged on the basis of sales in 1959, the fifth-biggest company in the country. It also drew a higher total of fines ($437,500) than any other company, and saw more of its executives sent to jail (three, with eight others receiving suspended sentences). Furthermore, as if to intensify in this hour of crisis the horror and shock of true believers—and the glee of scoffers—its highest-ranking executives had for years tried to represent it to the public as a paragon of successful virtue by issuing encomiums to the free competitive system, the very system that the price-fixing meetings were set up to mock. In 1959, shortly after the government's investigation of the violations had been brought to the attention of G.E.'s policymakers, the company demoted and cut the pay of those of its executives who admitted that they had been involved; one vice-president, for example, was informed that instead of the $127,000 a year he had been getting he would now get $40,000. (He had scarcely adjusted himself to that blow when Judge Ganey fined him four thousand dollars and sent him to prison for thirty days, and shortly after he regained his freedom, General Electric eased him out entirely.) The G.E. policy of imposing penalties of its own on these employees, regardless of what punishment the court might prescribe, was not adopted by Westinghouse, which waited until the judge had disposed of the case and then de-

cided that the fines and prison sentences he had handed out to its stable of offenders were chastisement enough, and did not itself penalize them at all. Some people saw this attitude as evidence that Westinghouse was condoning the conspiracies, but others regarded it as a commendable, if tacit, admission that management at the highest level in the conniving companies was responsible—morally, at least—for the whole mess and was therefore in no position to discipline its erring employees. In the view of these people, G.E.'s haste to penalize the acknowledged culprits on its payroll strongly suggested that the firm was trying to save its own skin by throwing a few luckless employees to the wolves, or—as Senator Philip A. Hart, of Michigan, put it, more pungently, during the hearings—"to do a Pontius Pilate operation."

Embattled days at 570 Lexington Avenue! After years of cloaking the company in the mantle of a wise and benevolent corporate institution, the public-relations people at G.E. headquarters were faced with the ugly choice of representing its role in the price-fixing affair as that of either a fool or a knave. They tended strongly toward "fool." Judge Ganey, by his statement that he assumed the conspiracies to have been not only condoned but approved by the top brass and the company as a whole, clearly chose "knave." But his analysis may or may not have been the right one, and after reading the Kefauver Subcommittee testimony I have come to the melancholy conclusion that the truth will very likely never be known. For, as the testimony shows, the clear waters of moral responsibility at G.E. became hopelessly muddied by a struggle to communicate—a struggle so confused that in some cases, it would now appear, if one of the big bosses at G.E. *had* ordered a subordinate to break the law, the message would somehow have been garbled in its reception, and if the subordinate *had* informed the boss that he was holding conspiratorial meetings with the competitors, the boss might well have been under the impression that the subordinate was gossiping idly about lawn parties or pinochle sessions. Specifically, it would appear that a subordinate who received a direct oral order from his boss had to figure out whether it meant what it seemed to or the exact opposite, while the boss, in conversing with a subordinate had to figure out whether he should take what the man *told* him at face value or should attempt to translate it out of a secret code to which he was by no means sure he had the key. That was the problem in a nutshell, and I state it here thus baldly as a suggestion for any potential beneficiary of a foundation who may be casting about for a suitable project on which to draw up a prospectus.

How could it happen?

For the past eight years or so, G.E. has had a company rule called Directive Policy 20.5, which reads, in part, "No employee shall enter into any understanding, agreement, plan or scheme, expressed or implied, formal or informal, with any competitor, in regard to prices, terms or conditions of sale, production, distribution, territories, or customers; nor exchange or discuss with a competitor prices, terms or conditions of sale, or any other competitive information." In effect, this rule is simply an injunction to G.E.'s personnel to obey the federal antitrust laws, except that it is somewhat more concrete and comprehensive in the matter of price than they are. It is almost impossible for executives with jurisdiction over pricing policies at G.E. to be unaware of 20.5, or even hazy about it, because to make sure that new executives are acquainted with it and to refresh the memories of old ones, the company formally reissues and distributes it at intervals, and all such executives are asked to sign their names to it as an earnest that they are currently complying with it and intend to keep on doing so. The trouble—at least during the period covered by the court action, and apparently for a long time before that as well—was that some people at G.E., including some of those who regularly signed 20.5, simply did not believe that it was to be taken seriously. They assumed that 20.5 was mere window dressing; that it was on the books solely to provide legal protection for the company and for the higher-ups; that meeting illegally with competitors was recognized and accepted as standard practice within the company; and that often when a ranking executive ordered a subordinate executive to comply with 20.5, he was actually ordering him to violate it. Illogical as it might seem, this last assumption becomes comprehensible in the light of the fact that, for a time, when some executives orally conveyed, or reconveyed, the order, they

were apparently in the habit of accompanying it with an unmistakable wink. In May of 1948, for example, there was a meeting of G.E. sales managers during which the custom of winking was openly discussed. Robert Paxton, an upper-level G.E. executive who later became the company's president, addressed the meeting and delivered the usual admonition about antitrust violations, whereupon William S. Ginn, then a sales executive in the transformer division, under Paxton's authority, startled him by saying, "I didn't see you wink." Paxton replied firmly, "There was no wink. We mean it, and these are the orders." Asked by Senator Kefauver how long he had been aware that orders issued at G.E. were sometimes accompanied by winks, Paxton replied that he had first observed the practice way back in 1935, when his boss had given him an instruction along with a wink or its equivalent, and that when, some time later, the significance of the gesture dawned on him, he had become so incensed that he had with difficulty restrained himself from jeopardizing his career by punching the boss in the nose. Paxton went on to say that his objections to the practice of winking had been so strong as to earn him a reputation in the company for being an antiwink man, and that he, for his part, had never winked.

Although Paxton would seem to have left little doubt as to how he intended his winkless order of 1948 to be interpreted, its meaning failed to get through to Ginn, for not long after it was issued, he went out and fixed prices to a fare-thee-well. (Obviously, it takes more than one company to make a price-fixing agreement, but all the testimony tends to indicate that it was G.E. that generally set the pattern for the rest of the industry in such matters.) Thirteen years later, Ginn—fresh from a few weeks in jail, and fresh out of a $135,000-a-year job—appeared before the Subcommittee to account for, among other things, his strange response to the winkless order. He had disregarded it, he said, because he had received a contrary order from two of his other superiors in the G.E. chain of command, Henry V. B. Erben and Francis Fairman, and in explaining why he had heeded their order rather than Paxton's he introduced the fascinating concept of degrees of communication—another theme for a foundation grantee to get his teeth into. Erben and Fairman, Ginn said, had been more articulate, persuasive, and forceful in issuing their order than Paxton had been in issuing his; Fairman especially, Ginn stressed, had proved to be "a great communicator, a great philosopher, and frankly, a great believer in stability of prices." Both Erben and Fairman had dismissed Paxton as naïve, Ginn testified, and, in further summary of how he had been led astray, he said that "the people who were advocating the Devil were able to sell me better than the philosophers that were selling the Lord."

It would be helpful to have at hand a report from Erben and Fairman themselves on the communication techniques that enabled them to prevail over Paxton, but unfortunately neither of these philosophers could testify before the Subcommittee, because by the time of the hearings both of them were dead. Paxton, who was available, was described in Ginn's testimony as having been at all times one of the philosopher-salesmen on the side of the Lord. "I can clarify Mr. Paxton by saying Mr. Paxton came closer to being an Adam Smith advocate than any businessman I have met in America," Ginn declared. Still, in 1950, when Ginn admitted to Paxton in casual conversation that he had "compromised himself" in respect to antitrust matters, Paxton merely told him that he was a damned fool, and did not report the confession to anyone else in the company. Testifying as to why he did not, Paxton said that when the conversation occurred he was no longer Ginn's boss and that, in the light of his personal ethics, repeating such an admission by a man not under his authority would be "gossip" and "talebearing."

Smoke-filled rooms

Meanwhile, Ginn, no longer answerable to Paxton, was meeting with competitors at frequent intervals and moving steadily up the corporate ladder. In November, 1954, he was made general manager of the transformer division, whose headquarters were in Pittsfield, Massachusetts—a job that put him in line for a vice-presidency. At the time of Ginn's shift, Ralph J. Cordiner, who has been chairman of the board of General Electric since 1949, called him down to New York for the express purpose of enjoining him to comply strictly and undeviatingly with Directive Policy 20.5. Cordiner communicated this idea so successfully that it was clear enough to Ginn at the mo-

ment, but it remained so only as long as it took him, after leaving the chairman, to walk to Erben's office. There his comprehension of what he had just heard became clouded. Erben, who was head of G.E.'s distribution group, ranked directly below Cordiner and directly above Ginn, and according to Ginn's testimony, no sooner were they alone in his office than he countermanded Cordiner's injunction, saying, "Now keep on doing the way that you have been doing, but just be sensible about it and use your head on the subject." Erben's extraordinary communicative prowess again carried the day, and Ginn continued to meet with competitors. "I knew Mr. Cordiner could fire me," he told Senator Kefauver, "but also I knew I was working for Mr. Erben."

At the end of 1954, Paxton took over Erben's job and thereby became Ginn's boss again. Ginn went right on meeting with competitors, but, since he was aware that Paxton disapproved of the practice, didn't tell him about it. Moreover, he testified, within a month or two he had become convinced that he could not afford to discontinue attending the meetings under any circumstances, for in January, 1955, the entire electrical-equipment industry became embroiled in a drastic price war—known as the "white sale," because of its timing and the bargains it afforded to buyers—in which the erstwhile amiable competitors began fiercely undercutting one another. Such a manifestation of free enterprise was, of course, exactly what the intercompany conspiracies were intended to prevent, but just at that time the supply of electrical apparatus so greatly exceeded the demand that first a few of the conspirators and then more and more began breaking the agreements they themselves had made. In dealing with the situation as best he could, Ginn said, he "used the philosophies that had been taught me previously"—by which he meant that he continued to conduct price-fixing meetings, in the hope that at least *some* of the agreements made at them would be honored. As for Paxton, in Ginn's opinion that philosopher was not only ignorant of the meetings but so constant in his devotion to the concept of free and aggressive competition that he actually enjoyed the price war, disastrous though it was to everybody's profits. (In his own testimony, Paxton vigorously denied that he had enjoyed it.)

Within a year or so, the electrical-equipment industry took an upturn, and in January, 1957, Ginn, having ridden out the storm relatively well, got his vice-presidency. At the same time, he was transferred to Schenectady, to become general manager of G.E.'s turbine-generator division, and Cordiner again called him into headquarters and gave him a lecture on 20.5. Such lectures were getting to be a routine with Cordiner; every time a new employee was assigned to a strategic managerial post, or an old employee was promoted to such a post, the lucky fellow could be reasonably certain that he would be summoned to the chairman's office to hear a rendition of the austere creed. In his book *The Heart of Japan,* Alexander Campbell reports that a large Japanese electrical concern has drawn up a list of seven company commandments (for example, "Be courteous and sincere!"), and that each morning, in each of its thirty factories, the workers are required to stand at attention and recite these in unison, and then to sing the company song ("For ever-increasing production/Love your work, give your all!"). Cordiner did not require his subordinates to recite or sing 20.5—as far as is known, he never even had it set to music—but from the number of times men like Ginn had it read to them or otherwise recalled to their attention, they must have come to know it well enough to chant it, improvising a tune as they went along.

Remorse and doubt

This time, Cordiner's message not only made an impression on Ginn's mind but stuck there in unadulterated form. Ginn, according to his testimony, became a reformed executive and dropped his price-fixing habits overnight. However, it appears that his sudden conversion cannot be attributed wholly to Cordiner's powers of communication, or even to the drip-drip-drip effect of repetition, for it was to a considerable extent pragmatic in character, like the conversion of Henry VIII to Protestantism. He reformed, Ginn explained to the Subcommittee, because his "air cover was gone."

"Your what was gone?" Senator Kefauver asked.

"My air cover was gone," replied Ginn. "I mean I had lost my air cover. Mr. Erben wasn't around

any more, and all of my colleagues had gone, and I was now working directly for Mr. Paxton, knowing his feelings on the matter. . . . Any philosophy that I had grown up with before in the past was now out the window."

If Erben, who had not been Ginn's boss since late in 1954, had been the source of his air cover, Ginn must have been without its protection for over two years, but, presumably, in the excitement of the price war he had failed to notice its absence. However that may have been, here he now was, a man suddenly shorn not only of his air cover but of his philosophy. Swiftly filling the latter void with a whole new set of principles, he circulated copies of 20.5 among his department managers in the turbine-generator division and topped this off by energetically adopting what he called a "leprosy policy"; that is, he advised his subordinates to avoid even casual social contacts with their counterparts in competing companies, because "once the relationships are established, I have come to the conclusion after many years of hard experience that the relationships tend to spread and the hanky-panky begins to get going." But now fate played a cruel trick on Ginn, and, all unknowing, he landed in the very position that Paxton and Cordiner had been in for years—that of a philosopher vainly endeavoring to sell the Lord to a flock that declined to buy his message and was, in fact, systematically engaging in the hanky-panky its leader had warned it against. Specifically, during the whole of 1957 and 1958 and the first part of 1959 two of Ginn's subordinates were piously signing 20.5 with one hand, and with the other, briskly drawing up price-fixing agreements at a whole series of meetings—in New York; Philadelphia; Chicago; Hot Springs, Virginia; and Skytop, Pennsylvania, to name a few of their gathering places.

It appears that Ginn had not been able to impart much of his shining new philosophy to others, and that at the root of his difficulty lay that old jinx, the problem of communicating. Asked at the hearings how his subordinates could possibly have gone so far astray, he replied,

I have got to admit that I made a communication error. I didn't sell this thing to the boys well enough. . . . The price is so important in the complete running of a business that, philosophically, we have got to sell people not only just the fact that it is against the law, but . . . that it shouldn't be done for many, many reasons. But it has got to be a philosophical approach and a communication approach. . . . Even though . . . I had told my associates not to do this, some of the boys did get off the reservation.. . . . I have to admit to myself here an area of a failure in communications . . . which I am perfectly willing to accept my part of the responsibility for.

In earnestly striving to analyze the cause of the failure, Ginn said, he had reached the conclusion that merely issuing directives, no matter how frequently, was not enough; what was needed was "a complete philosophy, a complete understanding, a complete breakdown of barriers between people, if we are going to get some understanding and really live and manage these companies within the philosophies that they should be managed in."

Senator Hart permitted himself to comment, "You can communicate until you are dead and gone, but if the point you are communicating about, even though it be a law of the land, strikes your audience as something that is just a folklore . . . you will never sell the package."

Ginn ruefully conceded that that was true.

The concept of degrees of communication was further developed, by implication, in the testimony of another defendant, Frank E. Stehlik, who had been general manager of the G.E. low-voltage-switchgear department from May, 1956, to February, 1960. (As all but a tiny minority of the users of electricity are contentedly unaware, switchgear serves to control and protect apparatus used in the generation, conversion, transmission, and distribution of electrical energy, and around $125 million worth of it is sold annually in the United States.) Stehlik received some of his business guidance in the conventional form of orders, oral and written, and some—perhaps just as much, to judge by his testimony—through a less intellectual, more visceral medium of communication that he called "impacts." Apparently, when something happened within the company that made an impression on him, he would consult a sort of internal metaphysical voltmeter to ascertain the force of the jolt that he had received, and, from the reading he got, would attempt to gauge the true drift of company policy. For example, he testified that during 1956, 1957, and most of 1958 he believed that G.E. was frankly and fully in favor of complying with 20.5. But then, in the autumn of 1958, George E. Bu-

rens, Stehlik's immediate superior, told him that he, Burens, had been directed by Paxton, who by then was president of G.E., to have lunch with Max Scott, president of the I-T-E Circuit Breaker Company, an important competitor in the switchgear market. Paxton said in his own testimony that while he had indeed asked Burens to have lunch with Scott, he had instructed him categorically not to talk about prices, but apparently Burens did not mention this caveat to Stehlik; in any event, the disclosure that the high command had told Burens to lunch with an archrival, Stehlik testified, "had a heavy impact on me." Asked to amplify this, he said, "There are a great many impacts that influence me in my thinking as to the true attitude of the company, and that was one of them." As the impacts, great and small, piled up, their cumulative effect finally communicated to Stehlik that he had been wrong in supposing the company had any real respect for 20.5. Accordingly, when, late in 1958, Stehlik was ordered by Burens to begin holding price meetings with the competitors, he was not in the least surprised.

Wages of sin

Stehlik's compliance with Burens' order ultimately brought on a whole new series of impacts, of a much more crudely communicative sort. In February, 1960, General Electric cut his annual pay from $70,000 to $26,000 for violating 20.5; a year later Judge Ganey gave him a three-thousand-dollar fine and a suspended thirty-day jail sentence for violating the Sherman Act; and about a month after *that* G.E. asked for, and got, his resignation. Indeed, during his last years with the firm Stehlik seems to have received almost as many lacerating impacts as a Raymond Chandler hero. But testimony given at the hearings by L. B. Gezon, manager of the marketing section of the low-voltage-switchgear department, indicated that Stehlik, again like a Chandler hero, was capable of dishing out blunt impacts as well as taking them. Gezon, who was directly under Stehlik in the line of command, told the Subcommittee that although he had taken part in price-fixing meetings prior to April, 1956, when Stehlik became his boss, he did not subsequently engage in any antitrust violations until late 1958, and that he did so then only as the result of an impact that bore none of the subtlety noted by Stehlik in his early experience with this phenomenon. The impact came directly from Stehlik, who, it seems, left nothing to chance in communicating with his subordinates. In Gezon's words, Stehlik told him "to resume the meetings; that company policy was unchanged; the risk was just as great as it ever had been; and that if our activities were discovered, I personally would be dismissed or disciplined [by the company], as well as punished by the government." So Gezon was left with three choices: to quit, to disobey the direct order of his superior (in which case, he thought, "they might have found somebody else to do my job"), or to obey the order, and thereby violate the antitrust laws, with no immunity against the possible consequences. In short, his alternatives were comparable to those faced by an international spy.

Although Gezon did resume the meetings, he was not indicted, possibly because he had been a relatively minor price-fixer. General Electric, for its part, demoted him but did not require him to resign. Yet it would be a mistake to assume that Gezon was relatively untouched by his experience. Asked by Senator Kefauver if he did not think that Stehlik's order had placed him in an intolerable position, he replied that it had not struck him that way at the time. Asked whether he thought it unjust that he had suffered demotion for carrying out the order of a superior, he replied, "I personally don't consider it so." To judge by his answers, the impact on Gezon's heart and mind would seem to have been heavy indeed.

The other side of the communication problem—the difficulty that a superior is likely to encounter in understanding what a subordinate tells him—is graphically illustrated by the testimony of Raymond W. Smith, who was general manager of G.E.'s transformer division from the beginning of 1957 until late in 1959, and of Arthur F. Vinson, who in October, 1957, was appointed vice-president in charge of G.E.'s apparatus group, and also a member of the company's executive committee. Smith's job was the one Ginn had held for the previous two years, and when Vinson got *his* job, he became Smith's immediate boss. Smith's highest pay during the period in question was roughly $100,000 a year, while Vinson reached a basic salary of $110,000 and also got a variable bonus, ranging from $45,000 to $100,000. Smith testified that on January 1, 1957, the very day he took charge of the transformer division—and a holiday, at that—he met with Chairman Cordiner and Executive Vice-President Paxton, and Cordiner gave him the familiar admonition about living up to 20.5. However, later that year, the competitive going got so rough that transformers were selling at discounts of as much as 35 percent, and Smith decided on his own hook that the time had come to begin negotiating with rival firms in the hope of stabilizing the market. He felt that he was justified in doing this, he said, because he was convinced that both in company circles and in the whole industry negotiations of this kind were "the order of the day."

By the time Vinson became his superior, in October, Smith was regularly attending price-fixing meetings, and he felt that he ought to let his new boss know what he was doing. Accordingly, he told the Subcommittee, on two or three occasions when the two men found themselves alone together in the normal course of business, he said to Vinson, "I had a meeting with the clan this morning." Counsel for the Subcommittee asked Smith whether he had ever put the matter more bluntly—whether, for example, he had ever said anything like "We're meeting with competitors to fix prices. We're going to have a little conspiracy here and I don't want it to get out." Smith replied that he had never said anything remotely like that—had done nothing more than make remarks on the order of "I had a meeting with the clan this morning." He did not elaborate on why he did not speak with greater directness, but two logical possibilities present themselves. Perhaps he hoped that he could keep Vinson informed about the situation and at the same time protect him from the risk of becoming an accomplice. Or perhaps he had no such intention, and was simply expressing himself in the oblique, colloquial way that characterized much of his speaking. (Paxton, a close friend of Smith's, had once complained to Smith that he was "given to being somewhat cryptic" in his remarks.) Anyhow, Vinson, according to his own testimony, had flatly misunderstood what Smith meant; indeed, he could not recall ever hearing Smith use the expression "meeting the clan," although he did recall his saying things like "Well, I am going to take this new plan on transformers and show it to the boys." Vinson testified that he had thought the "boys" meant the G.E. district sales people and the company's customers, and that the "new plan" was a new marketing plan; he said that it had come as a rude shock to him to learn—a couple of years later, after the case had broken—that in speaking of the "boys" and the "new plan," Smith had been referring to competitors and a price-fixing scheme. "I think Mr. Smith is a sincere man," Vinson testified. "I am sure Mr. Smith . . . thought he was telling me that he was going to one of these meetings. This meant nothing to me."

The bliss of ignorance

Smith, on the other hand, was confident that his meaning had got through to Vinson. "I never got the impression that he misunderstood me," he insisted to the Subcommittee. Questioning Vinson later, Kefauver asked whether an executive in his position, with thirty-odd years' experience in the electrical industry, could possibly be so naïve as to misunderstand a subordinate on such a substantive matter as grasping who the "boys" were. "I don't think it is too naïve," replied Vinson. "We have a lot of boys. . . . I may be naïve, but I am certainly telling the truth, and in this kind of thing I am sure I am naïve."

SENATOR KEFAUVER: Mr. Vinson, you wouldn't be a vice-president at $200,000 a year if you were naïve.

MR. VINSON: I think I could well get there by being naïve in this area. It might help.

Here, in a different field altogether, the communication problem again comes to the fore. Was Vinson really saying to Kefauver what he seemed to be saying—the naïveté about antitrust violations might be a help to a man in getting and holding a $200,000-a-year job at General Electric? It seems unlikely. And yet what else could he have meant? Whatever the answer, neither the federal antitrust men nor the Senate investigators were able to prove that Smith succeeded in his attempts to communicate to Vinson the fact that he was engaging in price-fixing. And, lacking such proof, they were unable to establish what they gave every appearance of going all out to establish if they could: namely, that at least some one man at the pinnacle of G.E.'s management—some member of the sacred executive committee itself—was impli-

cated. Actually, when the story of the conspiracies first became known, Vinson not only concurred in a company decision to punish Smith by drastically demoting him but personally informed him of the decision—two acts that, if he had grasped Smith's meaning back in 1957, would have denoted a remarkable degree of cynicism and hypocrisy. (Smith, by the way, rather than accept the demotion, quit General Electric and, after being fined three thousand dollars and given a suspended thirty-day prison sentence by Judge Ganey, found a job elsewhere, at ten thousand dollars a year.)

This was not Vinson's only brush with the case. He was also among those named in one of the grand jury indictments that precipitated the court action, this time in connection not with his comprehension of Smith's jargon but with the conspiracy in the switchgear department. On this aspect of the case, four switchgear executives—Burens, Stehlik, Clarence E. Burke, and H. Frank Hentschel—testified before the grand jury (and later before the Subcommittee) that at some time in July, August, or September of 1958 (none of them could establish the precise date) Vinson had had lunch with them in Dining Room B of G.E.'s switchgear works in Philadelphia, and that during the meal he had instructed them to hold price meetings with competitors. As a result of this order, they said, a meeting attended by representatives of G.E., Westinghouse, the Allis-Chalmers Manufacturing Company, the Federal Pacific Electric Company, and the I-T-E Circuit Breaker Company was held at the Hotel Traymore in Atlantic City on November 9, 1958, at which sales of switchgear to federal, state, and municipal agencies were divvied up, with General Electric to get 39 percent of the business, Westinghouse 35 percent, I-T-E 11 percent, Allis-Chalmers 8 percent, and Federal Pacific Electric 7 percent. At subsequent meetings, agreement was reached on allocating sales of switchgear to private buyers as well, and an elaborate formula was worked out whereby the privilege of submitting the lowest bid to prospective customers was rotated among the conspiring companies at two-week intervals. Because of its periodic nature, this was called the phase-of-the-moon formula—a designation that in due time led to the following lyrical exchange between the Subcommittee and L. W. Long, an executive of Allis-Chalmers:

SENATOR KEFAUVER: Who were the phasers-of-the-mooners—phase-of-the-mooners?

MR. LONG: As it developed, this so-called phase-of-the-moon operation was carried out at a level below me, I think referred to as a working group. . . .

MR. FERRALL [counsel for the Subcommittee]: Did they ever report to you about it?

MR. LONG: Phase of the moon? No.

Vinson told the Justice Department prosecutors, and repeated to the Subcommittee, that he had not known about the Traymore meeting, the phase-of-the-mooners, or the existence of the conspiracy itself until the case broke; as for the lunch in Dining Room B, he insisted that it had never taken place. On this point, Burens, Stehlik, Burke, and Hentschel submitted to lie-detector tests, administered by the F.B.I., and passed them. Vinson refused to take a lie-detector test, at first explaining that he was acting on advice of counsel and against his personal inclination, and later, after hearing how the four men had fared arguing that if the machine had not pronounced them liars, it couldn't be any good. It was established that on only eight business days during July, August, and September had Burens, Burke, Stehlik, and Hentschel all been together in the Philadelphia plant at the lunch hour, and Vinson produced some of his expense accounts, which, he pointed out to the Justice Department, showed that he had been elsewhere on each of those days. Confronted with this evidence, the Justice Department dropped its case against Vinson, and he has stayed on as a vice-president of General Electric. Nothing that the Subcommittee elicited from him cast any substantive doubt on the defense that had impressed the government prosecutors.

Above the madding crowd

Thus, the uppermost echelon at G.E. came through unscathed; the record showed that participation in the conspiracy went fairly far down in the organization but not all the way to the top. Gezon, everybody agreed, had followed orders from Stehlik, and Stehlik had followed orders from Burens, but that was the end of the trail, because although Burens said he had followed orders from Vinson, Vinson denied it and made the denial stick. The government, at the end of its investigation, stated in court that it could not prove, and did not claim, that either Chairman Cordiner or President Paxton had authorized, or even known about, the conspiracies, and thereby officially ruled out the possibility that they had resorted to at least a figurative wing. Later, Paxton and Cordiner showed up in Washington to testify before the Subcommittee, and its interrogators were similarly unable to establish that they had ever indulged in any variety of winking.

After being described by Ginn as General Electric's stubbornest and most dedicated advocate of free competition, Paxton explained to the Subcommittee that his thinking on the subject had been influenced not directly by Adam Smith but, rather, by way of a former G.E. boss he had worked under—the late Gerard Swope. Swope, Paxton testified, had always believed firmly that the ultimate goal of business was to produce more goods for more people at lower cost. "I bought that then, I buy it now," said Paxton. "I think it is the most marvelous statement of economic philosophy that any industrialist has ever expressed." In the course of his testimony, Paxton had an explanation, philosophical or otherwise, of each of the several situations related to price-fixing in which his name had earlier been mentioned. For instance, it had been brought out that in 1956 or 1957 a young man named Jerry Page, a minor employee in G.E.'s switchgear division, had written directly to Cordiner alleging that the switchgear divisions of G.E. and of several competitor companies were involved in a conspiracy in which information about prices was exchanged by means of a secret code based on different colors of letter paper. Cordiner had turned the matter over to Paxton with orders that he get to the bottom of it, and Paxton had thereupon conducted an investigation that led him to conclude that the color-code conspiracy was "wholly a hallucination on the part of this boy." In arriving at that conclusion, Paxton had apparently been right, although it later came out that there had been a conspiracy in the switchgear division during 1956 and 1957; this, however, was a rather conventional one, based simply on price-fixing meetings, rather than on anything so gaudy as a color code. Page could not be called to testify because of ill health.

Paxton conceded that there had been some occasions when he "must have been pretty damn dumb." (Dumb or not, for his services as the company's president he was, of course, remunerated on a considerably grander scale than Vinson—receiving a basic annual salary of $125,000, plus annual incentive compensation of about $175,000, plus stock options designed to enable him to collect much more, at the comparatively low tax rate on capital gains, if General Electric's stock should go up.) As for Paxton's attitude toward company communications, he emerges as a pessimist on this score. Upon being asked at the hearings to comment on the Smith-Vinson conversations of 1957, he said that, knowing Smith, he just could not "cast the man in the role of a liar," and went on:

When I was younger, I used to play a good deal of bridge. We played about fifty rubbers of bridge, four of us, every winter, and I think we probably played some rather good bridge. If you gentlemen are bridge players, you know that there is a code of signals that is exchanged between partners as the game progresses. It is a stylized form of playing. . . . Now, as I think about this—and I was particularly impressed when I read Smith's testimony when he talked about a "meeting of the clan" or "meeting of the boys"—I began to think that there must have been a stylized method of communication between these people who were dealing with competition. Now, Smith could say, "I told Vinson what I was doing," and Vinson wouldn't have the foggiest idea what was being told to him, and both men could testify under oath, one saying yes and the other saying no, and both be telling the truth. . . . [They] wouldn't be on the same wavelength. [They] wouldn't have the same meanings. I think, I believe now that these men did think that they were telling the truth, but they weren't communicating between each other with understanding.

Here, certainly, is the gloomiest possible analysis of the communications problem.

Chairman Cordiner's status, it appears from his testimony, was approximately that of the Boston Cabots in the celebrated jingle. His services to the company, for which he was recompensed in truly handsome style (with, for 1960, a salary of just over $280,000, plus contingent deferred income of about $120,000, plus stock options potentially worth hundreds of thousands more), were indubitably many and valuable, but they were performed on such an exalted level that, at least in antitrust matters, he does not seem to have been able to have any earthly communication at all. When he emphatically told the Subcommittee that at no time had he had so much as an inkling of the network of conspiracies, it could be deduced that his was a case not of faulty communication but of no communication. He did not speak to the Subcommittee of philosophy or philosophers, as Ginn and Paxton had done, but from his past record of ordering reissues of 20.5 and of peppering his speeches and public statements with praise of free enterprise, it seems clear that he was *un philosophe sans le savoir*—and one on the side of selling the Lord, since no evidence was adduced to suggest that he was given to winking in any form. Kefauver ran through a long list of antitrust violations of which General Electric had been accused over the past half-century, asking Cordiner, who joined the company in 1922, how much he knew about each of them; usually, he replied that he had known about them only after the fact. In commenting on Ginn's testimony that Erben had countermanded Cordiner's direct order in 1954, Cordiner said that he had read it with "great alarm" and "great wonderment," since Erben had always indicated to him "an intense competitive spirit," rather than any disposition to be friendly with rival companies.

Throughout his testimony, Cordiner used the curious expression "be responsive to." If, for instance, Kefauver inadvertently asked the same question twice, Cordiner would say, "I was responsive to that a moment ago," or if Kefauver interrupted him, as he often did, Cordiner would ask politely, "May I be responsive?" This, too, offers a small lead for a foundation grantee, who might want to look into the distinction between being responsive (a passive state) and answering (an act), and their relative effectiveness in the process of communication.

Guilt denied

Summing up his position on the case as a whole, in reply to a question of Kefauver's about whether he thought that G.E. had incurred "corporate disgrace," Cordiner said, "No, I am not going to be responsive and say that General Electric had corporate disgrace. I am going to say that we are deeply grieved and concerned. . . . I am not proud of it."

Chairman Cordiner, then, had been able to fairly deafen his subordinate officers with lectures on compliance with the rules of the company and the laws of the country, but he had not been able to get all those officers to comply with either, and President Paxton could muse thoughtfully on how it was that two of his subordinates who had given radically different accounts of a conversation between them could be not liars but merely poor communicators. Philosophy seems to have reached a high point at G.E., and communication a low one. If executives could just learn to understand one another, most of the witnesses said or implied, the problem of antitrust violations would be solved. But perhaps the problem is cultural as well as technical, and has something to do with a loss of personal identity that comes from working in a huge organization. The cartoonist Jules Feiffer, contemplating the communication problem in a nonindustrial context, has said, "Actually, the breakdown is between the person and himself. If you're not able to communicate successfully between yourself and yourself, how are you supposed to make it with the strangers outside?" Suppose, purely as a hypothesis, that the owner of a company who orders his subordinates to obey the antitrust laws has such poor communication with himself that he does not really know whether he wants the order to be complied with or not. If his order is disobeyed, the resulting price-fixing may benefit his company's coffers; if it is obeyed, then he has done the right thing. In the first instance, he is not personally implicated in any wrong-doing, while in the second he is positively involved in *right*doing. What, after all, can he lose? It is perhaps reasonable to suppose that such an executive might communicate his uncertainty more forcefully than his order. Possibly yet another foundation grantee should have a look at the reverse of communication failure, where he might discover that messages the sender does not even realize he is sending sometimes turn out to have got across only too effectively.

Expensive retribution

Meanwhile, in the first year after the Subcommittee concluded its investigation, the defendant companies were by no means allowed to forget their transgressions. The law permits customers who can prove that they have paid artificially high prices as a result of antitrust violations to sue for damages—in most cases, triple damages—and suits running into many millions of dollars soon began piling up. (By January, 1962, they had piled up so high that Chief Justice Warren set up a special panel of federal judges to plan how they should all be handled.) Needless to say, Cordiner was not allowed to forget about the matter, either; indeed, it would be surprising if he was allowed a chance to think about much else, for in addition to the suits, he had to contend with active efforts by a minority group of stockholders to unseat him. Paxton retired as president in April, 1961, because of ill health dating back at least to the previous January, when he underwent a major operation. As for the executives who pleaded guilty and were fined or imprisoned, most of those who had been employed by companies other than G.E. remained with them, either in their old jobs or in similar ones. Of those who had been employed by G.E., none remained there. Some retired permanently from business, others settled for comparatively small jobs, and a few landed big ones—most spectacularly Ginn, who in June, 1961, became president of Baldwin-Lima-Hamilton, manufacturers of heavy machinery. And as for the future of price-fixing in the electrical industry, it seems safe to say that what with the Justice Department, Judge Ganey, Senator Kefauver, and the triple-damage suits, the impact on the philosophers who guide corporate policy has been such that they, and even their subordinates, are likely to try to hew scrupulously to the line for quite some time. Quite a different question, however, is whether they have made any headway in their ability to communicate.

Imperfect Competition and Antitrust Policy

Readings 43, 44, and 45   Debate on Antitrust

Economists recognize that perfect competition is a good thing and deviations from it bad. Since, however, the real world rarely meets the strictest requirements of perfect competition as defined by the economist, the cause of antitrust needs more than these generalities to be useful and effective. The authors in the first reading propose a positive and practical approach to the subject. They do not believe laissez faire can itself provide an approximation to workably perfect competition. They do think economic analysis furnishes guides for legislation, prosecution, and adjudication, and for business conduct itself.

This first reading represents the collaboration of a top-notch economist and a top-notch lawyer. Carl Kaysen left the Harvard Economics Department to become Director of the Institute for Advanced Study in Princeton. He combines government service with scholarship and had the opportunity to be the first economist to serve as a "clerk" to a judge in an important antitrust case: Judge Charles Wyzanski, Jr., made history when he forced the United Shoe Company to sell, as well as to rent, its machinery. Donald Turner of the Harvard Law School used to be head of President Johnson's Antitrust Division in the Justice Department.

In contrast to Kaysen and Turner, who favor evolutionary reform of present antitrust policy, John Kenneth Galbraith in the second reading provides the Senate Committee on Small Business with a lecture on the new industrial state. No one is surprised when right-wing writers defend the corporation. Recall for example the Schumpeter Reading 41. But when the liberal critic Galbraith comes to defend the corporation and to play down the role of antitrust prosecution, that is a more surprising fact and one with which experts in that field disagree vociferously.

Opposed to Galbraith's acceptance of big business, Michigan Senator Philip A. Hart in the third reading proposes a sweeping Industrial Reorganization Act to reinstate competition, at long last, in our seven most basic industries.

Questions to guide the reading

Why would significant and never-ending economies of large-scale production tend, under laissez faire, to be destructive of competition? What optimistic evidence do the authors give in this regard?

What acts tend to enhance the market power of sellers? What penalties and attitudes do the authors propose to help limit market power?

Would you agree that Dr. Galbraith is offering a false choice when he says Either accept the modern large corporation or break it up? Can't one agree that the large corporation is here to stay and still advocate militant enforcement of antitrust legislation? Does Galbraith perhaps confuse "what is" with "what is right"? Even if the large corporation does do some good things, couldn't it be made to do even better things by vigorous antitrust enforcement? Look forward to M. A. Adelman's Reading 49 giving the grim details of the Mideast oil monopoly to remind Galbraith of what might be the shape of things to come if people fell for his advice to go easy in antitrust policy.

If Senator Hart thinks antitrust has been ineffective up to now, what makes him think his Industrial Reorganization Act will succeed any better in reinstating competition?

Reading 43

A Policy for Antitrust Law

Carl Kaysen and Donald F. Turner

This analysis of United States antitrust policy has two aims: the proposal of a strengthened antitrust policy, worked out in enough detail to indicate the changes in law and administration necessary to apply it; and a statement of the logic of the policy proposal—in terms of the presumptions, factual judgments, and analytical reasoning on which it rests—in such a way that it will be useful even to those who disagree with the value judgment inevitably involved in it.

Some underlying assumptions

Certain broad propositions must be taken as true to warrant any antitrust policy. We make these explicit here, in part to indicate our justification of them, in part to set bounds to the scope of our discussion.

As the context of our discussion we take for granted the present mixed economy, in which the largest part is organized on the decentralized lines of private property and private enterprise. The market is thus the central institution regulating economic activity. The use to a significantly greater extent than at present of other methods of economic organization—including nationalization, direct government control in detail of individual firms, consumer cooperation, or worker-manager guild organization—is ruled out as a real policy alternative. Indeed, only in this context is it worth while to place much emphasis on antitrust policy.

Further, we assume that the sectors of the economy in which government monopoly, or private monopoly controlled in more or less detail by government (to which antitrust policy is not applicable), are limited, and are not growing rapidly relative to the rest of the economy. Thus we posit a market-controlled sector and a distinct and identifiable government-controlled sector, in the first of which antitrust policy is the primary form of extra-market regulation, while in the second various kinds of more specific controls apply. Although the boundaries between the two sectors cannot be easily specified in general terms, we must be able to say of any specific industry or industrial activity that it falls on one or the other side of the boundary. We further assume that the size of the government-controlled sector and its interrelations with the market-controlled one are not, and will not become, such as to make a successful antitrust policy impossible. This is by no means an obvious truth. The government-regulated sector is not so large in a crude sense as to leave no room for market forces, but the problem of interrelations between regulation in the one area and competition in the other is more complex. Here we can only point out the difference between the existence of regulated monopoly in an industry like electric power, which does not affect the structure or market operations of power-users, although it does affect their costs; and the kind of regulation involved in crude-oil prorationing, or in collective bargaining as now established, which may have powerful impacts on industrial markets, in the first case in the oil industry, in the second case, generally.

We assume that some kind of antitrust policy is necessary or desirable. Again, though this proposition is often taken as obvious, it is not necessarily so. Other industrial nations, with few exceptions, have not had such policies in the past, although in recent years interest in them has grown. Belief in the need for a procompetitive public policy rests on two propositions. First, there is some minimum level of competition which it is necessary to achieve in the market-controlled sector if that sector is to be allowed to remain a market-regulated rather than a government-controlled one. Second, this level is not self-maintaining: in the absence of antitrust, the level of competition will sink below the minimum. While there are substantial economic arguments for the first proposition, it rests basically on a political judgment. In our democratic, egalitarian society, large areas of uncontrolled private power are not tolerated. The continued freedom of most industries from detailed government regulation rests on their subjection to the control of market forces. This means some level of competition, sufficient to prevent at least the accumulation of visible, unchecked private economic power. A complete absence of positive public policy would lead to a drastic decline in the competitiveness of business. A much more widespread pattern of growth by merger, an efflorescence of collusive arrangements of all sorts, and the use of various exclusionary, and otherwise anticompetitive practices now forbidden would all follow on the abandonment of a procompetitive public policy. In general, these changes in the structure of markets and the conduct of business firms would lead to declining economic efficiency and shifts in income distribution of a sort which are usually viewed as undesirable.

Next, we assume that enforcement of some kind of anti-trust policy is worth its cost. This means that the level of competition which would persist in the absence of any policy is far enough away from what could be achieved so that the administrative, political, and economic costs of government intervention involved in a procompetitive policy are worth incurring. One way of justifying this assumption is to point to the present antitrust policy, and its application—in changing ways— over the past sixty years. It is fairly clear from the cases that the antitrust law sets a standard of business conduct in respect to anticompetitive practices that is more stringent than would exist in its absence.

Bigness not necessarily better

At a deeper level, the assumption that an effective antitrust policy is worth while involves several complex judgments of fact. First, economies of scale under present technology do not indicate the desirability of a radically *greater* concentration of output in a small number of large firms, so that antitrust policy is not hopelessly at variance with the underlying cost situation. Several kinds of evidence support this conclusion.

First is the importance of mergers in explaining the present relative size distribution of industrial firms. Second is the fact that all of the technical economies of scale are achieved at the level of the plant rather than of the firm, and the greatest part of the size difference between very large and large firms (say $500 million and over assets in the first class, and $50 to $500 million in the second) lies in the number of plants they operate rather than in the size of the plants themselves. Technical economies of scale are not the only kind; economies at the level of the firm in selling, advertising, research, production planning, personnel recruitment, etc., are also possible. Third is the large variation in size within the group of "large" firms with modern management organizations, highly developed research and marketing activities, multiplant and multimarket activity. Among integrated steel producers the range is ten to one; among "major" oil producers, twenty to one; among chemical manufacturers it is perhaps fifty to one. This variation shows no tendency to diminish over time; giant firms are not generally outcompeting smaller ones, by any tests now available.

What is now true must be expected to continue in the future: no sharp change in technology, including the introduction of largescale rapid computation and automatic control techniques, will in the near future dictate a substantial increase in concentration among market-controlled firms. The truth of this is, of course, a speculative matter; inventions not now foreseen may lead to radical changes in all our ideas. But insofar as we have any basis of speculation, there appears to be no reason to expect any radical change in the character of scale economies.

Need for competition

In singling out the relation between size and efficiency for discussion, we are acknowledging that competition requires the existence of competitors, in the plural. The vexing question is "how many?" We begin exploring this question by observing that the rigorous model of the perfectly competitive market is the appropriate starting point of any definition, but it cannot be the end of any practically useful one. The model provides us with two important notions: first, a market in which each seller acts as if his own decisions had no influence on any significant market variable—price, supply, the number of other sellers and their sales, etc.; second, a definition of economic efficiency in terms of the relations between costs and prices characteristic of the model. The second result, the efficient use of resources in meeting the demands of consumers, depends on the first and on the logic of profit maximization. In the model, the first result comes about because sellers are many in number and individually of insignificant size relative to the total market, the product of any seller is a perfect substitute for that of any other, and new sellers enter and old ones leave freely and quickly in response to profits and losses. In real markets— with very few exceptions—these conditions do not hold. The existence of significant economies of scale at both the plant and the firm level over some size range means that firms are not generally insignificant in relation to the market. The geography of production and consumption reinforces this result: for many products there are local or regional markets in which the number of sellers is relatively small, and which are to a substantial extent isolated from other local and regional markets by the barriers of transport cost. The outputs of one seller are usually only imperfect substitutes for the outputs of another: product differentiation, advertising, and locational differences among sellers which bring about this result must be taken as permanent features of the economy, answering in some measure to real preferences of consumers. Neither entry nor exit is universally free and speedy. All sorts of barriers to entry, from large capital requirements to high advertising costs and closely held patented technology, are widely characteristic of the economy, though in varying measure in different industries. Frictions, and the influence of uncertainty and risk aversion on business decisions, mean that entry and exit often take place with substantial lags after the changes in profitability which occasion them.

Concentration and market power

Nonetheless, though the model of competitive market structure is not usable as such in our definition of competition, other concepts of the model are. Where firms can persistently behave over substantial periods of time in a manner which differs from the behavior that the competitive market would impose on competitive firms facing similar cost and demand conditions, they can be identified as possessing market power. Conversely, where, on the average and viewed over long periods of time, the relations of prices, costs, outputs, capacities, and investments among a group of rivalrous firms are such as would be expected in a competitive model, then it can be inferred that the market does constrain the scope of the individual firm's decisions sufficiently to be called competitive. The existence of such constraints depends on many features of a market. In general, numbers and conditions of entry are the most important of these features. There is a high correlation between concentration of output in the hands of a small number of large producers and the existence of firms with significant degrees of market power. This is the basic reason for singling out the relation between size and efficiency for rather extended discussion at this point. Were they such as to dictate a very small number of sellers—two, three, four— in most markets, antitrust policy would make little sense.

On the same ground, we must be concerned with differences in the levels of cost curves among enterprises. We must assume that it is not the case that a few firms, managed by men of superior gifts, can and will continue to attract the small number of superior managers, and thus will be enabled to outperform all rivals in all fields, were they permitted and motivated to do so. This proposition implies something about the distribution of business ability in the population at large and the nature of business activity. On the first point it is assumed that first-grade managerial talent exists sufficient to man a few hundred companies such as Du Pont, General Motors, Standard Oil of New Jersey, etc.: there is a chairman of the board's gavel in the attaché case of every division manager. On the second, it is assumed that where a particular firm does have an advantage in men and methods, rivals can and will copy the methods and hire away the men, and that incentives of pay and promotion will suffice to do so, in that employee loyalties to particular firms will not prove so strong as to make this impossible. It is hard to support this proposition with concrete evidence, and, while we believe it accords with experience, others have expressed different views. Perhaps it is best to label this assumption as an article of democratic faith and leave it at that.[1]

Finally, we must assume that the dependence of business initiative and vigor on the degree of *laissez faire* is not so intimate and important that variations in the amount of government intervention and supervision of the kind involved in antitrust

[1] Some light is cast on the general subject by an examination of an American Institute of Management survey of excellently managed firms, entitled "Manual of Excellent Managements." The 1955 edition lists 389 firms, of which 199 are in manufacturing. The size distribution of these was examined by comparison with the FTC list of 1000 largest manufacturing corporations (1948). The results showed that, while there was a significant correlation between size and the proportion of excellently managed firms, the largest firms were not all listed, nor were all those listed giants. The distribution by groups of 50 was:

The 1000 largest manufacturing firms, by size	Number of excellently managed firms (AIM)
1st 50	26
2nd	31
3rd	20
4th	26
5th	17
6th	11
7th	15
8th	9
9th	7
10th	5
11th	35
12th	2
13th	4
14th	2
15th	4
16th	11
17th	4
18th	2
19th	1
20th	3

A variance analysis of the distribution by groups of 10 among 250 firms showed no correlation between size and the proportion of excellently managed firms over this part of the size range. The assets of the 10th firm on the list were about $1150 million, of the 50th firm, $288 million; the 100th, $139 million; the 200th, $68 million; the 250th, $54 million; the 500th, $23 million; and the 1000th, $9 million.

These figures are compatible with the hypothesis suggested above that rational management practices historically began in large corporations, but have been spreading to smaller and smaller ones. (We do not think it necessary to examine the content of the AIM definition of "excellent management" for the present purposes.)

policy will significantly affect it. This is not to say that particular antitrust measures will not vary in their effects on business incentives, and that such variation is not relevant to the choice among them. Rather it is an assertion that over-all we need not fear that the possibility of any effective antitrust policy is foreclosed because of unfavorable repercussions on business vigor. This proposition is broadly supported by the history of the last three (or the last seven) decades, which have witnessed a progressive increase in the scope and detail of federal government intervention in business decisions with no worth-while evidence that overall business effort has been noticeably diminished.

A policy for antitrust law

Antitrust policy may serve a variety of ultimate aims. We can divide the aims against which any policy proposal may be tested into four broad classes: (1) limitation of the power of big business; (2) performance (efficiency and progressiveness); (3) "fair dealing"; and (4) protection of competitive processes by limiting market power. For reasons to be set forth in detail hereafter, we select (4) as the most desirable and feasible guide, though willy-nilly and by design, the others will necessarily play some part.

A review of existing antitrust law indicates what to us are some important gaps in coverage. Since the existing law is primarily oriented toward conduct, it does not effectively deal—or at least has not effectively dealt in the past—with undue market power that cannot be associated with bad or unduly restrictive conduct. It seems clear that there now exist significant concentrations of undue market power, some individually held, some collectively "shared" in the sense that the members of the industry behave nonrivalrously for mutual benefit. It also seems clear to us that present law (1) has not been and cannot be fairly construed to cover the mere nonrivalrous actions of members of a noncompetitive industry, i.e., the "parallel" behavior of firms in a classic oligopoly is not "conspiracy"; and (2) may not cover all situations of individual market power that could be attacked without upsetting competitive goals. In addition, we believe that the law on conduct should be tightened in several respects if the prevention of undue market power is taken as a central guiding light.

In sum, we are suggesting that the primary goal of antitrust policy be the limitation of undue market power to the extent consistent with maintaining desirable levels of economic performance. To carry this out, we propose amendments of the antitrust laws that would (1) enable a direct attack on undue market power without regard to the presence or absence of conspiracy in the legal sense, and (2) severely limit forms of conduct that contribute to, or are likely to contribute to, the creation of undue market power.

The policy goals

Almost any policy proposal resolves itself into a statement of a hierarchy of ends, ordered to indicate which should prevail in situations where they conflict. In proposing that the primary goal of antitrust policy be the limitation of market power, we do not make it our sole goal; we also give great weight to the achievement of desirable economic performance. Indeed, in so far as reduction of market power is incompatible with efficiency and progressiveness, we subordinate the first goal to the second. If, for example, the efficient scale of operation in a particular market is so large in relation to the size of the market that efficient firms are so few in number as to make their possession of market power likely, and the reduction of market power cannot be achieved except at the cost of a substantial loss in efficiency, our policy would call for no action against the power itself. But where market power exists and can be reduced without sacrifices in performance, then such action is desirable without reference to the question of how good over-all performance may have been.

The other two of the broad classes of goals— promoting "fair" business conduct and the redistribution of social power between large and small business—occupy a much lower position in our hierarchy of policy aims. We expect that some degree of regulation of business conduct in the interest of "fair dealing" may be necessary. As we have already indicated, the policy of limiting market power will not be pressed to the point of reducing it to negligible dimensions everywhere (and indeed, this is not possible, even if it were viewed as desirable). Thus there may be some case for limiting the way in which residual market power is used. To the extent that some methods of using market power will be controlled on grounds that they are likely to contribute to the perpetuation of market power or to its increase, the area of regulation on pure "fair dealing" grounds will be correspondingly narrowed. But some kinds of conduct which will require such regulation do exist, and where it can be achieved without too high a price in efficiency, we deem it desirable. The following is a brief summary of our recommendations.

Limitation of market power.

1. We propose statutory authorization for the reduction of undue market power, whether individually or jointly possessed; this to be done normally by dissolution, divorcement, or divestiture. We would except market power derived from economies of scale, valid patents, or the introduction of new processes, products, or marketing techniques.

2. We suggest, in the alternative, that the program be either (a) a permanent feature of antitrust policy, thus applying both to existing concentrations of market power and to concentrations that may later arise through inadequacies in the law, or in enforcement of the law, concerning conduct; or (b) a program limited to the time required to deal with existing undue concentrations of market power.

3. With respect to either of the above alternatives, we suggest that the policy might be carried out either (a) under a statute in which market power is defined in general terms, requiring a fairly extensive economic inquiry for determination of each case; or (b) under a statute in which market power is more arbitrarily defined, which would facilitate the disposition of cases and more clearly identify the "targets," but could possibly be applied to firms that, in fact, lacked market power.

Limitations on conduct contributing to market power.

1. *Mergers.* Particularly if the proposals as to market power are deemed unwise or undesirable, and perhaps in any event, we propose tightening the law on mergers. Some means of making enforcement more effective than it now is seems of paramount importance. We propose, as one step in this direction, a requirement of advance reporting of all mergers involving firms of more than a

certain absolute size in assets or more than a certain share of any market in which they operate. We also suggest the possibility of a more arbitrary standard for illegality, in line with the similar suggestion as to market power stated above.

2. *Price-fixing or price-influencing agreements.* Regarding trade association and similar activities, we propose specific statutory prohibition of agreements:

(a) to abide by reported list prices,

(b) to report offers at which no sales are made,

(c) to inform each other of the individual buyers and sellers in all transactions,

(d) to refuse to make reports, submitted to each other, available to buyers or buyers' trade associations,

(e) to submit books and accounts to the inspection of any member of the group or representative thereof; or

(f) to report transactions to each other, or to a representative of the group, within a period of seven days or less after said transactions take place.

3. *Collective refusals to deal.* Apart from those incidentally resulting from productive joint ventures, we would make collective refusals to deal illegal per se.

4. *Patents and patent licensing.* Proceeding on the basic premise that patentees' realizable rewards can be lowered without significantly reducing the flow of useful inventions and innovations, we propose:

(a) that the patent laws be revised to create a class of "petty" patents, with monopoly rights for five years only, and to raise the standard of invention for seventeen-year patents;

(b) that on restrictive clauses in patent licensing agreements,

(1) price-fixing clauses be made illegal per se,

(2) clauses providing for grant-backs of new patents or exclusive licenses thereunder be made illegal per se,

(3) covenants not to contest patent validity be invalid in any licensing agreement containing restrictions in addition to a uniform royalty provision,

(4) cross-licensing and pooling agreements contain no restrictions beyond that for a uniform royalty charge on each patent from all licenses (except that the owner may restrict the use), and

(5) all licensing agreements be registered with the Federal Trade Commission (but not made public);

(c) that Section 7 of the Clayton Act be revised to cover acquisitions of patents from individuals as well as from corporations.

5. *Price discrimination.* We propose that the Robinson-Patman Act be repealed, in favor of a statute dealing separately with (a) price discrimination directed against competing sellers and (b) price discrimination that harms particular buyers. In each case, we would make some substantive changes in the existing law. In both cases, we would liberalize the "cost" defense and specifically exclude from the law all geographic price discrimination that is accounted for entirely by differences in transportation cost.

Procedural and related recommendations.

1. We propose that criminal penalties be limited to the so-called per se offenses.

2. We propose that treble damages also be limited to the per se offenses; that no private suit be maintainable under a market power statutory provision; and that judgment under the market power provision would not constitute prima facie proof of anything under Section 5 of the Clayton Act.

3. We suggest the creation of a special court for adjudicating monopoly cases and other Sherman Act cases in which divestiture is part of the relief sought. For an extended program against undue market power, we propose a special court, with the prosecuting function placed in the hands of a new administrative agency. We also propose certain procedural steps designed to clarify and speed the trial of economic issues of fact.

Our reasons for giving primary emphasis to the fourth of the general goals of policy stated above and for making the above recommendations are partly positive and partly negative. Our positive reasons rest ultimately on a value judgment. The most important aspect of the competitive process is that it is self-controlling with regard to private economic power. For all the important qualifications and limitations of the doctrine of the invisible hand which modern economic analysis has produced, that doctrine remains the basic political justification for an enterprise economy in which major economic decisions are compelled and coordinated through the market. It is the fact that the competitive market *compels* the results of its processes which is the ultimate defense against the demand that economic decisions be made or supervised by politically responsible authorities. Without such market compulsion, that demand appears ultimately irresistible in a society committed to representative government. It is our preference for the kind of autonomy in economic life which a market-organized society makes possible that forms the particular judgment we make.

Our negative reasons are more objective, and less subject to dogmatic acceptance or rejection. In essence, they amount to the proposition that the alternative standards present definitional and administrative problems of such magnitude that consistent and sensible enforcement would be well-nigh impossible. While similar difficulties would attend the carrying out of a market power standard, we conclude that they would be much less severe. Moreover, we believe it is possible to formulate arbitrary tests designed to reduce administrative problems under a market power standard with considerably more confidence in the results than if similar steps were taken in order to carry out the other designated goals.

Reading 44

In My New Industrial State Trust Busting Not Needed

J. Kenneth Galbraith

I am very happy to be here this morning. I have long been a close and admiring student of [Assistant] Attorney General Turner's writings, as equally those of Professor Adams. As will become evident, Mr. Turner's position, fully explored, provides comprehensive and much appreciated support for mine. In the lectures that precipitated this discussion and the book I have just published [*The New Industrial State 1967*], I took it for granted that American business has become very big.

The element of surprise in this conclusion is very small; I doubt that this conclusion will be much disputed. There are still a large number of small firms and small farms in the United States. They are, however, no longer characteristic of the American economy. In 1962, the *five largest* industrial corporations in the United States, with combined assets in excess of $36 billion, possessed *over 12 percent* of all assets used in manufacturing. The *50 largest* corporations had *over a third* of all manufacturing assets. The *500 largest* corporations had well *over two-thirds*. Corporations with assets in excess of $10 million, some 2,000 in all, accounted for about 80 percent of all the resources used in manufacturing in the United States.

In the mid-1950's, 28 corporations provided approximately 10 percent of all employment in manufacturing, mining, and retail and wholesale trade. Twenty-three corporations provided 15 percent of all the employment in manufacturing. In the first half of that decade—June 1950–June 1956—a hundred firms received two-thirds by value of all defense contracts; 10 firms received one-third. In 1960 four corporations accounted for an estimated 22 percent of all industrial research and development expenditure. Three hundred and eighty-four corporations employing 5,000 or more workers accounted for 85 percent of these research and development expenditures; 260,000 firms employing fewer than 1,000 accounted for only 7 percent.

If I might continue this somewhat exaggerated dose of statistics for just a minute, in 1965, three industrial corporations, General Motors, Standard Oil of New Jersey, and Ford Motor Co., had more gross income than *all* of the farms in the country. This is relevant to my statement that these are the typical, characteristic parts of the economy. The income of General Motors, of $20.7 billion, about equalled that of the 3 million smallest farms in the country—around 90 percent of all farms. The gross revenues of each of the three corporations

From U.S. Senate, 90th Congress, 1st Session, Hearing before Subcommittees of the Select Committee on Small Business, June 29, 1967.

just mentioned far exceed those of any single State. The revenues of General Motors in 1963 were 50 times those of Nevada, eight times those of New York, and slightly less than one-fifth those of the Federal Government.

These figures, like all statistics, are subject to minor query on matters of detail. As orders of magnitude they are not, I believe, subject to any serious question. Nor are the consequences.

Bigness brings market power

The large firms that dominate the nonservice and nonagricultural sector of the economy have extensive power over their prices. They have large influence over the prices that they pay—at least those costs that are important to their operations. And also the wages they pay. They supply themselves with capital; some three-quarters of all savings now come from the retained earnings of corporations, which is to say that the latter have largely exempted themselves from dependence on the capital market. And, with varying degrees of success, firms with the resources to do so go beyond the prices that they set *to persuade their customers as to what they should buy.* This is a persuasion that, in various and subtle ways, extends to the State [the "military-industrial" complex]. There is great room for difference of opinion, and accordingly for debate, on how decisive are these several manifestations of power. But nearly all will agree that "There is a large correlation between the concentration of output in the hands of a small number of large producers and the existence of firms with significant degrees of market power." The observation just cited is that of Carl Kaysen and Donald F. Turner in their authoritative volume, "A Policy for Antitrust Law."

They add, as would I, that a policy that deals with "the existence and significance of market power is not aimed at merely marginal or special phenomena, but at phenomena spread widely through the economy."

In my own volume I have gone on, at no slight length, to argue that this trend to the large corporation and this resulting exercise of substantial power over the prices, costs, wages, capital sources, and consumers is part of the broad sweep of economic development. Technology; the extensive use of capital; affluent and hence *malleable* customers; the imperatives of organization [the techno-structure]; the role of the union; the requirements imposed by public tasks, including arms development and space exploration, have all weakened the authority of the market. At the same time, these developments have both enabled and required firms to *substitute planning with its management of markets* for a simple response to the market. Bigness and market power, in other words, are but one part of a much larger current of change. To see them in isolation from other change is artificial. In part it is what results when a social discipline passes however partially from the custody of scholars to that of specialists and mechanics.

I have also been concerned in this book with the problem of how we are to survive, and in civilized fashion, in a world of great organizations which, not surprisingly, impose both their values and their needs on the society they are assumed to serve [the military-industrial complex]. But these further matters are not directly at issue this morning. In any case they do not directly involve the question of the antitrust laws.

The issue of the antitrust laws arises in response to a prior question. That question is whether we can escape the concentration and the attendant market control and planning which I have outlined and whether the antitrust laws, as now used, are an effective instrument for this escape. The present hearings materialized when *I* urged the contrary—when *I* said that the trend to great size and associated control was immutable, given our desire for economic development, and that the present antitrust efforts to deal with size and market power were a charade. *I* noted that the antitrust laws legitimatize the real exercise of market power on the part of the large firms by a rather diligent harassment of those who have less of it. Thus, they serve to reassure us on the condition they are assumed to correct.

The facts which lead to the foregoing conclusions are not at all obscure. Nor are they matters of great subtlety. They are accepted by most competent economists and lawyers, including the very distinguished men here this morning. Only the rather obvious conclusions to be drawn from these facts encounter a measure of resistance. This, no doubt, is purely temporary, but while it persists it does cause a measure of confusion.

To him who hath

The most effective manifestation of economic power, all must agree, is simply the big firm. To be big in general and big in an industry is by far the best way of influencing prices and costs, commanding capital, having access to advertising, and selling resources, and possessing the other requisites of marked power. And, as we have seen, by common agreement the heartland of the industrial economy is now dominated by large firms. The great bulk of American business is transacted by very large corporations.

And here enters the element of charade in the antitrust laws. If a firm is *already* large it is substantially immune under the antitrust laws. If you *already* have the basic requisite of market power, you are safe. The assistant Attorney General in Charge of the Antitrust Laws [Donald F. Turner, since 1968 at the Harvard Law School] argues that the market power of the large firm should *now* be made subject to the antitrust laws. This indeed is the main thrust of Mr. Turner's and Mr. Kaysen's book. And in responding to the questions of this committee on May 2 of this year he affirmed the point, if in slightly more cautious language:

It is more difficult under present law to bring a case attacking *existing* concentration in an industry than to prevent further concentrations which firms attempt to realize through merger.

But this we see is no minor qualification. If firms are already large—if concentration is already great—if the resulting power, to use Mr. Turner's own words, is not "merely marginal" but is "spread widely through the economy" as he says, then it means that all so favored have won immunity or virtual immunity from the antitrust laws. And this, of course, is the case.

Meanwhile, the antitrust laws are effective in two instances where the firms do not have market power but are seeking to achieve it. Where firms are few and large they can, without overt collusion, establish and maintain a price that is generally satisfactory to all participants. Nor is this an especially difficult calculation, this exercise of power. This is what we economists with our genius for the neat phrase have come to call oligopolistic rationality. And this market power is *legally immune* or very nearly so. It is everyday practice in autos, steel, rubber, and virtually every other industry shared or dominated by, relatively, a few large firms. But if there are 20 or 30 or more significant firms in the industry, this kind of tacit pricemaking—this calculation as to what is mutually advantageous but without overt communication—becomes more difficult, may be very difficult. The same result can only be achieved by having a meeting or by exchanging information on prices and costs and price intentions. But this is illegal. It is also legally vulnerable. And it is, in fact, an everyday object of prosecution as the Department of Justice will confirm. *What the big firm in the concentrated industry can accomplish legally and effortlessly because of its size, the small firm in the unconcentrated industry does at the pain of civil and even criminal prosecution. Moreover, with this my colleagues will, I believe, agree.*

The second manifestation of the charade has to do with mergers. If a firm is *already* large, it has as a practical matter nothing to fear under antimerger provisions of the Clayton Act. It will not be demerged. It can continue to grow from its own earnings; if discreet, it can even, from time to time, pick up a small and impecunious competitor, for it can reasonably claim that this does little to alter the pattern of competition in the industry. But if two medium-sized firms unite in order to deal more effectively with this giant, the law will be on them like a tiger. Again if large, you are exempt. If you seek to become as large, or even if you seek to become somewhat larger, although still much smaller, you are in trouble.

Here we have the nature of modern antitrust activity. *It conducts a fairly effective war on small firms which seek the same market power that the big firms already, by their nature, possess.* Behind this impressive facade the big participants who have the most power bask in early total immunity. And since the competitive market, like God and a sound family life, is something that no sound businessman can actively oppose, even the smaller entrepreneurs who are the natural victims of this arrangement do not actively protest. It is possible that they do not know how they are being used.

My defense of bigness

As I say all of this is agreed—or at least is supported by the past writings and speeches of participants in this discussion. All I have done—I wish I could lay claim to greater novelty—is to state the rather disagreeable conclusion flowing from this agreement. The antitrust laws give the impression of protecting the market and competition by attacking those who exercise it most effectively. I wonder if the committee thinks that charade is an unjust word?

Now let me clear up two or three secondary matters which may seem to affect this discussion but really do not. The first requires me, I think for the first time—in substance as distinct from terminology—to quit company with Attorney General [sic] Turner. Mr. Turner, while conceding that the law is largely helpless in attacking achieved as distinct from aspired-to power, holds that it is important to act *preventatively* to keep smaller firms from getting larger. This he has emphasized in his responses to this committee. It will surely have occurred to the committee, as it must have occurred to Mr. Turner, that this does not meet the issue of gross discrimination as between those who already have and those who aspire to market power. Nor, one imagines, can a major law officer of the Government be entirely happy about such discrimination. It condones professional and accomplished wrongdoing, as it were, but stresses the importance of cracking down on amateur wickedness. Surely this is bad law. Also, given the size and market power that has already been achieved, and given its immunity, it will be evident that this justification amounts to locking the stable door not alone after the horse has been stolen but after the entire stud has been galloped away.

Next, I must correct a misapprehension of Attorney General Turner. His responses to the committee and his extremely interesting lecture attacking my general position in London convey the impression that I am concerned with making the economic case for the large corporation. I am, he suggests, especially concerned to defend its efficiency and technical virtuosity. To this he responds by arguing that, while the big corporation is more efficient than the small firm, there is no great difference between the big corporation and the giant corporation. He doesn't make altogether clear, incidentally, how a big as distinct from a giant corporation is. All would, I imagine, be among the five hundred or thousand firms that dominate industrial activity. But I have a more fundamental objection. He attacks me on a point that concerns me little and which is of no importance for my case.

I am not concerned with making the case for big business. Nor am I especially concerned about its efficiency or inefficiency. Doubtless efficiency is worth having. But, like truth, regular bathing and better traffic regulation, it has an adequate number of exponents. I have always thought it unwise to compete with the commonplace. Mr. Turner may be correct in his conclusions about the giants. I am content to argue that we have big business, and that the antitrust laws notwithstanding we will continue to have it, and that they give an impression of alternative possibilities that do not exist.

I conclude also that while big business and giant business may not be more efficient, their market power as manifested only on what they sell and what they buy and over buyers does *give them advantages in planning their own future and insuring their own survival.* Since big business is inevitable and will not be affected by the antitrust laws, I naturally go on to consider how we may come to terms with it. Much of my book is concerned with that. If my colleagues this morning disagree, as is their right, they must tell you how the antitrust laws are to be brought effectively to bear on the large corporation. Otherwise—and here let me interpolate an important point—there is no escape from the conclusion that the antitrust laws, so far from being a threat to business are a facade behind which it operates with yet greater impunity. They create the impression, the antitrust laws, that the market is a viable control. Then, if a drug firm has exorbitant profits, it can say this is what the market allows. Or if an automobile firm does not want to install safety appliances, it can say that the market does not demand it. Or if there is resistance to Government price guideposts to prevent inflation, it can be said that these interfere with the market.

In each case, the antitrust laws effectively protect the large business from social pressure or regulation by maintaining the myth that the market does the regulating instead.

Finally, I agree that the antitrust laws have purposes other than those related to the structure of industry and the resulting power and planning. I agree in particular they are a code of what is deemed fair and decent as between seller and buyers. They exclude the resort to activities—naked aggression, as in the case of the old Standard Oil Co. in the last century—based on superior economic resources, favoritism, surreptitious and unfair discounts, numerous other practices which the civilized commercial community holds in disesteem. I have no complaint about these aspects of the antitrust laws. On the contrary, I consider them serviceable. But only in the most marginal fashion do they thus affect the structure of industry. They are, in large part, a separate matter and do not affect the discussion here.

Put up or shut up

To what then does this all lead? It is possible that my distinguished colleagues here this morning will call for an all-out attack on achieved market power along the lines which Attorney General Turner has adumbrated in his book, which Prof. Walter Adams has long favored, and which I have just said would be necessary if they disagree with my conclusions on the inevitability of market power. This means action, including enabling legislation leading to all-out dissolution proceedings against General Motors, Ford, the oil majors, United States Steel, General Electric, IBM, Western Electric, Du Pont, Swift, Bethlehem, International Harvester, North American Aviation, Goodyear, Boeing, National Dairy Products, Procter & Gamble, Eastman Kodak, and all of comparable size and scope. For there can be no doubt: All are giants. All have market power. All enjoy an *immunity* not accorded to those who merely aspire to their power. Such an onslaught, tantamount, given the role of the big firms in the economy as I described it, to declaring the heartland of the modern economy illegal, would go far to make legitimate the objections to my position. It would mean that achieved market power was subject to the same legal attack as that which is only a matter of aspiration.

But I will be a trifle surprised if my distinguished colleagues from the Government are willing to proclaim such a crusade. I am frank to say I would not favor it myself; as I indicated at the outset, I do not think that the growth of the modern corporation can be isolated from other and intricately related changes in modern economic development. I doubt that one can operate on one part of this fabric. The political problems in proclaiming much of the modern economy illegal will also strike many as impressive.

If this crusade is not to be launched, then my good friends have no alternative but to agree with me. They are good men; they cannot acquiesce in a policy which by their own admission attacks the small man for seeking what the big firm enjoys with impunity.

The great myth

I readily concede that it would be quixotic to ask the repeal of the antitrust laws although other industrial countries function quite competently without them. But the antitrust laws are part of the American folklore. They receive strong support from the legal profession and vice versa. They have a reserve value for dealing with extreme and sanguinary abuse of power as occasionally occurs. I would be content were we simply to withdraw our faith from the antitrust laws—were we to cease to imagine that there is any chance that they will affect the structure of American industry or its market power and, having in mind the present discrimination in their application, were we then to allow them quietly to atrophy. Then we would face the real problem, which is how to live with the vast organizations—and the values they impose—that we have and will continue to have. This being so, nostalgia will no longer be a disguise for that necessity.

Reading 45

New Antitrust Policy

Senator Philip Hart

The Industrial Reorganization Act seeks to bring closer to reality what this country has pretended to have for years: a competitive economy. It grew out of years of study by the Antitrust and Monopoly Subcommittee. It is not a perfect bill. But it does represent perhaps the greatest effort which

Abridged from the *Congressional Record,* Proceedings and Debates of the 92d Cong., 2d Sess., July 24, 1972, vol. 118, no. 115.

has been put to finding a solution for economic concentration. And it may bear the seeds for producing an economy in which inflation and high unemployment are not a way of life. It also could be a giant step toward eliminating some of the feeling that opportunities no longer exist for the individual and that the economic life of the Nation will always be dominated by a few. We all recognize that too much power in too few hands is bad for social and political reasons, as well as for economic reasons.

Past investigations

Trotting out the specter of excessive economic power is not a new game. The Pujo Committee was at it before World War I and various other groups have been chewing on the problem since. The TNEC—1938-41—reached essentially the same conclusions as to the need for restructuring the economy. However, its effects were aborted by the advent of World War II, when we centralized our economy through the War Production Board to meet the demands of our Armed Forces.

Despite all this knowledge, we have taken no significant steps to remodel the economic structure of our country. Perhaps we lacked the courage—or the vision—or the patience to wade through the problem to the point of remedies.

There are really only two choices for a country: a regulated economy or a free economy. It is perfectly clear which road we are now on. We are operating under phase II of government regulation. It is showing no spectacular success—and because it is not, many persons in and out of Government now tell us that only far more pervasive regulation of wages, prices, and profits will straighten out the Nation's economic problems.

What a dangerous road that is to follow! Once we start with limited controls, and they do not work, it is a little too tempting to add some more controls, and eventually to end up with an economy based on big business, planned and controlled by the Federal Government.

Really free markets

This bill offers an alternative to Government regulation and control. It involves changing the life styles of many of our largest corporations, even to the restructuring of whole industries. It involves restore competition and freedom of enterprise in the economy.

Government regulation is not the way for a democracy. The tradeoff—less power in the hands of a few citizens for more power in the hands of government—to me is a bad bargain.

How much better if we could have an economy where the marketplace is the regulator, the rules are fair for all, and the more efficient and more diligent do the best.

Under this system, freedom prevails—freedom for companies to succeed and fail—freedom of movement for employees—freedom for beginning new companies—freedom for government from the will of superpowerful corporations—freedom for consumers to make companies respond to their desires.

Past failures

This is the type of freedom that has been the traditional goal of the antitrust laws, beginning in 1890 with the Sherman Act, the granddaddy of them all. This law sought to wipe out the power over men's lives—as well as the economy—exercised by the trusts.

By the time the Clayton Act was passed in 1914, Congress had recognized that economic power in and of itself was a thing to fear. The Clayton Act was designed to prevent the acquisition of monopoly power, not merely its abuse. In 1950, Congress reiterated its intent to prevent concentration brought about by mergers which tend to substantially lessen competition or to create a monopoly in any line of commerce in any section of the country.

Unfortunately, the philosophy of Congress—thrice stated—was generally ignored in enforcement of the antitrust laws. In most cases, the Government sought chiefly to prove that the power was or could be used to harm competition. Seldom were the laws applied so as to wipe out monopoly or obligopoly power just because it was there.

Indeed, the laws were not even vigorously applied as Congress had intended to prevent the development of monopoly power. The Sherman Act was followed by the first great wave of mergers in our economy, beginning around the turn of the century. DuPont put together nearly 100 companies to get a near monopoly on the explosives industry. United States Steel put together 180 companies. United States Rubber, General Motors, American Can, International Harvester and a host of other giants were products of this era. The merger movement was halted not by the antitrust authorities but by a 1903 [sic.] stock market crash and financial panic.

The Clayton Act was followed by the second great merger wave in the 1920's. This too was halted by the stock market crash of 1929 and the Great Depression, not by the Antitrust Division or the Federal Trade Commission.

We have just experienced the third great merger movement in our history, from the mid-1950's through the 1960's. Again it was more the stock market than the antitrust agencies which, hopefully, halted it or at least slowed it down considerably.

While I still believe that the antitrust laws could go a long way toward eliminating much of the concentrated economic power. I have given up hope that—absent a new congressional mandate— any attorney general will bring the necessary cases to undo the concentration which has already taken place.

New strong measures needed

We seemingly are caught in our own web: Popular reasoning is that while dismantling some of these corporations is theoretically in the public interest, the effect of the dismantling would be too disastrous.

To accept that is to accept that we must allow Government to be increasingly the handmaiden of the corporations and must sit back while we watch public government be replaced by private.

The Industrial Reorganization Act offers a reasonable approach to getting ourselves out of this problem.

It is really a very simple bill. It outlaws monopoly power, establishes a special Commission— which dies in 15 years—to devise means of eliminating economic concentration and establishes a special court to handle the cases resulting from the Commission's work. The Commission is also to determine the effect of collective bargaining practices on competition in designating industries and make recommendations to Congress for action.

The big seven. Top priority is given to reorganizing seven industries: First, chemical and drugs;

second, electronic computing and communication equipment; third, electrical machinery and equipment; fourth, energy; fifth, iron and steel; sixth, motor vehicles; and seventh, nonferrous metals.

These industries were selected because—based on our research and all available to us—we determined that they have the greatest impact on the persistent inflation eating away at the Nation and contribute most to the unemployment problems.

The seven industries account for nearly 40 percent of the total value created in U.S. manufacturing.

One hundred and forty of the top 200 corporations participate in these industries.

Concentrated industries not only display little price competition but tend to maintain or increase prices as demand falls—in order not to erode profits. Thus, Government steps to halt inflation by cutting demand tend in these industries to backfire. Cuts in demand too frequently result in higher prices—and more layoffs—as the companies seek to make the target profits.

Curing cost-push inflation

The situation has been all too familiar the past 4 years. Government used all the traditional tools in its arsenal to fight inflation, but inflation and high unemployment have flourished.

I suggest this is because we were applying medication designed for a competitive enterprise system when concentrated industries had wiped out much of the competition.

Competition must exist before fiscal and monetary policies can work effectively.

That is the best road to controlling inflation and easing unemployment.

Price controls may have had some impact, although it might be hard to convince consumers of this. But what the control system overlooks is that the prices which have been frozen in concentrated industries were too high in the first place. Price ceilings tend to become price floors, in the absence of competitive pressures to bring prices down.

Transitional harm? Some workers will be concerned that restructuring of industries may cost jobs. I believe that this will not be the case. The evidence is clear that firms in concentrated industries faced with a slackening of demand cut output and employment rather than prices. Competition will improve both the stability and the growth of jobs.

It is true, however, that restructuring of major industries could lead or even require some alterations in existing collective bargaining relationships. The Commission is specifically directed to study collective bargaining practices in the industries designated, to determine the effects of those practices on competition, and to report its findings and recommendations to the Congress.

Will not deconcentration result in further unemployment?

Yes—and no. But more no than yes. As I said, concentration itself tends to cut employment because a company that dominates its market can get higher prices per unit on less production. Also, mergers—which created much of this concentration—cut employment.

If the industries became competitive, it is likely that companies would be forced to increase production at lower prices. To do this, they obviously need more—not fewer—workers.

Also, under competitive conditions there is a better chance for new companies to start up—which would add to employment. Further, if we get to a competitive economy, fiscal and monetary policies can work so they could be used to hold down the overall rate of unemployment.

Why we need a new approach

Why create a special mechanism to enforce the traditional philosophy of the antitrust laws?

In the past, the enforcement agencies have built a poor record for attacking existing concentration. In a way that is understandable because even if an existing agency could find the time and personnel to present the big case—of which there may have been only 10 in the history of antitrust—they would not likely face a court equipped to handle the case.

To quote from a man who has lived through the experience, Judge Wyzanski who handled the United Shoe case:

Judges in prescribing remedies have known their own limitations. They do not, ex officio, have economic or political training. Their prophecies as to the economic future are not guided by unusually subtle judgment. . . . Judicial decrees must be fitted into the framework of what a busy, and none too expert, court can supervise.

That considerations of this type have always affected antitrust courts is plain from the history of the Standard Oil, American Tobacco and Alcoa cases. To many champions of the antitrust laws these cases indicate judicial timidity, economic innocence, lack of convictions, or paralysis of resolution.

But more important, because proving abusive use of economic power—or the positive potential for such abuse—was uppermost in the agencies' minds, little thought was given to remedies. A look at the cases will show that proposed remedy was often boilerplate language.

Seeking remedy.   Under the Industrial Reorganization Act, the remedy is the major goal of the Commission—and the court. Each is equipped with means to gather sufficient information and expert testimony to guide them to just and reasonable outcomes for the cases. Further, companies involved are themselves allowed to make suggestions.

Isn't the approach of this bill extremely radical?

No. It merely restates the philosophy which has been the bedrock of the antitrust laws for 82 years: Monopoly power is a danger to the public interest.

Second, the instructions are to put competition back in each industry in the best possible way. Several different steps might be taken—of which divestiture is the most drastic.

Divestiture itself is not unheard of for this country. It was the keystone of the Public Utility Holding Act of 1935 and was imposed with a heavy hand on Japan by the United States after World War II.

In both cases, experience was good.

Are you not penalizing firms for greater efficiency? What about the innocent parties—such as shareholders?

Competition the goal, not punishment

It is true that reorganization would take away the benefits firms got from controlling markets to their own advantage—and to the detriment of the public. Success in restraining trade would be penalized but efficiency definitely would not. In fact, if the Commission should file a "monopoly power" complaint that company could escape sanction if it could show that this power came either from legal use of valid patents or that reorganization would not make economic sense.

In truth, many companies would be treated better under this approach than under existing antitrust law. There are many who feel several companies in the target industries should be sued criminally for monopolization. This statute, however, is not a criminal one—nor would it open up the companies to treble damage claims from customers or competitors. In that sense, it is an amnesty statute. There is no accusation of wrongdoing—just the goal of establishing competition.

As for stockholders, clearly if they have been with the company long they have been enjoying what some might call "ill-gotten gains" of monopoly. Those we need not be fearful for.

But stockholders who bought into these companies just before enactment of the act need not be hurt. Again, the Public Utility Holding Act has led the way. Here, divestiture in general was accomplished by stock swaps—generally to the benefit of the stockholder.

Just what would happen under the bill? What sort of remedies would be imposed?

Let me start by saying I do not expect any remedy to be as simplistic as one that has constantly come up for years when talk turned to eliminating concentration: break up General Motors into two, three or even eight separate auto companies.

The Commission's remedies should grow out of the sort of sophisticated search which thus far has been conducted by no one. I expect the remedies to reflect this sophistication.

A company could spin off subsidiaries—or replace long-term supply contracts with frequently negotiated contracts—or alter its financial backing commitments—or eliminate exclusive dealerships—or alter its advertising expenditures—or license patents and trademarks—or actually divest.

The remedy could be one, several, or all of the above—or many others which the Commission may recommend.

No matter what plan the Commission proposed, it would be subject to full hearings before the Industrial Reorganization Court, which would make the final decision. At the hearings, the company would have a chance not only to attack the Commission's plan but to make its own proposal. The Commission is charged with prosecuting companies which have monopoly power—and to draft reorganization plans in the designated industries. The Commission is indeed a prosecutor. But it has

another—equally important function as a meaningful investigator and thinktank. Indeed, it must every 2 years report to Congress on the status of its studies and reorganization plans. But more important, it must make recommendations on how labor practices should be altered, on how Government itself, by law or practice, may be hampering competition and on what legislation may be needed in order to improve competition generally or specifically.

In this way, it is sort of a revival of the Temporary National Economic Commission.

This legislation does propose reformation of our economic structure. This is nothing to be taken on hastily. However, the need to move is great. This bill may not be the answer. But it can start us talking responsibly of solutions to a problem that must be solved.

This may not be the most important problem facing us, but it ranks high on the list. I see it as a question not only of economic—but human—freedom.

EXHIBIT 1: PREAMBLE
S. 3832

Be it enacted by the Senate and House of Representatives of the United States of America in Congress assembled. That this Act may be cited as the "Industrial Reorganization Act". The Congress finds and declares that (1) the United States of America is committed to a private enterprise system and a free market economy, in the belief that competition spurs innovation, promotes productivity, preserves a democratic society, and provides an opportunity for a more equitable distribution of wealth while avoiding the undue concentration of economic, social, and political power; (2) the decline of competition in industries with oligopoly or monopoly power has contributed to unemployment, inflation, inefficiency, an underutilization of economic capacity, and the decline of exports, thereby rendering monetary and fiscal policies inadequate and necessitating government market controls subverting our basic commitment to a free market economy; (3) the preservation of a private enterprise system, a free market economy, and a democratic society in the United States of America requires legislation to supplement the policy of the antitrust laws through new enforcement mechanisms designed to responsibly restructure industries dominated by oligopoly or monopoly power; (4) the powers vested in these new enforcement mechanisms are to be exercised to promote competition throughout the economy to the maximum extent feasible, and to protect trade and commerce against oligopoly or monopoly power.

4

DISTRIBUTION
OF INCOME: THE
PRICING OF THE
PRODUCTIVE
FACTORS

Reading 46

Output depends on labor, land, and capital—as determined by technical knowledge. Pessimists think economic growth cannot be stimulated. Uninformed optimists go to the other extreme and talk of long-term U.S. growth rates of 5, 6, and even larger percentages per annum.

Dr. Edward F. Denison, now of the Brookings Institution, formerly served as economist for the U.S. Department of Commerce and the Committee for Economic Development. He estimates numerically the realistic growth goals suggested by our historical experiences.

Questions to guide the reading

Do you agree that a country which starts out from a position of much unemployment and unused capacity can be made initially to grow at a much faster rate than it can permanently grow once it has achieved (and maintains) full employment?

How fast can manpower grow? Land acreage? Capital goods? What are likely limits on technical change?

Sources of United States Economic Growth

Edward F. Denison

It is absolutely essential to distinguish between the growth of the nation's "potential" production, its ability or capacity to produce marketable goods and services, and changes in the ratio of actual production to "potential" production. The growth of potential production depends on changes in the quantity and quality of available labor and capital, the advance of knowledge, and similar factors, while the ratio of actual to potential production is governed mainly by the relationship between aggregate demand and potential production.

The fact that the growth of actual national product since 1956 or 1957 has fallen short of our average past record stems from the partial failure of United States business cycle or economic stabilization policy, not in policies affecting the growth of our productive potential. Since 1956 or 1957 our ability to produce has increased at least as fast as it did, on the average, in the past. Moreover, it is now clear that this failure is not related in significant degree to any change in the rate of technological progress or any structural change in the economy. It is a failure in meeting the old problem of equating changes in aggregate demand with changes in productive potential and unit costs. I am convinced that, given appropriate fiscal and monetary policy, the maintenance of high employment need not be made more difficult in this country by the rate at which productive potential advances; rather, if there is any connection, rapid growth of output per man eases the problem by allowing a more rapid advance of wage rates without inflation.

We should move vigorously to reduce unemployment and use our productive capacity fully, and to continue to do so in the future. The loss of income and other costs imposed upon those unemployed or working short hours, upon proprietors and others dependent on profits, is ample reason to do so. The main tools open to the federal government are fiscal and monetary policy, and I believe they are adequate.

From "United States Economic Growth" by Edward F. Denison, *Journal of Business,* Vol. XXXV, No. 2, April, 1962. Reprinted with kind permission of the author and publisher, The University of Chicago Press. Copyright 1962 by the University of Chicago. All rights reserved. Published January, April, October, 1962.

Past growth

What are the sources of our past growth? From 1929 to 1957 the real national income or product increased at an average annual rate of 2.93 percent. I have tried to break this rate down among its sources. The results, shown in Table 1, are rough estimates, and their derivation required some strong assumptions, but I think they provide correct perspective.

The table distinguishes broadly between the contribution of increases in factor inputs and increases in output per unit of input. To derive the former, I start (in the left-hand columns of Table 1) with estimates of the share breakdown of the national income. I estimate that in the 1929-57 period, the earnings of labor (including the labor of proprietors) represented 73 percent of the national income; earnings of land, 4.5 percent; and earnings of reproducible capital, 22.5 percent. The last amount is divided in the table among types of capital.

The center section of the table provides estimates of the rate at which the various factor inputs increased, computed from indexes of their amount. The most familiar number here is that shown for employment on line 7. The series used, the Office of Business Economics estimates of persons engaged in production, increased at an average annual rate of 1.31 percent from 1929 to 1957. Over the same period, as shown on line 9, annual hours of work declined at an average rate of 0.73 percent a year. All the other entries under labor represent an attempt to adjust for changes in its quality.

The quantity of *land* available for use did not change during the period considered and, therefore, appears with a zero growth rate in line 14.

More and better capital and economies of scale

Capital input, which is restricted to privately owned capital, is measured in five parts. Input of structures and equipment other than residences is shown in line 17 to have increased at an average annual rate of 1.85 percent, much less than the national product.

Line 16 and lines 18-20 measure the growth rates of the deflated value of the gross stock of residences, of the deflated value of inventories, of the deflated value of United States owned invest-

ments abroad, and of foreign-owned investments in the United States.

The right side of the table gives the number of percentage points in the total growth rate that I estimate was contributed by each source of growth. Except for three small refinements, the upper portion of the right side of Table 1, referring to the increase in inputs, count be derived from the left and center sections by simple multiplication.

Most of the possible sources considered do not appear in the table at all, either because they appeared not to have changed over the period or because their effect on the growth rate was calculated at less than 0.01. In a few cases it was impossible to decide whether changes were favorable or unfavorable to growth. Also, some changes that might affect a "truer" measure of national income or product do not affect the national product as it is actually measured.

Various private and governmental restrictions prevent the optimum allocation and most efficient use of resources. Most did not change appreciably over the period, but some cost us more output in 1957 than in 1929. I estimate that they subtracted 0.07 points from the growth rate over that period, as shown in line 22. Line 23 refers to the fact, or what I believe to be the fact, that labor nominally employed but ineffectively utilized in agriculture was a smaller fraction of all labor, though a larger fraction of farm labor, in 1957 than in 1929. Line 24 arises because, even after eliminating excessive resources from the computation, resources in agriculture earned less than resources of equal quality in the rest of the economy in the base year of the real product estimates, 1954, because they were in oversupply. The shift out of agriculture thus contributed to a statistical rise in the national product estimated at 0.05 points in the growth rate.

Skip now to the last line, economies of scale associated with the growth of the national market. In the absence of any satisfactory procedure to arrive at a figure statistically, my effort here was to set down a number representing a sort of norm of expert opinion. I assume—and this is the third major assumption of the study—that in the 1929-57 period, economies of scale added 10 percent to the increment to output that would otherwise be provided by all other sources. Consequently, I allocate one-eleventh of the total growth rate in the

Table 1 Sources of Growth of Real National Income

Line	Source of growth	Share of national income (percent distribution)		Growth rates (percent per year)		Contribution to growth rate of real national income (percentage points)	
		1909–29	1929–57	1909–29	1929–57	1909–29	1929–57
1	Real national income	100.0	100.0¹	2.82²	2.93	2.82²	2.93
2	Increase in total inputs, adjusted	—	—	2.24	1.99	2.26	2.00
3	Adjustment	—	—	−0.09	−0.11	—	—
4	Increase in total inputs, unadjusted	—	—	2.33	2.10	—	—
5	Labor, adjusted for quality change	68.9	73.0	2.30	2.16	1.53	1.57
6	Employment and hours	—	—	1.62	1.08	1.11	0.80
7	Employment	—	—	1.58	1.31	1.11	1.00
8	Effect of shorter hours on quality of a man-year's work	—	—	0.03	−0.23	0.00	−0.20
9	Annual hours	—	—	−0.34	−0.73	−0.23	−0.53
10	Effect of shorter hours on quality of a man-hour's work	—	—	0.38	0.50	0.23	0.33
11	Education	—	—	0.56	0.93	0.35	0.67
12	Increased experience and better utilization of women workers	—	—	0.10	0.15	0.06	0.11
13	Changes in age-sex composition of labor force	—	—	0.01	−0.01	0.01	−0.01
14	Land	7.7	4.5	0.00	0.00	0.00	0.00
15	Capital	23.4	22.5	3.16	1.88	0.73	0.43
16	Nonfarm residential structures	3.7	3.1	3.49	1.46	0.13	0.05
17	Other structures and equipment	14.6	15.0	2.93	1.85	0.41	0.28
18	Inventories	4.8	3.9	3.31	1.90	0.16	0.08
19	United States owned assets abroad	0.6	0.7	4.20	1.97	0.02	0.02
20	Foreign assets in United States (an offset)	0.3	0.2	−1.85	1.37	0.01	0.00
21	Increase in output per unit of input	—	—	0.56	0.92	0.56	0.93
22	Restrictions against optimum use of resources	—	—	—	—	³	−0.07
23	Reduced waste of labor in agriculture	—	—	—	—	³	0.02
24	Industry shift from agriculture	—	—	—	—	³	0.05
25	Advance of knowledge	—	—	—	—	³	0.58
26	Change in lag in application of knowledge	—	—	—	—	³	0.01
27	Economies of scale—independent growth of local markets	—	—	—	—	³	0.07
28	Economies of scale—growth of national market	—	—	—	—	0.28	0.27

¹ For 1930–40 and 1942–46, interpolated distributions rather than the actual distributions for these dates were used. Estimates are 1929–58 averages.
² This rate, like that for 1929–57, derives from Department of Commerce estimates. Estimates by John W. Kendrick, based on adjustment to Department of Commerce concepts of estimates by Simon Kuznets, yield a growth rate of 3.17, which would result in a figure for output per unit of input (line 21) of 0.91.
³ Not estimated.

1929–57 period, or 0.27 percentage points, to this source. I use a slightly higher fraction in the earlier period since economies of scale presumably decline as the size of the economy increases.

Much, probably most, of this contribution, of course, is the result of the expansion of local and regional markets that automatically accompanies the growth of the national economy. In addition, however, local markets grew independently as a result of increasing concentration of population and especially of the adaptation of the trade and service industries to the general ownership of automobiles. The contribution of this independent development is represented in line 27.

Invention and technical productivity

Finally, we come to the contribution to growth of the advance of knowledge and the speed with which it is incorporated into production. I believe that, as indicated in line 26, the change in the lag of the average practice behind the best known was of negligible importance.

The estimate in line 25 for the contribution of the advance of knowledge is obtained as a residual, and has the usual weakness of a residual. It is intended to measure the contribution to the growth rate of the advance of knowledge of all types relevant to production, including both managerial and technological knowledge. Many will find the contribution of 0.58 percentage points, or 20 percent, of the total 1929–57 growth rate that I attribute to the advance of knowledge surprisingly small.

If expectation of a larger figure is based on previous studies, there is no basis for surprise. The term "technological progress" has often been applied to all the sources of growth except changes in man-hours, land, and capital. That definition would embrace everything in Table 1 except lines 7, 9, 14, and 15. These accounted for only three-tenths of the growth rate, so my estimates would leave seven-tenths of total growth for attribution to "technological progress" if that broad definition were used. If the calculation were confined to the private economy, the fraction would be still larger. The main object of these calculations has been to divide up the contribution to growth of what has been vaguely termed technological progress.

Nevertheless, the figure for the contribution of

knowledge is rather small even if expectations are based on *a priori* observation. The explanation is that much of what usually is thought of as the fruits of technological progress is simply not caught in the growth rate of the national product as measured because of the character of the price indexes used in deflation.

In general, the advance of knowledge can contribute to the measured growth rate only by reducing production costs for already existing final products, or through improvements in business organization at levels other than those serving the final purchaser.

Once these characteristics of the output measure are understood, it is not, I think, surprising that the contribution of the advance of knowledge to the measured growth rate is not larger.

Summary of past growth

Space limitations prohibit extended discussion of the results of this part of the study, but the table speaks for itself. In summary, from 1929 to 1957 five sources contributed an amount equal to 101 percent of the growth rate, out of a total of 109 percent contributed by all sources making a positive contribution. These were: increased employment (34 percent); increased education (23 percent); increased capital input (15 percent); the advance of knowledge (20 percent); and economies of scale associated with the growth of the national market (9 percent). The reduction of working hours accounted for −7 percent of the total "contribution" of −9 percent to the growth rate provided by sources adverse to growth, and increased restrictions against the optimum use of resources for the remainder.

The breakdown in the 1909–29 period was, of course, different. Increases in capital and in employment contributed more than in the period after 1929, and improvements in the quality of the labor force, much less.

But whatever period we examine, it is clear that economic growth, occurring within the general institutional setting of a democratic, largely free-enterprise society, has stemmed and will stem mainly from an increased labor force, more education, more capital, and the advance of knowledge, with economies of scale exercising an important, but essentially passive, reinforcing influence. Since

1929 the shortening of working hours has exercised an increasingly restrictive influence on the growth of output.

Future rate of growth

The second question is: *What rate of growth can we reasonably anticipate in the future?* Opinions on this vary, as they must, because the future is inherently uncertain. My own projection, derived by summing estimates of the contribution anticipated from each of the sources affecting past growth, is that if we are reasonably successful in maintaining high employment, avoid a major war, and otherwise maintain existing policies and conditions in fields affecting growth importantly, we can look forward to a growth rate in our productive potential of 3.33 percent over the period from 1960 to 1980. The rate is about 3.5 percent if we start the calculation from the recession-reduced actual national product in 1960 and assume 1980 will be a prosperous year. The 3.33 percent rate for productive potential is almost one-seventh above the actual rate from 1929 to 1957. It implies an average annual percentage increase in potential output per person employed of 1.62 percent per year, just slightly above that experienced from 1929 to 1957, and of 2.17 in output per man-hour.

The third question is: *Will the projected growth rate be high enough?* This obviously cannot be answered without establishing criteria, which I shall not attempt, but three things can be said.

First, the growth rate projected would yield a large improvement in living standards unless the proportion of output required for defense increases enormously. If the fraction of national product devoted to consumption does not change, per capita consumption in 1980 would be above 1960 by 38–46 percent on the basis of the two middle population projections of the Census Bureau.

Second, if it should be considered necessary or desirable to increase expenditures for defense and other essential public purposes, they could be doubled in twenty years without changing the proportion of national product they absorb, and by changing the proportion such expenditures could be enormously increased while still allowing a sizable advance in living standards.

Third, a growth rate of 3.33 or 3.5 percent is not likely to win any statistical growth race with the Soviet Union or any other industrial country that is presently substantially behind us in productivity and that has established institutional conditions equally favorable to growth. Mainly this is because the possibilities open to us of quick gains by imitation are so much more limited. Whether a statistical growth race is important to impress world opinion is a matter of dispute. But for us to accept a challenge for a growth-rate race with Russia or Japan would be as sensible as for Roger Bannister, the day he ran the four-minute mile, to have wagered a promising high-school sophomore on which of them could reduce his best time by the larger percentage.

Policy Implications

I come now to the last and most interesting of the four questions that I shall consider. *Should we try to change the future growth rate, and if so what courses are open to us?*

This is a real and legitimate issue. A large national product in the future is desirable, but measures to raise the growth rate significantly involve costs. Certainly, a democratic society is *entitled* to make a collective decision to use the instruments of government and other institutions to promote rapid growth, and there are many steps that might be taken. But to say that a democratic society *can* decide to accelerate growth is not the same as to say that it would be wise for it to do so. If such a decision is to represent a rational choice, it must be based on a comparison of the benefits with the costs that are imposed.

What choices are open to us if we wish to raise the growth rate over the next twenty years above what it would otherwise be? I shall indicate what I conclude would be necessary to raise the growth rate by 0.1 percentage point, as from 3.3 to 3.4 percent. Such a change would yield a national product in 1980 higher than otherwise by about 2 percent of $20 billion. Put the other way around, to change the growth rate over the next twenty years by 0.1 of a percentage point requires some action that will make the 1980 national product 2 percent larger than it would be in the absence of that action.

This requires that we increase either the quantity or quality of the total input of labor, land, and capital into the productive system or else increase its productivity.

To raise the national product 2 percent by increasing inputs would require slightly less than a 2 percent increase in total inputs because of the existence of economies of scale. I estimate total input in 1980 would have to be increased about 1.83 percent. One way to do this would be to increase all kinds of input by 1.83 percent. The other would be to increase only one kind of input by a larger percentage. I estimate that in 1954–58 labor comprised 77 percent of total input, capital 20 percent, and land 3 percent. It follows that we could raise *total* input by 1.83 percent in 1980 if we could raise labor input alone by 2.4 percent over what it would otherwise be, or capital input alone by 9.3 percent, or land alone by 61.0 percent.

Suppose we wish to add 0.1 to the growth rate by increasing the quantity or the average quality of *labor* input in 1980 by 2.4 percent, over and above what it would otherwise be. This could be done if we wished, and could find ways to achieve any of the following changes:

Prevent half the deaths that will otherwise occur from 1960 to 1980 among individuals less than sixty-five years of age; or

Cut in half time lost from work because of sickness and accidents; or

Draw into the labor force one-tenth of all able-bodied persons over twenty years of age who will not otherwise be working in 1980; or

Double the rate of net immigration over the next twenty years; or

Operate with a work week one hour longer than otherwise; or

Eliminate two-thirds of the loss of work resulting from seasonal fluctuations in non-farm production; or

Reduce cyclical unemployment below what it would be otherwise by 2 percent of the labor force—an impossibility unless the total unemployment rate would otherwise be above 4 percent; or

Add one and a half years to the average time that would otherwise be spent in school by everyone completing school between now and 1980, or make an equivalent improvement in the quality of education.

To raise the growth rate one-tenth of a percentage point by increasing the *capital stock* more rapidly would require devoting an additional 1 percent of the national income to net saving and investment throughout the next twenty years. This would be an increase of about one-sixth in the nation's net saving rate.

To increase *land* input offers no significant possibilities.

The alternative to increasing the quantity or quality of inputs is to increase productivity by accelerating the advance of knowledge or the efficiency with which the economy works. One important source of increase in productivity, the economies of scale that occur when the economy grows for other reasons, cannot be affected directly. I have taken it into account in estimating the yield from increasing inputs, and will also do so in examining other ways of increasing productivity. Let us consider the others.

My projection assumes the advance of knowledge will contribute 0.8 to the 1960–80 growth rate, more than in 1929–57. We could thus add 0.1 to the growth rate if we could raise by one-eighth the rate at which knowledge relevant to production advances. But many discoveries and inventions originate abroad, and many are not the result of deliberate research. On possible assumptions, we would have to increase by one-half the annual increment to knowledge that originates in the United States and is subject to being affected by deliberate action.

We could also add 0.1 to the growth rate over the next twenty years if we could reduce the lag of average production practices behind the best known by two and two-thirds years, in addition to any reduction that would otherwise take place. This would be a huge reduction in the world's most advanced country.

There are a number of smaller possibilities which we could combine to add 0.1 to the growth rate.

Thus, we might eliminate all the misallocation and wasteful use of resources that result from barriers to international trade (which I estimate costs us 1.5 percent of the national income) *and* misallocation resulting from private monopoly in markets for products.

Or we might eliminate state resale price maintenance laws *and* racial discrimination in hiring. (I estimate these cost us 1 percent and 0.8 percent of the national income, respectively.)

Or we might shift to other uses of resources going into the production of unwanted or little-wanted farm products *and* also eliminate unemployment and underemployment resulting from long-term declines in individual industries and areas by re-employing workers immediately upon their becoming surplus.

Or we might eliminate all formal obstacles imposed by labor unions against use of the most efficient production practices *and* also consolidate local school districts and firms in regulated industries, particularly the railroads, wherever this would reduce unit costs.

There are, of course, other possibilities but they appear small.

Doubts and debits

It is not at all clear that we know *how* to do some of these things; and even where we do, they involve costs. Some, such as those leading to more investment in private or public capital, or to a faster rate of advance in knowledge through more research, require that the nation consume less than it otherwise could. Others, such as diversion of resources to provide more education or better medical care, which are classified as consumption in the national product, require that the nation consume less in other forms. Still others, such as longer hours of work or enlargement of the labor force, require that more work be done. Except for increasing immigration, all of the changes that would permanently raise the growth rate by any considerable amount impose costs of one of these types.

Costs of this kind are not imposed by changes that would make the economy operate more efficiently with given resources and given knowledge. Also, the means by which such changes could be brought about are frequently obvious, often simply requiring the repeal of existing laws that prevent the best allocation and use of resources. From a broad standpoint, such changes consequently are

particularly attractive, even though their possible stimulus to long-term growth is temporary and rather small. Even these, however, require some real or imagined sacrifice on the part of some members of society. Were it not so, these changes would already have been made.

Decisions on whether or not to try to affect the growth rate by any of the means I have suggested cannot sensibly be made without full consideration of their costs.

Almost any policy to affect growth also has other consequences. Some of these consequences, such as improvement of health, or a better educated citizenry, will be widely accepted as desirable. Others, especially any appreciable sacrifice of individual freedoms, will be as widely regarded as undesirable. Still others, including notably changes in the distribution of income, will be regarded as desirable by some individuals and undesirable by others. Among all the policies that might be adopted that would affect growth, there are few indeed where the effect on growth is, or should be, the primary consideration in their appraisal.

A serious effort to stimulate growth significantly would not, in my opinion, concentrate on one or two approaches but would be broadly based. This view is reinforced in the case of steps to increase factor inputs by the phenomenon of diminishing returns. Large increases in either labor or capital input, but especially the latter, without increases in the other, would yield a proportional increase in the growth rate smaller than is implied by calculations used to arrive at the results I have just presented.

If there is one point to be stressed above all, it is that faster growth is not a free good, not something that can be achieved by wishing or by speeches. To change the growth rate requires that something be done differently, and this entails costs in every significant case. Whether the gain is worth the cost can be judged only by careful consideration of each particular proposal.

Land and Resource Rents

Reading 47

What accounts for the share of income going to the use of land? One classic answer to this question came from one of the towering figures in the history of economic thought, David Ricardo (1772–1823). Son of a merchant-banker and himself a phenomenal success in business and the stock market, Ricardo brought a gloomier view to British economics than his predecessor, Adam Smith, had done.

This brief excerpt offers the fundamental logic of Ricardo's answer to the rent question. In this view, rent is the return paid to the landlord for the original, indestructible powers of the soil. Land is fixed in quantity, but varies in quality, since the less productive land is brought into use by an expanding population, and extra return necessarily accrues from farming on the best lands. This extra return goes not to the laborer, nor to the capitalists, but rather to the landlords who are the beneficiaries of the land distribution system.

The argument here is historically important for two reasons. It gave rise to the school of thought, most often associated with Henry George in the United States, that wanted to place all of society's taxes on the landlords to offset their gains from rent. And it represented an early model of abstract, elegant, but somewhat difficult reasoning in economics.

Questions to guide the reading

How does the concept of rent here compare with the current usage of the term when a tenant pays rent to his landlord or a driver rents a car from an agency?

Building on the Ricardian argument, followers of Henry George argue that taxes placed on land to recover for society the extra returns from more desirable land will not have a disincentive effect. A man cannot, for example, withdraw his land from the market without suffering zero returns. Is this argument valid, and does it support the wisdom of moving to heavier reliance on land taxes today rather than on buildings, machinery, or labor?

On Rent

David Ricardo

Definition

Rent is that portion of the produce of the earth, which is paid to the landlord for the use of the original and indestructible powers of the soil.

It is often, however, confounded with the interest and profit of capital and, in popular language, the term is applied to whatever is annually paid by a farmer to his landlord. If, of two adjoining farms of the same extent, and of the same natural fertility, one had all the conveniences of farming buildings, and, besides, were properly drained and manured, and advantageously divided by hedges, fences, and walls, while the other had none of these advantages, more remuneration would natu-

From David Ricardo, *Principles of Political Economy and Taxation* (George Bell and Sons, London, 1891, 3d ed.).

rally be paid for the use of one, than for the use of the other; yet in both cases this remuneration would be called rent. But it is evident, that a portion only of the money annually to be paid for the improved farm, would be given for the original and indestructible powers of the soil; the other portion would be paid for the use of the capital which had been employed in ameliorating the quality of the land, and in erecting buildings. In the future, then, whenever I speak of the rent of land, I wish to be understood as speaking of that compensation, which is paid to the owner of land for the use of its original and indestructible powers.

Land scarcity and rent

On the first settling of a country, in which there is an abundance of rich and fertile land, a very small proportion of which is required to be cultivated for the support of the actual population, or indeed can be cultivated with the capital which the population can command, there will be no rent; for no one would pay for the use of land, when there was an abundant quantity not yet appropriated, and, therefore, at the disposal of whosoever might choose to cultivate it.

On the common principles of supply and demand, no rent could be paid for such land, for the reason stated why nothing is given for the use of air and water, or for any other of the gifts of nature which exist in boundless quantity. In the same manner the brewer, the distiller, the dyer, make incessant use of the air and water for the production of their commodities; but as the supply is boundless, they bear no price. If all land had the same properties, if it were unlimited in quantity, and uniform in quality, no charge could be made for its use, unless where it possessed peculiar advantages of situation.

It is only, then, because land is not unlimited in quantity and uniform in quality, and because in the progress of population, land of an inferior quality, or less advantageously situated, is called into cultivation, that rent is ever paid for the use of it. When in the progress of society, land of the second degree of fertility is taken into cultivation, rent immediately commences on that of the first quality, and the amount of the rent will depend on the difference in the quality of those two portions of land.

When land of the third quality is taken into cultivation, rent immediately commences on the second, and it is regulated as before, by the difference in their productive powers. At the same time, the rent of the first quality will rise, for that must always be above the rent of the second, by the difference between the produce which they yield with a given quantity of capital and labour. With every step in the progress of population, which shall oblige a country to have recourse to land of a worse quality, to enable it to raise its supply of food, rent, on all the more fertile land, will rise.

Diminishing returns

It often, and, indeed, commonly happens, that before No. 2, 3, 4, or 5, or the inferior lands are cultivated, capital can be employed more productively on those lands which are already in cultivation. It may perhaps be found, that by doubling the original capital employed on No. 1, though the produce will not be doubled, it may be increased by [more than] what could be obtained by employing the same capital on land No. 3.

If, then, good land existed in a quantity much more abundant than the production of food for an increasing population required, or if capital could be indefinitely employed without a diminished return on the old land, there could be no rise of rent; for rent invariably proceeds from the employment of an additional quantity of labour with a proportionally less return.

Rent not price determining

The most fertile, and most favourably situated, land will be first cultivated, and the exchangeable value of its produce will be adjusted in the same manner as the exchangeable value of all other commodities, by the total quantity of labour necessary in various forms from first to last, to produce it, and bring it to market. When land of an inferior quality is taken into cultivation, the exchangeable value of raw produce will rise, because more labour is required to produce it.

The reason then, why raw produce rises in comparative value, is because more labour is employed in the production of the last portion obtained, and not because a rent is paid to the landlord. The value of corn is regulated by the quantity of labour bestowed on its production on that quality of land, or with that portion of capital, which pays no rent. Corn is not high because a rent is paid, but a rent is paid because corn is high; and it has been justly observed, that no reduction would take place in the price of corn, although landlords should forego the whole of their rent. Such a measure would only enable some farmers to live like gentlemen, but would not diminish the quantity of labour necessary to raise raw produce on the least productive land in cultivation.

If the high price of corn were the effect, and not the cause of rent, price would be proportionally influenced as rents were high or low, and rent would be a component part of price. But that corn which is produced by the greatest quantity of labour is the regulator of the price of corn; and rent does not and cannot enter in the least degree as a component part of its price.

Reading 48

Henry George (1838–1897), printer and self-taught economist, noted the increment to land values caused by the California gold rush. His *Progress and Poverty* has sold millions of copies and serves as bible to the single-tax movement; in fact, George was almost elected mayor of New York City. George goes beyond the Ricardian argument that increased population will raise land rent. He concludes that all the gains of progress will go to rent unless this is taxed away by the state.

Questions to guide the reading

If God gave the land, why should man collect rent for it?

Would the same argument for taxation apply to buildings and various improvements made on the land? Why not? If your grandfather paid good money for land, in reasonable anticipation that the single-tax movement would not succeed in taxing all its unearned increment, would it be fair to tax away your inherited wealth in the form of land? Suppose your cousin was left by his grandfather the same amount of wealth in nonland form? Why tax you more than him?

Denison (Reading 46) shows that pure land rent is probably today less than 5 per cent of the GNP. Since government needs at a minimum at least 25 per cent, would Henry George, if he were alive today, call his movement the *Single* Tax—or merely the Land Tax Movement?

Progress and Poverty

Henry George

The law of rent

Rent or land value does not arise from the productiveness or utility of land. No matter what are its capabilities, land can yield no rent and have no value until some one is willing to give labor or the results of labor for the privilege of using it; and what any one will thus give depends not upon the capacity of the land, but upon its capacity as compared with that of land that can be had for nothing. I may have very rich land, but it will yield no

From Henry George, *Progress and Poverty* (Appleton-Century-Crofts, Inc., New York, 1883).

rent and have no value so long as there is other land as good to be had without cost. But when this other land is appropriated, and the best land to be had for nothing is inferior, either in fertility, situation, or other quality, my land will begin to have a value and yield rent. Rent, in short, is the price of monopoly, arising from the reduction to individual ownership of natural elements which human exertion can neither produce nor increase.

To put the law of rent in algebraic form:

As Produce = Rent + Wages + Interest, Therefore,

Produce − Rent = Wages + Interest.

Thus wages and interest do not depend upon the produce of labor and capital, but upon *what is left* after rent is taken out; or, upon the produce which they could obtain without paying rent— that is, from the poorest land in use. And hence, no matter what be the increase in productive power, if the increase in rent keeps pace with it, neither wages nor interest can increase.

The moment this simple relation is recognized, a flood of light streams in upon what was before inexplicable, and seemingly discordant facts range themselves under an obvious law. The increase of rent which goes on in progressive countries is at once seen to be the key which explains why wages and interest fail to increase with increase of productive power. For the wealth produced in every community is divided into two parts by what may be called the rent line, which is fixed by the margin of cultivation, or the return which labor and capital could obtain from such natural opportunities as are free to them without the payment of rent. From the part of the produce below this line wages and interest must be paid. All that is above goes to the owners of land. Thus, where the value of land is low, there may be a small production of wealth, and yet a high rate of wages and interest, as we see in new countries. And, where the value of land is high, there may be a very large production of wealth, and yet a low rate of wages and interest, as we see in old countries. And, where productive power increases, as it is increasing in all progressive countries, wages and interest will be affected, not by the increase, but by the manner in which rent is affected. If the value of land increases proportionately, all the increased production will be swallowed up by rent, and wages and interest will remain as before. If the value of land

increases in greater ratio than productive power, rent will swallow up even more than the increase; and while the produce of labor and capital will be much larger, wages and interest will fall. It is only when the value of land fails to increase as rapidly as productive power, that wages and interest can increase with the increase of productive power. All this is exemplified in actual fact.

The persistence of poverty amid advancing wealth

The great problem, of which recurring seasons of industrial depression are but peculiar manifestations, is now, I think, fully solved, and the social phenomena which all over the civilized world appall the philanthropist and perplex the statesman, which hang with clouds the future of the most advanced races, and suggest doubts of the reality and ultimate goal of what we have fondly called progress, are now explained.

The reason why, in spite of the increase of productive power, wages constantly tend to a minimum which will give but a bare living, is that, with increase in productive power, rent tends to even greater increase, thus producing a constant tendency to the forcing down of wages.

The true remedy

We have traced the unequal distribution of wealth which is the curse and menace of modern civilization to the institution of private property in land. We have seen that so long as this institution exists no increase in productive power can permanently benefit the masses; but, on the contrary, must tend still further to depress their condition.

There is but one way to remove an evil—and that is, to remove its cause. Poverty deepens as wealth increases, and wages are forced down while productive power grows, because land, which is the source of all wealth and the field of all labor, is monopolized. To extirpate poverty, to make wages what justice commands they should be, the full earnings of the laborer, we must therefore substitute for the individual ownership of land a common ownership. Nothing else will go to the cause of the evil—in nothing else is there the slightest hope.

This, then, is the remedy for the unjust and unequal distribution of wealth apparent in modern civilization, and for all the evils which flow from it:

We must make land common property.

But a question of method remains. How shall we do it?

We should satisfy the law of justice, we should meet all economic requirements, by at one stroke abolishing all private titles, declaring all land public property, and letting it out to the highest bidders in lots to suit, under such conditions as would sacredly guard the private right to improvements.

Thus we should secure, in a more complex state of society, the same equality of rights that in a ruder state were secured by equal partitions of the soil, and by giving the use of the land to whoever could procure the most from it, we should secure the greatest production.

But such a plan, though perfectly feasible, does not seem to me the best. Or rather I propose to accomplish the same thing in a simpler, easier, and quieter way, than that of formally confiscating all the land and formally letting it out to the highest bidders.

To do that would involve a needless shock to present customs and habits of thought—which is to be avoided.

To do that would involve a needless extension of governmental machinery—which is to be avoided.

It is an axiom of statesmanship, which the successful founders of tyranny have understood and acted upon—that great changes can best be brought about under old forms. I do not propose either to purchase or to confiscate private property in land. The first would be unjust; the second, needless. Let the individuals who now hold it still retain, if they want to, possession of what they are pleased to call *their* land. Let them continue to call it *their* land. Let them buy and sell, and bequeath and devise it. We may safely leave them the shell, if we take the kernel. *It is not necessary to confiscate land; it is only necessary to confiscate rent.*

We already take some rent in taxation. We have only to make some changes in our modes of taxation to take it all.

What I, therefore, propose, as the simple yet sovereign remedy, which will raise wages, increase the earnings of capital, extirpate pauperism, abolish poverty, give remunerative employment to whoever wishes it, afford free scope to human powers, lessen crime, elevate morals, and taste, and intelligence, purify government and carry civilization to yet nobler heights, is—*to appropriate rent by taxation.*

Now, insomuch as the taxation of rent, or land values, must necessarily be increased just as we abolish other taxes, we may put the proposition into practical form by proposing—

To abolish all taxation save that upon land values.

Reading 49

The media shout out, "An Energy Crisis!" Professor Morris A. Adelman of M.I.T., expert on monopoly and industrial organization, says, Nonsense. It's a case of Asia Minor monopoly, in which the big oil companies act as their tax collectors. If governments would wise up and resist the monopoly, abundant oil with marginal costs of 5 to 10 cents a barrel wouldn't sell for almost $2 a barrel.

And there is worse to come. Hundreds of billions of dollars will be going in the decades ahead to governments that will, for the most part, not be using such funds for peaceful development purposes. All this is analyzed in greater detail in the Adelman book, *The World Petroleum Market* (Johns Hopkins University Press, Baltimore, Maryland, 1972).

Questions to guide the reading

Does Adelman worry sufficiently about future depletion of oil? Socially, should oil sell at 5 to 10 cents per barrel, which Adelman reckons to be its incremental costs? If oil fell like manna from heaven, would that justify a zero price?

Is the author perhaps overly optimistic that getting the big oil companies out of crude-oil marketing will, miraculously, undermine the OPEC monopoly?

In what ways does all this depart from the traditional theory of imperialism—according to which the United States and other affluent nations would dictate to the Mid-East nations and would favor them at the expense of oil-poor Israel?

Oil Shortage a Myth Created by Mideast Monopoly and "Tax-Collecting" Giant Corporations

M. A. Adelman

Brief Summary

The United States currently consumes more energy than any other country. Over the next dozen years, our energy consumption may double. Oil and gas provide three-fourths of our energy. Domestic reserves could supply this projected demand only at excessive costs, and large-scale supply of nuclear energy is more than a decade away. By the end of this decade, we will probably be importing very substantial quantities of our oil.

It is widely believed that this situation will constitute a major foreign policy problem in the coming decade with implications ranging from adverse effects on our balance of payments to a changed political balance in the Middle East. Negotiations between oil companies and oil-producing countries have been front page news almost continuously for the past two years, with the companies recently agreeing to producing country "participation" in ownership.

Given these views, it is rather startling to find a highly respected M.I.T. economist and oil expert stating that there is "absolutely no basis to fear an acute oil scarcity over the next 15 years." Professor Adelman, while acknowledging that the United States is confronted with a local exhaustion of its low cost oil and gas, nevertheless argues in the following article that not only is the world energy crisis "a fiction," but that to the extent that there is a foreign policy problem, it is in considerable part caused by inept policies of the U.S. government.

In Adelman's view, the State Department's interest in "stability" has reinforced the oil companies' and producing-countries' ability to maintain a monopoly price at 10 to 20 times the long-run incremental cost of producing oil. The only question that matters is whether the monopoly will flourish or fade.

In the meantime, contrary to popular myth, the multinational companies turn out to be agencies for taxing people in consuming countries—both rich and poor—and transferring the lion's share of the proceeds to the governments of the oil-producing countries. The amount of the resources transferred by this transnational system exceeds the amounts of resources transferred in bilateral governmental aid programs.

The new monopoly

The multinational oil companies have become, in the words of the board chairman of British Petroleum, the "tax collecting agency" of the producing nations. In 1972, the companies operated the greatest monopoly in history and transferred about $15 billion from the consuming countries to their principals. If the arrangement continues, a conservative estimate for 1980 collection is over $55 billion per year. Much of that wealth will be available to disrupt the world monetary system and promote armed conflict. Oil supply is now much more insecure. Monopoly, the power to overcharge, is the power to withhold supply. Among nations, an embargo is an act of war, and the threat of an oil embargo ushered in the Organization of Petroleum Exporting Countries (OPEC) cartel.

Willing pawns. The oil companies are now the agents of a foreign power. They will be blamed for impairing the sovereignty of the consuming countries, and quite unjustly. They only did the will of

From M. A. Adelman, "Is the Oil Shortage Real? Oil Companies as OPEC Tax-Collectors," *Foreign Policy*, Winter 1972–1973. Reprinted in abridgment with the kind permission of the author and the publisher.

the OPEC nations and of the consuming countries themselves, notably the United States. The consumers' "strange and self-abuse" is the key to how the events of 1970-71 turned a slowly retreating into a rapidly advancing monopoly.

The most important player in the game is the American State Department. This agency is deplorably poorly informed in mineral resource economics, the oil industry, the history of oil crises and the participation therein of the Arabs with whom it is obsessed; in fact, State cannot even give an accurate account of its own recent doings.

Myths of shortage.   The unanimous opinion issuing from companies and governments in the capitalist, Communist, and Third Worlds is that the price reversal of 1970 and 1971 resulted from a surge in demand, or change from surplus to scarcity, from a buyers' to a sellers' market. The story has no resemblance to the facts. The 1970 increase in consumption over 1969 was somewhat below the 1960-1970 average in all areas. The increase in 1971 over 1970, in Western Europe and Japan, was about half the decade average. In the first quarter of 1972, Western European consumption was only 1.5 percent above the previous year. By mid-1972, excess producing capacity, a rarity in world oil (i.e., outside North America) was almost universal and had led to drastic government action, especially in Venezuela and Iraq. The industry was "suffering from having provided the facilities for an increase in trade which did not materialize." A drastic unforeseen slowdown in growth and unused capacity would make prices fall, not rise, in any competitive market.

Enter monopoly

Some powerful force has overridden demand and supply. This force did not enter before the middle of 1970, at the earliest. Up to that time the trend of prices had been downward, and long-term contracts had been at lower prices than short-term, indicating that the industry expected still lower prices in the future, even as far as 10 years ahead.

If demand exceeds supply at current prices, sellers and buyers acting individually make new bargains at higher prices. When supply exceeds demand yet prices are raised, the conclaves, joint actions, and "justifications" are strong evidence of collusion, not scarcity.

More precisely: in a competitive market, a surge in demand or shrinkage in supply raises price because it puts a strain on the productive apparatus. To produce additional output requires higher costs; unless compensated by higher prices, the additional output will not be supplied.

If there were increasing long runs scarcity at the Persian Gulf, discoveries falling behind consumption, the reservoirs would be exploited more intensively to offset decline, and to maintain and expand production. More capital and more labor would be required per additional barrel of producing capacity. In fact, between 1960 and 1970 (the last year available), the investment needed per unit of new crude oil capacity fell by over 50 percent, despite a rising general price level. Labor requirements (which are both for construction and operation) have fallen even more drastically. Supply has not only not tightened, it has been getting easier.

The world "energy crisis" or "energy shortage" is a fiction.[1] But belief in the fiction is a fact. It makes people accept higher oil prices as imposed by nature, when they are really fixed by collusion. And sellers of all fuels, whatever their conflicts, can stand in harmony on the platform of high oil prices.

[1] The United States "energy crisis" is a confusion of two problems. First, environmental costs are slowing down electric power growth and threatening blackouts. The worse the slowdown, the less the drain on fuel supply. Second, there has been gradual exhaustion of lower-cost oil and gas resources in the Lower 48 States. Natural gas deserves special mention, for the world has been deeply impressed by American business executives and cabinet members rocketing about the world like unguided missiles in search of gas supplies; particularly coming hat in hand to beg gas of the Soviet Union. One folly has led to another. Prices of American natural gas have been held at a level well below what would clear the market, generating a huge excess demand, all channeled overseas. Import prices have soared and will probably rise further if domestic price-fixing is not abolished. Profits to the overseas producing nations who own the gas will be lush. American companies have tried to arrange deals and obtain a part of the gains; American government officials have helped the stampede. The gas shortage could be abolished by the simple expedient of abandoning price ceilings. Gas might still be imported, but at lower prices, in smaller amounts. The strain on coal and oil resources would actually be less, since higher domestic prices would increase domestic supply of natural gas.

Twenty years ago, the Paley Commission made the classic statement of the problem:

Exhaustion is not waking up to find the cupboard is bare but the need to devote constantly increasing efforts to acquiring each pound of materials from natural resources which are dwindling both in quality and quantity. . . . The essence of the materials problem is costs.

Depletion of reserves at the Persian Gulf is only about 1.5 percent a year. It is uneconomic to turn over an inventory so slowly. But Persian Gulf operators have not been free to expand output and displace higher cost production from other areas because this would wreck the world price structure. Therefore, it is meaningless to average production-reserve ratios for the whole world, as is too often done. A barrel of reserves found and developed elsewhere in the world is from five to seven times as important in terms of productive capacity as a barrel at the Persian Gulf.

In other words, one could displace production from the entire Persian Gulf with reserves from one-fifth to one-seventh as large. Today at the Persian Gulf, capital and operating costs are each about 5 cents per barrel; under our extreme assumptions, they are roughly double [not remotely near the almost $2 per barrel usually charged]. The difference between 10 and 20 cents measures the value of discovering new fields: it takes the strain off the old.

No basis for fears

There is no more basis for fears of acute oil scarcity in the next 15 years than there was 15 years ago—and the fears were strong in 1957. The myth that rising imports (of the United States) will "turn the market around" is only the latest version of the myth that rising imports of Europe and Japan would "dry out the surplus in 1957-70."

More generally: supply and demand are registered in incremental cost, which is and long will be a negligible fraction of the current crude oil price of about $1.90 per barrel. Hence *supply and demand are irrelevant to the current and expected price of crude oil.* All that matters is whether the monopoly will flourish or fade.

Libya begins the squeeze. In Europe and Japan, there was a mild and temporary shortage of refin-

ing capacity in early 1970. At the same time, a tanker shortage put rates at the highest level since shortly after the closing of the Suez Canal, and raised product prices.

In May 1970 the trans-Arabian pipeline was blocked by Syria to obtain higher payments for the transit rights, while the Libyan government began to impose production cutbacks on most of the companies operating there, to force them to agree to higher taxes. Although the direct effect of the cutback and closure was small, the effect on tanker rates was spectacular, and product prices and profits shot up.

The companies producing in Libya speedily agreed to a tax increase. The Persian Gulf producing countries then demanded and received the same increase, whereupon Libya demanded a further increase and the Persian Gulf countries followed suit. Finally, agreements were signed in Tehran in February 1971, increasing tax and royalty payments at the Persian Gulf as of June 1971 by about 47 cents per barrel, and rising to about 66 cents in 1975. North African and Nigerian increases were larger. In Venezuela the previous 1966 agreement was disregarded and higher taxes were simply legislated.

Government and company accessories

The multinational companies producing oil were amenable to these tax increases because as was openly said on the morrow of Tehran, they used the occasion to increase their margins and return on investment in both crude and products. In Great Britain the object was stated: to cover the tax increase "and leave some over," and the February 1971 tax increase was matched by a product price increase perhaps half again as great. The best summary of the results was by a well known financial analyst, Kenneth E. Hill, who called the agreements "truly an unexpected boon for the worldwide industry."

Mr. Hill rightly emphasized product price increases, but arm's length crude prices also increased by more than the tax increases. When the producing countries made fresh demands later in 1971, an American investment advisory service (United Business Services) remarked that tax increases were actually favorable to oil company profits. And 1971 was easily the best year for company profits since 1963, although there was a profit slide off later in the year, as competition in products though not yet in crude again reasserted itself.

Worse to come. The price pattern is set for the 1970's. From time to time, either in pursuance or in violation of the Tehran-Tripoli "agreements," the tax is increased, whereupon prices increase as much or more, but then tend to erode as the companies compete very slowly at the crude level and less slowly at the products level. Thus prices increase in steps, yet at any given moment there is usually a buyer's market, i.e., more is available than is demanded at the price, which is under downward pressure.

The companies' margin will therefore wax and wane, but they benefit by the new order. They cannot, even if they would, mediate between producing and consuming nations. As individual competitors, they are vulnerable to producing-nation threats to hit them one at a time. As a group, they profit by a higher tax through raising prices in concert, for the higher tax is that clear signal to which they respond without communication. The Secretary General of OPEC, Dr. Nadim Pachachi, said truly that there is no basic conflict between companies and producing nations. The then head of Shell, Sir David Barran, spoke of a "marriage" of companies and producing governments. Most precise of all was Sir Eric Drake, the chairman of BP, who called the companies a "tax collecting agency," for both producing and consuming country governments.

Leading role of the United States

Without active support from the United States, OPEC might never have achieved much. When the first Libyan cutbacks were decreed, in May 1970, the United States could have easily convened the oil companies to work out an insurance scheme whereby any single company forced to shut down would have crude oil supplied by the others at tax-plus-cost from another source. (The stable was possibly locked a year after the horse was stolen.) Had that been done, all companies might have been shut down, and the Libyan government would have lost all production income. It would have been helpful but not necessary to

freeze its deposits abroad. The OPEC nations were unprepared for conflict. Their unity would have been severely tested and probably destroyed. The revenue loses of Libya would have been gains to all other producing nations, and all would have realized the danger of trying to pressure the consuming countries.

Before January 20, an open threat by the OPEC nations would not have been credible, in view of the previous failure of even mild attempts at production regulation in 1965 and 1966. But after the capitulation, threats were credible and were made often.

The United States Under Secretary of State arrived in Tehran January 17 [1971], publicly stating his government's interest in "stable and predictable" prices, which in context meant higher prices. He told the Shah of Iran the damage that would be done to Europe and Japan if oil supplies were cut off. Perhaps this is why the Shah soon thereafter made the first threat of a cutoff of supply. It is hard to imagine a more effective incitement to extreme action than to hear that this will do one's opponents great damage.

Resistance to the OPEC demands would have shattered the nascent cartel. As late as January 24, the Shah told the press: "If the oil producing countries suffer even the slightest defeat, it would be the death-knell for OPEC, and from then on the countries would no longer have the courage to get together."

When the Tehran agreement was announced, another State Department special press conference hailed it, referring many times to "stability" and "durability." They "expected the previously turbulent international oil situation to calm down following the new agreements." They must really have believed this! Otherwise they would not have claimed credit for Mr. Irwin or for Secretary Rogers, or induced President Nixon's office to announce that he too was pleased. We now live with the consequences.

Scraps of paper. The oil companies knew better than to take the "agreements" seriously; they had been there before. To be sure, one could cite many a statement by an oil executive about the "valuable assurances of stability," but this was ritual. The London *Economist,* always in close touch with the industry, expected any agreements to last only a few months, given the "persistent bad faith." The best summary was made by *Petroleum Intelligence Weekly:* "If such agreements were worth anything the present crisis wouldn't exist."

Onward and upward with taxes and prices

The genie is out of the bottle. The OPEC nations have had a great success with the threat of embargo and will not put the weapon away. The turbulence will continue as taxes and prices are raised again and again. The producing nations are sure of oil company cooperation and consuming-country nonresistance. This is a necessary condition. There are two purely economic reasons why the situation cannot be stable.

1. The crude oil price can go much higher before it reaches the monopoly equilibrium or point of greatest profit.

The average price in Europe of a barrel of [finished] oil products in 1969–70 was about $13 per barrel. It is higher today. If the new tax rates were doubled, say from $1.50 to $3 per barrel at the Persian Gulf, a straight pass-through into product prices would be an increase of only 10–14 percent. It is doubtful that such an increase would have any noticeable effect on oil consumption. Moreover, about half of the European price consists of taxes levied by the various consuming-country governments. The producing nations have long insisted that in justice they *ought* to receive some or most of this amount. Be that as it may, most or all of this tax *can* be transferred from consuming to producing nations, with help from consuming-country governments who dislike unpopularity through higher fuel prices.

The current price of oil, however far above the competitive level, is still much less than alternatives. The producing nations are not a whit displeased by big expensive projects to produce oil or gas from coal or shale or tar sands, which are a constant reminder of what a bargain crude is, even at higher prices. Particularly outside the United States, nuclear power sets a high ceiling, coal a much higher ceiling. The price of British coal has long and well served sellers of fuel oil in Britain, who priced at or slightly below coal-equivalent. Small wonder that the head of Shell appealed in October 1971 for the maintenance of a British coal industry.

There has therefore been much discussion, mostly oral, of the goal for the Persian Gulf nations being the U.S. price; or $5 per barrel, etc. These are attainable goals, and we must therefore expect attempts to reach them.

2. The producing nations cannot fix prices without using the multinational companies. All price-fixing cartels must *either* control output *or* detect and prevent individual price reductions, which would erode the price down toward the competitive level. The OPEC tax system accomplishes this simply and efficiently.

It is essential for the cartel that the oil companies continue as *crude oil marketers,* paying the excise tax before selling the crude or refining to sell it as products.

Were the producing nations the sellers of crude, paying the companies in cash or oil for their services, the cartel would crumble. The floor to price would then be not the tax-plus-cost, but only bare cost.

* * *

We may therefore conclude: the producing countries can raise prices and revenues further by jacking up the excise tax floor, in concert. Conversely, if and when the consuming countries want to be rid of the cartel, they can take their companies out of crude oil marketing. To avoid taxation, they can decommission the tax collecting agents who are their own creation.

So far, the consuming countries have gone in precisely the opposite direction. As they develop high cost substitutes, and strive to get their respective companies, public or "private," into crude oil production and marketing, they will rivet the tax collection agency more firmly on their necks. It is time to ask why they do this, and whether the policy may change.

Reasons why.   One can only guess at the unstated reasons why the United States has put OPEC in the driver's seat. First, American companies have a large producing interest in the world market. In 1971, American companies produced about 6.5 billion barrels outside the United States. For every cent of increase in prices above that in tax, there is an additional $65 million in profit. Second, the higher energy costs will now be imposed on competitors in world markets; and in petrochemicals, higher raw material costs as well. Third, the United States has a large domestic oil producing industry. The less the difference between domestic and world prices, the less the tension between producing and consuming regions.

Fourth, the United States desired to appease the producing nations, buying popularity with someone else's money and trying to mitigate the tension caused by the Arab-Israel strife, which, however, is irrelevant to oil. If the Arab-Israeli dispute were settled tomorrow, the producing nations would not slow down for one minute their drive for ever-higher prices and taxes. The acknowledged leader of the Persian Gulf nations in early 1971 was Iran, which has in one important respect—the Trans-Israel Pipe Line—actually cooperated with Israel more than the United States, which in 1957 and 1968 discouraged the pipeline.

The changing American interest

First, security has been greatly impaired for all importing countries by the cohesion of the OPEC nations which made an embargo feasible.

Second, the balance of payments impact will soon turn unfavorable to us, as it is to all other importers.

The fact will slowly be recognized, that nearly all of the oil deficit could be abolished by getting American companies out of crude oil marketing, to produce on contract for the producing countries, who could then compete the price way down. The companies' profits (and contribution to the balance of payments) would not be much less, and in the long run they might be greater, as the experience in Venezuela proves: the companies producing there are at or over the loss line.

Larger American imports will if anything tend to put the world price down. The process was seen on a small scale after 1966, when quotas on (heavy) residual fuel imports were lifted. Imports increased considerably, and the price *decreased*. Moreover, concern over air pollution was growing rapidly, and alarm was felt over possible loss of markets for residual fuel oil. Hence the Venezuelan government made agreements with Esso and Shell granting them lower taxes on production of low-sulfur fuel oil. This bit of history was too rapidly forgotten.

The declining price of fuel oil in the face of greater demand would be inexplicable in a competitive market, but is to be expected when the price is far above cost. It is exactly what happened in Europe to embarrass coal. The hope of greater profits on increased sales, and the knowledge that large buyers have now an incentive to roam the market and look for every chance of a better deal, means that one must reduce the price before one's rivals tie up the good customers. As American quotas are relaxed, refiners who have a crude deficit will become exactly the kind of large-scale buyer whom Sheik Yamani rightly fears.

The prospect of world prices rising because of large-scale American imports has alarmed Europe and Asia, and the United States government has gladly fanned those fears. But they have no basis in theory or experience.

Let the reader excuse our saying again what needs to be said often: larger consumption only raises price in a competitive market, by raising marginal cost. In so awesomely noncompetitive a market, cost is not relevant because price is 10 to 20 times cost. Supply and demand have nothing to do with the world price of oil: only the strength of the cartel matters.

A look ahead

Oil supply is threatened by one and only one danger: a concerted shutdown by the OPEC nations. No single nation can do any harm. The fewer the sellers and the larger their market shares, the easier for them to collaborate and act as one. The central question is their union or disunion. If a single large seller breaks away, or a few minor ones, the cartel breaks down in a stampede for the exit. The cartel is only needed, only exists, to thwart the basic condition of massive potential excess capacity—ability to expand output at costs below prices—and prevent it from becoming actual. Hence lower prices and secure supply are the two sides of the same coin: absence of monopoly, or impotence of disunion.

The monopoly may still have its finest hours before it, and prices should rise well into the decade. The important consuming countries show no sign of understanding their plight.

The LDCs.   The less-developed nations will suffer the most, with no offsets. For example, India today consumes about 150 million barrels per year, and is expected to use about 345 in 1980. The burden of monopoly pricing is direct (paying higher prices for imports) and indirect (being forced to find and produce higher-cost domestic oil). It amounts in total to about $225 million ($1.50 × 150 million) per year, and increasing rapidly. Yet at the 1972 UNCTAD meeting there was no breath of criticism of the oil-producing nations. Solidarity prevailed: things were felt to be going well "on the oil front," and, said *Le Monde,* the same ought to happen on other fronts.

This favorable public attitude also holds in the developed countries. A private monopoly which extracted $1.5 billion per year from consumers would be denounced and probably destroyed; were they American, some executives would be in jail. An intergovernmental monopoly 10 times as big is viewed as a bit of redress by the Third World.

Now one may approve this double standard, or deplore it, or laugh to keep from crying, but it is a truth.

Breaking the vicious circle. The larger the reserves piled up by the OPEC nations, the greater their power to withhold oil. Hence the higher the price, and the greater the insecurity, the easier for the OPEC nations to make it still more expensive and insecure.

The consuming countries can have cheapness and security only by a clean break with the past: get the multinational oil companies out of crude oil marketing; let them remain as producers under contract and as buyers of crude to transport, refine and sell as products. The real owners, the producing nations, must then assume the role of sellers and they should be assisted in competing the price of crude oil down.

Need for sanity in analysis

It is a simple and elegant maneuver to destroy the cartel by removing an essential part—the multinational company as crude oil marketers fixing the price on a firm excise tax floor. But this would only minimize conflict and confrontation; it is too late to avoid them. The producing countries, like many raw troops, have been welded by success

into a real force, and the huge sums they receive and accumulate will be both the incentive and the means to fight, by embargo, monetary disruption, or even local wars. There will be non-negligible damage. To have put the power and the motive into the producers' hands was light-minded folly by the American government.

Moreover, clean breaks with past policy are rare. The honest confession of error is less likely than anger at the cartel's local agents, the multinational companies, and attempts to restrict and penalize them. Yet this misconception is exactly what has led to past mistakes. Bypassing the companies to make direct deals with producing nations can be helpful only when the objective is clearly seen: to mobilize national buying power, encourage domestic oil buyers to avoid established channels, and help compete prices down. More usually such deals sacrifice all buying independence in a vain attempt to get a good "connection," or placate a producing nation, and only raise costs.

The multinational companies will probably survive the crisis. Yet there is a real danger that they will be forced out of crude oil production. This would be a grievous waste of resources and could precipitate a genuine shortage of crude oil.

It's up to us

What happens to oil in the 1970's depends altogether on the consuming countries. If they are as slow to learn as they have been, then the projection of $55 billion annual tribute paid the OPEC nations by 1980 may be surpassed. But they may also learn that transferring those billions is not only dangerous but *unnecessary*. Their energy economics would need to be updated at least to 1952, when the Paley Commission explained that shortage means only cost; they might then see that the "world energy shortage" is a myth, that crude oil continues in oversupply, as the Venezuelans, the Iraqis, and the Saudi Arabs have recognized.

And the consuming nations' strategic thinking would need to be updated at least to 1914, when Winston Churchill, who was then a young fox, not an old lion, explained to the House of Commons that access to oil is only a special case of monopoly; the power to withhold is the power to overcharge.

Competitive Wages and Collective Bargaining

Reading 50

"The road to hell is paved with good intentions." So argues Milton Friedman of Chicago. Although minimum wages are favored by liberals and unions in order to help the poor who need help most, Dr. Friedman argues that they will hurt precisely this group by excluding them from jobs altogether. In his brief and trenchant remarks, this leading exponent of economic libertarianism and laissez faire does not list both the pros and cons of the subject: e.g., the argument that all the low-paid who *continue* to hold jobs will receive more adequate incomes; the argument that what this group gains may, if the demand for labor is inelastic rather than elastic, more than make up for the wage loss from lower employment; the argument that the higher wage may enable the worker to be better fed, better motivated, and hence, so much more productive that both he and the employer (and, we may add, society) will be better off; the argument that imposing higher wage rates may have a "shock effect" on the employer's efficiency in the use of labor, making the company, the consumer, and the worker all better off; finally, the argument that in our affluent society no one should have to work below some decent wage, even if that means that society must help provide him with minimum income, or better training or (through more aggressive fiscal and monetary policies) greater job opportunities.

Whatever the merits of these pros, the fundamental fact remains that economists of widely differing political opinions agree that the higher the minimum wage is set in comparison with the supply- and demand-level set by the market, the more powerful become the harmful effects on the groups most in need.

Questions to guide the reading

If a "decent wage" is $3 an hour, why stop at $2? Why not $4 or $5. Why do many experts favor a minimum wage just a bit above the market, as a spur, but not as too great a deterrent?

Since black youth unemployment did not rise to 30 per cent, is the author's argument invalidated? How can you decide? Five arguments ignored by Friedman are listed in the introduction above. Evaluate each of them, as he might do, and as you *would* do.

Minimum-wage Rates

Milton Friedman

Congress has just acted to increase unemployment. It did so by raising the legal minimum-wage rate from $1.25 to $1.60 an hour, effective in 1968, and extending its coverage. The result will be and must be to add to the ranks of the unemployed.

Does a merchant increase his sales by raising prices? Does higher pay of domestic servants induce more housewives to hire help? The situation is no different for other employers. The higher wage rate decreed by Congress for low-paid workers will raise the cost of the goods that these workers produce—and must discourage sales. It will

From Milton Friedman, "Minimum-wage Rates," *Newsweek*, September 26, 1966. Reprinted with kind permission of the author and publisher.

also induce employers to replace such workers with other workers—either to do the same work or to produce machinery to do the work.

Some workers who already receive wages well above the legal minimum will benefit—because they will face less competition from the unskilled. That is why many unions are strong supporters of higher minimum-wage rates. Some employers and employees in places where wages are already high will benefit because they will face less competition from businessmen who might otherwise invest capital in areas that have large pools of unskilled labor. That is why Northern manufacturers and unions, particularly in New England, are the principal sources of political pressure for higher legal minimum-wage rates.

It's anti-Negro

The groups that will be hurt the most are the low-paid and the unskilled. The ones who remain employed will receive higher wage rates, but fewer will be employed. As Prof. James Tobin, who was a member of President Kennedy's Council of Economic Advisers, recently wrote: "People who lack the capacity to earn a decent living need to be helped, but they will not be helped by minimum-wage laws, trade-union wage pressures or other devices which seek to compel employers to pay them more than their work is worth. The more likely outcome of such regulations is that the intended beneficiaries are not employed at all."

The loss to the unskilled workers will not be offset by gains to others. Smaller total employment will result in a smaller total output. Hence the community as a whole will be worse off.

Women, teen-agers, Negroes and particularly Negro teen-agers will be especially hard hit. I am convinced that the minimum-wage law is the most anti-Negro law on our statute books—in its effect not its intent. It is a tragic but undoubted legacy of the past—and one we must try to correct—that on the average Negroes have lower skills than whites. Similarly, teen-agers are less skilled than older workers. Both Negroes and teen-agers are only made worse off by discouraging employers from hiring them. On-the-job training—the main route whereby the unskilled have become skilled—is thus denied them.

Who is helped?

The shockingly high rate of unemployment among teen-age Negro boys is largely a result of the present Federal minimum-wage rate. And unemployment will be boosted still higher by the rise just enacted. Before 1956, unemployment among Negro boys aged 14 to 19 was around 8 to 11 per cent, about the same as among white boys. Within two years after the legal minimum was raised from 75 cents to $1 an hour in 1956, unemployment among Negro boys shot up to 24 per cent and among white boys to 14 per cent. Both figures have remained roughly the same ever since. But I am convinced that, when it becomes effective, the $1.60 minimum will increase unemployment among Negro boys to 30 per cent or more.

Many well-meaning people favor legal minimum-wage rates in the mistaken belief that they help the poor. These people confuse wage *rates* with wage *income*. It has always been a mystery to me to understand why a youngster is better off unemployed at $1.60 an hour than employed at $1.25. Moreover, many workers in low wage brackets are supplementary earners—that is, youngsters who are just getting started or elderly folk who are adding to the main source of family income. I favor governmental measures that are designed to set a floor under *family income*. Legal minimum-wage rates only make this task more difficult.

The rise in the legal minimum-wage rate is a monument to the power of superficial thinking.

Reading 51

Many economists are concerned over the power of unions in our economy. One of the most articulate of these was the late Edward H. Chamberlin of Harvard University. Here he presents the case that a number of immunities of unions under federal law give labor leaders excessive opportunities to push wages up too fast, to coerce neutrals, and to interfere with the healthy functioning of competitive pressures. Because Chamberlin was father of the theory of imperfect competition, his views gain interest.

Questions to guide the reading

Chamberlin argues that excessive power in today's unions does not stem from collective bargaining per se. Would collective bargaining itself be affected if his proposals for curbing union power were adopted?

To what extent does the union power which Chamberlin fears come from the labor market itself? From the existence of high levels of employment? From disorganization or shortsightedness on management's part? From the political climate of the nation?

Can Union Power Be Curbed?

Edward H. Chamberlin

Professor Sumner H. Slichter has pointed out that we live not, as we used to think, in a capitalistic society but in a laboristic one. Certainly most of us have a time lag in our thinking, and the economist's distrust of power has not yet been transferred in any substantial degree to labor. But I do believe that such a transfer is in process. Indeed, the most disturbing thing to my mind is not so much that people are unaware of the significance of this growth in labor union power but that so many seem to think that nothing can be done about it. I do not believe that anything in the field of social policy is inevitable, and we ought to stop saying that it is, however great the difficulties to be overcome.

The belief that nothing can be done about labor union power reduces to the belief that nothing *will* be done about it. This kind of fatalism is particularly evident with respect to the inflationary problem. Creeping inflation, we are told, is inevitable—all we can do is to accept it and learn to live with it.

Cost-push inflation

Now the doctrine that inflation is inevitable is very closely linked with a particular kind of inflation, namely the cost-push type. We know a great deal about how to control inflation of the demand-pull variety by well-established monetary and fiscal techniques. No one believes that such inflation is inevitable, though it may approach inevitability in

wartime. If the war years are omitted, prices have risen very little in the United States over the last hundred and fifty years. Years of rising prices have been fewer than those of falling or stable prices, and many of these latter have been years of prosperity.

Inflation of the cost-push variety is held to be inevitable partly because the conventional methods of control are not effective against it. For many reasons, the upward pressure on wages exerted by individual unions is strikingly insensitive to fiscal and credit restraints. And so, when one limits his thinking to fiscal and monetary measures, it is easy to conclude either that nothing can stop the upward cost push or that it can be stopped only at an unacceptable social cost of rising unemployment and lost production. By holding demand in check, the economy is indeed slackened, cost increases are harder to pass on, employer resistance to wage demands is increased, strikes are harder to win, and wage demands are correspondingly reduced. And so economists like to speculate on how high unemployment must go before it begins to act as a brake on wage demands. The great mistake, I think, is in trying to control wage-push inflation by methods which are inappropriate for the job.

It becomes necessary to go back and ask a very simple and fundamental question: What is the source of the problem? If it is excessive power in the hands of labor, the most obvious way to seek a remedy would be to reduce the power, and this is in fact the gist of my proposal. An alternative proposal would be to strengthen management by such devices, for example, as the pooling arrangement among airlines which has recently received so much publicity. Perhaps we might have some of both. But strangely enough I have found in discussing these matters that many who are horrified at the thought of weakening unions have no objection whatever to strengthening management. They would prefer to equalize power at a higher level, for bigger and better struggles, whereas I should prefer a measure of disarmament.

Monopoly is monopoly

Inflation is only one aspect of the general problem. The basis of labor union power is similar to that of any monopoly power—control of a market through collective action—but with the superimposition of decisive elements unique to the labor market.

The monopoly problem is simply one of maximum gain, both by the suppression of internal competition and by closing the path of entry to any from outside who would by their participation tend to break down the monopoly. This is precisely the method of monopoly in both the industrial and the labor areas. The striking difference between them is that monopoly in industry has been recognized as a matter of public concern for a long time and has been subjected, with at least partial success, to a program of regulation; whereas labor monopoly, hidden by the attractive phrase "collective bargaining," has hardly been recognized, let alone brought under control.

The control of monopoly generally involves the application of some standard of fairness, and in industry this standard has usually been found by a reference to competitive markets. Two procedures in applying the competitive criterion have been developed. In the case of public utilities and certain forms of transportation, monopoly is permitted and subjected to direct regulation. Here the lack of alternatives open to the consumer is recognized by imposing the obligation of service on the company. Here too, public commissions, subject to court review, regulate rates and earnings in accord with principles designed to bring about a rough correspondence between earnings in the regulated and in the competitive sectors of the economy, with allowance for such special factors as stability of income, risk, and so forth.

For the great bulk of the industrial area which remains, the attempt is made to preserve competition by forbidding agreements in restraint of trade, forbidding mergers under certain conditions, and outlawing certain specific practices which are regarded as detrimental to healthy competition. The expectation seems to be that enough competition can be preserved to give the public at least a reasonable protection against the abuses of concentrated private power and against the consequences of government regimentation.

The success of these policies may be questioned; I think everyone would agree that there is room for improvement. We get perspective on the policy, however, by comparing the prevailing spirit of American industry with that of Continental Europe, where cartelization is generally accepted and where, since agreements in restraint of trade are not forbidden, all manner of informal and tacit agreements and a generally restrictive mentality dominate the picture. I once heard the contrast put in this form: If a European retailer has an item on his shelf for some months without its being sold, he is likely to raise the price because of the cost he has incurred in keeping it for that time; the American retailer, on the contrary, will lower the price so as to get rid of it and make room for something else. The notion of not engaging too vigorously in price competition is a universal phenomenon in some degree, but a willingness to gain business at a rival's expense is fairly well developed in the United States, and I think the antitrust laws in this country are an important part of the reason why this is so.

Concentration of economic power in the labor field is paradoxically very great, partly because few people are aware of it. It is hidden because the gains which are made, say in terms of wages or so-called fringe benefits, are made immediately, speaking from the employer instead of from the public.

There is a common belief that higher wages come out of profits; and this is often superficially the case as a short-run proposition. Yet such a belief is in direct conflict with a fundamental long-run principle of economics as hoary and as generally respectable as the famous law of supply and demand, namely, the law of cost: that prices tend to conform to cost of production, including a normal allowance for profits. The principle is a rough one, and it ought to be elaborated if space permitted, especially as to the *amount* of profit which it includes. But there is no reason to expect wage increases, any more than increases in the cost of raw materials, to be met out of profits; both are paid in the end by the public in the form of higher prices.

The new despots

Through the law of costs, the power of labor to raise money wages, and so indirectly to raise prices, is fundamentally no different from the power of business to raise prices directly. Monopoly wages, like monopoly prices, are paid in the end by the public; and it is for this reason that there is exactly as much public interest involved in the regulation of monopoly in the labor field as in the field of industry.

Now the problem of industrial monopoly power, even at those times in history when it has been of the greatest public concern, has never been associated with inflation. How is it therefore that such an association is made in the labor field? There are several reasons for this: the practice of wage settlements over wide areas on a pattern basis, so that one increase means many more; the institution of the annual wage increase, augmented by the growing practice of embodying it in long-term contracts; competition among labor leaders to outdo their rivals—and we must include competition from employers in nonunionized areas to do even better, so as to avoid unionization; and finally the fact that wages are more important than profits as an element in prices. The role of union power in cost inflation would seem to indicate that the control of this general inflationary force may be achieved only by putting a damper on thousands of individual wage and price increases.

How then to hold them in check? The decisive elements unique to the labor market which are mainly responsible for the fact that labor has too much power are not a part of collective bargaining per se. They are accretions of power which have developed partly through specific exemptions by Congress and through court interpretations, partly through a failure to understand the problem, but mostly through an uncritical public indulgence which can only be explained by a confused belief that since the labor cause is good, the more power in the hands of labor the better. As a practical matter, it seems to me that progress could be made in reducing union power by attacking directly those accretions which clearly rest upon privileges and immunities of laborers as compared with other citizens, and which it is therefore reasonable and fair to correct on the simple ground of equal treatment for all.

A recent booklet entitled *The Legal Immunities of Labor Unions* by [the late] Dean Emeritus Roscoe Pound of the Harvard University Law School analyzes an impressive list of such immunities. They are treated under the headings of torts (civil wrongs), contracts, restraint of trade, duties of public service, the right to work, racketeering, centralized power, and irresponsibility. Legal immunities are related to economic power, and each such immunity therefore contributes its bit to wage-push inflation. Certainly the appeal of equal treatment for all is a strong one in a democracy. Why should it not apply in this area?

On the more purely economic front, the power accretions are startling. The practice of making a deal with the teamsters to "honor" a picket line has nothing to do with free speech, as the Supreme Court seems to think it has because it involves picketing, and it has nothing to do with collective bargaining. It is simply a power gadget to deprive an employer not only of the services of his own workers who are on strike but of all other goods and services as well. The old legal principle that a service of such vital public necessity as transportation must not be closed or obstructed clearly corresponds to the economic realities. Yet it has not been adapted to developments of recent decades in the transportation field. Most firms in modern times are heavily if not totally dependent for their existence on private trucking. In fact, the teamsters derive most of their power not from the racketeering with which they are ridden but from their control over transportation, including the freedom with which they can choke off this vital service from any specific business enterprise they please.

The threat of potential violence and intimidation through the device of the picket line are powerful factors—so powerful, in fact, that nowadays a firm rarely attempts any operations at all if a strike has been called, although it would be within its legal rights to do so. For all practical purposes the alternative of making a bargain with anyone other than the union has been removed. Even the attempts in the 1959 bus strike in Massachusetts to run a few buses operated by supervisors for school children were successfully blocked by masses of pickets surrounding the buses. Boycotts, hot cargo rules, refusals to work with nonunion labor or on materials produced by nonunion labor or by the wrong union are used with impunity to close the channels of trade and commerce. These and other privileges and immunities which tremendously augment union monopoly power are unique to the labor market.

Curbing the monarchs

Many of these developments are a logical conclusion of what seems to be the overriding principle that a union's economic power must not be compromised. In the further matter of agreements and alliances, for instance, anything is legal so long as only labor groups are involved. No—there is one qualification of mock seriousness. A union may restrain trade as much as it pleases and combine with others against other unions, against nonunion laborers, against some particular employer, or against the general public, provided only—in the quaint language of the Hutcheson decision—it is acting in its own self-interest.

I have seen a statement by an important labor leader before the Joint Economic Committee of Congress to the effect that even to raise the question of whether unions have too much power is to question their very right to exist. This is the union point of view, and it seems to be widespread. Yet what could be more absurd? Has anyone ever held that to reduce and regulate monopoly power in the business area was to question the right of business to exist?

We need only to make the distinction between collective bargaining and the application of further pressures, to make clear that such pressures may be reduced as the public interest and ordinary fairness require, without imperiling the existence of unions. Should a union be allowed to strangle a business economically by arranging with the teamsters to cut off its transportation? It seems to me we might as well ask if a physically strong cus-

tomer in a retail shop should be allowed to twist the arm of the shopkeeper in order to drive a better bargain with him.

I suggest as a good general rule that no employer should have brought against him pressures exerted by anyone other than his own employees.[1] To implement such a principle fully may seem too much to hope for, but it should not be overlooked that there is an opening wedge in the outlawing of the secondary boycott by Congress in the Taft-Hartley Act. It remains, after closing some of the loopholes which have developed in this prohibition, to make progress in applying the general principle more widely. There seems every reason to think that the questions of alliances in the labor field, interunion relationships, and the extent of single-union control are as much a matter of public concern and of regulation as are intercorporate relationships and agreements in industry.

A national policy of encouraging collective bargaining, adopted in the middle thirties in the belief that labor's bargaining power was weak and needed to be strengthened, has encouraged not merely collective bargaining but the development of a wide power complex. The careless view that labor must have enough power to win may have been understandable when labor was the underdog. But pilots who can close down airlines in negotiating for top salaries of well over $20,000 a year are not underdogs. And when a few hundred workers in New York who merely deliver newspapers after they have been produced can deprive ten million readers of printed news and inflict losses, not only on their employers but on a whole community, estimated at $50 million, it seems clear that the time has come for a reevaluation of where the power now lies.

As this article is being written (1959), the fast-approaching crisis in the steel industry provides an example on a national scale of where the power lies. However one may judge the demands of the steel workers and wage-price relationships in the industry, the simple fact remains that the nation will be offered its choice between a long-drawn-out strike which would deal a heavy blow to eco-

[1] EDITOR'S NOTE: Since this was written, some tightening up of the restrictions on union power over third parties was passed by Congress in the Landrum-Griffin Act of 1959.

nomic recovery or an inflationary increase in costs. Indeed, it may very well get both.

The increase in wages (or fringe benefits) will be inflationary for two reasons: 1) whether at once or after an interval, steel prices will be higher, and so will the prices of all things made of steel; 2) less obvious but much more important, an increase in steel wages (already among the highest) must be followed by other wage increases. This is so because of the pattern phenomenon: if steel workers get more, inexorable pressures are created to bring other wages in the whole structure into line. So the wage-price spiral works not only vertically from wages to prices but horizontally from wages to other wages, and especially so when a key industry like steel is involved. With these considerations in mind, the question of whether or not certain steel companies could increase wages without raising their own prices (whatever the answer) recedes into proper perspective.

The choice between a disastrous closing down of the steel industry and another round of inflation is indeed a hard one, and if unions had less power other alternatives with a measure of concern for the public interest might have a hearing.

Unions have achieved their present position largely through public indulgence, and if the public becomes less indulgent, union power can be curbed. What is needed is a general awakening to the real nature of the problem. In its fundamentals monopoly power is the same whether used by laborers or by businessmen, and it has the same adverse effect on the rest of society, with an inflationary influence to be added in the case of labor. It has been subjected to regulation in business; how much longer will it go unregulated in the labor area? Will the rest of society continue to accept the principle that a labor union's freedom in the pursuit of its own self-interest shall be unrestrained?

5

INTERNATIONAL TRADE AND FINANCE

Tariffs and Free Trade

Reading 52

The advantages of free trade in furthering the international division of labor and thereby raising living standards for both rich and poor nations can be demonstrated by logical argumentation. Frederic Bastiat (1801–1850) fought for this cause with the weapons of satire and wit, and the results were often devastating. In his *Economic Sophisms* he deliberately took the protectionists' case somewhat further than they intended to go and, in so doing, made the whole case teeter.

Questions to guide the reading

How closely do the arguments which Bastiat builds into this petition correspond to the most frequently used arguments for tariffs today?

How might the protectionists argue in response to this satire? Does the free-trade case lend itself equally well to this treatment?

Petition of the Candlemakers—1845

Frederic Bastiat

To the Honorable Members of the Chamber of Deputies:

GENTLEMEN,—You are in the right way: you reject abstract theories; abundance, cheapness, concerns you little. You are entirely occupied with the interest of the producer, whom you are anxious to free from foreign competition. In a word, you wish to secure the *national market* to *national labor*.

We come now to offer you an admirable opportunity for the application of your—what what shall we say—your theory? No, nothing is more deceiving than theory;—your doctrine? your system? your principle? But you do not like doctrines; you hold systems in horror; and, as for principles, you declare that there are no such things in political economy. We will say, then, your practice; your practice without theory, and without principle.

We are subjected to the intolerable competition of a foreign rival, who enjoys, it would seem, such superior facilities for the production of light, that he is enabled to *inundate* our *national market* at so

exceedingly reduced a price, that, the moment he makes his appearance, he draws off all custom for us; and thus an important branch of French industry, with all its innumerable ramifications, is suddenly reduced to a state of complete stagnation. This rival is no other than the sun.

Our petition is, that it would please your honorable body to pass a law whereby shall be directed the shutting up of all windows, dormers, skylights, shutters, curtains, in a word, all openings, holes, chinks, and fissures through which the light of the sun is used to penetrate into our dwellings, to the prejudice of the profitable manufactures which we flatter ourselves we have been enabled to bestow upon the country; which country cannot, therefore, without ingratitude, leave us now to struggle unprotected through so unequal a contest.

We foresee your objections, gentlemen; but there is not one that you can oppose to us which you will not be obliged to gather from the works of the partisans of free trade. We dare challenge you to pronounce one word against our petition, which

From Frederic Bastiat, *Economic Sophisms* (G. P. Putnam's Sons, New York, 1922).

is not equally opposed to your own practice and the principle which guides your policy.

Do you tell us, that if we gain by this protection, France will not gain because the consumer must pay the price of it?

We answer you: You have no longer any right to cite the interest of the consumer. For whenever this has been found to compete with that of the producer, you have invariably sacrificed the first. You have done this to *encourage labor,* to *increase the demand for labor.* The same reason should now induce you to act in the same manner.

You have yourselves already answered the objection. When you were told, "The consumer is interested in the free introduction of iron, coal, corn, wheat, cloths, etc.," your answer was, "Yes, but the producer is interested in their exclusion." Thus, also, if the consumer is interested in the admission of light, we, the producers, pray for its interdiction.

You have also said, "The producer and the consumer are one. If the manufacturer gains by protection, he will cause the agriculturist to gain also; if agriculture prospers, it opens a market for manufactured goods." Thus we, if you confer upon us the monopoly of furnishing light during the day, will as a first consequence buy large quantities of tallow, coals, oil, resin, wax, alcohol, silver, iron, bronze, crystal, for the supply of our business; and then we and our numerous contractors having become rich our consumption will be great, and will become a means of contributing to the comfort and competency of the workers in every branch of national labor.

Will you say that the light of the sun is a gratuitous gift, and that to repulse gifts is to repulse riches under pretense of encouraging the means of obtaining them?

Take care,—you carry the death blow to your own policy. Remember that hitherto you have always repulsed foreign produce *because* it was an approach to a gratuitous gift, and *the more in proportion* as this approach was more close. You have, in obeying the wishes of other monopolists, acted only from a *half-motive;* to grant our petition there is a much *fuller inducement.*

Labor and nature concur in different proportions, according to country and climate, in every article of production. The portion of nature is always gratuitous. If a Lisbon orange can be sold at half the price of a Parisian one, it is because a natural and gratuitous heat does for the one what the other only obtains from an artificial and consequently expensive one. When, therefore, we purchase a Portuguese orange, we may say that we obtain it half gratuitously and half by the right of labor; in other words, at *half price* compared with those of Paris.

Now it is precisely on account of this *demi-gratuity* (excuse the word) that you argue in favor of exclusion. How, you say, could national labor sustain the competition of foreign labor, when the first has everything to do, and the last is rid of half the trouble, the sun taking the rest of the business upon himself? If then the *demi-gratuity* can determine you to check competition, on what principle can the *entire gratuity* be alleged as a reason for admitting it? Choose, but be consistent. And does it not argue the greatest inconsistency to check as you do the importation of coal, iron, cheese, and goods of foreign manufacture, merely because and even in proportion as their price approaches *zero,* while at the same time you freely admit, and without limitation, the light of the sun, whose price is during the whole day at *zero?*

Reading 53

Some 106 years after Frederic Bastiat published his satirical petition to the French National Assembly, a real-world group of candlemakers offered their serious petition to the Finance Committee of the United States Senate. They were silent on the subject of the sun, but they did argue vigorously, though briefly, on some other grounds for modern-day protectionism.

Questions to guide the reading

How does foreign competition in candles differ from, say, new domestic competition in its impact on our economy?

What criteria should our government use to decide whether or not a particular product ought to be given tariff protection?

Assuming that society feels some sort of obligation to a domestic industry being harmed by foreign competition, are there remedies other than those advocated here that might better fulfill this obligation?

Petition of the Candlemakers—1951

Congressional Hearings

February 27, 1951

Re: Extension of the Trade Agreements Act, H.R. 1612

Chairman, Senate Finance Committee,
United States Senate, Washington, D.C.

SIR: This brief is filed in behalf of the candle manufacturers in the United States in protest against an extension of the Trade Agreement Act of 1934 as amended by the House of Representatives, H.R. 1612. In spite of our brief presented in opposition to tariff cuts (which are a matter of record and available to your committee) we have been given the maximum reduction possible up to this point.

The facts upon which we have based our previous briefs are as important and as pertinent as they were when first presented. Rather than take the time of the committee by repetition of the entire argument we are listing the facts (all of which we have previously substantiated) in the hope that this time we will reach some one who has the understanding to interpret these facts intelligently and the power to act in the light of those facts.

1. An industry stemming from Colonial times.

2. A product required in national defense to such an extent as to utilize the full capacity of the industry.

3. High essentiality of labor and materials under war conditions.

4. An overcapacity of more than five to one.

5. Increased labor costs of 25 percent from 1946-50 with labor rates well above those prevailing in competitive countries.

6. A decline in sales of 17.45 percent since 1946.

7. A 63 percent increase in number of manufacturers since 1933.

8. With plants operating one shift, present production well above demand.

9. Full impacts of currency devaluations, abnormal conditions, pending legislation in countries not yet felt in our markets.

The record of imports for last year has shown a steady increase through the first 11 months from 12 countries, most of whom have not supplied candles to the United States for many years if ever. These are the countries mentioned in our earlier briefs from whom we feared this type of low-cost-labor competition. As a result of current untenable conditions one of the oldest manufacturers—representing a substantial percentage of the total candle business—had been forced to close and demolish its plant.

It is evident that the purposes of the act outlined in the preamble are not being fulfilled: "Overcoming domestic unemployment," "increasing purchasing power of the American public," "maintaining a better relationship among various branches of American agriculture, industry, mining and commerce." This country should forgo the trade agreement policy until normal times return during which the benefits or ill effects of this act can be given a fair test. The expanded economy resulting from World War II has precluded any normal business operations and because of the Korean war we are still in an abnormal economy.

Competent legal opinion has proven that the entire act is illegal and unconstitutional.

We are requesting outright repeal of the act at this time. Failing that, we ask that any extension at least carry with it the following recent provi-

From *Trade Agreements Extension Act of 1951, Hearings before the Committee on Finance, United States Senate, on H.R. 1612,* 82d Cong., 1st Sess. (1951).

sions of the House amendments as well as incorporate the points outlined above.

1. Tie in reductions with parity price levels.

2. Reinstate the peril points empowering the Tariff Commission to fix a point below which the tariff on any item cannot be cut.

3. Reinstate the right of judicial review of grievances and arbitrary decisions which may be imposed upon the citizens by the negotiators.

4. End all the tariff concessions to communist countries.

Respectfully submitted.

The Candle Manufacturing Industry
by H. R. Farker

Exchange Rates

Readings 54 and 55   Debate on Stable Exchange Rates

According to classical economics, foreign exchange rates could be stable provided that prices and wages could move flexibly upward and downward to correct any chronic disequilibria in the balance of payments. However, in a modern mixed economy it is rarely possible to engineer downward flexibility of wages and costs without producing great social disorder; and there are grave social objections to engineering inflationary upward movements when such are called for to remove international disequilibria.

In consequence, Professor Milton Friedman, who was introduced in previous readings and as the ideological spokesman for the "Chicago School" of Libertarians who espouse reliance on free-market pricing, puts forward the case for floating exchange rates. Many economists of all political persuasions agree with this view. The objections to it and the case for a stable exchange rate are presented by Henry C. Wallich, a Yale professor, columnist, and Republican economic adviser.

Questions to guide the reading

Would international trade, the division of labor, and the process of foreign investment be inhibited if importers and investors had to face the uncertainty of not knowing from day to day what the foreign exchange rate would be? Could speculators be expected to provide a broad market that would promote stability and enable traders to *hedge* their international transactions?

Reading 54

The Case for Flexible Exchange Rates

Milton Friedman

Discussions of U.S. policy with respect to international payments tend to be dominated by our immediate balance-of-payments difficulties. I should like today to approach the question from a different, and I hope more constructive, direction. Let us begin by asking ourselves not merely how we

From Milton Friedman, "The Case for Flexible Exchange Rates," *Essays in Positive Economics,* The University of Chicago Press, 1953, pp. 157–203. © 1953 by the University of Chicago. Reprinted with the kind permission of the author and the publisher.

can get out of our present difficulties but instead how we can fashion our international payments system so that it will best serve our needs for the long pull; how we can solve not merely this balance-of-payments problem but the balance-of-payments problem.

A shocking, and indeed, disgraceful feature of the present situation is the extent to which our frantic search for expedients to stave off balance-of-payments pressures has led us, on the one hand, to sacrifice major national objectives; and, on the other, to give enormous power to officials of foreign governments to affect what should be purely domestic matters.

Foreign payments amount to only some 5 percent of our total national income. Yet they have become a major factor in nearly every national policy.

I believe that a system of floating exchange rates would solve the balance-of-payments problem for the United States far more effectively than our present arrangements. Such a system would use the flexibility and efficiency of the free market to harmonize our small foreign trade sector with both the rest of our massive economy and the rest of the world; it would reduce problems of foreign payments to their proper dimensions and remove them as a major consideration in governmental policy about domestic matters and as a major preoccupation in international political negotiations; it would foster our national objectives rather than be an obstacle to their attainment.

Bringing down tariffs

Suppose that we succeed in negotiating far-reaching reciprocal reductions in tariffs and other trade barriers with the Common Market and other countries. To simplify exposition I shall hereafter refer only to tariffs, letting these stand for the whole range of barriers to trade, including even the so-called voluntary limitation of exports. Such reductions will expand trade in general but clearly will have different effects on different industries. The demand for the products of some will expand, for others contract. This is a phenomenon we are familiar with from our internal development. The capacity of our free enterprise system to adapt quickly and efficiently to such shifts, whether produced by changes in technology or tastes, has been a major source of our economic growth. The only

additional element introduced by international trade is the fact that different currencies are involved, and this is where the payment mechanism comes in; its function is to keep this fact from being an additional source of disturbance.

An all-around lowering of tariffs would tend to increase both our expenditures and our receipts in foreign currencies. There is no way of knowing in advance which increase would tend to be the greater and hence no way of knowing whether the initial effect would be toward a surplus or deficit in our balance of payments. What is clear is that we cannot hope to succeed in the objective of expanding world trade unless we can readily adjust to either outcome.

Many people concerned with our payments deficits hope that since we are operating further from full capacity than Europe, we could supply a substantial increase in exports whereas they could not. Implicitly, this assumes that European countries are prepared to see their surplus turned into a deficit, thereby contributing to the reduction of the deficits we have recently been experiencing in our balance of payments. Perhaps this would be the initial effect of tariff changes. But if the achievement of such a result is to be *sine qua non* of tariff agreement, we cannot hope for any significant reduction in barriers. We could be confident that exports would expand more than imports only if the tariff changes were one-sided indeed, with our trading partners making much greater reductions in tariffs than we make. Our major means of inducing other countries to reduce tariffs is to offer corresponding reductions in our tariff. More generally, there is little hope of continued and sizable liberalization of trade if liberalization is to be viewed simply as a device for correcting balance-of-payments difficulties. That way lies only backing and filling.

Suppose then that the initial effect is to increase our expenditures on imports more than our receipts from exports. How could we adjust to this outcome?

Floating rates in history

Floating exchange rates is the method which the United States used from 1862 to 1879, and again, in effect, from 1917 or so to about 1925, and again from 1933 to 1934. It is the method which Britain used from 1918 to 1925 and again from 1931 to

1939, and which Canada used for most of the interwar period and again from 1950 to May 1962. Under this method, exchange rates adjust themselves continuously, and market forces determine the magnitude of each change. There is no need for any official to decide by how much the rate should rise or fall. This is the method of the free market, the method that we adopt unquestioningly in a private enterprise economy for the bulk of goods and services. It is no less available for the price of one money in terms of another.

With a floating exchange rate, it is possible for Governments to intervene and to try to affect the rate by buying or selling, as the British exchange equalization fund did rather successfully in the 1930's, or by combining buying and selling with public announcements of intentions, as Canada did so disastrously in early 1962. On the whole, it seems to me undesirable to have government intervene, because there is a strong tendency for government agencies to try to peg the rate rather than to stabilize it, because they have no special advantage over private speculators in stabilizing it, because they can make far bigger mistakes than private speculators risking their own money, and because there is a tendency for them to cover up their mistakes by changing the rules—as the Canadian case so strikingly illustrates—rather than by reversing course. But this is an issue on which there is much difference of opinion among economists who agree in favoring floating rates. Clearly, it is possible to have a successful floating rate along with governmental speculation.

The great objective of tearing down trade barriers, of promoting a worldwide expansion of trade, of giving citizens of all countries, and especially the underdeveloped countries, every opportunity to sell their products in open markets under equal terms and thereby every incentive to use their resources efficiently, of giving countries an alternative through free world trade to autarchy and central planning—this great objective can, I believe, be achieved best under a regime of floating rates. All countries, and not just the United States, can proceed to liberalize boldly and confidently only if they can have reasonable assurance that the resulting trade expansion will be balanced and will not interfere with major domestic objectives. Floating exchange rates, and so far as I can see, only floating exchange rates, provide this assurance. They do so because they are an automatic mechanism for protecting the domestic economy from the possibility that liberalization will produce a serious imbalance in international payments.

False objections

Despite their advantages, floating exchange rates have a bad press. Why is this so?

One reason is because a consequence of our present system that I have been citing as a serious disadvantage is often regarded as an advantage, namely, the extent to which the small foreign trade sector dominates national policy. Those who regard this as an advantage refer to it as the discipline of the gold standard. I would have much sympathy for this view if we had a real gold standard, so the discipline was imposed by impersonal forces which in turn reflected the realities of resources, tastes, and technology. But in fact we have today only a pseudo gold standard and the so-called discipline is imposed by governmental officials of other countries who are determining their own internal monetary policies and are either being forced to dance to our tune or calling the tune for us, depending primarily on accidental political developments. This is a discipline we can well do without.

A possibly more important reason why floating exchange rates have a bad press, I believe, is a mistaken interpretation of experience with floating rates, arising out of a statistical fallacy that can be seen easily in a standard example. Arizona is clearly the worst place in the United States for a person with tuberculosis to go because the death rate from tuberculosis is higher in Arizona than in any other State. The fallacy in this case is obvious. It is less obvious in connection with exchange rates. Countries that have gotten into severe financial difficulties, for whatever reason, have had ultimately to change their exchange rates or let them change. No amount of exchange control and other restrictions on trade have enabled them to peg an exchange rate that was far out of line with economic realities. In consequence, floating rates have frequently been associated with financial and economic instability. It is easy to conclude, as many have, that floating exchange rates produce such instability.

This misreading of experience is reinforced by the general prejudice against speculation; which has led to the frequent assertion, typically on the basis of no evidence whatsoever, that speculation in exchange can be expected to be destabilizing and thereby to increase the instability in rates. Few who make this assertion even recognize that it is equivalent to asserting that speculators generally lose money.

Floating exchange rates need not be unstable exchange rates—any more than the prices of automobiles or of Government bonds, of coffee or of meals need gyrate wildly just because they are free to change from day to day. The Canadian exchange rate was free to change during more than a decade, yet it varied within narrow limits. The ultimate objective is a world in which exchange rates, while free to vary, are in fact highly stable because basic economic policies and conditions are stable. Instability of exchange rates is a symptom of instability in the underlying economic structure. Elimination of this symptom by administrative pegging of exchange rates cures none of the underlying difficulties and only makes adjustment to them more painful.

The confusion between stable exchange rates and pegged exchange rates helps to explain the frequent comment that floating exchange rates would introduce an additional element of uncertainty into foreign trade and thereby discourage its expansion. *They introduce no additional element of uncertainty.* If a floating rate would, for example, decline, then a pegged rate would be subject to pressure that the authorities would have to meet by internal deflation or exchange control in some form. The uncertainty about the rate would simply be replaced by uncertainty about internal prices or about the availability of exchange; and the latter uncertainties, being subject to administrative rather than market control, are likely to be the more erratic and unpredictable. Moreover, the trader can far more readily and cheaply protect himself against the danger of changes in exchange rates, through hedging operations in a forward market, than he can against the danger of changes in internal prices or exchange availability. Floating rates are therefore more favorable to private international trade than pegged rates.

Our current deficit

Though I have discussed the problem of international payments in the context of trade liberaliza-

tion, the discussion is directly applicable to the more general problem of adapting to any forces that make for balance-of-payments difficulties. Consider our present problem, of a deficit in the balance of trade plus long-term capital movements. How can we adjust to it? By one of the three methods outlined: first, drawing on reserves or borrowing; second, keeping U.S. prices from rising as rapidly as foreign prices or forcing them down; third, permitting or forcing exchange rates to alter. And, this time, by one more method: by imposing additional trade barriers or their equivalent, whether in the form of higher tariffs, or smaller import quotas, or extracting from other countries tighter "voluntary" quotas on their exports, or "tieing" foreign aid, or buying higher priced domestic goods or services to meet military needs, or imposing taxes on foreign borrowing, or imposing direct controls on investments by U.S. citizens abroad, or any one of the host of other devices for interfering with the private business of private individuals that have become so familiar to us since Hjalmar Schacht perfected the modern techniques of exchange control in 1934 to strengthen the Nazis for war and to despoil a large class of his fellow citizens.

Fortunately or unfortunately, even Congress cannot repeal the laws of arithmetic. Books must balance. We must use one of these four methods. Because we have been unwilling to select the only one that is currently fully consistent with both economic and political needs—namely, floating exchange rates—we have been driven, as if by an invisible hand, to employ all the others, and even then may not escape the need for explicit changes in exchange rates.

We affirm in loud and clear voices that we will not and must not erect trade barriers—yet is there any doubt about how far we have gone down the fourth route? After the host of measures already taken, the Secretary of the Treasury has openly stated to the Senate Finance Committee that if the so-called interest equalization tax—itself a concealed exchange control and concealed devaluation—is not passed, we shall have to resort to direct controls over foreign investment.

We affirm that we cannot drain our reserves further, yet short-term liabilities mount and our gold stock continues to decline.

The final solution

Even all together, these measures may only serve to postpone but not prevent open devaluation—if the experience of other countries is any guide. Whether they do, depends not on us but on others. For our best hope of escaping our present difficulties is that foreign countries will inflate.

In the meantime, we adopt one expedient after another, borrowing here, making swap arrangements there, changing the form of loans to make the figures look good. Entirely aside from the ineffectiveness of most of these measures, they are politically degrading and demeaning. We are a great and wealthy Nation. We should be directing our own course, setting an example to the world, living up to our destiny. Instead, we send our officials hat in hand to make the rounds of foreign governments and central banks; we put foreign central banks in a position to determine whether or not we can meet our obligations and thus enable them to exert great influence on our policies; we are driven to niggling negotiations with Hong Kong and with Japan and for all I know, Monaco, to get them to limit voluntarily their exports. Is this posture suitable for the leader of the free world?

It is not the least of the virtues of floating exchange rates that we would again become masters in our own house. We could decide important issues on the proper ground. The military could concentrate on military effectiveness and not on saving foreign exchange; recipients of foreign aid could concentrate on how to get the most out of what we give them and not on how to spend it all in the United States; Congress could decide how much to spend on foreign aid on the basis of what we get for our money and what else we could use it for and not how it will affect the gold stock; the monetary authorities could concentrate on domes-

tic prices and employment, not on how to induce foreigners to hold dollar balances in this country; the Treasury and the tax committees of Congress could devote their attention to the equity of the tax system and its effects on our efficiency, rather than on how to use tax gimmicks to discourage imports, subsidize exports, and discriminate against outflows of capital.

Demise of gold

A system of floating exchange rates would render the problem of making outflows equal inflows unto the market where it belongs and not leave it to the clumsy and heavy hand of Government. It would leave Government free to concentrate on its proper functions.

In conclusion, a word about gold. Our commitment to buy and sell gold for monetary use at a fixed price of $35 an ounce is, in practice, the mechanism whereby we maintain fixed rates of exchange between the dollar and other currencies—or, more precisely, whereby we leave all initiative for changes in such rates to other countries. This commitment should be terminated. The price of gold should be determined in the free market, with the U.S. Government committed neither to buying gold nor to selling gold at any fixed price. This is the appropriate counterpart of a policy of floating exchange rates. With respect to our existing stock of gold, we could simply keep it fixed, neither adding to it nor reducing it; alternatively, we could sell it off gradually at the market price or add to it gradually, thereby reducing or increasing our governmental stockpiles of this particular metal. In any event, we should simultaneously remove all present limitations on the ownership of gold and the trading in gold by American citizens. There is no reason why gold, like other commodities, should not be freely traded on a free market.

Reading 55

A Defense of Fixed Exchange Rates

Henry C. Wallich

Flexible rates have achieved a high measure of acceptance in academic circles, but very little among

public officials. This raises the question whether we have a parallel to the famous case of free trade:

From *The United States Balance of Payments, Hearings before the Joint Economic Committee,* 88th Cong., 1st Sess., pt. 3.

almost all economists favor it in principle, but no major country ever has adopted it. Does the logic of economics point equally irrefutably to flexible rates, while the logic of politics points in another direction?

The nature of the case, I believe, is fundamentally different. Most countries do practice free trade within their borders, although they reject it outside. But economists do not propose flexible rates for the States of the Union, among which men, money, and goods can move freely, and which are governed by uniform monetary, fiscal, and other policies. Flexible rates are to apply only to relations among countries that do not permit free factor movements across their borders and that follow, or may follow, substantially different monetary and fiscal policies. It is the imperfections of the world that seem to suggest that flexible rates, which would be harmful if applied to different parts of a single country, would do more good than harm internationally.

The question is, Do we want to look upon the world as quite different from the United States, as hopelessly divided into self-contained units where cooperation and efforts to coordinate policies are doomed to frustration? In that case, flexible rates may be the best way to avoid a very bad situation. But should we not try to establish within the world something that begins to approximate the conditions that prevail within a country, in the way of coordination of policies, freer flow of capital and of goods and so try to achieve the benefits of one large economic area within the world?

Advantages

The proponents of flexible rates argue, in effect, that flexible rates can help a country get out of almost any of the typical difficulties that economies experience. This is perfectly true. If the United States has a balance-of-payments deficit, a flexible exchange rate allows the dollar to decline until receipts have risen and payments fallen enough to restore balance. If the United States has unemployment, flexible rates can protect it against the balance-of-payments consequences of a policy of expansion. We would then have less unemployment. If the United States has suffered inflation and fears that it will be undersold internationally, flexible rates can remove the danger.

All of these advantages are quite clear.

Other countries have analogous advantages. If Chile experiences a decline in copper prices, flexible rates can ease the inevitable adjustment. If Germany finds that other countries have inflated while German prices have remained more nearly stable, flexible rates could help to avoid importing inflation. If Canada has a large capital inflow, a flexible rate will remove the need for price and income increases that would otherwise be needed to facilitate the transfer of real resources.

There are other adjustments, however, that must be made in all of these cases. If a country allows its exchange rate to go down, some price adjustments still remain to be made. Furthermore, each time a country makes this kind of adjustment, allowing its exchange rate to decline, other countries suffer. If the U.S. dollar depreciates, we undersell the Europeans. It could be argued that if the U.S. price levels go down instead of the exchange rate, we also undersell the Europeans, and if because of a declining price level we have unemployment we would be buying still less from them. Nevertheless, there is a difference. A price adjustment tends to be slow and is likely to be no greater than it need be and tends to be selective for particular commodities. In contrast, an exchange rate movement is unpredictable. It can be large—we could easily have a drop of 10 or 20 percent in an exchange rate. It comes suddenly. And it compels other countries to be on their guard.

Need for discipline

Why, given the attractions of flexible rates, should one advise policymakers to stay away from them? Since the dollar problem is the concrete situation in which flexible rates are being urged today, it is in terms of the dollar that they must be discussed. In broadest terms, *the reason why flexible rates are inadvisable is that their successful functioning would require more self-discipline and mutual forbearance than countries today are likely to muster.* Exchange rates are two sided—depreciation for the dollar means appreciation for the European currencies. To work successfully, a flexible dollar, for instance, must not depreciate to the point where the Europeans would feel compelled to take counteraction. I believe that the limits of tolerance, before counteraction begins today are narrow and that a flexible dollar would invite retaliation almost immediately.

In the abstract, the European countries perhaps ought to consider that if the United States allows the dollar to go down, it is doing so in the interests of all-around equilibrium. They ought perhaps to consider that with a stable dollar rate the same adjustment might have to take place through a decline in prices here and a rise in prices there. In practice, they are likely to be alive principally to the danger of being undersold by American producers if the dollar goes down, in their own and third markets. The changing competitive pressure would fall unevenly upon particular industries, and those who are hurt would demand protection.

The most likely counteraction might take one of two forms. The Europeans could impose countervailing duties, such as the United States also has employed at times. They could alternately also depreciate European currencies along with the dollar or, what would amount to almost the same thing, prevent the dollar from depreciating. This might involve the European countries in the purchase of large amounts of dollars. If they are to peg the dollar, they could minimize their commitment by imposing a simple form of exchanging control that the Swiss practiced during the last war. The Swiss purchased dollars only from their exporters, also requiring their importers to buy these dollars thereby stabilizing the trade dollar, while allowing dollars from capital movements—finance dollars—to find their own level in the market.

The large volume of not very predictable short-term capital movements in the world today makes such reactions under flexible rates particularly likely.

A sudden outflow of funds from the United States, for instance (because of the fear of budget deficits or many other things that could happen), would tend to drive the dollar down. As a result, American exporters could undersell producers everywhere else in the world. It seems unlikely that foreign countries would allow a fortuitous short-term capital movement to have such far-reaching consequences. It would not even be economically appropriate to allow a transitory fluctuation in the capital account of the balance of payments to have a major influence on the current account. Such a fluctuation should not alter the pattern of trade, because the situation is likely to be reversed. Other countries therefore would probably take defensive action to make sure that no industry is destroyed and after several years may have to be rebuilt because of the ups and downs of short-term capital movements.

Destabilizing speculation

It can be argued that under flexible rates the effects of such a movement would be forestalled by stabilizing speculation on a future recovery of the dollar. This is possible. It is possible also, however, that speculation would seek a quick profit from the initial drop in the dollar, instead of a longer run one from its eventual recovery. Then short-run speculation would drive the dollar down farther at first. In any case there is not enough assurance that speculators will not make mistakes to permit basing the world's monetary system upon the stabilizing effects of speculation.

In the case of countries which import much of what they consume, such as England, a temporary decline in the local currency may even be self-validating. If the cost of living rises as the currency declines, wages will rise. Thereafter, the currency may never recover to its original level.

This points up *one probable consequence of flexible exchange rates: A worldwide acceleration of inflation.* In some countries the indicated ratchet effect of wages will be at work. If exchange rates go down, wages will rise, and exchange rates cannot recover. In the United States the rise in the cost of imports would not be very important. But the removal of balance-of-payments restraints may well lead to policies that could lead to price increases. The American inflation of the 1950's was never defeated until the payments deficit became serious. Elsewhere, the removal of balance-of-payments disciplines might have the same effect. Rapid inflation in turn would probably compel governments to intervene drastically in foreign trade and finance.

It is quite clear that the discipline of the balance of payments has made for a more restrictive policy in this country than would have been followed in the absence of this discipline. It is quite conceivable that the absence of balance-of-payments disciplines would have strong inflationary effects in some countries. In that case governments would be compelled immediately to intervene drastically in foreign trade and finance; in other words, flexible exchange rates would contribute to their own extinction or to exchange control.

Costs of uncertainty

The prospect that flexible rates would greatly increase uncertainty for foreign traders and investors has been cited many times. It should be noted that this uncertainty extends also to domestic investment decisions that might be affected by changing import competition or changing export prospects. It has been argued that uncertainties about future exchange rates can be removed by hedging in the future market. This, however, involves a cost even where cover is readily available. The history of futures markets does not suggest that it will be possible to get cover for long-term positions. To hedge domestic investment decisions that might be affected by flexible rates is in the nature of things impracticable.

The picture that emerges of the international economy under flexible rates is one of increasing disintegration. Independent national policies and unpredictable changes in each country's competitive position will compel governments to shield their producers and markets. The argument that such shielding would also automatically be accomplished by movements in the affected country's exchange rate underrates the impact of fluctuations upon particular industries, if not upon the entire economy. That international integration and flexible rates are incompatible seems to be the view also of the European Common Market countries, who have left no doubt that they want stable rates within the EEC. The same applies if we visualize the "Kennedy round" under the Trade Expansion Act. I think if we told the Europeans that, after lowering our tariffs, we were going to cast the dollar loose and let it fluctuate, we would get very little tariff reduction. They would want to keep up their guard.

If the disintegrating effects of flexible rates are to be overcome, a great deal of policy coordination, combined with self-discipline and mutual forbearance, would be required. The desired independence of national economic policy would in fact have to be foregone—interest rates, budgets, wage and prices policies would have to be harmonized. If the world were ready for such cooperation, it would be capable also of making a fixed

exchange rate system work. In that case, flexible rates would accomplish nothing that could not more cheaply and simply be done with fixed rates. It seems to follow that flexible rates have no unique capacity for good, whereas they possess great capacity to do damage.

Wider "points"

A modified version of the flexible rates proposal has been suggested. This version would allow the dollar and other currencies to fluctuate within a given range, say 5 percent up and down. This "widening of the gold points" is believed to reduce the danger of destabilizing speculation. It might perhaps enlist speculation on the side of stabilization, for if the dollar, say, had dropped to its lower limit, and if the public had confidence that that limit would not be broken, the only movement on which to speculate would be a rise. The spectacle of a currency falling below par may induce, according to the proponents, a strong political effort to bring it back.

This proposal likewise strikes me as unworkable. For one thing, I doubt that people would have a great deal of confidence in a limit of 5 percent below par, if par itself has been given up. Political support for holding this second line would probably be less than the support that can be mustered to hold the first. For another, the execution of the plan would still require the maintenance of international reserves, to protect the upper and lower limits. But with fluctuating rates, dollar and sterling would cease to be desirable media for monetary reserves. International liquidity would become seriously impaired. A third objection is that under today's conditions, the complex negotiations and legislation required, in the unlikely event that the plan could be negotiated at all, could not go forward without immediate speculation against the dollar before the plan goes into effect.

Conclusions

It remains only to point out that, even in the absence of a high degree of international cooperativeness, a system of fixed exchange rates can be made to work. It can be made to work mainly because it imposes a discipline upon all participants, and because within this discipline there is nevertheless some room for adjustment. The principal sources of flexibility are productivity gains and the degree to which they are absorbed by wage increases. Wages cannot be expected to decline. But their rise can be slowed in relation to the rate of productivity growth, in which case prices would become more competitive relative to other countries. With annual productivity gains of 2 to 3 percent in the United States and more abroad, it would not take many years to remove a temporary imbalance.

International Monetary Reform

Reading 56

Convertibility of the dollar into gold was suspended by President Nixon in 1971. The 1971 Smithsonian parity rearrangement had broken down by February 1973, and the dollar had to be devalued by another 10 per cent. Many of the principal currencies of the world are floating.

The Nixon Team worked out the following proposals for long-run international reform. Although many of these programs for greater flexibility of currency parities were stubbornly resisted by France, increasingly economists all over the world have been moving in these directions. (You might look back to Reading 35 on the fluctuations in the price of free gold, in connection with this item; and also to the Friedman-Wallich debate on fixed exchange rates.)

Questions to guide the reading

Why should reform preserve freedom of trade? Why are adjustments in exchange rates needed, and why should they be made early and frequently? Do you see an analogy between the United States proposal that exchange rate parities be adjusted whenever a country's reserves fall below some specified ratio and the customary practice within a country of requiring banks to achieve certain reserve ratios in their process of creating demand-deposit money?

Why is it important for symmetry of adjustment as between surplus and deficit countries? Do you agree with the ultimate phasing out of gold from the international monetary system?

Reforming the International Economic System: The Nixon Proposals

Economic Report of the President, 1973

Changes are required in monetary arrangements, in trading arrangements and in procedures for dealing with policies usually considered to be "domestic" but having a significant impact on international transactions. The United States has strongly emphasized not only that reform is needed in all

Abridged from *The Economic Report of the President,* United States Government Printing Office, Washington, D.C., 1973.

these areas but also that the reforms in all must be considered as part of a single package, since policies adopted in one field may complement or conflict with policies in the others. However, thinking is now farthest advanced with respect to monetary reform.

The international monetary system

The suspension of the convertibility of the dollar into gold on August 15, 1971, gave public recognition to the fact that the postwar international monetary arrangements, known as the Bretton Woods system, had become untenable. Interim arrangements, including the negotiation of a multilateral realignment of exchange rates at the Smithsonian Institution in December 1971 [and the February 1973 10 per cent devaluation of the dollar by Nixon] have been developed, but they do not provide a long-term solution to the problems which made changes in the rules of the Bretton Woods system inevitable. They do not constitute an adequate system of rules for the international monetary system in the long run.

Requirements. A stable international monetary system must meet several major requirements if it is to serve as the basis for the continued expansion of world trade and investment. First, it should be *market-oriented.* For the sake of both efficiency and equity, the mechanism for balancing each country's total foreign exchange receipts and payments over the long run should function in such a way as to minimize interference with individual market transactions.

Second, the settlement of payments balances among countries should be *multilateral,* so that every country can offset its deficits with some countries by means of surpluses with others. To fulfill this condition, the system must provide [for some kind of "convertibility"] for the ultimate settlement of claims in terms of commonly accepted reserve assets. Such a generalized payments system makes possible a far higher level of international trade and investment transactions than would be feasible if each country had to balance its payments bilaterally with every other country in a network of barter relationships.

Third, the system should be *stable.* International commerce frequently entails long-run commitments and hence requires stable expectations about conditions affecting the future profitability of international transactions.

Functioning. In order to meet these requirements the international monetary system must fulfill certain specific functions. It must provide an effective and equitable mechanism for *adjustment* of payments imbalances among countries, so that external payments imbalances are not allowed to persist and accumulate. It must also provide international monetary reserves in adequate amounts and in forms acceptable to the participants in the system, i.e., international *liquidity* has to be adequate. If the system permits the creation of too much international money, international inflationary pressures will be created; if too little international money is created, deflationary pressure or pressures for restrictions on international transactions will result. Finally, the system must operate in such a way as to create and maintain *confidence* in its continued viability and in the value of the international reserve assets associated with it.

Characteristics of the Bretton Woods system

The Articles of Agreement which established the International Monetary Fund (IMF) in the immediate postwar period reflected a heavy emphasis on the need for stability and confidence in the international monetary system.

Under the Articles of Agreement, governments were obligated to support their exchange rates at agreed parity levels in either of two ways—by buying or selling their own currency in the foreign exchange market whenever the rate rose 1 percent above or fell 1 percent below parity, or by making their currency convertible into gold or other reserve assets at the request of a foreign official institution. In practice, all countries but the United States have supported their currencies by buying or selling them for dollars, while the United States has maintained the convertibility of dollars into gold or other reserve assets tied to gold.

Rigidity. The rules permitted changes in a country's parity when its balance of payments was in fundamental disequilibrium. In practice the parities were changed only infrequently, generally after a prolonged period of disequilibrium in external payments.

There was also a widespread belief that, because

of the importance of the United States in world trade and the central role of the dollar in the international monetary system, the United States could not change its exchange rate. In any case, since most other countries were pegging their rates to the dollar in the foreign exchange market, the United States could not be certain that a change in the price of gold would actually result in a change in the value of the dollar in terms of foreign currencies.

The Articles of Agreement did not address themselves explicitly to the question of liquidity. The expectation was that, as in the past, newly mined gold would provide the major source of new official reserves. It was also implicitly assumed that countries would hold certain currencies as additional reserves. There were no arrangements, however, for reviewing or influencing the growth of liquidity. The growth of reserves was thus dependent on the vagaries of gold markets and on deficits in the balance of payments of reserve currency countries. In practice, the U.S. deficits provided the bulk of new reserves for the rest of the world.

Paper gold.   The inadequacies of the system with respect to the process of liquidity creation led to an important step forward with the recent creation of Special Drawing Rights (SDR's), an internationally created obligation of the International Monetary Fund. With the establishment of SDR's, the system no longer had to rely on a persistent deficit in the U.S. balance of payments for the creation of new reserves. The creation of SDR's could not in itself restore equilibrium to international payments, however, since provisions for the adjustment of payments imbalances remained inadequate.

Postponed adjustments.   The Articles of Agreement were not very explicit about the circumstances under which countries should take action to remove balance-of-payments deficits or surpluses. The assumption was that deficit countries would sooner or later run out of reserves or borrowing facilities and therefore would have to adjust. However, surplus countries could postpone adjustment as long as they were willing to accumulate reserves. Since the major deficit country, the United States, could not adjust its exchange

rate without endangering the operation of the system, and since most of the surplus countries were persistently reluctant to change their own rates, the disequilibrium in world payments increased through the latter half of the 1960's until it reached a breaking point in mid-1971.

At that time, the disequilibrium became so large that speculative pressures caused billions of dollars to be exchanged for foreign currencies within a few days. These currency movements greatly increased U.S. liabilities to foreign offical institutions and further reduced the stock of U.S. reserve assets. This brought to a head a problem which had been developing for some time: how to maintain convertibility as the stock of dollars held by foreign official institutions grew and the United States' own stock of reserve assets, mainly gold, shrank.

On August 15, the President announced a suspension of the convertibility of the dollar into gold or SDR's. This action withdrew U.S. support from the old exchange rates between the dollar and other foreign currencies, and in effect put the dollar on a floating basis. Subsequently, a new set of exchange rates was agreed upon at the Smithsonian Institution, and as part of that realignment the United States agreed to increase the U.S. official price of gold from $35 to $38 an ounce. This 8.5-percent increase in the price of gold was signed into law on March 31, 1972. The United States has not resumed the convertibility of the dollar, but has said that it will undertake appropriate convertibility obligations in the context of a suitably reformed international monetary system, provided that the U.S. balance-of-payments and reserve positions improve sufficiently to make such an undertaking viable.

United States ideas on international monetary reform

The member countries of the International Monetary Fund agreed to create a committee to conduct negotiations on reform. This committee, the Committee of Twenty, is patterned after the representational system used in the Executive Board of the International Monetary Fund.

In order to help get the negotiation process underway, the United States has advanced some general proposals on reform. The U.S. approach is evolutionary, seeking to build on existing principles and practices where they have proved useful and have met with international approval. At the same time, it proposes certain important changes to ensure the viability of the new system.

The primary emphasis is on the creation of an effective and evenhanded mechanism for the adjustment of payments imbalances that would place all countries, surplus and deficit alike, under agreed and broadly symmetrical rules and responsibilities for taking action to restore equilibrium.

Reserve levels as triggers for changes in exchange rates. In the U.S. view, the most promising approach is a system in which disproportionate changes in a nation's reserves in either direction indicate the need for measures to eliminate the payments imbalance. Within such a system of symmetrical adjustment discipline, the U.S. approach would allow considerable diversity in the choice of instruments for bringing about adjustment. One way to widen the choice of adjustment tools would be to allow increased flexibility of exchange rates.

With respect to international liquidity, the U.S. proposal envisages an increase in the importance of the SDR and the elimination of various encumbrances which reduce its usefulness as a reserve asset. At the same time, the U.S. proposal contemplates a gradual diminution of the role played by gold in the international monetary system. Holdings of foreign currency reserves would be neither banned nor encouraged, but it is expected that they would become a smaller proportion of total international reserve assets than they are today.

Reserves as objective indicators for adjustment

The U.S. [proposes] that disproportionate changes in reserves in either direction be used as the primary indicator of the need for balance-of-payments adjustment. In summary, the proposal is that certain points should be established above and below each country's "base," or "normal" level of reserves, and that movements in reserves beyond these points would signal the need for balance-of-payments adjustment.

Symmetry on surplus as well as deficit countries. The U.S. proposal is based on the recognition that countries experiencing a persistent deterioration in

their reserve positions have always had to devalue their currencies or to take other adjustment measures. The U.S. proposal would make this discipline symmetrical for both deficit and surplus countries by providing that a disproportionate gain in reserves would indicate the need for adjustment actions by (1) surplus countries to the same extent that disproportionate reserve losses now impose pressure on (2) deficit countries to adjust.

Symmetry in the adjustment process, as provided for in the U.S. proposal, is desirable for several reasons. Adjustment policies frequently entail political costs. And it may sometimes involve economic costs of adjustment as well. Thus, a balanced distribution of the responsibility for initiating adjustment is in part a question of equity.

Such symmetry also makes the process of international adjustment more efficient. If countries on both the deficit and the surplus sides of a payments imbalance follow active policies for the restoration of equilibrium the process is likely to be easier than if the deficit countries try to bring about adjustment by themselves.

A link between adjustment measures and reserve changes is essential if a generalized system of convertibility of national currencies into international reserve assets is to be sustainable. In the long run, convertibility can be maintained only if the adjustment mechanism prevents the development of large and persistent imbalances which would inevitably prevent a deficit country from providing conversion of its own currency into primary reserve assets.

Reserve indicators have several other advantages as compared to other conceivable adjustment guides. They are comprehensive, quickly available, and relatively unambiguous. Furthermore, they do not discriminate between one set of transactions and another. They leave the relation between specific types of transactions to market forces, focusing only on the overall level of the balance of payments. In a system based on the market principle, it would be inappropriate to base judgments about the need for adjustment solely on trade, or the current account, or the capital account.

Adoption of reserve criteria as a primary indicator of the need for adjustment does not imply automaticity. The system would operate in the context of a multilateral review procedure.

Short-term capital movements may present a problem in managing any system of adjustment, including one based on reserve indicators. Large movements of such funds in response to differences in interest rates, or the expectation of future changes in exchange rates, could bring about large changes in reserves. This could signal the need for adjustment actions even though they might not otherwise be thought appropriate. It should be possible, however, to identify such cases in the multilateral review and to override the signal by international agreement.

Greater flexibility in the exchange rate

An important feature of the U.S. proposals is that they would make exchange rate changes a more useful internationally acceptable instrument of adjustment. The U.S. suggestions regarding the exchange rate mechanism assume that most countries will generally choose to continue their practice of maintaining established values for their currencies. At the same time, the United States recognizes that the difficulties caused by prolonged maintenance of inappropriate exchange rates can be avoided only if countries adjust their parities more promptly than was usual in the past.

The U.S. proposal recognizes the current evolution of more flexible techniques of exchange rate management. For example, despite the fact that floating a currency—suspending the maintenance of its value by exchange market intervention—is technically a violation of the Bretton Woods Agreement, a number of important countries have done so. Such floats may be either transitional, as a way of utilizing market signals in determining a new rate, or indefinite in their duration. The Canadians have floated during long intervals for more than two decades, the Germans have floated twice in recent years, and the British have been floating since mid-1972. [In 1973, the Swiss, Italians, and Japanese joined in the floating of currencies.] The U.S. proposal would permit either transitional or indefinite periods of floating, but it would impose standards on countries adopting floating regimes to guard against their use as instruments for competitive devaluation.

Widened bands for all. The United States also proposes that countries which maintain parity ex-

change rates adopt wider margins within which the market exchange rate is allowed to fluctuate. The Smithsonian Agreement temporarily increased the permissible margins from 1 percent on either side of dollar parity to $2\frac{1}{4}$ percent above or below dollar parity, implying a maximum spread of $4\frac{1}{2}$ percent between any two nondollar currencies. A number of countries have adopted these wider margins. The United States favors the permanent adoption of margins for all currencies, including the dollar, that are in the same range as those permitted for nondollar currencies under the Smithsonian Agreement.

A larger zone within which fluctuation can take place without government intervention implies more opportunity for the operation of market forces and can facilitate small changes in parities. Wider margins can also lessen the incentives for short-term capital flows in response to interest rate differentials by increasing the scope for forward premiums or discounts in the exchange markets, thus neutralizing such differentials.

Other techniques of adjustment. Under the U.S. proposal a variety of mechanisms for restoring payments balance would be available, among them changes in monetary and fiscal policy. Furthermore, in keeping with the goal of the international monetary system to encourage a freer flow of resources, surplus countries would be encouraged to remove barriers to imports and capital outflows, while deficit countries would be encouraged to remove barriers to exports and capital inflows.

The U.S. proposal would in extreme circumstances permit the imposition of direct restraints for balance-of-payments purposes. Their use, however, would be appropriately circumscribed to ensure that controls remained temporary and caused the least possible distortion in the pattern of trade and investment. Controls or surcharges on some transactions and not on others distort economic relationships, and for that reason broad adjustment measures are generally preferable. And where selective measures are used, price-based barriers such as taxes or surcharges are generally preferable to quantitative barriers such as quotas. Taxes on some transactions and not on others change relative prices, but they do not insulate such transactions from market pressures, as quotas do. This view contrasts with the present rules of the General Agreement on Tariffs and Trade (GATT), which specifically authorize quantitative restrictions but not surcharges for balance-of-payments purposes.

Getting rid of capital controls.

The U.S. proposal furthermore reflects the view that controls on capital transactions for balance-of-payments purposes should not be encouraged and certainly should not be required in lieu of other measures of adjustment, nor should they become the means of maintaining an undervalued or overvalued exchange rate.

This position is based on a belief that restrictions have a distorting influence whether they are focused on trade in commodities, in services, or in assets (the capital account), and that this parallelism should be recognized in the rules governing the reformed international monetary system. In contrast, the provisions of the earlier system made a sharp distinction between controls on trade and other current transactions and controls on capital transactions.

International liquidity

The magnitude, composition, and distribution of world liquidity have undergone substantial changes in recent years. From the end of 1969 to the end of October 1972, gross international official reserves increased almost 100 percent. Part of this increase was in newly created Special Drawing Rights, but most of it was in dollars. Gold and reserve positions in the International Monetary Fund remained at approximately the same level as in 1969. As a result, a significant change occurred in the proportional composition of international reserves. Gold dropped from 50 percent to 26 percent, reserve positions in the IMF dropped from 9 percent to 4 percent, foreign exchange rose from 41 percent to 64 percent, and SDR's, which did not exist in 1969, provided 6 percent of world reserves.

For the future, the United States supports movement toward increasing reliance on the SDR as the primary source of world reserve growth and toward progressive reduction in the role of gold as a reserve asset. The U.S. proposal also assumes that currencies will play a much smaller role in reserve holdings in the future than they do today.

Phasing out gold.

The United States believes that the role of gold in the international monetary system should continue to diminish, and would support orderly procedures to facilitate that process. A declining role for gold is fully consistent with the long-term trend of monetary history. Governments long ago recognized the inadequacy of gold as a basis for national monetary systems, and in recent decades the dependence of the international economy on that metal has diminished sharply. With the physical supply of gold limited; with its commodity uses competing inevitably and increasingly with its monetary uses; and with residual noncommercial availability in no way related to the liquidity needs of a prosperous and expanding international economy, the world has naturally developed supplements and substitutes.

The current situation—where speculative pressures on a thin and volatile commodity market have led to a [free gold] price much higher than the official gold price—is evidence of the instabilities and tensions inherent in a system based on gold or other commodities.

The international trading system

A new round of multilateral trade negotiations within the framework of the GATT is scheduled to begin in the fall of 1973. The purpose of these negotiations will be both to expand the scope for international trade and to improve the institutional process for resolving international trade disputes. The world as a whole, including the United States, has benefited substantially from the expansion of trade made possible by previous multilateral reductions of trade barriers.

World trade expanded more than fivefold in the last 20 years, and this expansion has been accompanied by an equivalent expansion of world output. The average annual growth in the value of both world trade and economic output during this period was about 8 percent. While the expansion of trade was only one reason for these output gains, it was undoubtedly an important source of growth. Trade not only allows each country to produce what is best suited to its capabilities, it also provides competition which stimulates everyone to produce goods more cheaply and to improve their quality.

Although the United States is less dependent on trade than most other nations, the role of trade in the economy has grown. Over the last two decades, GNP in the United States has increased about three and one-half times, while trade has increased more than four times. Exports have become a more significant source of employment and income for those sectors in which the United States has a comparative advantage, particularly agriculture and high technology manufactures, while imports are becoming more important as the source both of the raw materials and fuels used by U.S. industry and of consumer goods whose production requires much use of relatively unskilled labor.

Aims of trade negotiations

The trade negotiations look to the longer term. Their goal is to remove the sources of difficulties that have arisen under present trading arrangements and to provide for the expansion of trade on the basis of mutual advantage and mutual commitment with reciprocity. However, results from the negotiations in the form of concrete changes affecting the world trading system are likely to be gradual and will not begin to take effect for several years.

In approaching these negotiations the United States seeks, as it has since the end of World War II, a more open and equitable world trading system. A freer movement of goods, services, and capital throughout the world in response to market forces is in the U.S. interest for several reasons. To the extent that trade is undistorted by artificial barriers, our producers can sell what they make best and our consumers will reap the benefits of efficient production and competition on a worldwide basis. These benefits to the United States will not conflict with the interests of other countries. All countries can expect gains from expanded world trade on a nondiscriminatory basis.

A world trading system that minimizes trade distortions is also one of the important prerequisites for a smoothly functioning international monetary system. The more barriers that countries erect to the flow of goods, services, and capital, the more the adjustment of payments imbalances is focused on the narrower range of economic activity which remains free to respond to market forces. The result is to place heavy and uneven burdens of adjustment on particular sectors, often forcing countries to choose between accepting severe economic dislocations and postponing overall adjustment.

Freeing agriculture too. In view of the increasing importance of nontariff barriers as tariff barriers are reduced, it is crucial that the movement toward a more open trading system be comprehensive, encompassing all forms of barriers to trade. Among the major types that distort trade are quantitative import restrictions [i.e., quotas], export subsidies, restrictive government procurement policies, and discriminatory design and performance standards.

Further steps toward trade liberalization should also be comprehensive in the sense that they encompass all economic sectors. From the point of view of the United States, it is particularly important that such negotiations include agricultural as well as industrial trade. Abundant natural resources and advanced farm management and technology give this country a comparative advantage which makes our farm products highly competitive in world markets.

Industrialized and developing economies. One of the important objectives of reform is to create a more stable and mutually beneficial framework for economic relations between developed and developing countries. Both groups of countries can benefit from reducing the degree of arbitrariness in national decisions affecting international trade, investment, and aid.

Trade with socialist countries. Trade between market and centrally planned economies can be advantageous for both sides, and with a relaxation of political tensions this trade can be expected to grow significantly. In the past the United States has engaged in less trade with the centrally planned economies than has western Europe. Recently, however, the United States has taken a number of steps to expand its trade with these countries; among such moves have been the signing of trade agreements with the Soviet Union and Poland and the elimination of the embargo on bilateral trade with the People's Republic of China.

Finale

In advancing proposals for reform, the United States has kept in mind the necessity of building on commonly accepted principles. Foremost among these principles is the belief that an open exchange of goods, services, and capital based on market relationships can benefit all countries. Moreover, if all countries are to remain committed to freer trade and investment, the international rules must give everyone a chance to share in the benefits.

Recent experience has shown the need for cer-tain reforms in current rules and practices. The rules should more explicitly define international standards of conduct and yet provide greater flexibility in the means of discharging these international responsibilities. Lastly, any stable and well-functioning international economic system must rest upon sound domestic policies to promote domestic growth and price stability in the major countries.

6

CURRENT ECONOMIC PROBLEMS

Stages of Growth

Readings 57 and 58

To controvert the nineteenth-century Marxian theory of capitalist development, Walt Whitman Rostow presented a five-stage theory of economic growth and development. The "take-off" stage, in which an economy finally moves into accelerated growth and abundance, has captured the public imagination of the readers of this "non-Communist Manifesto."

Every brilliant construction of the imagination must, in a social science like economics, be subjected to the cold confrontation with the statistical facts of historical experience. In the second of these readings, a master economic historian and statistician carefully audits the Rostow thesis.

W. W. Rostow, Yale graduate and Rhodes Scholar, has been a professor at Oxford, Cambridge, and M.I.T. An early adviser to President Kennedy, Dr. Rostow has been a major planner in the State Department and White House, and is now a professor at the University of Texas. Simon Kuznets is a professor emeritus at Harvard, having earlier been at Johns Hopkins, the University of Pennsylvania, and the National Bureau of Economic Research. Aside from his seminal works in quantitative economic history and development, Kuznets pioneered the statistical measurement of national income for the United States. He was awarded the Nobel Prize in Economics in 1971.

Questions to guide the reading

How many hairs does it take to make a beard? By what test can one decide whether there was or was not an industrial revolution in England during the eighteenth century or at any other time? Is it a useful approximation to divide the history of a country into five—or more, or less—distinct stages?

If a dramatic device, such as the take-off, is only approximately valid, might it still be a useful analytical device? Under what conditions could it do more harm than good?

Reading 57

Stages of Growth and the Take-off: Yes

W. W. Rostow

Traditional society

A traditional society is one whose structure is developed within limited production functions, based on pre-Newtonian science and technology, and on pre-Newtonian attitudes towards the physical world. Newton is here used as a symbol for that watershed in history when men came widely to believe that the external world was subject to a

From W. W. Rostow, *The Stages of Economic Growth,* abridged (Cambridge University Press, New York, 1960). Reprinted with kind permission of the author and publisher.

few knowable laws, and was systematically capable to productive manipulation.

The conception of the traditional society is, however, in no sense static; and it would not exclude increases in output. But the central fact about the traditional society was that a ceiling existed on the level of attainable output per head. This ceiling resulted from the fact that the potentialities which flow from modern science and technology were either not available or not regularly and systematically applied.

In terms of history then, with the phrase "traditional society" we are grouping the whole pre-Newtonian world: the dynasties in China; the civilization of the Middle East and the Mediterranean; the world of medieval Europe. And to them we add the post-Newtonian societies which, for a time, remained untouched or unmoved by man's new capability for regularly manipulating his environment to his economic advantage.

To place these infinitely various, changing societies in a single category, on the ground that they all shared a ceiling on the productivity of their economic techniques, is to say very little indeed. But we are, after all, merely clearing the way in order to get at the subject; that is, the post-traditional societies, in which each of the major characteristics of the traditional society was altered in such ways as to permit regular growth: its politics, social structure, and (to a degree) its values, as well as its economy.

Period of transition

The second stage of growth embraces societies in the process of transition; that is, the period when the preconditions for take-off are developed; for it takes time to transform a traditional society in the ways necessary for it to exploit the fruits of modern science, to fend off diminishing returns, and thus to enjoy the blessings and choices opened up by the march of compound interest.

The preconditions for take-off were initially developed, in a clearly marked way, in Western Europe of the late seventeenth and early eighteenth centuries as the insights of modern science began to be translated into new production functions in both agriculture and industry, in a setting given dynamism by the lateral expansion of world markets and the international competition for them.

But all that lies behind the break-up of the Middle Ages is relevant to the creation of the preconditions for take-off in Western Europe. Among the Western European states, Britain, favored by geography, natural resources, trading possibilities, social and political structure, was the first to develop fully the preconditions for take-off.

The more general case in modern history, however, saw the stage of preconditions arise not endogenously but from some external intrusion by more advanced societies. These invasions—literal or figurative—shocked the traditional society and began or hastened its undoing.

The idea spreads not merely that economic progress is possible, but that economic progress is a necessary condition for some other purpose, judged to be good. Education, for some at least, broadens and changes to suit the needs of modern economic activity. New types of enterprising men come forward—in the private economy, in government, or both—willing to mobilize savings and to take risks in pursuit of profit or modernization. Banks and other institutions for mobilizing capital appear. Investment increases, notably in transport, communications, and in raw materials in which other nations may have an economic interest. The scope of commerce, internal and external, widens. But all this activity proceeds at a limited pace within an economy and a society still mainly characterized by traditional low-productivity methods, by the old social structure and values, and by the regionally based political institutions that developed in conjunction with them.

In many recent cases, for example, the traditional society persisted side by side with modern economic activities, conducted for limited economic purposes by a colonial or quasi-colonial power.

The transition we are examining has, evidently, many dimensions. A society predominantly agricultural—with, in fact, usually 75 per cent or more of its working force in agriculture—must shift to a predominance for industry, communications, trade and services.

A society whose economic, social and political arrangements are built around the life of relatively small—mainly self-sufficient—regions must orient its commerce and its thought to the nation and to a still larger international setting.

The view towards the having of children—ini-

Table 1   Some Tentative, Approximate Take-off Dates

Country	Take-off	Country	Take-off
Great Britain	1783–1802	Russia	1890–1914
France	1830–60	Canada	1896–1914
Belgium	1833–60	Argentina	1935–
United States	1843–60	Turkey	1937–
Germany	1850–73	India	1952–
Sweden	1868–90	China	1952–
Japan	1878–1900		

tially the residual blessing and affirmation of immortality in a hard life, of relatively fixed horizons—must change in ways which ultimately yield a decline in the birth-rate, as the possibility of progress and the decline in the need for unskilled farm labor create a new calculus.

The income above minimum levels of consumption, largely concentrated in the hands of those who own land, must be shifted into the hands of those who will spend it on roads and railroads, schools and factories rather than on country houses and servants, personal ornaments and temples.

Men must come to be valued in the society not for their connection with clan or class, or, even, their guild; but for their individual ability to perform certain specific, increasingly specialized functions.

And, above all, the concept must be spread that man need not regard his physical environment as virtually a factor given by nature and providence, but as an ordered world which, if rationally understood, can be manipulated in ways which yield productive change and, in one dimension at least, progress.

All of this—and more—is involved in the passage of a traditional to a modern growing society.

The take-off

The beginning of take-off can usually be traced to a particular sharp stimulus. The stimulus may take the form of a political revolution which affects directly the balance of social power and effective values, the character of economic institutions, the distribution of income, the pattern of investment outlays and the proportion of potential innovations actually applied. Such was the case, for example, with the German revolution of 1848, the Meiji restoration in Japan of 1868, and the more recent achievement of Indian independence and the Communist victory in China. It may come about through a technological (including transport) innovation, which sets in motion a chain of secondary expansion in modern sectors and has powerful external economy effects which the society exploits. It may take the form of a newly favourable international environment, such as the opening of British and French markets to Swedish timber in the 1860's or a sharp relative rise in export prices and/or large new capital imports, as in the case of the United States from the late 1840's, Canada and Russia from the mid-1890's; but it may also come as a challenge posed by an unfavourable shift in the international environment, such as a sharp fall in the terms of trade (or a wartime blockage of foreign trade) requiring the rapid development of manufactured import substitutes, as with the Argentine and Australia from 1930 to 1945.

What is essential here is not the form of stimulus but the fact that the prior development of the society and its economy result in a positive, sustained, and self-reinforcing response to it: the result is not a once-over change in production functions or in the volume of investment, but a higher proportion of potential innovations accepted in a more or less regular flow, and a higher rate of investment.

As indicated in the accompanying table, we believe it possible to identify at least tentatively such take-off periods for a number of countries which have passed into the stage of growth.

For the present purposes the take-off is defined as requiring all three of the following related conditions:

1. a rise in the rate of productive investment from, say, 5% or less to over 10% of national income (or net national product [NNP]);

2. the development of one or more substantial manufacturing sectors, with a high rate of growth;

3. the existence or quick emergence of a political, social and institutional framework which exploits the impulses to expansion in the modern sector and the potential external economy effects of the take-off and gives to growth an on-going character.

The third condition implies a considerable capability to mobilize capital from domestic sources. Some take-offs have occurred with virtually no capital imports, for example, Britain and Japan. Some take-offs have had a high component of foreign capital, for example, the United States, Russia and Canada.

Whatever the role of capital imports, the preconditions for take-off include an initial ability to mobilize domestic savings productively, as well as a structure which subsequently permits a high marginal rate of savings.

This definition is designed to isolate the early stage when industrialization takes hold rather than the later stage when industrialization becomes a more massive and statistically more impressive phenomenon. In Britain, for example, there is no doubt that it was between 1815 and 1850 that industrialization fully took hold. If the criterion chosen for take-off was the period of most rapid overall industrial growth, or the period when large-scale industry matured, all our take-off dates would have to be set later; Britain, for example, 1819–48.

With a sense of the considerable violence done to economic history, we are here seeking to isolate a period when the scale of productive economic activity reaches a critical level and produces changes which lead to a massive and progressive structural transformation in economies and the societies of which they are a part, better viewed as changes in kind than merely in degree.

Causal process at work

Whatever the importance and virtue of viewing the take-off in aggregative terms—embracing national output, the proportion of output invested, and an aggregate marginal capital/output ratio—

that approach tells us relatively little of what actually happens and of the causal processes at work in a take-off; nor is the investment-rate criterion conclusive.

Perhaps the most important thing to be said about the behaviour of these variables in historical cases of take-off is that they have assumed many different forms. There is no single pattern.

The purpose of the following paragraphs is to suggest briefly, and by way of illustration only, certain elements of both uniformity and variety in the variables whose movement has determined the inner structure of the take-off.

By and large, the loanable funds required to finance the take-off have come from two types of source: from shifts in the control of income flows, including income-distribution changes and capital imports; and from the plough-back of profits in rapidly expanding particular sectors.

The shift of income flows into more productive hands has, of course, been aided historically not only by government fiscal measures but also by banks and capital markets. Virtually without exception, the take-off periods have been marked by the extension of banking institutions which expanded the supply of working capital; and in most cases also by an expansion in the range of long-range financing done by a central, formally organized, capital market.

Although these familiar capital-supply functions of the State and private institutions have been important to the take-off, it is likely to prove the case, on close examination, that a necessary condition for take-off was the existence of one or more rapidly growing sectors whose entrepreneurs (private or public) ploughed back into new capacity a very high proportion of profits. Put another way, the demand side of the investment process, rather than the supply of loanable funds, may be the decisive element in the take-off, as opposed to the period of creating the preconditions, or of sustaining growth once it is under way.

What can we say, in general, about the supply of financing during the take-off period? First, as a precondition, it appears necessary that the community's surplus above the mass-consumption level does not flow into the hands of those who will sterilize it by hoarding luxury consumption or low-productivity investment outlays. Second, as a precondition, it appears necessary that institutions be developed which provide cheap and adequate working capital. Third, as a necessary condition, it appears that one or more sectors of the community must grow rapidly, inducing a more general industrialization process; and that the entrepreneurs in such sectors plough back a substantial proportion of their profits in further productive investment, one possible and recurrent version of the plough-back process being the investment of proceeds from a rapidly growing export sector.

The devices, confiscatory and fiscal, for ensuring the first and second preconditions have been historically various. And the types of leading manufacturing sectors which have served to initiate the take-off have varied greatly. Finally, foreign capital flows have, in significant cases, proved extremely important to the take-off, notably when lumpy overhead capital construction of long gestation period was required; but take-offs have also occurred based almost wholly on domestic sources of finance.

Leading sectors

The overall rate of growth of an economy must be regarded in the first instance as the consequence of differing growth rates in particular sectors of the economy, such sectoral growth-rates being in part derived from certain overall demand factors (for example, population, consumers' income, tastes, etc.); in part, from the primary and secondary effects of changing supply factors, when these are effectively exploited.

On this view the sectors of an economy may be grouped in three categories:

1. Primary growth sectors, where possibilities for innovation or for the exploitation of newly profitable or hitherto unexplored resources yield a high growth-rate and set in motion expansionary forces elsewhere in the economy.

2. Supplementary growth sectors, where rapid advance occurs in direct response to—or as a requirement of—advance in the primary growth sectors; for example, coal, iron and engineering in relation to railroads. These sectors may have to be tracked many stages back into the economy.

3. Derived-growth sectors, where advance occurs in some fairly steady relation to the growth of total real income, population, industrial production or some other overall, modestly increasing variable. Food output in relation to population and housing in relation to family formation are classic derived relations of this order.

In the earlier stages of growth, primary and supplementary growth sectors derive their momentum essentially from the introduction and diffusion of changes in the cost—supply environment (in turn, of course, partially influenced by demand changes); while the derived-growth sectors are linked essentially to changes in demand (while subject also to continuing changes in production functions of a less dramatic character).

At any period of time it appears to be true even in a mature and growing economy that forward momentum is maintained as the result of rapid expansion in a limited number of primary sectors, whose expansion has significant external economy and other secondary effects. From this perspective the behaviour of sectors during the take-off is merely a special version of the growth process in general; or, put another way, growth proceeds by repeating endlessly, in different patterns, with different leading sectors, the experience of the take-off. Like the take-off, long-term growth requires that the society not only generate vast quantities of capital for depreciation and maintenance, for housing and for a balanced complement of utilities and other overheads, but also a sequence of highly productive primary sectors, growing rapidly, based on new production functions. Only thus has the aggregate marginal capital/output ratio been kept low.

Once again history is full of variety: a considerable array of sectors appears to have played this key role in the take-off process.

What can we say, then, in general about these leading sectors? Historically, they have ranged from cotton textiles, through heavy-industry complexes based on railroads and military end-products, to timber, pulp, dairy products and finally a wide variety of consumers' goods. There is, clearly, no one sectoral sequence for take-off, no single sector which constitutes the magic key. Four basic factors must be present:

1. There must be enlarged effective demand for the product or products of sectors which yield a foundation for a rapid rate of growth in output. Historically this has been brought about initially by the transfer of income from consumption or hoarding to productive investment; by capital im-

ports; by a sharp increase in the productivity of current investment inputs, yielding an increase in consumers' real income expended on domestic manufactures; or by a combination of these routes.

2. There must be an introduction into these sectors of new production functions as well as an expansion of capacity.

3. The society must be capable of generating capital initially required to detonate the take-off in these key sectors; and especially there must be a high rate of plough-back by the (private or state) entrepreneurs controlling capacity and technique in these sectors and in the supplementary growth sectors they stimulated to expand.

4. Finally, the leading sector or sectors must be such that their expansion and technical transformation induce a chain of requirements for increased capacity and the potentiality for new production functions in other sectors, to which the society, in fact, progressively responds.

Reading 58

Stages of Growth and the Take-off: No

Simon Kuznets

The very ease with which separate segments can be distinguished in the historical movement from non-modern to modern economic growth and within the long span of the latter should warn us that any sequence of stages, even if offered as a suggestive rather than a substantive scheme, must meet some minimum requirements—if it is to be taken seriously.

The following requirements are relevant:

(a) A given stage must display *empirically testable characteristics,* common to all or to an important group of units experiencing modern economic growth. This means the specification of modern economic growth; identification of the units that have manifested such growth; and establishment of empirically testable characteristics claimed to be common to those units at the given stage.

(b) The characteristics of a given stage must be *distinctive* in that, not necessarily singly but in combination, they are *unique* to that stage. Mere precedence (or succession) in time does not suffice: given the unidirectional character of growth (by definition), any period is necessarily characterized by larger economic magnitudes than earlier ones and by the structural shifts that accompany such larger magnitudes (particularly a rise in per capita income). Stages are presumably something more

than successive ordinates in the steadily climbing curve of growth. They are segments of that curve, with properties so distinct that separate study of each segment seems warranted.

(c) *The analytical relation to the preceding stage must be indicated.* This naturally involves more than saying that the preceding stage is one of preparation for the given. More meaningfully, we need identification (again in empirically testable terms) of the major processes in the preceding stage that complete it and, with the usual qualifications for exogenous factors, make the next (our given) stage highly probable. Optimally, this would permit us to diagnose the preceding stage *before* the given stage is upon us, and thus would impart predictive value to the whole sequence. But even short of this difficult aim, it means specifying the minimum that must happen in the preceding stage to allow the given stage to emerge.

(d) The analytical relation *to the succeeding stage* must be indicated. Here too a clear notion (again in empirically testable terms) must be given of the occurrences in the given stage that bring it to a close—aside from mere passage of time. Optimally, such knowledge would permit us to predict, *before* the given stage is finished, how long it still has to run. But even short of such precision, we

From Simon Kuznets, "Notes on the Take-off," paper presented at the International Economic Association's Conference at Konstanz in September, 1960, on "The Economics of Take-off into Sustained Growth." Reprinted with kind permission of the author and St. Martin's Press, Inc., The Macmillan Co. of Canada, Limited, and Macmillan & Co., Ltd., London.

should know the essentials that occur during a given stage to bring about its end and clear the ground for the next stage.

(e) These four requirements relate to the common and distinctive characteristics of a given stage, viewed as one in an analytical (and chronological) sequence that links successive stages. However, these common and distinctive characteristics may differ among important groups of units undergoing modern economic growth. Consequently, the fifth requirement is for a clear *indication of the universe for which generality of common and distinctive characteristics is claimed;* and for which the analytical relations of a given stage with the preceding and succeeding ones are being formulated.

Against the background of the requirements just stated, we may consider Professor Rostow's discussion of the common and distinctive characteristics of the take-off stage, and the relations between it and the contiguous stages.

Shortcomings

How distinctive are these characteristics? Do they occur in combination only in the take-off stage and not in any other stage—particularly the preceding transition or pre-conditions stage and the succeeding self-sustained growth or drive to maturity stage? Professor Rostow is not explicit on this point. Presumably the transition stage does not see a rise in the investment proportion from 5 to 10 per cent or more. Yet much of what Professor Rostow would attribute to the take-off has already occurred in the pre-conditions stage. Thus, the agricultural revolution assigned to the pre-conditions stage "must supply expanded food, expanded markets, and an expanded supply of loanable funds to the modern sector"; much of social overhead capital is already invested in transport and other outlays—in the pre-conditions stage; and, in general, "the essence of the transition can be described legitimately as a rise in the rate of investment to a level which regularly, substantially and perceptibly outstrips population growth." In short, one wonders whether the three specifically stated characteristics of take-off could not be found in the pre-conditions—unless explicit qualifications are attached, e.g., that the investment proportion in that earlier stage must stay

below 5 per cent; that the marked agricultural revolution does not immediately call for, and in fact is possible without, a contemporaneous rapid growth in some manufacturing sector; and that investment in overhead capital in transport, etc., is not necessarily accompanied by a rapid growth of one or more modern manufacturing sectors. Finally, one should note that [a] characteristic of the take-off mentions both the *existence* and the *quick emergence* of the political, social, and institutional framework favorable to exploiting "the impulses to expansion in the modern sector" as admissible alternatives.

The line of division between the take-off and the following stage of self-sustained growth or drive to maturity is also blurred. Presumably the latter stage is marked by the existence of the proper social and institutional framework—which also exists during the take-off. Presumably this later stage also witnesses the rapid growth of one or more modern manufacturing sectors. Indeed, the only characteristics that are distinctly appropriate to the take-off and not to the next stage are the rise in the rate of productive investment to over 10 per cent of national income or net national product; and the implicit rise in the rate of growth of total and per capita income. But are we to assume that both the rate of investment and the rate of growth of product (total and per capita) level off at the high values attained at the end of the take-off stage? And is it this leveling off, the cessation of the rise in the rate of investment and in the rate of growth, that terminates the take-off stage?

Indictment

Given this fuzziness in delimiting the take-off stage and in formulating its distinctive characteristics; given the distinctiveness only in the statistical level of the rate of productive investment (and the implicit rate of growth), there is no solid ground upon which to discuss Professor Rostow's view of the analytical relation between the take-off stage and the preceding and succeeding stages. At any rate, the brief comments that can be made within the scope of this paper will follow the review of the empirical evidence.

I do not know what "a political, social and institutional framework which exploits the impulses to expansion in the modern sector, etc." is; or how to identify such a framework except by hindsight and conjecture; or how to specify the empirical evidence that would have to be brought to bear to ascertain whether such a framework is in "existence or in quick emergence." It seems to me that the passage just cited defines these social phenomena as a complex that produces the effect Professor Rostow wishes to explain; and then he treats this definition as if it were a meaningful identification.

It is easier to define the characteristic that specifies "the development of one or more substantial manufacturing sectors with a high rate of growth" once "high" is explained. But a review of empirical evidence on this point holds little interest if I am correct in assuming that the major distinctive characteristic of the take-off is a marked rise in the rate of growth of per capita and hence of total income. If the rate of growth does accelerate, some sectors are bound to grow more rapidly than others, as has been demonstrated in Arthur F. Burns' and my own work on production trends—partly in response to the differential impact of technological opportunities (including raw material supplies), and partly in response to the different income elasticities of the demand for various goods. Under these conditions, one or more manufacturing sectors, and one or more sectors of agriculture, transportation, services, etc., are bound to show high rates of growth. The pertinent question is *why* manufacturing—rather than agriculture, transport, or any other rapidly growing industry—should be specified as the leading sector.

In considering this question, the two constitutive characteristics of a leading sector must be kept in mind. First, sector A leads, rather than follows, if it moves not in response to sectors B, C, D, etc., within the country, but under the impact of factors which, relative to the given national economy, may be considered autonomous. The point to be noted is that the autonomous nature of this characteristic, relative to the given national economy, rests upon the origin of the stimulus, not upon the scope of the response. The latter may depend largely upon many other factors besides the stimulus, factors that are part and parcel of a given economy and society.

This brings us to the second constitutive characteristic of a leading sector, the magnitude of its effects; or more specifically, the magnitude of its contribution to a country's economic growth. Sector A may be leading in the sense of responding to an autonomous stimulus, but unless its contribution to the country's economic growth is substantial, it does not "lead" the country's economic growth—no matter how high its own rate of growth. After all, a thousandfold rise in the production of plastic hula hoops over a decade does not make it a leading industry.

Leadership of sectors, or any other element in the acceleration of the rate of growth can be established only after careful analysis of the particular circumstances preceding and during the period of acceleration—country by country, and by the application of statistical, theoretical, and other tools to the historical evidence.

Negative verdicts

The failure of aggregative data to reveal the characteristics claimed by Professor Rostow as common to the take-off stage, at least in countries that did not experience the drastic and forced transformation associated with Communist revolutions, is disturbing. *It casts serious doubt on the validity of the definition of the take-off as a generally occurring stage of modern economic growth, distinct from what Professor Rostow calls the "pre-conditions" or "transition" stage preceding it and the "self-sustained" growth stage following it.*

The evidence used to test Professor Rostow's scheme is not conclusive. Some non-Communist countries for which we have no data may have experienced a period of growth conforming with Professor Rostow's take-off stage. Also, his scheme may fit the Communist "take-offs," but my knowledge of them is inadequate for checking. *All that is claimed here is that aggregative data for a number of countries do not support Professor Rostow's distinction and characterization of the take-off stage.* On the other hand, the fact that the evidence is confined to aggregative data does not limit their bearing. Economic growth is an aggregative process; sectoral changes are interrelated with aggregative changes, and can be properly weighted only after they have been incorporated into the aggregative framework; and the absence of required aggregative changes severely limits the likelihood of the implicit strategic sectoral changes.

My disagreement with Professor Rostow is *not* on the value and legitimacy of an attempt to suggest some pattern of order in the modern economic growth experience of different countries. On the contrary, I fully share what I take to be his view on the need to go beyond qualitative and quantitative description to the use of the evidence for a large number of countries and long periods, in combination with analytical tools and imaginative hypotheses, to suggest and explain not only some common patterns but also, I would add, the major deviations from them. However, for reasons clearly indicated above, I disagree with the sequence of stages he suggests.

Urban and Minority Problems

Reading 59

The nonwhite population, which is more than 10 per cent of the total number of people in the U.S., gets much less than 10 per cent of the total income. Unemployment of blacks, particularly of black youths, is vastly greater than that of whites. Education and skills are less and wage rates are lower.

What can be done to improve this inequitable and inefficient situation? James Tobin, a realistic liberal and economists' expert, presents a definitive survey.

Questions to guide the reading

Confronted with the facts about inequality of education, training, and opportunity for blacks, can you maintain that economic positions reflect genetic inferiority?

Can some measures which aim to help blacks—such as minimum-wage rates—actually hurt him sometimes?

On Improving the Economic Status of the Black-American

James Tobin

I start from the presumption that the integration of Negroes into the American society and economy can be accomplished within existing political and economic institutions. I understand the impatience of those who think otherwise, but I see nothing incompatible between our peculiar mixture of private enterprise and government, on the one hand, and the liberation and integration of the Negro, on the other. Indeed the present position of the Negro is an aberration from the principles of our society, rather than a requirement of its functioning. Therefore, my suggestions are directed to the aim of mobilizing existing powers of government to bring Negroes into full participation in the main stream of American economic life.

The economic plight of individuals, Negroes and whites alike, can always be attributed to specific handicaps and circumstances: discrimination, immobility, lack of education and experience, ill health, weak motivation, poor neighborhood, large family size, burdensome family responsibilities. Such diagnoses suggest a host of specific rem-

From James Tobin, "On Improving the Economic Status of the Negro," *Daedalus,* Journal of the American Academy of Arts and Sciences, Fall, 1965. Reprinted with kind permission of the author and publisher.

edies, some in the domain of civil rights, others in the war on poverty. Important as these remedies are, there is a danger that the diagnoses are myopic. They explain why certain individuals rather than others suffer from the economic maladies of the time. They do not explain why the over-all incidence of the maladies varies dramatically from time to time—for example, why personal attributes which seemed to doom a man to unemployment in 1932 or even in 1954 or 1961 did not so handicap him in 1944 or 1951 or 1956.

Public health measures to improve the environment are often more productive in conquering diseases than a succession of individual treatments. Malaria was conquered by oiling and draining swamps, not by quinine. The analogy holds for economic maladies. Unless the global incidence of these misfortunes can be diminished, every individual problem successfully solved will be replaced by a similar problem somewhere else. That is why an economist is led to emphasize the importance of the over-all economic climate.

Over the decades, general economic progress has been the major factor in the gradual conquest of poverty. Recently some observers, J. K. Galbraith and Michael Harrington most eloquently, have contended that this process no longer operates. The economy may prosper and labor may become steadily more productive as in the past, but "the other America" will be stranded. Prosperity and progress have already eliminated almost all the easy cases of poverty, leaving a hard core beyond the reach of national economic trends. There may be something to the "backwash" thesis as far as whites are concerned. But it definitely does not apply to Negroes. Too many of them are poor. It cannot be true that half of a race of twenty million human beings are victims of specific disabilities which insulate them from the national economic climate. It cannot be true, and it is not. Locke Anderson has shown that the pace of Negro economic progress is peculiarly sensitive to general economic growth. He estimates that if nationwide per capita personal income is stationary, nonwhite median family income falls by .5 per cent per year, while if national per capita income grows 5 per cent, nonwhite income grows nearly 7.5 per cent.

National prosperity and economic growth are still powerful engines for improving the economic status of Negroes. They are not doing enough and they are not doing it fast enough. There is ample room for a focused attack on the specific sources of Negro poverty. But a favorable over-all economic climate is a necessary condition for the global success—as distinguished from success in individual cases—of specific efforts to remedy the handicaps associated with Negro poverty.

The importance of a tight labor market

But isn't the present over-all economic climate favorable? Isn't the economy enjoying an upswing of unprecedented length, setting new records almost every month in production, employment, profits, and income? Yes, but expansion and new records should be routine in an economy with growing population, capital equipment, and productivity. The fact is that the economy has not operated with reasonably full utilization of its manpower and plant capacity since 1957.

The most important dimension of the over-all economic climate is the tightness of the labor market. In a tight labor market unemployment is low and short in duration, and job vacancies are plentiful. People who stand at the end of the hiring line and the top of the layoff list have the most to gain from a tight labor market. It is not surprising that the position of Negroes relative to that of whites improves in a tight labor market and declines in a slack market. Unemployment itself is only one way in which a slack labor market hurts Negroes and other disadvantaged groups, and the gains from reduction in unemployment are by no means confined to the employment of persons counted as unemployed. A tight labor market means not just jobs, but better jobs, longer hours, higher wages. A tight labor market will not only employ more Negroes; it will also give more of those who are employed full-time jobs. In both respects, it will reduce disparities between whites and Negroes.

Labor-force participation. In a tight market, of which a low unemployment rate is a barometer, the labor force itself is larger. Job opportunities draw into the labor force individuals who, simply because the prospects were dim, did not previously regard themselves as seeking work and were therefore not enumerated as unemployed. For the economy as a whole, it appears that an expansion of job opportunities enough to reduce unemployment by one worker will bring another worker into the labor force.

This phenomenon is important for many Negro families. Statistically, their poverty now appears to be due more often to the lack of a breadwinner in the labor force than to unemployment. But in a tight labor market many members of these families, including families now on public assistance, would be drawn into employment. Labor-force participation rates are roughly 2 per cent lower for nonwhite men than for white men, and the disparity increases in years of slack labor markets. The story is different for women. Negro women have always been in the labor force to a much greater extent than white women. A real improvement in the economic status of Negro men and in the stability of Negro families would probably lead to a reduction in labor-force participation by Negro women. But for teenagers, participation rates for Negroes are not so high as for whites; and for women twenty to twenty-four they are about the same. These relatively low rates are undoubtedly due less to voluntary choice than to the same lack of job opportunities that produces phenomenally high unemployment rates for young Negro women.

Duration of unemployment.   In a tight labor market, such unemployment as does exist is likely to be of short duration. Short-term unemployment is less damaging to the economic welfare of the unemployed. More will have earned and fewer will have exhausted private and public unemployment benefits. In 1953 when the over-all unemployment rate was 2.9 per cent, only 4 per cent of the unemployed were out of work for longer than twenty-six weeks and only 11 per cent for longer than fifteen weeks. In contrast, the unemployment rate in 1961 was 6.7 per cent; and of the unemployed in that year, 17 per cent were out of work for longer than twenty-six weeks and 32 per cent for longer than fifteen weeks. Between the first quarter of 1964 and the first quarter of 1965, over-all unemployment fell 11 per cent, while unemployment extending beyond half a year was lowered by 22 per cent.

Migration from agriculture.   A tight labor market draws the surplus rural population to higher pay-ing non-agricultural jobs. Southern Negroes are a large part of this surplus rural population. Migration is the only hope for improving their lot, or their children's. In spite of the vast migration of past decades, there are still about 775,000 Negroes, 11 per cent of the Negro labor force of the country, who depend on the land for their living and that of their families. Almost a half million live in the South, and almost all of them are poor.

Migration from agriculture and from the South is the Negroes' historic path toward economic improvement and equality. It is a smooth path for Negroes and for the urban communities to which they move only if there is a strong demand for labor in towns and cities North and South. In the 1940's the number of Negro farmers and farm laborers in the nation fell by 450,000 and one and a half million Negroes (net) left the South. This was the great decade of Negro economic advance. In the 1950's the same occupational and geographical migration continued undiminished. The movement to higher-income occupations and location should have raised the relative economic status of Negroes. But in the 1950's Negroes were moving into increasingly weak job markets. Too often disguised unemployment in the countryside was simply transformed into enumerated unemployment, and rural poverty into urban poverty.

Quality of jobs.   In a slack labor market, employers can pick and choose, both in recruiting and in promoting. They exaggerate the skill, education, and experience requirements of their jobs. They use diplomas, or color, or personal histories as convenient screening devices. In a tight market, they are forced to be realistic, to tailor job specifications to the available supply, and to give on-the-job training. They recruit and train applicants whom they would otherwise screen out, and they upgrade employees whom they would in slack times consign to low-wage, low-skill, and part-time jobs.

Wartime and other experience shows that job requirements are adjustable and that men and women are trainable. It is only in slack times that people worry about a mismatch between supposedly rigid occupational requirements and supposedly unchangeable qualifications of the labor force. As already noted, the relative status of the Negroes improves in a tight labor market not only in respect to unemployment, but also in respect to wages and occupations.

Cyclical fluctuation. Sustaining a high demand for labor is important. The in-and-out status of the Negro in the business cycle damages his long-term position because periodic unemployment robs him of experience and seniority.

Restrictive practices. A slack labor market probably accentuates the discriminatory and protectionist proclivities of certain crafts and unions. When jobs are scarce, opening the door to Negroes is a real threat. Of course prosperity will not automatically dissolve the barriers, but it will make it more difficult to oppose efforts to do so.

I conclude that the single most important step the nation could take to improve the economic position of the Negro is to operate the economy steadily at a low rate of unemployment. We cannot expect to restore the labor market conditions of the second world war, and we do not need to. In the years 1951–1953, unemployment was roughly 3 per cent, teenage unemployment around 7 per cent, Negro unemployment about 4.5 per cent, longterm unemployment negligible. In the years 1955–57, general unemployment was roughly 4 per cent, and the other measures correspondingly higher. [In the summer of 1966 unemployment finally dipped below 4 per cent. Ed.] But society and the Negro can benefit immensely from tightening the labor market still further, to 3.5 or 3 per cent unemployment.

Increasing the earning capacity of Negroes

Given the proper over-all economic climate, in particular a steadily tight labor market, the Negro's economic condition can be expected to improve, indeed to improve dramatically. But not fast enough. Not as fast as his aspirations or as the aspirations he has taught the rest of us to have for him. What else can be done? I shall confine myself to a few comments and suggestions that occur to a general economist.

Even in a tight labor market, the Negro's relative status will suffer both from current discrimination and from his lower earning capacity, the result of inferior acquired skill. In a real sense

both factors reflect discrimination, since the Negro's handicaps in earning capacity are the residue of decades of discrimination in education and employment. Nevertheless for both analysis and policy it is useful to distinguish the two.

Discrimination means that the Negro is denied access to certain markets where he might sell his labor, and to certain markets where he might purchase goods and services. Elementary application of "supply and demand" makes it clear that these restrictions are bound to result in his selling his labor for less and buying his livelihood for more than if these barriers did not exist. If Negro women can be clerks only in certain stores, these storekeepers will not need to pay them so much as they pay whites. If Negroes can live only in certain houses, the prices and rents they have to pay will be high for the quality of accommodation provided.

Successful elimination of discrimination is not only important in itself but will also have substantial economic benefits. Since residential segregation is the key to so much else and so difficult to eliminate by legal fiat alone, the power of the purse should be unstintingly used. I see no reason that the expenditure of funds for this purpose should be confined to new construction. Why not establish private or semi-public revolving funds to purchase, for resale or rental on a desegregated basis, strategically located existing structures as they become available?

The effects of past discrimination will take much longer to eradicate. The sins against the fathers are visited on the children. They are deprived of the intellectual and social capital which in our society is supposed to be transmitted in the family and the home. We have only begun to realize how difficult it is to make up for this deprivation by formal schooling, even when we try. And we have only begun to try, after accepting all too long the notion that schools should acquiesce in, even re-enforce, inequalities in home backgrounds rather than overcome them.

Upgrading the earning capacity of Negroes will be difficult, but the economic effects are easy to analyze. Economists have long held that the way to reduce disparities in earned incomes is to eliminate disparities in earning capacities. If college-trained people earn more money than those who left school after eight years, the remedy is to send a larger proportion of young people to college. If machine operators earn more than ditchdiggers, the remedy is to give more people the capacity and opportunity to be machine operators. These changes in relative supplies reduce the disparity both by competing down the pay in the favored line of work and by raising the pay in the less remunerative line. When there are only a few people left in the population whose capacities are confined to garbage-collecting, it will be a high-paid calling. The same is true of domestic service and all kinds of menial work.

This classical economic strategy will be hampered if discrimination, union barriers, and the like stand in the way. It will not help to increase the supply of Negro plumbers if the local unions and contractors will not let them join. But experience also shows that barriers give way more easily when the pressures of unsatisfied demand and supply pile up.

It should therefore be the task of educational and manpower policy to engineer over the next two decades a massive change in the relative supplies of people of different educational and professional attainments and degrees of skill and training. It must be a more rapid change than has occurred in the past two decades, because that has not been fast enough to alter income differentials. We should try particularly to increase supplies in those fields where salaries and wages are already high and rising. In this process we should be very skeptical of self-serving arguments and calculations—that an increase in supply in this or that profession would be bound to reduce quality, or that there are some mechanical relations of "need" to population or to Gross National Product that cannot be exceeded.

Such a policy would be appropriate to the "war on poverty" even if there were no racial problem. Indeed, our objective is to raise the earning capacities of low-income whites as well as of Negroes. But Negroes have the most to gain, and even those who because of age or irreversible environmental handicaps must inevitably be left behind will benefit by reduction in the number of whites and other Negroes who are competing with them.

Conclusion

By far the most powerful factor determining the economic status of Negroes is the over-all state of the U.S. economy. A vigorously expanding economy with a steadily tight labor market will rapidly raise the position of the Negro, both absolutely and relatively. Favored by such a climate, the host of specific measures to eliminate discrimination, improve education and training, provide housing, and strengthen the family can yield substantial additional results. In a less beneficent economic climate, where jobs are short rather than men, the wars against racial inequality and poverty will be uphill battles, and some highly touted weapons may turn out to be dangerously futile.

The forces of the market place, the incentives of private self-interest, the pressures of supply and demand—these can be powerful allies or stubborn opponents. Properly harnessed, they quietly and impersonally accomplish objectives which may elude detailed legislation and administration. To harness them to the cause of the American Negro is entirely possible. It requires simply that the federal government dedicate its fiscal and monetary policies more wholeheartedly and singlemindedly to achieving and maintaining genuinely full employment. The obstacles are not technical or economic. One obstacle is a general lack of understanding that unemployment and related evils are remediable by national fiscal and monetary measures. The other is the high priority now given to competing financial objectives.

In this area, as in others, the administration has disarmed its conservative opposition by meeting it halfway, and no influential political voices challenge the tacit compromise from the "Left." Negro rights movements have so far taken no interest in national fiscal and monetary policy. No doubt gold, the federal budget, and the actions of the Federal Reserve System seem remote from the day-to-day firing line of the movements. Direct local actions to redress specific grievances and to battle visible enemies are absorbing and dramatic. They have concrete observable results. But the use of national political influence on behalf of the goals of the Employment Act of 1946 is equally important. It would fill a political vacuum, and its potential long-run pay-off is very high.

Reading 60

Daniel Patrick Moynihan is one of the most colorful social scientists of our day. As assistant secretary of labor in the Kennedy administration, he wrote a controversial report which attributed much of the ills of the blacks to the absence of fathers in so many ghetto homes. Then he became director of the Joint Center for Urban Studies of M.I.T. and Harvard University, and was known as a strong advocate of children's allowances by the federal government. Although a liberal himself, Moynihan became increasingly critical of the social interpretations of liberals. The present trenchant essay may have been partially instrumental in making him acceptable to Nixon's Republican administration. In any case he took leave from Harvard to serve in the White House, and there he has been a strong and effective fighter for the cause of the negative income tax, in the modified form of Nixon's proposed family-allowance system. Dr. Moynihan, in 1973, became American Ambassador to India.

Questions to guide the reading

Are good intentions enough in the field of economics and the social sciences? How would you contrast the Newark and the Detroit situations? The government as employer of last resort does sound noble, but what might some of the problems be if hundreds of hard-core unemployed youths are brought together and made to go through the motions of pretending to do useful work when even they can see the purposelessness of what is being done? Aside from scolding liberals, has Moynihan really new and better suggestions to offer for what are undoubtedly difficult problems?

Race Riots and Poverty

Daniel P. Moynihan

The past is prologue

Nothing that we could say could add to the impressiveness of the lesson furnished by the events of the past year as to the needs and dangerous conditions of the neglected classes in our city. Those terrible days in July—the sudden appearance, as from the bosom of the earth, of a most infuriated and degraded mob; the helplessness of property owners and the better classes; the boom of cannon and rattle of musketry in our streets; the sky lurid with conflagrations; the inconceivable barbarity and ferocity of the crowd . . . the immense destruction of property were the first dreadful revelations to many of our people of the existence among us of a great, ignorant, irresponsible class, who were growing up without any permanent interest in the welfare of the community, of the success of the government . . . of the gradual formation of this class and the dangers to be feared from it, the agents of this society have incessantly warned the public for the past 11 years. (Draft riots in New York, c. 1863)

This description of New York in 1863 could be of Newark or Detroit, or of a dozen other American cities in which violence has raged in the streets this summer. But it describes the aftermath of the great Civil War draft riots in which the Irish masses of the city exploded in blind fury at what they perceived to be the injustices of the society in which they found themselves.

The nation was then in the midst of the great crisis of slavery. We are now in the midst of an-

From Daniel P. Moynihan, "Poverty, Welfare, and Jobs," *Republican Papers,* Melvin Laird (ed.), (Doubleday & Company, Inc., New York, 1968). Reprinted with kind permission of the author and editor.

other moment of maximum danger that has evolved from our failure fully to resolve that first crisis, and our unwillingness to see that this second one was developing in an urban setting for which the attitudes, and to some degree the machinery, of American government are desperately ill-suited.

The streets of the Negro slums contain the wreckage of a generation of good intentions on the part of American liberals, and good people generally, who have foreseen this outcome or at least insisted on the urgency of the problems that we must suppose have led to it. Many of our proudest achievements are a ruin as well.

Consideration for liberals

Liberals, to be sure, are not the only people in America who have been hurt and damaged by the violence of this summer. But they, and the poor themselves, are the only ones who deserve much consideration. The racists and reactionaries and so-called conservatives in Congress, the shrewd careerists in the administration who have learned so well how to get along with them while keeping up appearances, and the great indifferent American mass who wanted it that way: for them there need be no sympathy.

When one reads the Democratic chairman of the House Appropriations Committee, describing Mayor Cavanagh of Detroit as "this arrogant man" for daring to suggest that the federal government was not facing up to the needs of our cities, it becomes clear that the leaders of Congress have not only learned nothing from their failure, but that neither do they propose to forgive anyone who warned them against it. They had all but destroyed the legislative program of John F. Kennedy when he was murdered, and only thereafter relented somewhat.

Now that American cities are being assaulted one after another across the land, they appear to have decided against any further display of weakness. These are familiar men in history. They are the ones who lose wars, waste opportunities, squander time and destroy civilizations.

They will commonly do so, while invoking the Chairman's principles of "discipline, self respect . . . law and order." Yet it is not ordained that they should prevail, and in the great crises of the American past they have not. Whether they shall do so now is the issue before the nation.

The outcome is likely to be determined now by persons of good will—who actively desire to see American society continue to succeed, who accept the fact that it has in ways failed, and realize that only great and costly effort can reverse the course of events.

Sources of failure

We liberals must inquire into the sources of our own failure, for surely we have not succeeded in bringing the nation along with us. It is not only useless and tasteless to get into a name-calling contest with our presumed opponents; it is also a sure way to avoid facing the possibility that we have some explaining to do about the sources of the present crisis.

We ourselves have lost battles and opportunities, and with time growing short we would do well to ask "why?"

First, in our concern to protect the good name of the poor, especially perhaps the Negro poor, we have entangled ourselves in positions that have led us into preventing effective action to help them.

Second, in our eagerness to see some progress made we have been all too willing to accept the pathetically underfinanced programs which have normally emerged from Congress, and then to oversell them both to ourselves and to those they are designed to aid.

Third, in our desire to maintain public confidence in such programs, we have tended to avoid evidence of poor results, and in particular we have paid too little heed to the limited capacities of government to bring about social change.

These failings have been accompanied, moreover, by a formidable capacity for explaining them away.

In the aftermath of the Newark riots one could already detect our self-defense system at work. Newark, we were beginning to say, was after all a backward city, doubtless run by the Mafia. Unemployment was high. The mayor was fighting with the poverty program. The police were brutal and corrupt. Newark, we were almost saying, deserved a riot. But Detroit . . . what have we to say after Detroit?

Detroit had everything the Great Society could wish for a municipality; a splendid mayor and a fine governor. A high-paying and, thanks to the fiscal policies of the national government, a booming industry, civilized by and associated with the hands-down leading liberal trade union of the world.

Moreover, it was a city whose Negro residents had every reason to be proud of the position they held in the economy and government of the area. Two able and promising Negro Congressmen are from Detroit. Relations between the Negro community and City Hall could hardly have been better. Detroit Negroes held powerful positions throughout the city administration, and to cap matters, the city was equipped with the very model of a summer task force, with a solid program and a twenty-four-hour watch to avert violence.

Urban under class

How then could Detroit riot? The answer lies in the question, "Who rioted?" The rioting was begun and probably largely continued by *young persons whom sociologists would describe as an urban under class.* They happened in this case to be Negro and American, yet their counterparts are to be found in the slums and in the literature of nations throughout the Western world.

Marx despaired of getting any help for his revolution from persons whose main impulses seemed to be so destructive, both to themselves and the society around them.

Most agree that the life of this stratum of society is profoundly different from that of most working people, and certainly most middle-class people. As one middle-aged Negro declared on television, at the height of the Detroit disturbances, "You don't see a family man out here." He may or may not have been right about that moment, but his understanding was sound: violent and criminal behavior set this group apart from the rest of society.

Where did this under class come from? How did it form? There does not seem to be any satisfactory answer, save that something like it has always been present in most cities in America, and that there are reasonably good signs by which to detect it. The Children's Aid Society of New York had foreseen the formation of such a class among the Catholic immigrants of the city, and indeed was formed to help the wretched young people—orphans and foundlings—involved. Their first annual report, dated 1854, said:

It should be remembered that there are no dangers to the value of property or to the permanency of our institutions so great as those from the existence of such a class of vagabond, ignorant, and ungoverned children. This dangerous class has not begun to show itself as it will in 8 or 10 years when these boys and girls are matured. Those who were too negligent or too selfish to notice them as children will be fully aware of them as men. They will poison society. They will perhaps be embittered at the wealth and luxuries they never share. Then let society beware, when the outcast vicious, reckless multitude of New York boys, swarming now in every foul alley and low street come to know their power and use it.

A decade or so ago we began to detect the formation of a Negro version of this class growing up in our northern cities. Just as certain, we did little or nothing about it.

The basic conditions that would appear necessary for the formation of such a class have clearly existed in our cities for a generation now. *First, and uppermost, is unemployment.* The Depression has never ended for the slum Negro.

To unemployment, add low wages, add miserable housing, add vicious and pervasive forms of racial discrimination, compound it all with an essentially destructive welfare system and a social scientist would have every ground on which to predict violence in this violent country. Moreover, there were many specific warnings.

1. The increase in welfare dependency. Something like six out of every ten Negro youths reaching eighteen have at some time been supported by the Federal Aid to Dependent Children program.

2. The increase in certain types of crime. For the crimes of burglary, larceny, and auto theft, the Negro crime rate increased 33 percent between 1960 and 1965. White rates also increased but not as much.

3. The missing men in the census count. At least three years ago we began to realize that the number of Negro males enumerated in the 1960 census was far fewer than it should have been. We now know that altogether we missed 10 percent of the Negro population, with a much higher loss

rate in young adult males. *Something like one male in six, in effect, had simply dropped out of organized society.*

4. Educational failure. For five years or more, we have known that Negro children were doing very badly even in schools that would have to be described as quite good. For some time we have known that the net results, the failure rates on Selective Service examinations, were horrendous: until recently, something like 56 percent of Negro youth called up for the draft have been failing the mental test—a sixth-grade examination.

5. The steady deterioration of family structure in low-income neighborhoods. *Probably not more than a third of the children of low-income Negro families who now reach eighteen have lived all their life with both their parents.*

This last point is often misunderstood. Probably the best available evidence we have of the increase or decrease in the size of lower-class populations lies in the statistics about family life. Breakdown in family relations among poor persons is a pretty good clue that an under class is forming. Many persons—the more liberal a person is the more likely he will be to react this way—interpret the statement to mean that the plight of the poor is being blamed on the state of their families. In other words, that the poor are to blame for their troubles. But just the opposite is the truth; the state of the families is the best evidence of what is happening to the poor.

Available evidence

It happens that this evidence was available not only for the nation but specifically for Detroit. It would be outrageous and unforgivable at this moment to pretend to understand more than we do, but we do know that these were signs of trouble coming. The Negro community was splitting: on the one hand, there was a large and growing group for whom progress was real and unmistakable. On the other hand, there was another group for whom things were not working.

Relatively they grew worse off, not just when compared with white society but also when compared with other Negroes.

Negro leaders have naturally and properly wished to draw attention to their great achievements and even greater potential. Trapped in their own decencies, liberals have agreed; and so in a hundred ways, great and small, the problem of the burgeoning urban lower class was concealed.

If there was delinquency in the slums, we told ourselves that well-to-do kids in the suburbs were just as unruly but were never brought to law—which is not true, but which leaves everyone feeling better. If there were fatherless children in the slums, we told ourselves that white middle-class fathers were never at home either—which is true, but has nothing to do with the matter. It also, somehow, leaves those children in the slums needing help and not getting it.

A crucial opportunity

When the new frontier began formulating its programs, these were designed for an essentially different class of person; *the competent, reasonably well-motivated individual who happened to be out of work or out of skills, and who would surely take advantage of opportunities offered him.* Our one crucial opportunity came with the major amendments to the welfare system in 1962, but we did nothing then except to confirm the conventional wisdom that, for example, portrayed the typical mother requiring aid for dependent children as a West Virginia miner's widow. The system was enlarged somewhat but not changed.

Last summer, with something like one New York City child in five living on welfare, Dr. Mitchell Ginsberg of the Lindsay administration declared the system "bankrupt. It was just as bankrupt five years ago, but somehow we could not, would not, see it then."

There has been a massive loss of confidence on the part of Negroes as to white sincerity. Two years ago, during the rioting in Watts, comedian Dick Gregory tried to help calm things. He was shot for his troubles, and told the young man who had done it, "All right; you shot me. Now go home." Two months ago at a Black Power rally in Washington, Gregory was shouting over and over again: "Watts was legal!"

Our programs might have had far greater impact if only they had been of sufficient size. *The amounts of money going to cities and to the poor increased, but in nothing like the amounts or for the purposes demanded by the situation.*

Anyone who was involved with the establishment of the War on Poverty knows that it was put together by fiscal mirrors; scarcely a driblet of new money was involved. Even an element of fraud entered the picture: the Bureau of the Budget began calculating interstate highway funds as part of the financial aid going to cities.

Such money is of considerable aid to General Motors and the United Automobile Workers, and to the Association of General Contractors, but as for the poor, the best that can be said for it is that it destroys a lot of bad housing.

Here again it was fear of, and after a point too sophisticated a knowledge of, the fiscal conservatism, and also social complacency in the Congress that held us back, that even somehow kept us from telling ourselves the truth.

Huge-sounding bills were passed, but mini-appropriations followed, and after a point both ends of Pennsylvania Avenue were co-operating in this process. Instead of taking what we could get, but insisting that it was not enough, liberals both within and without the administration gave in to an orgy of tub thumping.

It does not automatically follow that we raised hopes out of all proportion to our capacity to deliver on our promises, but if we did, and we *must* have, we have only ourselves to blame.

Ourselves and the federal bureaucracy. *Somehow liberals have been unable to acquire from life what conservatives seem to be endowed with at birth, namely, a healthy skepticism of the powers of government agencies to do good.*

The American national government is a superb instrument for redistributing power and wealth in our society. One person in ten in the United States, for example, now gets a Social Security check every month. But as an instrument for providing services, especially to urban lower-class Negroes, it is a highly unreliable device.

The more programs, the less impact. The 1966 White House conference "to fulfill these rights" produced a hundred pages of recommendations,

which meant that the conference was a failure and a disaster. If it had produced three recommendations, it might have been a success. I shall propose three.

First. The United States government must become the employer of last resort, so that anyone looking for work and not finding it is automatically given a job. Put to work. If this is done stupidly it will turn out to be a WPA, but with just a little administrative energy it can be worked out that such jobs are distributed throughout the labor market, so that in fact they are not visible as such. The government must see to it that everyone looking for work finds work, and correspondingly that those without work have no excuse for their situation.

Second. We have got to get more money directly into the hands of the poor. The best way to do this, or at least the best known way, is through a family (or children's) allowance. The United States is the only industrial democracy in the world that does not have such a system of automatic payments for families who are raising minor children. We are also the only industrial democracy whose streets are filled with rioters each year. The connection may not be direct, or may not exist at all, but then it may.

Such a payment would have the advantage that everyone would get it, not just a special segment artificially defined as below a certain income line or across a certain racial line.

It has worked well all over the world, including Canada, and for $9 billion a year, it would be a sound investment in the future as well as in the present.

Third. We must rebuild, or at least clear, the burnt-out neighborhoods. The federal government has a dozen ways to do this, and it must. Otherwise the ruins remain a symbol of the injustices that led to them. Accompanying such a clearance and rebuilding program, we simply must enact a form of federal reinsurance of small business in such areas. Otherwise they will become deserts.

Reading 61

The rise and fall of the city is nowhere better displayed than in New York. Every tool of economic analysis—and some social science generally—can be used in this problem area.

Nathan Glazer, a sociologist at Harvard, was coauthor with David Riesman and Reuel Denney of the classic, *The Lonely Crowd;* and with Daniel Patrick Moynihan of the perhaps overoptimistic study on race and ethnic relations in New York City, *Beyond the Melting Pot*. Many regard him—like Irving Kristol, Daniel Bell, and Moynihan himself—as a conservative or, if there is a difference, as a disillusioned liberal.

The accompanying piece was abridged from the Introduction Professor Glazer wrote to a 1972 study of New York City prepared by the Economics Department of the First National City Bank, the second largest bank in the world (which had itself, earlier, been the object of a critical study by a regiment of Ralph Nader's roving raiders).

Whether this business sponsorship affects the author's view of business's role in helping solve urban problems, the forewarned reader must judge from his own reading of the text.

Questions to guide the reading

Is New York City really typical? Mightn't a critical size make a difference in kind? Is "the liberal government of Mayor Lindsay" an accident in a city with Puerto Ricans and blacks? (If not, what about Chicago's Mayor Daley?)

Why so little treatment of "unsafety" in New York life? What evidence is there that "Americans used to pride themselves . . . that . . . it was not true that the best jobs were with government . . ."? How many thought about this issue at all?

When Dr. Glazer speaks of "business," does he mean *big* business? The liquor store or pawnshop down the street?

M.I.T.'s Jay Forrester, electric engineer turned world dynamicist, sought to solve the city problem by forcing problem people out of the city. Should Glazer have endorsed this solution? At the opposite pole, to keep people of means from running away from the city's problems, mustn't the federal government take over the main financial burden?

New York City: A Paradigm for Urban Economics Everywhere

Nathan Glazer

There are three aspects of studies of a great city—New York, at the turn of the seventies—that should make it of the first importance to all of us who are concerned with the future of American cities.

First, despite the exclusive concern with the problems of New York, the specifics of the New York situation, the figures and numbers of New York, what these report is generally true of all large American cities.

Pollution and poverty

It is obvious that the issue of pollution is found in every large city of the United States, and the hard choices affecting how we deal with it—choices between convenience and low cost on the one hand as against a higher standard in the environment on the other—will have to be dealt with everywhere.

It is clear the peculiarly intractable problems of poverty and welfare are to be found almost every-

From Nathan Glazer, "Introduction," *Profile of a City* (prepared by members of the Economics Department, First National City Bank, New York), McGraw-Hill Book Company, New York, 1972. Reprinted in abridgment with the kind permission of the author and the publisher.

where. As the welfare population shot up in the second half of the 1960s, there was a common early reaction that something special was going on in New York City: perhaps the rise was due to its distinctive immigration mix of blacks and Puerto Ricans, its special job structure, the liberal government of Mayor Lindsay. Many other special reasons were suggested.

Alas, it turned out the explosion in welfare was a national phenomenon, as marked in Mayor Yorty's Los Angeles and in Mayor Daley's Chicago as in New York. And indeed, early in President Nixon's administration it became a national priority to introduce some basic reform into the welfare system.

Education and housing

Education in New York City has some distinctive features: the enormous power of the teachers' union, for example; the special ethnic composition of the teaching force and the higher administrators; the distinctive history of excellence, still carried on by the specialized high schools and perhaps in other parts of the system. But here too, whatever is distinctive about New York City is fast fading in a general national crisis over urban education: its rapidly increasing cost, its inability to show substantial progress in educating the new urban minorities, its loss of authority in the face of challenges from militant communities and rebellious students. These are no longer distinctive New York City problems, if they ever were.

One would think, if anything was uniquely distinctive of New York City, marking it off from all other American cities, it is its housing. New York stands alone among American cities in the very high proportion of its housing stock that is in multiple dwellings and the very high proportion that is rental housing. And for these reasons, it remained the only American city to maintain rent control without a break from World War II until the present. A few years ago a striking phenomenon—one never seen before in any American city, or perhaps in any other cities, since the decline of the urbanism of the ancient world—appeared in New York: the abandonment of sound housing. The suddenness and scale of this phenomenon left all analysts for a while dumbfounded, even if moviemakers rapidly added to their gallery of visual images

scenes in the abandoned and burned-out apartment houses in New York, where drug addicts and other down-and-outers might occasionally shelter themselves. It seemed clear to many that rent control explained housing abandonment.

The fact is that housing abandonment has now spread to other large cities, with rather different characteristics of housing stock and housing administration. Even here New York is not completely unique.

Subway versus auto

Alongside the characteristics of its housing stock, the most distinctive feature of New York in contrast to other American cities is its system of mass transportation. The density of family units in large apartment houses and the density of jobs in large office buildings and factory lofts made it economic to provide mass-transportation facilities expensive to build and to maintain, and they survived in New York during a time when in other cities some equivalent facilities were abandoned.

The cycle of limited service, less use, less income, and less service was to be found in New York City, too, as ownership and use of the automobile rose, even in the crowded city. But it did not reach the point where, as in Los Angeles, a remarkable system of street railways was completely abandoned.

All mass transit is increasingly limited to the journey to and from work. And how can these enormously expensive facilities be maintained for maximum use for only a few hours a day? New York is now struggling with the same issues other cities are now pondering—how the mass transit is to be financed, how taxes can be levied on users of automobiles to encourage a shift to mass transit.

Welfare costs and cushy public jobs

Finally, the issues of municipal finance are now almost everywhere in the country the same. In every city, there is enormous increase in municipal costs, tremendous pressure on tax resources, a desperate search for new taxes, and increasing insistence that state and federal governments take over the costs of large branches of municipal services. Welfare is the leading candidate. In some cases, states pay all or most of the burden (in New York, there is still a very large city share). And the federal government, in the Family Assistance Plan reform, begins to accept the responsibility of taking on a larger share, and perhaps ultimately the total cost. Even if this plan does not become law, any plan that succeeds it must move in the direction of the federal government paying a larger share or all of welfare costs. There are now demands that the federal government take on the costs of education.

The financial crisis of the cities is universal. What still perhaps remains distinctive about New York, and what the analysis of its budget indicates most clearly, is the enormous role of increases in costs of municipal labor as a factor in increasing the costs of city government.

Here indeed is one area where some change is necessary if the cities are to become viable. Americans used to pride themselves on the fact that in this productive society it was not true that the best jobs were with government, as was true in developing countries where everyone scrambled to get on the government payroll. It is a wry commentary on recent developments that municipal jobs, in New York City at least, have become, in salary, in fringe benefits, and in seniority, better than jobs in the private sector.

These studies of New York demonstrate the remarkable advance that we saw in the sixties in the application of the tools of economic analysis to various problems, a development which has permitted us a much better insight into our urban problems. Admittedly not all our problems are to be illuminated by these techniques. Political scientists, sociologists, and historians, and even philosophers, have a good deal of light to shed on our present situation. Yet to my mind the economists have the most important light: they tell us which of the things we are doing simply don't seem to be worthwhile, to "pay." Political scientists, sociologists, and historians may give us reasons why we nevertheless keep on doing them, but at least the first step to improvement is to know whether they are worthwhile, not what interests they serve, or what role satisfaction they give, or how they got started.

Thus, when we learn, as we do in the education chapter, how much more we pay for the very modest improvement in achievement recorded by students in the More Effective Schools program, we have certainly learned something very useful. Perhaps we maintain this program as a means of employing more teachers or teacher aides as a means of responding to parental demands to do something, or because the teachers' union demands it. But let us at least know what it does for educational achievement.

Similarly, it is useful to discover that it is easier to secure funds for capital investment on our subways than to acquire the amounts needed for adequate maintenance—millions for new equipment, relatively little for upkeep. Again there are reasons for this in the political realm. But the location of a problem of a misuse of resources in terms of efficiency is certainly by itself a contribution to our capacity to act.

Economics to the rescue?

The style of analysis demonstrates a marked advantage over most discussions of urban problems, which characteristically take the form of the denunciation of one villain (the mayor, his party, the machine, the unions, the state government, the federal government, the property owners and taxpayers, the banks, the minorities, and so on), and the proposal of one solution (ban automobiles, community control of schools, public low-cost housing, federal tax sharing, and so on). There are many variants which these simpler approaches to urban problems take.

Even the very knowledgeable John Kenneth Galbraith was recorded as saying a few years ago that New York City has no problems that another billion dollars will not solve, or words to that effect. In the few years since that statement was made, New York City has been able to find another three or four billion to spend every year, with no discernible impact on its problems. No one should dismiss the importance of money in dealing with urban problems; but even great sums of money may achieve nothing in the absence of a sound analysis and understanding.

When one reviews the range of programs and proposals that have been made—and in fact implemented—to improve the situation of cities since

1960, [an] important theme becomes apparent: there are no simple solutions anymore. There seems to be no one crux of the matter which, once grasped, gives us understanding and solution.

The range of problems in our great cities is complex indeed and comes from many different sources: changes in demographic patterns, in the economy, in migration, in ethnic composition, in the scope and capacity of government, in mismatches between governmental responsibilities and resources, and many others. The catalog is endless. And the unfortunate conclusion of recent years is: it is hard to argue this or that part of it is unimportant.

There is unfortunately no way of making the problem simple.

A role for business?

One element that is suggested by this complexity is that solutions are to be found in many quarters. Inevitably, government, at its various levels, must take the largest responsibility for solutions. Yet again and again in recent years we have seen important potential roles for business organization.

Admittedly the more extravagant hopes that were placed on a business commitment to help solve the problems of cities have not been realized. Business investment in the ghettos has not stopped their decline. Investment in job training has not dried up the pool of those who cannot or will not work; investment in educational technology has not done much for educational problems. But one can say pretty much the same about governmental programs, and it would be hard to say that one has been more successful than the other.

The notion of a business role in dealing with the problems of our cities—whether in pollution, education, poverty, housing, transportation, or strengthening of the general economic base of cities—is not a simple one. The business role emerges in many different ways. As our faith in single, simple solutions—even if of monumental scale—declines, since the experience of the sixties shows that such faith is poorly founded, inevitably we look more sympathetically on other sources of contributions to urban problems. These analyses suggest a place for the business role. They scarcely exhaust its possibilities. But in each of the areas of

concern dealt with in these studies there is a persuasive case that the remarkable resources of American business enterprise, resources of knowledge, organization, capacities for implementation, can be put to better use in attacking urban problems.

Too-high hopes

This book appears at a time when American morale is low—low because of what are quite properly seen as foreign and domestic failures. It is my judgment that morale is probably presently lower than the best analysis would justify.

Our environmental problems, severe as they are, also represent a remarkable success in making available automobiles and other energy-using devices to vast numbers of people and in opening up to people, more than any other nation has, the ability to realize individual desires for homes, transportation, recreation. This is not to gainsay the frightful environmental problems that have followed. But there must be a way of utilizing the resources of intelligence and organization that have produced the first in the service of the second.

Our educational problems in part derive from our ambitions, which aim to bring many years of education to all people. Inevitably, this extension, which few other countries have attempted, brings a good number of problems in its wake.

Our housing problems derive from our success in building so many better houses on the outskirts of our cities. Abandonment reflects terrible problems, but they are not so much problems of insufficiency of housing as problems of its upgrading—problems of better housing and neighborhood competing with worse housing and neighborhood. And our problems of public transportation derive from the fact that so many Americans have private transportation.

I do not mean to downgrade the urgency of the problems. I mean to suggest that perhaps our morale is lower than it should be, and that there are many approaches and many sources of power, those of private business as well as principally those of government, which it is now incumbent upon us to develop and implement.

Reading 62

Half of our population has for so long been discriminated against economically that it almost escaped our attention. Only recently has our consciousness become elevated.

Marina von Neumann Whitman is a professor of economics at the University of Pittsburgh and an expert on international matters. (Her father was the mathematical genius John von Neumann.) Dr. Whitman was appointed by President Nixon as a member of the Council of Economic Advisers.

The present reading is taken from the 1973 Economic Report. It aroused some controversy when privately circulated in first draft. Excessive complacency was alleged to be its fault. Despite the cautious prose of official documents, the revised version points clearly to the fact that we have a long way to go before sexual equality and nondiscrimination are approached.

Questions to guide the reading

What corrections must be made before we can fairly compare the average female wage with the average male wage? *Hint:* More women work part time; more women move in and out of the labor force; etc.

Does it seem really plausible to you that, after all corrections are made, women's incomes average out to be as much as 80 per cent of men's?

Are careers and marriage compatible? Careers and children? Will partnership responsibilities of fathers and mothers evolve?

Is the problem of day care centers a hard or an easy one to solve?

The Economic Role of Women and Sex Discrimination

Economic Report of the President, 1973 (Marina von Neumann Whitman et al.)

One of the most important changes in the American economy in this century has been the increase in the proportion of women who work outside the home. This increase is the most striking aspect of the expansion of the role of women in the economy.

The addition of millions of women to the labor force has contributed substantially to the increase of total output. Most of the benefits of this additional output accrue to the women who produce it, and to their families. There are, however, also direct benefits to the society at large, including the taxes paid on the women's earnings.

Concern is sometimes expressed that the increase in women in the labor force will reduce the employment opportunities for men and raise their unemployment. There is no reason to think that would happen and there is no sign that it has happened. The work to be done is not a fixed total. As more women enter employment and earn incomes they or their families buy more goods and services which men and women are employed to produce. A sudden surge of entrants into the labor force might cause difficulties of adjustment and, consequently, unemployment, but the entry of women into the labor force has not been of that character.

Reprinted in abridgment from "The Economic Role of Women," *Economic Report of the President,* United States Government Printing Office, Washington, D.C., 1973.

Why women work

Women work outside the home for the same reasons as men. The basic reason is to get the income that can be earned by working. Whether—for either men or women—work is done out of necessity or by choice is a question of definition. If working out of necessity means working in order to sustain biologically necessary conditions of life, probably a small proportion of all the hours of work done in the United States, by men or women, is necessary. If working out of necessity means working in order to obtain a standard of living which is felt by the worker to be desirable, probably almost all of the work done by both men and women is necessary.

The Employment Act of 1946 sets forth a goal of "maximum employment." This goal applies equally to men and to women.

Although the goals apply equally to men and women, some of the obstacles to their achievement apply especially to women. Women have gained much more access to market employment than they used to have, but they have not gained full equality within the market in the choice of jobs, opportunities for advancement, and other matters related to employment and compensation.

To some extent the cause of this discrepancy is direct discrimination. But it is also the result of more subtle and complex factors originating in cultural patterns that have grown up in most societies through the centuries. In either case, because the possibilities open to women are restricted, they are not always free to contribute a full measure of earnings to their families, to develop their talents fully, or to help achieve the national goal of "maximum production."

Special problems. Among the topics [relevant to the economic role of women] are job training and counseling in the schools, special problems of minority women, problems related to child care, women's performance at work, the extent of job discriminations, women's access to credit, and legislative action on taxes and social security that may have a different effect on women than on men.

Another, more fundamental, issue affecting women in the economy underlies many of the others. The roles played by women and men have been sharply differentiated. It is obvious that only women are capable of childbearing. But along with this biologically determined role, women have by tradition come to assume primary responsibility for child care and home management, while men have primary responsibility for the family's financial support. Until very recently this division of labor within the family has had such general acceptance as to impose limitations on women's work outside the home. The way in which the economic role of women evolves thus hinges on the most fundamental societal patterns, and the extent to which social action can and should influence further change in these patterns will be one of the most difficult and important questions the committee must consider.

By way of an introduction to the problem, this chapter looks at job-related aspects of the economic role of women.

Participation in the labor force

In 1900 about 20 percent of all women were in the work force (Table 1). In the succeeding decades this percentage hardly increased, reaching about 25 percent by 1940.

With World War II, however, the movement rapidly accelerated, and by 1972 the percentage of women 16 years and older in the work force had risen to 43.8. Single women and women widowed, divorced, or separated, have always had higher labor force participation rates than married women living with their husbands. By 1950, the participation of women in the two former groups had already reached levels close to those of today.

Thus, the upward trend in labor force participation since World War II has been due almost entirely to the changed behavior of married women (Table 2). The first to respond were the more mature married women beyond the usual childbearing years. More recently there has also been a sharp upturn in the labor force participation of younger married women.

Male withdrawal? The record for men has tended to run in the opposite direction. A secular reduction in time spent in paid work over most men's lifetimes has taken place: A man spends more years at school and enters the labor force later than formerly; he retires earlier, works fewer hours a week, and has longer vacations. Of course these changes have also affected women, but for

Table 1   Women in the Labor Force, Selected Years, 1900–72

Year	Women in labor force (thousands)	Women in labor force as percent of	
		Total labor force	All women of working age
1900	5,114	18.1	20.4
1910	7,889	20.9	25.2
1920	8,430	20.4	23.3
1930	10,679	22.0	24.3
1940	12,845	24.3	25.4
1945	19,270	29.6	35.7
1950	18,412	28.8	33.9
1955	20,584	30.2	35.7
1960	23,272	32.3	37.8
1965	26,232	34.0	39.3
1970	31,560	36.7	43.4
1972	33,320	37.4	43.8

Note.—Data for 1900 to 1940 are from decennial censuses and refer to a single date; beginning 1945 data are annual averages.
For 1900 to 1945 data include women 14 years of age and over; beginning 1950 data include women 16 years of age and over.
Labor force data for 1900 to 1930 refer to gainfully employed workers.
Data for 1972 reflect adjustments to 1970 Census benchmarks.
Sources: Department of Commerce, Bureau of the Census, and Department of Labor, Bureau of Labor Statistics.

them the increase in years worked has far outweighed the other work-reducing factors.

In one very important respect, however, the working life patterns of men and women have not merged. The typical man can expect to be in the labor force continuously, for an unbroken block of some 40 years between leaving school and retirement. Of men in the 25–54 year age group, 95.2 percent were in the labor force in 1972. For most women, this continuity in participation is the exception rather than the rule.

The historical pattern

What are the causal factors that induced women to enter the labor force? One might have expected that the strong increases in husbands' real incomes

which occurred during the period would have provided an incentive to women not to enter the labor force. This seeming puzzle is resolved, however, when one considers that by entering the labor force women did not leave a life of leisure for work, but rather changed from one kind of work, work at home, to another kind of work, work in the market.

The incentive for women to make this dramatic occupational change came from several developments which made paid work outside the home the increasingly more profitable alternative.

Rapidly rising earnings and expanded job opportunities for women gave a strong impetus to the change. The expansion of job opportunities for women was undoubtedly influenced by the expansion of the service sector of the economy, where employment increased by 77 percent from 1950 to 1970, compared to the increase of 26 percent in the goods-producing industrial sector over the same period. Women have always been more heavily represented in services than in industry, since the service sector offers more white-collar employment and provides more opportunities for part-time work, an especially important feature for women with small children. On the other hand, the increasing supply of women workers perhaps itself contributed to the rapid expansion in the service sector.

The increase in women's educational attainments has also helped to raise the amount they can earn by working. Education may make women more productive in the home, that is, more efficient housekeepers, consumers, and mothers, but education appears to increase still more their productivity in work outside the home. Women with more education earn more, and they are more likely than less educated women to seek work in the market.

Because life expectancy has increased considerably over the century (and more for women than for men), and because most women complete their childbearing at a younger age, women can look forward with more certainty to a longer uninterrupted span of years in the labor force. This lengthening of a woman's expected working life is significant because it increases her return on her investment in training and education: the greater the number of years in which to collect the return the greater is the return.

Table 2   Labor Force Participation Rates of Women by Marital Status and Age, 1950, 1960, and 1972 (percent [1])

Marital status and year	Total	Age					
		Under 20 years	20–24 years	25–34 years	35–44 years	45–64 years	65 years and over
Single:							
1950	50.5	26.3	74.9	84.6	83.6	70.6	23.8
1960	44.1	25.3	73.4	79.9	79.7	75.1	21.6
1972	54.9	41.9	69.9	84.7	71.5	71.0	19.0
Married, husband present:							
1950	23.8	24.0	28.5	23.8	28.5	21.8	6.4
1960	30.5	25.3	30.0	27.7	36.2	34.2	5.9
1972	41.5	39.0	48.5	41.3	48.6	44.2	7.3
Widowed, divorced, or separated:							
1950	37.8	(²)	45.5	62.3	65.4	50.2	8.8
1960	40.0	37.3	54.6	55.5	67.4	58.3	11.0
1972	40.1	44.6	57.6	62.1	71.7	61.1	9.8

[1] Labor force as percent of noninstitutional population in group specified.
[2] Not available.
Note.—Data relate to March of each year.
Data for 1950 and 1960 are for women 14 years of age and over; data for 1972 are for women 16 years of age and over.
Source: Department of Labor, Bureau of Labor Statistics.

These increases in the income a woman could potentially earn meant essentially that time spent producing goods and services at home was coming at a higher and higher cost in terms of the income foregone by not working in the market. It made sense then to buy available capital equipment (such as washing machines) which would substitute for some of the housewife's time and free her to go to work. And changes in technology which lowered the cost and increased the array of time-saving devices facilitated the substitution.

Fewer children

The most difficult home responsibility to find a good substitute for is child care; and, although the labor force participation of women with children under 6 years has increased from 12 percent in 1950 to 30 percent in 1971, child-rearing is probably the major factor causing some women to interrupt and others to curtail their careers.

The long-term decline in the average number of children in the family has undoubtedly had a strong influence on the proportion of women entering the labor force. Advances in birth control techniques permit parents not only to reduce the number of births but also to control their timing to suit a mother's working career. Declines in infant and child mortality may also have encouraged a reduction in births by increasing the parents' expectation that all their children would survive to adulthood. On the other hand, reductions in family size may themselves be influenced by the desire of women to work.

Childbearing has a very noticeable effect on the patterns of women's labor force participation by age. Based on census data, Chart 1 traces the lifetime changes in labor force participation by groups of women born at different times, the earliest group consisting of women born between 1886 and 1895. The chart therefore simulates the actual work history of particular cohorts of women followed longitudinally. According to this chart, the various forces in the economy that have induced women to work have generally had a more powerful effect on women beyond the childbearing ages than on younger groups.

Those increases in labor force participation that have occurred for groups of women reaching the childbearing ages of 20–34 years have been closely associated with declining fertility rates. Thus labor force participation for the group reaching 25–34 years increased substantially from 1930 to 1940, and again between 1960 and 1970, while there was

a decline between 1940 and 1950 in the participation of those reaching this age group—the baby boom mothers.

Whether the young women now in their twenties have simply postponed having children and will later drop out of the labor force or whether many will continue to work, choosing to have small families or remain childless is, of course, a question of great interest.

The working woman today

Although the decisions of individual women to work outside the home are undoubtedly based on many different factors, there are some economic factors which seem to be of overriding importance. The necessity to support oneself or others is one

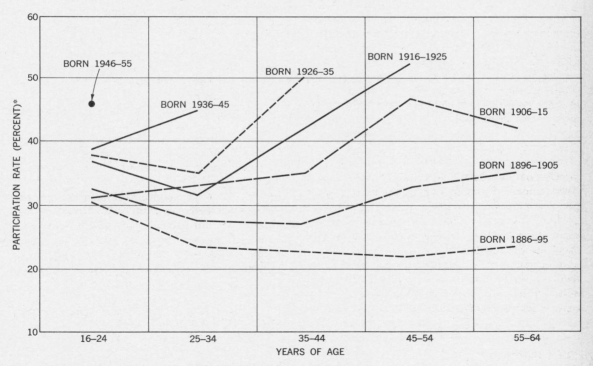

*Total labor force as percent of total noninstitutional population in group specified.

NOTE: For women born between 1886 and 1915, the first age plotted is 14–24 years. Cohorts reach age interval according to the midpoint of their birth years. Thus, the cohort born 1886–95 reached ages 25–34 in 1920 and ages 55–64 in 1950; the cohort born 1916–25 reached ages 25–34 in 1950 and ages 45–54 in 1970.

Chart 1 Labor force participation over a working life of cohorts of women born in selected time intervals, 1886–1955.
Source: Department of Commerce

obvious reason and, not surprisingly, adult single women and women who have been separated from husbands or widowed are highly likely to work.

The increase in earnings opportunities, which proved to be such a powerful factor influencing the secular growth of women's participation in the labor force, is a similarly powerful factor influencing the pattern of women's participation at any given time. Thus, education and other training which affect the amount a woman can earn are strongly related to women's work patterns.

The importance of education is such that, whether a woman is single, married or separated, the more education she has, the more likely she is to work. (One striking exception to this pattern is that, among mothers of children under 6 years old, there is scarcely any relation between education and labor force participation. Thus, the rearing of children of preschool age causes all women, regardless of education, to curtail their work outside the home. However, the drop in participation during this child-rearing period is most pronounced for highly educated women who in other circumstances have much higher participation rates.)

Although for most women the childbearing period has been reduced, childbearing still means an interruption of outside work. A longitudinal survey of the lifelong work experience of women indicates that among all women who were 30–44 years old in 1967, only 7 percent had worked at least 6 months out of every year since leaving school. Among married women with children the proportion was still lower, dropping to 3 percent. By contrast, 30 percent of childless married women in the same group had worked at least 6 months out of every year.

Information on job tenure collected by the Bureau of Labor Statistics illustrates much the same phenomenon. Job tenure increases with age for both men and women. Since women tend to change jobs less frequently than men, their shorter time spent on any given job is the result of a higher propensity to leave the labor force at least temporarily. A survey of women who had dropped out of the labor force and had not yet reentered was undertaken by the Labor Department in an effort to find out why they had left. Pregnancy was most frequently cited as the primary reason—by 74 percent of the 18- to 24-year-olds and 56 percent of the 25- to 34-year-olds.

Among married women, husband's income does not have a very pronounced effect on work patterns. The median annual income of husbands with working wives was $8,070 in 1971 compared to $8,330 for husbands of wives not in the labor force. Only when husbands' incomes reach the $10,000 and over category does wives' participation decline to any noticeable extent. However, many other things vary with husbands' incomes, such as wives' education and age as well as family size. These other factors are sufficiently important to obscure the simple relation between husband's income and a wife's tendency to work.

Working wives of the unemployed and minorities

It should be noted, however, that during a time of hardship, such as when a husband experiences a prolonged spell of unemployment, wives who usually do not work may be compelled to work. Thus, the labor force participation of women with unemployed husbands is generally above that of women with employed husbands.

Although the probability that a black woman will work seems to vary with education and presence of children in much the same way as it does for all women, there is one very striking difference. The labor force participation of black women is higher.

Particularly pronounced differences are observed when the comparison of labor force participation is confined to married women living with their husbands. In March 1971, about 53 percent of black wives were in the labor force compared to 40 percent of white wives. One important reason why this difference prevails may be that the earnings of black wives are closer to their husbands' than is the case among white married couples. Black married women who worked year-round, full-time earned 73 percent as much as black married men who worked year-round, full-time. Among whites the percentage was only 51 percent.

Behind these relationships is the fact that black men earn considerably less than white men, while black women's earnings are much closer to white women's earnings.

Unemployment

Women have generally experienced more unemployment than men and this differential has been more pronounced in recent years.

Some of the difference arises from the way people are classified in our unemployment statistics. Thus, a woman who may in a real sense be clearly employed in the home while she searches for a job, will be counted as unemployed, unlike the man who searches while on his job.

Most adult men are continuously in the labor force and therefore become unemployed because they have either quit or lost their jobs. For women, the picture is different: labor force participation is frequently interrupted, sometimes for several years, but sometimes just for several weeks during the year. This high rate of labor force turnover generates unemployment, and it is not surprising to find that in both the tight labor market of 1969 and the looser labor market of 1972 a considerable portion of unemployed women were labor force entrants. People entering or reentering the labor force tend, however, to be unemployed for relatively short periods, and this is one of the reasons why the duration of unemployment is in general shorter for women than for men.

In order to know what significance to attach to the observation that the greater unemployment of women appears to be related to their greater labor force turnover, it is of course necessary to know more about the causes of the turnover. Some have stressed that excessive labor force turnover indicates a poor job market. According to this view, women drop out of the labor market because lack of opportunities has discouraged them from continuing the search.

Another school of thought, however, stresses that the labor force turnover of women and the unemployment it generates is largely induced by factors external to the current labor market, such as the uneven pressures of home responsibilities.

It would of course be interesting to know more about the unemployment experience of women who do remain continuously in the labor force. Some evidence from the Labor Department's longitudinal survey indicates that women who were in the labor force in both 1967 and 1969 had considerably lower unemployment in 1969 than those who were in the labor force in 1969 but not in 1967. The unemployment rate in 1969 for the group who were also in the labor force 2 years previously was 2.9 percent, compared to the rate of 6.9 percent for the women who were in the labor force only in 1969. However, this was still above the rate of 2.1 percent for men 20 years old and over in 1969, as measured by the household survey.

Although movement in and out of the labor force is probably the most important factor leading to higher unemployment for women compared to men, two other factors seem to be important. Women with less time on a job and in whom the employer had made negligible training investments are more vulnerable to layoffs. Finally, one additional factor which doubtless contributes to unemployment of married women is the difficulty in maximizing employment opportunities for both the husband and the wife. A wife seldom is free to migrate to wherever her own prospects are best.

It is important to emphasize, because the point is often misunderstood, that to explain the unemployment of women is not to excuse it or belittle it or to place blame on the women who are unemployed. The unemployment of women who seek work is costly, to themselves, their families, and the Nation. Our goal should be to reduce this unemployment wherever that can be done.

Education and the occupational stratification

Some of the hesitancy of women to enter or to stay in the labor force is undoubtedly the result of societally determined factors that restrict the possibilities open to them. The low representation of women in positions of responsibility is striking. Despite gradual gains, progress has not been sufficient to alter the picture significantly (Table 3). Exactly how much of this situation has been imposed on women because of prejudice and how much of it derives from a voluntary adjustment to a life divided between home responsibilities and work remains obscure.

The existence of discriminatory barriers may discourage women from seeking the training or adopting the life style it would take to achieve a responsible and highly demanding job. On the other hand, women who expect to marry and have

Table 3   Women as a Percent of Persons in Several Professional and Managerial Occupations, 1910–70 (Percent)

Occupational group	1910	1920	1930	1940	1950	1960	1970
Clergymen	.6	1.4	2.2	2.4	4.0	2.3	2.9
College presidents, professors, and instructors[1]	18.9	30.2	31.9	26.5	23.2	24.2	28.2
Dentists	3.1	3.3	1.9	1.5	2.7	2.3	3.5
Editors and reporters	12.2	16.8	24.0	25.0	32.0	36.6	40.6
Engineers	(2)	(2)	(2)	.4	1.2	.8	1.6
Lawyers and judges	.5	1.4	2.1	2.5	3.5	3.5	4.9
Managers, manufacturing industries	1.7	3.1	3.2	4.3	6.4	7.1	6.3
Physicians	6.0	5.0	4.4	4.7	6.1	6.9	9.3

[1] Data for 1920 and 1930 probably include some teachers in schools below collegiate rank. The Office of Education estimates the 1930 figure closer to 28 percent.
[2] Less than one tenth of 1 percent.
Note.—Data are from the decennial censuses. Data for 1910 and 1920 include persons 10 years of age and over; data for 1930 to 1970 include persons 14 years of age and over.
Source: Department of Commerce, Bureau of the Census.

children and who also put their role at home first are subject to considerable uncertainty about their future attachment to the labor force. In the latter case, incentives to train extensively for a career would be few; and, once such women started working, the restrictions imposed by home responsibilities could limit their ability to take a job requiring long hours or the intensive commitment that most high-status positions demand. At the same time, changes in the accepted social roles of men and women would alter current patterns if they changed women's expectations about their future in the labor force.

Sex bias in schooling. For whatever reasons, from school onward the career orientation of women differs strikingly from that of men. Most women do not have as strong a vocational emphasis in their schooling; and for those who do, the preparation is usually for a stereotyped "female" occupation.

Although the probability of graduating from high school has been somewhat greater for women than for men, it is less probable that a woman will complete college, and still less that she will enter graduate school. The representation of women consequently declines as they move upward through the stages of education beyond high school. In 1971, 50 percent of all high school graduates were women and 45 percent of first-year college students were women. During 1971 women earned 44 percent of the bachelor's degrees granted, 40 percent of the master's degrees, and 14 percent of the doctorates.

Even more striking are the differences in the courses taken. At both the undergraduate and advanced levels, women are heavily represented in English, languages, and fine arts—the more general cultural fields. They are poorly represented in disciplines having a strong vocational emphasis and promising a high pecuniary return. In 1970, 9.3 percent of the baccalaureates in business and 3.9 percent of the master's in business went to women. In the biological sciences, women had a larger share, taking about 30 percent of the bachelor's and master's degrees and 16 percent of the doctorates. But only 8.5 percent of the M.D.'s and 5.6 percent of the law degrees went to women. Most of these percentages, low as they are, represent large gains from the preceding year.

The situation is quite different in the so-called women's occupations. In 1971 women received 74 percent of the B.A.'s and 56 percent of the M.A.'s given in education. In library science, which is even more firmly dominated by women, they received 82 percent of all degrees in 1971. And in nursing, 98 percent of all the degrees went to women.

Sex bias in jobs. It is not surprising, then, to find that women do not have anything like the same occupational distribution as men. Even within an educational level, significant differences remain in the distribution across broad occupational categories. Although 77 percent of women college graduates in 1970 were in the professions, mostly as teachers, only 4.8 percent, compared to 20 percent for men, were classified as managers. At high school levels, the proportion of women working as skilled craftsmen is minuscule, although a substantial proportion of women are blue-collar workers in the lower paying operative categories.

Although women are found in all occupations, the extent of occupational segregation by sex is large. In broad outline, this situation does not appear to have undergone any dramatic change between 1950 and 1970, although there are several examples of large increases in the proportion of women in less typically "female" occupations (for example busdrivers, bartenders, and compositors and typesetters).

Earnings

In 1971 annual median earnings for women 14 years old and over were $2,986, or 40 percent of the median earnings of men. But women work fewer hours per week and fewer weeks per year. If the comparison is restricted to year-round, full-time workers, women's earnings are 60 percent of men's, that is, $5,593 compared to $9,399. An additional adjustment for differences in the average full-time workweek—full-time hours for men were about 10 percent higher than for women—brings the female-male ratio to 66 percent in 1971.

Differentials of this order of magnitude appear to have persisted since 1956. Indeed, a slight increase in the differential seems to have occurred from 1956 to 1969. Part of the source of the increasing differential was the relatively low rate of growth in the earnings of female clerical workers and female operatives, who in 1970 accounted for 32 percent and 14 percent, respectively, of all women workers. On the other hand, the rate of

growth of earnings of women in the professions was high (a 5.1-percent annual compound rate between 1955 and 1968) relative to all workers; more recently it was even high relative to male professionals.

A large differential is also evident when the comparison is restricted to men and women of the same age and education. As Chart 2 indicates, the incomes of women do not increase with age in anything like the same way men's do. Thus the differential widens with age through much of the working life.

One important factor influencing the differential is experience. The lack of continuity in women's attachment to the labor force means that they will not have accumulated as much experience as men at a given age. The relatively steeper rise of men's income with age has been attributed to their greater accumulation of experience, of "human capital" acquired on the job. Since very few women have participated in the labor force to the same degree as men, it is difficult to set up direct comparisons between the earnings of men and women with the same lifetime pattern of work.

Among women 30-44 years old the gain from continuous work was apparently very large. Thus the women who had worked less than half of the years since leaving school earned only 49 percent as much as men, while the small group of women who had worked each year earned 75 percent as much as men.

Interestingly, single women who had worked each year since leaving school earned slightly more than single men.

More sophisticated comparisons, adjusting for additional differences in training, continuity at work, and education, can be made. One recent study found that the earnings differential was reduced to below 20 percent after taking account of such differences.

Direct discrimination versus role differentiation

A differential, perhaps on the order of 20 percent, between the earnings of men and women remains after adjusting for factors such as education, work experience during the year, and even lifelong work experience. How much of this differential is due to differences in experience or in performance on the job which could not be measured adequately, and

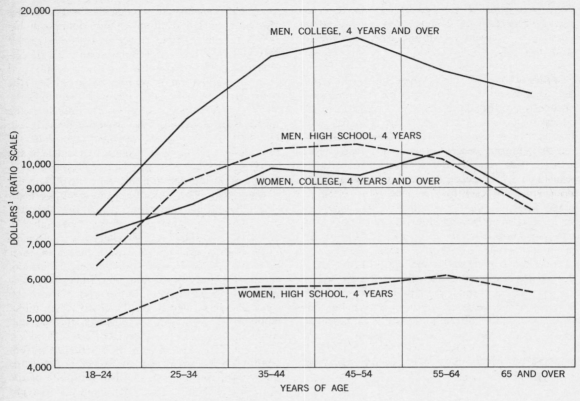

DOLLARS[1] (RATIO SCALE)

20,000

MEN, COLLEGE, 4 YEARS AND OVER

MEN, HIGH SCHOOL, 4 YEARS

10,000
9,000
WOMEN, COLLEGE, 4 YEARS AND OVER
8,000

7,000

6,000
WOMEN, HIGH SCHOOL, 4 YEARS

5,000

4,000

18–24   25–34   35–44   45–54   55–64   65 AND OVER

YEARS OF AGE

1 Median income of full-time, year-round workers, 1971.

Chart 2   Annual income for male and female high school and college graduates.
Source: Department of Commerce

how much to discrimination? The question is difficult to answer, in part because there are differences of opinion about what should be classified as
discrimination.

Some studies have succeeded in narrowing the
male-female differential well below 20 percent. Indeed, Department of Labor surveys have found
that the differential almost disappears when men's
and women's earnings are compared within detailed job classifications and within the same establishment. In the very narrow sense of equal pay
for the same job in the same plant there may be
little difference between women and men. However, in this way the focus of the problem is shifted
but not eliminated. For then we must explain why
women have such a different job structure from
men and why they are employed in different types
of establishments.

Prejudice.   There is clearly prejudice against
women engaging in particular activities. Some patients reject women doctors, some clients reject
women lawyers, some customers reject automobile
saleswomen, and some workers reject women
bosses. Employers also may have formulated discriminatory attitudes about women, exaggerating
the risk of job instability or client acceptance and
therefore excluding women from on-the-job training which would advance their careers.

In fact, even if employers do estimate correctly
the average job turnover of women, women who
are strongly committed to their jobs may suffer
from [stereotype] "statistical discrimination" by
being treated as though their own behavior resem-
bled the average. The extent to which this type of
[stereotype] discrimination occurs depends on how
costly it is for employers to distinguish women

who will have a strong job commitment from those who will not. Finally, because some occupations restrict the number of newcomers they take in and because women move in and out of the labor force more often, more women than men tend to fall into the newcomer category and to be thus excluded. For example, restrictive entry policies may have kept women out of the skilled crafts.

Type casting. On the other hand, as discussed above, some component of the earnings differential and of the occupational differential stems from differences in role orientation which start with differences in education and continue through marriage, where women generally are expected to assume primary responsibility for the home and subordinate their own outside work to their household responsibilities.

It is not now possible to distinguish in a quantitative way between the discrimination which bars women from jobs solely because of their sex, and the role differentiation whereby women, either through choice or necessity, restrict their careers because of the demands of their homes. Some may label the latter as a pervasive societal discrimination which starts in the cradle; nonetheless, it is useful to draw the distinction.

One other missing link in our chain of understanding of these problems is the value of the work done at home by women. One study has found that women college graduates tend to reduce their outside work when their children are small more than less educated women, and that they also devote more time to the training of their children. Of course this pattern is undoubtedly facilitated by the higher income of their husbands. However, this pattern also results in a considerable sacrifice of earnings, and one may infer that these women have therefore placed a very high value on the personal attention they can give their children. Without more information, it is difficult to evaluate the full extent to which women's capabilities have actually been underutilized by society.

Special problems: the female-headed household

In 1971, some 6 million families, about 11.5 percent of all families, were headed by women. These women are widowed, divorced, separated, or single, and many have responsibilities for the support of children in fatherless families or of other rela-

tives. Close to two-thirds of all female-headed families include children; the average number of children under 18 years of age in a female-headed family with children was about 2.3 in 1971, about the same as in male-headed families with children.

As a result of the division of labor within families, the average woman who has been married has not had the same labor market experience or vocationally oriented training as her husband. Unless she has a substantial alimony or pension, she is likely to face financial difficulties. The median income of female-headed families was $5,116 in 1971, less than half the income of male-headed families ($10,930). When women who head families were full-time, year-round workers, the family's median income was $7,916; but only 32 percent of women heading families were able to be full-time, year-round workers. And the woman who heads a family and works has additional expenses of child care and other home care expenses.

Black female family heads. The problems faced by the woman who heads a household are particularly acute if the woman is black, and 27 percent of women heading households are black. For this group, median family income was only $3,645 in 1971. Although, at higher education levels, black women now earn amounts comparable to white women, those black women who head families are at a disadvantage compared to white women. The median personal income of white women heading households and working year-round, full-time was $6,527 in 1971, compared to $5,227 for black women in the same position.

As a result of the combination of a large number of dependents and the difficulty of maintaining the dual responsibility of monetary support and home care, many female-headed families fall below the low-income level. In 1971, 34 percent of female-headed families were below the low-income level, compared to 7 percent for male-headed families. Among black households with a female head, 54 percent were below the low-income level. A large proportion receive public assistance. In 1971, 30 percent of the women heading households received public assistance payments.

Welfare assistance bias. It has been suggested, though not proved, that widespread availability of public assistance has encouraged husbands to desert their wives or wives to leave their husbands in families where the husband earns little more than the amount of welfare benefits his family would be entitled to in his absence. Remarriage may also be discouraged because the low-income mother would then lose her entire public stipend, including the child support portion, and without some outside child support a man might be reluctant to marry a woman with several children.

Among the women who are now welfare recipients many are handicapped by lack of education and training and are not in a position to earn an income that would lift them and their families above poverty levels. A program established in 1967, the Work Incentive Program, now gives many mothers currently on welfare, training and placement assistance so that they can improve their ability to support themselves and their dependents.

The income tax

The tax treatment of working wives is one of the more difficult problems. The income tax law as such treats men and women equally and, indeed, its effects on single men and single women are the same. However, the tax structure [has] unequal effects on the second earner of a married couple, who is usually the wife.

Only income arising from market transactions is taxed. Indeed, there is no practical way to assign a market value to the unpaid work performed at home and then subject it to the tax. As a result, the tax system imposes a general bias in the economy favoring unpaid work at home compared to paid work in the market. However, the bias and the resulting disincentive toward market work are particularly relevant for the married woman who traditionally has done more work at home.

An equity problem also arises from this situation. To use a hypothetical example, a husband and wife each earning $8,000 would pay the same income tax as a couple where the husband alone works and earns $16,000, although the couple with two earners will have the additional expenses of buying the services which would be produced at home and untaxed if the wife did not work.

Remedies for the situation are not easy to find. One suggestion has been to allow working wives to deduct a given percentage of their earnings from their income for tax purposes. However, this would be unfair to single persons, who also incur expenses of going to work. A general earned income credit has also been suggested, but this creates a bias against investments in capital and in favor of wage income.

As discussed below, the Revenue Act of 1971 has given expanded tax relief to working wives with children by allowing more liberalized child care deductions to couples within a given income range. This provision, however, does not affect couples without children or couples with combined incomes outside the allowable income range.

Child care: a crying need

Provision for child care is a cost to working mothers and a major obstacle to the employment of many other mothers who would work outside the home if they could find satisfactory arrangements for taking care of their children. As more mothers have taken jobs outside the home, and more weigh the possibility of doing so, several major questions about child care have become intense national issues.

One question is whether the Government should pay for part or all of the cost of child care. This question is usually raised about the Federal Government, but it could be equally asked about State or local governments. According to one view of the matter parents have chosen to have children, which implies a certain allocation of their resources, therefore they have no reason to burden other taxpayers to look after the children. Another view of the matter is that Government subsidies can be justified and different groups have cited different reasons. The point has been made that the pressures of custom result in a bias against the wife going to work while the husband stays home with the children. A child care subsidy for working mothers would help remove any harmful effects of this cultural bias. Another reason given is that there is a national interest in the proper care of children, who are, of course, the future nation, and that this case justifies Government subsidies. The analogy commonly given is to public education.

Government has given subsidies to families with children but there has been no consistent philosophy behind them. At the extreme, with respect to children in very poor families, we have long recognized the need for public assistance in the form of the program of Aid to Families with Dependent Children. This program is not specifically addressed to children with working mothers. In fact, until recently it was tilted *against* helping working mothers. The Federal Government also provides a form of assistance for child care through the income tax. With the Revenue Act of 1971, a much more liberal deduction than had ever been provided was instituted specifically for child care expenses incurred by working wives. Below a combined husband-wife income of $18,000, a working wife can now deduct up to $400 a month for child care expenses. The deduction is scaled downwards to zero as combined income goes from $18,000 to $27,600. The two groups not covered are women whose family income is too low to benefit from a tax deduction and women at the other end of the income scale.

Public discussion of Government support for child care has not clearly distinguished among several possible objectives:

(a) To reward and assist the care of all small children;

(b) To assist the care of small children whose parents might not be otherwise able to care for them;

(c) To assist the care of the small children of working mothers;

(d) To assist in the care of small children in a particular way—through day-care institutions, or at home, etc.

Both the amount of Government support that is desirable, and the form it should take if it is to be provided, depend on the choice made among these objectives.

Unavailability of day care centers

Recently, publicly supported institutional group care, or day care, has received considerable attention as one approach to helping the working mother. Some have also stressed day care as a developmental program. It may be noted that a very small proportion of working women have depended on group day care in an institutional center. A Government-sponsored survey of 1965 found that, among employed mothers of children under 6, only 6.4 percent depended on school or

group care centers. About 47 percent of the women arranged to have their children cared for at home, often by a relative. The rest mainly arranged for care in someone else's home (31 percent) or looked after the child while working (15 percent).

Some have attributed the low use of day care to a failure of the market to provide a service that would be utilized if financing were available. Others have interpreted it as an indication that the true demand for institutional day care is low. Even among more affluent and knowledgeable working mothers who presumably could afford it, dependence on institutional group care is low. A survey of college graduates found that in 1964, among those who worked and who had children under 6 years, 9 percent used group care, which included nursery schools, kindergartens, and day-care centers. Most (73 percent) arranged for care in their own home.

Whether institutional day care provides the best use of dollars spent on child care has yet to be established. While this issue has not been resolved, it is clear that the problems of mothers who want and need to work require serious attention and a continuing search for new solutions.

Government action

Government has been profoundly concerned with promoting full equality of opportunity for women within both the public and the private sectors.

A number of laws have been passed and Executive Orders issued which deal with discrimination by employers. Included are the Equal Pay Act of 1963, requiring employers to compensate men and women in the same establishment equally for work of equivalent skill and responsibility, and Title VII of the Civil Rights Act of 1964, which prohibits discrimination in hiring, discharging, compensation, and other aspects of employment. Title VII is administered by the Equal Employment Opportunity Commission (EEOC). The Equal Employment Opportunity Act, signed by the President in 1972, gave the EEOC enforcement power through the courts in sex-discrimination cases. In December 1971, Order No. 4, under Executive Order 11246, was extended to women. This Order requires Federal contractors employing more than 50 workers and holding contracts of $50,000 or more to formulate written affirmative action plans, with goals and timetables, to ensure equal opportunities. Title IX of the Education Amendments of 1972 prohibits discrimination in educational programs or activities on the basis of sex.

The Equal Rights Amendment to the Constitution, which was strongly supported by the President, passed the Senate on March 22, 1972, and has now been ratified by 22 States. The proposed amendment would provide that "equality of rights under the law shall not be denied or abridged by the United States or by any State on account of sex," and would authorize the Congress and the States to enforce the amendment by appropriate legislation. The purpose of the proposed amendment would be to provide constitutional protection against laws and official practices that treat men and women differently.

It is only in the past few years that the problems women face as a group have been given the widespread recognition they deserve. There is much to be learned before we can even ask all the appropriate questions. Many of the problems involve profound issues of family and social organization. By listening to diverse groups and to the discussion of the public it is hoped that Government will be able to find its appropriate role.

Quality of Life

Reading 63

A century ago John Ruskin was a lone voice criticizing political economy for its preoccupation with money and material growth, and for its neglect of human values. Today economics has a mighty army of such critics.

Instead of denying the merits of such charges, modern economics is beginning to tackle these genuine issues. Professors William Nordhaus and James Tobin of Yale start with the inadequacies of the GNP as conventionally measured. They develop the theoretical adjustments needed to transform GNP into a measure of Net Economic Welfare (NEW). Equally important, they prepare numerical estimates.

Apparently NEW is still growing. But it grows at only two-thirds the annual rate of per capita real GNP. And unless we do more about urban blight, environmental pollution, and ecological recycling, NEW will fall increasingly short of conventional GNP growth.

Questions to guide the reading

Would the authors agree that "war makes for economic prosperity"? That a move to a four-day week would kill off a fifth of NEW? That the earnings of working wives are a clear gain to NEW? From their analysis, do they think, "Yes, growth is obsolete"?

Is Growth Obsolete?

William Nordhaus and James Tobin

New campaign against growth

A long decade ago economic growth was the reigning fashion of political economy. It was simultaneously the hottest subject of economic theory and research, a slogan eagerly claimed by politicians of all stripes, and a serious objective of the policies of governments.

The climate of opinion has changed dramatically. Disillusioned critics indict both economic science and economic policy for blind obeisance to aggregate material "progress," and for neglect of its costly side effects. Growth, it is charged, distorts national priorities, worsens the distribution of income, and irreparably damages the environment.

Paul Erlich speaks for a multitude when he says, "We must acquire a life style which has as its goal maximum freedom and happiness for the individual, not a maximum Gross National Product."

Growth was in an important sense a discovery of economics after the Second World War. Of course economic development has always been the grand theme of historically minded scholars of large mind and bold concept, notably Marx, Schumpeter, Kuznets. But the mainstream of economic analysis was not comfortable with phenomena of change and progress.

Last decade's standard growth theory.
By now modern growth theory is well enough formulated to have made its way into textbooks. It is a theory of the growth of potential [or full employment] output. The theory relates potential output to three determinants: the labor force, the state of technology, and the stock of human and tangible capital. Simple as it is, the model fits the observed trends of economic growth reasonably well.

In the early 1960s growth became a proclaimed objective of government policy, in this country as elsewhere. Who could be against it?

To economists schooled in postwar growth theory, growth policy meant deliberate effort to speed up the growth of potential output itself, specifically to accelerate the productivity of labor: measures that advanced technological knowledge and measures that increased the share of potential output devoted to accumulation of physical or human capital.

Sacrificing now for the future.
Growth measures nearly always involve diversions of current resources from other uses, sacrifices of current consumption for the benefit of succeeding generations of consumers. Enthusiasts for faster growth are advocates of the future against the present. Their case rests on the view that in a market economy left to itself, the future would be shortchanged because too small a fraction of current output would be saved. We mention this point now because we shall return later to the ironical fact that the anti-growth men of the 1970s believe that it is they who represent the claims of a fragile future against a voracious present.

Needed: Not GNP but Net Economic Welfare (MEW, or NEW)

We have chosen to direct our attention to important problems raised by those who question the desirability and possibility of future growth: How good are measures of output currently used for evaluating the growth of economic welfare? Does the growth process inevitably waste our national resources? How does the rate of population growth affect economic welfare? In particular, what would be the effect of zero population growth?

Adjusting GNP.
Gross national product is not a measure of economic welfare. Erlich is right in

From William Nordhaus and James Tobin, "Is Growth Obsolete?" *Economic Growth* (Fiftieth Anniversary Colloquium V), National Bureau of Economic Research, New York, 1972. Reprinted in abridgment with the kind permission of the authors and the National Bureau of Economic Research.

claiming that maximization of GNP is not a proper objective of policy. Economists all know that, and yet their everyday use of GNP as the standard measure of economic performance apparently conveys the impression that they are evangelistic worshipers of GNP.

An obvious shortcoming of GNP is that it is an index of production, not consumption. The goal of economic activity, after all, is consumption. The economic profession has been slow to develop, either conceptually or statistically, a measure of economic performance oriented to consumption, broadly defined and carefully calculated. We have constructed a primitive and experimental "measure of economic welfare" (MEW) [or Net Economic Welfare (NEW)], in which we attempt to allow for the more obvious discrepancies between GNP and economic welfare.

In proposing a welfare measure, we in no way deny the importance of the conventional national income accounts or of the output measures based upon them. Our MEW is largely a rearrangement of items of the national accounts.

1. Reclassification of GNP final expenditures

Our purposes are first, to subtract some items that are better regarded as instrumental and intermediate than as final output, and second, to allocate all remaining items between consumption and net investment. Since the national accounts do not differentiate among government purchases of goods and services, one of our major tasks will be to split them among the three categories: intermediate, consumption, and net investment. We will also reclassify some private expenditures.

Intermediate products are goods and services whose contributions to present or future consumer welfare are completely counted in the values of other goods and services. To avoid double counting they should not be included in reckoning the net yield of economic activity. Thus all national income accounts reckon as final consumption the bread but not the flour and as capital formation the finished house but not the lumber.

Capital consumption. The depreciation of capital stocks is a cost of production, and output required to offset the depreciation is intermediate as surely as materials consumed in the productive process.

For most purposes, including welfare indexes, NNP is preferable to GNP. Only the difficulties and lags in estimating capital consumption have made GNP the popular statistic.

However, NNP itself fails to treat many durable goods as capital, and counts as final their entire output whether for replacement or accumulation. These elementary points are worth repeating because some of our colleagues are telling the public that economists glorify wasteful "through-put" for its own sake. Focusing on NNP, and accounting for all durables as capital goods, would avoid such foolish paradoxes as the implication that deliberate efforts to make goods more perishable raise national output. We estimate, however, that proper treatment of consumer durables has little quantitative effect.

The other capital consumption adjustments we have made arise from allowing for government capital and for the educational and medical capital embodied in human beings. In effect, we have reclassified education and health expenditures, both public and private, as capital investments.

Growth requirements. In principle net national product tells how much consumption the economy could indefinitely sustain. GNP does not tell that; consuming the whole GNP in any year would impair future consumption prospects. But *per capita* rather than aggregate consumption is the welfare objective; neither economists nor other observers would as a rule regard sheer increase in the numbers of people enjoying the same average standard of living as a gain in welfare. Even NNP exaggerates sustainable *per capita* consumption, except in a society with stationary population—another example of pervasiveness of the "stationary" assumption in the past. Per capita consumption cannot be sustained with zero net investment; the capital stock must be growing at the same rate as population and the labor force. This capital-widening requirement is as truly a cost of staying in the same position as outright capital consumption.

This principle is clear enough when growth is simply increase in population and the labor force. Its application to an economy with technological progress is by no means clear. Indeed, the very concept of national income becomes fuzzy. Should the capital-widening requirement then be interpreted to mean that capital should keep pace with output and technology, not just with the labor force? If so, the implied sustainable consumption per capita grows with the rate of technological progress. This is the point of view which we have taken in what follows. On the other hand, a given level of consumption per capita could be sustained with a steady decline in the capital-output ratio, thanks to technological progress.

The growth requirement is shown on line 7 of Table 1. This is clearly a significant correction, measuring about 16 per cent of GNP in 1965.

Our calculations distinguish between actual and sustainable per capita consumption. *Actual MEW* may exceed or fall short of *sustainable MEW,* the amount that could be consumed while meeting both capital consumption and growth requirements. If these requirements are met, per capita consumption can grow at the trend rate of increase in labor productivity. When actual MEW is less than sustainable MEW, the economy is making even better provision for future consumers; when actual MEW exceeds sustainable MEW, current consumption in effect includes some of the fruits of future progress.

Instrumental expenditures.   Since GNP and NNP are measures of production rather than of welfare, they count many activities that are evidently not directly sources of utility themselves but are regrettably necessary inputs to activities that may yield utility. Some consumer outlays are only instrumental, for example, the costs of commuting to work. Some government "purchases" are also of this nature—for example, police services, sanitation services, road maintenance, national defense. Expenditures on these items are among the necessary overhead costs of a complex industrial nation-state, although there is plenty of room for disagreement as to necessary amounts. We are making no judgments on such issues in classifying these outlays as intermediate rather than final uses of resources. Nevertheless, these decisions are difficult and controversial.

Excluding defense expenditures and other "regrettable" items.   The issues are clearly illustrated in the important case of national defense. We exclude defense expenditures. We see no direct effect of defense expenditures on household economic welfare. No reasonable country (or household)

buys "national defense" for its own sake. If there were no war or risk of war, there would be no need for defense expenditures and no one would be the worse without them. Conceptually, then, defense expenditures are gross but not net output.

The second reason is that defense expenditures are input rather than output data. Measurable output is especially elusive in the case of defense. Conceptually, the output of the defense effort is national security. Has the value of the nation's security risen from $0.5 billion to $50 billion over the period from 1929 to 1965? Obviously not. It is patently more reasonable to assume that the rise in expenditure was due to deterioration in international relations and to changes in military technology. The cost of providing a given level of security has risen enormously. If there has been no corresponding gain in security since 1929, the defense cost series is a very misleading indicator of improvements in welfare.

The economy's ability to meet increased defense costs speaks well for its productive performance. But the diversion of productive capacity to this purpose cannot be regarded simply as a shift of national preferences and the product mix. Just as we count technological progress, managerial innovation, and environmental change when they work in our favor (consider new business machines or mineral discoveries) so we must count a deterioration in the environment when it works against us (consider bad weather and war). From the point of view of economic welfare, an arms control or disarmament agreement which would free resources and raise consumption by 10 per cent would be just as significant as new industrial processes yielding the same gains.

In classifying defense costs—or police protection or public health expenditures—as regrettable and instrumental, we certainly do not deny the possibility that given the unfavorable circumstances that prompt these expenditures consumers will ultimately be better off with them than without them. This may or may not be the case. The only judgment we make is that these expenditures yield no direct satisfactions. Even if the "regrettable" outlays are rational responses to unfavorable shifts in the environment of economic activity, we believe that a welfare measure, perhaps unlike a production measure, should record such environmental change.

We must admit, however, that the line between final and instrumental outlays is very hard to draw. For example, the philosophical problems raised by the malleability of consumer wants are too deep to be resolved in economic accounting. Consumers are susceptible to influence by the examples and tastes of other consumers and by the sales efforts of producers. Maybe all our wants are just regrettable necessities; maybe productive activity does no better than to satisfy the wants which it generates; maybe our net welfare product is tautologically zero. More seriously, we cannot measure welfare exclusively by the quantitative flows of goods and services. We need other gauges of the health of individuals and societies. These, too, will be relative to the value systems which determine whether given symptoms indicate health or disease. But the "social indicators" movement of recent years still lacks a coherent, integrative conceptual and statistical framework.

We estimate that overhead and regrettable expenses, so far as we have been able to define and measure them, rose from 8 per cent to 16 per cent of GNP over the period 1929-65 (Table 1, line 4).

2. Imputations for capital services, leisure, and nonmarket work

In the national income accounts, rent is imputed on owner-occupied homes and counted as consumption and income. We must make similar imputations in other cases to which we have applied capital accounting. Like owner-occupied homes, other consumer durables and public investments yield consumption directly, without market transactions. Our measure understates economic welfare and its growth to the extent that education and medical care are direct rather than indirect sources of consumer satisfaction.

The omission of leisure and of nonmarket productive activity from measures of production conveys the impression that economists are blindly materialistic. Economic theory teaches that welfare could rise, even while NNP falls, as the result of voluntary choices to work for pay fewer hours per week, weeks per year, years per lifetime.

These imputations unfortunately raise serious conceptual questions, discussed at some length in section 3, below. Suppose that in calculating aggregate dollar consumption the hours devoted to leisure and nonmarket productive activity are val-

ued at their presumed opportunity cost, the money wage rate.

In Table 1 we provide calculations for MEW.

3. Disamenities of urbanization

The national income accounts largely ignore the many sources of utility or disutility that are not associated with market transactions or measured by the market value of goods and services. If one of my neighbors cultivates a garden of ever-increasing beauty, and another makes more and more noise, neither my increasing appreciation of the one nor my growing annoyance with the other comes to the attention of the Department of Commerce.

Likewise there are some socially productive assets (for example, the environment) that do not appear in any balance sheets. Their services to producers and consumers are not valued in calculating national income. By the same token no allowance is made for depletion of their capacity to yield services in the future.

External diseconomies. Many of the negative "externalities" of economic growth are connected with urbanization and congestion. The secular advances recorded in NNP figures have accompanied a vast migration from rural agriculture to urban industry. Without this occupational and residential revolution we could not have enjoyed the fruits of technological progress. But some portion of the higher earnings of urban residents may simply be compensation for the disamenities of urban life and work. If so we should not count as a gain of welfare the full increments of NNP that result from moving a man from farm or small town to city. The persistent association of higher wages with higher population densities offers one method of estimating the costs of urban life as they are valued by people making residential and occupational decisions.

We have tried to estimate by cross-sectional regressions the income differentials necessary to hold people in localities with greater population densities. As can be seen [in Table 1 line 5C], the estimated disamenity premium is quite substantial, running about 5 per cent of GNP. Nevertheless, the urbanization of the population has not been so rapid that charging it with this cost significantly reduces the estimated rate of growth of the economy.

Table 1   Gross National Product and MEW, Various Years, 1929–65 (billions of dollars, 1958 prices)

	1929	1935	1945	1947	1954	1958	1965
1. Gross national product	203.6	169.5	355.2	309.9	407.0	447.3	617.8
2. Capital consumption, NIPA	−20.0	−20.0	−21.9	−18.3	−32.5	−38.9	−54.7
3. Net national product, NIPA	183.6	149.5	333.3	291.6	374.5	408.4	563.1
4. NIPA final output reclassified as regrettables and intermediates							
a. Government	−6.7	−7.4	−146.3	−20.8	−57.8	−56.4	−63.2
b. Private	−10.3	−9.2	−9.2	−10.9	−16.4	−19.9	−30.9
5. Imputations for items not included in NIPA							
a. Leisure	339.5	401.3	450.7	466.9	523.2	554.9	626.9
b. Nonmarket activity	85.7	109.2	152.4	159.6	211.5	239.7	295.4
c. Disamenities	−12.5	−14.1	−18.1	−19.1	−24.3	−27.6	−34.6
d. Services of public and private capital	29.7	24.2	31.0	36.7	48.9	54.8	78.9
6. Additional capital consumption	−19.3	−33.4	−11.7	−50.8	−35.2	−27.3	−92.7
7. Growth requirement	−46.1	−46.7	−65.8	+5.4	−63.1	−78.9	−101.8
8. Sustainable MEW	543.6	573.4	716.3	858.6	961.3	1,047.7	1,241.1

NIPA = national income and product accounts.
Note: Variants A, B, C in the table correspond to different assumptions about the bearing of technological progress on leisure and nonmarket activities. Variant A assumes that neither has benefited from technological progress at the rate of increase of real wages; variant C assumes that neither has so benefited; variant B assumes that leisure has not been augmented by technological progress but other nonmarket activities have benefited. See section 3 for explanation.
Source: Appendix Table A.17 of ibid.

The adjustments and the relations of GNP, NNP, and MEW are summarized in Table 1. For reasons previously indicated, we believe that a welfare measure should have the dimension *per capita*. We would stress the per capita MEW figures computable from the data of Table 1.

*   *   *

Summary.   Although the numbers presented here are very tentative, they do suggest the following observations. First, MEW is quite different from conventional output measures. Some consumption items omitted from GNP are of substantial quantitative importance. Second, our preferred variant of per capita MEW has been growing more slowly than per capita NNP (1.1 per cent for MEW as against 1.7 per cent for NNP, at annual rates over the period 1929–65). Yet MEW has been growing. The progress indicated by conventional national accounts is not just a myth that evaporates when a welfare-oriented measure is substituted.

Readings 64 and 65   Debate on Doomsday

Zero Population Growth (ZPG), Zero Economic Growth (ZEG)—these have replaced the former fad for GNP growth unlimited. Undoubtedly, the Los Angeles smog and the Lake Erie pollution have elevated people's consciousness of the dangers to ecological balance. Urban blight spreads and urban sprawl shrinks the countryside. No wonder the fear of Malthus has returned.

The first reading is taken from the much publicized *Limits to Growth,* a study by an M.I.T. team of systems analysts commissioned by the so-called Club of Rome, a consortium of private and public leaders concerned with world problems. Dennis Meadows, leader of the team and now at Dartmouth College, has been a student of M.I.T.'s Jay Forrester, inventor of the ceramic memory bank for computers and author of *Industrial Dynamics,* of *Urban Dynamics,* and of *World Dynamics.*

The second reading is by the brilliant and versatile Robert Solow of M.I.T., whom we've already met in earlier Readings.

Questions to guide the reading

Will new science keep ahead of eventual shortages? If the Club of Rome had written in 1873 or 1800, what mistakes might they have made? Would you take even odds to bet that, by 1999, world growth will have substantially declined?

Why are less-developed nations resentful of attempts to curb growth? Should they be? Will the United States reduce its per capita standard of living—by, say, one-half—in order that a limited world GNP can provide better minimum subsistence for the billions who still live in abject poverty?

Notice how economists jump on engineers and biologists who fail to realize that scarcity of resources will raise their prices to the point of rationing their use, induce use of substitutes, and promote new inventions. Is necessity always "the mother of invention"?

How do you draw the line between "hysteria" and "complacency"? If doomsdayers exaggerate, is it still in a good cause?

Reading 64

The Limits to Growth

Donella H. Meadows
Dennis L. Meadows
Jørgen Randers
William W. Behrens III

Our world model was built specifically to investigate five major trends of global concern—accelerating industrialization, rapid population growth, widespread malnutrition, depletion of nonrenewable resources, and a deteriorating environment. These trends are all interconnected in many ways, and their development is measured in decades or centuries, rather than in months or years. With the model we are seeking to understand the causes of these trends, their interrelationships, and their implications as much as one hundred years in the future.

The model we have constructed is, like every other model, imperfect, oversimplified, and unfinished. We are well aware of its shortcomings, but we believe that it is the most useful model now available for dealing with problems far out on the space-time graph. To our knowledge it is the only formal model in existence that is truly global in scope, that has a time horizon longer than thirty

From Donella H. Meadows, Dennis L. Meadows, Jørgen Randers, and William W. Behrens III, *The Limits to Growth* (A report for the Club of Rome's project on the Predicament of Mankind), Universe Books, New York, 1972. Reprinted in abridgment with the kind permission of the authors and publishers (Universe books, Potomac Associates, and Earth Inland Ltd.).

years, and that includes important variables such as population, food production, and pollution, not as independent entities, but as dynamically interacting elements, as they are in the real world.

Since ours is a formal, or mathematical, model it also has two important advantages over mental models. First, every assumption we make is written in a precise form so that it is open to inspection and criticism by all. Second, after assumptions have been scrutinized, discussed, and revised to agree with our best current knowledge, their implications for the future behavior of the world system can be traced without error by a computer, no matter how complicated they become.

We feel that the advantages listed above make this model unique among all mathematical and mental world models available to us today. But there is no reason to be satisfied with it in its present form. We intend to alter, expand, and improve it as our own knowledge and the world data base gradually improve.

Opening up debate

In spite of the preliminary state of our work, we believe it is important to publish the model and our findings now. Decisions are being made every day, in every part of the world, that will affect the physical, economic, and social conditions of the world system for decades to come. These decisions cannot wait for perfect models and total understanding. They will be made on the basis of some model, mental or written, in any case. We feel that the model described here is already sufficiently developed to be of some use to decision-makers. Furthermore, the basic behavior modes we have already observed in this model appear to be so fundamental and general that we do not expect our broad conclusions to be substantially altered by further revisions.

It is not the purpose of this book to give a complete, scientific description of all the data and mathematical equations included in the world model. Such a description can be found in the final technical report of our project. Rather, in *The Limits to Growth* we summarize the main features of the model and our findings in a brief, nontechnical way. The emphasis is meant to be not on the equations or the intricacies of the model, but on what it tells us about the world. We have used a computer as a tool to aid our own understanding of the causes and consequences of the accelerating trends that characterize the modern world, but familiarity with computers is by no means necessary to comprehend or to discuss our conclusions. The implications of those accelerating trends raise issues that go far beyond the proper domain of a purely scientific document. They must be debated by a wider community than that of scientists alone. Our purpose here is to open that debate.

Preliminary conclusions

The following conclusions have emerged from our work so far. We are by no means the first group to have stated them. For the past several decades, people who have looked at the world with a global, long-term perspective have reached similar conclusions. Nevertheless, the vast majority of policy-makers seems to be actively pursuing goals that are inconsistent with these results.

Our conclusions are:

1. If the present growth trends in world population, industrialization, pollution, food production, and resource depletion continue unchanged, the limits to growth on this planet will be reached sometimes within the next one hundred years. The most probable result will be a rather sudden and uncontrollable decline in both population and industrial capacity.

2. It is possible to alter these growth trends and to establish a condition of ecological and economic stability that is sustainable far into the future. The state of global equilibrium could be designed so that the basic material needs of each person on earth are satisfied and each person has an equal opportunity to realize his individual human potential.

3. If the world's people decide to strive for this second outcome rather than the first, the sooner they begin working to attain it, the greater will be their chances of success.

These conclusions are so far-reaching and raise so many questions for further study that we are quite frankly overwhelmed by the enormity of the job that must be done. We hope that this book will serve to interest other people, in many fields of study and in many countries of the world, to raise the space and time horizons of their concerns and to join us in understanding and preparing for a period of great transition—the transition from growth to global equilibrium.

How to improve matters

We have seen that positive feedback loops operating without any constraints generate exponential growth. In the world system two positive feedback loops are dominant now, producing exponential growth of population and of industrial capital.

In any finite system there must be constraints that can act to stop exponential growth. These constraints are negative feedback loops. The negative loops become stronger and stronger as growth approaches the ultimate limit, or carrying capacity, of the system's environment. Finally the negative loops balance or dominate the positive ones, and growth comes to an end. In the world system the negative feedback loops involve such processes as pollution of the environment, depletion of nonrenewable resources, and famine.

The delays inherent in the action of these negative loops tend to allow population and capital to overshoot their ultimately sustainable levels. The period of overshoot is wasteful of resources. It generally decreases the carrying capacity of the environment as well, intensifying the eventual decline in population and capital.

The growth-stopping pressures from negative feedback loops are already being felt in many parts of human society. The major societal responses to these pressures have been directed at the negative feedback loops themselves. Technological solutions have been devised to weaken the loops or to disguise the pressures they generate so that growth can continue. Such means may have some short-term effect in relieving pressures caused by growth, but in the long run they do nothing to prevent the overshoot and subsequent collapse of the system.

Another response to the problems created by growth would be to weaken the *positive* feedback loops that are generating the growth. Such a solution has almost never been acknowledged as legitimate by any modern society, and it has certainly never been effectively carried out. What kinds of policies would such a solution involve? What sort of world would result? There is almost no historical precedent for such an approach, and thus there is no alternative but to discuss it in terms of mod-

els—either mental models or formal, written models. How will the world model behave if we include in it some policy to control growth deliberately? Will such a policy change generate a "better" behavior mode?

The state of global equilibrium

We are searching for a model output that represents a world system that is:

1. sustainable without sudden and uncontrollable collapse; and
2. capable of satisfying the basic material requirements of all of its people.

Now let us see what policies will bring about such behavior in the world model.

Deliberate constraints on growth

The overwhelming growth in world population caused by the positive birth-rate loop is a recent phenomenon, a result of mankind's very successful reduction of worldwide mortality. There are only two ways to restore the resulting imbalance. Either the birth rate must be brought down to equal the new, lower death rate, or the death rate must rise again. All of the "natural" constraints to population growth operate in the second way—they raise the death rate. Any society wishing to avoid that result must take deliberate action to reduce the birth rate.

In a dynamic model it is a simple matter to counteract runaway positive feedback loops. We need only add to the model [the requirement] that the number of babies born each year be equal to the expected number of deaths in the population that year. As the death rate decreases, because of better food and medical care, the birth rate will decrease simultaneously. Such a requirement, which is as mathematically simple as it is socially complicated, is for our purposes an experimental device, not necessarily a political recommendation.

Stabilizing population alone is not sufficient to prevent overshoot and collapse; a similar run with constant capital and rising population shows that stabilizing capital alone is also not sufficient. We can stabilize the capital stock in the model by requiring that the investment rate equal the depreciation rate, with an additional model link exactly analogous to the population-stabilizing one.

Population and capital reach constant values at a relatively high level of food, industrial output, and services per person. Eventually, however, resource shortages reduce industrial output and the temporarily stable state degenerates.

What model assumptions will give us a combination of a decent living standard with somewhat greater stability? We can improve the model behavior greatly by combining technological changes with value changes that reduce the growth tendencies of the system. Different combinations of such policies give us a series of computer outputs that represent a system with reasonably high values of industrial output per capita and with long-term stability.

The policies that produced [such] behavior:

1. Population is stabilized by setting the birth rate equal to the death rate in 1975. Industrial capital is allowed to increase naturally until 1990, after which it, too, is stabilized, by setting the investment rate equal to the depreciation rate.

2. To avoid a nonrenewable resource shortage, resource consumption per unit of industrial output is reduced to one-fourth of its 1970 value. (This and the following five policies are introduced in 1975.)

3. To further reduce resource depletion and pollution, the economic preferences of society are shifted more toward services such as education and health facilities and less toward factory-produced material goods.

4. Pollution generation per unit of industrial and agricultural output is reduced to one-fourth of its 1970 value.

5. Since the above policies alone would result in a rather low value of food per capita, some people would still be malnourished if the traditional inequalities of distribution persist. To avoid this situation, high value is placed on producing sufficient food for *all* people. Capital is therefore diverted to food production even if such an investment would be considered "uneconomic."

6. This emphasis on highly capitalized agriculture, while necessary to produce enough food, would lead to rapid soil erosion and depletion of soil fertility, destroying long-term stability in the agricultural sector. Therefore the use of agricultural capital has been altered to make soil en-

richment and preservation a high priority. This policy implies, for example, use of capital to compost urban organic wastes and return them to the land (a practice that also reduces pollution).

7. The drains on industrial capital for higher services and food production and for resource recycling and pollution control under the above six conditions would lead to a low final level of industrial capital stock. To counteract this effect, the average lifetime of industrial capital is increased, implying better design for durability and repair and less discarding because of obsolescence. This policy also tends to reduce resource depletion and pollution.

The stable world population is only slightly larger than the population today. There is more than twice as much food per person as the average value in 1970, and world average lifetime is nearly 70 years. The average industrial output per capita is well above today's level, and services per capita have tripled. Total average income per capita (industrial output, food, and services combined) is about $1,800. This value is about half the present average US income, equal to the present average European income, and three times the present average world income. Resources are still being gradually depleted, as they must be under any realistic assumption, but the rate of depletion is so slow that there is time for technology and industry to adjust to changes in resource availability.

The numerical constants that characterize this model run are not the only ones that would produce a stable system. Other people or societies might resolve the various trade-offs differently, putting more or less emphasis on services or food or pollution or material income. This example is included merely as an illustration of the levels of population and capital that are *physically maintainable* on the earth, under the most optimistic assumptions. The model cannot tell us how to attain these levels. It can only indicate a set of mutually consistent goals that are attainable.

We do not suppose that any single one of the policies necessary to attain system stability in the model can or should be suddenly introduced in the world by 1975. A society choosing stability as a goal certainly must approach that goal gradually. It is important to realize, however, that the longer exponential growth is allowed to continue, the fewer possibilities remain for the final stable state.

Many people will think that the changes we have introduced into the model to avoid the growth-and-collapse behavior mode are not only impossible, but unpleasant, dangerous, even disastrous in themselves. Such policies as reducing the birth rate and diverting capital from production of material goods, by whatever means they might be implemented, seem unnatural and unimaginable, because they have not, in most people's experience, been tried, or even seriously suggested. Indeed there would be little point even in discussing such fundamental changes in the functioning of modern society if we felt that the present pattern of unrestricted growth were sustainable into the future. All the evidence available to us, however, suggests that of the three alternatives—unrestricted growth, a self-imposed limitation to growth, or a nature-imposed limitation to growth—only the last two are actually possible.

Accepting the nature-imposed limits to growth requires no more effort than letting things take their course and waiting to see what will happen. The most probable result of that decision, as we have tried to show here, will be an uncontrollable decrease in population and capital. The real meaning of such a collapse is difficult to imagine because it might take so many different forms. It might occur at different times in different parts of the world, or it might be worldwide. It could be sudden or gradual. If the limit first reached were that of food production, the nonindustrialized countries would suffer the major population decrease. If the first limit were imposed by exhaustion of nonrenewable resources, the industrialized countries would be most affected. It might be that the collapse would leave the earth with its carrying capacity for animal and plant life undiminished, or it might be that the carrying capacity would be reduced or destroyed. Certainly whatever fraction of the human population remained at the end of the process would have very little left with which to build a new society in any form we can now envision.

Achieving a self-imposed limitation to growth would require much effort. It would involve learning to do many things in new ways. It would tax the ingenuity, the flexibility, and the self-discipline of the human race. Bringing a deliberate, controlled end to growth is a tremendous challenge, not easily met.

Reading 65

"Doomsday Models" and the "Chicken Little" Syndrome: or "The Computer That Cried 'Wolf'"

Robert M. Solow

I would like to state, briefly and bluntly, why I think the various "Doomsday Models" are worthless as science and as guides to public policy. I hope it will not be deduced that I believe problems of population control, environmental degradation, and resource exhaustion to be unimportant, or that I think an adequate response to them is a vague confidence that something will turn up.

They are important problems and, for that very reason, public policy had better be based on sound and careful analysis. I do not think that the global models under discussion provide even the beginnings of that kind of foundation. What follows are some of my reasons.

Structure of the models: assuming one's conclusion

The characteristic conclusion of the models in question is that the natural evolution of the world economy is overshoot of its possible equilibrium output, followed by collapse, and that the collapse is likely to happen within the next 30–70 years unless special and drastic changes are made in the behavior of the system. I call this a "conclusion"

From Robert M. Solow, "Notes on 'Doomsday Models,'" *Proceedings of the National Academy of Sciences USA,* vol. 69, no. 12, December, 1972. Reprinted in abridgment with the kind permission of the author and the editor.

of the models, but it is actually practically an assumption. That is to say, the step from the assumptions to the conclusion that collapse is imminent is so short and so obvious that it hardly needs "an M.I.T. computer" to do the logic and tell the bad news.

Finite, depletable resources. The basic assumption is that the stocks of things like natural resources and the waste-disposal capacity of the environment are finite, that the world economy tends to consume the stocks at an increasing rate, and that there are no mechanisms by which approaching exhaustion tends to turn off consumption gradually. Then, to show how the forecast of overshoot and collapse is resistant against optimism, one is told:

Imagine that the stock of natural resources were actually twice as big as we now believe it to be, or imagine that the annual amount of pollution were once halved and then set to growing again, all that would happen is that the date of collapse is postponed by T years, where T is not a large number.

No economies in resource use?

The annual output of any production process, large or small, divided by the annual employment of labor is called the productivity of labor. Symmetrically, though the usage is less common, one could call output per unit of some particular natural resource (or per unit of natural resources in general) the productivity of natural resources. We usually think of the productivity of labor as rising exponentially, say at 2 or 3% per year, because that is the way it has behaved in the past century or so since the statistics began. But all the Doomsday Models are prepared to allow is a once-for-all increase in the productivity of natural resources from one constant level to another. Why shouldn't the productivity of any given natural resource rise steadily through time, like the productivity of labor?

In fact, though the figures have been less studied, Gross National Product (GNP) per unit of natural resources does seem to rise slowly through time. It is easy to understand why labor productivity rises faster. Labor costs amount to some three-quarters of all costs of producing the real GNP; an increase of 1% in the productivity of labor saves

0.75% of the cost of producing GNP. Resource costs are a much smaller fraction of GNP (about 5%). Therefore, industry and engineering have a much stronger motive to reduce labor requirements per unit of output by 1% than to reduce resource requirements per unit of output by 1% (assuming, which may or may not be true, that it is intrinsically about as hard to do one as to do the other).

But if this is the explanation, then, as the earth's supply of natural resources nears exhaustion and as natural resources become more and more valuable, and as the resource-cost component of GNP rises, the motive to economize resources should become at least as strong as the motive to economize labor. One could imagine that the productivity of resources might begin to increase more rapidly than in the past and to increase fairly steadily.

But then the characteristic assumption-conclusion of the Doomsday Models fails and overshoot-collapse is no longer the inevitable trajectory of the system. Please note that I am not asserting the truth of this counter-story, but only claiming that the overshoot-collapse pattern is built into the models by assumption, very near the surface, and not deduced from any more compelling set of postulates.

Absence of a price system

The most glaring defect of the Forrester-Meadows models is the absence of any sort of functioning price system. The price system is, after all, the main device evolved by capitalist (and, to an increasing extent, even socialist) economies for registering and reacting to relative scarcity. I have already mentioned one way that a price system might radically alter the behavior predicted by the models—by inducing more active search for resource-saving innovations as resource costs bulk larger in total costs and appear to be increasing. There are other, more pedestrian, modes of operation of the market mechanism. Higher and rising prices of exhaustible resources can be expected to lead to the substitution of other, more plentiful, and, therefore, cheaper materials. To the extent that it is impossible to design around or substitute away from expensive natural resources, the prices of commodities containing a lot of them will rise relative to the prices of other goods and services.

Consumers will be driven to buy fewer resource-intensive goods and more of other things. All these effects work automatically to increase the productivity of natural resources, i.e., to reduce resource requirements per unit of GNP, and steadily, not once-and-for-all—indeed, one might say "exponentially" as first approximation.

To forestall misunderstanding, let me say that this is not an argument for *laissez-faire*. Many markets are "imperfect"; they contain substantial elements of monopoly; information is of different quality and spread unevenly among participants; and private interests, to which prices respond, may be in conflict with the public interest. Since the proper response depends to some extent on what is expected to happen and not on what has already happened, uncoordinated activity may lag too far behind events, and even become perverse. Public agencies can try to shorten the lag by providing the best available information about future supplies and demands.

But I don't see how one can have the slightest confidence in the predictions of models that seem to make no room for everyday market forces.

Actual past trends. As a matter of fact, the relative prices of natural resources and resource products have shown no tendency to rise over the past half-century. This means there have been offsets to any progressive impoverishment of deposits—improvements in extraction technology, savings in use, the availability of cheaper substitutes. The situation could, of course, change. If the expert participants in the market now believed that resource prices would be sharply higher at some time in the future, prices would *already* be rising.

Empirical foundations

This raises the question of the reliability of the functional relationships that make up the models. Economics has a long history of experience in constructing determinate dynamic models of a national economy, to be used for simple forecasting and for estimating the effects of alternative public policies. These econometric models range in size from a couple of equations to hundreds. They are usually intended for seeing ahead at most six or eight quarters of a year, but there are many models, based on annual data, that are meant to look

as much as 5 years ahead, perhaps a bit more. Occasionally, such models are allowed to run for 20 or 30 years with plausible forcing functions, but these exercises are usually part of an exploration of the nature of the model as a dynamical system and not genuine forecasts.

I think it is the general experience of econometricians that these models positively devour empirical parameters. They require the estimation of very many coefficients describing the response of one economic variable to changes in another. Because economics is not an experimental science, the only source of parameter values is statistical analysis of the historical record of economic behavior. Econometricians invest much of their effort in the statistical exploitation of time series and whatever other relevant data they can find.

Casual empiricism. So far as one can tell, the Doomsday Models do none of this. There is no trace of detailed statistical estimation of behavior parameters. There is not even any clear standard of goodness of fit, or any reasonably objective test of whether a particular model is any good or not. And indeed, so far as one can tell, some of the important behavior relations that are actually employed appear to be nonsensical, to fly in the face of the facts or to contradict earlier work on the basis of no evidence whatever.

This is a matter of some importance. Econometricians modelling a national economy often have the following experience. Two alternative models—not necessarily radically different, but slightly different in formulation and using slightly different parameter estimates—will fit the observed facts of recent history reasonably well, and about equally well. Moreover, they give forecasts of the immediate future that more or less agree, and which have similar implications for policy. Nevertheless, if you let the models run for many years they will diverge quite considerably, and even may behave in unbelievable ways. One of the reasons for this is that economic quantities are often related to one another with substantial "distributed lags." These lag relationships are extraordinarily difficult to estimate from time series, yet the long-run characteristics of the model may be fairly sensitive to the lag structure.

Long lags play a crucial role in the Doomsday Models. So far as one can tell, the particular lag structures are essentially invented and then made the basis of long extrapolations. One can perhaps excuse this on the grounds that the underlying configuration of the trajectory has already been imposed by *fiat*—as discussed above—so the rest is mere detail.

The Chicken Little syndrome

I have heard it said that, even if the Doomsday Models are all balderdash, the publicity surrounding them has served an important social purpose in drawing the world's attention to the possibility that Spaceship Earth is about to abort. Maybe so.

It seems to me more likely, however, that the net effect will be a minus. A sound analysis of the dynamics of population growth, resource use, and environmental pollution might provide the basis for public policy. It might, that is, suggest a list of things to do that can actually be done, and say what will happen if they are done or if they aren't.

My impression is that the Doomsday Models divert attention from remedial public policy by permitting everyone to blame "the predicament of mankind." Who could pay attention to a humdrum affair like legislation to tax sulfur emissions when the date of the Apocalypse has just been announced by a computer?

Cost-Push Inflation

Readings 66, 67, and 68   Debate on Incomes Policy

"How to get full employment while preserving reasonable price stability?" That is the question confronting every mixed economy today.

Arthur F. Burns, long-time professor at Columbia University and head of the National Bureau of Economic Research, is Chairman of the Federal Reserve Board. Since preparing this Reading, Dr. Burns has changed his mind and is believed to have been one of the most important influences on President Nixon, persuading him in 1971 to abandon his policy of "benign neglect" in the realm of incomes policy. This Nixon decision led to Phases I, II, and III, bringing the Nixon administration pretty much full circle back to the Kennedy-Johnson wage-price guidelines. These guidelines are defended here by Harvard's Otto Eckstein, former Johson Economic Adviser and head of the economic research firm Data Resources, Inc.

John Kenneth Galbraith, who needs no introduction here, states the case for going all the way to permanent mandatory price-wage controls.

Questions to guide the reading

Is there room for industrial statesmanship, presidential exhortation, and union responsibility in a competitive society? In a mixed economy do large corporations and national unions have discretionary market power?

Why are stabilized monetary and fiscal policies indispensable adjuncts to an incomes policy of the guidepost type? If you reject guideposts, what do you put in their place as an incomes policy to reconcile full employment and price stability?

If conditions of supply and demand are constantly shifting, what will be the longer-run consequences of freezing relative prices and wages? If established businesses honestly satisfy the letter of the law, with the passing of time will not there be a premium on those who are less honest and more skillful in finding legal loopholes? Underline in pencil those passages in which you think the author is providing proof rather than assertion for what he is saying.

Reading 66

Wage-Price Guideposts: No

Arthur F. Burns

. . . . Let us try to visualize a little more definitely how the CEA's wage-price guideposts, if they were generally and fully respected, would work out in practice.

Wages and prices

Statistical records stretching back into the nineteenth century demonstrate that, although the over-all productivity of our economy occasionally declines, its trend has been steadily upward. If this continues to be true, as we may reasonably suppose, general observance of the guidelines will result in higher wages every year, regardless of the stage of the business cycle or the level of unemployment or the state of the balance of payments. The rise of wages will be the same, on the average, in years of recession as in years of prosperity; but in any given recession the rise of wages could easily be larger than in the preceding years of prosperity. Furthermore, the average wage will tend to rise in any given year by the same percentage in every firm, regardless of its profitability or the state of the market for different kinds of labor.

However, general observance of the guidepost for prices will not freeze individual prices or the relations among them. What it would tend to freeze is (1) the general level of prices and (2) the ratio of individual prices to unit labor costs of production. The tendency of the price-cost ratio to remain constant will be stronger in some industries than in others. Strictly speaking, the guidepost for prices specifies merely that the ratio of price to unit labor cost of production should not rise; it

does not argue against a decline of the price-cost ratio. Hence, firms or industries experiencing a weak demand for their products or keen foreign competition may need to be content with prices that decline relative to their unit labor costs. On the other hand, firms or industries that are favored in the marketplace would be unable to raise prices relative to their unit labor costs even if their incoming orders were many times as large as their production. Nor would they be able to raise prices to compensate for increases in costs of production other than those of labor.

Income shares

The broad effect of these tendencies would be to keep more or less constant the percentage share of the national income—or of national output—going to labor. Changes in the use of capital relative to the use of labor, whether upward or downward, could still have a large influence on the size of national income but not on the proportion of income accruing to labor. Unless major shifts occurred in the occupational or industrial distribution of employment, any fluctuation in labor's percentage share of the national income would be due primarily to the discrepancy between the movement of over-all productivity in a particular year and the corresponding trend increase. Nonlabor income, in the aggregate, would also tend to be a constant percentage of the national income.

It is well to bear in mind, however, that since profits are only a fraction of nonlabor income, the share of profits in the total national income could either rise or decline. In the postwar period, the amount paid by corporations on account of excises, customs duties, property taxes, licensing fees, and other indirect taxes has risen more rapidly than their net output. If this trend continues, the income share of investors in the corporate sector will tend to undergo a persistent decline, while that of labor will tend to remain constant. . . .

Throttling of competition

The *fundamental* point of the preceding analysis is that general observance of the guideposts would throttle the forces of competition no less effectively than those of monopoly. The point is important because, unlike much of the rest of the world, the rivalry among U.S. business firms is very keen. Even in industries where a few corporations dominate the market—as in the case of automobiles, steel, and aluminum—each corporation competes actively against the others in its industry, against rival products of other industries, and against foreign suppliers. Competition in labor markets is also stronger than casual references to labor monopoly may suggest. After all, only a little over a fourth of the population working for wages or salaries is unionized, and many of the trade unions are weak. By and large, it is competition—not monopoly—that has vast sweep and power in our everyday life. Since free competitive markets would virtually cease to exist in an economy that observed the guidelines, this transformation of the economy merits serious reflection.

To be sure, compliance with the guidelines would be voluntary in the economy we are considering. That, however, may not mean much. For when economic freedom is not exercised, it is no longer a part of life. As far as I can see, an economy in which wages and prices are set voluntarily according to a formula suggested by the government would be almost indistinguishable from an economy in which wages and prices are directly fixed by governmental authorities. In either case—

• the movement of resources toward uses that are favored by the buying public would be impeded;

• the tendency to economize on the use of what happens to be especially scarce, whether it be materials or labor or equipment, would be weakened;

• since prices will no longer tend to equate demand and supply in individual markets, some form of rationing would need to be practiced.

In all likelihood, therefore, a shift from our present market economy to one of voluntary compliance with the guidelines would adversely affect efficiency. It would also adversely affect the rate of economic growth and the rate of improvement of the general standard of living. . . .

Are the guides workable?

This theoretical sketch of how our economy would work if the guidelines were generally and fully observed has blinked institutional factors—such as the adjustments caused by the disappearance of auction markets, the new role of trade unions, and so on. Moreover, our theoretical sketch has tacitly assumed that voluntary compliance with the guidelines is merely a matter of will. Life is not that simple. Even if everyone responded to the government's plea for "cooperation" and sought faithfully to act in accordance with the guidelines, it would frequently be difficult or actually impossible to do so.

There is, first of all, a vast gap in our statistical arsenal. To comply with the guideline for *wages,* businessmen would need to know the trend increase of the over-all output of the nation per man-hour. . . .

Compliance with the *price* guideline would be infinitely harder. For this purpose, every company would need to know the trend increase in the productivity of its own industry and how this increase compares with the trend increase of over-all productivity of the economy. Such information is not generally available, nor is it readily usable.

The productivity indexes now being published, besides being often out of date, lump together a great variety of products. In time, more detailed and more current indexes of productivity will doubtless be constructed, but there are limits to what is statistically feasible. Even if measures of this type become available for each of a thousand or ten thousand industries, much confusion or perlexity will still remain. Better statistics on productivity will reduce these difficulties; however, they cannot possibly remove them.

Other pitfalls and puzzles

Another puzzling problem would be posed by changes in the composition of labor that is used in industry. Consider, for example, the case of a company that has recently decided to employ more skilled workers of different sorts and less unskilled labor. . . .

In view of modern trends that emphasize the use of higher skills, this sort of difficulty would be bound to occur frequently in an economy of voluntary compliance. . . .

Another problem that businessmen and trade-union leaders would need to face is whether the modifications of the guideposts that the Council of Economic Advisers has officially sanctioned apply in a particular case. In assuming, as I have, a general willingness to comply with the guidelines, I have not meant to abstract from human nature entirely. Since the modifications suggested by the Council are phrased in very general terms, men acting in good faith may feel that their situation is precisely the kind of rare case that permits some departure from the guidelines. But will business managers and labor leaders always or even frequently agree in their interpretation of what modifications are permissible? In any event, is it not likely that the modifications will turn out to be numerous, rather than, as now intended by the Administration, relatively few?

In view of these and many other problems that are bound to arise in practice, guidelines would prove unworkable over a very large segment of industry, even if everyone sought conscientiously to observe them. To deal with this critical difficulty, a new governmental apparatus might need to be established; its function would be to spell out detailed rules and to interpret them in individual cases. Although there is no way of telling just how such an agency would work, it seems reasonable to expect that not a few of its clarifying rules and interpretations would be arbitrary, that its advisory rulings would at times involve considerable delay and thereby cause some economic trouble, and that the rulings themselves would have at least some inflationary bias. These factors inevitably cast a cloud over the preceding analysis of how an economy of voluntary compliance would function, but they hardly make the prospect more inviting.

Specter of controls

I have as yet said nothing about the aspect of guidepost policy that has aroused the most skepticism—namely, the likelihood of general observance on a voluntary basis. In recent years unemployment has been fairly large, and many industries have had sufficient capacity to increase output readily. Under such conditions, upward pressure on prices cannot be great. Even so, the guidelines have been sharply criticized or defied by powerful segments of the business and labor community. The critical test of the inhibiting power of the guidelines will come, of course, when both labor and commodity markets become appreciably tighter—and this test may come soon. If the recent wage settlement in the automobile industry is at all indicative, expectations of a high degree of compliance with the guidelines are hardly warranted. Similar experiments in other countries also suggest that general price stability will not long be maintained through voluntary restraint.

But once the government in power has committed itself to a policy, it may become difficult to move off in a new direction. A strong commitment to the policy of the guidelines inevitably means that any extensive private defiance would, besides frustrating the government's anti-inflation policy, injure its prestige. There is always a possibility, therefore, that failure to comply voluntarily with the guidelines will be followed by some coercive measure. This might initially take the form, as has frequently been proposed, of a review by a governmental board of the facts surrounding the price or wage changes that are being contemplated. The thought behind proposals of this nature is that once the facts are clearly developed, the force of public opinion will ordinarily suffice to ensure "responsible" action by corporations and trade unions.

No one can be sure whether this expectation will be fulfilled. But if it is, the governmental review board will have virtually become an agency for fixing prices and wages. If, on the other hand, the board's reports were flouted with any frequency, the next step might well be outright price and wage fixing by the government. It would seem, therefore, that from whatever angle we examine the guidelines, direct controls pop up dangerously around the corner.

Incipient realities

This danger must not be dismissed as an illusion. Although the guidelines are still in their infancy, they have already hardened. Nor has the evolution of the Administration's thinking concerning the guidelines been confined to a literary plane. In April 1962, only three months after the announcement of the guidelines, the Administration moved sternly to force the leading steel companies to cancel the price increases that they had just posted. This interference with the workings of a private market had no clear sanction in law, and it caused consternation in business circles. Fortunately, a crisis was avoided by a prompt and concerted effort of the Administration, in which President Kennedy himself took the leading part, to restore business confidence.

Since then, the government has been more cautious. But it has continued to espouse the need for moderation in the matter of wages and prices, and now and then has even gently rattled its sword. Early in 1964 President Johnson requested the Council to reaffirm the guideposts. He emphasized his commitment to this policy by adding that he would "keep a close watch on price and wage developments, with the aid of an early warning system which is being set up." Last summer, when intimations of a rise in the price of steel appeared in the press, the President lost no time in declaring that such action would "strongly conflict with our national interest in price stability."

Toward sounder policies

As this account of recent history suggests, the guidepost policy may, under the pressure of events, move our nation's economy in an authoritarian direction. The danger may not yet be large, in view of prevailing political attitudes, but it could become serious in a time of trouble or emergency. And this is not the only risk, as I shall presently note. However, the fact that many citizens both within and outside government favor the guidelines must also be considered, for it means that they see smaller risks or larger advantages in this policy than I do.

It may readily be granted that the guidepost policy has the meritorious objective of blunting the power of monopolists to push up the price level. This is the feature of the policy that its proponents often stress. Indeed, they are apt to argue that it matters little in practice whether or not the bulk of the economic community pays any attention to the guidelines—as long as the major corporations and trade unions do so.

But if the guidelines are circumscribed in this fashion, they are still subject to the criticism of interfering with the competitive forces of the markets in which many major corporations actually operate. Moreover, the absence of a precise indication of what firms, industries, or trade unions are covered by the guidelines can create a mood of uncertainty that will militate against compliance. Not least important, the effectiveness of the guidelines in curbing inflation becomes doubtful when their application is restricted. For the very limitation on wage and price increases in the guideline sector of the economy would facilitate increases in the uncovered sector whenever an expansive economic policy generated a monetary demand that grew faster than the supply of goods and services.

Another argument frequently advanced in favor of the guideposts is that if they were in fact respected on a sufficient scale, then profit margins would tend to be maintained and the chances of prolonging the current business expansion would therefore be improved. This consideration is bound to count in men's thinking at a time when our nation is striving to reduce unemployment and to spread prosperity.

We must not, however, become so absorbed in today's problems that we overlook those that will haunt us in a later day. If the guidelines may stretch out the expansion now by helping to maintain the relatively high profit margins of prosperity, may they not at some later time stretch out contraction by serving to maintain the low profit margins of recession?

Let me add, also, that I recognize that the guideline policy was adopted by the Administration only after it had given serious consideration to alternatives. The thought of its economists apparently is that, in general:

1. Monetary and fiscal tools must be used to promote expansion as long as the economy is not operating at full employment.

2. Other devices must therefore be employed (in the absence of full employment) to prevent inflation.

3. Policies aiming to increase competition or to improve productivity cannot accomplish much in the short run or cannot be pushed hard for political reasons.

4. Direct controls of wages and prices cannot

and should not be seriously considered under peacetime conditions.

5. Consequently, there is only one major way left for curbing immediate inflation—namely, through devices of exhortation.

6. And the guidelines for wages and prices are merely a promising specific application of the technique of exhortation.

Locus of responsibility

Space will not permit me to unravel this complicated argument, but I at least want to suggest why I think it may be faulty. Once the government looks to trade unions and business firms to stave off inflation, there is a danger that it will not discharge adequately its own traditional responsibility of controlling money supply and of maintaining an environment of competition. In the past our own and other governments have often found it convenient to blame profiteers, corporations, or trade unions for a rising price level. Only rarely have they pointed the finger of blame at their own policies—such as flooding the economy with newly created currency or bank deposits.

To the extent that the government relies on private compliance with its guidelines for prices and wages, it may more easily be tempted to push an expansive monetary and fiscal policy beyond prudent limits. Besides, it may fail to resist strongly enough the political pressure for higher minimum wages, larger trade union immunities, higher farm price supports, higher import duties, more import quotas, larger stockpiling programs, and other protective measures that serve either to raise prices or to prevent them from falling.

One of the major needs of our times is to give less heed to special interest groups and to reassert the paramount interest of consumers in vigorous competition. The political obstacles to reducing artificial props for prices are undoubtedly formidable. However, reforms of this type—supplemented by more stringent antitrust laws, effective enforcement of these laws, and reasonable steps to curb featherbedding—are likely to contribute more to the maintenance of reasonable stability in the general price level than will the guidelines for wages and prices on which we have recently come to rely. . . .

Reading 67

Wage-Price Guideposts: Yes

Otto Eckstein

Much is at stake for all Americans in continued, *sustainable* expansion. Prosperity will not solve all our domestic problems. But when firing on all eight cylinders, our economy is a mighty engine of social progress, the greatest man has so far devised.

To the technical analyst, there is little mystery in this. Fiscal and monetary policies were designed to promote full use of our potential, through expenditure increases and three rounds of tax reduction. The private economy responded to the growth of markets with more efficient operations which produced a high rate of productivity growth. Prudent purchasing, investment and hiring policies helped keep markets in balance. Re-

sponsible wage increases generally within the productivity guideposts, and responsible price policies helped preserve our excellent cost and price record. Our balance of trade improved despite rising prosperity and an inevitable expansion of imports. Our goods strengthened their position in foreign markets, as other countries failed to combine prosperity with price-cost stability.

The history of the 1950s

This experience [since 1961] is in sharp contrast to the record of the preceding two short-lived expansions in the 1950's. In those years, the economy's growth was about half of the recent rate. Markets

From Otto Eckstein, "Guideposts and the Prosperity of Our Day," *Proceedings of a Symposium on Business–Government Relations,* sponsored by the American Bankers Association, Apr. 1, 1966. Reprinted with kind permission of the author and the ABA.

were not allowed to expand to match the economy's rising ability to produce.

Slack developed, unemployment increased, and profits became depressed because the operating rates of industry were far below the preferred levels. Yet, the country suffered from creeping inflation, which at least in part must be blamed on cost-push elements. The inflationary experience from 1956 to 1958 was deeply disturbing and gave rise to wide fears that this economy could not prosper unless it also had inflation—yet inflation inevitably made expansion unsustainable because of its effect on our international position.

Costs, prices, and guideposts in the current situation

This country is determined not to repeat the record of the 1950's. To avoid a repetition of this experience—to allow this society to achieve full use of resources without inflation—the Administration adopted the guideposts for noninflationary price and wage behavior in 1962. They are a bold and vital innovation—still only imperfectly understood, still in process of evolution, with business, labor and government now learning to live within them. They are a heavy bet that we can measure up to the new opportunities, that private and public leadership can manage their affairs responsibly, so that the American people will obtain the full benefit from the productivity of their labor and of their invested capital.

Innovation is clearly necessary, for history is not at all reassuring. Since World War II every period of full employment was also a period of inflation.

While unemployment was too high and operating rates too low, economic conditions strongly reinforced the guideposts. But today the margins are largely gone. The challenge to public and private policies is greater.

The price-cost record is still good, considering the rapid recent progress. I am sure that few or no observers would have predicted that we could score such gains and reach such levels with industrial prices rising by just 1.4% in the last 12 months, with unit labor costs in manufacturing lower than at the beginning of the expansion and still showing little rise. To be sure there are trouble spots and our price record is no longer perfect. Nonferrous metals have been in short supply in the last 18 months and are sharply up in price. Scattered price increases are now found in most

industries and are no longer offset by decreases. More important, farm and food prices are up about 10% in the last 12 months due to low marketings of meat and rising demands. Housewives are keenly aware of their grocery bills and are adding to inflation fears. But the outlook on prices generally remains good despite the great prosperity and the disappearance of margins of unutilized resources. So long as unit labor costs and order-shipments relations show little change, industrial price increases will remain moderate, not of the sort experienced in the creeping inflation of the mid-fifties. Needless to say, the key indicators of excess demand and cost pressures need the closest watching week-by-week.

Federal responsibility to sustain prosperity

All branches of our society, public and private, have their part to play to sustain this great prosperity.

The most important responsibility of the federal government in the present situation is to pursue fiscal and monetary policies that will keep total demand within the economy's capacity to produce.

Without such policies, guideposts and other measures cannot succeed.

Private responsibilities and guideposts

The main private responsibilities for cost-price stability are these: First, to continue the prudent decision-making that has characterized these last five years; and second, to give full weight to the guideposts.

The general wage guidepost states that the annual rate of increase of total employee compensation (wages and fringe benefits) per manhour worked should not exceed the national trend rate of increase in output per manhour. If wages follow this guidepost, average unit labor costs in the economy will remain stable—the most fundamental for a requisite for price stability.

The general guidepost for prices states that prices should remain stable in those industries where the increase of productivity equals the national trend; that prices can appropriately rise in those industries where the increase of productivity is smaller than the national trend; and that prices should fall in those industries where the increase in productivity exceeds the national trend. In essence, it says that prices can be expected to rise in low productivity industries where labor costs will be rising; that prices should fall in high productivity industries on the basis of their falling labor costs.

Some exceptions to these general guideposts have always been recognized. On the wage side, increases beyond the 3.2% general guidepost may be desirable for an industry to attract its necessary share of the labor force, or to bring up wages if they are near the bottom of the economy's wage scales, or to help defray the human costs associated with productivity boosting changes in work rules. This year's Economic Report adds, "Because the industries in which unions possess strong market power are largely high-wage industries in which job opportunities are relatively very attractive, the first two of these exceptions are rarely applicable."

On the price side, increases beyond the general guideposts "may be appropriate to reflect increases in unit material costs, to the extent that such increases are not offset by decreases in other costs, and significantly impair gross profit margins on the relevant range of products, or to correct an inability to attract needed capital." This year's Economic Report adds "the large firms to which guideposts are primarily addressed typically have ready access to sources of capital; moreover, the profits of virtually every industry have risen sharply and are at record levels as a by-product of the general prosperity of the economy. The second exception is thus not widely applicable in the present environment."

From confrontation to accommodation

The guideposts, like any new social instrument, are gradually evolving as we accumulate experience and understanding. In their early years the role of the guideposts was mainly educational. They taught business that not all wage increases are inflationary, but only those which exceed the rate of increase of productivity. They taught labor that wages are not only income, but also costs. And they taught all Americans that a rising price level serves no purpose and that a stable price level requires stable unit labor costs and appropri-

ate price decreases to offset necessary price increases.

While the economy had general slack in product and labor markets, this general educational role sufficed. The guideposts were breached occasionally, and sometimes in quite important situations, but the overall record of wages and prices so closely corresponded to the guideposts that one could take deep satisfaction in it.

As the economy approached full utilization of its potential, and particularly when the commitment of resources for Vietnam became large, the government's concern had to be expressed more directly. In the steel negotiations last summer the government helped to achieve a guidepost settlement. And in the several episodes in metal prices last fall and winter the government made its concern with stability of basic industrial prices very clear.

These government interventions created considerable uncertainty and led to some criticism of the guideposts. But I think this was a transitional phase. Both sides have learned a great deal about guideposts: government about operating them without creating unnecessary uncertainty; business about achieving desirable changes of relative prices while following guidepost principles. The two sides have learned from each other and have acquired a finer appreciation of each other's problems and viewpoints.

I doubt that we shall see many more confrontations that make banner headlines. I do expect that business and government will increase their informal contacts, that understanding of price behavior within the guideposts will become general. In other words, I expect that the contribution of guideposts to industrial price stability will continue and even become greater, but through a spirit of partnership and harmony. Of course, for guideposts to play this role, overall fiscal and monetary policy must contain the total demand within the economy's capacity to produce, and the extremes of sectoral imbalance must be avoided.

On the labor side, guideposts have not moved toward sweetness and light within the last few months. To be sure, the labor movement has never endorsed guideposts, and indeed has periodically criticized them throughout their existence. Nonetheless, the guideposts have been a very real factor in a number of important labor negotiations, and I am sure that they will play an increasingly important role.

The discontent of the labor movement with guideposts is easy to understand. The necessity of formulating fair labor standards policy within the guidepost framework—even with some allowance for the low-wage exception—runs counter to labor's normal aspirations. During years of expansion the rate of profit per unit of capital has increased substantially more than the rate of wages paid per hour. This disparity is inevitable during a period of cyclical recovery, for profits always fluctuate more than wages: they fall more in recession, rise more in expansion.

The guideposts are geared to long-term trends. With wages rising by the long-term productivity trend and prices stable on the average, a cyclical swing in the distribution of income between profits and wages is to be expected.

Now that the economy has completed its cyclical recovery, little further change in the division of income between profits and wages can be expected to occur within the guideposts. This source of friction should therefore disappear.

Labor, like business, understands that the continuation of uninterrupted progress depends upon the preservation of general price-cost stability. As tempers cool and the risks to prosperity become clear, a rapprochement between labor and the Administration on the guidepost question is the most sensible policy.

There is as much need to move from confrontation to accommodation on the labor side as has already occurred on the business side.

Alternatives to guideposts

The guideposts may fail because of misunderstanding, or inability or unwillingness of private and public leadership to generally abide by them. But make no mistake: we shall all be the worse for it. No incantation of the theories appropriate to an atomistic society of tiny business enterprises and unorganized workers is going to solve this problem. If guideposts are not pleasing, we must turn to alternative approaches. What are the alternatives?

Open inflation.   One view occasionally advanced is to relax and enjoy it, suffer a bit of inflation, and

reduce the social injustices by tying all forms of income to the rising cost of living. For example, wage contracts would generally contain escalator clauses. Social security would rise by formula, and so on.

This is not only bad, but indeed impossible advice to follow. Our balance of payments cannot stand a rising cost structure at this time. The dollar remains in deficit. We are in the middle of important international negotiations to reform the monetary system, and the United States must deal from strength in these negotiations. A stable price-cost situation is fundamental to our international financial strength. Further, such a situation could easily deteriorate into accelerating inflation.

Antitrust alternative?   Another alternative—and the most respectable in academic circles—is to convert the economy to perfect competition through escalated anti-trust policies and other measures. If the economy has cost-push problems, if there is ability to exercise market power to raise prices and wages even when demand does not exceed supply, then break up these concentrations, so it is argued. Now I believe in a firm, solid anti-trust policy. It has played a large role in restraining the growth of monopoly.

But it is a wholly unrealistic—and indeed a very radical—counsel to suggest that the gigantic enterprises of our economy should be broken up. This economy relies on our large corporate firms to channel much of its savings into productive investments, to search out new growth opportunities, to make innovations and to operate the large scale productive units which technology requires in many fields. To urge that we break up these enterprises is to propose a change in our economic system far more fundamental than any that has occurred in this century. It would move us into unknown territory which would have new problems that we cannot foresee. It is a solution far more radical than the guideposts. As the Economic Report of 1965 stated, the guideposts "are an attempt to operate our economy as it is—without controls, without wholesale fragmentation of our large, successful enterprises."

Permanent wage-price controls.   Finally, controls are another solution, by direct regulation of wages and prices.

Some people maintain that even guideposts constitute controls, but this is altogether an unrealistic view.

When you look at the alternatives, guideposts look pretty good.

Reading 68

Mandatory and Permanent Wage-Price Controls

J. Kenneth Galbraith

Control of the wage-price spiral

A complete attack on inflation requires that both causes of inflation—both the *excess of demand,* or spending, and the *wage-price spiral* [cost-push]—be brought under control.

The line of attack on excess spending is obvious. It calls primarily for heavy—very heavy—taxation. It calls for intelligent economy in expenditures by government. It calls for postponement of business investment. It calls for increased voluntary saving. This means that Americans must be assured for the future, as they have so long been assured in the past, that their dollars are good. They must be assured that the dollar they save instead of spend and put in a bank account or government bonds will have as high a purchasing power in the future as in the present. Nothing will serve this end more effectively than evidence of a strong determination by the administration and the Congress to check inflation.

I should like to make one comment concerning taxes. We shall need higher personal-income taxes and higher corporate-income taxes. We shall certainly have to have more and higher excise taxes. But I especially hope that doctrinaire opposition to the idea of sales taxes will not prevent us from looking carefully at the possibilities of this tax. I would not be in favor of a flat across-the-board levy on food, clothing, and other essentials. I do feel that the sales tax has great possibilities if it is properly designed. The British made extremely effective use of the sales tax in World War II—they called it the purchase tax—as a way of taxing expensive or luxury goods. These are the goods which place the greatest drain on scarce materials, labor, and skills and plant. A sales tax directed toward these goods—toward expensive lines of clothing, for example—can be actually helpful in keeping lower priced lines of goods cheap and abundant. It can also raise a lot of revenue.

The defense against the wage-price spiral—the second of the inflationary forces which work in our economy—are the *direct controls over prices and wages.* These direct controls are not a substitute for a strong fiscal policy; they perform a different task. Taxes and other fiscal measures dry up the excess of purchasing power; wage and price controls keep wages from shoving up prices and prices from shoving up wages. We cannot, under conditions we now face, be sure that any tax or fiscal policy will control the wage-price spiral. No more can we look upon wage- and price-fixing as a defense, in itself, against inflation. *Both* lines of attack are necessary because each deals with a different cause of inflation.

Because the primary purpose of the direct controls is to check the wage-price spiral, the controls we invoke must accomplish that purpose. It is not necessary, however, assuming no one wants control for the sake of control, to do more than necessary to achieve this end. To tie down the wage-price spiral, with reasonable justice and equity, we need to do three things. They are:

1. Effectively *stabilize basic living costs.* This is necessary if wages are to be stabilized.

2. Maintain a *general ceiling on wages and prices* in that part of the economy where wages are determined by collective-bargaining contracts and where prices normally move in response to wage movements. I have reference here to what may properly be called the great industrial core of the American economy—the steel, automobile, electri-

From *Hearings before the Joint Committee on the Economic Report,* 82d Cong., 1st Sess., pp. 354–356.

cal goods, construction, transport, and like industries.

3. As a contribution to over-all stability, placing of firm *ceiling prices on basic raw materials.*

Had we approached the problem of controls with a view to having as few of them as possible (though as many as necessary) and had the action been timely, we would have started out along the above lines. It is a system of controls with which, if necessary, we could live for a long time. It would not require a large administrative or enforcement staff.

Stabilizing the wage-price spiral is the central task of the direct controls. Fixing *all* prices [including] a great many prices that do not need to be controlled provides no guaranty of stable living costs. There is danger that administrative energies will be dissipated over a large number of products when, in fact, the key danger to wage-price stability lies in a relatively *few* —in food, basic clothing, and rents. None of these latter is now securely controlled. While we managed, although not without difficulty, to keep such a general ceiling in effect throughout World War II and for a period thereafter, it is not the kind of regulation which is right for the long pull. In World War II we, in effect, improvised for a particular set of circumstances of *limited duration.* For those circumstances it was the thing to do. We now face a *long* period of inflationary tension. For that a different line of action is called for. Energies should now be concentrated on getting the kind of stabilization program with which we can live, if we must, for a long time. This requires that we control strongly where control is necessary and not at all where it isn't.

The first step is a fundamental attack on living costs. Apart from rent I do not see this as, primarily, a problem in price-fixing. The ceilings, which undoubtedly should be kept on basic clothing and on food, should be viewed as merely an adjunct to more fundamental action. In the case of clothing, for example, a far more effective approach than price-fixing would be to use government allocation powers to direct generous quantities of fiber and textiles into standard low-priced goods—into work

clothing, household textiles, children's clothing, and the lower priced lines of men's and women's clothing. These should be made abundant, and so kept cheap. I would not worry if expensive lines of clothing became more expensive and scarce; freedom from ceilings on such clothing should readily be conceded in return for a substantial tax. If we rely on ceilings on clothing we will get too much expensive clothing and not enough of the cheap. We all remember during World War II when gay sports shirts were plentiful and ordinary ones not to be had.

The key to our problem is meat. I very much doubt if present ceilings, even when buttressed by slaughter controls, will hold meat prices even at their present astronomical levels. And even if they should, the attempt to meet the demand at these prices will place a heavy drain on our feed supplies. Rising feed prices will mean higher costs for dairy and poultry farmers, higher milk, poultry, and egg prices, and also more expensive cereals for direct consumption. Barring crop failure and full-scale war, our food position is strong. Could the demand for meat be effectively restrained, feed prices would be easier, and other animal products would be cheaper and more abundant. The necessary steps are not easy. It may be necessary to control here in order to have fewer controls elsewhere. And a policy of minimizing controls may well take more vigor and imagination than one which merely fixes ceilings and hopes for the best.

Action along these commodity lines in the cost-of-living area—coupled with the necessary fiscal policy—will lessen our reliance on price controls as such while greatly increasing our security against inflation. I should not want you to think I am arguing for a soft policy. I regard the threat of inflation as extremely grave. We are currently in much greater danger of demoralization of the economy as a result of inflation than we ever were from the great depression which the Russians were presumed to be counting upon to finish off American capitalism after World War II. It will take a stronger and more sure-footed policy to minimize reliance on ceilings than to multiply them.

Problems in the Mixed Economy

Readings 69, 70, and 71   Second Debate on Monetarism

What the Lincoln-Douglas debates were to politics, the 1968 Heller-Friedman debate at N.Y.U. was to modern economics. Both men are eloquent and witty speak-
ers. Each represents a point of view. The audience got its money's worth. But
brilliance of the repartee does not make a science. Therefore, reproduced below
are not the pyrotechnics of the N.Y.U. debate, but rather the solid and substantive
writings of Friedman and Heller—and also a brief Samuelson summing up for an
English audience.

We have already met in Readings 30 and 31 by Friedman and Samuelson a discussion of the Quantity Theory of Money and its limitations. Before 1929 most
economists thought there was nothing to macroeconomics except the Quantity
Theory. Then during the Great Depression of the 1930s, fiscal policy was discovered, and in one extreme version of the Keynesian system it was held that money
did not matter. That this belief still lingers on in England is shown by the Radcliffe
Committee Report of 1959, in which scorn was shown for the role of money. Actually, however, post-Keynesians (and for that matter Lord Keynes himself) stressed in
an eclectic fashion the vital importance of *both* monetary and fiscal policy.

Professor Friedman has been led by his scholarly studies to reject this eclectic
view. The present account summarizes his broad findings on the role of money.
Having no hesitation in setting himself up as a target, he insisted that to affect
aggregate dollar demand, only money matters—not fiscal policy, not budget policy,
not tax-rate policy, and (in other than the shortest run) not public expenditure policy. At N.Y.U. he said, "I believe . . . the government budget . . . matters a great
deal—for some things . . . [for] what fraction of the nation's income is spent through
the government . . . [for] the level of our taxes. . . . If the federal government runs a
large deficit, that . . . tends to raise interest rates." [But here is Friedman's] "main
point—in my opinion, the state of the budget by itself has no significant effect on
the course of nominal [i.e., money] income, on inflation, on deflation, or on cyclical
fluctuations." No statement could be more clear-cut, but to clarify exactly the sense
in which it is money alone that is alleged to matter for inflation and deflation, Friedman explains: "The crucial words . . . are 'by itself' because the whole problem of
interpretation is precisely that you are always having changes in monetary policy
[and at the same time] changes in fiscal policy. And if you want to think clearly
about the two separately, you must somehow try to separate the influence of fiscal
policy from the influence of monetary policy. The question you want to ask yourself
is, 'Is what happened to the government budget the major factor that produced a
particular change, or is it what happened to monetary variables?'" These quotations, which are taken from the Friedman-Heller debate, are reinforced by his subsequent reference to a November, 1968 statistical study by the Federal Reserve
Bank of St. Louis. This Andersen-Jordan study, using multiple-correlation techniques, concluded that GNP changes were significantly affected by lagged M
changes, but insignificantly affected by tax-rate changes; and the positive effects of
recent public-expenditure changes were washed out by negative effects in the
longer run. (See also the Samuelson Reading 31 for more detailed evaluation of
monetarism and its poorer forecasting performance in the 1970s.)

Walter Heller at N.Y.U. correctly fingered the key contention of "monetarism" as against "eclectic post-Keynesianism," saying: "At the outset, let's clarify what is and what isn't at issue in today's discussion of fiscal-monetary policy. The issue is not whether money matters—we all grant that—but whether only money matters [for inflation], as some Friedmanites would put it."

Heller argues that *both* fiscal and monetary policies count for inflation-deflation analysis. He criticizes automatic reliance on a rigid monetary rule, in which the Federal Reserve keeps some *M* magnitude always growing at some fixed rate—say, 4 to 5 per cent per annum, and does nothing else.

Milton Friedman has already been identified in earlier Readings. Dr. Heller is a Regent Professor at the University of Minnesota. From 1961 to 1965 he was chairman of the Kennedy and Johnson Council of Economic Advisers, and is widely regarded as the spokesman for the "New Economics." As a scholar, Dr. Heller is an expert in the field of public finance. He is co-author of the Heller-Pechman-Friedman plan for automatic tax-revenue sharing by the federal government with the state and localities, a plan which was partially put into effect by the Nixon Administration after 1972.

Questions to guide the reading

Can you check off those sentences in the Friedman argument which are evidence for the view that it is *only* money that matters for the purpose of appraising the aggregate of inflationary or deflationary spending? Could every one of his allegations be true and still not prove the impotence of fiscal policy or the unimportance of nonmonetary disturbances in creating business instability?

Suppose the causal mechanisms of monetarism were assumed for the sake of argument to be true. Do you think a strong case could still be made for departing from a steady growth in the money supply in favor of a policy of "leaning against the wind"—i.e., expanding money faster when the year ahead looked to be one of too little demand and slowing down money growth when the year ahead looked to be one of too much inflation? What proofs are offered for the assertion that steadiness is the best policy under all circumstances?

Should the wit and eloquence of a speaker be important in judging the merits of his case? Is economics an exact science so that a controlled experiment can be made to see how much (*a*) fiscal and (*b*) monetary variables were responsible for the long expansion of the 1960s? Can statistics take the place of controlled experiments? Does correlation prove causation?

To get a fair hearing for money, may one have to *exaggerate* its importance? If *M*'s effects are not perfectly predictable, does Heller agree that a fixed rate of growth of *M* is the best feasible rule?

Is the debate "much ado about nothing" in view of Dr. Friedman's 1970 statement: "Of the instruments available to the government to affect normal income, I believe that changes in the quantity of money are far and away the most important."? But that is a far cry from saying that they are the unique cause.

Reading 69

Monetarism, Yes

Milton Friedman

Long-run money-price relations

There is perhaps no empirical regularity among economic phenomena that is based on so much evidence for so wide a range of circumstances as the connection between substantial changes in the stock of money and in the level of prices. To the best of my knowledge *there is no instance in which a substantial change in the stock of money per unit of output has occurred without a substantial change in the level of prices in the same direction.* Conversely, I know of no instance in which there has been a substantial change in the level of prices without a substantial change in the stock of money per unit of output in the same direction. And instances in which prices and the stock of money have moved together are recorded for many centuries of history, for countries in every part of the globe, and for a wide diversity of monetary arrangements.

There can be little doubt about this statistical connection. The statistical connection itself, however, tells nothing about direction of influence, and it is on this question that there has been the most controversy. It could be that a rise or fall in prices, occurring for whatever reasons, produces a corresponding rise or fall in the stock of money, so that the monetary changes are a passive consequence. Alternatively, it could be that changes in the stock of money produce changes in prices in the same direction, so that control of the stock of money would imply control of prices. The variety of monetary arrangements for which a connection between monetary and price movements has been observed supports strongly the second interpretation, namely, that substantial changes in the stock of money are both a necessary and a sufficient condition for substantial changes in the general level of prices. But of course this does not exclude a reflex influence of changes in prices on the stock of money. This reflex influence is often important, almost always complex, and, depending on the monetary arrangements, may be in either direction.

The relationship between changes in the stock of money and changes in prices, while close, is not of course precise or mechanically rigid. Two major factors produce discrepancies: changes in output, and changes in the amount of money that the public desires to hold relative to its income.

A wide range of empirical evidence suggests that the ratio which people desire to maintain between their cash balances and their income is relatively stable over fairly long periods of time aside from the effect of two major factors:

1. The level of real income per capita, or perhaps of real wealth per capita;
2. the cost of holding money.

The cost of holding cash balances depends mainly on the rate of interest that can be earned on alternative assets—thus if a bond yields 4 per cent while cash yields no return, this means that an individual gives up $4 a year if he holds $100 of cash instead of a bond—and on the rate of change of prices—if prices rise at 5 per cent per year, for example, $100 in cash will buy at the end of the year only as much as $95 at the beginning so that it has cost the individual $5 to hold $100 of cash instead of goods. The empirical evidence suggests that while the first factor—the interest rate—has a systematic effect on the amount of money held, the effect is rather small. The second factor, the rate of change of prices, has no discernible effect in ordinary times when price changes are small—on the order of a few per cent a year. On the other hand, it has a clearly discernible and major effect when price change is rapid and long continued, as during extreme inflations or deflations. A rapid inflation produces a sizable decline in the desired ratio

From *The Relationship of Prices to Economic Stability and Growth*, 85th Cong., 2d sess., Joint Economic Committee Print, Washington, D.C.: U.S. Government Printing Office (1958).

of cash balances to income; a rapid deflation, a sizable rise.

Short-run money-price relations

Over the longer periods considered in the preceding sections, changes in the stock of money per unit of output tend to dominate price changes, allowance being made for the effect of the growth of real income per head. This is less so over the shorter periods involved in the fluctuations we term business cycles, though the general and average relationship is very similar. The reason for the looser connection in such periods presumably is that movements in both the stock of money and in prices are smaller. Over longer periods, these movements cumulate and tend to swamp any disturbance in the relation between desired cash balances, real income, and the cost of holding money; in the ordinary business cycle, the disturbances, though perhaps no more important in an absolute sense, are much more important relative to the movements in money and prices.

There can be little doubt on the basis of this evidence that there is a close link between monetary changes and price changes over the shorter periods within which business cycles run their course as well as over longer periods and during major wartime episodes. But important considerations must be borne in mind if this fact is not to be a misleading guide to policy. [One] has to do with the timing of the changes in the money supply and in income and prices. The generally upward trend in the money supply which accounts for its continuing to rise, though at a slower rate, during most contractions in economic activity as well as during expansions makes it difficult to judge timing relations from ups and downs in the money supply itself. For this and other reasons, we have found it most useful to examine instead the ups and downs in the rate at which the money supply is changing. The rate of change of the money supply shows well-marked cycles that match closely those in economic activity in general and precede the latter by a long interval. On the average, *the rate of change of the money supply* has reached its *peak nearly 16 months before the peak in general business and has reached its trough over 12 months before the trough in general business.*

This is strong though not conclusive evidence for the independent influence of monetary change. But it also has a very different significance. It means that it must take a long time for the influence of monetary changes to make themselves felt—apparently what happens now to the rate of change of the money supply may not be reflected in prices or economic activity *for 12 to 16 months, on the average.* Moreover, the timing varies considerably from cycle to cycle—since 1907, the shortest time span by which the money peak preceded the business cycle peak was 13 months, the longest, 24 months; the corresponding range at troughs is 5 months to 21 months. From the point of view of scientific analysis directed at establishing economic regularities on the basis of the historical record—the purpose for which the measures were computed—this is highly consistent behavior; it justifies considerable confidence in the reliability of the averages cited and means that they cannot easily be attributed simply to the accident of chance variation. But *from the point of view of policy directed at controlling a particular movement such as the current recession, the timing differences are disturbingly large*—they mean that monetary action taken today may, on the basis of past experience, affect economic activity within 6 months or again perhaps not for over a year and 6 months; and of course past experience is not exhaustive; the particular episode may establish a new limit in either direction.

The long time lag has another important effect. It leads to misinterpretation and misconception about the effects of monetary policy, as well as to consequent mistakes in monetary policy. Because the effects of monetary change do not occur instantaneously, monetary policy is regarded as ineffective.

Output relations

Over the cycle, prices and output tend to move together—both tend to rise during expansions and to fall during contractions. Both are part of the cyclical process and anything, including a monetary change, that promotes a vigorous expansion is likely to promote a vigorous rise in both and conversely. Over the longer period, the relation between price changes and output changes is much less clear. Now this seems clearly valid, not only as an expository device but also as a first approximation to reality. What happens to a nation's output over long periods of time depends in the first instance on such basic factors as resources available, the industrial organization of the society, the growth of knowledge and technical skills, the growth of population, the accumulation of capital and so on. This is the stage on which money and price changes play their parts as the supporting cast.

One proposition about the effect of changes in the stock of money and in prices that is widely accepted and hardly controversial is that large and unexpected changes in prices are adverse to the growth of output—whether these changes are up or down. At one extreme, the kind of price rise that occurs during hyperinflation seriously distorts the effective use of resources.[1] At the other extreme, sharp price declines such as occurred from 1920 to 1921 and again from 1929 to 1933 certainly produce a widespread and tragic waste of resources.

So much is agreed. The more controversial issue is the effect of moderate change in prices. One view that is widely held is that slowly rising prices stimulate economic output and produce a more rapid rate of growth than would otherwise occur. A number of reasons have been offered in support of this view. (1) Prices, and particularly wages, are, it is said, sticky. In a market economy, the reallocation of resources necessitated by economic growth and development requires changes in relative prices and relative wages. It is much easier, it is argued, for these to come about without friction and resistance if they can occur through rises in some prices and wages without declines in others. If prices were stable, some changes in relative wages could still come about in this way, since economic growth means that wages tend to rise

relative to prices, but changes in relative prices could not, and, of course, there would not be as much scope even for relative wage changes. (2) Costs, and in particular, wages, are, it is argued, stickier than selling prices. Hence generally rising prices will tend to raise profit margins, giving enterprises both a bigger incentive to raise output and to add to capital and the means to finance the capital needed. (3) The most recently popular variant of the preceding point is that costs are not only sticky against declines but in addition have a tendency to be pushed up with little reference to the state of demand as a result of strong trade unions. If the money stock is kept from rising, the result, it is claimed, will be unemployment as profit margins are cut, and also a higher level of prices, though not necessarily a rising level of prices. Gently rising prices, it is argued, will tend to offset this upward pressure by permitting money wages to rise without real wages doing so. (4) Interest rates are particularly slow to adapt to price rises. If prices are rising at, say, 3 per cent a year, a 6 per cent interest rate on a money loan is equivalent to a 3 per cent rate when prices are stable. If lenders adjusted fully to the price rise, this would simply mean that interest rates would be 3 percentage points higher in the first case than in the second. But in fact this does not happen, so that productive enterprises find the cost of borrowing to be relatively low, and again have a greater incentive than otherwise to invest, and the associated transfer from creditors to debtors gives them greater means to do so.

In opposition to this view, it has been argued that generally rising prices reduce the pressure on enterprises to be efficient, stimulate speculative relative to industrial activity, reduce the incentives for individuals to save, and make it more difficult to maintain the appropriate structure of relative prices, since individual prices have to change in order to stay the same relative to others. Furthermore, it is argued that once it becomes widely recognized that prices are rising, the advantages cited in the preceding paragraph will disappear: escalator clauses or their economic equivalent will eliminate the stickiness of prices and wages and the greater stickiness of wages than of prices; strong unions will increase still further their wage demands to allow for price increases; and interest

---

[1] However, even open hyperinflations are less damaging to output than suppressed inflations in which a wide range of prices are held well below the levels that would clear the market. The German hyperinflation after World War I never caused anything like the reduction of production that was produced in Germany from 1945 to the monetary reform of 1948 by the suppression of inflation. And the inflationary pressure suppressed in the second case was a small fraction of that manifested in the first.

rates will rise to allow for the price rise. If the advantages are to be obtained, the rate of price rise will have to be accelerated and there is no stopping place short of runaway inflation.

Historical evidence on the relation between price changes and output changes is mixed and gives no clear support to any of these positions. All in all, perhaps the only conclusion that is justified is that either rising prices or falling prices are consistent with rapid economic growth, provided that the price changes are fairly steady, moderate in size, and reasonably predictable. The mainsprings of growth are presumably to be sought elsewhere. But unpredictable and erratic changes of direction in prices are apparently as disturbing to economic growth as to economic stability.

Policy Implications

Past experience suggests that something like a 3 to 5 per cent per year increase in the stock of money is required for long-term price stability. For cyclical movements, a major problem is to prevent monetary changes from being a source of disturbance. If the stock of money can be kept growing at a relatively steady rate, without erratic fluctuations in short periods, it is highly unlikely if not impossible that we would experience either a sharp price rise—like that during World Wars I and II and after World War I—or a substantial price or output decline—like those experienced from 1920-21, 1929-33, 1937-38.

A steady rate of growth in the money supply will not mean perfect stability even though it would prevent the kind of wide fluctuations that we have experienced from time to time in the past. It is tempting to try to go farther and to use monetary changes to offset other factors making for expansion and contraction. The available evidence casts grave doubts on the possibility of producing any fine adjustments in economic activity by fine adjustments in monetary policy—at least in the present state of knowledge.

There are thus serious limitations to the possibility of a discretionary monetary policy and much danger that such a policy may make matters worse rather than better. Federal Reserve policy since 1951 has been distinctly superior to that followed during any earlier period since the establishment of the System, mainly because it has avoided wide fluctuations in the rate or growth of the money supply. At the same time, I am myself inclined to believe that in our present state of knowledge and with our present institutions, even this policy has been decidedly inferior to the much simpler policy of keeping the money supply growing at a predesignated rate month in and month out with allowance only for seasonal influences and with no attempt to adjust the rate of growth to monetary conditions.[2]

To avoid misunderstanding, it should be emphasized that the problems just discussed are in no way peculiar to monetary policy. Fiscal action also involves lags. Indeed the lag between the recognition of need for action and the taking of action is undoubtedly longer for discretionary fiscal than for discretionary monetary action: the monetary authorities can act promptly, fiscal action inevitably involves serious delays for congressional consideration. Hence the basic difficulties and limitations of monetary policy apply with equal force to fiscal policy.

Political pressures to "do something" in the face of either relatively mild price rises or relatively mild price and employment declines are clearly very strong indeed in the existing state of public attitudes. The main moral to be drawn from the two preceding points is that *yielding to these pressures may frequently do more harm than good.* The goal of an extremely high degree of economic stability is certainly a splendid one; our ability to attain it, however, is limited; we can surely avoid extreme fluctuations; we do not know enough to avoid minor fluctuations; the attempt to do more than we can will itself be a disturbance that may increase rather than reduce instability. But like all such injunctions, this one too must be taken in moderation. It is a plea for a sense of perspective and balance, not for irresponsibility in the face of major problems or for failure to correct past mistakes.

---

[2] The extensive empirical work that I have done has given me no reason to doubt that the simple policy suggested above would produce a very tolerable amount of stability. This evidence has persuaded me that the major problem is to prevent monetary changes from themselves contributing to instability rather than to use monetary changes to offset other forces.

Reading 70

Both Fiscal and Monetary Policy, Yes

Walter W. Heller

My intent today is neither to praise nor to bury that towering iconoclast Milton Friedman, for to praise him and his works would absorb far too much of my limited time, and to bury him is, in a word, impossible.

Also, a word about the title, "Is Monetary Policy Being Oversold?" You should keep in mind that a speech title, like a biblical text, is a point of departure—and depart from it I shall. In one sense, in striving for symmetry with Milton's title, I may have made it too broad. It might better have read "Is Money Supply Being Oversold?" But since the twin topics under review are really fiscal versus monetary policy and discretionary versus automated policy, this title may be too narrow. In this sense, it might better have read "The Future of Discretionary Fiscal—and Monetary—Policy."

Money only?

At the outset, let's clarify what is and what isn't at issue in today's discussion of fiscal-monetary policy.

The issue is *not* whether money matters—we all grant that—but whether *only* money matters, as some Friedmanites, or perhaps I should say Friedmanics, would put it. Or really, whether only money matters *much,* which is what I understand Milton Friedman to say—he is more reasonable than many of the Friedmanites.

It's important in this connection, too, to make clear that the economic policy of the 1960's, the "new economics" if you will, assigns an important role to *both* fiscal and monetary policy. Indeed, the appropriate mix of policies has often been the cornerstone of the argument.

In short, to anyone who might fear that the "new economics" is all fiscal policy, the record offers evidence, and the new economists offer assurance, that money *does* matter.

ists confront us: First, should money supply be the sole or primary guide to Federal Reserve policy? Should it, at the very least, be ranged side by side with interest rates and credit availability in the Fed's affections? Second, should we rely on the Federal Reserve authorities to adapt monetary policy flexibly to changing economic events and to shifts in fiscal policy, or should we instead not only enthrone money supply but encase it in a rigid formula specifying a fixed increase of 3, 4, or 5 per cent a year? In other words, should we adopt the Friedman rule and replace the Fed with an exponential curve?

Intelligent discretion vs. inflexible formulas

Again, in the fiscal field, the issue is not *whether* fiscal policy matters—even some monetarists, perhaps in unguarded moments, have urged budget cuts or tax changes for stabilization reasons. The issues are *how much* it matters, and how heavily we can lean on discretionary changes in taxes and budgets to maintain steady economic growth in a dynamic economy: Is the close correlation of activist fiscal policy and strong expansion—which has brought our economy into the narrow band around full employment—a matter of accident or causation? Does a fair balancing of the successes and shortcomings of active fiscal policy suggest (a) that we should now take refuge in rigid fiscal rules like the lock-stop tax cuts espoused by Barry Goldwater and Milton Friedman, or rather (b) that we need to modify our fiscal institutions—especially our procedures for cutting or boosting taxes—to step up their speed and precision, especially in dealing with inflation?

From Walter W. Heller, "Is Monetary Policy Being Oversold?" *Monetary vs. Fiscal Policy, A Dialogue,* Milton Friedman and Walter W. Heller (W. W. Norton & Company, Inc., New York, 1969). Reprinted in abridgment with the kind permission of the authors and the publisher.

Weighing evidence

Now, turning to doubts, unresolved questions, and unconvincing evidence, I group these into conditions that must be satisfied—if not completely, at least more convincingly than they have been to date—before we can even consider giving money supply sovereignty, or dominance, or greater prominence in economic policy. These conditions center on such questions as: Which money-supply indicator do you believe? Can one read enough from money supply without weighing also shifts in demand and interest rates—that is, don't both quantity *and* price of money count? Don't observed variations in monetary time lags and velocity cast serious doubt on any simple relation between money supply and GNP? Can a rigid monetary rule find happiness in a world beset with rigidities and rather limited adjustment capabilities? That is, is the rigid Friedman rule perhaps a formula made in heaven, that will work only in heaven?

I claim no originality in my catalogue of doubts. My debt to people like James Tobin, John Kareken, Lyle Gramley, and others, whose painstaking research and analysis I draw on, is virtually complete.

Let me turn now to the more positive side of my assignment. Two important tasks remain. The first is to remind you of the potency and effectiveness of fiscal policy. The second is to restate the case for continued and expanded use of discretionary, man-made policy in preference to rigid monetary and fiscal rules.

Again, we need to stop, look, and listen lest we let simplistic or captious criticism operate to deny us the benefits of past experience and thwart the promise of future discretionary action on the monetary and fiscal fronts.

Perhaps the best way to begin is to move back from a day-by-day or month-by-month perspective to ask this broad question: What has been the course of the American economy during the postwar period of an increasingly active and self-conscious fiscal-monetary policy for economic stabilization? Or, for that matter, let's broaden it: What has been the course of the world's advanced industrial economies during this period? The correlation is unmistakable: the more active, informed, and self-conscious fiscal and monetary policies have become, by and large, the more fully employed and stable the affected economies have become. Casual empiricism? Perhaps—yet a powerful and persuasive observation.

Witness the conclusion of the two-and-a-half-year study for the OECD by a group of fiscal experts from eight industrial countries:

The postwar economic performance of most Western countries in respect of employment, production and growth has been vastly superior to that of the pre-war years. This, in our view, has not been accidental. Governments have increasingly accepted responsibility for the promotion and maintenance of high employment and steady economic growth. The more conscious use of economic policies has undoubtedly played a crucial role in the better performance achieved—an achievement which, from the point of view of the ultimate social objectives of policy, is of paramount importance.

The term "fine tuning" brings an important issue into focus. For policy tolerances become much narrower in the high-employment economic zone. Fiscal and monetary actions must not only pack a punch, but that punch has to be delivered with greater speed and precision—and with greater courage as well, since inflation is so often the foe in a high-employment, high-growth economy.

That throws the issue of man versus rules, discretion versus automaticity, into bold relief. The monetarists tell the policy maker, in effect, "Don't do something, just stand there." They doubt that we have the economic wisdom, the strength of character, and the institutional capability to operate a successful discretionary policy. In their view, rigid rules would outperform mortal man.

Case for discretion

Time and space do not permit a full review here of the case for discretionary and flexible policy. [There is a] basic flaw in the concept of living by rules alone—namely, that there is no escape from discretion, if only in setting the rules and changing them from time to time.

I have already suggested a couple of practical defects. (1) In anything but a world of flexible price, cost, and exchange adjustments, fixed rates of change in the money stock and tax levels are more likely to be destabilizing than stabilizing. (2) It offends common sense to say that policy should (or would) deny itself the increasingly broad, prompt, and reliable current economic information available to us, let alone, the forecasts grounded in this growing fund of information and knowledge of economic relationships.

Reasonable forecasting ability. One of Milton Friedman's main charges against discretionary policy is that economic forecasting is a weak reed on which to lean in guiding policy action. The contrary view, which I hold, is that we cannot operate intelligent economic policies—public or private—without forecasts. We have to make the most reasonable forecast of the future and then be as nimble and flexible as possible in adjusting to unforeseen events and forces.

What's the right test to apply in judging whether forecasting can carry the burden that is required for discretionary policy? The right test, I submit, is not whether annual GNP forecasts are accurate to the nearest $5 or $10 billion, but whether they are sufficiently right in predicting the direction and intensity of change, first, to avoid *wrong* policy advice (for if they do no more than that, they have already at least matched automatic, or lockstep, policy); second, to lead to the *right* policy advice, if not every time, at least a very high proportion of the time.

Now by that reasonable standard, I submit that official forecasts since 1960 [through 1968] have fallen from grace for only four brief periods.

The rest of the time, official economic forecasts have correctly led the President's economic advisers to urge [corrective] action.

Summing up

We need to bend every effort to make fiscal policy—and particularly tax policy—more responsive and flexible. Indeed, if tax rates can be adjusted quickly and flexibly to ebbs and flows of aggregate demand, the penalties for errors in forecasting would be correspondingly reduced. We must find a way to make tax rates more adaptable to economic circumstances, either by granting the President standby power to make temporary cuts and increases in the income tax (subject to Congressional veto); or by setting up speedier Congressional procedures to respond to Presidential requests for quick tax changes to head off recession or inflation; or by developing the executive practice (proposed by a Nixon task force) under which the President would, as part of his budget message each January, propose a positive or negative income surtax (for stabilization purposes).

In winding up these comments, let me say that just as the monetarists have a great deal still to clarify, establish, and correct before they can lay claim to an only-money-matters-much economic policy, so the economic activists—I won't say "fiscalists," because economic activism implies a balanced policy of fiscal and monetary discretion—still have a great deal to learn about operating in the narrow band around full employment; a great deal more to do in improving forecasting; and important worlds to conquer in speeding up the executive and legislative processes and developing the skills to manage the fiscal dividend so as not to let it retard normal expansion, and yet, when the economy overheats, to let it become a welcome fiscal drag.

In my comments today, I referred to the brilliance of the Chicago School. I should also comment on their great consistency over the years. The rest of us—responding to new analysis and evidence, observing basic changes in the economy, and conditioned (or perhaps "burned") by experience and on-the-job training—adapt and modify our views from time to time on such key issues as (a) the role and desirability of government tax incentives for investments; (b) the independence of the Fed; (c) the proper mix of tax cuts, government budget increases, and tax sharing; and (d) yes, even the relative roles of fiscal and monetary policy. In short, we have yet to encounter the revealed and immutable truth.

But the Chicago school just goes rolling along. Miraculously, all the evidence—I really mean, all the admissible evidence—strengthens their conviction, held for decades, that to err is human, and to live by rules is divine. In spite of vast improvements in the promptness, breadth, and accuracy of economic statistics, in spite of important advances in forecasting techniques and performance, in spite of vast strides in public understanding and acceptance of positive economic policy, in spite of encouraging signs of greater responsiveness of executive and legislative officials to informed economic policy advice, the Chicago School still adheres to the proposition that we should put our trust in stable formulas, not in unstable men and institutions.

That's a bit of a caricature, but only a bit. The monetarists have taught us much. We are far richer for their analyses and painstaking research. But we would be far poorer, I believe, for following their policy prescription. It is high time that they stop trying to establish a single variable—money supply—as all-powerful, or nearly so, and stop striving to disestablish another variable—fiscal policy—as impotent, or nearly so.

The path to progress in economic policy lies, instead, in a mutual undertaking to work out the best possible combination of fiscal, monetary, and wage-price policies—coupled with measures to speed the rise in productivity—for reconciling sustained high employment with reasonable price stability.

Reading 71

Monetarism Pure and Neat, No

Paul A. Samuelson

Monetary policy seems to have been underrated by British economists in recent decades. Now there seems to be a real danger that financial opinion is veering to the opposite extreme of a crude monetarism. And that would be a pity.

Rediscovery of money

The new impetus appears, in the first instance, to be an import from America. Money was, so to speak, "rediscovered" in my country around 1950. We are all post-Keynesians now. And that means, among other things, that we believe national income can be significantly affected by monetary as well as fiscal policy.

I believe this. Walter Heller, chief economic adviser to Presidents Kennedy and Johnson, believes it. Paul McCracken, newly appointed as chairman of Nixon's Council of Economic Advisers, believes in the potency of both tools of policy—monetary as well as fiscal.

I could go down the list of our experts. Professor Tobin of Yale. Professor Modigliani of M.I.T. All are agreed on this eclectic position.

The new prophet

All? Well, almost all. Professor Milton Friedman is an exception. His is a voice that says the rate of growth of the money supply is vastly more important than any changes in tax rates or fiscal expenditures. And Friedman's voice is like the voice of ten.

Like Billy Graham, Dr. Friedman has been making converts throughout the land. The Federal Reserve Bank of St. Louis has seen the light. Senator Proxmire's Joint Economic Committee has requested the Federal Reserve to keep the money supply growing within the range of 2 to 6 per cent per year. [In the 1970s, it backed down on this.]

At the First National City Bank in New York and the Harris Trust Company in Chicago, vice presidents prepare their forecasts on the basis of the New Quantity Theory of Money.

Within the academic community, Professors Allen Meltzer of Carnegie, Karl Brunner of Rochester, Richard Seldon of Virginia, Phillip Cagan of the National Bureau of Economic Research and Columbia, all play up the importance of money.

At the distance of 3,000 miles, all this might look like the general American position and the wave of the future. In my view it is neither of those.

The brute facts

Let me review the evidence, very briefly—all too briefly.

First, the current [1968] strength of the American economy is indeed greater than was predicted by those who believed that fiscal restraint in the form of the 10 per cent mid-year tax surcharge would greatly slow up our rate of growth.

It is naive to infer from this that fiscal potency is nil, or that the discrepancy is explicable in terms of the New Quantity Theory, or the old one for that matter.

Abridged from Paul A. Samuelson, "Don't Make Too Much of the Quantity Theory," *London Sunday Telegraph*, December, 1968. Reprinted with kind permission of the publisher.

For every monetarist who predicted pretty much what happened, I can give you one who predicted greater current weakness than did the fiscal enthusiasts; and another who declared that the divergences between growth rates of alternative definitions of the money supply make all predictions difficult. (The same diversity of analysis held for the slowdown following the 1966 "money crunch": some of the greatest errors in 1967 forecasts were made by Chicago economists. And, in 1973, one can add that the post-1968 forecasts by monetarists showed the same wide errors of estimate as other methods.)

Finally, there is the appeal to authority. None of the non-Chicago authorities have succumbed to the disease of monetarism. Not even one governor of the Federal Reserve Board can endorse its monism, and usually you can find one in seven in favour of anything.[1]

[1] Paradoxically, the "Keynesians" on the Federal Reserve Board—Sherman Maisel and George Mitchell—are the advocates of having the agents of the Open-Market Committee replace chief reliance on "interest-rate and orderly-market-targets" by greater reliance on "aggregative" targets dealing with the M supply. I, as a Keynesian eclectic, also favor this—while rejecting pure "monetarism."

When Professor Friedman formulates his system in generality—with the velocity of circulation of money a function of the rate of interest and all the rest—it coincides with the post-Keynesianism of the Tobin-Modigliani type. When he speaks less guardedly, the consensus is rudely shattered.

It was in connection with such less-guarded utterances that Professor Tobin once properly remarked—Proving that "Money does not matter" is false only proves that "Money does matter," not that "Money alone matters."

I may reverse the Tobin syllogism to point out the fundamental and fatal *non sequitur* of the Radcliffe Committee—Proving that "It is not money alone that matters (and matters in a simple quantity-theory proportionality)" does not at all establish the proposition that "Money does not matter."

Britain does seem in need of greater recognition that monetary and credit policies count, and can count for much.

But why should it be necessary to go overboard and import crude monetarism?

Gresham's Law does operate in the realm of ideology: "Strong ideology drives out weak—among the gullible, that is." But why fall into such company?

Competing Economic Ideologies

Readings 72 and 73

Capitalism has changed, claims England's Andrew Shonfield. Economic planning by governments underlies the post-World War II production miracles of Germany, France, Japan, the Netherlands, Italy, Sweden, and Europe generally. Only Britain has failed. And, according to Shonfield, the United States could use considerably more planning.

Agreeing that the mixed economy differs from old-fashioned capitalism, Charles P. Kindleberger nevertheless argues that Shonfield exaggerates the role that planning has played in the Common Market and other miracles.

Andrew Shonfield is director of studies at the Royal Institute of International Affairs, London; C. P. Kindleberger is professor of international economics at M.I.T.

Questions to guide the reading

Must planning involve a sacrifice of personal freedoms? Can one distinguish fiscal and monetary policies from "planning"? What would you recommend for the United States?

Reading 72

Modern Capitalism

Andrew Shonfield

The advanced industrial countries of the Western world have during the 1950s and early 1960s enjoyed an extended period of prosperity for which it is impossible to find a precedent. Three major factors can be identified which are responsible for the distinctive economic flavour of the postwar period.

First, economic growth has been much steadier than in the past. It has not been completely even, but the recessions, when they have come, have been very mild and shallow by historical standards. In several countries they have resulted in nothing more than the temporary slowing down of a continuing advance. There has been no halt or reversal. In others, where production has fallen back in recessions, these interruptions have been shortlived and have had relatively little effect on the level of employment.

Secondly, the growth of production over the period has been extremely rapid. It is true that in the United States there have been periods in the past, notably from 1900 to 1913, when the average rate of economic growth was even higher than in the 1950s. But the American case was exceptional in the postwar Western world. It was accompanied by many features which had no parallel elsewhere—notably a rising level of unemployment and a declining level of business investment, measured as a proportion of the national product. In Western Europe the pace of economic advance after the middle of the century was much faster, as well as being less interrupted, than in any known comparable period of peacetime history.

Thirdly, the benefits of the new prosperity were very widely diffused. In the conditions of full employment and rising demand for labour established in almost all areas of Western Europe during the 1950s, average wage earnings rose as fast as, or faster than, the national product. In the United States too consumption rose fairly steadily and the upward trend was barely interrupted even by business recessions. What distinguished Western Europe was the deliberate effort to widen the spread of consumer benefits, by means of welfare services and pension schemes, to those members of society who cannot rely on automatic gains as a result of the rise in wage-earnings.

Pre-Kennedy doldrums

It is noteworthy that this diffusion of rising incomes over the population as a whole has not reduced the flow of savings required to support a high level of investment. On the contrary, Western Europe has set aside a larger proportion of its resources for investment than ever before. Again the United States is different: there the rate of investment was somewhat lower than in the period of expansion immediately preceding the First World War. One of the aims of the Democratic Administration which took office in 1961 was to raise the level of American investment, with the help of fiscal incentives and the promise of sustained economic expansion uninterrupted by serious recessions.

The evidence suggests that a continuing 'recession psychology' in the United States has been a major reason for the contrast between American and West European economic experience in recent years. Analysis of the actual recessions which have occurred since the war suggests that they have been aggravated in the United States by government financial policies. There have been more recessions in the United States than in Western Europe, and they have been allowed to go further before the government intervened decisively to boost demand.

There is an alternative explanation of the postwar contrast between North America and Western Europe, which sees the latter as enjoying an exceptional and transient expansion while the former is closer to the long-term economic norm. An impor-

From Andrew Shonfield, *Modern Capitalism* (published under the auspices of the Royal Institute of International Affairs by Oxford University Press, New York and London, 1965). Reprinted with kind permission of the author and publisher.

tant school of economic historians argues on the basis of the experience of the past century that the favourable conditions from 1950 onwards reflected a 'long upswing' (of about ten years' duration) of a kind which has been seen regularly, alternating with downswings of about equal duration, in the past. On this view there has been no decisive change of trend in the Western capitalist world leading to a sustained high rate of economic growth. The reason why appearances suggest that there has been is that a number of extremely favourable conditions have fortuitously combined to accelerate the expansion of the 1950s; the lucky combination is unlikely to endure.

How the West grew

Two powerful economic forces have played a major part in raising the tempo of economic growth in the West. They are: (1) the sustained expansion of international trade, and (2) the great building boom of the 1950s. Some economists, among whom Simon Kuznets and Arthur Lewis are outstanding, maintain these are transient phenomena; both residential building and international trade in manufactured goods are believed to have been subjected to a species of forced growth, which will be matched by a markedly slower rate of expansion later on.

[My] central thesis is that there is no reason to suppose that the patterns of the past, which have been ingeniously unravelled by the historians of trade cycles, will reassert themselves in the future. To begin with, the advent of full employment, and its conscious pursuit in the advanced industrial countries as an act of policy, have added a new dimension to international trade. When countries are operating constantly at the margin of their available resources, their imports of manufactured goods tend to rise faster than their domestic output of manufactures. This tendency is particularly marked during a period of rapidly advancing technology.

The distinctive features of the new era of capitalism which has opened since the end of the Second World War are first, the conscious pursuit of full employment, and secondly, the accelerated pace of technological progress. The latter has made possible a high and steady increase from year to year in output per manhour. This process will continue and may accelerate.

The early stages of the new capitalism were sustained in several countries with the help of ample supplies of additional labour moving into industry. The 1960s show a marked change in the trend. This has reinforced the emphasis on technological innovation in general and on higher education in particular.

Thus far the argument has tried to show only that continuing prosperity and uninterrupted growth on the scale of recent years are possible in the future. The underlying conditions in the second half of the twentieth century are more favourable than at any time in the history of capitalism. The more interesting question, however, is whether success is probable. The answer to this depends very largely on political will and skill: specifically on the management of the institutional apparatus which guides Western economic life.

Keynes to the rescue

There is an alternative approach which sees this whole issue as a technical problem, and one that was solved some time ago as a result of the advance in economic techniques. Once Keynes showed how an economy should be handled when it produced the recurrent signs of debility, there was little more to it, it is averred, than following the instructions in the new guide book. You might find yourself with a little more inflation than you had bargained for, but you could always rely on having plenty of economic growth.

Control over the business cycle, which owes so much to Keynes's work, has been one of the decisive factors in establishing the dynamic and prosperous capitalism of the postwar era. Indeed, it is probably the single most important factor in this change. So many other developments flow from it, notably the reduction of business risks and the incentive to speed up the process of investment. My point is only that if the change from old-style capitalism to the new style had depended solely on a process of intellectual conversion to the system of economic doctrines developed by Keynes, it is unlikely that it would have got as far as it has. Moreover, the future would by now be looking highly uncertain. After all, there have been many occasions since the war when we have seen people in authority, who believe themselves to have penetrated the truths of Keynesian economics, being guided in an emergency by quite other, and often contradictory, policies.

What is characteristic of the postwar period is that a variety of independent forces have combined to increase the available powers of control over the economic system and at the same time to keep the volume of demand constantly at a very high level. Governments have therefore been given time to learn how to intervene with increasing skill, without causing disaster in the course of educating themselves.

There is indeed an element of paradox in the fact that the two nations which had earliest and most readily absorbed the Keynesian message— Britain and the United States—were also the least successful among the Western capitalist countries in managing their economies after the Second World War. This contrast would itself be sufficient to suggest that the purely intellectual change, which is popularly labelled the 'Keynesian revolution', is not the decisive factor. Something more is evidently required than a knowledge of techniques. On the continent of Europe during the period immediately following the war, the Keynesian message was not generally accepted. Yet there were other more powerful factors which allowed these countries to avoid any serious cyclical fluctuations and to maintain a significantly higher rate of economic growth than either Britain or the United States.

The miraculous Common Market

This success of the continental Europeans was so glaring that by the early 1960s it had become a significant factor in both British and American domestic politics. At any rate both countries embarked on policies which were intended to mark a deliberate break with the past, while copying some feature, real or imagined, of the European experience. In Britain the effort was concentrated on avoiding 'stop-go' measures, which had interfered with an even rate of growth; the formula adopted was economic planning on the French model which, by making progress more even, would also,

it was expected, make it more rapid. In the United States, after the Democratic Administration took office in 1961, following eight years of Republican rule, the whole focus of economic policy shifted: it came to concentrate on the objective of full employment, which was to be achieved by deliberately pushing up the demands on the country's productive apparatus.

It is worth noting that when the United States came to set itself its new objective, it did not turn to Britain for its model, despite the fact that the British had successfully maintained a state of full employment, without interruption, for two decades. It was the experience of continental Europe in the 1950s which beckoned to the Americans. What had been achieved there was the combination of full employment with a high rate of growth and international competitive power which had notably eluded the British.

I shall try to identify the characteristic institutional features of the economic order which has gradually emerged in postwar capitalism. There are big differences between the key institutions and economic methods of one country and another. The differences are often the subject of sharp ideological cleavages. Yet when the total picture is examined, there is a certain uniformity in the texture of these societies. In terms of what they do, rather than of what they say about it, and even more markedly in terms of the pattern of their behaviour over a period of years, the similarities are striking. This may be because nations exchange their experiences nowadays, including the intimate experiences of management both in the public sphere and in business, more actively than ever before. That may also be one of the reasons why the design of the pattern has become clearer in the 1960s than it was in the 1950s.

Shape of things to come

Some of its outstanding features may be usefully listed:

1. There is the vastly *increased influence* of the *public authorities* on the management of the economic system. This operates through different mechanisms in different countries: in one the control of the banking system is decisive, in another it is the existence of a wide sector of publicly con-

trolled enterprise. In all of them the government's expenditure has been enormously enlarged and determines directly a large segment of each nation's economic activities.

2. The *preoccupation with social welfare* leads to the use of public funds on a rising scale, most notably to support people who do not earn, either because they are young and being educated or old and retired. Public welfare policies, of course, have a long history in several European countries; what is, however, characteristic of the postwar period is the steady advance of social welfare measures over wide areas of the Western world. This is most obviously reflected in the fact that education and pensions together have been absorbing an increasing proportion of the national income of the advanced capitalist countries. (Again a proviso must be made about the United States in the 1950s.)

3. In the private sector the *violence of the market has been tamed*. Competition, although it continues to be active in a number of areas, tends to be increasingly regulated and controlled. The effort to secure an enlarged area of predictability for business management, in a period in which technological change is very rapid and individual business investments are both larger in size and take longer to mature, has encouraged long-range collaboration between firms. Governments in their anxiety to increase the area of the predictable for purposes of economic planning have encouraged firms within an industry to evolve agreed policies on the basis of their common long-range interests. The classical market of the textbooks in which firms struggle with one another and disregard any possible effect that their actions may have on the market as a whole has become more remote than ever.

4. It has now come to be taken for granted, both by governments and by the average person in the Western capitalist countries, that *each year should bring a noticeable increase in the real income per head of the population*. The accepted procedure of annual wage claims in most countries reflects this expectation. It is, in fact, capable of being fulfilled, at any rate for a long time to come, as a result of the accelerated pace of technological innovation in industry. But to secure the full benefits of the enlarged industrial potential requires new forms of organization, (a) in the sphere of research and development, and (b) for the training of workers and generally for the more efficient deployment of scarce resources of skilled manpower. A conscious effort has begun to be applied in both fields since the late 1950's. The purpose of (a) is to reduce the time span from the inception of novel ideas to their development into usable models ready to be absorbed into the process of production; while (b) aims to reduce the bottlenecks caused by the shortage of trained labour capable of responding to new technology. There is increasing realization that in a full employment economy, rapid technical progress can be sustained only if there is an active public policy designed to speed up the transfer of people from jobs in which they are established to new forms of employment.

5. The characteristic attitude in large-scale economic management, both inside government and in the private sector, which has made itself increasingly felt during the postwar period, is the *pursuit of intellectual coherence*. Its most obvious manifestation is in long-range national planning. Lengthening the time horizon used in making economic decisions also means extending the range of data that have to be studied in the present; more current facts become relevant. Thus the framework of systematic analysis has to be extended in two dimensions. Techniques and institutions, different in the various countries and varying in efficiency, have been developed to meet the demand for both explicitness and coherence in those economic decisions which have a significant impact on national production or public welfare. Once again the motive is at least partly the desire, in the face of greatly accelerated change, to try to reduce the area of the unpredictable to a manageable series of clear alternatives.

Last questions

Finally, how far are the methods being adopted for the efficient management of the new capitalism compatible with the ideas and practice of traditional parliamentary democracy? How much of the original objective of government by popular consent can be sustained in a system in which the sphere of active government has been greatly enlarged and is likely to become more so?

Reading 73

The Best Laid Plans

Charles P. Kindleberger

It is somewhat ironic that Shonfield's book was published in January, 1966, after the United States had assumed the growth lead over Japan and the nations of North America and Europe. Part of his thesis is that traditional capitalism is flawed for purposes of growth because it relies on government only to stabilize demand and on the market to produce the supply response, whereas under "modern" capitalism it is necessary, above all, to plan, coordinate or organize supply through government or through governmental surrogates. Like Baum and Luethy, who wrote off French economic vitality prematurely only to have the patient flex his muscles before their books reached print—a point which Shonfield does not miss—the author falls victim to printer's lag, and his ideas are in some part overtaken by the fast pace of events.

Thesis

Shonfield's major theme is that modern capitalism needs government and centralization. (Incidentally, he fails to note that what modern socialism seems to need, judging from Yugoslav and Soviet experience, is decentralization.) Adam Smith is stood on his head. People do not know their best interest. Markets are "violent," and "market prices generally fail to measure either social costs or benefits." Enterprise needs "tutelary" (a favorite word of his) direction.

Government, on the other hand, has produced the dazzling performance of capitalism since World War II, in all but the United States and Britain, by its activity as an entrepreneur, by guiding private enterprise and by both stimulating technical change and producing coherence in disparate private decisions.

Planning is all, even though in some environments it is disguised as anti-planning. The period since 1945 is not a Kuznets cycle, in which a burst of energy sparked by technological change produces a once-and-for-all reallocation of resources and dies away. The very nature of the system has changed, and growth is built in on a permanent basis. This overstates the thesis perhaps, but not by much.

Antithesis

If Shonfield had been content to say that the horizons of households, firms and governments had been extended in time one could hardly fault him.

On all sides, it is clear that the short-run profit maximizer, interested in separate, discrete "deals," has been superseded by (or converted to) the manager calculating returns over extended periods, and that this changes the nature of capitalism. Maximizing profits at low rates of implicit interest over the long run is indistinguishable from maximizing survival.

If supply bottlenecks or undesirable social consequences of present action can be foreseen by government, governmental steps may be taken. Government, having in mind the future consequences of present action, is readier today to intervene in the public interest. In limited areas there are external economies and diseconomies, where market prices do not reflect social values; in a world of pollution, overcrowding and aggressive commercialization, it is clearly not true to maintain that man always advances the common welfare in pursuit of his own interest.

One can even go further and say that the governmental problem changes, from the macroeconomic or aggregative steps required in an economy with unemployment, to the difficult micro as well as macro problems under full employment. But Shonfield wants to say more. He wants to in-

From Charles P. Kindleberger, "The Best Laid Plans," Reprinted from *Challenge*, The Magazine of Economic Affairs, a publication of Challenge Communications, Inc., May–June, 1966. Reprinted with kind permission of the author and publisher.

sist on the inescapable necessity of some elusive technique called planning.

I applaud the attention to supply. Keynesians have been right about the United States up to now and, during the 1950s, about Belgium, but they are totally wrong about England, for example. So are the anti-Keynesians. The point is not that there has been too little, or too irregular or too much demand. What they have slighted or ignored is supply.

But Shonfield is certainly not right in implying that all supply problems are basically the same. In France it was the structure of industry; in Italy structural unemployment; in Britain the immobility (and occasionally the intransigence) of labor. German rapid growth until 1965 was helped by the inflow of refugees and later immigrants who provided a peculiarly mobile labor force. In the United States, enterprise did respond quickly to demand, though pockets of poverty have remained. It is hard to generalize about the nature of the bottlenecks and social problems; and even harder about the therapy that will cope with them.

False synthesis

To attempt such generalization leads to error. Shonfield is persuaded that the wide-ranging intervention of governments and monopoly banks in European capital markets is a source of strength. He refers derisively to the "grossly inefficient structure of American Banking," and hankers after a system in which the Reconstruction Finance Corporation was the allocator of capital, like the "Caisse" in France or the "Kreditanstalt fuer Wiederaufbau" (plus the "Lastungsausgleich-fond," which he neglects) in Germany. (He even hints that the United States went off the track in scrapping NRA, and has a good word to say for the Nazi industrial associations.)

Students of the subjects will have a hard time with his views on capital markets on both sides of the Atlantic. What is a reasonable test of the efficiency of capital markets: the level of rates, the spread between lenders' and borrowers' returns, the need to depend on profits for investment? By any of these tests, the Shonfield verdicts would be reversed.

Semantics of planning

An interpretation which gives me great trouble is implied in the reference to Sweden's "central planning." But Swedish policy is distinguished first by its short-run stabilization of demand through investment reserves, and second by its governmental assistance to labor and capital markets. This is making private markets work better, not replacing them. Resources are not directed so much as made more mobile. There is no "coherence" imposed on resource allocation, even though such might logically follow from the investment reserve scheme. Similarly in Austria, which grew with nationalized industry but with no plan, it is hardly a point for planning that Austrian socialists "have come to see" the need for planning. The task is rather to explain why the Austrian economy grew so rapidly without it.

Planning in Shonfield's usage, turns out to be merely intervention. He insists that this is not so: *ad hoccery* is excluded. The case is not persuasive. Planning focuses on key industries here, structural objectives there, factor markets in this setting, allocating capital in that. In France planning has weak statistics but strong action; in the Netherlands it is the contrary. It may have been that planning was a dirty word as capitalism is an O.K. word in the United States, but if the first condition is going to be changed, we must know what we mean by planning if it is O.K., and this is not made clear.

This sounds uniformly negative. It is not meant to be. The book is rich in information, historical insights, suggestive asides and good writing. It is the standard revenge of the economist who writes mouthfilling jargon to accuse the fluent economist of lack of rigor. Shonfield will have to suffer from the envy of his less articulate brethren, as Galbraith and Rostow have done. But while I envy his prose style, I really differ with Shonfield's analysis.

The new era

European growth at 8 to 10 per cent a year from 1950 to 1963 cannot be sustained. It was the consequence of a backlog of demand, a technological backlog to be made up in investment, and excess supplies of labor on the Continent, not to mention the useful start of the Marshall Plan. Once the excess labor supply runs out, as it has done, supergrowth is over, and there is nothing that planning can do to restore it.

This is partly so because the interruption of growth, to hold down prices, alters the expectations of enterprise that demand will expand each year in five, not only four out of five.

There is now a risk of overinvestment whereas previously the only possible error was from underinvestment. Governments may plan and push, haul, nudge, apply body-English in trying to make enterprise conform to the plan, but without the same effect when demand and supply are expanding in unison with a mobile labor supply. Italy has been trying now for 18 months to restimulate private investment—with all the apparatus of which Shonfield makes so much, and with planning too—and is finding it difficult indeed.

It would be pleasant to subscribe to his central thesis, that the patterns of the past will not reassert themselves. But while it is true that government will respond to any lapse from growth with more speed and understanding than ever before in history, I cannot adhere to the view that the major danger for European growth stems from lack of international monetary reserves. The era of European supergrowth after World War II is over already, and one of the first victims of the change is this highly useful and stimulating book.

Reading 74

William Graham Sumner was a famous Yale professor at the turn of the century. His defense of laissez faire in terms of a crude social Darwinism—or, in fairness to Darwin, perhaps we should say in terms of Herbert Spenser's simplistic philosophy—has to be read to be believed. Will Milton Friedman sound so bizarre to future readers as Graham does today? Will Ayn Rand? Will J. K. Galbraith?

Perhaps it is not surprising that Yale, then the habitat of the privileged elite, should have a Sumner as one of its most popular lecturers. Yet truth is more complex: William Graham Sumner was an important contributor to sociology by his *Folkways.* And he was an outspoken opponent of McKinley's imperialism in the Philippines and Cuba. He began as an Episcopalian minister and ended assuring Yale students that in feathering their own nests they would be adding to God's grace.

The second of these pieces is Sumner's famous parable of The Forgotten Man. Ironically, Franklin Roosevelt purloined the expression in the New Deal, using it not to apply to Sumner's industrious taxpayer, but to any one of us who gets thrown out of work in the Great Depression and suffers economic misfortune. Roosevelt's forgotten men banded together in the mutual reinsurance that constitutes the modern welfare state. "There but for the grace of God go I," we each say to ourselves and vote for Medicare and social security. When Sumner quotes history against new progress, today's unforgotten man is reminded of those who say: "If God had intended us to fly, He'd have given us wings." Such an argument is always open to the riposte, "If He hadn't wanted us to fly, He could have fixed the laws of gravity to make that impossible. Who are you to tell Him His business?"

Questions to guide the reading

Just as Nietzsche, the creator of the superman, himself went mad, Sumner, the extoller of the strong as against the weak, had a breakdown of health at the age of fifty. Is this coincidence or nemesis? Does Sumner give proofs that biological inequalities can justify the skewness of the income distribution of his time or ours? How about Kropotkin's demonstration that altruism—mother love and group cohesion—is a powerful force conducive to natural survival and evolution of the species?

If Sumner's logic can justify getting rid of the police, what miracles can it not accomplish? And what does that suggest for his less absurd positions?

Social Darwinism and The Forgotten Man

William Graham Sumner

Biological moonshine

The assertion that all men are equal is perhaps the purest falsehood in dogma that was ever put into human language; five minutes' observation of facts will show that men are unequal through a very wide range of variation. Men are not simple units; they are very complex; there is no such thing as a unit man. Therefore we cannot measure men. If we take any element of man and measure men for it, they always fall under a curve of probable error.

Inferiority of women. When we say "man" for human being, we overlook distinctions of age and sex. Males of different ages are not equal; men and women are not equal in the struggle for existence. Women are handicapped by a function which causes disabilities in the struggle for existence, and this difference produces immense disparity in the sexes as to all interests through all human life.

The ground is then shifted to say that all men should be equal before the law, as an ideal of political institutions. They never have been so yet in any state; practically it seems impossible to realize such a state of things. It is an ideal. If this doctrine is a fighting doctrine, if it means that the law should create no privileges for one, or some, which others do not obtain under the same legal conditions, we should all take sides with it for the purposes of the fight. Even this, however, would remain an ideal, an object of hope and effort, not a truth.

Complaints of the envious

When we come nearer to the real thing which men have in mind we find that they actually complain of inequality of fortune, of realization, of earthly lot, of luxury and comfort, of power and satisfaction. This is what they want and this craving is what is in the mores. Nearly all, when they say that they want equality, only use another form of expression to say that they want more welfare than they have, because they take as a standard all which any one has and they find many who have more than themselves.

The eighteenth-century rhetoric about natural rights, equal rights, etc., gradually took on the form of a demand for the materialistic equality of enjoyment. Every change by which rhetorical phrases are set aside and real meaning is revealed is a gain. The fact of the mores of present-day society is that there is in them an intense craving for something which is a political phantasm.

History says, "No."

There is no reason whatever why it should be expected that men should enjoy equally, for that means that all should have means of enjoyment equal to the greatest which any one has; there is nothing in history, science, religion, or politics which could give warrant for such an expectation under any circumstances. We know of no force which could act for the satisfaction of human desires so as to make the satisfaction equal for a number of men, and we know of no interference

Abridged from William Graham Sumner, *Selected Essays,* Yale University Press, 1924, and *What Social Classes Owe to Each Other,* Harper and Brothers, New York, 1883.

by "the State," that is, by a committee of men, which could so modify the operation of natural forces as to produce that result. There is an old distinction between commutative and distributive justice which goes back to the Greeks, and which some writers of the nineteenth century have brought out again. Distributive justice is justice in which all personal circumstances are duly allowed for so that all are made "equal" on an absolute standard. Of course equality must necessarily be carried to some such conception at last. It is evident that God alone could give distributive justice; and we find, in this world in which we are, that God has not seen fit to provide for it at all.

*   *   *

The Forgotten Man
[Sumner's, not Roosevelt's]

The type and formula of most schemes of philanthropy or humanitarianism is this: A and B put their heads together to decide what C shall be made to do for D. The radical vice of all these schemes, from a sociological point of view, is that C is not allowed a voice in the matter, and his position, character, and interests, as well as the ultimate effects on society through C's interests, are entirely overlooked.

I call C the Forgotten Man.

For once let us look him up and consider his case, for the characteristic of all social doctors is, that they fix their minds on some man or group of men whose case appeals to the sympathies and the imagination, and they plan remedies addressed to the particular trouble; they do not understand that all the parts of society hold together, and that forces which are set in action act and react throughout the whole organism, until an equilibrium is produced by a re-adjustment of all interests and rights.

Capital the creator

They therefore ignore entirely the source from which they must draw all the energy which they employ in their remedies, and they ignore all the effects on other members of society than the ones

they have in view. They are always under the dominion of the superstition of government, and, forgetting that a government produces nothing at all, they leave out of sight the first fact to be remembered in all social discussion—that the State cannot get a cent for any man without taking it from some other man, and this latter must be a man who has produced and saved it. This latter is the Forgotten Man.

Pets

The friends of humanity start out with certain benevolent feelings toward "the poor," "the weak," "the laborers," and others of whom they make pets. They generalize these classes, and render them impersonal, and so constitute the classes into social pets. They turn to other classes and appeal to sympathy and generosity, and to all the other noble sentiments of the human heart.

Action in the line proposed consists in a transfer of capital from the better off to the worse off. Capital, however, as we have seen, is the force by which civilization is maintained and carried on. The same piece of capital cannot be used in two ways. Every bit of capital, therefore, which is given to a shiftless and inefficient member of society, who makes no return for it, is diverted from a reproductive use; but if it was put to reproductive use, it would have to be granted in wages to an efficient and productive laborer.

Hence the real sufferer by that kind of benevolence which consists in an expenditure of capital to protect the good-for-nothing is the industrious laborer. The latter, however, is never thought of in this connection. It is assumed that he is provided for and out of the account. Such a notion only shows how little true notions of political economy have as yet become popularized.

There is an almost invincible prejudice that a man who gives a dollar to a beggar is generous and kind-hearted, but that a man who refuses the beggar and puts the dollar in a savings-bank is stingy and mean. The former is putting capital where it is very sure to be wasted, and where it will be a kind of seed for a long succession of future dollars, which must be wasted to ward off a

What Social Classes Owe to Each Other, Harper and Brothers, New York, 1883.

greater strain on the sympathies than would have been occasioned by a refusal in the first place. Inasmuch as the dollar might have been turned into capital and given to a laborer who, while earning it, would have reproduced it, it must be regarded as taken from the latter.

When a millionnaire gives a dollar to a beggar the gain of utility to the beggar is enormous, and the loss of utility to the millionnaire is insignificant. Generally the discussion is allowed to rest there. But if the millionnaire makes capital of the dollar, it must go upon the labor market, as a demand for productive services. Hence there is another party in interest—the person who supplies productive services.

There always are two parties. The second one is always the Forgotten Man, and any one who wants to truly understand the matter in question must go and search for the Forgotten Man. He will be found to be worthy, industrious, independent, and self-supporting. He is not, technically, "poor" or "weak"; he minds his own business, and makes no complaint. Consequently the philanthropists never think of him, and trample on him.

One up, one down

For our present purpose it is most important to notice that if we lift any man up we must have a fulcrum, or point of reaction. In society that means that to lift one man up we push another down. The schemes for improving the condition of the working classes interfere in the competition of workmen with each other. The beneficiaries are selected by favoritism, and are apt to be those who have recommended themselves to the friends of humanity by language or conduct which does not betoken independence and energy. Those who suffer a corresponding depression by the interference are the independent and self-reliant, who once more are forgotten or passed over; and the friends of humanity once more appear, in their zeal to help somebody, to be trampling on those who are trying to help themselves.

Trades-unions adopt various devices for raising wages, and those who give their time to philanthropy are interested in these devices, and wish them success. They fix their minds entirely on the workmen for the time being *in* the trade, and do not take note of any other *workmen* as interested

in the matter. It is supposed that the fight is between the workmen and their employers, and it is believed that one can give sympathy in that contest to the workmen without feeling responsibility for anything farther.

Trade unions lower wages.   It is soon seen, however, that the employer adds the trades-union and strike risk to the other risks of his business, and settles down to it philosophically. If, now, we go farther, we see that he takes it philosophically because he has passed the loss along on the public. It then appears that the public wealth has been diminished, and that the danger of a trade war, like the danger of a revolution, is a constant reduction of the well-being of all. So far, however, we have seen only things which could *lower* wages—nothing which could raise them. The employer is worried, but that does not raise wages. The public loses, but the loss goes to cover extra risk, and that does not raise wages.

It is not upon the masters nor upon the public that trades-unions exert the pressure by which they raise wages; it is upon other persons of the labor class who want to get into the trades, but, not being able to do so, are pushed down into the unskilled labor class. These persons, however, are passed by entirely without notice in all the discussions about trades-unions. They are the Forgotten Men. But, since they want to get into the trade and win their living in it, it is fair to suppose that they are fit for it, would succeed at it, would do well for themselves and society in it; that is to say, that, of all persons interested or concerned, they most deserve our sympathy and attention.

Leave vice to nature

The cases already mentioned involve no legislation. Society, however, maintains police, sheriffs, and various institutions, the object of which is to protect people against themselves—that is, against their own vices. Almost all legislative effort to prevent vice is really protective of vice, because all such legislation saves the vicious man from the penalty of his vice. Nature's remedies against vice are terrible. She removes the victims without pity. A drunkard in the gutter is just where he ought to be, according to the fitness and tendency of things. Nature has set up on him the process of decline and dissolution by which she removes things which have survived their usefulness. Gambling and other less mentionable vices carry their own penalties with them.

Now, we never can annihilate a penalty. We can only divert it from the head of the man who has incurred it to the heads of others who have not incurred it. A vast amount of "social reform" consists in just this operation. The consequence is that those who have gone astray, being relieved from Nature's fierce discipline, go on to worse, and that there is a constantly heavier burden for the others to bear. Who are the others? When we see a drunkard in the gutter we pity him. If a policeman picks him up, we say that society has interfered to save him from perishing. "Society" is a fine word, and it saves us the trouble of thinking. The industrious and sober workman, who is mulcted of a percentage of his day's wages to pay the policeman, is the one who bears the penalty. But he is the Forgotten Man. He passes by and is never noticed, because he has behaved himself, fulfilled his contracts, and asked for nothing.

The fallacy of all prohibitory, sumptuary, and moral legislation is the same. A and B determine to be teetotalers, which is often a wise determination, and sometimes a necessary one. If A and B are moved by considerations which seem to them good, that is enough. But A and B put their heads together to get a law passed which shall force C to be a teetotaler for the sake of D, who is in danger of drinking too much. There is no pressure on A and B. They are having their own way, and they like it. There is rarely any pressure on D. He does not like it, and evades it. The pressure all comes on C. The question then arises, Who is C? He is the man who wants alcoholic liquors for any honest purpose whatsoever, who would use his liberty without abusing it, who would occasion no public question, and trouble nobody at all. He is the Forgotten Man again, and as soon as he is drawn from his obscurity we see that he is just what each one of us ought to be.

Reading 75

The *magnum opus* of Karl Marx, *Das Kapital* (or, in English, *Capital*), runs to almost 2 million words and appears in three volumes (1867, 1885, 1894), two of them posthumously edited by Marx's friend and collaborator Friedrich Engels. Few who call themselves Marxists have read through this work in its entirety. Indeed, many of today's New Left have reversed the earlier evaluation of Marx: they now attach primary importance to his youthful writings of the period prior to the 1849 *Communist Manifesto* and to the pre-*Das Kapital* incomplete book called the *Grundrisse* (or *Outline*) of 1857–1858, a work that was not known until deep into the twentieth century and which has still not been completely translated into English. Marx and Engels themselves, however, naturally attached prime importance to the mature economics of Marx, in which he believed he had laid bare the nature of capitalistic exploitation and the laws of motion of developing and decaying capitalism.

No serious reader can hope to pass judgment on Marx if he has not at least sampled the first volume of *Capital*. The present selection strips to the bone Marx's arguments (i) to demonstrate that labor provides a needed absolute common denominator between commodities of different physical properties and different kinds of usefulness; and (ii) his claim that the exchanging of goods for goods and of labor for goods gives rise under the special modes of production and relationships of competitive capitalism to "Fetishism" akin to the fetishisms of the superstitious and "mist-enveloped" region of the religious world. Also presented is (iii) Marx's analysis that normal barter of commodities for commodities, C—C, can be effectively handled by means of selling one good for money and using that money to buy a desired other good, C—M—C; but that, by contrast under competitive profit-seeking capitalism, there ensues a perversion of means and ends, so that the capitalist starts with money, exchanges it for commodities or the labor power of the toolless workers—in order to sell more dearly than he bought and end up with more than the M he started with, namely with M′. (I.e., we now have M—C—M′.)

Finally, (iv) Marx thought he had identified the essence of wage exploitation by his discovery that labor must allegedly accept in the wage market its minimum cost of production and reproduction just like any other thing, and that hence the capitalist can pocket the difference between what labor produces in the full working day and what it produces in the fraction of the working day needed under modern technology to produce its minimum food, clothing, and shelter. If it takes 6 hours of the 12-hour day to produce the minimum-subsistence wage, the capitalists garner 100 per cent in surplus value: so to speak, 6 hours of unpaid labor divided by 6 hours of paid labor.

It is perhaps not surprising that the Left today has tended to play down this analysis in favor of such notions as alienation of workers under modern market economies. Clearly, real wages did *not* stagnate in the hundred years after 1867 at any level remotely like that of an iron ration of subsistence. Marxism's principal tenet was falsified by the historical fact of steadily rising real wages of skilled and unskilled labor—in England, on the Continent, and in America. Careful economic analysis shows that this is no surprise: Karl Marx never did *cogently deduce* why a grasping capitalist, who must compete with other capitalists to get the workers who can allegedly produce so much, is able to find any worker to hire at the low minimum-subsistence iron wage.

To be sure, as Paul Baran and Paul Sweezy have argued in our time, Marx might have stressed the role of monopoly rather than persisting in the attempt to demonstrate that competitive capitalism must result in absolute or relative poverty for the worker. Or, like Malthus, Marx might have stressed the role of too-high birth rates in the resource-poor less-developed world. These, however, are might-have-beens.

The fact is that Marx is a difficult writer to read, and even he was not able to ferret out the non sequiturs in his logical syllogisms. (To help understand Marx, as you read selections i, ii, iii, and iv, consult the accompanying question guides to i, ii, iii, and iv.)

Questions to guide the reading

i. Who in the twentieth century feels the need for an *absolute* common denominator for commodities—to be found in labor or in anything else (such as marginal utility)? Why don't goods have in common such attributes as atoms, molecules, electrons, neutrons, protons, and other physics particles rather than allegedly "socially necessary labor"? Manna from heaven would have great dollar value in exchange to capitalist or worker: why, then, stress labor?

Coming closer to practical life, oil is where you find it, and labor costs are unimportant in the Kuwait or Libyan GNP. Why look to oil's labor cost only? The best red wine cannot be produced by any amount of labor except on certain French acres. If communism prevails in France, could such claret be sold in a future utopia at its labor cost? Would that be "fair"? Would it be "efficient"? As natural resources get depleted and polluted in the future, will mere labor costs dwindle in relative importance? And does it matter if a communist abandons the dogmatic labor theory of value, provided that he expropriates all private ownership of oil lands, vineyard lands, and other sources of great incomes?

ii. Imagine two capitalistic countries. In one every school child learns about commodity fetishism under capitalism. The blindfolds are removed from their eyes. In the other, the blindfolds remain, preserved in a shroud of pseudo-mystical capitalistic apologetics. But both economies have similar antitrust laws and post-Keynesian macro policies. What difference does it then make that Karl Marx developed his theory of commodity fetishism? Would it be itself "fetishistic" to attach much significance to the theory if it really makes no real difference to the Lorenz curve of inequality or to the rate of real growth of Net Economic Welfare (NEW) or of Gross National Product (GNP)?

iii. Would replacing C—M—C by M—C—M′ matter if vigorous antitrust laws hold down monopoly and preserve "effective competition"? And if post-Keynesian fiscal and monetary policies succeed in keeping total purchasing power high enough to avoid great depressions?

If, because of heavy inheritance taxation and new small-family patterns, every rich man arranged to spend his wealth *by the time he died,* would M—C—M′ be shifted back to C—C, perhaps through the longer chain C—M—C—M′—C′? Would the poor in America or Europe or India be likely to be any better off if habits changed to convert M—C—M′ into M—C—M′—C′? (*Hint:* At the Versailles Peace Conference, Maynard Keynes feared that capitalists would "eat up the cake"—i.e., the accumulated machinery and raw materials—upon which high wages depended.) Which macroeconomic chapters of your economics textbook do you think would be improved by stressing Marx's M—C—M′ analysis? Why?

iv. Test Marx's alleged demonstration that the real wage *must,* under capitalistic competition, sink to the minimum of subsistence and stay there. Assume birth control keeps the average family at a two-child level. Assume that modern technology is "very productive" and that there exist many known ways of producing more goods with the same labor if only that labor is embodied in the form of more intricate machinery. (Assume also that there are less efficient ways of producing that would become profitable if a bombing of all the existent supplies of raw materials and machinery required mankind to start from lower levels of capital goods.) Notice that, under *some* such circumstances that could be outlined in detail, the view that Marx was trying to refute *might* actually be correct—namely, just as abstinence in China and Russia on the part of one generation could make it possible for a later generation to have more and better capital goods and higher real-wage standards. Hence, under *some* forms of capitalism, abstinence might result in a rising trend of real wages like that in Western Europe after 1867. What happens then to Marx's assertion that labor power must *sell* at its minimum cost of reproduction—in terms of food, fuel, clothing, and furniture?

Did the United States real wage in 1928 exceed that of 1908 because workers had raised their minimum standard of living at which they would reproduce? (*Hint:* United States unions were weak then. Modern medicine was raising life expectancy and the size of the labor force, despite a drop in birth rates attributable to noneconomic factors.)

In terms of conventional supply and demand curves, *ss* and *dd,* Marx evidently posits a horizontal supply curve for labor at an alleged minimum wage. (*Note:* Physiology is concrete; but once the minimum could be determined by history and custom, it might mean high 1973 wages of $12,000 per year.) For Western Europe and North America, birth rates were dropping after 1870. What happened then to Marx's alleged horizontal *ss* curve? Did this negate his "laws of motion of developing capitalism"?

The Essence of *Das Kapital*

Karl Marx

I. Labour theory of value

Use value. Every useful thing, such as iron, paper, etc., may be looked at from the two points of view of quality and quantity. The utility of a thing makes it a use-value. A commodity, such as iron, corn, or a diamond, is therefore, so far as it is a material thing, a use-value, something useful. This property of a commodity is independent of the amount of labour required to appropriate its useful qualities.

Exchange value. Exchange value, at first sight, presents itself as a quantitative relation, as the proportion in which values in use of one sort are exchanged for those of another sort, a relation constantly changing with time and place.

Let us take two commodities, e.g., corn and iron. The proportions in which they are exchangeable, whatever those proportions may be, can always be represented by an equation in which a given quantity of corn is equated to some quantity of iron: e.g., 1 quarter corn = x cwt. iron. What does this equation tell us? It tells us that in two different things—in 1 quarter of corn and x cwt. of iron, there exists in equal quantities something common to both. The two things must therefore be equal to a third, which in itself is neither the one nor the other. Each of them, so far as it is exchange value, must therefore be reducible to this third.

A simple geometrical illustration will make this clear. In order to calculate and compare the areas of rectilinear figures, we decompose them into triangles. But the area of the triangle itself is expressed by something totally different from its visible figure, namely, by half the product of the base into the altitude. In the same way the exchange values of commodities must be capable of being expressed in terms of something common to them all, of which thing they represent a greater or less quantity.

This common "something" cannot be either a geometrical, a chemical, or any other natural property of commodities.

Labour, the common element. Let us now consider the residue of each of these products; it consists of the same unsubstantial reality in each, a mere congelation of homogeneous human labour, of labour-power expended without regard to the mode of its expenditure. All that these things now tell us is that human labour-power has been expended in their production, that human labour is embodied in them. When looked at as crystals of this social substance, common to them all, they are—Values.

The common substance that manifests itself in the exchange value of commodities, whenever they are exchanged, is their value. The progress of our investigation will show that exchange value is the only form in which the value of commodities can manifest itself or be expressed.

A use-value, or useful article, therefore, has value only because human labour in the abstract has been embodied or materialised in it. How, then, is the magnitude of this value to be measured? Plainly, by the quantity of the value-creating substance, the labour, contained in the article. The quantity of labour, however, is measured by its duration, and labour time in its turn finds its standard in weeks, days, and hours.

We see then that that which determines the magnitude of the value of any article is the amount of labour socially necessary, or the labour time socially necessary for its production.

II. The Fetishism of commodities and the secret thereof

A commodity is therefore a mysterious thing, simply because in it the social character of men's labour appears to them as an objective character stamped upon the product of that labour; because the relation of the producers to the sum total of their own labour is presented to them as a social relation, existing not between themselves, but be-

From Karl Marx, *Capital*, vol. I (1867). Abridged.

tween the products of their labour. There is a physical relation between physical things.

Social relations. But it is different with commodities. There the existence of the things *qua* commodities, and the value relation between the products of labour which stamps them as commodities, have absolutely no connection with their physical properties and with the material relations arising therefrom. There it is a definite social relation between men that assumes, in their eyes, the fantastic form of a relation between things. In order, therefore, to find an analogy, we must have recourse to the mist-enveloped regions of the religious world. In that world the productions of the human brain appear as independent beings endowed with life, and entering into relation both with one another and the human race. So it is in the world of commodities with the products of men's hands. This I call the Fetishism which attaches itself to the products of labour, so soon as they are produced as commodities, and which is therefore inseparable from the production of commodities.

This Fetishism of commodities has its origin, as the foregoing analysis has already shown, in the peculiar social character of the labour that produces them.

III. Money circulation

We saw in a former chapter the differentiation of commodities into commodities and money.

Rational barter or exchange. The exchange of commodities is therefore accompanied by the following changes in their form:

$$\text{Commodity—Money—Commodity}$$
$$\text{C—M—C}$$

The result of the whole process is, so far as concerns the objects themselves, C—C, the exchange of one commodity for another, the circulation of materialised social labour. When this result is attained, the process is at an end.

The goal of profit, not usefulness

The simplest form of the circulation of commodities is C—M—C, the transformation of commodities into money, and the change of the money back again into commodities; or selling in order to buy. But alongside of this form we find another specifically different form: M—C—M, the transformation of money into commodities, and the change of commodities back again into money; or buying in order to sell. Money that circulates in the latter manner is thereby transformed into, becomes capital, and is already potentially capital.

The circuit C—M—C starts with one commodity, and finishes with another, which falls out of circulation and into consumption. Consumption, the satisfaction of wants, in one word, use-value, is its end and aim. The circuit M—C—M, on the contrary, commences with money and ends with money. Its leading motive, and the goal that attracts it, is therefore mere exchange value.

To exchange £ 100 for cotton, and then this same cotton again for £ 100, is merely a roundabout way of exchanging money for money, the same for the same, and appears to be an operation just as purposeless as it is absurd. The cotton that was bought for £ 100 is perhaps resold for £ 100 + £ 10 or £ 110. The exact form of this process is therefore M—C—M′, where M′ = M + ΔM = the original sum advanced, plus an increment. This increment or excess over the original value I call "surplus-value." The value originally advanced, therefore, not only remains intact while in circulation, but adds to itself a surplus-value or expands itself. It is this movement that converts it into capital.

M—C—M′ is therefore in reality the general formula of capital as it appears prima facie within the sphere of circulation.

IV. Demonstration of wage exploitation by capital

In order that our owner of money may be able to find labour-power offered for sale as a commodity, various conditions must first be fulfilled.

Renting out one's labour. Labour-power can appear upon the market as a commodity only if, and so far as, its possessor [is] the untrammelled owner of his capacity for labour, i.e., of his person. He and the owner of money meet in the market, and deal with each other as on the basis of equal rights, both equal in the eyes of the law. The continuance of this relation demands that the owner of the labour-power should sell it only for a definite period, for if he were to sell it rump and stump, once for all, he would be selling himself, converting himself from a free man into a slave.

Workers lack tools and sustenance.   The labourer instead of being in the position to sell commodities in which his labour is incorporated, must be obliged to offer for sale as a commodity that very labour-power which exists only in his living self. [To be able to avoid having to sell his labor power to a capitalist employer] he must of course have the means of production, such as raw material, implements, etc. No boots can be made without leather. He requires also the means of subsistence. Nobody—not even "a musician of the future"— can live upon future products or upon use-values in an unfinished state; and ever since the first moment of his appearance on the world's stage, man always has been and must still be a consumer, both before and while he is producing. In a society where all products assume the form of commodities, these commodities must be sold after they have been produced; it is only after their sale that they can serve in satisfying the requirements of their producer. The time necessary for their sale is superadded to that necessary for their production.

For the conversion of his money into capital, therefore, the owner of money must meet in the market with the free labourer, free in the double sense, that as a free man he can dispose of his labour-power as his own commodity, and that on the other hand he has no other commodity for sale, is short of everything necessary for the realisation of his labour-power.

Cost of production and reproduction of labour-power.   We must now examine more closely this peculiar commodity, labour-power. Like all others it has a value. How is that value determined?

The value of labour-power is determined, as in the case of every other commodity, by the labour time necessary for the production, and consequently also the reproduction, of this special article. So far as it has value, it represents no more than a definite quantity of the average labour of society incorporated in it. Labour-power exists only as a capacity, or power of the living individual. Its production consequently presupposes his existence. Given the individual, the production of

labour-power consists in his reproduction of himself or his maintenance.

For his maintenance he requires a given quantity of the means of subsistence. Therefore labour time requisite for the production of labour-power reduces itself to that necessary for the production of those means of subsistence; in other words, the value of labour-power is the value of the means of subsistence necessary for the maintenance of the labourer.

His means of subsistence must therefore be sufficient to maintain him in his normal state as a labouring individual. His natural wants, such as food, clothing, fuel, and housing, vary according to the climatic and other physical conditions of his country.

Subsistence not merely physiological.   On the other hand, the number and extent of his so-called necessary wants, as also the modes of satisfying them, are themselves the product of historical development, and depend therefore to a great extent on the degree of civilization of a country, more particularly on the conditions under which, and consequently on the habits and degree of comfort in which, the class of free labourers has been formed. In contradistinction therefore to the case of other commodities, there enters into the determination of the value of labour-power a historical and moral element. Nevertheless, in a given country, at a given period, the average quantity of the means of subsistence necessary for the labourer is practically known.

The owner of labour-power is mortal. If then his appearance in the market is to be continuous, and the continuous conversion of money into capital assumes this, the seller of labour-power must perpetuate himself, "in the way that every living individual perpetuates himself, by procreation" (Petty). The labour-power withdrawn from the market by wear and tear and death must be continually replaced by, at the very least, an equal amount of fresh labour-power. Hence the sum of the means of subsistence necessary for production of labour-power must include the means necessary for the labourer's substitutes, i.e., his children, in order that this race of peculiar commodity owners may perpetuate its appearance in the market.

The value of labour-power resolves itself into the value of a definite quantity of the means of subsistence. It therefore varies with the value of these means or with the quantity of labour requisite for their production—the means of subsistence, such as food and fuel, such as clothes and furniture.

Technology's bounty: half a day's work produces a full day's subsistence.

Suppose that in this mass of commodities requisite for the average day there are embodied 6 hours of social labour, then there is incorporated daily in labour-power half a day's average social labour, in other words, half a day's labour is requisite for the daily production of labour-power. This quantity of labour forms the value of a day's labour-power or the value of the labour-power daily reproduced. If its owner therefore offers it for sale at its value, our friend Moneybags, who is intent upon converting his [investment outlays] into capital, pays this value.

On leaving this sphere of simple circulation or of exchange of commodities, which furnishes the "Free-trader Vulgaris" with his views and ideas, and with the standard by which he judges a society based on capital and wages, we think we can perceive a change in the physiognomy of our dramatis personæ. He who before was the money owner now strides in front as capitalist; the possessor of labour-power follows as his labourer. The one with an air of importance, smirking, intent on business; the other, timid and holding back, like one who is bringing his own hide to market and has nothing to expect but—a hiding.

Surplus value and exploitation

[Suppose the capitalist were to give workers such high real wages that they have to work for him only half the 12-hour day to produce their needed minimum-of-subsistence wages. Then no surplus would be available for the capitalist.] Our capitalist, who is at home in his vulgar economy, exclaims: "Oh! but I advanced my money for the express purpose of making more money." The way to Hell is paved with good intentions, and he might just as easily have intended to make money without producing at all. He threatens all sorts of things. He won't be caught napping again. In future he will buy the commodities in the market, instead of manufacturing them himself. But if all his brother capitalists were to do the same, where would he find his commodities in the market? And his money he cannot eat. He tries persuasion. "Consider my abstinence; I might have played ducks and drakes with the 15 shillings; but instead of that I consumed it productively, and made yarn with it."

He now gets obstinate. "Can the labourer," he asks, "merely with his arms and legs, produce commodities out of nothing? Did I not supply him with the materials, by means of which, and in which alone, his labour could be embodied? And as the greater part of society consists of such ne'er-do-wells, have I not rendered society incalculable service by my instruments of production, my cotton and my spindle, and not only society, but the labourer also, whom in addition I have provided with the necessaries of life? And am I to be allowed nothing in return for all this service?"

Capitalists appropriate surplus over subsistence.

The means of subsistence that are daily required for the production of labour-power cost half a day's labour. But the past labour that is embodied in the labour-power and the living labour that it can call into action; the daily cost of maintaining it and its daily expenditure in work, are two totally different things. The former determines the exchange-value of the labour-power, the latter is its use-value. The fact that half a day's labour is necessary to keep the labourer alive during 24 hours does not in any way prevent him from working a whole day. Therefore, the value of labour-power and the value which that labour-power creates in the labour process are two entirely different magnitudes; and this difference of the two values was what the capitalist had in view, when he was purchasing the labour-power. The useful qualities that labour-power possesses, and by virtue of which it makes yarn or boots, were to him nothing more than a *conditio sine qua non;* for in order to create value, labour must be expended in a useful manner. What really influenced him was the specific use-value which this commodity possesses of being *a source not only of value, but of more value than it has itself.* This is the special service that the capitalist expects from labour-power, and in this transaction he acts in accordance with the "eternal laws" of the exchange of commodities. The seller of labour-power, like the seller of any other commodity, realises its exchange-value and parts with its use-value. He cannot take the one without giving the other. The use-value of labour-power, or in other words, labour, belongs just as little to its seller as the use-value of oil after it has been sold belongs to the dealer who has sold it. The owner of the money has paid the value of a day's labour-power; his, therefore, is the use of it for a day; a day's labour belongs to him. The circumstance that on the one hand the daily sustenance of labour-power costs only half a day's labour, while on the other hand the very same labour-power can work during a whole day, that consequently the value which its use during one day creates is double what he pays for that use, this circumstance is,

without doubt, a piece of good luck for the buyer. The trick has at last succeeded; money has been converted into capital.

Profit at labour's expense. By turning his money into commodities that serve as the material elements of a new product, and as factors in the labour process, by incorporating living labour with their dead substance, the capitalist at the same time converts value, i.e., past, materialised, and dead labour into capital, into value big with value, a live monster that is fruitful and multiplies.

Since the production of surplus-value is the chief end and aim of capitalist production, it is clear that the greatness of a man's or a nation's wealth should be measured not by the absolute quantity produced, but by the relative magnitude of the surplus-produce.

Reading 76

Few Marxists are to be found in the economics departments of American universities. The late Paul Baran, professor of economics at Stanford, was one of the rare exceptions. His earlier book, *The Political Economy of Growth* (Monthly Review Press, New York, 1957), is critical of capitalistic colonialism and enjoys considerable audience abroad. Dr. Sweezy, trained at Exeter, Harvard, and the London School of Economics, has written a definitive work on Marxian economics, *The Theory of Capitalist Development* (Oxford University Press, New York, 1942), and is the editor of the *Monthly Review*.

The present excerpt was selected by the surviving author. The chapter from which it is taken claims much more than that America's attitude toward the Cuban revolution is primarily determined by the pecuniary interests of Standard Oil and other large corporations that hope to profit from a nonrevolutionary colony.

Questions to guide the reading

Had Cuba never offered a foothold for American business, would the American public still have been unconcerned to have a self-styled Marxist-Leninist government 90 miles from our shores? Is opposition to the Soviet Union and to what was regarded as expansion of the communist sphere of interest attributable only, or even primarily, to threatened loss of profits? Reversing roles, does the U.S.S.R. get material economic benefit from Cuba? Is Russia interested primarily in helping the peasants of Cuba? In all this do power politics, nationalism, balance of power, and xenophobia play important roles? Would a *reapprochement* between Nixon and Castro change the essentials? How can one test the validity of conflicting theses?

American Imperialism: A Marxian View

Paul Baran and Paul M. Sweezy

It is often said that capitalism cannot exist without foreign trade and that every advance of socialism means a constriction of capitalism's trading area. Hence, the argument continues, for the leading capitalist countries, even if they are not threatened by powerful internal socialist movements, the struggle against socialism is quite literally a struggle for survival. Put in this form, the reasoning from capitalist interests involves a *non sequitur*. It is true that capitalism is inconceivable without foreign trade, but it is not true that socialist countries are unwilling or unable to trade with capitalist countries. Hence the spread of socialism, taken by itself, does not imply any reduction of the trading area open to the capitalist countries. One can even go further. Bourgeois economists never tire of repeating that the more industrially developed a country is, the greater its potential as a trading partner. Since underdeveloped countries industrialize more rapidly under socialism than under capitalism, the leading capitalist countries, on this argument, should welcome the spread of socialism in the underdeveloped parts of the capitalist world. That they do not but instead resist it tooth and nail must be explained on other grounds.

The problem is in reality much more complex and can only be fruitfully posed in quite different terms. Capitalist governments do not, in general, trade with each other. Most trade in the capitalist world is carried on by private enterprises, mainly by large corporations. What these corporations are interested in is not trade as such but profits: the reason they and the governments they control are opposed to the spread of socialism is not that it necessarily reduces their chances of importing or exporting (though of course it may), but that it does necessarily reduce their opportunities to profit from doing business with and in the newly socialized area. And when account is taken of the fact that for corporations in the leading capitalist countries, profit rates from doing business with and in the less developed and underdeveloped countries are generally higher than domestic profit rates, the reason for the vehemence of opposition to the spread of socialism in precisely those areas will be appreciated.

We advisedly use the general term "doing business with and in" rather than the more limited "buying from and selling to." The international relationships and interests of the typical giant corporation today are likely to be diverse and extremely complex, much more so than mere exporting or importing. There is perhaps no better way to make this clear than by summarizing the world-wide scope and character of what is unquestionably the leading United States "multinational corporation"—Standard Oil of New Jersey [in 1973, Exxon Corporation]. The facts and figures which follow are taken from official publications of the company.[1]

In terms of dollar assets, Jersey Standard is the largest industrial corporation in the United States, the total at the end of 1962 amounting to $11,488 million. Aggregate revenues for the same year were $10,567 million and net income (profit) $841 million. It is only when these figures are broken down geographically, however, that the crucial importance of foreign operations becomes clear. As of the end of 1958, the percentage distribution of assets and profits by regions was as follows:

	Assets	Profits
United States and Canada	67	34
Latin America	20	39
Eastern Hemisphere	13	27
Total	100	100

[1] *Notice of Special Stockholders' Meeting* (October 7, 1959); *Form 10-K for the Fiscal Year Ended December 31, 1962* (filed with the Securities and Exchange Commission pursuant to Section 13 of the Securities Act of 1934); and 1962 *Annual Report.*

While two thirds of Jersey's assets were located in North America, only one third of its profits came from that region. Or to put the point differently, Jersey's foreign investments were half as large as its domestic investments but its foreign profits were twice as large as its domestic profits. The indicated profit rate abroad is thus four times the domestic rate.

That Jersey's operations are truly worldwide can be gathered from the facts that in 1962 the company sold its products in more than a hundred countries and owned 50 percent or more of the stock in 275 subsidiaries in 52 countries. Summarizing by regions, we find that Jersey had 114 subsidiaries in the United States and Canada, 77 in Europe, 43 in Latin America, 14 in Asia, 9 in Africa, and 18 elsewhere.

The tremendous variety and scope of Jersey's foreign operations might lead one to suppose that over the years the company has been a large and consistent exporter of capital. Nothing could be further from the truth. Apart from a small initial export of capital many years ago, the expansion of Jersey's foreign assets has been financed from the profits of its foreign operations. Moreover, so great have been these foreign profits that after all foreign expansion needs have been taken care of, there have still been huge sums left over for remittance to the parent company in the United States. Separate figures on the amount of these remittances from foreign profits are not published, but an idea of the orders of magnitude is conveyed by the following figures for 1962. In that year, as already noted, total profits were $841 million. Of this sum, $538 million were paid out as dividends to stockholders, the vast majority of whom are residents of the United States. The remaining $303 million were added to the company's investments, at home and abroad. Elsewhere in the same Annual Report that records these figures we learn that profits from operations in the United States in 1962 were $309 million. This figure, it will be seen, is $229 million less than the amount of dividends paid. In other words, approximately 40 percent of dividends paid to stockholders plus whatever net investment was made in the United States during the year were financed from the profits of foreign operations. In a word: Standard Oil of New Jersey is a very large and consistent *importer* of capital.

At this point, however, we must pause and ask whether Standard Oil of New Jersey is really an ideal type which helps us to distill the essence of capitalist reality, or whether on the contrary it may not be an exceptional case which we should ignore rather than focus attention on.

Up to the Second World War, it would have been correct to treat Standard Oil as a sort of exception—a very important one, to be sure, exercising tremendous, and at times even decisive, influence on United States world policy. Nevertheless in the multinational scope and magnitude of its operations not only was it far ahead of all the others; there were only a handful which could be said to be developing along the same lines. Many United States corporations of course had large interests in import and export trade, and quite a few had foreign branches or subsidiaries. In neither respect, however, was the situation much different in 1946 from what it had been in 1929. Indeed, direct foreign investments of United States corporations actually declined from $7.5 billion to $7.2 billion, or by 4 percent, between these two dates.[2] Most of the giant corporations which dominated the American economy in those years were, in the words of *Business Week,* "domestically oriented enterprises with international operations" and not, like Standard Oil, "truly world oriented corporations."[3]

A big change took place during the next decade and a half. To quote *Business Week* again, "In industry after industry, U.S. companies found that their overseas earnings were soaring, and that their return on investment abroad was frequently much higher than in the U.S. As earnings abroad began to rise, profit margins from domestic operations started to shrink. This is the combination that forced development of the multinational company."[4] As a result, of course, foreign direct investments of American corporations shot up—from

[2] United States Department of Commerce, Office of Business Economics, *U.S. Business Investments in Foreign Countries: A Supplement to the Survey of Current Business,* Washington, 1960, p. 1.

[3] "Multinational Companies," *Business Week,* April 20, 1963. It is interesting to note that in the United States the business press is often far ahead of the economics profession in recognizing, and even trying to analyze, the latest developments in the capitalist economy.

[4] *Ibid.*

Table 1 Growth of Foreign and Domestic Manufacturing Sales and Merchandise Exports, 1957–1962 (billions of dollars)

	Sales of foreign manu- facturing affiliates	Total domestic manu- facturing sales	Merchandise exports (excluding foodstuffs)
1957	18.3	341	16.8
1958	n.a.	314	13.8
1959	21.1	356	13.7
1960	23.6	365	16.6
1961	25.6	368	16.9
1962	28.1	400	17.3

n.a. = not available
Sources: Foreign sales, Fred Cutler and Samuel Pizer, "Foreign Operations of U.S. Industry," *Survey of Current Business,* October 1963; domestic sales and exports, *Economic Indicators,* current issues.

$7.2 billion in 1946 to $40.6 billion in 1963, a more than fivefold increase in the years since the Second World War.[5] Parallel to this growth in foreign investments has gone an increase in the sales and profits of foreign branches and subsidiaries. In manufacturing (excluding petroleum and mining), sales of such affiliates amounted to $18.3 billion in 1957 (the first year for which figures are available) and to $28.1 billion in 1962, an increase of 54 percent in six years.[6]

Some idea of the growing relative importance of these foreign operations of American corporations may be gathered from Table 1, which presents data on the sales of foreign manufacturing affiliates, total domestic manufacturing sales, and non-agricultural merchandise exports.

It would of course be preferable to compare the foreign and domestic sales and exports of those corporations which have foreign branches or subsidiaries; and it would be still better if we could include the profits of these corporations from foreign and domestic operations respectively. If such data were available, we could form a very clear

[5] *Survey of Current Business,* August 1964, p. 10.
[6] Fred Cutler and Samuel Pizer, "Foreign Operations of U.S. Industry: Capital Spending, Sales, and Financing," *Survey of Current Business,* October 1963, p. 19.

picture of the degree of involvement of the United States giant corporations in foreign activities. But even the figures presented in Table 1 bear eloquent testimony to the rapid growth of that involvement. In the six years beginning with 1957, the sales of foreign affiliates grew by 54 percent, while total domestic manufacturing sales expanded only 17 percent and non-agricultural exports hardly changed at all.

So much for the record of recent years. If we look ahead, we find that American corporate business, far from regarding its expansion abroad as having come to an end, is relying heavily for its future prosperity on the continued penetration of other countries' economies. "America as the 'land of opportunity' is beginning to lose that title in the eyes of many U.S. businessmen," says a Special Report in *U.S. News & World Report.*[7] And the Report goes on to tell why:

These businessmen increasingly are deciding that markets abroad—not those in this country—offer the biggest potential for future growth. The feeling grows that the U.S. market, while huge, is relatively "saturated."

It is overseas that businessmen see the big, untapped market with hundreds of millions of customers wanting—and increasingly able to buy—all kinds of products and services.

To go after this market, U.S. firms are building and expanding factories all around the world. Since 1958, more than 2,100 American companies have started new operations in Western Europe alone.

All types of businesses—from autos to baby foods—predict a glowing future for markets outside the U.S.

It thus appears both from the record of the past and from the plans and hopes for the future that American corporate business has irrevocably embarked on the road long since pioneered by Standard Oil. Standard is still the model of a multinational corporation, but it is no longer an exception. It simply shows us in the most devel-

[7] "For New Opportunities: Now, the Word Is 'Go Abroad,'" *U.S. News & World Report,* June 1, 1964. In order to gather material for this report, "members of the International Staff of *U.S. News & World Report* talked with scores of U.S. firms abroad. Added material was gathered from corporations in the U.S. heavily engaged in the foreign field."

oped form what the other giants either already are or are in the process of becoming.

As it happens, the recent history of Standard Oil of New Jersey [now Exxon] also supplies us with a textbook example of why multinational corporations are profoundly hostile to the spread of socialism. Before the Cuban Revolution, Jersey was heavily involved in Cuba in several ways. It owned refining facilities on the island and operated an extensive distribution system, involving altogether properties valued at $62,269,000.[8] In addition, Jersey's Cuban subsidiary bought its crude from Creole Petroleum, Jersey's Venezuelan subsidiary, at the high prices maintained by the international oil cartel. The company therefore reaped profits in two countries and on three separate operations—sale of crude, refining of crude, and sale of finished products. As a result of the Revolution, the company's properties in Cuba were nationalized without compensation, and Creole lost its Cuban market. More than $60 million in assets and all three sources of current profit were lost in one blow—and without in any way involving exports from or imports to the United States.

It might be argued that if Jersey and the United States government had pursued different policies toward Cuba, the revolutionary regime would have been glad to continue buying oil from Venezuela, which after all is the nearest and most rational source of supply. This is no doubt true—but with a big proviso. The revolutionary regime would have been glad to continue buying oil from Venezuela, but it would not have been glad to continue paying prices and meeting terms of payment dictated by Standard Oil. And since it could turn to the Soviet Union as an alternative source of supply, it was no longer obliged to go on submitting to the cartel's terms. Hence to remain in the Cuban market, Jersey would at the least have had to cut its prices and offer better credit terms. This not only would have meant less profits on sales to Cuba but would have threatened the whole structure of cartel prices. Jersey and Washington decided instead to make war on the Cuban Revolution.

That what is at stake in the conflict between the United States and Cuba is not trade between the

[8] Standard and Poor, *Standard Corporate Descriptions,* July 24, 1961.

two countries is confirmed by Cuba's relations with other capitalist countries. Long after the socialization of the Cuban economy, the Havana government was vigorously promoting its trade with Britain, France, Spain, Canada, Japan—in short, with any country willing and able to do business with Cuba. It is true, of course, that Cuba's capacity to export and import has been seriously curtailed by the disorganization and other difficulties of the early years of the change-over to socialism, but there seems to be no reason to doubt the Cubans' own contention that in a few years the island will be a much better trading partner than it was under the old neo-colonial regime. Nor is there any reason to doubt that the United States could capture a major share of the Cuban trade if the blockade were called off and normal relations re-established between the two countries.

But this is not what really interests the giant multinational corporations which dominate American policy. What they want is *monopolistic control* over foreign sources of supply and foreign markets, enabling them to buy and sell on specially privileged terms, to shift orders from one subsidiary to another, to favor this country or that depending on which has the most advantageous tax, labor, and other policies—in a word, they want to do business on their own terms and wherever they choose. And for this what they need is not trading partners but "allies" and clients willing to adjust their laws and policies to the requirements of American Big Business.

Against this background, one can see that Cuba's crime was to assert, in deeds as well as in words, her sovereign right to dispose over her own resources in the interests of her own people. This involved curtailing and, in the struggle which ensued, eventually abrogating the rights and privileges which the giant multinational corporations had previously enjoyed in Cuba. It was because of this and not because of a loss of trade, still less because of any irrational fears or prejudices, that the corporations and their government in Washington reacted so violently to the Cuban Revolution.

It might perhaps be thought that since Cuba is a small country, the violence of the reaction was out of all proportion to the damage suffered. But this would be to miss the main point. What makes

Cuba so important is precisely that she is so small, plus the fact that she is located so close to the United States. If Cuba can defect from the "free world" and join the socialist camp with impunity, then any country can do so. And if Cuba prospers under the new setup, all the other underdeveloped and exploited countries of the world will be tempted to follow her example. The stake in Cuba is thus not simply the exploitability of one small country but the very existence of the "free world" itself, that is to say, of the whole system of exploitation.

It is this fact that has dictated the Cuban policy of the United States. The strategy has been to damage and cripple the Cuban economy in every possible way, with a threefold objective. First, it is hoped that the Cuban people will sooner or later become disillusioned with their revolutionary leadership, thus setting the stage for a successful counter-revolution. Second, the peoples of the underdeveloped countries are to be taught that revolution does not pay. And third, the burden of supporting the Cuban economy thrown on the rest of the socialist camp, and especially on the Soviet Union as its economically most developed member, is to be maximized so that these other socialist countries may be induced to use their influence to restrain any new revolutions which might place further burdens on their already overstrained economies.

Readings 77 and 78   A Debate on Alienation

That real wages have been rising this past century is no longer subject to debate. But are people happier? Polls show that people with more money today report they are happier than those with less money. But the polls do not demonstrate that, over the decades, a general increase in real income shared by both rich and poor makes people consciously happier than they used to be.

Affluence can bring boredom, ennui, and neurosis. Even if the factory worker is well paid and subject to shorter hours per week, the tension and boredom of the modern assembly line may make him more nervous and bored than were past craftsmen working on more self-fulfilling tasks. In a word, modern man may have become increasingly "alienated."

Karl Marx had emphasized alienation. But as Ernest Mandel, a leading interpreter of Marx in our time, points out, there is much more to Marx's analysis of alienation than mere boredom with factory specialization.

Irving Kristol, Henry Luce Professor of Urban Values at New York University, who delights in puncturing what he regards as radical and liberal bubbles, attacks belief in the pervasiveness of alienation as a myth of the intellectual that workers themselves deny.

Questions to guide the reading

If workers abhor boring work under authoritarian conditions, will competition begin to force employers to make working conditions more attractive? Is a prior revolution *inevitable*? Is it a *probable* requirement to lessen alienation? After a revolution, could people still feel alienated—in Esthonia, Czechoslovakia, Russia, Romania, or China? Could a Swiss feel less alienated than a Swede? Than a Chinese? How would one go about trying to settle debate about a question like this?

Could a French Kristol, writing just before the university and workers' revolts of 1968, have argued that Frenchmen are generally prosperous and contented? Why, then, the revolt? Are hard hats who vote for George Wallace unhappy people? Why the university unrests of recent years when allegedly "students never had it so good before"?

Reading 77

The Marxist Theory of Alienation

Ernest Mandel

Hegel and young Marx

It was by studying Hegel that Marx first came across the concept of alienation. But, oddly enough, it was not the theory of alienated labor that he originally picked up from Hegel's works. It was the alienation of man as a citizen in his relationship with the state that became the starting point of Marx's philosophical, political and social thought.

When Marx takes up definitions of alienated labor given by Hegel, he contradicts them. He says that the discrepancy between needs and material resources, the tension between needs and labor, is a limited one, conditioned by history.

Alienation results from a certain form of organization of society. More concretely, only in a society which is based on commodity production and only under the specific economic and social circumstances of a market economy, can the objects which we project out of us when we produce acquire a socially oppressive existence of their own and be integrated in an economic and social mechanism which becomes oppressive and exploitative of human beings.

The tremendous advance in human thought which I referred to in this critique of Hegel consists in the fact that Marx rejects the idea of the alienation of labor as being an anthropological characteristic, that is, an inherent and ineradicable curse of mankind. He says that the alienation of labor is not bound to human existence in all places and for all future time. It is a specific result of specific forms of social and economic organization. In other words, Marx transforms Hegel's notion of alienated labor from an eternal anthropological into a transitory historical notion.

This reinterpretation carries a message of hope for mankind. Marx says that mankind is not condemned to live "by the sweat of his brow" under alienated conditions throughout his whole term on earth. He can become free, his labor can become free, he is capable of self-emancipation, though only under specific historical conditions.

The mature Marx and alienation

Another major work of Marx, *Gründrisse der Kritik der Politischen Ökonomie* (Fundamental Outlines of a Critique of Political Economy), a thirteen-hundred-page work written in 1857–58, which is a kind of laboratory where all the major ideas of *Capital* were first elaborated and tested, was not published until a century after it was written. Anybody who reads it can at once see that a Marxist theory of alienation exists because in the *Gründrisse* the word, the concept, and the analysis appear dozens and dozens of times.

What then is this theory of alienation as it was developed by the mature Marx, not by the young Marx? And how can we relate it to what is set down in *Capital*?

Let us start this analysis with a definition of economic alienation. I must immediately state that in the comprehensive Marxist theory of alienation, economic alienation is only one part of a much more general phenomenon which covers practically all fields of human activity in class society. But it is the most decisive element. So let's start from economic alienation. We will approach it in successive stages. The first and most striking feature of economic alienation is the separation of men from free access to the means of production and means of subsistence. This is a rather recent development in human history. As late as the nineteenth century free access to the means of production in agriculture survived in some countries of the world, among others, in the United States and Canada. Until after the American Civil War it was not impossible for masses of people to find some unpreempted spot of land and to establish themselves on that acreage as free farmers, as homesteaders. In Europe that possibility had ceased to exist for two hundred years, and in some countries there even three or four hundred years earlier.

The second stage in the alienation of labor came about when part of society was driven off the land, no longer had access to the means of production and means of subsistence, and, in order to survive, was forced to sell its labor power on the market. That is the main characteristic of alienated labor. In the economic field it is the institution of wage labor, the economic obligation of people who cannot otherwise survive to sell the only commodity they possess, their labor power, on the labor market.

Wage slavery: invention of the age of capitalism

What does it mean to sell your labor power to a boss? In Marx's analysis, both in his youthful and his mature work, behind this purely formal and legal contractual relation—you sell your labor power, part of your time, to another for money to live on—is in reality something of deepgoing consequence for all human existence and particularly for the life of the wage laborer. It first of all implies that you lose control over a large part of your waking hours. All the time which you have sold to the employer belongs to him, not to you. You are not free to do what you want at work. It is the employer who dictates what you will and will not do during this whole time. He will dictate what you produce, how you produce it, where you produce it. He will be master over your activity.

And the more the productivity of labor increases and the shorter the workweek becomes, the stricter will be the control of the employer over every hour of your time as a wage laborer. In time and motion studies—the ultimate and most perfected form of this control—the boss even tries to control every second, *literally* every second, of the time which you spend in his employ.

Alienation thereupon acquires a third form. When a wage earner has sold his labor power for a certain part of his life to his employer, the products of his labor are not his own. The products of his labor become the property of the employer.

The fact that the modern wage earner owns none of the products of his own labor, obvious as it may appear to people who are accustomed to bourgeois society, is not at all so self-evident from the viewpoint of human history as a whole. It was not like that for thousands upon thousands of years of human existence. Both the medieval handicraftsman and the handicraftsman of antiquity were the proprietors of their own products. The peasant, and even the serf of the middle ages, remained in possession of at least 50 per cent, sometimes 60 and 70 per cent, of the output of their own labor.

The machine: man's enemy

Under capitalism not only does the wage earner lose possession of the product of his labor, but these products can function in a hostile and injurious manner against him. This happened with the machine. This remarkable product of human ingenuity becomes a source of tyranny against the worker when the worker serves as an appendage of the machine and is forced to adapt the cadence of his life and work to the operation of the machine. This can become a serious source of alienation in shift work when part of the working class has to work during the night or at odd hours in conflict with the normal rhythm of human life between day and night. Such an abnormal schedule causes all sorts of psychological and nervous disorders.

Another aspect of the oppressive nature which the products of labor can acquire once society is divided into hostile classes of capitalists and wage workers are the crises of overproduction, depressions or, as it is nowadays more prudently put, recessions. Then people consume less because they produce too much. And they consume less, not because their labor in inadequately productive, but because their labor is too productive.

Creativity versus money

We come now to a final form of alienated labor in the economic field which derives from the conclusions of the points I have noted. The alienation of the worker and his labor means that something basic has changed in the life of the worker. What is it? Normally everybody has some creative capacity, certain talents lodged in him, untapped potentialities for human development which should be expressed in his labor activity.

However, once the institution of wage labor is prevalent, these possibilities become nullified. Work is no longer a means of self-expression for anybody who sells his labor time. Work is just a means to attain a goal. And that goal is to get money, some income to be able to buy the consumer goods necessary to satisfy your needs.

In this way a basic aspect of man's nature, his capacity to perform creative work, becomes thwarted and distorted. Work becomes something which is not creative and productive for human beings but something which is harmful and destructive. Catholic priests and Protestant pastors who have worked in factories in Western Europe, the so-called "worker-priests," who have written books about their experiences, have arrived at conclusions on this point that are absolutely identical with those of Marxism. They declare that a wage earner considers the hours passed in factories or in offices as time lost from his life. He must spend time there in order to get freedom and capacity for human development outside the sphere of production and of work.

Alienation of the consumer

Once socially necessary labor time became shorter and leisure time greater, a commercialization of leisure took place. The capitalist society of commodity production, the so-called "consumer society" did its utmost to integrate leisure time into the totality of economic phenomena at the basis of commodity production, exploitation and accumulation.

At this point the notion of alienation is extended from a purely economic to a broader social phenomenon. The first bridge to this wider application is the concept of alienation of the consumer. Thus far we have spoken only about the consequences of alienated labor. But one of the cardinal characteristics of capitalist society, as Marx understood as early as 1844, is its built-in contradiction regarding human needs. On the one hand, each capitalist entrepreneur tries to limit the human needs of his own wage earners as much as possible by paying as little wages as possible. Otherwise he would not make enough profit to accumulate.

On the other hand, each capitalist sees in the work force of all the other capitalists not wage earners but potential consumers. He would therefore like to expand the capacity of consumption of these other wage earners to the limit or otherwise he cannot increase production and sell what his own workers produce. Thus capitalism has a tendency to constantly extend the needs of people.

Up to a certain point this expansion can cover genuine human needs, such as the elementary requirements of feeding, housing and clothing everybody in more or less decent circumstances. Very quickly, however, capitalism in its efforts to commercialize everything and sell as many gadgets as possible, goes beyond any rational human needs and starts to spur and stimulate artificial needs in a systematic, large-scale manner.

Crime, frustration, and capitalism

Such alienation is no longer purely economic but has become social and psychological in nature. For what is the motivation of a system for constantly extending needs beyond the limits of what is rational? It is to create, purposely and deliberately, permanent and meretricious dissatisfactions in human beings. Capitalism would cease to exist if people were fully and healthily satisfied. The system must provoke continued artificial dissatisfaction in human beings because without that dissatisfaction the sales of new gadgets which are more and more divorced from genuine human needs cannot be increased.

A society which is turned toward creating systematic frustration of this kind generates the bad results recorded in the crime pages of the daily newspapers. A society which breeds worthless dissatisfaction will also breed all kinds of antisocial attempts to overcome this dissatisfaction.

Humans "reified" into things

Beyond this alienation of human beings as consumers, there are two very important aspects of alienation. One is the alienation of human activity in general. The other is the alienation of human beings in one of their most fundamental features, the capacity to communicate.

What is meant by the extension of the concept of alienation to human activity in general? We live in a society based on commodity production and a social division of labor pushed to the limits of overspecialization. As a result, people in a particular job or doing a certain type of activity for a living will incline to have an extremely narrow horizon. They will be prisoners of their trade, seeing only the problems and preoccupations of their specialty. They will also tend to have a restricted social and political awareness because of this limitation.

Along with this shut-in horizon will go something which is much worse, the tendency to transform relations between human beings into relations between things. This is that famous tendency toward "reification," the transformation of social relations into things, into objects, of which Marx speaks in *Capital*.

This habit of reification is not the fault of the inhumanity or insensitivity of the workers. It results from a certain type of human relation rooted in commodity production and its extreme division of labor where people engaged in one trade tend to see their fellows only as customers or through the lenses of whatever economic relations they have with them.

Noncommunication across class lines

I come now to the ultimate and most tragic form of alienation, which is alienation of the capacity to communicate. The capacity to communicate has become the most fundamental attribute of man, of his quality as a human being. Without communication, there can be no organized society because without communication, there is no language, and without language, there is no intelligence. Capitalist society, class society, commodity-producing society tends to thwart, divert and partially destroy this basic human capacity.

The Marxist notion of alienation extends far beyond the oppressed classes of society, properly speaking. The oppressors are also alienated from part of their human capacity through their inability to communicate on a human basis with the majority of society. And this divorcement is inevitable as long as class society and its deep differentiations exist.

Another terrible expression of this alienation on the individual scale is the tremendous loneliness which a society based on commodity production and division of labor inevitably induces in many human beings. Ours is a society based on the principle, every man for himself. Individualism pushed to the extreme also means loneliness pushed to the extreme. Capitalism tends to extend the zone of this extreme loneliness with all its terrible implications.

If the curve of mental sickness has climbed parallel with the curve of material wealth and income in most of the advanced countries of the West, this dismal picture has not been invented by Marxist critics but corresponds to very deep-rooted aspects of the social and economic reality in which we live.

Withering away of alienation under classless socialism

This grim situation is not at all without hope. Our optimism comes from the fact that, after all this analysis of the roots of the alienation of labor and the specific expressions of the alienation of man in bourgeois society is completed, there emerges the inescapable conclusion that a society can be envisaged in which there will be no more alienation of labor and alienation of human beings. This is a historically produced and man-made evil, not an evil rooted in nature or human nature. Like everything else which has been made by man, it can also be unmade by man. This condition is a product of history and it can be destroyed by history or at least gradually overcome by further progress.

Thus the Marxist theory of alienation implies and contains a theory of disalienation through the creation of conditions for the gradual disappearance and eventual abolition of alienation. I stress "gradual disappearance" because such a process or institution can no more be abolished by fiat or a stroke of the pen than commodity production, the state, or the division of society into classes can be eliminated by a government decree or proclamation.

Marxists understand that the social and economic preconditions for a gradual disappearance of alienation can be brought about only in a classless society ushered in by a world socialist revolution. And when I say a classless socialist society, I obviously do not mean the societies which exist in the Soviet Union, Eastern Europe or China. In the best cases these are transitional societies somewhere halfway between capitalism and socialism. Though private property has been abolished, they have not yet abolished the division of society into classes, they still have different social classes and different social layers, division of labor and commodity production. As a consequence of these conditions, they still have alienated labor and alienated men.

The prerequisites for the disappearance of human alienation, of alienated labor and the alienated activities of human beings, can only be created precisely through the continuation of those processes I have just named: the withering away of commodity production, the disappearance of economic scarcity, the withering away of social division of labor through the disappearance of private ownership of the means of production and the elimination of the difference between manual and intellectual labor, between producers and administrators.

All of this would bring about the slow transformation of the very nature of labor from a coercive necessity in order to get money, income and means of consumption into a voluntary occupation that people want to do because it covers their own internal needs and expresses their talents. This transformation of labor into all-sided creative human activity is the ultimate goal of socialism. Only when that goal is attained will alienated labor and all its pernicious consequences cease to exist.

Reading 78

Myth of the Alienated Worker Meets the Fact of Workers Who Deny It

Irving Kristol

All of a sudden, we are being inundated by learned accounts of the "blue collar blues." What happened? Why the intense interest in this subject at this time? Are the workers rioting in the streets? Burning down the factories?

No, nothing so spectacular has occurred. What did happen is really quite prosaic: a great many workers decided to vote for George Wallace and subsequently for Richard Nixon, and for some liberal social scientists and politicians this "perverse" behavior requires deep sociological and psychological explanation.

One such explanation, derived from a faded neo-Marxism, is that American workers are so frustrated by their monotonous and "soulless" work that they become exceedingly vulnerable to racist or chauvinist demagoguery. With such an explanation in hand, liberals need not worry about whether or not *they* alienated the workers from the Democratic Party; the workers had already been alienated from reality by industrial capitalism, and in a fit of unreason—a proper Marxist would call it a spasm of "false consciousness"—they bit the hand that tried to feed them.

The predestined conclusion is clear enough: we must "redesign" our economy and society so as to "humanize" work, and thereby permit American workers to vote "rationally," i.e., for left-of-center candidates.

Too dumb to know?

But an obvious precondition on such a reformation is that the workers have to *know* they are alienated. Senator McGovern tried to get this message across in some of his TV commercials, with little apparent effect. The most recent effort takes the form of a report by an HEW task force—a report which made front-page news, which our television reporters hailed as a significant event, and which some Senators seem to think is terribly important. The document, entitled "Work in America," finds that both "blue collar blues" and

From Irving Kristol, "Is the American Worker Alienated?" *The Wall Street Journal*, Jan. 18, 1973. Reprinted with the kind permission of the author and *The Wall Street Journal*.

"white collar blues" are endemic in our labor force.

Some odd "conclusions"

About 85% of American workers, when asked if they are satisfied with their jobs, answer in the affirmative. "Work in America" tries to show that they don't mean what they say. Thus, if an employe tells an interviewer that he finds his work satisfying, but also says that he would like to change his job for something better, "Work in America" promptly concludes that he is not "really" satisfied with, but is rather really "alienated" from, his work. Similarly, if factory workers or file clerks indicate that they are not as fascinated with their daily tasks as are doctors and professors, this too is taken as an unmistakable sign of "alienation."

And when a worker says he would choose a different line of work if he could start out all over again, "Work in America" finds still another illuminating index of "alienation." One gets the firm impression that the authors of this study believe that to have unfulfilled aspirations, to daydream, to engage in wishful thinking, or to express regret for lost opportunities (real or imaginary) is less than human. It apparently never occurs to them that these activities may be all too human. It also apparently never occurs to them that it is utopian to expect ordinary working people to be as content with their jobs as the most successful surgeon or lawyer. Why should they be? How could they be? Where and when have they ever been? Perhaps once in Arcadia—but not in the recorded history of the human race.

Substance and ideology

Does this mean that all such discussion of work and its discontents is so much political froth? No, that would be going much too far. Though there is less here than meets the partisan sociological eye, the issue is not an entirely empty one. Only, one must be careful to distinguish substance from ideological shadow.

One immense difficulty in making any such distinction is that our upper-middle classes—whose offspring populate the mass media and staff the offices of politicians—have so little first-hand knowledge of that world of work which is inhabited by ordinary people. Their heads are full of old and irrelevant stereotypes.

Most of them are sincerely convinced, for instance, that Charlie Chaplin's "Modern Times" gives a true picture of factory work, with the worker forced to become a robot-like slave to the assembly line. Tell them that *fewer than 2%* of American workers are on the assembly line—a fact duly (if fleetingly) recorded in "Work in America"—and they are incredulous.

Undue attention to Detroit

In this, as in so many other respects, undue attention to Detroit and the automobile industry makes for gross distortion. General Motors is a huge corporation which fascinates our social critics. But GM, which has about one-third of its 550,000 employes on the assembly line, is not a typical firm and the automobile industry is not a typical industry. A much more accurate picture of what is fast becoming the typical manufacturing firm is provided by the Bendix Corporation, which has less than 10% of its 57,000 employes on the assembly line, while 50% are white-collared workers and 30% are professional and technical staff.

And even this picture, taken by itself, is skewed, since the average American worker does not work for a manufacturing firm. Indeed, a majority of blue-collar workers are now outside manufacturing—they are in transportation, construction, utilities, trade, etc.

The post-industrial service state

More and more, as the American economy becomes a "post-industrial," service-oriented economy, fewer and fewer people are engaged in blue-collar factory work, in blue-collar work of any kind, in manufacturing altogether. The factory is following the farm as *yesterday's* typical place of employment.

Today, there are more insurance salesmen than blue-collar steelworkers in America, and the insurance "industry" as a whole probably employs more people than does automobile manufacturing. There are more white-collar than blue-collar workers in the American labor force, and by 1980 the ratio will reach an overwhelming 5:3. Moreover, by 1980, some 25% of these white-collar workers will be either in the "professional-technical" category (teachers, engineers, scientists, etc.) or in the "managerial" (public and private) category.

It is quite true, as many are fond of pointing out, that today's young worker is likely to have at least a high school education, and will therefore have a lower threshold of boredom. (To create such a lower threshold of boredom is, of course, what education is all about.) But the changing shape of our economy is producing jobs for precisely such better-educated people—indeed, it *needs* such better-educated people. Which is why those who are better educated have lower unemployment rates than the less well-educated.

A key assumption

The HEW report is not insensitive to these trends, which is why it tries so hard to uncover a set of "white-collar blues" to complement the more familiar notion of "blue-collar blues." Its key assumption here is that these white-collar workers are more likely than before to work for large, impersonal bureaucratically-organized corporations or government departments (which is true enough) and that therefore they *ought* to experience "alienation."

This inference, however, turns out to be fiendishly difficult to substantiate, and "Work in America" has little success at it.

Upon reflection, one is not surprised. Office work, even of the most routine kind, is rarely utterly routine: the complexities and subtleties of a service organization are constantly disrupting all efforts at routinization. In addition, the office, much more than the factory, seems to be a place where conviviality and personal intimacies can

prosper—to a degree, sometimes, where it is conviviality rather than "alienation" that threatens efficiency or morale. An office love affair can be disastrous for all concerned, but somehow it doesn't seem right to describe it as an instance of "alienation."

Rising expectations?

There is, however, one aspect of workers' morale that "Work in America" mentions which is indeed worthy of serious attention. This has less to do with the nature of work in the abstract than with the specific nature of the young men and women who are now entering the labor force. As Daniel Bell has emphasized, the young American worker of today is more likely to be the child of native-born parents and to be distanced from the older, immigrant ethos. This means that his economic and social expectations will be higher and he may well be more "militant" in seeking that middle-class income and middle-class status which Americans tend to regard as being due them "by right." Those reared in the immigrant ethos could take immense satisfaction in ultimately owning their own homes; their children will want home ownership quickly, and may well want a country place—or at least expensive vacations—as well.

This will create a problem, to be sure—but it is the kind of problem that American society has long been familiar with, and which an expanding American economy has been so very good at solving. The fact that young workers are more insistently demanding a middle-class life style will hardly suggest, to the disinterested observer, that they are an "alienated" class. To reach such a conclusion, you have to be an "alienated" sociologist. Of these, alas, we seem to have an abundant supply.

Readings 79, 80 and 81   Debate on New Left Economics

We need the outsider to tell us what we are like. Last century it was De Tocqueville who insightfully interpreted American life. Thirty years back Gunnar Myrdal, a Swede, wrote the definitive study of America's race problem in *The American Dilemma*. Similarly, Professor Assar Lindbeck of Stockholm University spent a year as a visiting professor in the Columbia economics department in the late 1960s. Being himself a supporter of the ruling Swedish Labour Party, he was naturally interested in the college unrest then sweeping our campuses. So, like Margaret Mead studying the sex life of the natives in Samoa, Lindbeck made a serious study of the economics of the New Left. He talked to students. He visited campuses at Berkeley, Yale, M.I.T., Harvard, and throughout the country. He read the burgeoning literature.

Back in Sweden, Lindbeck wrote a paperback (in Swedish) called *Economics of the New Left: An Outsider's View.* This was soon translated into Danish and Finnish. American publishers, hearing of this unique book, competed for it. The author himself prepared an English version, which was published in 1971 by Harper & Row. Seldom has a paperback received such thoughtful attention—both in economics classes and by the general reader.

Reproduced here is a debate, occasioned by the Lindbeck book, in the pages of the *Quarterly Journal of Economics* of Harvard University. Professor George L. Bach of Stanford University, who is an important mainstream economist and also author of a widely used elementary textbook, led off the debate. Professors Stephen Hymer and Frank Roosevelt of the New School for Social Research replied vigorously for the camp of radical economists. Paul Sweezy, a leading exponent of both Old and New Left, also replied (in an essay not reproduced here). Finally, Lindbeck gave his rebuttal.

The reader is invited to this no-holds-barred intellectual battle.

Questions to guide the reading

Has an outsider the right to butt in? Is he necessarily at a disadvantage? At an advantage? Is it surprising that the guinea pigs don't always relish the anthropologist who observes them?

Which of Lindbeck's five points dealing with alleged shortcomings of traditional economics appeals to you most? More important, which of the six criticisms of "the modern capitalist system"—the present-day mixed economy—do you think is best taken? Which do you think least justified? Why?

Can a rational person be *against both the market and the bureaucracy?* What about Thoreau? What would life expectancy and living standards be like, do you think, if we all decided to live in Walden-like *Kibbutzim?* How can one form an intelligent view on this complicated question?

College radicals are often accused of being affluent kids who feel guilty about their affluence in a world where many are poor and underprivileged. Would Hymer and Roosevelt disagree? Would they think this grounds for disapprobation or for approval?

What do you think of the view, expressed by Sweezy as well as Hymer-Roosevelt, that people who look at the same problems through different theoretical glasses— i.e., by means of different theoretical systems, or Kuhn "paradigms"—can't possibly be expected to agree on the same objective answers? Can a union auto worker be regarded as exploited by a Sweezy while a Bach thinks he is making a pretty good real income? Is *his own* testimony to be the relevant criterion? Or would you agree with Herbert Marcuse that people can be so exploited that they don't even realize that they are being exploited?

Which parts, if any, of the Marxian paradigm impress you as giving a superior approach to the important problems mentioned? Which, if any, seem to you to involve little beyond emotive rhetoric? Would you say the same about some or all of mainstream economic's formulations?

Was the debate worthwhile?

Reading 79

Yes to Lindbeck on New Left

G. L. Bach

The Political Economy of the New Left falls into three parts. First, Lindbeck examines the New Left's critique of "traditional" economics. Then he presents a more detailed picture of its critique of the present (capitalist) U.S. economy. And finally, he asks, "Where does the New Left's economics lead?"

It is important to recognize that he writes of the economics of some members of the New Left who are not economists, ranging at times as far as Castro, Mao, and Marcuse. Thus, most but not necessarily all, of his criticisms apply to the economics of the economists of the New Left, who often identify themselves as "radical economists."

Indictment of traditional economics

Lindbeck finds that the New Left's critique of "traditional economics" centers on five points.

1. The traditional economics pays too little attention to the uneven distribution of income, wealth, and power.

2. It largely takes consumer tastes as given in analyzing resource allocation, whereas the real problem is the domination of consumer tastes by large sellers.

3. It grossly underemphasizes the quality of life, as distinct from quantity of output.

4. It takes as given the social and economic system and concerns itself largely with small, marginal changes, whereas it should be concerned with massive changes in the entire structure of the system.

5. And, last, it grossly underemphasizes political considerations—it should be concerned with *political* economy rather than with the merely "economic" issues that are the center of traditional economic analysis.

Lindbeck has considerable sympathy with each of these criticisms, as, indeed, do I. But they are hardly novel with the New Left. Much of modern economic analysis, in the journals and in textbooks, has been concerned with fine points of professional debate, rather than with major issues of social policy. No doubt too little attention has been given to many of the big issues raised by the New Left, and some reallocation of effort by the best minds in the profession to these bigger issues might well have contributed a substantial net marginal product to our understanding of the way the system works and how it might work better. But, as Lindbeck points out, merely to raise the critical points is easy; the hard part is to show how a different approach could contribute more to our understanding of the operation of the system and to its improvement.

Talk of "power." For example, the New Left says, perhaps most of all, that we should be more concerned with the issues of power in our society and with the factors that determine the distribution of income and power. But the New Left literature seems to Lindbeck, and to me, strangely barren of concrete, scientifically testable propositions on the relations between classes, "the power structure," and income distribution—or even of concrete suggestions as to how such a testable theory might be developed.

Critique of modern mixed economy

Lindbeck finds the main contribution of the New Left to be its critique of the operations of the modern capitalist system, more than its critique of traditional economics. He summarizes this main critique as centering on six issues.

1. Shall the economic system be organized through markets, through a political bureaucracy, or how? 2. Shall the system be centralized or decentralized in its decision-making processes?

From G. L. Bach, "Comment (Symposium: Economics of the New Left)," *The Quarterly Journal of Economics*, vol. 86, no. 4. Reprinted in abridgment with the kind permission of the author and the editor.

While the New Left is far from monolithic, Lindbeck correctly emphasizes that it generally criticizes the use of markets to organize economic activity—and also the centralization of power in political bureaucracies. But if we deny both, how is a complex economy like ours to be organized? Lindbeck's few pages on this issue (pp. 32–57) ought to be required reading for every student in elementary economics.

With moderation, he stresses that we have to have some way to gain information about preferences, to allocate resources in accordance with some set of preferences, to create incentives, to coordinate the decisions of millions of individuals in the society and make them consistent, and to allocate incomes. He looks in vain for the New Left's solution to the problem if we reject both bureaucracy and the market; the best he can find is such formulations as "A society can be developed in which the individual would be formed, influenced, and educated . . . by a system of rationally planned production for use, by a universe of human relations determined by the oriented toward solidarity, cooperation and freedom."[1]

Similarly, Lindbeck's put-down of the more extreme claims that human wants are now "fabricated" by modern advertising and big corporations is a masterpiece of good sense and perception, not rejecting the fact that advertisers do significantly influence the pattern of human wants, but warning against easy acceptance of overstatements and citing both empirical evidence and analytical reasoning that underline the extremity of many New Left statements.

Force of economic reasoning.   And, strikingly, all he uses throughout are the most elementary and fundamental of economic concepts and reasoning. Properly used, they are powerful tools, and he shows how. There is not an equation or a graph, not an intricate piece of economic reasoning, in the book.

3. Who shall own capital? 4. How shall we manage material incentives and the distribution of incomes? Lindbeck sympathizes with the egalitarian inclinations of the New Left. He agrees, more than I would, that the concentration of income and

wealth in the United States carries with it a comparable concentration of political power. But again, he finds much of the New Left literature stronger on rhetoric than on analysis and evidence.

Most important, Lindbeck insists on facing up to the fundamental difficulty of somehow achieving adequate incentives for initiative in a society without private ownership of capital and substantial income inequalities. He suspects that we can get a better mix than we now have in the United States, involving less inequality and, I gather, a larger public sector. But again he rejects simplistic arguments (advanced by some New Left writers) that all we need to do is get rid of private property and abolish the evil capitalist system, and all will be solved. He writes: "This problem—of encouraging initiative—is probably the basic unsolved problem of completely (or largely) nationalized economies, along with the problem of avoiding bureaucratization and strong concentration of economic, political, and military power in the same hands." Lindbeck has a pervading distrust of concentration of political power to solve our economic problems, and he refuses to accept easy solutions that abolish the market without facing up to the dangers of such bureaucratization.

5. Shall we have competition or cooperation? 6. What is the real meaning of "development," and how much of it do we need?

The New Left's argument against competition seems to be primarily an ethical one; competition is less moral than cooperation. Although Marx and many of his followers found in competition and the capitalist state an impressively productive arrangement, the New Left believes it would be a "better" society if we cooperated rather than competed.

Where from here?

Where does the New Left's economics lead? Lindbeck searches for an answer—Anarchism? A liberal-democratic society? A nonmarket system with collective ownership? Market socialism? He finds no real answer.

Turnover of the oppressors?   Marx's influence on the New Left has certainly increased in recent

[1] Paul Baran, *The Political Economy of Growth* (New York: Monthly Review Press, 1958), p. xvii.

years, and perhaps this means stronger movement toward a nonmarket system with collective ownership. Some New Left economists are struggling with these issues. But Lindbeck has grave doubts about such a system. "Is it not rather likely," he asks, "that leaders emerging as a result of this type of selection process may often be both authoritarian and cruel? The possibility that revolution, in fact, only means the substitution of oppressors hardly lacks historical illustrations."

Complexity. He continues: "What a social scientist misses most of all in the New Left literature is an awareness of the enormous difficulties involved in solving the problems which arise in *any* social and economic system. . . . On most of these difficult and important problems, the New Left is generally silent or superficial."

Useful reminders. He concludes that its main contribution has been to remind us once more of a "number of eternal problems in the political debate—issues of ownership, distribution of income and power, externalities, public participation, and social values in general—aspects which have sometimes tended to disappear from the political debate during the postwar period, perhaps especially in the United States."

Summing up

In conclusion, what of the New Left? From this outsider's inexpert view, it is an important challenge to conventional economics and to modern mixed capitalist systems, representing a modern, mixed evolution from Marxism, Veblenism, and utopianism. (1) It challenges our (implicit or explicit) social welfare functions as improperly narrow and discipline-bound. (2) It (with the exception of some of the economists) insists that we substitute the New Left's own values in such welfare functions for those widely accepted in our (western capitalist) societies, and that we adopt revolutionary, if only vaguely specified, changes in the structure and operations of the existing economy. (3) It shows the beginnings of serious scientific research by some radical economists on the acceptability and practicality of its propositions compared to those of "traditional economics." I doubt that the New Left will fade away soon, nor should it. But a rising ratio of reason to rhetoric will make it a more productive challenge in the future.

Reading 80

In Defense of New Left Economics

Stephen Hymer and Frank Roosevelt

Failure of communication

Radicals usually have trouble communicating with economists. The reason is that the two are generally interested in different questions. At the moment, however, we are fortunate enough to have an economist who is interested in the same questions that activate radicals. For this reason, Assar Lindbeck's *The Political Economy of the New Left—An Outsider's View* is a useful book for presenting the radical critique of economics and setting the stage for further dialogue.

The questions being asked by the New Left are (1) what is the connection between corporate capitalism and the obvious evils in our society, and (2) how do we go beyond capitalism towards the achievement of a decent society? Lindbeck begins his book explicitly accepting the validity of these questions: "The salient features of New Left economics are . . . its critique of present-day capitalist societies, with the important role played by large corporations, and the vision of how the economy should be reorganized."

From Stephen Hymer and Frank Roosevelt, "Comment (Symposium: Economics of the New Left)," *The Quarterly Journal of Economics*, vol. 86, no. 4. Reprinted in abridgment with the kind permission of the authors and the editor.

The fact that Lindbeck begins with the right questions enables us to avoid sterile arguments about the internal consistency of his presentation and to concentrate instead on the general usefulness of economics in dealing with the questions we agree on. Along the way, however, we shall have to examine whether the method favored by Lindbeck does not in fact lead him to change the questions themselves—or dodge them altogether.

Alternative visions. In evaluating the relationship between Lindbeck's economics and the questions raised by the New Left, we will use the now familiar notion of a "paradigm" developed by Thomas Kuhn.[1] A paradigm provides a fixed conceptual framework for scientific research, placing limits on the type of *questions* that can be asked, the *methods* that can be used, and the *answers* that are acceptable. Thus a paradigm is like a flashlight in that it allows the scientist to shed light on certain questions, while at the same time leaving large areas in the dark. It is our contention that Lindbeck, while pointing with one hand at the right questions, holds in his other hand a flashlight (the economics paradigm) that is shining in the wrong direction. Hence, he must either change the questions or point his flashlight in another direction (i.e., adopt a new paradigm). We shall find that insofar as he illuminates anything, he has changed the questions.

But the New Left will not tolerate changing the questions. For they have arrived at their questions not, as Lindbeck suggests most economists choose theirs, "by considerations of available analytical techniques," but through their experience. This experience began, as a rule, in the comfortable homes of the middle class. As Adam Smith noted, "Before we can feel much for others, we must in some measure be at ease ourselves." Having been reared in conditions of relative affluence and security, a new generation naturally became sympathetic to the plight of others subject to poverty, prejudice, and colonialism.

The class struggle. In what follows, we will argue that it is essential to take into account the class struggle—i.e., the fact of antagonistic relationships between groups of people—if one wishes to understand what is going on in the world. With Marx, we see this struggle occurring in modern society mainly between workers and capitalists. And it is important to observe, again following Marx, that capitalists and workers confront each other in two separate but interconnected realms: (1) the sphere of circulation, and (2) the sphere of production. The sphere of circulation is the realm of the market where the various actors meet each other as owners of commodities intent on exchanging them. The sphere of production is the more important realm where we find not only the production of commodities going on but also the capital-labor relationship itself being reproduced.

We have introduced these distinctions at this point because they help to explain the differences between the economic and the Marxian paradigms. They also help, in our opinion, to account for the different degrees of usefulness of the two paradigms in providing answers to the questions raised by the New Left.

A balance sheet

Let us draw up Lindbeck's balance sheet for economics in a table. It is our contention that the items on the positive side of the balance sheet that form the basic tool kit of economics are insufficient for dealing with the New Left's questions. They relate exclusively to the sphere of circulation and thus cover only an arbitrarily circumscribed area of economic phenomena.

But the capitalist process of production taken as a whole represents a synthesis of production and circulation. If we wish to understand the roots of the evils in our society and assess the possibilities of going beyond capitalism, we must be able to move also in the second dimension of production relations. This involves an analysis of the excluded items on Lindbeck's balance sheet, which, taken together, form the basis of the Marxian paradigm.

The Marxian paradigm

The Marxian system begins with the process of production. In every mode of production, labor and means of production are united to produce output. But it is the specific manner in which this union is accomplished that distinguishes the differ-

[1] *The Structure of Scientific Revolutions* (University of Chicago Press, Chicago, 1962).

Question	Included in economics	Excluded from economics
Distribution	Marginal productivity theory	Distribution of power Class struggle

Tastes—allocation	Assumption of given preferences
	  exogenously determined
	Theory of efficient allocation of
	  resources
		Endogenous preference change
		Development of needs through
		  productive activity

The quality of life:
  environment
  working conditions
  decision making
	Theory of external effects	Drive to accumulate capital
		Capital-labor relationship

Large vs. small changes	Marginal analysis Comparative economic systems	Transformation of systems Contradictions (dialectical analysis)
Political considerations		Distribution of power and its role in the economy

ent socioeconomic formations from one another. Under capitalism they are united through the wage-labor contract under which the laborer alienates his labor power and agrees to submit to the control of the capitalist or his representative during the process of production.

In the market the laborer was a "free agent" who owned his own labor power and dealt with the capitalist on equivalent footing in pursuit of his own private interest. The bargain completed, however, he finds himself no longer free or equal or a property owner or an individual but a subordinate in an authoritarian hierarchy working with and on materials he does not own in a collective process of production.

The dualism between freedom in the marketplace and authoritarianism in the workplace is the essential characteristic of capitalist society. If the marketplace furnishes the economist with the model to justify capitalism in terms of freedom, equality, possession, and individualism, the actual conditions of work furnish the New Left with the critique of capitalism (with its nonfreedom and nonequality) as well as the clues to a future society (with a nonpossessive and nonindividualistic organization of work).

When the worker sells his labor, he in effect surrenders his freedom; but this does not mean that he passively accepts capitalist production. The laborer's daily work is involuntary, and so each day

involves a struggle between capital and laborer. The capitalist tries to get the worker to do something he or she does not want to do; the worker tries to resist doing it. In Volume I of *Capital,* Marx analyzes the capitalist system of production in terms of this constant struggle, showing the forms of resistance put up by the workers and the types of pressure (e.g., organization, introduction of machinery, social legislation) devised by the capitalist to maintain control over the workers' labor time. These problems, which lie outside the market sphere, are hardly touched on at all in the modern economics curriculum. Although detailed and explicit discussion of them can be found in the literature of corporate organization, personal relations, industrial sociology, and psychology, they are always approached from the point of view of control rather than resistance. One of the tasks of radical social scientists is to turn this literature on its head and develop counter-organization theories in continuation of Marx's work.

Inequality and dominance. Since capitalism requires unequal relations of dominance and subordination in production, the game of the market must be a loaded game. The players begin with unequal endowments of wealth and education and at the end of play find themselves in much the same relative position as before. Of course a certain degree of mobility exists: a small number of people change ranks; but in cycle after cycle over the last two hundred years, the pyramid has remained a pyramid. In each round the top 10 percent of the population gets from 30 to 40 percent of the take, the bottom two thirds get only one third. The players are then ready to play again in production—the poor to work, the middle to manage, the rich to accumulate.

Much force was needed to bring this system into being. Though economists have generally overlooked its brutal origins during the period of primitive accumulation in the sixteenth and seventeenth centuries, we can today see in the underdeveloped countries a replay of the violence of modernization. Pacification of the countryside, the police state, the pass system are the seeds and fertilization from which a free market is growing in the "backward" areas.

Once free markets are established, force takes on more respectable forms. One of these respectable forms is the education system where people are trained to accept competition, discipline, authoritarianism, rigid schedules in preparation for life in capitalist production. This form of coercive socialization has been of particular interest to the New Left and is being extensively investigated by radical economists using the tools of class analysis rather than the market methodology of human capital.

Conclusion

The Marxian paradigm offers an alternative perspective and produces a different set of answers. It shows that capitalism, because it is based on private property and promotes an individualist point of view, places strict limits on how much government interference it will tolerate. It argues that as the system advances, the contradiction between its social nature and its private organization becomes increasingly intense. And it recommends that we supersede the mode of production based on wage labor by striving consciously to control our own everyday life in production as well as in consumption.

Reading 81

Response to Debate on New Left Economics

Assar Lindbeck

Are the weaknesses of traditional economics the strength of Marxism?

A main point in the Sweezy paper, as well as in Hymer-Roosevelt's, is that academic economists and New Leftists are interested in completely different questions. There is some truth in this statement. One of the main points in my book was to show that we *should* be interested in the same questions. There are at least two reasons for this: (1) we are all living in the same world; and (2) every economic system has to solve very much the same problems.

Common problems. Hymer-Roosevelt try to defend their lack of interest in and appreciation for traditional economics by talking about the existence of different "paradigms." Traditional economic theory is said to be a "flashlight" (or "paradigm") "which is shining in the wrong direction." Sweezy goes even further when he says that traditional economists and radical economists "see two totally different realities," which difference is said to make my book "as irrelevant and boring as most neoclassical economics" is to radical (revolutionary) economists. Sweezy tries, in fact, to make his ideas invulnerable to criticism from outsiders, when he implies that Marxism cannot be understood by those who lack "empathy for the radical position." It would seem that Sweezy is quite close to the opinion that Marxism is so delicate that it is

From Assar Lindbeck, "Response (Symposium: Economics of the New Left)," *The Quarterly Journal of Economics*, vol. 86, no. 4. Reprinted in abridgment with the kind permission of the author and the editor.

impossible for those who do not *believe* in it to understand it.

I cannot accept this position, which is basically antiintellectual. If the impossibility of intellectual communication between different groups of social scientists is accepted, these groups belong in (different) divinity schools rather than in social science faculties of universities.

It is quite possible that the academic tradition in economics is partly responsible for the relative neglect of several of these important problems. However, there may very well be another reason for the underdeveloped state of scientific methods and knowledge in several of these fields: they may be particularly difficult to handle.

It would seem that both Sweezy and Hymer-Roosevelt, on the basis of the rather reasonable assertion that traditional economic theory has not been particularly successful in dealing with several of these problems, draw two main conclusions: that economic theory has practically *nothing* of interest to tell about them; and that Marxism, or New Leftism, has *much* to teach us about these very problems. Are these conclusions well founded?

Proof of the pudding

It is quite possible, of course, that some tools and insights developed by Marx and his successors have a bearing on some of these problems. For instance, the Marxian emphasis on the *interrelations* between technology, the forms of economic and social organization, and politics is certainly helpful in analyzing long-term changes in social, economic, and political systems. In fact, this emphasis is shared by many non-Marxian scholars.

To explain transformations of societies over time by the inconsistencies between different structures in a society, and by the competition between classes, certainly may be of great interest also. Thus, Marxian theory has undoubtedly supplied some interesting, though *partial,* hypotheses about long-term historical processes—a problem dealt with only slightly by most neoclassical economists, though certainly by a number of other non-Marxian social scientists, from Adam Smith, David Ricardo, Thomas Malthus, and John Stuart Mill to Max Weber, Joseph Schumpeter, Friedrich

Hayek, Arnold Toynbee, and a number of contemporary historians and sociologists.

I think the Marxists should admit more readily that their approach to the philosophy of long-term historical processes is only one among many, and that it is very difficult to discriminate among different hypotheses in this very field.

Moreover, if we look at "neglected" subjects in economics it would seem to me that many achievements in recent years in these fields have been made by economists with a rather traditional kit of tools. Some examples of such contributions are

Analyses of the determinants of the distribution of income and wealth and its change over time, using the theory of investment in human capital and allowing for such factors as family background, education, and training

The economics of information and learning-by-doing

The development over time of consumption patterns, including changes in preferences

Studies of poverty, discrimination, and urban decay, and the analysis of externalities and their bearing on the "quality of life"

The implications of centralization and decentralization in economic systems and studies of "the politics" of economic policy, the relation between economic and political factors

Empirical studies of the economic relations between rich and poor countries, for instance with respect to capital movements and trade

Etc.

There is certainly a long way to go before we can say that we understand these problems very well. But on what grounds do Marxists and New Leftists claim that *they* have the answer to, or a better understanding of, these difficult and important problems?

Hard questions? Do Marxist economists have better explanations, for instance, of

Why the share of labor income has been rising during the postwar period in many highly developed capitalist countries

Why wage differentials between industries have tended to rise in some countries (such as the United States), while they have tended to be constant in other countries (such as Sweden)

Why certain minority groups are discriminated

against in some countries but privileged in other countries

Are Marxists able to give a more powerful explanation for the deterioration of the environment, and to show methods to improve it, than are provided by the theory of externalities?

Have the Marxists solved, or even dealt with, the problems about the optimum mix of centralization and decentralization in economic systems?

Have the Marxists developed models, other than market systems, to avoid centralization, bureaucratization, and an enormous concentration of power in the context of highly developed societies?

Can they explain why and how consumption patterns have changed just the way they have—in the United States and the USSR (without relying at least partly on neoclassical tools such as income and price elasticities and theories of learning processes)?

In the field of interaction between political and economic factors on an international level, for instance imperialism, have Marxists really given convincing, specific, and empirically based explanations for the U.S. presence in Vietnam and the Soviet presence in Eastern Europe?

Has the New Left given us particularly good explanations of the conflict between the Soviet Union and China?

The list of questions can be extended ad infinitum.

Rhetoric, not analysis

So far as I can see, Marxian economists have at most made *general statements* about some *concepts* that are *asserted* to be both useful and necessary for explanations about these phenomena. If Marxian economists really have *specific and empirically founded* answers to questions of this type, why do they not present them, if possible in forms susceptible to empirical tests? Before it has been demonstrated that Marxian theory gives particularly powerful explanations for these problems, it seems

rather pretentious to assert that Marxian theory has the answers.

General talk about class struggle, distribution of power, development of needs through production activity, a drive for capitalists to accumulate, capital-labor relations, contradictions, and dialectics is surely not enough, until these concepts have been made concrete and used to explain *specific* empirically observable phenomena. Until some indication has been given of the power of Marxian theory to explain these specific issues, or similar ones, I think it is necessary to assume that we are all rather ignorant about many aspects of these difficult problems.

Thus, when Hymer-Roosevelt present a table of problems on which traditional theory is particularly silent—a list in fact derived from my study—this is hardly evidence that Marxian concepts will open the doors for an understanding of these topics. The fact that traditional theory has important lacunae hardly proves that *Marxism* (or Hinduism, fascism, mysticism, "Toynbeeism") is necessary to understand these issues. Just to present a column vector of general Marxist *terms* is certainly not enough.

Hope for the future

These reflections are, of course, no denial of the fact that a number of young economists calling themselves "radical economists" or "revolutionaries," are making or will make important contributions to economic research, including empirical studies. However, much of the methodology of this research has, as Bach points out, a rather conventional flavor. In fact, it is often difficult to see what is radical, Marxist, or revolutionary in this research—except possibly some tendencies in the choice of topic, some emphasis on competition among socioeconomic power groups, and sometimes an inclination to add personal, subjective value terms (occasionally borrowed from Marxist jargon) to the analysis.

Alternative Economic Systems

Reading 82

In the mid-1960s Russian administrators and economists rediscovered the price system. Centralized decision making could scarcely cope with the million and one variables that had to be resolved each month. In consequence, profitability began to replace purely physical and technical quotas. Nevertheless, there was a tendency for westerners to exaggerate the degree of change in the Russian ideology and practice.

Abram Bergson, professor of economics at Harvard University, is one of the best-known of the American economists specializing in Russian affairs, and the passing years have conformed remarkably well with his predictions. One of his numerous books and monographs on the Soviet economic system has been his study for the nonprofit RAND Corporation. That study earned the supreme compliment of being translated by the Russians to help their bureaucrats understand their own system.

Time has also confirmed the predictions made here. The slowdown observed earlier in the final table seems to have continued in 1966–1973.

Questions to guide the reading

To run an economic system optimally, is it not enough to replace the motive "production for profit" by the goal "production for use"? Why is the problem of economic organization so much more complicated than this? Why does profitability have a role to play even in a system that is not run for private profit? If consumers are to have a range of free choices and if production is still to be organized with efficiency, why does pricing have a role to play?

Planning and the Market in the U.S.S.R.

Abram Bergson

Recently announced decisions of the Soviet government to reform its planning system have been greeted in the West as a momentous international event. The changes being made are surely not quite as dramatic as this assumes, but the government is reorganizing, often in novel ways, its proverbially centralized arrangements for industrial planning, and it has good reason to do so.

To refer only to bare essentials, the agency at the lowest bureaucratic level in Soviet industry and hence the one immediately in charge of opera-

tions is the *predpriiatie,* or enterprise. Under centralized planning, enterprise management has not been subject to control from above to quite the minute degree often supposed, but its authority has been severely limited. Under the new program, such authority is to be expanded. This will occur through a reduction in the number of the enterprise's plan targets that must be approved by superior agencies, and also in other ways. Thus, in utilizing available wage funds, enterprise management previously was much constrained by targets

From Abram Bergson, "The Current Soviet Planning Reforms," in Alex Balinky et al., *Planning and the Market in the USSR* (Rutgers University Press, New Brunswick, N.J., 1967). Reprinted with kind permission of the author and publisher.

for wage payments, for employment and for average earnings for different categories of workers. Now management will be subject to only one such target, for total wages paid to all workers. Within the limits of the total fund assigned it, the management may employ labor as it wishes. Scales of basic wage rates for different categories of workers, however, will continue, as in the past, to be determined primarily by superior agencies. Dismissals of workers presumably will still require, as they have since 1958, the consent of the trade union factory committee.

Again, decisions on capital investments hitherto have been especially centralized, but through charges to profits and depreciation, each enterprise is now to establish a "fund for the growth of production," which it may use with some discretion to finance modernization, automation and various other capital investment projects. Since, for industry generally, funds for the growth of production are expected to finance about 20 per cent of state capital investment in 1966, the additional authority gained at this point could be of some consequence.

Enterprise management is also to be allowed greater discretion in some other, related ways. Thus, it may now decide whether and to what extent piece (rather than time) work is to be employed in determining wages; it has more authority than before in respect to custom production, and so on.

Targets and Incentives

Plan targets in the USSR constitute at once standards of performance, in effect, "success criteria," for enterprise management, but necessarily not all targets can have equal weight. Interestingly, then, not only are targets approved by superior agencies being reduced in number. To some extent they are also being changed in character, and apparently also in their relative importance. Among other things, targets for output, including unfinished goods and stocks, which were previously stressed are to give way to one for "realized production," or sales. Contrary to many reports, profits have long been calculated in the USSR, but now the target for profits is also to become an important test of performance.

Along with success criteria, changes are also be-

ing made in arrangements for managerial bonuses. These affect managerial behavior under Soviet socialism hardly less than elsewhere. Thus, bonuses, which hitherto have been based chiefly on performance relatively to the plan target for output, or a variant thereof, are henceforth to depend primarily on performance relatively to the plan targets for sales and profits.

Then, too, such managerial bonuses, together with some premia for workers generally, are now to be paid out of a new "fund for material encouragement," which is to be maintained to a considerable extent through charges from profits. Appropriations will depend not only on sales and profits, but on other indicators of performance, including "profitability," a Soviet euphemism for the rate of return on capital. Regarding sales and profits, what will count is performance relatively not only to the plan but to pre-plan levels. The government is also establishing new arrangements for rewarding the introduction of new products, and hopes to heighten interest in satisfactory performance generally through diverse changes in procedures for financing of housing, nurseries, and the like, that are administered by the enterprise.

Last but not least, the changes in success criteria are to be accompanied by revisions in financial and price-fixing practices. According to a strange but long-standing policy, new capital hitherto has been made available to enterprises for the most part in the form of interest-free grants from the government budget. In future, however, enterprises will have to pay out of their profits a charge, typically 6 per cent, on their capital. The enterprises will also have to finance their capital needs increasingly through repayable loans. A firm which enjoys an especially favorable position regarding natural resources may also be subjected to a fixed "rental" payment.

For the rest, the manner in which price-fixing practices will be changed is still under study. Apparently, industrial wholesale prices, which usually are fixed to allow a standard mark-up over average branch cost, but which for the most part have not been changed since July 1, 1955, are at long last to be up-dated. In the process, the prices presumably will also be altered to allow for the novel charges on capital, and rental payments.

In sum, in industrial planning the Soviet government is scarcely dismantling wholesale its system of centralized planning, as sometimes has been suggested in the West, but it is adapting this system measurably in the direction of decentralization and increased use of market-type controls.

Bad effects of centralization

Why is the government at long last initiating such changes?

The USSR, it has been reported,[1] is "going through a crisis as profound, if not as eye-catching, as capitalism's crisis in the 1930's." Though eye-catching, this is hardly accurate, but the government is manifestly concerned about the onerous responsibilities which under centralized planning superior agencies in the bureaucratic structure must bear. Subject to approval at the highest level, such agencies must among other things determine in essentials the volume and direction of capital investment. They also have major responsibilities for the coordination of myriads of plan targets, and for the control of current factor inputs, especially of materials, fuel, power and machinery that are required to implement the plan.

With such responsibilities, the superior agencies understandably find it difficult to cope, and one must read partly in this light complaints that lately have become commonplace even in the USSR, such as this:

because of the absence of equipment, there are now about 1.5 million square meters of deserted productive floor space. In the textile department of the Kursk Synthetic Fiber Kombinat more than 3000 square meters of floor space have been empty since 1960. In the "Tadzhiktekstilmash" Factory around 5000 square meters of productive floor space . . . have been idle for more than two years because of the lack of specialized equipment.

The government understandably is now seeking to lighten responsibilities of superior agencies. Since managers of enterprises have often complained of the "petty tutelage" to which they are subject, it is also hoped that the authority transferred to them will be exercised more effectively than it was by their superiors.

The government has no less reason to reform managerial success criteria, however, for within

their limited sphere enterprise managers also act wastefully, and curiously they are even impelled to do so by the success criteria that have prevailed. Even with a "visible hand" replacing an "invisible" one, as it has turned out, what is good for the individual enterprise is by no means always good for the country.

Thus, the infamous "safety factor" which is also a familiar theme in the USSR: Enterprise managers of necessity are allowed to negotiate with superior agencies regarding their plan targets, and in doing so seek to limit their assignments. In this way they hope more easily to earn bonuses for plan fulfillment. To the same end, the managers also hesitate to overfulfill targets, for fear that subsequent goals will only be made the higher.

In trying especially to fulfill the target for gross output, managers also often find it possible, and even expedient, to stress inordinately goods that bulk large physically. Alternatively, where gross output is calculated in value terms, emphasis may be placed rather on products that have relatively high ruble prices, but such prices too have their limitations, so the resulting assortment again may be strange. Thus the unending reports of difficulties of the Soviet consumer in shopping for particular items: for example, in buying large-size boy's shoes, as distinct from small-size men's shoes; of shirt as distinct from bandage cloth; of small-size as distinct from large-size electric bulbs, and so on.

Almost inevitably short-cuts are also taken regarding quality: as in the RSFSR, where among products examined by inspectors of the Ministry of Trade in the first half of 1962, 32.7 per cent of the clothing articles, 25 per cent of the knitwear, and 32.6 per cent of the leather shoes were rejected or reclassified in a lower quality category; or in the Ukraine where 20 to 25 per cent of the clothing and knitwear examined by the Ministry of Trade during 1963 had to be condemned as defective; or as where a factory manufacturing tractor parts found it advantageous to overfulfill its output goal by 60 per cent while lowering the quality of its products and so reducing their useful life by 40–50 per cent. In order to fulfill the current target for output, managers also hesitate to introduce new products, and find it profitable to abuse their machinery.

[1] *The Economist*, March 19, 1966, p. 1100.

Reasons for change

The foregoing deficiencies in centralized planning are hardly new; they had already become manifest in the early five year plans under Stalin. Why is the government only now taking any consequential action to alleviate them? Reform might have been in order long ago, but it has become especially so lately because of the ever-increasing complexity of the task with which the cumbersome system of industrial planning must grapple.

The complexity is also greater because the government's own aim is no longer simply to produce steel and then more steel, as it was in essentials under Stalin. In his famous attack on Gosplan men in "steel blinkers" Khrushchev, of course, meant to urge not merely a greater use of plastics, but a more flexible outlook on alternative industrial branches generally. Despite their criticism of him, Khrushchev's successors probably will hesitate to abandon altogether this particular policy. Moreover, the government, which in the face of crop shortages has been importing about 20 million tons of grain since mid-1963, is also more attentive to consumers than it was under Stalin. For the dictator, food shortages did not even preclude exports. And the task of directing economic activity has become the more intricate because, though still not affluent, the consumers themselves have become more choosy; as witness the quite new phenomenon in the USSR of overstocks of consumers' goods of less desirable sizes, styles, and so on.

If prevailing priorities reflect a greater awareness of alternatives, this must be due partly to another development which has also been favorable to economic reform in other ways as well. The government has now found it expedient to allow economists generally to explore [economic] questions. In doing so, the economists are even permitted to use forms of analysis, especially of a mathematical sort, formerly regarded as bourgeois, and so tabu.

The invigorated economics that has quickly emerged not surprisingly has itself been a factor in the equation indicating economic reform. Thus, much of the Soviet criticism of planning procedures is to be found in the writings of Soviet economists themselves.

Scarcely less momentous than these developments, however, has been another: as reported, the rate of economic growth has declined; and markedly, according to both Soviet official and Western calculations, though the former as usual seem inflated:

Even the reduced rates are still respectable, but the decline must be disconcerting for proponents of a social system whose asserted economic superiority is held to be observable, above all, in its ability to generate rapid growth. And, still worse, the rival capitalist system in the West lately has itself shown unexpected capabilities in this regard, first in Western Europe and most recently even in the United States. To "overtake and surpass" the advanced capitalist countries economically can no longer seem the easy task that the ebullient Khrushchev assumed not so long ago.

By all accounts, economic growth has declined in the USSR for diverse reasons, and among these some of the most important, such as those causing the continued stagnation in agriculture, are remote from deficiencies in industrial planning. By repairing these deficiencies, however, the government hopes to assure an increasingly effective use of productive factors in industry, and on this basis to offset more successfully retarding forces affecting the economy generally.

The government is not about to restore capitalism, and Soviet economists have rightly criticized commentators, both in China and the West who have suggested as much, but it may not be easy to

	Real national income, average annual % increase	
	Soviet official data	Western data
1950–58	10.9	7.0
1958–59	7.5	4.2
1959–60	7.7	4.9
1960–61	6.8	6.8
1961–62	5.7	4.3
1962–63	4.1	2.6
1963–64	9.0	7.2
1964–65*	6.0	3.0

* In 1966–73, the slowdown observed earlier seems to have continued.

confine the market to limits now being observed. Another characterization of the current reforms also suggested, therefore, may not really be amiss: "creeping capitalism." It will be fascinating to see how in the years ahead the government grapples with its complex problem of planning organization.

Reading 83

Dr. Kissinger and President Nixon began a new United States-China era. Among the many recent first-hand accounts by travelers to China is this analysis by Yale's James Tobin. Here we see his creative estimating of the Chinese GNP and its implied structure for that economy.

Questions to guide the reading

The hopes raised by China's "Great Leap Forward" were dashed by the setbacks of "The Cultural Revolution." Might the present euphoria about China meet a similar fate? During what we now know were the worst years of the Stalin terror and purges, many visitors to Russia wrote home glowing accounts of the new utopia they found there. Does this suggest caution? Or is this paranoiac thinking?

Would you rather be born in India with freedom and poverty and a short life expectancy, or in the new China where no one starves but where all work hard at the tasks set by the community?

The Economy of China: A Tourist's View

James Tobin

I visited the People's Republic of China for two weeks, September 8–22, 1972, together with Professors John Kenneth Galbraith and Wassily Leontief, in the first of a series of visits by U.S. academicians and scientists arranged by the Federation of American Scientists and the Chinese Academy of Sciences.

We visited an arts and crafts workshop, a cotton textile factory, a machine tool plant, a rural people's commune, a grocery supermarket, a large department store, an industrial exposition, a high school, and a hospital. We found all of these visits and discussions extremely informative. Nevertheless, we are acutely aware of the vast gaps in our information about the Chinese economic system. Very few macro-economic data were available to us, and we were not able to talk to economists and other responsible officials in the planning and operating agencies of the government.

In this report I have tried to summarize my impressions. They are personal ones, which my traveling companions may not share. Moreover, I am fully aware of the extraordinary margins of uncertainty which surround them, particularly the numerical speculations I have attempted. To write about so large and complex a subject on such short and fragmentary acquaintance is certainly presumptuous. It is justified only by the tremendous interest and ignorance in the West concerning a country with which we have had so little contact for a quarter of a century.

China's GNP

There really is no information on Chinese national accounts. Indeed, as orthodox Marxists, the Chinese do not recognize bourgeois national accounting concepts. They subscribe to a materialist defi-

From James Tobin, "The Economy of China: A Tourist's View," *Challenge,* March/April 1973. Reprinted in abridgment with the kind permission of the author and the editor.

nition of national output and regard the provision of services as "unproductive" activity. Figures are scanty even for their definition.

Nevertheless, I have thought it a worthwhile exercise of imagination to try to construct some plausible, consistent, primitive national accounts from the hints and scraps of data we were able to pick up. Needless to say, the standard errors of these guesses are vast, but the numbers may be indicative of orders of magnitude. One purpose of the exercise is to see how it is possible to reconcile the evidence that labor productivity is seven to eight times as high in industry as in agriculture with indications that industrial wage incomes are only three to four times as high as agricultural earnings.

Population. First, as to population and labor force, I begin with the UN estimate of the 1971 population, 773 million. I have no information on labor force participation, or even on the age distribution of the population. One may assume a high participation rate because it is customary for women to work both in city and country, and because neither tradition nor life expectancy (50 years, according to the UN) suggests that there are many retired people. Arbitrarily, I have taken the labor force to be 500 million.

Rural-urban division. Second, I have divided the labor force among producing sectors. I have set the agricultural fraction of the labor force somewhat lower, 75 percent.

The other 25 percent of the labor force cannot be fully assigned to industry, because a substantial number are occupied in service trades, general government, and the armed forces. According to materialist economic accounting, these latter activities are "unproductive." With no statistics to support or contradict me, I have placed 15 percent of the labor force in industry and 10 percent in services and government.

GNP benchmark. Third, a figure of $90 billion U.S. was floating around as an estimate of China's GNP for 1970 or 1971. I was told this by the "principal responsible person" of the Institute of Economics, and he indicated that it came from an interview of Chou En-lai with a foreign journalist, probably Edgar Snow. My informants could not, or would not, give details.

There are difficulties of interpretation. One arises from the dual system of agricultural prices. Is agricultural output valued at the prices paid by the state to the producers or at the lower prices charged by the state in sales to industrial users of raw materials and to consumers of food? I have assumed the latter.

The second difficulty is the standard problem of conversion into foreign currency. I assume this is done at the official rate, 45 cents U.S. per yuan. Judging from the informal sample of prices I observed in shops or collected in conversational inquiries from our Chinese escorts, I presume the official rate is not out of the "purchasing power parity" ball park. If anything it understates the dollar value of the yuan in buying a Chinese market basket. It is just not possible, of course, to buy an American market basket in China.

Final GNP picture

The $90 billion figure implies a per capita output of $116. Previous guesses in World Bank and UN publications are $85 for 1965 and $78 for 1968. The implied rate of growth of 6 percent a year in per capita output since 1965 seems high, and it is possible that the earlier figures are conceptually different. But the qualitative picture is plausible.

A decline to 1968 is attributable to the economic damage incident to the Great Cultural Revolution of the years 1966–69. A rapid increase since 1968 is consistent with the impression that the political reorganization, consolidation, and stabilization which terminated the Cultural Revolution in 1969 and 1970 have been a great success. They appear to have given the country not only efficient and dedicated administration but also very high morale and community of purpose.

Work ethic. Work and production, more work and more production, are the current Maoist keynotes. All the patriotic zeal with which an authoritarian regime can indoctrinate a population is now channeled to this end. That represents a big change since the Cultural Revolution, when the country and its leadership were confused and divided, when Mao himself was struggling for political and ideological supremacy, and when eradication of elitism, intellectualism, revisionism, and bourgeois cultural survivals took precedence over production.

Agricultural output has grown at 4 percent a year since 1953; and there is no reason to assume that industry has done better, given the vicissitudes of the Greap Leap Forward and the Cultural Revolution. In producing materialist GNP, then, my guess is that an industrial labor force one-fifth the size of the agricultural labor force produces 150 percent as much output, implying an average productivity in industry seven and a half times that in agriculture.

State budget. Income differences between the two sectors are, as I have already indicated, much less than the apparent difference in productivity. The main reason is that the state deliberately and systematically redistributes income in favor of the peasants. This brings me to the fifth part of the imaginative exercise, the state budget.

Effective taxes on agricultural output have been reduced from 13.2 percent of output in 1952 to 6 percent in 1971. The deliberate policy is to keep absolute aggregate taxes on agriculture constant. The figures therefore imply that output has increased two and two-tenths times in twenty years, the average growth rate of 4 percent per annum which I already mentioned. On the other hand, there are substantial subsidies to agriculture, probably exceeding the taxes collected. The most important are the price subsidies already referred to. While food prices to consumers have been stable for twenty years, the prices paid producers for major foodstuffs have risen 90 percent. Evidently the concept of agricultural-industrial parity is a universal one, transcending ideology and social organization. We were told that the "disparity" had been reduced 40 percent by government effort since the liberation.

State control. As for industry, I would guess the state takes 50 percent of industrial output, possibly more. In the first place, there are heavy turnover taxes on gross value of production. The textile factory we visited paid 18 percent in taxes; the machine tool factory, 5 percent. Our informants agreed that the tax rate is generally higher for consumer goods than for capital goods.

In any case, turnover taxes, levied on total value of output including costs of materials, pyramid into substantial rates on gross value added, the concept used in GNP estimates. In the second

place, a substantial fraction of depreciation charges are commandeered by the state. The textile enterprise, for example, retained discretion over only half of its replacement allowances. In the third place, industrial enterprises seem to make large net profits, which are turned over to the state in full. The textile factory reported its profit as 19 percent of the value of its output. The machine tool factory would not say, but it must have been large, given that their payroll and turnover tax together accounted for only 10 percent of the value of their shipments and that their profits were said to be ten times the amount of their gross investments—and this in an expanding industry with high priority in the plan.

My guess of 50 percent-plus is consistent with information given us that 90 percent of state revenues come from state enterprises, the remaining 10 percent from agricultural communes, collectives in the service trades, and miscellaneous sources. Of course a substantial part of the state's take from industry is returned in investment appropriations. But industry also pays for "nonproductive" investments—housing, hospitals, roads, sewers, etc.—and for some appropriations of investment funds to agriculture.

In addition to taxes and profits, the state, through its People's Bank, disposes of the people's savings. The only assets, other than small consumer durables, which households can acquire are currency and deposits, on which miniscule interest is paid. The Bank also receives deposits of the working balances of communes and collectives—which could be regarded as indirect deposits of member households—and of state enterprises and state agencies. I have estimated annual household saving at about 6 percent of household income, but this is a wild guess. The Bank makes mainly short-term loans, to finance inventory-building, seasonal agricultural expenses, and the like. Again, interest charges are nominal. Longer-term investments evidently are handled mainly by state appropriations.

Balanced-budget philosophy

The state does no other borrowing. Its budget is balanced, and the pride the Chinese take in this fact would make Herbert Hoover and Dwight Eisenhower happy. China has no debt, external or internal. The debt to the Soviet Union incurred during the Korean war was repaid in advance when the two countries parted diplomatic and ideological ways. Internal bonds were issued prior to 1958, but by the end of 1968 had all been repaid as due from budget surpluses.

As for investments, we were told that in 1957 gross investment took 24 percent of materialist GNP—productive investment, 15 percent; unproductive, 9 percent. Should these proportions still hold, they imply gross investments totaling $22 billion in 1971. Not all of this would come from the state budget; some investments are made directly by communes and state enterprises. Our Shanghai commune invests about 5 percent of the value of its output, 7 percent of its value added. Our Peking textile factory reinvests directly half of its depreciation charges.

Finally, to complete the imaginative tableau requires some numbers for the so-called unproductive sectors, for which we have even fewer statistical clues than for industry and agriculture. I guessed above that 10 percent of the labor force might be engaged in service and governmental activities. Some of these workers are in modern employment where they earn wages at least comparable to industrial wages: civil servants, teachers, bus drivers, medical workers, department store clerks, etc. Their average productivity—measured in terms of value of output at *market prices*—is, however, perhaps only half that in industry, since in these activities the markups for taxes and profits are much smaller.

Many other workers in these sectors are closer to agricultural workers in their productivity and earnings. They use technology equally as primitive. Most local transportation, for example, is powered by back-breaking human effort. The streets are full of old men and women conveying incredibly heavy loads by pulling two-wheeled carts, or slowly pumping pedicabs or tricycle pickups, or simply piling cargo on their backs or their bicycles.

In addition, I should make some other bourgeois imputations, in particular rents for the homes people occupy. Only nominal rents are charged by the state, surely no more than costs of upkeep. The same principle applies to hospital beds, another facility whose use is priced in a market economy but is virtually free in China. I have quite arbitrarily placed the value of such imputations at $10 billion, or $13 a year per person. This

Table 1   Imaginative Construction of China's GNP 1971: Producing Sector

	Agriculture	Industry	Services & government	Housing & other consumer capital	Total
(1) Labor force (millions)	375	75	50	0	500
(2) Value added (billions $U.S.)	36	54	12	10	112*
(3) Av. productivity (2)/(1)($U.S.)	96	720	240	—	224
(4) Payments to govt.: taxes & profits (billions)	3	28	1	—	32
(5) Govt. subsidy ($ billion)	6	—	—	—	6
(6) Undistributed gross profit ($ billion)	2	2	1	—	5
(7) Wage payments (2) + (5)-(4)-(6)	37	24	10	—	71
(8) Av. wage ($U.S.) (7)/(1)	99	320	200	—	142

Memoranda: GNP per capita = 112/773 = 145 where $112 billion is the total GNP from row (2) and 773 million is the UN estimated population, giving a GNP per capita of $145 per year.
Wage income per capita = 71/773 = 92 where $71 billion wage income is the total from row (7) and 773 is the population figure in millions, giving a wage income per capita of $92.
[* In terms of final purchases, household consumption gets 78/112, government purchases 29/112, and "Business investment" 5/112.]

is probably conservative; the implied proportion of consumer income devoted to housing is low, compared with other countries. It is also obvious, even to the casual sightseer, that the quality of the housing is very poor; this is clearly one of China's biggest economic challenges.

All these guesses are summarized in Table 1. We end up with a Chinese GNP, Western style, of $145 per capita. More important, perhaps, we get some picture of the interrelationships of agriculture, industry, and government.

Hard-money ideology

I have already noted the proud commitment of Communist China to pre-Keynesian budgetary orthodoxy. The same old-fashioned bourgeois rectitude guides monetary policy. The note issue is carefully confined to the needs of an expanding volume of transactions at stable wages and declining prices. Standard wage rates are held constant —although an individual's wages will rise with experience, seniority, skill, and effort. There is full employment, but no trade unions, no free labor market, no Phillips dilemma. China follows the old prescription that productivity increases over time should be translated into real wages by falling prices rather than rising money wages.

Of course, if prices are not reduced to the extent that productivity improves, the revenues of the state automatically grow. No doubt this avenue is partly responsible for the apparently comfortable budgetary position of the state. By this process it would be easy for the state to raise the share of resources devoted to investment and collective consumption.

Our impression, however, is that there is great official resistance to this temptation. Current policy and party line, in contrast to earlier five-year plans and the Great Leap Forward, favor private consumption. The emphasis is on lowering consumer prices—for industrial rather than agricultural products—and on increasing the variety and quality of consumer goods available. Certainly the shops, small and large, were well stocked in every city we visited; and the customer queues often noted in other socialist countries were completely absent.

The dual economy in China

For most countries, a principal feature of economic development is the transfer of population from countryside to city, from agriculture to industry and commerce. This is an important source of growth, because labor productivity is much higher in industry than in agriculture. Moreover, the process raises labor productivity in agriculture as well. Industry provides tractors, combines, fertilizers, electricity. With the help of capital and new technology, crop yields per acre rise while direct human labor per acre declines. During the process of transfer, growth rates are very high. Once the shift is largely completed, as in a mature economy like that of the United States, growth depends solely on the slower processes of capital accumulation and technological advance *within* the two sectors.

Industrialization brings growth; but as we know all too well, it brings social disruption and misery as well. This was true in England's Industrial Revolution, and even in the United States we are experiencing the social convulsions incident to the last wave of migration from Southern agriculture to cities. In many developing countries, high wages and glittering city lights attract hordes from the countryside to take their chances on a scarce supply or urban jobs. In these countries the cities are crowded with people unemployed or unproductively occupied in nuisance jobs on the fringes of urban society. Their housing is squalid, and they overwhelm the capacities of municipal services, as the incidence of begging and crime attests.

Controlled migration. China is not undergoing economic development in this sense, and by the same token is not suffering from the social problems that accompany it. There is no unemployment in China. The Chinese proudly make this claim, and I find it easy to credit. Individual Chinese do not have free choice of occupation, job, and place of residence. Neither adults nor young people just completing school can leave the countryside of their own volition. On reaching adulthood, a young man or woman simply becomes a full working member of the commune in which he has grown up, gone to school, and worked right along. A rural resident could get nowhere in the city even if he were permitted to travel there, because no factory or other employer would have the right to hire him.

Factories and urban employers do recruit in the countryside when the planning authorities have licensed them to add to their work force. They go to the country "middle schools," junior and senior high schools, in search of promising and interested talent. But my impression is that they do so only when they have exhausted the supply of school-leavers within the city itself.

As a result of this policy, the relative distribution of population between countryside and city has remained stable, roughly 80 percent of the population being rural. Since the rate of natural increase is higher for the rural population, stability implies some industrial and urban recruitment of rural youth. But the classic process of development by shift of labor force has yet to begin. China has not succeeded in expanding the number of urban jobs much faster than the natural increase of urban population itself.

No urban ghettos.
The happy consequence of strict central control of the labor market is that Chinese cities do not exhibit the distressing urban pathologies from which so many cities elsewhere suffer, and for which some Chinese cities were notorious before the revolution. There are no beggars on the streets, no idlers on the corners, no derelicts without beds or roofs, no sidewalk clamor of peddlers and vendors. Litter goes into litter cans with a regularity that would astound and delight Mayor Lindsay of New York. Streets, parks, and public lavatories are clean and well kept. In all these public places, as well as in your home or hotel, your person and property are secure day and night. The careless foreign traveler can count on speedy recovery of the full Hongkong shopping bag left behind in the railway coach.

Inherited poverty.
But China is still a miserably backward and poor country, especially rural China. One can travel two days on the train through fields of rice, cotton, jute, maize, wheat, and sorghum and see no tractors and surprisingly few draft animals. Water pumps are fairly frequent, but the main sources of power in agricul-

tural work are the peasants themselves. Even human-powered farm implements, beyond the simplest tools, are rarely in evidence.

Our impression through the train window was somewhat misleading, because of the time of year. The people's commune we visited near Shanghai had 84 tractors for the 4,700 households (20,500 people) farming 1,700 hectares, and claimed that 95 percent of the area was mechanically cultivated. The commune also had some rice-transplanters and small, simple threshers.

Nevertheless, there can be no doubt that Chinese agriculture is extremely labor-intensive—according to my fellow traveler, former Ambassador to India, much more so than Indian agriculture. Likewise, chemical fertilizer is very little used, again much less than in India. Even in the model commune we visited, chemical fertilizer is only 30–40 percent of all the fertilizer used.

Urban-rural differentials.
As in most developing countries, industrial wages are substantially higher than peasants' incomes. My guess in the first section of this report was a factor of three.

As I explained above, redistribution through the state budget explains why industrial wages may be only two to four times peasants' earnings, while industrial productivity is seven or eight times higher. I think it is safe to conclude that the marginal productivity of a worker in agriculture (measured by the loss of output if one typical worker is withdrawn) is less than his consumption. In this sense there is surplus labor in agriculture, in China as in many other underdeveloped countries; and industrial wages are well above the shadow price of labor. But in China strict control of personal movement and residence prevents this problem from taking the form of urban unemployment.

Regional stability.
I should note that our Chinese hosts, both economists and others, would disagree with this diagnosis. They repeatedly claimed that there was a shortage of labor in agriculture, a remark I could make sense of only by interpreting it to mean that the marginal product of labor in agriculture exceeds zero. Moreover, they regarded it as entirely natural that people should grow up to work in the locales where they were born, even if their marginal products—my word, of course, not

theirs—might be higher somewhere else. The principle militates not only against rural-urban migration but also against rural-rural migration. Our suggestion that it might be desirable gradually to shift people from poorer land to better land was stoutly resisted. If for historical reasons people happen to live on unpromising terrain, they and their children must simply put more Maoist energy and ingenuity into improving the situation, with the help of the state.

The people's communes

The Chinese countryside is organized into people's communes, which are geographical and administrative subdivisions of government as well as economic units for agricultural, and some nonagricultural, production. The communes vary in size from 5,000 to 40,000 persons. They are in turn divided into production brigades of roughly 1,000 members, and these in turn into production teams of 150-200 members. The team is the basic unit of production, responsible for cultivating its assigned land and for allocating and organizing the work of its members. A part of the proceeds of each team is appropriated by the brigade and the communes for local public services, administrative costs, welfare benefits, and investments. These levies are of the order of 10-15 percent. In addition, there is the 6 percent state tax previously referred to. The brigades and communes own certain equipment—tractors, threshers, transplanters. Teams are charged rent for their use.

After all these charges are met, the remainder is available for distribution to the members of the team, although the team itself may decide to appropriate some for collective purposes. Distribution among team members follows what the Chinese describe as the socialist principle of remuneration: "to each according to his work." Specifically, each member accumulates work points each day he works, up to a maximum of 13 per day. Distributions are in proportion to accumulated points. These are meant to reflect strength, skill, diligence, and "attitude."

The scores are publicly determined at meetings once a month. Each peasant suggests his own score, and his suggestion usually prevails without dissent. Sometimes his colleagues argue that his score should be higher. Less frequently, we were told, they try to persuade him it should be lower. It was hard to pin down how decisions are made in these cases, but we were told that it was done by "democratic centralism." In the commune we visited near Shanghai, the average daily score was said to be about 11.

The teams, brigades, and communes also operate their own social security systems. The sick, disabled, and elderly are first of all the responsibility of their kinfolk, by eternal tradition. But in case of need, they become a collective responsibility.

Evidently the process of organizing the entire countryside into teams, brigades, and communes was largely accomplished during the Cultural Revolution and its aftermath. But it is not yet complete in all areas of the country; for it is not yet known in Peking, at least by our informants, how many communes there are altogether and how many people are members.

Gray markets? Peasants in communes are allowed small plots for personal gardens and, in the commune we saw, may keep two pigs. Private output is meant for personal consumption, not for sale, certainly not for sale in the city. But the regime is anxiously conscious of what are termed the "spontaneous forces" of the rural economy, by which I understood the instinct of peasants for private trading and arbitrage. The concerns expressed on this count suggest that private sales may be more frequent than anyone cares to admit.

Normally, the commune keeps what it wants for internal consumption and sells the rest to the state for distribution to factories or retail outlets. There is discretion here as long as the delivery targets specified in the plan are met. A grocery store we visited in Peking maintained direct telephonic contact day and night with neighboring communes, to order deliveries of fresh vegetables and fruits. In the case of grain crops—the only foodstuffs rationed in China are grain and vegetable oil—the commune is expected to limit its internal consumption and sell the excess, no matter how much it is overachieving its "tasks," to the state.

No free supply-demand. Prices are set by the state and are extremely stable. The notion that prices fluctuate with supply and demand is regarded as a bourgeois doctrine inappropriate to a planned economy. Worse still, it is regarded as a revisionist heresy, associated with Eastern European experiments with market socialism and the hated Khrushchev's gestures in the same direction. The ideological heroes in China, one may judge from the portraits that adorn every meeting room in every institution, are Marx, Engels, Lenin, Stalin, and of course Mao. One of the early victims of the Cultural Revolution was an economist—Sun Yeh-fung—who evidently aspired to be China's Liberman.

At first our queries about seasonal fluctuations in prices of fresh produce were met with insistent denials that these even occurred, but searching inquiry revealed that they do happen. Prices are still, of course, planned rather than market-determined. Two other factors evidently contribute to making fairly stable prices workable. One is the rationing of grain in the form of rice, flour, bread, etc. Although the rations are generous—15 kg per person per month for a normal adult—there is presumably an unsatisfied demand at the controlled price. The same observation may also apply to another major crop, cotton, because cotton cloth is also rationed. The other factor is that most of China's consumers are peasants who can find a way to consume whatever supplies of many products are not purchased for urban consumption. If they have a big harvest of apples and prices are held stable or reduced insufficiently to attract extra urban consumption to match, the peasants can simply eat the apples or preserve them. If the apple harvest is poor while urban demand says high, the peasants will simply have fewer apples to consume or preserve. The elasticity of their demand with available supplies provides a buffer that makes controlled prices workable.

This is possible in China because agricultural markets are local and segmented, not national in scope. Every city is served mainly by a surrounding hinterland of diversified agriculture, and only to a minor degree by shipments from distant regions specialized in particular crops.

In the commune we visited, the strongest and best workers earned perhaps 40 percent more than the weaker members. In the textile factory the lowest wage was 35 yuan per month; the average was 60; the highest wage for workers was a bit more than 100; engineers and technicians earned 130–140. In a Peking arts and crafts workshop, wage rates varied from 40 to 102 yuan, and some very special experienced craftsmen earned 200. In the department store, wages ranged from 36 to 80 yuan and averaged 63. In a Shanghai hospital, average wages were 67 yuan for all staff members, and only 85 for doctors. But some physicians and surgeons earned 200 yuan and even 300. Young university teachers are being paid 50 yuan, but the salaries of some veteran professors are 200 or more.

One of the aims of the anti-elitist, anti-intellectual Cultural Revolution was to narrow income differentials, especially those that gave educated people superior status to workers and peasants. We were given to understand that the high wages paid to older engineers, doctors, craftsmen, and professors are obsolete vestiges of the past, maintained for present incumbents out of humanity and charity but certainly not anticipated for their successors. At the hospital, for example, it was implied that the current generation of physicians, properly inculcated and motivated by Maoist thought, would not expect to advance much beyond 100 yuan.

China really is at the beginning of an experiment to see if nonpecuniary incentives can be substituted for substantial income differences as inducements for high-quality professional, scientific, and administrative performance. Of course the chances of success are facilitated by the state's control of job allocations and the denial of free choice of jobs and occupations. Once a university student, for example, chooses his field of study, he has in effect lost control of his career. The engineering student will go where he is assigned, just like an officer newly graduated from a military academy. In conversation with our Chinese companions, I was surprised at how easily and cheerfully they accepted this fact of their lives, and how little value they placed on the freedom of choice they lack. One after another simply said, "I go where the state needs me most." But the high morale inspired by a strong sense of national duty will also have to be sustained to make the experiment a success.

State of intellectual life

Universities, and intellectual life in general, took quite a beating from the Cultural Revolution. The universities were shut in 1967, the students were not enrolled again until 1970. As in all Chinese institutions, the Cultural Revolution ended with new administrations in charge, invariably called Revolutionary Committees. The university is run by a Revolutionary Committee of professors, young teachers, students, army representatives, party delegates, workers, and administrators. So is every subdivision, the economics department, for example.

The new university leaders are presiding over what they regard as an educational revolution. Its main elements are these:

1. The university is politicized. All subjects are taught and studied with homage to Mao's thoughts.

2. Students and teachers must not set themselves apart from or above workers and peasants. Students will not be admitted until they have two years of practical manual work on farm or in factory. Moreover, students must spend a third of every academic year in such work.

3. Subjects must be taught and learned in ways that combine theory and practice. The message is to get outside the cloistered walls and learn by getting your hands dirty.

4. The length of courses of study has been cut.

5. The university is supposed to be less hierarchical and authoritarian in structure than in the old days.

These last strands of reform sound like the academic revolutions in the 1960s all over the world. But I found the general anti-intellectualism and political dogmatism of the university reforms frightening.

I cannot be optimistic about Chinese universities in general, or about economics as a scientific discipline in China in particular. Although we engaged in much brave talk about exchanges of academicians and scientists, I am afraid it will be some time before we talk the same language in economics, and even longer before "a hundred flowers" are allowed once more to bloom in Chinese universities.

A new order. Whether these developments in academia are any long-run threat to the Chinese economy is another matter. Meanwhile, the Chinese are stressing the universalization of primary and secondary education. It, too, is strongly ideological; but the new generation will be literate as well as Maoist.

Since one cannot escape the impression that the Chinese are a very able and industrious people, who were kept in misery and ignorance by centuries of misrule and, more recently, by a century of foreign exploitation, stable government and elementary literacy may set the stage for remarkable progress for several decades to come.

The Future?

Reading 84

In the midst of the Great Depression, the most important economist of this century was able to glimpse into the future. Decades before J. K. Galbraith, Keynes foresaw the "affluent society." Although Keynes knew that laissez faire could not be counted upon to do so, he was optimistic that macroeconomic policies could secure full employment and rapid growth for the mixed economy. Keynes gave the simple Marxian notion of the inevitable collapse of capitalism in a final depression its fatal rebuttal. Under affluence, economics would cease to be Man's master and become his useful servant. That is the vision of Lord Keynes, genius and economist.

Questions to guide the reading

Do men need the goad of economic scarcity to keep life from becoming dull? William James once spoke of the need for "a moral equivalent of war"—e.g., the Peace Corps or the vigorous battle against poverty, which was to engage the energies bred into man by the evolutionary struggle for existence. Can you construct a "moral equivalent" for economic scarcity? Foreign aid? Adult cultural enrichment?

Economic Possibilities for Our Grandchildren (1930)

John Maynard Keynes

I

We are suffering just now from a bad attack of economic pessimism. It is common to hear people say that the epoch of enormous economic progress which characterised the nineteenth century is over; that the rapid improvement in the standard of life is now going to slow down—at any rate in Great Britain; that a decline in prosperity is more likely than an improvement in the decade which lies ahead of us.

I believe that this is a wildly mistaken interpretation of what is happening to us. We are suffering, not from the rheumatics of old age, but from the growing-pains of over-rapid changes, from the painfulness of readjustment between one economic period and another. The increase of technical efficiency has been taking place faster than we can deal with the problem of labour absorption; the improvement in the standard of life has been a little too quick; the banking and monetary system of the world has been preventing the rate of interest from falling as fast as equilibrium requires. And even so, the waste and confusion which ensue relate to not more than 7½ per cent of the national income; we are muddling away one and sixpence in the £, and have only 18s. 6d., when we might, if we were more sensible, have £ 1; yet, nevertheless, the 18s. 6d. mounts up to as much as the £ 1 would have been five or six years ago. We forget that in 1929 the physical output of the industry of Great Britain was greater than ever before, and that the net surplus of our foreign balance available for new foreign investment, after paying for all our imports, was greater last year than that of any other country, being indeed 50 per cent greater than the corresponding surplus of the United States. Or again—if it is to be a matter of comparisons—suppose that we were to reduce our wages by a half, repudiate four-fifths of the national debt, and hoard our surplus wealth in barren gold instead of lending it at 6 per cent or more, we should resemble the now much-envied France. But would it be an improvement?

The prevailing world depression, the enormous anomaly of unemployment in a world full of wants, the disastrous mistakes we have made, blind us to what is going on under the surface—to the true interpretation of the trend of things. For I predict that both of the two opposed errors of pessimism which now make so much noise in the world will be proved wrong in our own time—the pessimism of the revolutionaries who think that things are so bad that nothing can save us but violent change, and the pessimism of the reactionaries who consider the balance of our economic and social life so precarious that we must risk no experiments.

My purpose in this essay, however, is not to examine the present or the near future, but to disembarrass myself of short views and take wings into the future. What can we reasonably expect the level of our economic life to be a hundred years hence? What are the economic possibilities for our grandchildren?

From the earliest times of which we have record—back, say, to two thousand years before

From John Maynard Keynes, *Essays in Persuasion* (Macmillan and Co., London, 1933). Reprinted with kind permission of Rupert Hart-Davis Limited.

Christ—down to the beginning of the eighteenth century, there was no very great change in the standard of life of the average man living in the civilised centres of the earth. Ups and downs certainly. Visitations of plague, famine, and war. Golden intervals. But no progressive, violent change. Some periods perhaps 50 per cent better than others—at the utmost 100 per cent better—in the four thousand years which ended (say) in A.D. 1700.

This slow rate of progress, or lack of progress, was due to two reasons—to the remarkable absence of important technical improvements and to the failure of capital to accumulate.

The absence of important technical inventions between the prehistoric age and comparatively modern times is truly remarkable. Almost everything which really matters and which the world possessed at the commencement of the modern age was already known to man at the dawn of history. Language, fire, the same domestic animals which we have to-day, wheat, barley, the vine and the olive, the plough, the wheel, the oar, the sail, leather, linen and cloth, bricks and pots, gold and silver, copper, tin, and lead—and iron was added to the list before 1000 B.C.—banking, statecraft, mathematics, astronomy, and religion. There is no record of when we first possessed these things.

At some epoch before the dawn of history—perhaps even in one of the comfortable intervals before the last ice age—there must have been an era of progress and invention comparable to that in which we live to-day. But through the greater part of recorded history there was nothing of the kind.

The modern age opened, I think, with the accumulation of capital which began in the sixteenth century. I believe—for reasons with which I must not encumber the present argument—that this was initially due to the rise of prices, and the profits to which that led, which resulted from the treasure of gold and silver which Spain brought from the New World into the Old. From that time until to-day the power of accumulation by compound interest, which seems to have been sleeping for many generations, was re-born and renewed its strength. And the power of compound interest over two hundred years is such as to stagger the imagination.

Let me give in illustration of this a sum which I

have worked out. The value of Great Britain's foreign investments to-day is estimated at about £ 4,000,000,000. This yields us an income at the rate of about 6½ per cent. Half of this we bring home and enjoy; the other half, namely, 3¼ per cent, we leave to accumulate abroad at compound interest. Something of this sort has now been going on for about 250 years.

For I trace the beginnings of British foreign investment to the treasure which Drake stole from Spain in 1580. In that year he returned to England bringing with him the prodigious spoils of the *Golden Hind*. Queen Elizabeth was a considerable shareholder in the syndicate which had financed the expedition. Out of her share she paid off the whole of England's foreign debt, balanced her Budget, and found herself with about £ 40,000 in hand. This she invested in the Levant Company—which prospered. Out of the profits of the Levant Company, the East India Company was founded; and the profits of this great enterprise were the foundation of England's subsequent foreign investment. Now it happens that £ 40,000 accumulating at 3¼ per cent compound interest approximately corresponds to the actual volume of England's foreign investments at various dates, and would actually amount to-day to the total of £ 4,000,000,000 which I have already quoted as being what our foreign investments now are. Thus, every £ 1 which Drake brought home in 1580 has now become £ 100,000. Such is the power of compound interest!

From the sixteenth century, with a cumulative crescendo after the eighteenth, the great age of science and technical inventions began, which since the beginning of the nineteenth century has been in full flood—coal, steam, electricity, petrol, steel, rubber, cotton, the chemical industries, automatic machinery and the methods of mass production, wireless, printing, Newton, Darwin, and Einstein, and thousands of other things and men too famous and familiar to catalogue.

What is the result? In spite of an enormous growth in the population of the world, which it has been necessary to equip with houses and machines, the average standard of life in Europe and the United States has been raised, I think, about fourfold. The growth of capital has been on a scale which is far beyond a hundredfold of what any previous age had known. And from now on we need not expect so great an increase of population.

If capital increases, say, 2 per cent per annum, the capital equipment of the world will have increased by a half in twenty years, and seven and a half times in a hundred years. Think of this in terms of material things—houses, transport, and the like.

At the same time technical improvements in manufacture and transport have been proceeding at a greater rate in the last ten years than ever before in history. In the United States factory output per head was 40 per cent greater in 1925 than in 1919. In Europe we are held back by temporary obstacles, but even so it is safe to say that technical efficiency is increasing by more than 1 per cent per annum compound. There is evidence that the revolutionary technical changes, which have so far chiefly affected industry, may soon be attacking agriculture. We may be on the eve of improvements in the efficiency of food production as great as those which have already taken place in mining, manufacture, and transport. In quite a few years—in our own lifetimes I mean—we may be able to perform all the operations of agriculture, mining, and manufacture with a quarter of the human effort to which we have been accustomed.

For the moment the very rapidity of these changes is hurting us and bringing difficult problems to solve. Those countries are suffering relatively which are not in the vanguard of progress. We are being afflicted with a new disease of which some readers may not yet have heard the name, but of which they will hear a great deal in the years to come—namely, *technological unemployment*. This means unemployment due to our discovery of means of economising the use of labour outrunning the pace at which we can find new uses for labour.

But this is only a temporary phase of maladjustment. All this means in the long run *that mankind is solving its economic problem.* I would predict that the standard of life in progressive countries one hundred years hence will be between four and eight times as high as it is to-day. There would be nothing surprising in this even in the light of our present knowledge. It would not be foolish to contemplate the possibility of a far greater progress still.

II

Let us, for the sake of argument, suppose that a hundred years hence we are all of us, on the average, eight times better off in the economic sense than we are to-day. Assuredly there need be nothing here to surprise us.

Now it is true that the needs of human beings may seem to be insatiable. But they fall into two classes—those needs which are absolute in the sense that we feel them whatever the situation of our fellow human beings may be, and those which are relative in the sense that we feel them only if their satisfaction lifts us above, makes us feel superior to, our fellows. Needs of the second class, those which satisfy the desire for superiority, may indeed be insatiable; for the higher the general level, the higher still are they. But this is not so true of the absolute needs—a point may soon be reached, much sooner perhaps than we are all of us aware of, when these needs are satisfied in the sense that we prefer to devote our further energies to non-economic purposes.

Now for my conclusion, which you will find, I think, to become more and more startling to the imagination the longer you think about it.

I draw the conclusion that, assuming no important wars and no important increase in population, the *economic problem* may be solved, or be at least within sight of solution, within a hundred years. This means that the economic problem is not—if we look into the future—*the permanent problem of the human race.*

Why, you may ask, is this so startling? It is startling because—if, instead of looking into the future, we look into the past—we find that the economic problem, the struggle for subsistence, always has been hitherto the primary, most pressing problem of the human race—not only of the human race, but of the whole of the biological kingdom from the beginnings of life in its most primitive forms.

Thus we have been expressly evolved by nature—with all our impulses and deepest instincts—for the purpose of solving the economic problem. If the economic problem is solved, mankind will be deprived of its traditional purpose.

Will this be a benefit? If one believes at all in the real values of life, the prospect at least opens up the possibility of benefit. Yet I think with dread of the readjustment of the habits and instincts of the ordinary man, bred into him for countless generations, which he may be asked to discard within a few decades.

To use the language of to-day—must we not expect a general "nervous breakdown"? We already have a little experience of what I mean—a nervous breakdown of the sort which is already common enough in England and the United States amongst the wives of the well-to-do classes, unfortunate women, many of them, who have been deprived by their wealth of their traditional tasks and occupations—who cannot find it sufficiently amusing, when deprived of the spur of economic necessity, to cook and clean and mend, yet are quite unable to find anything more amusing.

To those who sweat for their daily bread leisure is a longed-for sweet—until they get it.

There is the traditional epitaph written for herself by the old charwoman:—

Don't mourn for me, friends, don't weep for me never.
For I'm going to do nothing for ever and ever.

This was her heaven. Like others who look forward to leisure, she conceived how nice it would be to spend her time listening-in—for there was another couplet which occurred in her poem:—

With psalms and sweet music the heavens'll be ringing,
But I shall have nothing to do with the singing.

Yet it will only be for those who have to do with the singing that life will be tolerable—and how few of us can sing!

Thus for the first time since his creation man will be faced with his real, his permanent problem—how to use his freedom from pressing economic cares, how to occupy the leisure, which science and compound interest will have won for him, to live wisely and agreeably and well.

The strenuous purposeful money-makers may carry all of us along with them into the lap of economic abundance. But it will be those peoples, who can keep alive, and cultivate into a fuller perfection, the art of life itself and do not sell themselves for the means of life, who will be able to enjoy the abundance when it comes.

Yet there is no country and no people, I think,

who can look forward to the age of leisure and of abundance without a dread. For we have been trained too long to strive and not to enjoy. It is a fearful problem for the ordinary person, with no special talents, to occupy himself, especially if he no longer has roots in the soil or in custom or in the beloved conventions of a traditional society. To judge from the behaviour and the achievements of the wealthy classes to-day in any quarter of the world, the outlook is very depressing! For these are, so to speak, our advance guard—those who are spying out the promised land for the rest of us and pitching their camp there. For they have most of them failed disastrously, so it seems to me—those who have an independent income but no associations or duties or ties—to solve the problem which has been set them.

I feel sure that with a little more experience we shall use the new-found bounty of nature quite differently from the way in which the rich use it to-day, and will map out for ourselves a plan of life quite otherwise than theirs.

For many ages to come the old Adam will be so strong in us that everybody will need to do *some* work if he is to be contented. We shall do more things for ourselves than is usual with the rich to-day, only too glad to have small duties and tasks and routines. But beyond this, we shall endeavour to spread the bread thin on the butter—to make what work there is still to be done to be as widely shared as possible. Three-hour shifts or a fifteen-hour week may put off the problem for a great while. For three hours a day is quite enough to satisfy the old Adam in most of us!

There are changes in other spheres too which we must expect to come. When the accumulation of wealth is no longer of high social importance, there will be great changes in the code of morals. We shall be able to rid ourselves of many of the pseudo-moral principles which have hag-ridden us for two hundred years, by which we have exalted some of the most distasteful of human qualities into the position of the highest virtues. We shall be able to afford to dare to assess the money-motive at its true value. The love of money as a possession—as distinguished from the love of money as a means to the enjoyments and realities of life—will be recognised for what it is, a somewhat disgusting morbidity, one of those semi-criminal, semi-pathological propensities which one hands over with a shudder to the specialists in mental disease. All kinds of social customs and economic practices, affecting the distribution of wealth and of economic rewards and penalties, which we now maintain at all costs, however distasteful and unjust they may be in themselves, because they are tremendously useful in promoting the accumulation of capital, we shall then be free, at last, to discard.

Of course there will still be many people with intense, unsatisfied purposiveness who will blindly pursue wealth—unless they can find some plausible substitute. But the rest of us will no longer be under any obligation to applaud and encourage them. For we shall inquire more curiously than is safe to-day into the true character of this "purposiveness" with which in varying degrees Nature has endowed almost all of us. For purposiveness means that we are more concerned with the remote future results of our actions than with their own quality or their immediate effects on our own environment. The "purposive" man is always trying to secure a spurious and delusive immortality for his acts by pushing his interest in them forward into time. He does not love his cat, but his cat's kittens; nor, in truth, the kittens, but only the kittens' kittens, and so on forward for ever to the end of cat-dom. For him jam is not jam unless it is a case of jam to-morrow and never jam to-day. Thus by pushing his jam always forward into the future, he strives to secure for his act of boiling it an immortality.

Let me remind you of the Professor in *Sylvie and Bruno:*—

"Only the tailor, sir, with your little bill," said a meek voice outside the door.

"Ah, well, I can soon settle *his* business," the Professor said to the children, "if you'll just wait a minute. How much is it, this year, my man?" The tailor had come in while he was speaking.

"Well, it's been a-doubling so many years, you see," the tailor replied, a little gruffly, "and I think I'd like the money now. It's two thousand pound, it is!"

"Oh, that's nothing!" the Professor carelessly remarked, feeling in his pocket, as if he always carried at least *that* amount with him. "But wouldn't you like to wait just another year and make it *four* thousand? Just think how rich you'd be! Why, you might be a *king,* if you liked!"

"I don't know as I'd care about being a king," the man said thoughtfully. "But it *dew* sound a powerful sight o' money! Well, I think I'll wait—"

"Of course you will!" said the Professor. "There's good sense in *you,* I see. Good-day to you, my man!"

"Will you ever have to pay him that four thousand pounds?" Sylvie asked as the door closed on the departing creditor.

"*Never,* my child!" the Professor replied emphatically. "He'll go on doubling it till he dies. You see, it's *always* worth while waiting another year to get twice as much money!"

Perhaps it is not an accident that the race which did most to bring the promise of immortality into the heart and essence of our religions has also done most for the principle of compound interest and particularly loves this most purposive of human institutions.

I see us free, therefore, to return to some of the most sure and certain principles of religion and traditional virtue—that avarice is a vice, that the exaction of usury is a misdemeanour, and the love of money is detestable, that those walk most truly in the paths of virtue and sane wisdom who take least thought for the morrow. We shall once more value ends above means and prefer the good to the useful. We shall honour those who can teach us how to pluck the hour and the day virtuously and well, the delightful people who are capable of taking direct enjoyment in things, the lilies of the field who toil not, neither do they spin.

But beware! The time for all this is not yet. For at least another hundred years we must pretend to ourselves and to every one that fair is foul and foul is fair; for foul is useful and fair is not. Avarice and usury and precaution must be our gods for a little longer still. For only they can lead us out of the tunnel of economic necessity into daylight.

I look forward, therefore, in days not so very remote, to the greatest change which has ever occurred in the material environment of life for human beings in the aggregate. But, of course, it will all happen gradually, not as a catastrophe. Indeed, it has already begun. The course of affairs will simply be that there will be ever larger and larger classes and groups of people from whom problems of economic necessity have been practically removed. The critical difference will be realised when this condition has become so general that the nature of one's duty to one's neighbour is changed. For it will remain reasonable to be economically purposive for others after it has ceased to be reasonable for oneself.

The *pace* at which we can reach our destination of economic bliss will be governed by four things—our power to control population, our determination to avoid wars and civil dissensions, our willingness to entrust to science the direction of those matters which are properly the concern of science, and the rate of accumulation as fixed by the margin between our production and our consumption; of which the last will easily look after itself, given the first three.

Meanwhile there will be no harm in making mild preparations for our destiny, in encouraging, and experimenting in, the arts of life as well as the activities of purpose.

But, chiefly, do not let us overestimate the importance of the economic problem, or sacrifice to its supposed necessities other matters of greater and more permanent significance. It should be a matter for specialists—like dentistry. If economists could manage to get themselves thought of as humble, competent people, on a level with dentists, that would be splendid!